The Financial System

The Financial System

J. O. Light
William L. White

both of the
Graduate School of
Business Administration
Harvard University

1979

RICHARD D. IRWIN, INC. *Homewood, Illinois 60430*

Case material of the Harvard Graduate School of
Business Administration is made possible by the
cooperation of business firms who may wish to remain
anonymous by having names, quantities, and other
identifying details disguised while basic relationships
are maintained. Cases are prepared as the basis for
class discussion rather than to illustrate either effective
or ineffective handling of administrative situations.

ISBN 0-256-02120-1
Library of Congress Catalog Card No. 78–62626

Printed in the United States of America

6 7 8 9 0 MP 6 5 4 3

Preface

This book analyzes the processes at work within the U.S. financial system, its major participants, its responsiveness to economic activity, its continuous adaptation to changing needs, its procedures for assessing and pricing risk, and its role in the allocation of credit to different financial sectors. It is intended for both graduate-level courses in Financial Markets and Institutions and a wider professional audience.

In the course of teaching this material at the Harvard Business School, we have come to believe that there is a void in the spectrum of available books, which this book is intended to fill. There are excellent books which describe the principal actors and features of financial markets. There are excellent books which analyze money, banking and monetary policy. There are excellent books which derive the quantitative theory of risk and return in financial markets. While all of these describe important facets of the financial system, they do not seem to analyze the processes at work within the financial system itself. This book deals with each of the above topics, but it also attempts to introduce and to analyze them within the larger context of the processes at work in a changing, adaptable financial system.

A number of major themes are developed and explored throughout the book, among them:

The structure of financial markets and the financial system.

Financial markets as allocators of funds and distributors of risk.

The role and functions of financial intermediaries.

Risk and return: theories of financial asset pricing in competitive markets.

At its most basic level, the book strives to develop an understanding of the structural interrelationships among the important actors within the U.S. financial system including the demanders of funds, the suppliers of funds, the financial intermediaries, regulators, and the credit allocation programs of the federal government. The book also strives to develop an understanding of the dynamic processes at work within financial markets, the origins of credit demands and patterns of saving, the Federal Reserve's role in influencing the supply of money/credit, the role of interest rates, and the changing allocation of funds. The book explores financial risks and the ways in which they are distributed including an analysis of the changing financial condition of important borrowers, the uncertain future values of their financial obligations, and the risks assumed by different investors who hold these obligations. Throughout the book, the roles and functions of financial intermediaries are discussed, including their role as sources of funds, allocators of funds, risk-bearers, and risk-sharers. Finally, as the book proceeds, it develops alternative theories of financial asset pricing in the context of particular markets including the relationship between inflation and interest rates, the term structure of interest rates, and the capital asset pricing model of expected returns and risk.

The principal parts of the book, sequenced to build upon each other are:

I. Introduction
II. Primary Sectors and Their Financial Demands
III. Equilibrium Forces in Financial Markets
IV. Commercial Banks and the Federal Reserve
V. The Principal Financial Markets

After describing the function and structure of financial markets, the first chapter introduces the central intellectual issue around which the book is organized—the extent to which the interest rates or expected returns from different securities are determined by the balance of supply and demand for funds in the market for each of the securities, as opposed to being determined by a set of forces which operate across all markets to keep the expected returns from all securities in a risk-adjusted equilibrium relationship. Part II of the book analyzes the financial demands of each of the "primary financial sectors"—business corporations, households, the federal government, state and local governments, and the international sector. Each of these is analyzed in detail, focusing on its role as demanders of and/or suppliers of funds to the different financial markets. This section of the book ends with an introduction to the competition for funds among the primary financial sectors. Part III develops a number of the equilibrium relationships which affect the returns on securities—the connections between inflation, the expected real rate of interest, and the nominal rate of interest, between expected returns on long-term and short-term securities, and between risk and expected return. After introducing the idea of public and private markets, this section explores the roles which financial intermediaries can play in financial markets as well as how the structure of financial institutions has changed as a result of conflicts between the equilibrium forces and the forces of supply and demand.

After a discussion of the role of commercial banks and the Federal

Reserve, the final and largest part of the book is devoted to an analysis of each of the principal financial markets. For each market, the functions of the principal financial intermediaries, the supply and demand for funds, and the pricing of financial obligations are discussed. In considering each of these markets, particular attention is given to the role played by the forces of supply and demand and by the equilibrium forces in the determination of interest rates.

The book places special emphasis upon the external financial demands of business corporations and the competition for funds among the private sectors, principally between business corporations and households. With regard to commercial banks, the book deemphasizes their earlier image as simple demand deposit institutions. It accentuates instead the differences among banks from the very large international money-center banks to small local retail banks. The large money-center banks are depicted and analyzed as complex institutions with multiple channels for raising funds—institutions which play a central role in the market for short-term business credit. The retail banks and the thrift institutions are analyzed as the key institutions in the household deposit market, and along with the federally sponsored credit intermediaries, as the key institutions in the home mortgage market. Indeed, all of the principal nonbank financial intermediaries (thrift institutions, insurance companies, pension funds, federally sponsored credit intermediaries) are discussed in the chapters which deal with the markets in which these institutions operate. As a result, they are analyzed in the context of the financial markets in which they are most important rather than in a separate section on financial intermediaries.

A previous understanding of economics and corporate finance provides a useful foundation for this book, although they are not mandatory. In several sections we derive equations for the theoretical structure of financial asset prices. We have attempted to keep the quantitative analysis as simple and straightforward as possible, sacrificing some rigor for clarity, so that a knowledge of elementary algebra should be sufficient.

This book grew out of the materials developed initially for a course entitled Capital Markets. In this course we have used not only this book but also a variety of other materials. Within the financial markets sections, we have used outside readings, generally drawn from the financial community, describing and interpreting recent financial phenomena. Within the more theoretical sections, we have used a variety of articles drawn from current academic journals. Interspersed throughout the course we have used a set of cases and problems whose resolutions depend upon an understanding of issues within financial markets. A number of these cases are included at the end of this book. Our hope is that this book can be used by other instructors as the core of their Financial Markets and Institutions course. All instructors, of course, tend to develop their own very special type of Financial Markets and Institutions course, emphasizing and deemphasizing certain areas—among them the linkages with real economic activity, applied monetary policy, business financing decisions, the functions of financial intermediaries, theories of risk and return. We hope that with the proper choice of supplementary material, this book can become a useful part of many of these courses.

J. O. Light
William L. White

December 1978

Contents

Federal government financing demands. The changing composition of federal expenditures. The composition of federal receipts: *Inflation and federal tax receipts.* Factors affecting the balance in the federal budget and federal financing demands. The history of budget management. Other sources of treasury financial demands. Indirect effects of the federal government.

The connection between debt issues and capital outlays: *Short-term borrowing. Sensitivity to credit market conditions.* Debt issues in the overall financing of state and local governments: *State and local government receipts and expenditures. Inflation and state and local budgets. The effects of recessions on state and local governments. The history of budget deficits. Financial asset accumulation. Net funds raised in financial markets.*

Internal and external markets for dollar denominated financial claims. Nonresident demand for dollar denominated financial assets and liabilities: *Private parties. Official parties (central banks).* Gross and net financial investment: *Dollar outflows and inflows.* History of nonresident transactions in the U.S. financial markets: *1960–1965. 1966–1969. 1970–1971. 1972–1973. 1974–1976. 1977–1978.*

Interaction between private and federal government demands for funds. Competition for funds between business and households: *Fund flows to the home mortgage market during periods of high interest rates.*

PART III EQUILIBRIUM FORCES IN FINANCIAL MARKETS

The basic equilibrium relationship: Inflationary expectations and nominal interest rates. Divergences from the equilibrium relationship: Forces of supply and demand: *The connection between inflation and the forces of supply and demand.* Empirical tests of interest rates and inflationary expectations. An extension of the basic equilibrium relationship: The hypothesis of efficient markets: *Empirical tests of the efficient markets hypothesis.* A complicating factor: Income taxes and the Fisher effect. The alternative views revisited.

The basic equilibrium relationship: Expectations of future rates: *The forward rates imbedded in the yield curve. Forward rates as expected future rates. Risk aversion and liquidity premiums.* Divergences from the basic equilibrium relationship: The forces of supply and demand. An extension of the basic equilibrium relationship: Efficient markets: *Empirical studies of the term structure of interest rates.* Inflation and the term structure of interest rates: The combined theories. The notion of randomness in efficient markets. Concluding comments.

Prior probability distributions for future uncertain returns. The basic equilibrium relationship: A theory of risk premiums: *A security's contribution to portfolio risk. A theory of risk premiums.* An extension of the basic equilibrium relationship: Efficient markets. Validity and usefulness of the model.

The risk and return from different securities. Public versus private markets. Function of financial intermediaries—Suppliers' point of view. Function of financial intermediaries—Demanders' point of view. Pricing of securities in private markets.

Causal forces—supply and demand for funds from primary sectors. Equilibrium forces. Barriers to full equilibrium. Disequilibrium returns and incentive for change. Modes of financial adaptation. Wall Street's investment bankers in the adaptation process. The process of adaptation.

PART IV   COMMERCIAL BANKS AND THE FEDERAL RESERVE

The balance sheet of a commercial bank. Bank assets and credit demands of the primary sectors. Structure of the domestic banking system: *Correspondent banking. Interbank markets. Bank holding companies.* International expansion of the banking system. Evolution of banks' sources of funds: *Deposits as a source of funds. Borrowing as a source of funds. Capital as a source of funds. Liability management as a source of liquidity.* Asset and liability management in the banking system: *Evolution of asset and liability management. Bank capital as a constraint.*

The structure of the Federal Reserve System. Member bank reserves and the Federal Reserve. Impact of changes in bank reserves. The reaction of individual banks to reserve changes. The choice among the policy tools.

Managing monetary policy: *Interest rates and credit market conditions. The quantities of money and credit. Divergent movements in the indicators and the problems these pose.* Formulation and implementation of monetary policy: *Evolution of the Federal Reserve's monetary policy.*

PART V   THE PRINCIPAL FINANCIAL MARKETS

Supply and demand in the short-term corporate debt market. Large commercial banks as suppliers of short-term credit: *The changing role of large banks in the competition for funds. Negotiable CDs within the money markets. The Federal Reserve and the control of bank liabilities. Regulation Q and the CD market. The elements of competing for funds.* The commercial paper market as an alternative source of short-term debt for large corporations: *Commercial paper as a money-market instrument. Competition for funds in the money markets. Demand for funds in the commercial paper market. The events of 1970. Allocation of short-term corporate borrowing between the two markets.* Linkages between the internal and external dollar markets for bank loans and CDs: *Eurodollar and U.S. CD rates. Terms on Eurodollar versus U.S. dollar bank lending.* Short-term corporate debt and the financial system: A summary.

The primary bond market as a source of corporate funds: *The demand for funds. The supply of funds. Interest rates on corporate bonds. Bond market segments: Private placements and public issues. Adaptations of the corporate bond market. The bond market as a source of finance.* Pricing in the secondary market for corporate bonds: *The composition of outstanding corporate bonds. The variability of holding period returns for long-term corporate bonds. The basic equilibrium relationship—corporate bonds and stocks. Risk and the term structure of interest rates. The departures from equilibrium—the forces of supply and demand. The hypothesis of "efficient markets" in the bond market.*

The primary stock market as a source of corporate funds: *The demand for new equity capital. The supply of equity capital. The federal tax system and the equity market. Corporate pension funds, a consolidated perspective.* Pricing in the secondary market for common stock: *The valuation problem for common stocks. Holding period returns for common stocks. The basic equilibrium relationship among stocks: Risk-adjusted expected returns. The hypothesis of efficient markets in the stock market.*

part **I**

Introduction

1

Introduction to the financial system

FINANCIAL ASSETS AND LIABILITIES

Financial assets are future claims—claims against the prospective income or wealth of others. Financial liabilities are promises—promises to pay some specified portion of future income or wealth to others. Financial assets and liabilities, claims and promises, arise from the basic process of financing today's needs in exchange for some share of tomorrow's benefits. They provide the flexibility that allows our economic system to adapt to ever-changing needs and opportunities. They

3

spread the risks of various economic activities to a wide variety of financial participants. They promise expected returns in exchange for, and commensurate with, those risks.

There are a wide variety of financial promises and claims in our current financial system. Among them:

Demand deposits—promises to repay a specified sum upon the holder's demand.

Short-term debt—promises to repay a specified sum, plus some interest, in a relatively short period of time.

Long-term bonds—promises to pay a specified stream of income (coupons) over some longer period, and then repay a lump sum (the principal) at the conclusion of this period.

Common stock—ownership shares within a corporation with an implied promise to share in the pro-rata future income of the enterprise.

These financial assets, and others, have value today insofar as people believe they will have value in the future.

FINANCIAL MARKETS

Financial markets are the places where financial assets and liabilities are traded. Financial markets serve two important and related functions. First, they are the channels through which flows of savings are allocated to investment. For those who wish to save, they provide a variety of financial assets. For those who wish to raise funds for investment, they provide a variety of forms in which to raise those funds. Second, financial markets establish a pricing mechanism for financial assets, and this pricing mechanism plays a most important role in allocating saving to investment. Because of this pricing mechanism, funds can be raised by the private sector for relatively safe, profitable enterprises at a relatively moderate cost. More risky enterprises must be financed at higher costs. This pricing mechanism also assures that investors in riskier financial assets have the prospects of higher expected returns. This pricing mechanism tends to channel or allocate the scarce savings of a society toward the most profitable (and hopefully most productive) investments. It is a critical aspect of our overall economic and financial system.

Financial markets are often referred to as either primary markets or secondary markets. The *primary* financial markets are the media through which new financial assets are issued or generated. They are the media through which the demanders and suppliers of today's funds, the creators and acceptors of financial claims, meet. In these primary markets, financial assets are created and exchanged, satisfying in part the financial needs of both demands and suppliers of today's funds.

The *secondary* financial markets are the markets where many already outstanding financial assets are traded from old to new owners. These secondary markets provide "liquidity" for financial assets, making them more attractive to savers. Within these secondary markets, financial assets are priced such that they will be attractive to their prospective new owners. In particular, they seem to be priced such that their expected returns just compensate for their prospective risk.

The annual holding period returns from three very different types of financial assets (short-term U.S. Treasury bills, long-term U.S. Treasury bonds, and common stocks) are shown in Figure 1–1, for 1926–1976. Not

Figure 1–1
Annual returns for three different financial assets, 1926–1976 (In percent)

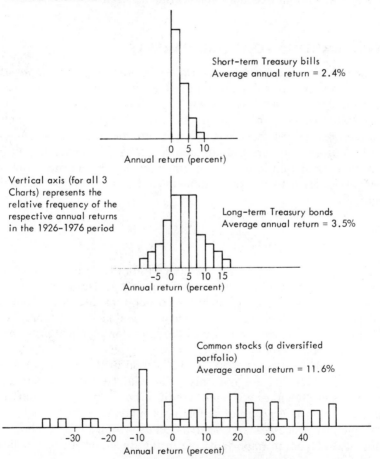

Relative frequency charts (histograms) represent the proportion of the years when the observed annual returns fell within certain ranges.

Source: Roger Ibbotson and Rex Sinquefield, *Stocks, Bonds, Bills and Inflation: The Past (1926–1976) and the Future (1977–2000)*, The Financial Analysts Research Foundation, 1977.

surprisingly, the annual holding period returns from common stocks have been quite variable, long-term Treasury bonds have been moderately variable, and short-term Treasury bills have been much less variable. By this measure, common stocks have been risky, long-term Treasury bonds have been moderately risky, and short-term Treasury bills have been safe. As we would expect, the average long-term returns from holding these alternative securities have also been quite different, compensating prospective investors over this long period for the different risks they have assumed. Figure 1–1 documents the fundamental dilemma of savers: relatively safe financial assets provide only modest returns (particularly after considering the effects of inflation), and larger expected returns appear to be available only in exchange for bearing a significant degree of risk.

PARTICIPANTS IN FINANCIAL MARKETS

The actors in the financial system are best analyzed by emphasizing a distinction between two major types of participants: the *primary financial sectors* and the *financial institutions*. The primary financial sectors are the participants engaged in the production, investment, and consumption of real economic goods and services. Their activities lead to important financial needs, and they are the ultimate suppliers and demanders of funds. The financial institutions, on the other hand, are intermediaries which channel funds between the suppliers and demanders of the primary sectors.

Primary financial sectors

The most important primary sectors within the domestic economy are business corporations, individuals (whom we will also refer to as "households"), and governments. Business corporations are one of the largest and most active demanders of credit in our financial system and have played a dominant role in many of the important cyclical processes and secular financial trends of recent years.

Individuals (or households) are the second of the important domestic sectors. Households are not only a large and important demander of credit, generally either consumer credit or home mortgages, but are also the most important group of suppliers of funds to our financial markets. The cyclical processes and secular trends within the household sector have also played an important role in the development of our financial markets.

Governments are the third and final domestic primary sector in our financial system. The spending programs of our federal, state, and local governments often exceed the tax revenues they raise. These activities are then financed through the financial markets, forming a third important demand for credit. In addition, these governments and their agencies hold a variety of financial assets so that governments can also be an important source of funds in our financial system.

To these three domestic primary sectors, the analyses of this book will often add a fourth: the international sector. The financial transactions associated with international trade give rise to inflows and outflows of funds in U.S. financial markets. Also, the special position of the dollar as an international currency has created a large foreign demand for dollar-denominated financial assets and liabilities. Much of this foreign demand for dollar financial assets and liabilities has resulted in credit flows in U.S. financial markets. For both these reasons, transactions with the rest of the world can have a major effect on U.S. financial markets.

Most of the important processes which will be described by this book will both originate with, and have important effects upon, these four primary sectors: business corporations, households, governments, and the international sector.[1]

Demand for funds in the primary sectors. Each of the four primary sectors has been an important demander of funds within recent years. The principal *flows* of credit to these sectors (the funds obtained from our domestic financial markets) are shown in Table 1–1, as the average annual flows for the period 1971–1975.[2] As Table 1–1 suggests, the credit flows in our financial markets in these years were dominated by the needs of our private sector participants: business corporations and households. Both the federal government and state/local governments borrowed somewhat less, on the average, although their borrowings were still substantial.

As Table 1–1 demonstrates, the two principal types of credit furnished to business corporations within recent years have been short-term and long-term debt.[3] The total borrowing of corporations has substantially exceeded their new equity issues. The household sector has been another large demander of credit within our markets in recent years. It has relied principally upon home mortgages to finance single-family

---

[1] Of course, the international participants in our financial markets could also be classified as either foreign individuals, corporations, or governments. But for analytical purposes, it will be most convenient to categorize all these within the primary "international" sector.

[2] The period 1971–1975 approximately spans a full economic cycle, and thus it is an appropriate set of years over which to compare the average flows of funds in the various sectors. By flow of funds, we mean that *net* increase in the outstanding financial liabilities of each of these sectors.

[3] Financial businesses (including any financial subsidiaries engaged in consumer financing for nonfinancial corporate parents) and unincorporated businesses have been excluded from these data for (nonfinancial) business corporations. In addition, farm businesses have also been excluded from these data and will continue to be throughout this book.

Table 1-1
Funds raised in financial markets by primary
sectors, average annual flows, 1971–1975
($ billions)

Nonfinancial business corporations	57.8
Short-term debt	17.4
Long-term debt	32.6
Equity (net new issues)	7.7
Households	58.4
Home mortgages	37.9
Consumer credit	14.7
Other...................................	5.9
Governments	43.7
Federal	29.1
State and local	14.6
International (rest of the world)	8.9

Source: Flow of Funds Accounts, Federal Reserve Board.

homes, and to a lesser extent upon consumer credit to finance other purchases.[4]

Net supply of funds from the primary sectors. Thus far, each of the primary financial sectors has been described as a demander of credit. In addition to being a demander of credit, each of the primary sectors also accumulates financial assets for various purposes and thus serves as a supplier of credit to the financial markets. Indeed, several of these sectors have been more important as suppliers of funds to our financial markets than as demanders of funds. The net financing supplied by each of these sectors in any given year is equal to the total funds it supplies to the financial markets through an increase in its holding of financial assets, minus the total funds it withdraws from the markets through an increase in its financial liabilities.[5] The average annual rates (for 1971–1975) of this supplied net financing are shown for each of the primary sectors in Table 1-2.

---

[4] For data purposes, it is difficult to estimate the actual credit demands and supplies of households. Most sources of data, including the Federal Reserve Board flow of funds data (upon which this work relies heavily), infer the financial transactions of households by treating them as the residual sector. This approach unfortunately includes several other entities, particularly personal trusts and nonprofit organizations such as churches, foundations, and schools. While this is regrettable for some purposes, there is no alternative in most instances but to rely upon these data. Fortunately, the flows of credit in these data are clearly dominated by actual households so that difficulties are minimized. Throughout this book, as we refer to households, however, we really mean the collection of households as individual units, personal trusts, and nonprofit organizations. Where this ambiguity might cause a special problem, it will be noted.

[5] Plus, in the case of corporations, through net new issues of equity.

Table 1–2
Net primary sector funds flows in financial markets, average annual flows, 1971–1975
($ billions)

	Funds raised	Funds supplied	Net supply
Nonfinancial business corporations	57.8	9.0	−48.8
Households	58.4	130.3	71.9
Federal government	29.1	6.5	−22.6
State and local governments	14.6	4.7	−9.9
International (rest of the world)	8.9	12.8	3.8

As the data indicate, the most important *net suppliers* of funds to the financial markets have been households. During the 1971–1975 period, the household supply of funds was supplemented, to a small extent, by funds from the international sector. The corporate and government sectors were *net demanders* of funds in the 1971–1975 period. The largest net demander of funds was the corporate sector.

Each new exchange of a financial claim between the suppliers and demanders of funds creates both a new liability and a new financial asset. Thus, the sum of the net funds supplied for all primary sectors should be approximately equal to zero in any given period. This is approximately true for the data compiled in Table 1–2.[6] Because the net financial supplies of all primary sectors must approximately balance each other in this way, it is clear that the financial activities of all primary sectors are inextricably related to each other. An expansion of the net external financing of one primary sector must be balanced by a roughly compensating increase in the funds supplied (or reductions in net external financing) of all other sectors and conversely.

Outstanding debt of the primary sectors. The continued accumulation over time of these flows of credit in the primary sectors results in a large outstanding stock of debt in our financial system. Figures 1–2 and 1–3 show the outstanding debt of the primary sectors from 1954 to 1977.[7] Figure 1–2 measures the outstanding debt in billions of dollars and dramatizes the rising debt levels—particularly in the early 1970s. These

[6] Actually, this concept of all net supplies of funds aggregating to zero has several difficulties. The net supply from smaller sectors, such as unincorporated business and farm business, has been excluded from Table 1–2, and in addition some small fraction of the financial assets can be transformed into real assets in financial intermediaries. Finally, there are some substantial statistical discrepancies in most data. For our purposes, though, the concept is still a useful and important one.

[7] Actually, these two figures document the total "credit market instruments" outstanding for each sector, which excludes various small amounts of short-term transient debt such as taxes payable and trade credit that arise in the course of various transactions and are not channeled through financial markets and/or institutions.

Figure 1–2
Outstanding debt obligations of primary financial sectors 1954–1977 ($ billions)

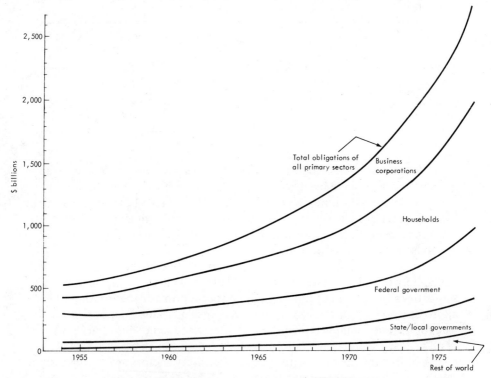

dollar totals can be quite misleading, however, given the expanding rate of inflation in latter period. Figure 1–3 measures the outstanding debt as a percent of GNP (gross national product), to indicate the debt relative to the size of the economic system and thus relative to the system's ability to repay.

As Figure 1–3 demonstrates, while the total debt of the primary sectors has grown substantially in absolute dollars, it has maintained a roughly constant relationship to GNP. This suggests that there has been no net accumulation or decumulation of total credit relative to current economic activity for the sum of all primary sectors in the overall economy. In view of the massive flows of new credit in the early 1970s, this relative stability is very surprising. As we shall later see, inflation was proceeding at a relatively rapid pace in these years, and this inflation was in part responsible for the large credit flows of recent years. But inflation was also eroding the value of prior financial promises relative to the current value of real goods and services as well as income. The size of debt burdens *relative* to GNP is affected by both of these factors; that is, it is affected not only by the rate at which new debt is being formed, but by the rate at

Figure 1–3
Outstanding debt obligations of primary financial sectors (As percent of current GNP)

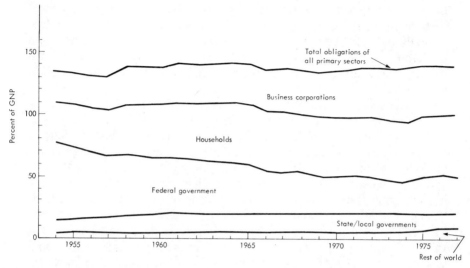

which old debt is being effectively "devalued" by inflation. As Figure 1–3 demonstrates, the level of all primary sector credit relative to GNP, that is, relative to national income, has remained approximately unchanged.

More importantly, as Figure 1–3 also demonstrates, there has been a substantial shift in the relative proportions of credit owed by the primary sectors. In 1954, the outstanding debt of the federal government, accumulated largely during World War II, dominated the outstanding debt. In subsequent years, however, the federal government undertook relatively little net new borrowing, and the federal government's proportion of total credit declined sharply. Whereas the outstanding federal debt represented almost half of all the outstanding debt of the primary sectors in 1954, it declined to only 19 percent of this same total by 1974. Between 1975 and 1977, the outstanding federal debt expanded rapidly because of the large federal financing needs associated with federal budget deficits. By the end of 1977 federal debt represented about 21 percent of total primary sector debt.

The long-term decline in the federal government's share of outstanding debt was almost exactly matched by the increasing debt of the private sectors. From 1954 to 1965, the outstanding debt of all sectors other than the federal government expanded, both in absolute dollars and, more importantly, relative to GNP. In this period, the increase in household debt was a particularly important force in the financial markets. In the 1965–1974 period, as the federal government's share of outstanding debt continued to erode, the credit demands of corporations led to a substantially increased level of debt in the corporate sector. During this period, the annual new credit demands of corporations were a most important force in our financial markets. In the 20-year period, the outstanding debt of state and local governments increased somewhat but remained at a moderate level relative to other sectors. The debt of the rest of the world (the international sector) in U.S. financial markets also remained small in relative terms.

The substantial shift away from federal government debt toward private sector debt has had important implications for all financial market participants. Because of the financial resources and powers of the federal government, its financial instruments are the least risky of our credit market instruments. On the other hand, the outstanding debt of the private financial sectors are perceived as much more risky, particularly during economic and/or financial crises, because of the very real uncertainties as to whether the promises embodied in these debts can be fulfilled. The shift from federal government debt to private debt has thus caused a shift in the average quality, or riskiness, of financial instruments available to savers. In large part, the development of our financial system in recent decades has revolved around the problems of managing this shift in the quality and perceived riskiness of financial instruments.

Financial institutions

One aspect of the reality of financial markets is the very large number of potential suppliers and demanders of funds. The logistics of managing these numbers would prove an enormous obstacle if all exchanges of financial assets had to be negotiated and completed directly between the ultimate demanders and suppliers of funds. Furthermore, the particular terms of the financial agreement acceptable to the suppliers of funds might often be incompatible with the credit needs of the borrowers. In response to these problems, a vast network of financial intermediaries has evolved.

These intermediaries accumulate funds by making promises to a very large number of potential suppliers, and they channel these funds to the various demanders of funds in today's markets. This process of "financial intermediation" has come to dominate our financial markets. Today most of the credit supplied by savers moves first through an intermediary and then to the financial markets. See Figure 1–4 for a diagram of this process.

As suggested above, the growth of financial institutions is due in part to the cumbersome logistics of the alternative: bringing large numbers of suppliers and demanders together directly. More fundamentally, however, financial intermediaries can (and often do) offer borrowers relatively long-term credit and yet offer individual savers the relatively short-term

Figure 1–4
Patterns of funds flows in financial markets

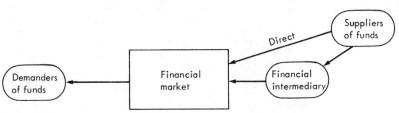

and liquid assets that they seem to prefer. In addition, by pooling large numbers of borrowers, financial intermediaries can offer a diversified, and thus relatively safer, set of financial assets to suppliers of credit. For all of these reasons, financial institutions have emerged as an essential part of our financial system.

Financial institutions compete with each other to provide the service of intermediating credit flows. Different types of financial institutions compete through the terms of the credit agreements they offer to potential borrowers. Financial institutions also compete to obtain the supplies of credit from potential savers by offering them attractive financial assets. Because most financial institutions are highly regulated by various state and federal regulatory bodies, success or failure in this competitive environment is often dependent upon the changing attitudes and decisions of the regulatory bodies. Throughout the postwar period, there have been substantial changes in the character of most of our financial institutions as they continue to compete with each other to provide intermediating functions.

Evolution of financial institutions.   A list of the important financial institutions in our economy is compiled in Table 1–3, along with the relative size of these institutions (as measured by total financial assets) in 1954, 1964, and 1976. Table 1–3 also shows these total financial assets as a percent of GNP in these respective years, thus relating the increasing size of financial institutions to the generally increasing size and scale of overall economic activity. For the sake of convenience, the set of all financial institutions has been divided into four general sectors in Table 1–3: the deposit institution sector, the insurance sector, the pension fund sector, and other special institutions. A thumbnail sketch of each of these institutions is offered in the Appendix to this chapter as a brief introduction to their role in the financial system. A detailed discussion of their behavior is contained in later chapters which analyze the financial markets in which the institutions operate.

As Table 1–3 suggests, the total assets of all financial institutions have been growing more rapidly than the underlying trends in economic activ-

Table 1–3
Total financial assets of various financial institutions (end of year, in $ billions)

	1954		1964		1976	
	$	Percent of GNP	$	Percent of GNP	$	Percent of GNP
Deposit institutions						
Commercial banks	$190	49	$306	48	$880	52
Savings and loan associations	32	9	119	19	392	23
Mutual savings banks	29	8	54	9	134	8
Insurance sector						
Life insurance companies	82	23	145	23	306	18
Property-casualty insurers	18	5	35	5	85	5
Pension fund sector						
Private penion funds	14	4	64	10	162	10
State/local govt. pension funds	9	3	30	5	120	7
Other institutions						
Mutual funds	6	2	29	5	41	2
Federally-sponsored credit agencies	4	1	16	3	98	6
Total		103		126		131

ity. This is due, in part, to the shift away from the relatively safe and liquid securities of the federal government to the relatively riskier and/or less liquid obligations of the private sectors. Hence, the need for inter-mediation is greater, and as a result, financial institutions have come to play a larger role in our credit markets. They now account for a substantial fraction of the outstanding amount of both debt and equity. The relative growth rates of different types of financial institutions is importantly affected by the composition of the financing demands of the primary sectors. For example, savings and loan associations grew very rapidly in the 1954–1964 period, in large part due to the rapid expansion of home mortgage credit in those same years. Similarly, commercial banks grew in the 1964–1976 period, due in part to the growth of business debt. Thus, the overall size and relative importance of different financial institutions depends upon the financial needs in the primary financial sectors.

There have also been substantial shifts in the relative mix of institutions' sources of funds—in response to both regulatory changes and the changing needs of fund's suppliers. As we shall see in later chapters, these shifts have been particularly rapid in the late 1960s and early 1970s—in response to the various strains in our financial markets.

Finally, as Table 1–3 suggests, commercial banks have continued to be by far the largest class of financial intermediaries in our economy. As opposed to other intermediaries which gather funds almost exclusively from domestic households, the commercial banks are engaged in lending to, and obtaining deposits from, all of the primary financial sectors: corporate business, households, governments, and the international sector. Banks are important because they are the most important source of short-term credit for corporations. They are also particularly important because their demand deposits form a major component of the economy's money supply, and as such, their activities are thought to have important interrelationships with the overall pace of economic activity. For all these reasons, commercial banks maintain a central position in the set of all financial intermediaries. This book will therefore devote considerable time to their evolution, regulation, and relationships with the rest of our financial and economic system.

Some important trends

The data on the behavior of the primary sectors and the financial institutions reveal four important trends:

1. Contrary to much popular belief, the debt levels within the overall financial system have remained quite stable when measured relative to GNP or national income (that is, relative to the size of the economic system and, hence our ability to repay).
2. There has been an important shift in the mix of outstanding debt (less U.S. Treasury debt and more private sector debt), lowering the average quality and increasing the average risk of the total debt.
3. Concomitantly, the private sectors (households and particularly business corporations) have become more highly leveraged; that is, they now have more debt relative to income and thus a riskier financial structure.
4. There has been a continual growth in the importance of financial intermediaries (as opposed to direct financing among the primary sectors), whether measured in absolute dollars or relative to the size of the economic and financial system. There have also been long-term shifts in the relative importance of different financial intermediaries.

We will return to these trends at several places throughout the remainder of this book.

THE FORCES AT WORK IN FINANCIAL MARKETS

Behavior in financial markets takes place in response to two types of forces. On the one hand, changes in the pace of real economic activity and in the rate of inflation create changing patterns in the demand and supply for funds in each of the different financial markets. These forces affect each primary actor, financial institution, and market differently. They can tend to drive apart the relative interest rates or expected returns on the different kinds of financial assets. These forces are often called the *forces of supply and demand* for specific types of credit.

On the other hand, there are a set of *equilibrium forces* which tend to keep the expected returns from different securities in a relationship that reflects only their relative risks and not their relative supplies. These forces arise in part as savers shift their funds to financial assets with higher (risk-adjusted) returns, and borrowers concentrate their financing in relatively "cheaper" markets. Financial institutions also play an important role in this process. They reallocate their existing assets to markets where prospective returns seem to be higher (in response to increased demands for funds) and away from markets where prospective returns seem to be lower (in response to excessive supply).

Thus, financial markets are subjected to a continually changing set of counteracting forces—the forces of supply and demand which can tend to drive relative interest rates apart—and to a set of equilibrium forces which tend to keep interest rates on different securities in a relationship reflecting (only) their relative risks.

Economic cycles, inflation, and the supply and demand for funds

Fluctuations in the pace of economic activity and inflation are two of the most important factors influencing the supply and demand for funds in the primary sectors. The recent growth rates of GNP in current dollars are shown in the top panel of Figure 1–5. These growth rates have been extremely variable, reflecting the substantial fluctuations in economic activity. A substantial fraction of this growth can be attributed to inflation. The lower line (in the top panel) has been adjusted for inflation such that it represents the growth rate of GNP measured in real terms.[8] Most of the fluctuations in the growth rate of nominal GNP have been caused by the changes in real GNP, though the process of inflation did become a major factor in the 1970s.

The second panel of Figure 1–5 shows the growth rate of total primary credit—the total amount of credit (debt) raised by all of the primary sectors. As the data demonstrate, these flows of new credit have also been quite variable. Furthermore, the fluctuations in total primary credit have been rather well correlated with the fluctuations in economic activity, as measured by the changes in nominal GNP. This suggests that a relatively constant amount of new credit has been used to finance each increment of dollar-valued economic growth, regardless of whether that nominal growth has reflected real growth or inflation.

---

[8] A broad measure of inflation designed particularly for this adjustment process, the GNP deflator, was used to produce the estimates of real GNP.

Figure 1–5

Rates of growth in real and nominal GNP, 1954–1977

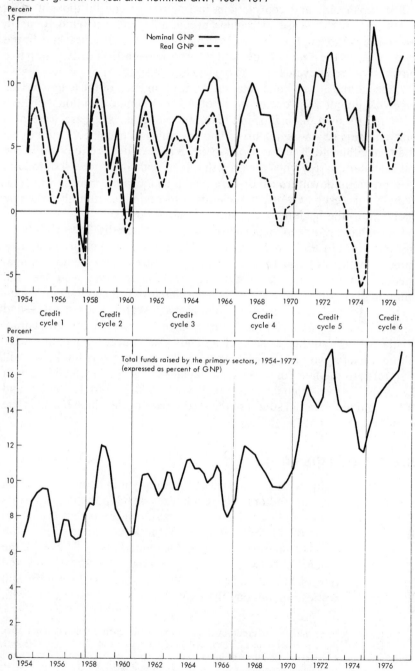

Concept of credit cycles

The expansions and contractions in Figure 1–5 can be thought of as cycles, not in the sense of regular predictable uniform fluctuations (a pendulum, for example), but in a less rigorous sense. The brackets in the lower panel of the figure divide the time period from 1954 to 1977 into five consecutive credit cycles and the beginning of a sixth. The detailed behavior of economic activity and total credit flows in each of these cycles was somewhat unique. The cycles were not only of unequal duration, but each cycle had its own distinguishing features. Nonetheless, there were also some common repeating features. The beginning of each new credit cycle (and hence the end of the previous cycle) has been defined to occur in the first calendar quarter when the growth rate in real GNP increased, following a previous downturn, and there was a significant expansion in total credit.[9] Thus, each new credit cycle tends to begin just after an economic recession, at the beginning of a subsequent expansion.

The behavior of economic activity and total credit flows follows a similar pattern in each credit cycle. At the beginning of each cycle, economic growth rates and total credit flows increase very rapidly. Somewhere in the middle of each cycle, they peak; later in the cycle they fall quite rapidly. More importantly, as later chapters will show, many financial variables (the credit needs of each primary sector, interest rates, and the flows through financial institutions) have behaved in certain characteristic patterns during these cycles. Thus, the concept of credit cycles will be a useful way of segmenting time. Throughout this book, we will often refer to the five complete credit cycles (1954–1975) which began in the following five calendar quarters 1954:3, 1958:2, 1961:1, 1967:2, and 1970:4, and to the initial stages of the sixth credit cycle which began in the second quarter of 1975 (1975:2).

OUTLINE OF THIS BOOK

This book begins with an analysis of the supply and demand for funds in each of the primary sectors. These analyses develop the determinants of these funds flows and examine their behavior in the recent credit cycles. The next part of this book introduces the three major equilibrium forces which influence interest rates in financial markets. It deals with the equilibrium relationship between the level of nominal interest rates and the expected rate of inflation; between interest rates on long-term and short-term securities; and among the expected returns on securities with

---

[9] Actually, the determination of credit cycles is arbitrary (for each is unique), and a good deal of judgment must be used to decide exactly where one cycle ends and another begins. Nonetheless, most observers would agree upon their approximate boundaries. This is much like the problem of defining economic cycles (expansions and recessions).

different risks. This part introduces the notion of private financial markets and discusses the functions that financial institutions perform in financial markets. Its final chapter presents an outline of the process which determines interest rates, credit flows, and changes in the structure of financial institutions. The next part deals with the rapidly changing structure of commercial banks, and the effect of the activities of the Federal Reserve System on funds flows and interest rates in the United States.

The final part presents a detailed analysis of the principal financial markets in the United States. It combines the behavior of the primary financial sectors, the equilibrium forces, and the role of the regulators in an explanation of interest rates and credit flows in these markets.

APPENDIX
BRIEF DESCRIPTIONS OF PRINCIPAL FINANCIAL INTERMEDIARIES

Deposit institutions: The commercial banks

Commercial banks not only comprise the largest single group of financial intermediaries in the United States, numbering about 15,000, but represent the largest asset holdings among financial intermediaries as well. They are a very heterogeneous group of financial intermediaries, ranging from a myriad of small local institutions serving the needs of their immediate geographic areas to a relatively small number of large money-center banks which compete worldwide in various financial service markets.

The main sources of funds of commercial banks are demand deposits (checking accounts), which constitute the bulk of the U.S. money supply, and time and savings deposits. In the postwar period, about half of all demand deposits and most of the time deposits have been supplied by households. Various regulatory authorities, particularly the Federal Reserve System, control the ability of banks to compete for deposit funds by controlling the maximum interest rates that they can offer to potential depositors. In general, no interest can be paid on demand deposits, though banks do offer various services for these deposits.

The assets of commercial banks are widely distributed among loans to business (mostly short-term), mortgages, consumer credit, federal government securities, and state and local government securities. In general, short-term loans to business are the most important asset of large money-center banks, while smaller local banks supply relatively more credit to households and governments in their respective communities.

Deposit institutions: The savings and loan associations

Savings and loan associations are the second largest group of financial intermediaries. They obtain their funds from time and savings deposits (often called savings shares) offered to households. Various regulatory authorities, particularly the Federal Home Loan Bank Board, control the maximum interest rates that can· be offered to potential depositors by savings and loans. The principal assets of savings and loans (S & Ls) are first mortgages on single-family homes located within 50 miles of the head office. To some extent, S & Ls have diversified into long-term mortgages on other types of real property in recent years, including multifamily residential and commercial mortgages.

Deposit institutions: Mutual savings banks

Mutual savings banks are state-chartered, state-supervised, deposit institutions operating for the benefit of their depositors. Most savings banks are located in the northeastern part of the United States. Like savings and loan associations, they draw funds from households by offering time and savings deposits. The maximum rates that savings banks can offer on their deposits are limited by various regulatory authorities. The principal assets of mutual savings banks are mortgages (chiefly residential mortgages), but to a lesser extent, savings banks have also become investors in corporate bonds and equities.

Insurance sector: Life insurance companies

Life insurance companies constitute the largest group of financial intermediaries in which the holding of financial assets is ancillary to their major activity—the provision of retirement income and death benefits. Nevertheless, as a result of the saving element (equal to the cash-surrender value of the contract) in all straight life insurance policies, these institutions have accumulated substantial pools of funds. Most of the funds of life insurance companies are provided by households via these long-term policy contracts. Most life insurance company assets are invested in long-term claims, primarily corporate bonds and mortgages.

Insurance sector: Property-casualty insurance companies

Property-casualty insurance companies, more commonly called fire and casualty companies, are primarily engaged in providing coverage against various kinds of risk. Coverage ranges from third-party liability, property damage, and theft to fidelity and surety bonds as well as accident and health insurance. While their main service from the consumer's point of view is coverage against risk, they also invest various funds in financial assets, including both the prepaid premiums from their customers' insurance policies and their own capital. In comparison with life insurance companies, they accumulate smaller asset holdings, but they are still important institutions in several parts of our financial markets.

Pension sector: Private pension funds

Private pension funds accumulate the annual contributions by employers (and to a smaller extent their employees) for eventual payment of employee retirement benefits. The postwar years have seen a general movement toward provision for retirement income as a concomitant of employment, and private pension funds have grown dramatically throughout the period. The details of most pension plans are complex, and they vary widely. Basically, the employer implicitly promises a stream of retirement benefits to the employees. This amount is often tied to the employee's final wage or salary level.

Pension sector: State/local government pension funds

State and local retirement systems (sometimes called "public pension funds") are designed to provide similar retirement benefits for employees of state and local governments. Unlike private pension funds, where the employer is the chief contributor, employers and employees contribute about equally to these public pension funds. Otherwise, in terms of their membership and operations, these systems are similar to private plans, except that they are administered by government officials. Like private plans, they have grown rapidly in the postwar period.

Investment companies: Mutual funds and closed-end funds

Mutual funds are the more important of two types of investment companies—the only type of financial institutions whose funds are chiefly raised by the sale of their own stock. These funds are then invested largely in stocks and bonds (of corporations they do not control or manage). Thus investment companies are primarily a device for indirect investment in common stock, or other securities, for individuals of limited means.

The two types of investment companies are the open-end, commonly known as the mutual fund, and the closed-end. By far the larger group, the shares of open-end investment companies are sold continuously. They are redeemable at any time at (or close to) asset value. Closed-end investment companies, on the other hand, operate like ordinary business corporations in that they acquire funds from time to time by making public fixed-price offerings of their securities.

Federally sponsored credit intermediaries

In addition to the private-sector institutions described above, there are special purpose credit agencies of the federal government. These credit agencies are another form of financial intermediary. They raise funds through the sale of their own securities in the federal agency securities market and channel those funds to various credit needs in the primary sectors. Most of the important credit agencies have been established to channel funds to the farm credit and home mortgage markets. These institutions have grown very rapidly in the postwar period, and they have become a major factor in the annual flows of credit in recent years.

QUESTIONS

1. How do the functions of the primary financial markets differ from those of the secondary markets?
2. What are the features which distinguish the primary sectors from the financial intermediaries?
3. What are the important trends in Figure 1–3 and Table 1–3?
   a. What forces have caused these trends? How might these trends be related to each other?
   b. What have been the most important consequences of these trends?
   c. What is the outlook for a continuation of these trends?
4. How might the movements in inflation and the pace of real economic activity affect the financial demands of the different primary sectors? The financial institutions?

REFERENCES

Arrow, Kenneth J. "The Role of Securities in the Optimal Allocation of Risk Bearing," *Review of Economic Studies,* vol. 31 (April 1964), pp. 91–96.

Goldsmith, Raymond W. *The Flow of Capital Funds in the Postwar Economy.* National Bureau of Economic Research, New York, 1965.

——. *Financial Intermediaries in the American Economy Since 1900.* Princeton, N.J.: Princeton University, 1958.

Gurley, John G. and Shaw, Edward S. *Money in a Theory of Finance.* Washington: The Brookings Institution, 1960.

part **II**

Primary Sectors and Their Financial Demands

2

Financing demands
of business corporations

The external financing of business corporations has had a clearly cyclical character as businesses have responded to the underlying cycles of real economic activity.[1] Inflation has also had a dramatic effect on the overall financing demands of business firms and on the channels through which they have raised funds. The business sector appears to be one of the primary forces which transmits the effects of changes in pace of real economic activity, and the effects of inflation, into pressures within credit markets. As we shall see throughout this book, the financing demands of business corporations have had an important impact upon the rest of the financial system.

---

[1] This chapter focuses on the financial behavior of nonfinancial business corporations. It does not deal with the financial choices of unincorporated business or of farm business, as the financing demands of these sectors are relatively much smaller. Neither does it deal with financial intermediaries.

In the short run, the financing demands of business corporations are determined by the relationship between their internally generated funds and their current rate of investment. In the long run, the pace of this investment is influenced by the prospective ability of corporations to generate profits. The financing demands of corporations are thus the complex time-varying result of the linkages between profitability, internal cash flows, and investment.

The net external financing demands of business corporations are shown in Figure 2–1. This external financing is defined as the net flow of funds to corporations from the financial system, that is, the increase in corporate financial liabilities plus net new issues of equity during the period, minus the increase in corporate liquid financial assets.[2] It is not only a measure of net corporate financing during the period but a measure of the net impact of the corporate sector upon the financial system.

As Figure 2–1 demonstrates, the net external financing demands of corporations have been highly variable.[3] Examining the 1950s first, we find external financing demands in this period were quite cyclical and fluctuated between 0 and 4½ percent of GNP. These fluctuations were roughly coincident with the fluctuations in the pace of economic activity in the economy as a whole. Beginning in the mid-1960s, however, a sharp uptrend was superimposed on this cyclicality. By 1973–1974, corporate external financing demands reached about 5 percent of GNP. This represented an extremely high, and probably unsustainable, level of external corporate financing.[4] That is, it would have been difficult for corporate financing to have remained at these very high levels for very long without enormous changes in the patterns of savings and economic activity. Indeed, as Figure 2–1 shows, corporate external financing soon collapsed (in 1975) back to the very low levels which had characterized the recessions of the 1950s.

A major source of this sharp increase in external financing demands was the substantial acceleration in the rate of inflation which took place during the late 1960s and early 1970s. The bottom panel of Figure 2–1

---

[2] To obtain net external financing demands, the increase in liquid financial assets has been subtracted from the total finance raised (net of refinancings) by corporations on the grounds that these funds are recycled back to the financial system. The external financing demands, as defined, are thus the best measure of *net* financing demands of corporations.

[3] In Figure 2–1, the external financing demands of business have been divided by GNP to measure them *relative* to the changing size of the economic and financial system.

[4] The net saving of the largest supplier of funds, households, has over this period averaged about 7½ percent of GNP. This sum is generally rather evenly divided between the net investment in consumer durables (auto, appliances, and so forth), the net investment in housing, the net financing of federal and state/local governments, and the net financing of corporations. In 1973–74, therefore, with corporate external financing demands at 5 percent of GNP, only very limited funds were available for satisfying these other important demands.

Figure 2–1

Net external financing demands of business corporations

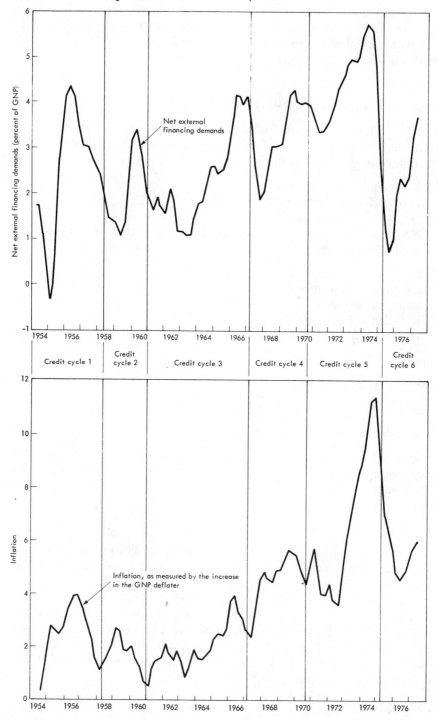

shows the recent behavior of the rate of inflation. Throughout this chapter, we will investigate the changing behavior of corporate external financing with special emphasis on its relationship to the pace of real economic activity and the rate of inflation.

DETERMINANTS OF CORPORATE FINANCING DEMANDS

The corporate demands for financing arise from the continual investment in new assets. The total financing demands of corporations can be attributed to increases in the following kinds of assets:

Increase in short-term assets
    Inventories (net new units of inventory)
    Net trade and consumer credit
    Net miscellaneous financial assets (excluding liquid financial assets, categorized separately below)

plus
Increase in long-term assets
    Plant and equipment
    Residential construction
    Direct foreign investment

plus

Increase in liquid financial assets

yields

Total financing demands

Figure 2–2 documents the recent patterns of total financing demands, highlighting two particular components: inventory investment, and plant and equipment investment.

Inventory investment

A substantial portion of the variability in the total financing demands is attributable to inventory investment. The region between the dotted and solid lines in Figure 2–2 shows the rate at which corporations have invested in new inventory. Inventory investment was a very cyclical component of total investment in the 1950s and early 1960s. In the late 1960s and early 1970s, however, the investment in new inventories was more stable. During the latter stages of the recession of 1974–1975, corporations sharply reduced their inventories, causing an extreme but short-lived plunge in new inventory investment.

Figure 2–2
Composition of total financing demands of business corporations

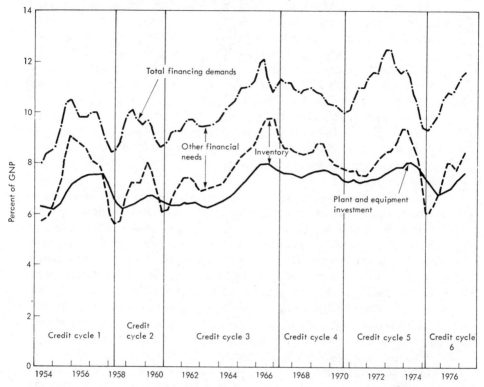

Net trade and consumer credit

For any particular firm, the difference between the trade credit granted to their customers and the trade debt accumulated from their suppliers is called *net trade credit.* As a rule, large corporations tend to extend substantial amounts of net trade credit, particularly to the smaller corporations that are their customers. Moreover, all nonfinancial corporations, taken as a group, are a net trade creditor to other economic participants—in particular, proprietorships, partnerships, and governments. In addition, corporations often extend credit to their retail customers in the form of consumer credit. In its role as a supplier of trade and consumer credit, the nonfinancial corporate sector functions to some extent as a financial institution by channeling funds to other economic sectors. As with inventories, there has been a substantial cyclical component to the increases in this class of financial asset. This has contributed to the cyclicality in total financing demands.

Plant and equipment and other long-term assets

For the corporate sector as a whole, the largest financing demand arises from investment in new plant and equipments as Figure 2–3 demonstrates. Expenditures on new capacity are critically dependent upon the current rate of market demand and businesses' expectations of the growth of these demands. As capacity utilization rises from a cyclical trough, there is often substantial slack capacity within an industry. Thus the rising demand generates relatively little need for plant and equipment additions. As an industry approaches full capacity, however, relatively small increases in market demand can generate relatively large percentage increases in the desired investment in new production capability. This process generates a clear cyclical component to plant and equipment additions.

For many types of plant and equipment, particularly large, more complex facilities, there can be substantial lead times involved in new capacity additions. In many corporations, a fairly long and time-consuming process is often involved in deciding to proceed with major capital investment plans. For many large projects there may also be substantial lead times involved in the actual construction of a facility once the decision to proceed has been made and the capital appropriated. Thus, while some plant and equipment spending adjusts rather quickly to changes in businesses' expectations of market demand and profitability, there is also a component which adjusts only slowly and with a lag to perceived market developments.

While the above process determines the *units* of new capacity added, the *actual dollar* spending on plant and equipment by business firms will also be dependent upon the prices of newly installed capacity. The prices of plant and capacity have recently been affected not only by the escalating prices of particular components, but by the substantially expanded environmental and other restrictions which can only be satisfied by more complex and costly equipment.

SOURCES OF BUSINESS FINANCE

Corporations meet some fraction of their financing demands from the cash flow generated by their own operations. These funds are called *internal funds* or *internal cash flow*. Internal cash flow is equal to retained profits plus depreciation (and any other noncash charges against income).[5]

---

[5] That is, internal cash flow is defined as sales revenues minus the outlays for production, marketing, and general administration, minus the reported cost of the inventories consumed by the production and sales processes, minus income taxes, interest, and dividends. In addition, a part of reported profits must often be used to replace consumed inventories at their new replacement cost. These funds are called the "inventory valuation adjustment," and they are not available to fund any of the new investment contained within our measure of "total financing demands." Hence, this inventory valuation adjustment (IVA) has been subtracted from retained profits when computing our measure of internal funds.

If the total financing demands exceed the internal funds, then corporations must obtain the remainder from external sources. The *externally raised funds* are the difference between total financing demands and internal funds.

Figure 2–3 shows the relationships among total financing demands, internal funds, and externally raised funds. As we have seen, there has been a clear but somewhat diminishing cyclical component in total financing demands through the last five credit cycles. There has also been an approximately synchronous cyclicality of internal funds. The significant cyclicality in the volume of funds raised externally by business corporations that was noted at the outset of this chapter has arisen because the magnitude of the swings in total demands has exceeded the magnitude of the swings in internal funds.

Table 2–1 shows these same data, averaged across the recent credit cycles. As Figure 2–3 and Table 2–1 demonstrate, there was an important

Figure 2–3
Changing balance between internal and external funds for business corporations

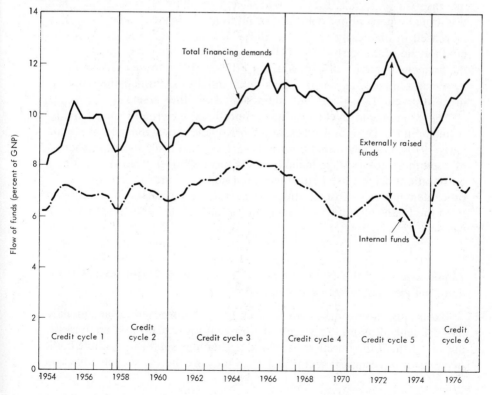

Table 2–1

Nonfinancial business corporations: internal funds versus externally raised funds*

	Credit cycle 1 1954:3 to 58:1	Credit cycle 2 1958:2 to 60:4	Credit cycle 3 1961:1 to 67:1	Credit cycle 4 1967:2 to 70:3	Credit cycle 5 1970:4 to 75:1
Total financing demands	9.4%	9.3%	10.4%	10.6%	11.2%
Internal funds	6.9	6.9	7.7	6.9	6.4
Externally raised funds	2.5	2.4	2.8	3.7	4.7
Ratio: external funds/ internal funds	36%	35%	36%	54%	73%

* All data are flows as a percent of GNP averaged over recent credit cycles.

set of diverging trends from the mid-1960s up through 1974. In the late 1960s and early 1970s, the flow of internal funds decreased substantially. Yet, investment (as measured by "total financing demands") continued to grow. This increased investment could be financed only with a sharp increase in external funds. Whereas externally raised funds had traditionally been about one third of internal funds (see Table 2–1), they increased dramatically to almost three fourths of internal funds in the credit cycle of the early 1970s. This represented a fundamental change in the financial behavior of corporations. In 1975–1976, these external funds demands plunged, as corporations substantially restrained their investment in inventories, plant and equipment, and other assets.

The pronounced cyclicality in corporations' externally raised funds. throughout the 1950s and 1960s, and the sizeable prolonged increase in the early 1970s, has meant that corporations have had a significant impact on all the other sectors in financial markets throughout this period. At times corporations have raised substantial amounts of funds, "crowding-out" other demanders. At other times, corporations have largely withdrawn from the financial markets, leaving these markets to other potential borrowers.

Liquid assets and the distinction between "externally raised funds" and "net external financing demands"

Externally raised funds can be used for two purposes: to accumulate liquid financial assets, or to invest in inventories, plant and equipment, and so forth. If they are used to build up liquid assets (for example bank deposits or government securities), then they are merely recycled back to the financial system to serve some other sector's financing demands. The impact of the corporate sector's financing demand on financial markets is thus best measured by their *net external financing demands,* which are externally raised funds minus the increase in liquid assets.

Figure 2–4 shows the recent history of externally raised funds and net external financing demands. For the most part, these two series have behaved similarly, experiencing a pronounced cyclicality in the 1950s, an enormous increase from the early 1960s up through 1974, and a plunge in 1975–1976. The two series do behave somewhat differently, however, due to the way firms manage their liquid assets. Corporations have traditionally used their liquid assets balances as a buffer in the financial process. As Figure 2–4 indicates, during the 1950s and 1960s, liquid assets were used as a *contra-cyclical* buffer, providing incremental finance during

Figure 2–4

External financing of business corporations*

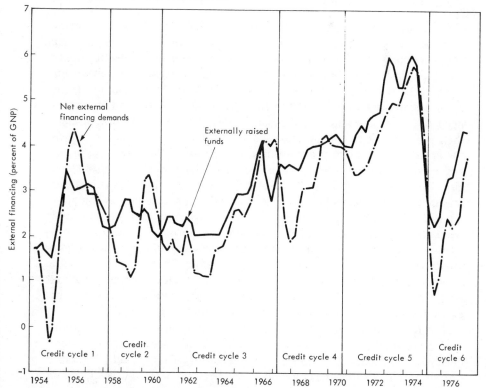

* Externally raised funds and net external financing demands (Seasonally adjusted, smoothed annual rates as percent of GNP).

periods of large financing demands and then being rebuilt during periods of smaller financing demands.

By the 1970s, however, liquid assets no longer played such a contra-cyclical role. Indeed, during the 1973–1974 period, when net external financing demands were very large, corporations chose to continue building their liquid asset buffers. As we shall document later, the dollar value of liquid asset balances had become small relative to various financial flows by the early 1970s. In these years, corporations believed that the reduced levels of liquid asset buffers were no longer sufficient relative to future uncertainties and thus could no longer be used to fund current total financing demands. As a result, the cyclical role of liquid assets changed in the 1971–1975 credit cycle, and contributed in an important way to the increase in externally raised funds at the peak period of net external financing.

THE IMPACT OF INFLATION ON NET EXTERNAL FINANCING DEMANDS

Inflation increases the financial demands of corporations in several important ways. Inflation raises the current nominal cost of any *new* plant and equipment, inventory, or financial asset investment needed to support real growth. In addition, inflation leads to higher wage rates, higher unit labor costs, and thus to increased production costs. In general, of course, these inflationary increases in the dollar value of expenses and investment need not pose a financing problem. If prices expand commensurately, then profit margins can be maintained and the dollar value of internal funds can be expanded proportionately. Unfortunately, however, in several recent inflations, corporations have not maintained their profit margins. For example, in the inflation of 1973–1974, unit labor costs and total unit costs grew faster than prices in the business sector (see accompanying table). As a result, operating profits fell sharply, and internal funds were unable to increase with the inflation. Furthermore, the pace of inflation in several key investment areas (inventories, and plant and equipment) was faster than the general pace of inflation. Thus, differences in the *relative* rates of inflation for investment, corporate revenues, and unit labor costs created a substantial external financing demand as investment expenditures increased faster than internal funds.

The forces which kept business firms from maintaining their margins during the inflation are complex and not fully understood. To some extent, corporate managers may have been misled by their high level of reported profits. Initially, at least, they might have been unaware that a significant portion of these reported profits was arising from understatement of the replacement costs of inventory and plant and equipment. Many corporations that were painfully aware of their true profitability and cash flow

Changes in unit costs, prices, and profits—nonfinancial
business sector, 1973–74

	Percent change			
Year	Unit labor costs	Total unit costs	Unit prices	Unit profits
1973	5.7	5.1	4.4	−1.7
1974	13.8	14.9	11.4	−18.9

problem, however, were still unable to raise prices on their products
enough to cover the increasing costs of investment. During an inflationary
period there are often enormous political pressures to hold down business
prices. These pressures can take either the form of implicit and subtle
"jawboning" from public officials or, as in recent periods, direct controls.
Furthermore, even without these constraints and pressures, corporations
may find it difficult to raise prices. The confidence of consumers is
adversely affected by rising inflation. An inflationary period may be a very
difficult time for a corporation to raise prices without adversely affecting
the final demand for its products. For a combination of these and other
reasons, the corporate sector has not raised prices rapidly enough during
inflationary periods to keep the growth in internal funds in line with the
growth in total financing demands. During these periods they have increasingly turned to external funds to fund their net new investment,
thereby swelling the demands they place on the financial system.

While thus far we have discussed only the corporate sector as a whole,
it is clear that the relative impact of inflation can be quite different for
different industries. In the first place, inflation itself does not proceed in a
uniform and homogeneous manner across all goods and services. More
typically, some particular prices and/or labor costs surge and are then
followed later by other prices and costs. In a rather uneven and heterogeneous manner, the inflation thus feeds through the economic system as a
whole. The extent to which corporations can raise prices in an inflationary
time varies unevenly across industries. At one extreme, in some of the
regulated industries, such as public utilities, there is very limited short-
run ability to respond to cost increases by raising prices. In some other
less-regulated and less price-sensitive industries, there is probably enough
flexibility to respond with price increases in the absence of explicitly
imposed price controls. However, for the corporate sector as a whole,
external financing demands appear to be clearly and directly related to the
changing pace of inflation.

The corporate income tax system compounds these difficulties. When
computing income for tax purposes, corporations are allowed to charge

depreciation only on the basis of historical costs (and some corporations choose to use a similar accounting system for inventories). Thus, income tax payments are based upon an overstated level of income. These increased corporate tax payments seriously erode after-tax internal cash flow during inflationary periods. Table 2–2 documents the importance of these tax effects during the inflationary period of the early 1970s. While reported profits grew throughout the period, the portion of these reported profits that arose from understatement of the replacement costs of inventory and plant and equipment grew to be very large. This was especially true in 1974.[6] As more and more of the funds represented by reported profits were necessary to replace existing inventory and plant and equipment, less and less was available to finance new investment in these areas. Since tax payments are based largely on reported profits, tax payments remained high and adjusted profits after tax fell precipitously. In 1974, the ratio of tax payments to profits available for new investment rose to 0.72. Because dividend payments continued to increase throughout the period, the volume of retained earnings (exclusive of the profits arising from the use of historic instead of replacement costs) was quite depressed. (Figure 2–5 documents in another way the substantial impact which inflation had on corporate profitability during this period.)

Table 2–2
Profits, taxes, and cash flows in the nonfinancial corporate sector 1973–1976 ($ billions)

	1973	1974	1975	1976
Reported profits	92.7	102.9	102.3	130.6
Inventory valuation adjustment (or "inventory profits")	−18.6	−40.4	−12.0	−14.1
Capital consumption adjustment	1.8	−3.0	−12.0	−14.5
Adjusted profits	76.0	59.5	78.3	101.9
Taxes	39.6	42.7	40.8	53.7
Adjusted profits after tax	36.4	16.8	37.5	48.2
Dividends	23.9	26.0	29.0	32.4
Adjusted retained earnings	12.5	−9.2	8.5	15.8
Ratio: Tax payments/adjusted profits	0.52	0.72	0.52	0.53

As a result of these factors related to inflation (depressed unit operating profits and large taxable inventory gains) and growing dividends, retained earnings were actually negative in 1974. Since total financing demands were large at that time, external demands were very large.

---

[6] As pointed out earlier, the part of reported profits that must be used to replace consumed inventories at their replacement cost is called the "inventory valuation adjustment" or "inventory profits."

Figure 2–5

Nonfinancial corporate profits after tax, reported and adjusted (as percent of GNP)

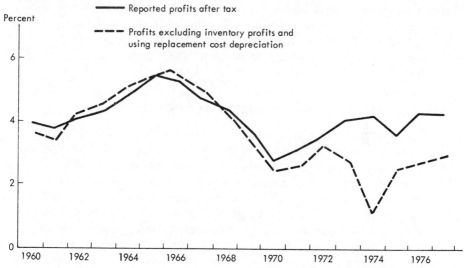

The process of inflation, particularly unanticipated inflation, is not without its blessings for corporations, however. The stock of corporate financial liabilities, their accumulated financial promises to others, are fixed in dollar amounts. Thus as the value of the dollar depreciates, the magnitude of these accumulated promises also depreciates relative to current financial flows and to the ability of corporations to generate income at the new higher price level. In a sense, an outburst of inflation actually generates additional potential debt capacity for a corporation. During an inflationary period, corporations can expand the rate at which they undertake new debt while still holding the levels of their outstanding debt constant relative to GNP and other measures of real or financial flows.

An outburst of current inflation can also affect the anticipated rates of future inflation. These anticipated rates of inflation will be reflected in the current terms on which corporations can extend new long-term promises. In particular, the long-term interest rates, or other terms of their financial liabilities, will be raised by expectations of future inflation.

An outburst of inflation thus appears to have several effects upon corporate financial flows: The external financing demands are increased, the ability to incur an enlarged stock of liabilities is increased; but to the extent that the inflationary burst raises expectations of future inflation, the interest costs of new long-term liabilities are increased. The effects of inflation upon the corporate sector are thus complex. For our purposes we will concentrate on the relationships between inflation, external financing demands, and interest rates. But these relationships are merely part of a larger and more complicated set of effects. Indeed, it is quite possible that the relationship between inflation and external financing demands will change in the future as corporations develop more adaptable pricing policies, and financial policies, to deal with the financial implications of inflation.[7]

SOURCES OF EXTERNALLY RAISED FUNDS

New external funds can be raised in financial markets by issuing financial promises, either in the form of increased short-term debt, increased long-term debt, or new equity issues. The principal source of short-term debt for corporations has been the commercial banking system. The principal sources of long-term debt for corporations are corporate bonds and mortgages. Corporate bonds, the general long-term debt obligations of corporations, have generally been the dominant source of long-term debt for manufacturing corporations. Mortgages have also been an important source of finance in the corporate sector, particularly for financing real property such as office buildings, shopping centers, and apartment buildings.

In addition, commercial banks have often made "term loans" to corporate business. Indeed, more than one third of all bank loans in recent years have been term loans. Term loans are generally considered to be intermediate-term finance, being longer than one year (the arbitrary break point for most definitions of short debt) and yet shorter than the typical 15-year to 30-year maturities of "long-term debt." Because of definitional problems and corresponding deficiencies in our data, we will include all bank loans within "short-term debt." However, a significant fraction of this bank debt would be more accurately described as "intermediate-term debt."

Historical pattern of new funds raised in financial markets

Figure 2–6 displays the changing patterns of externally raised funds. In addition to the cyclicality in the total of these new funds, which we have already discussed, there appears to be a clear cyclicality in the composition of these funds. In the early phases of each credit cycle, long-term sources of

---

[7] For further analysis of the impact of inflation on business firms see "Inflation Accounting and Nonfinancial Corporate Profits: Physical Assets" and "Inflation Accounting and Nonfinancial Corporate Profits: Financial Assets and Liabilities," J. B. Shoven and J. I. Bulow, Brookings Papers on Economic Activity, 3:1975 and 1:1976; G. M. von Furstenberg and B. G. Malkiel, "Financial Analysis in an Inflationary Environment," *Journal of Finance* (May 1977).

Figure 2–6
Composition of externally raised funds (Seasonally adjusted, smoothed flows as a percent of GNP)

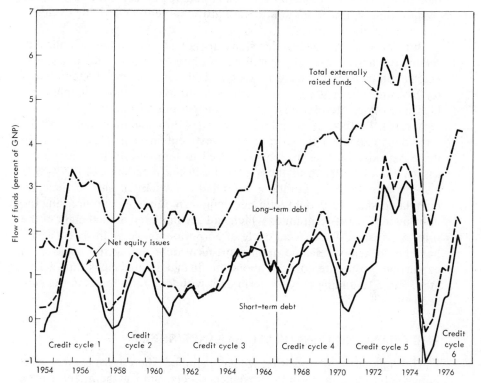

funds (particularly long-term debt) are the principal sources of new funds. Towards the middle of each credit cycle, as total new funds are usually accelerating rapidly, the increase in long-term debt actually declines. In this period, short-term debt becomes the principal source of funds raised in financial markets. And finally, toward the end of each credit cycle, in the economic recession or slow-down, the increase in short-term debt declines rapidly and long-term debt resumes its role as the principal source of external funds.

Alternative strategies for raising new funds

The clear cyclical patterns of raising new funds are attributable to corporate financial decision making. To a large extent, corporate financial managers attempt to match the "maturity" of their liabilities to the "maturity" of their assets. Thus, other things being equal, they attempt to fund increases in short-term assets with short-term debt and increases in long-term assets with long-term funds. To a large extent, the cycles in the composition of new funds sources are attributable to underlying cycles in the composition of assets.

But corporate financing decisions do not always follow a policy of relatively passive maturity matching. As interest rates in financial markets fluctuate, aggressive corporate financial managers may be tempted to try to "time" their long-term debt issues to avoid periods of relatively high long-term interest rates and exploit periods of relatively low long-term rates. In 1968–1969 and again in 1973–1974, the increases in short-term debt exceeded the corporate investment in short-term assets. In these periods, short-term debt was used to temporarily fund long-term assets. Following each of these periods, in the recessions of 1970–1971 and again in 1975, corporations refunded a substantial part of their accumulated short-term debt with new long-term funds, thus redressing the imbalance of short-term funds which had accumulated at the height of the prior expansion. The typical cycle of corporate financing in recent years has been a heavy reliance upon short-term debt during the peak of an expansion, corporate concern about the financial imbalances thus generated, and a refunding of short-term debt with long-term funds in the subsequent recession.

THE CHANGING CORPORATE BALANCE SHEET

Throughout the periods that we have studied, there have been several important trends in corporate balance sheets, among them: increasing levels of debt relative to equity and decreasing levels of liquid asset balances. These factors have contributed to a more financially leveraged, and perhaps a more fragile, corporate financial structure.

In the early 1950s, debt comprised a relatively modest fraction of the capital structure of corporations. Moreover, in the 1950s, the majority of the additions to capital came from equity (retained earnings and new issues of equity) instead of debt.

In the 1960s and 1970s, in contrast, the debt being added to corporate balance sheets far exceeded the equity being added. Throughout these several credit cycles, therefore, the balance sheets of business corporations have been evolving rapidly toward a more highly leveraged position.

In addition, in recent years corporate holdings of liquid assets have consistently declined as a percent of GNP. And relative to outstanding corporate debt, there has been a drastic erosion of liquid assets. Figure 2–7 shows liquid asset balances, and outstanding short-term and long-term debt, all as a percent of GNP over the past two decades.

Figure 2-7
Trends in the financial condition of business corporations (Levels, seasonally adjusted, as a percent of GNP)

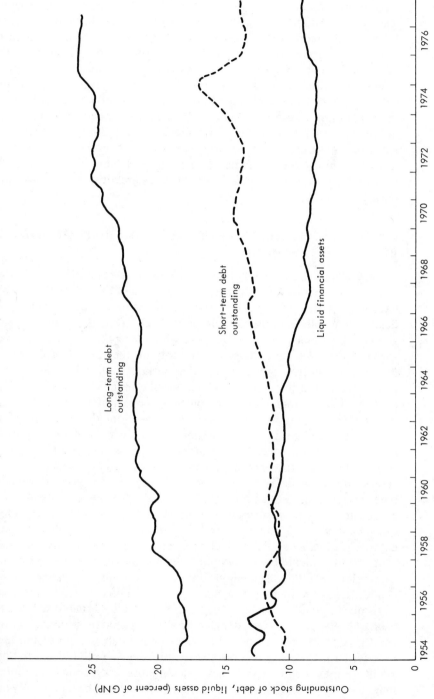

Corporate balance sheets have evolved toward this more leveraged and less liquid position for a variety of reasons. After the mid-1960's, total financing demands grew more rapidly than internal funds leading to a sustained increase in the demand for external funds. Faced with these large external demands, corporations chose to restrain the growth in their liquid assets and to raise large sums in the financial markets. Theoretically, most of these funds could have been raised by new equity issues, thus maintaining corporate debt positions at their historical level. Indeed in the 1971–1972 period, the new issues of equity did soar to new highs. But even these issues of new equity were insufficient to offset the trend toward more debt. On balance, corporations chose to fund most of their needs with debt, and corporate debt burdens grew rapidly throughout the period.

PROFITABILITY, THE MARKET VALUE OF THE FIRM, AND BUSINESS INVESTMENT

Throughout this chapter, business firms have been portrayed as relatively active demanders of credit. Our analysis of their financial decisions has suggested that businesses take the investment requirements of production and sales and the volume of internally generated funds as given, and use the financial markets to raise whatever volume of external funds is necessary. We have chosen to accentuate the impact of corporation investment patterns upon the financial markets, rather than the impact of conditions in the financial markets upon the investment plans of corporations. This characterization of business corporations is, in fact, quite different from the images we will develop of some other primary sectors, where we will instead accentuate their responsiveness to financial market conditions. By and large, the empirical evidence supports the accentuation we have chosen. The expenditures of the corporate sector on new assets appear to be relatively insensitive to current interest rates and other financial market conditions. Indeed, the periods of largest external corporate financing correspond closely with the periods of highest interest rates, and not vice versa, suggesting at the very least that corporate external financing is relatively undeterred by high nominal interest rates.

It is not difficult to understand why business firms are such active demanders of funds. Their investment needs frequently cannot be postponed, nor is the interest rate on borrowed funds a major factor in their decisions to invest. Consider, for example, a typical firm at the peak of an economic expansion. The demand for their products is high, and they need further inventory and other working capital to support the higher production rates consistent with their customers' needs. The cost of inventories may well be rising rapidly as inflation accelerates. The interest rates on short-term funds, however high, still seem to be a relatively small price to pay for the ability to keep their current plants operating at capacity. Furthermore, new capacity expansion programs seem quite attractive at this time, and the cost of funds seems to be a minor factor relative to the possible returns from new capacity.[8]

Also, the corporate debt markets have developed in such a way that they can supply the quite variable external financial demands of business. The short-term corporate debt markets, especially the market for bank loans, have become very effective conduits for raising large amounts of external funds on relatively short notice. Furthermore, the long-term corporate debt markets have also developed into effective conduits, at least for the financial demands of large creditworthy business firms. It was primarily through these two sets of markets that business firms obtained their external funds in periods of very large demands, such as 1973–1974.

In the long run, however, the pace of business investment is responsive to trends in current profitability and prospective profitability. It is this profitability which ultimately controls the pace of business investment and constrains the long-run financing demands of the corporate sector.

Profitability and rate of return on corporate assets

Corporate profitability is one of the most closely monitored and widely discussed financial variables. Yet, it is one of the most difficult to measure. In the final analysis, the rate of current "profitability," unlike cash flows, can be imputed only after some reasonably heroic assumptions, particularly regarding the appropriate rate of depreciation on capital equipment and the values of consumed inventories. Data on reported profits are readily available for all publicly held corporations, but as the field of financial accounting makes so clear, these reported profits are not necessarily an accurate reflection of underlying economic gains. The problems are compounded by inflation, which obfuscates many of the relationships and judgments that must be made.

For our purposes here, we will rely upon an estimate of *adjusted returns to total capital,* which is the sum of reported corporate profits after tax (with three separate adjustments) plus the interest paid to corporate debt-holders. The first adjustment to profits after tax subtracts the inventory valuation profits which occur when corporations impute a lower value to consumed inventories than their current replacement cost.[9] The

---

[8] Compare this to the situation faced by the business firms' major competitor for funds, the household borrower. For a prospective homeowner, the decision to move to a new, larger home (and incur mortgage debt) is quite postponable, and the interest cost of the mortgage is one of the major costs (perhaps *the* major cost) of prospective housing. Prospective mortgage borrowers may thus be very sensitive to high interest rates, preferring to wait until a more desirable time to purchase a new home. Indeed, as we shall see, they do appear to be much more sensitive to high interest rates than business firms.

[9] This adjustment is merely the "inventory valuation adjustment" which has been discussed before.

second adjustment subtracts the component of profits which occurs because corporations impute a lower value to the depreciation of their capital goods than the current replacement cost. The third adjustment adds back an additional component of profit which is omitted because corporations sometimes use accelerated depreciation methods rather than straight-line depreciation methods. In addition, as we have seen, business firms have been adding more debt to their financial structures. The interest paid on this debt is a return to the debt-holders. To analyze the behavior of the returns to capital when debt levels have been rising, therefore, we examine "adjusted returns to total capital," that is, the sum of adjusted profits after tax (the return to the equity holders) and interest paid (the return to the debt-holders).

Finally, in order to obtain a *rate of return* on total assets, that is, profitability as a percent of assets, we shall divide our measure of profits by a measure of the current value of these assets. The graph in Figure 2–8 shows the *adjusted returns to total capital* as a percent of the replacement cost of total assets for the corporate sector.[10]

Market value of corporations

An interesting perspective on estimates of future profitability can be obtained by examining the market value of corporations, that is, the sum of the market value of both their outstanding debt and equity. The full stream of prospective future corporate returns will accrue to either the debt-holders or the equity holders. Thus, the total market value of a company should be equal to the present value of the future returns that both groups of investors are expecting the underlying assets to produce. Rising market values should reflect rising estimates of future returns.[11]

Figure 2–9 shows the ratio of the total market value to the replacement costs of total assets for the nonfinancial corporate sector as a whole. When this ratio is greater than unity, investors are presumably expecting future returns whose present value is greater than the current cost of reproducing the corporate sector's total assets. Thus, when this ratio is greater than unity, investors are likely to believe that new investment is worthwhile, for the present value of its benefits are likely to exceed its

---

[10] For a discussion of this and other measures of profitability, see M. Feldstein and L. Summers, "Is the Rate of Profit Falling?" Brookings Papers on Economic Activity, 1:1977; and von Furstenberg and Malkiel, "Inflationary Environment," and Patrick J. Corcoran, "Inflation, Taxes, and Corporate Investment Incentives," Federal Reserve Bank of New York, *Quarterly Review* (Autumn 1977).

[11] For a discussion of these measures, see Daniel M. Holland and Stewart C. Myers, "Trends in Corporate Profitability and Capital Costs," Working Paper, Sloan School of Management, MIT, 1976.

Figure 2–8
Trends in corporate profitability

costs.[12] Unfortunately, when this ratio is less than unity, it indicates that new investment (identical to, or comparable to, the existing assets) is not likely to produce benefits which exceed its cost.[13]

From 1960–1965, the actual rates of profitability increased as shown in Figure 2–8. The data in Figure 2–9 suggest that investors seemed to extrapolate these rising profit rates into the future. They raised the market value of the assets owned by corporations well above their replacement cost. This provided a strong positive signal and incentive for businesses to expand their rate of investment. As actual profitability declined sub-

---

[12] For a discussion of the linkage between this ratio and investment, see James Tobin, "A General Equilibrium Approach to Monetary Policy," *Journal of Money, Credit, and Banking* (February 1969), pp. 15–29, and George M. von Furstenberg, "Corporate Investment: Does Market Valuation Matter in the Aggregate?" Brookings Papers on Economic Activity, 2:1977.

[13] Of course, at the margin there may always be new investments (whose characteristics are quite different from the existing assets) which appear to be worthwhile, regardless of the market value of the existing assets. Nonetheless, particularly in the aggregate, the almost continual decline in the ratio shown in Figure 2–9 (from 1965 to 1974) means that estimates of future profitability, and incentives for capital investment, were most likely being drastically reduced.

Figure 2–9
Market's expectation of future profitability

The ratio of the total market value of (nonfinancial) business corporations to the replacement cost of their net assets.

Source: Economic Report of the President, 1977. The data were obtained from the Council of Economic Advisors and other sources.

sequently, however, the market's estimate of the value of the assets held by corporations fell sharply relative to their replacement cost. By the mid-1970s, investors had such a depressed or uncertain outlook for future profitability that they were willing to pay much less for American business firms than it would cost to reproduce their assets at current replacement costs. The decline in profitability and in this ratio of market value to replacement cost raised serious questions about the market's outlook for the prospective profitability of new investment. It provided a strong negative or cautionary signal to business firms as they contemplated investing in new capacity or products.

Net investment

Figure 2–10 documents the recent patterns of business fixed investment (primarily plant and equipment). This time series shows some similarities to the time series of profitability and market value. But the differences are

Figure 2–10
Trend in corporate investment

Business fixed investment (in real terms) as a percent of GNP (in real terms) over time. Both business fixed investment and GNP have been deflated by their respective deflectors to put them in real (inflation-adjusted) terms.

Source: Economic Report of the President, 1977. Data obtained from Department of Commerce.

particularly interesting. Up through 1963, business investment remained at a relatively low level. Then, responding to rising current profitability and prospects of continued high profitability, investment rose sharply from 1964 to 1966. It declined somewhat from 1967 to 1971, but then rebounded in 1973 and 1974, only to decline again to relatively low levels in 1975–1976 (this same phenomenon was evident in Figure 2–2). Evidently, capital investment responded to current profitability and prospective profitability but with a lag. In view of the nature of capital spending (discussed earlier) this is not too surprising.

In retrospect, however, the rebound of capital investment in 1973–1974 was surprising. In the face of sharply declining profitability (after adjustment for inflation) and the sharply declining volume of internal funds, corporations actually increased their (real) capital spending. They continued to invest, indeed increased their investment plans, despite the shortage of profits and internal cash. To some extent, corporate managers may have been emphasizing growth and market share goals and paying relatively little attention to profitability and cash flows. To some extent, they may have been temporarily misled by the higher levels of reported profits despite the erosion of cash flows caused by inflation. To some extent, they may have believed in the future profitability of this investment despite the levels of current profitability and the clear signals from financial markets about expected future profitability. To some extent, the "scarcity" psychology of the times and concern over a potential "capital shortage" may have induced them to invest before the prices of capital equipment and the costs of financing rose even further. Indeed, the investment during these years may indeed turn out to have been a sensible choice, given the rising costs of capital equipment. Nonetheless, this persistent investment in the face of a decline in actual profitability was the source of the enormous external financing demands of those years.

The collapse of capital spending in 1975–1976 is also interesting. It is counterpart of the surprising increase in 1973–1974. Despite a rebounding economy, an increase in profitability and cash flows, and a turnaround in market values relative to replacement cost, capital spending slumped back to the low levels that characterized the early 1960s. Relative to other economic sectors, capital spending in these years was severely depressed.[14] Corporations were emphasizing the goals of improved profits and improved rates of return, and they curtailed new investment until these goals were met. The effect of the poor profitability in 1973–1974 was clearly evident in the investment expenditures in the following three years.

SUMMARY

Corporate external financing demands are determined by the relationship between total financing demands and internal funds. When these two series diverge, as the pace of investment and profitability diverge, the demand for external funds increases. In particular, when increased inflation has caused these two series to diverge, corporations have continued to invest in expanded inventories and capital equipment in the face of inflation-eroded internal cash flows. In the short run, there appears to be little immediate feedback causing a slowdown in the rapid pace of investment. Furthermore, in the short run, business investment and business demands for external finance seem to be quite unresponsive to rising interest rates. In the long run, however, the pace of investment seems to respond to current profitability and signals from the financial markets about future profitability. In the long run, then, it is unlikely that total financing demands and internal funds will diverge too far for too long. The long-run linkage between corporate investment plans and prospective

---

[14] See, for example, "How's the Recovery—Compared to What?" The Morgan Guaranty Survey (March 1977).

profitability is the equilibrium force that ultimately tends to limit the magnitude of external financing. In the future, financial shocks (like rapidly accelerating inflation) may once again dramatically expand corporations' external financing and place considerable strains upon financial markets. But these financing demands will be ultimately reduced by the decisions of corporate managers themselves, restoring a more normal relationship with the rest of the financial system.

Table 2A
Sources and uses of funds—nonfinancial corporate business sector (1972–1977) ($ billions)

	1972	1973	1974	1975	1976	1977
Total operational needs	129.3	152.5	156.3	123.3	171.4	208.0
Plant and equipment	86.9	102.2	113.0	107.4	120.1	146.1
Inventory investment	7.6	13.3	12.9	−12.1	13.8	17.2
Net trade credit	7.2	5.3	4.4	0.7	6.7	7.6
Other*	27.6	31.7	26.0	27.3	30.8	37.1
Plus increase in liquid financial assets	9.0	6.7	2.1	17.8	19.6	7.7
Yields total financing demands	138.3	159.2	158.4	141.1	191.0	215.7
Minus internal funds	80.8	83.8	75.7	107.8	125.8	135.9
Yields externally raised funds	57.5	75.4	82.9	33.3	65.2	79.8
Comprised of						
Short-term debt	16.9	38.0	43.6	−15.9	16.5	30.6
Bank loans	12.5	29.4	29.9	−12.4	1.6	20.7
Profit tax liabilities	−0.1	2.3	1.0	−3.2	6.8	−3.6
Other short-term debt†	4.5	6.3	12.7	−0.3	8.1	13.5
Long-term debt	29.7	29.5	35.0	39.4	38.1	45.5
Bonds	12.7	11.0	21.3	29.8	25.3	24.5
Mortgages	17.0	18.2	13.7	9.6	12.8	21.0
Equity	10.9	7.9	4.1	9.9	10.5	3.7
Memo:						
Net external financing (or						
net pressure on financial markets)	48.5	68.7	80.6	15.5	45.6	72.1
Net external financing as percent						
of GNP	4.1%	5.2	5.7	1.0	2.7	3.8

* Includes home and multifamily construction expenditures made by nonfinancial corporations plus their expenditures on mineral rights, consumer credit, miscellaneous assets minus miscellaneous liabilities, plus an account called discrepancy.
† Includes commercial paper, acceptances, finance company loans, and U.S. government loans.

QUESTIONS

Table 2A shows the sources and uses of funds in the nonfinancial business corporation sector from 1972 through 1977.

1. What caused net external financing demands to rise in 1973 and 1974?

2. Why did the overall volume of external financing shrink in 1975?

3. Why did the volume of long-term debt issues remain high in 1975 and 1976 while the volume of short-term financing collapsed?

4. What were the consequences of this financing behavior for the balance sheet of business, for commercial banks, for investment bankers?

5. How did inflation affect corporate profitability during the 1970s?

6. What has been the recent behavior of corporate profitability? Of business investment? Of the ratio of the market value of corporations to the replacement cost of their assets?

7. What is the outlook for the volume and composition of business financing demands today?

REFERENCES

Corcoran, Paul J. "Inflation, Taxes, and Corporate Investment Incentives," *Quarterly Review,* Federal Reserve Bank of New York, September 1976.

Feldstein, Martin, and Summers, Lawrence. "Is the Rate of Profit Falling?" *Brookings Papers on Economic Activity,* vol. 1 (1977).

von Furstenberg, George M. "Corporate Investment: Does Market Valuation Matter in the Aggregate?" *Brookings Papers on Economic Activity,* vol. 2 (1977).

"Recent Developments in Corporate Finance," *Federal Reserve Bulletin,* Board of Governors of the Federal Reserve System, June 1978.

3

Financial decisions
in the household sector

In their role as consumers, households provide the consumer demand that stimulates most real economic activity. Households are also very important forces in the financial markets. Their financing demands have given rise to the mortgage and consumer credit markets. In addition, the net supply of funds from households provides almost all of the net funds raised by the other primary sectors.

ACQUISITION OF ASSETS

Households acquire a wide variety of real and financial assets. Their real asset purchases are comprised of investments in housing and consumer durables. Their financial asset acquisitions take the form of deposits at commercial banks and thrift institutions, the purchase of the debt securities of corporations and governments, contractual retirement and savings plans, and corporate equities. There has been a substantial change in the relative amounts invested in each of these different types of assets over the past three decades. Table 3–1 presents some data on the pattern of household acquisition of assets.

Table 3–1
Household acquisition of assets (Data are flows as a percent of GNP averaged over five recent credit cycles)

	Credit cycle 1 1954:3 to 58:1	Credit cycle 2 1958:2 to 60:4	Credit cycle 3 1961:1 to 67:1	Credit cycle 4 1967:2 to 70:3	Credit cycle 5 1970:4 to 75:1
Net investment in real assets	5.32	3.85	3.49	2.99	3.60
Residential construction	3.79	3.04	1.96	1.32	1.82
Consumer durables	1.53	0.81	1.53	1.67	1.78
Increase in financial assets	6.37	6.40	7.30	7.40	9.27

The pace of household net investment in housing was much higher in the 1950s than it has been since. Net investment in new consumer durables has increased somewhat, although in an irregular way. The most significant change is that which has taken place in the pace of household financial asset acquisitions. It increased from slightly more than 6 percent of GNP in the early 1950s to over 9 percent of GNP by the early 1970s.

Several factors contributed to the decline in the rate of household investment in residential construction. Because of World War II and to a lesser extent the Korean involvement, consumers entered the 1950s with a substantial volume of financial assets, having found it difficult to buy homes and other goods during the war efforts. There was, therefore, a substantial rebuilding and enlarging of the housing stock in the 1950s. In addition, in the late 1960s and early 1970s, there was a substantial shift toward multifamily residences and away from single-family homes. As households decided to live in apartments rather than purchase homes, they have avoided a substantial new investment in real assets and substituted instead an annual cash outlay in the form of rent.

SOURCES OF EXTERNAL FINANCE

In order to fund their purchases of homes and durables, households have relied in part upon several forms of external borrowing. The net borrowings, that is, the net increases in various financial liabilities, are shown in Table 3–2 for recent credit cycles. As this table suggests, the net borrowings or credit demands of households have been dominated by home mortgages.[1] Consumer credit has been a smaller, but still important,

---

[1] Mortgages on family residential structures housing between one and four families.

Table 3–2
Sources of external finance for households (Data are flows as a percent of GNP averaged over five recent credit cycles)

	Credit cycle 1 1954:3 to 58:1	Credit cycle 2 1958:2 to 60:4	Credit cycle 3 1961:1 to 67:1	Credit cycle 4 1967:2 to 70:3	Credit cycle 5 1970:4 to 75:1
Total net borrowings	3.90	3.75	3.84	3.19	4.45
Increase in home mortgage debt	2.54	2.28	2.17	1.55	2.74
Increase in consumer credit	0.87	0.85	1.03	0.93	1.24
Increase in other financial liabilities	0.49	0.61	0.64	0.71	0.46

source of external finance. The other forms of borrowing, chiefly bank loans and security credit, have formed a relatively less significant percentage of the total.

CYCLICAL PATTERNS IN REAL ASSETS AND THEIR FINANCING

Household borrowing is closely tied to the purchase of specific real assets since these real assets are often used as the collateral for the borrowing. Thus, the cyclical fluctuations in these borrowings have been closely related to the cyclical fluctuations in household purchases. Figure 3–1 shows the net flows of new residential construction and new home mortgage borrowings for households over the last two decades. Similarly, Figure 3–2 shows net investment in consumer durables and increases in consumer credit over the same period.

Mortgages and housing

Figure 3–1 documents a clear cyclical relationship between interest rates, home mortgage borrowings, and household net investment in residential construction. This cyclical pattern has repeated itself in each of the five credit cycles. Mortgage borrowing and new residential construction have risen very rapidly in the early phases of each cycle, when interest rates have been low and funds plentiful. As interest rates have risen in the cycle and as the general pace of economic activity has expanded, mortgage borrowings and residential construction have reached their peaks. Toward the end of each cycle, as the pace of economic activity has neared its peak and interest rates have escalated to their highs, mortgage financing and particularly residential construction have collapsed.

When compared with other measures of general economic activity, mortgage financing and residential construction appear to lead the econ-

Figure 3–1

Net investment in housing and net increase in net home mortgage debt (Seasonally adjusted, smoothed annual rates as percent of GNP)

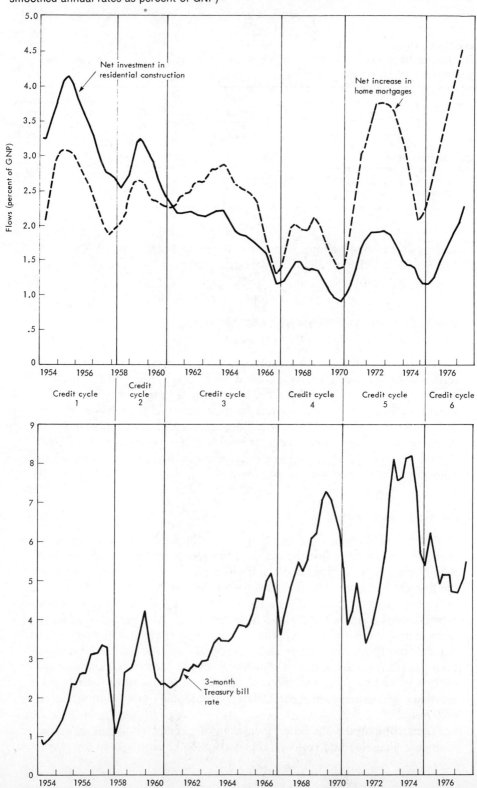

Figure 3–2

Net investment in consumer durables and net increase in consumer credit (Seasonally adjusted, smoothed annual rates as a percent of GNP)

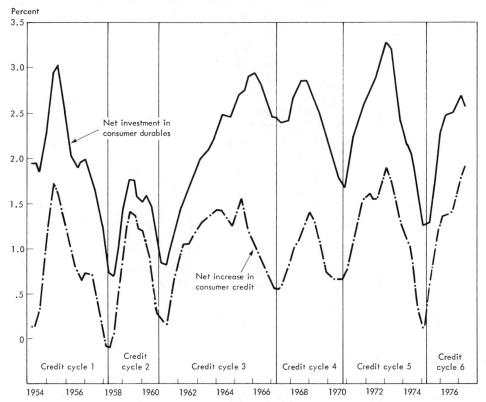

omy through its cycles, decreasing before the decline of a more general recession and rising again before general economic activity recovers. This is a cyclical pattern which contrasts sharply with the investment and financing patterns in other sectors. Recall, for example, that the net external financing of the corporate sector reaches its peak during the intervals of highest inflation and interest rates, a time when new debt financing and new residential investment of the household sector appear to be quickly dropping to their troughs. In one sense, this is not at all surprising, for the net external financing of all the primary sectors has to approximately add to zero. If the corporate sector is demanding and obtaining a larger and larger share of net external finance, the external financing of some other sectors must be dropping.

There are a number of reasons why the rate of mortgage borrowing is very sensitive to conditions in the financial markets. As general interest rates rise, mortgage rates also rise, and the potential home buyer is faced with higher annual costs for a given home purchase. In addition, as open-market interest rates rise, less money flows to the deposit institutions, which are so important in the financing of mortgages. Because deposit institutions have less funds to lend, they may respond either with the higher mortgage rates described above, more restrictive terms on mortgages (lower loan/value ratios or shorter maturities), or in some periods they may just run out of money to lend. In any event, the perceived cost and/or availability of mortgage funds will be affected and this, in turn, impacts housing decisions.

The conditions within financial markets, and their impact upon mortgage borrowing, are just one of the determinants of residential construction. A full examination of the causes of wide cyclical fluctuations in residential construction must also include the decisions of home builders and other participants in the construction process, changes in the size of the inventory of unsold houses, vacancy rates in rental housing, the cost of funds to builders, demographic factors, and other phenomena that are all part of this more complex process. We will delve into the residential mortgage markets in a later chapter. For our present purposes, however, the mortgage borrowing and residential construction expenditures of households appear to be relatively sensitive to interest rates and conditions within the financial markets. Thus they serve as an important link between financial markets and the pace of real economic activity.

Consumer credit and durables

The short-term changes in consumer credit and the net investment in consumer durables are also coincident, as shown in Figure 3–2. In fact, the amplitudes of their cyclical fluctuations have exceeded even the cyclical fluctuations in home mortgage credit and residential investment, suggesting that the demand for consumer credit plays an important role in the total demands for credit in the financial system. The cyclicality in the flows of consumer credit cannot be explained, however, by consumers' sensitivity to the fluctuations in interest rates. Since the assets (consumer durables) need to be financed for only a relatively short period of time, interest costs are probably a less important factor in the purchasing decision. Also, the interest rates charged for many types of consumer credit are regulated by various state usury laws and are quite insensitive to changes in open-market rates. For example, even during the wide swings in open-market interest rates in 1971–1976, interest rates for most forms of consumer credit barely moved. The sharp decreases in new consumer credit toward the end of each credit cycle have thus been attributable, not to consumers' reluctance to borrow during times of high nominal interest rates, but instead to other factors. Toward the end of the credit cycle, the growth in real personal incomes tends to falter, thus decreasing the demand for consumer durables and consumer credit. Furthermore, the profitability of supplying new consumer credit becomes severely constrained as lenders are caught between the inflexible returns from their assets on the one hand and rising financing costs and loan loss expectations on the other. The suppliers of consumer credit (for example, finance companies) have responded by tightening their credit standards, thus reducing the effective supplies (and increasing the "effective cost") of available consumer credit. For both of these reasons, the flows of new consumer credit have been, like the flows of new home mortgages, cyclical.

Some longer term trends

While the data in Figure 3–1 show a rather close cyclical relationship between mortgage flows and the volume of net investment in residential construction, there are additional forces influencing the long-run behavior of mortgage flows. In the early cycles, the investment in residential construction far exceeded the mortgage borrowing. But in later cycles, the net investment in new residential construction had actually become less than mortgage borrowing. This change in the relative magnitudes of increased home mortgages and new residential construction reflects, among other things, the rapid recent inflation and perhaps changing attitudes toward the assumption of debt. In the 1950s, a substantial fraction of net new home mortgage credit seemed to be associated with new home building. More recently, however, much of net new mortgage credit seems to have been used to finance the rising costs (prices) of existing homes. In addition, while new mortgage debt may be secured by a single-family home, the funds (once borrowed) are fungible and may be used for other household purposes as well. It appears that some households are using their ability to borrow against the value of their house to finance purchases other than housing. Since interest rates on home mortgages are usually much less than interest rates on other forms of consumer borrowing, this practice would seem quite sensible.

Also, there has been a general increase in the flows of new consumer credit throughout the period. Table 3–2 shows that flows of new consumer credit expanded at a 50 percent higher rate (relative to GNP) in the early 1970s than it did in the 1950s. In part, this increase may be due to developments in the institutional structure within the consumer credit markets, viz., the entry of commercial banks into the field, the increasing use of credit cards, and more liberalized attitudes of various retail outlets to charge accounts and other means of finance. But it must also be due to the increased willingness of consumers to extend promises against their future income in exchange for goods today.

HOUSEHOLD FINANCIAL ASSETS AND THE FLOW OF FUNDS TO FINANCIAL MARKETS

In addition to real assets and their associated financing, households also continuously acquire new financial assets. The increase in household financial assets, minus the increase in financial liabilities, is the rate of household *net financial investment*. This net financial investment is the analog of the external financing demand of the corporate sector. It is a measure of the net impact of the household sector on fund flows in financial markets. In this case it is a net supply of funds to the financial markets. The net financial investment of households is shown in Figure 3–3.

Net financial investment has always been positive; that is, households have always supplied more funds to the financial system than they have

Figure 3–3

Net financial investment and its determinants (Seasonally adjusted, smoothed annual rates as a percent of GNP)

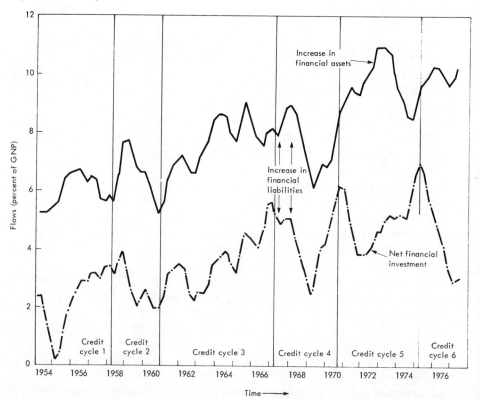

demanded in the form of new debt. Furthermore, there are clear cyclical fluctuations in the rate of net financial investment, particularly in the credit cycles in the 1960s and 1970s.

For example, in 1966, 1970, and 1974 (three periods of relatively high interest rates), the rate of net financial investment increased substantially. This was caused primarily by a decrease in net new borrowing. In each of these three time periods, the increase in funds supplied by households to financial markets occurred around the time when corporate external financing demands were large. While the correlation of household net financial investment and corporate net financing demand is not perfect, it is clear that the increases in the volume of funds supplied to the financial markets by households have been an important factor allowing corporations to raise increased amounts of external capital at several critical junctures.

NET FINANCIAL INVESTMENT AS A COMPONENT OF SAVING

Saving and wealth accumulation take place as households deal with the problem of allocating consumption over their lifetime such that the utility of this consumption stream is maximized. To do this, households save and accumulate wealth for use in later years. Saving is a purposeful decision of households, and is determined by the current levels of income and wealth, expectations of future income, and the returns available from financial and other assets.[2]

In addition to being the major source of funds for the financial system, the net financial investment of households is one of the two forms in which households save and hold their wealth. The accumulation of real assets is the other of these forms. Table 3–3 presents some data on household saving behavior. Disposable personal income has remained a large and fairly constant fraction of GNP, as have outlays for nondurables and services. Net personal saving as a percent of disposable personal income or GNP has also been relatively constant. In the period covered by Table 3–3, though, there has been a dramatic shift in the *composition* of net savings.

The proportion of net saving which has taken the form of net financial investment rose from 32 percent in the early 1950s to almost 60 percent in the early 1970s. This changed pattern of saving is another reflection of the

---

[2] There are many studies of the determinants and behavior of household consumption and saving behavior. A summary can be found in Robert Ferber, "Consumer Economics, A Survey," *Journal of Economic Literature* (December 1973).

Table 3–3

Determinants and composition of net savings for households (Data in Part I are flows as a percent of GNP averaged over the five recent credit cycles)

	Credit cycle 1 1954:3 to 58:1	Credit cycle 2 1958:2 to 60:4	Credit cycle 3 1961:1 to 67:1	Credit cycle 4 1967:2 to 70:3	Credit cycle 5 1970:4 to 75:1
Part I					
Disposable personal income (adjusted)*	70.5	70.7	69.8	69.9	71.1
Less: Consumer outlays for nondurables and services (including depreciation on durables and housing)	62.7	64.2	62.9	62.7	62.7
Equals: Net saving	7.8	6.5	6.9	7.2	8.4
Part II					
Net saving as percent of disposable personal income	11.0	9.2	9.9	10.3	11.8
Composition of net saving	100%	100%	100%	100%	100%
Net increase in consumer durables	20.0	12.0	22.0	23.0	21.0
Net increase in residential construction	49.0	47.0	28.0	18.0	21.0
Net financial investment	32.0	41.0	50.0	58.0	57.0

* Disposable personal income, as reported here, has been adjusted for capital gains distributions and the net accrual of equity in government insurance and pension funds to make it comparable with the Flow of Funds Accounts' definitions of savings and financial assets.

earlier mentioned sharp fall in the importance of household residential construction expenditures and sharp rise in net financial investment.[3]

THE CHANGING HOUSEHOLD BALANCE SHEET

It is difficult to compile accurate estimates for the market value of many important components of the balance sheet of the household sector. For example, accurate estimates of the market value of household debt securities, particularly long-term debt securities, are difficult to compile. Nor are there very reliable estimates of the market values of real assets, particularly homes. Furthermore, in one very practical sense, the household balance sheet is an incomplete portrayal of the household financial condition. Perhaps the greatest component of most households' financial condition is their human wealth, that is, their income-producing potential

[3] As a note of caution about these savings data, they describe the net flow of funds into various savings vehicles, but not necessarily the net change in wealth. The fluctuating market values of both real assets (particularly homes) and financial assets (particularly common stocks) are an important factor in the total change in wealth, and these have not been included in these data. For example, home prices rose rapidly in the 1973–1974 period. The fraction of total household wealth in family homes (one to four families) probably increased in this period, despite the fact that there was relatively little net new investment in residential construction.

in future years. This human wealth is not reflected at all in these balance sheet concepts. Nor is the potential value of future Social Security payments, an important source of post-retirement income. Thus for both conceptual and data-availability reasons, it is difficult to construct accurate representations of the changing household financial position.

Notwithstanding these difficulties, estimates of the stock of outstanding household financial assets and liabilities are shown in Table 3–4. In these

Table 3–4
Balance sheet of households

	1955 ratio to GNP		1965 ratio to GNP		1975 ratio to GNP	
Total financial assets........................	1.77		2.13		1.65	
Debt assets.................................	0.90		0.95		0.96	
Claims on intermediaries..................	0.60		0.70		0.73	
Demand deposits......................		0.17		0.12		0.11
Time and savings deposits..............		0.27		0.42		0.51
Life insurance reserves.................		0.17		0.15		0.10
Credit market instruments (debt obligations acquired directly)*.....	0.29		0.26		0.24	
Pension funds.............................	0.13		0.23		0.24	
Equities...................................	0.72		0.92		0.42	
Investment company shares..............		0.02		0.05		0.03
Other....................................		0.70		0.87		0.39

* For example, U.S. government securities, state/local government securities, corporate bonds, and so on.

data, all equities are valued at market value and all debt securities at book value (usually their original issue value). Several trends are important. First, the financial assets which households hold in the form of debt securities have grown about as fast as GNP (and therefore personal income.) Second, the fraction of these assets which are held as claims on financial institutions is large, and has risen from two thirds to three quarters. Within the claims on intermediaries, time and saving deposits account for all the relative growth, as the holding of demand deposits and life insurance reserves have fallen in relative importance. Third, pension fund reserves have doubled in their importance in household financial assets. Finally, the importance of equities has declined dramatically, in part because households have been net sellers of equities throughout the period, but more importantly because of the declining relative market value of equities from 1965 to 1975.

The large and growing role of time and saving deposits suggests that households have a strong preference for liquidity and safety. In addition, most household financial assets are rather well indexed to inflation. Their debt securities are rather short, and their pension promises are most often linked to the pay they earn in the final years of their work.

GROWTH AND COMPETITION AMONG
FINANCIAL INSTITUTIONS

The data in Table 3–4 document the continuation of the trend toward financial intermediation that has been underway for a very long time. During the first decades of this century, the *flows* into direct financial assets amounted to about 63 percent of all household financial savings. Intermediated forms of asset acquisition accounted for only 37 percent (see Table 3–5). By the 1950s, intermediated forms accounted for about

Table 3–5

Composition of financial asset acquisition in the household sector (All flows averaged over the respective time periods)

Flow of funds	1900–1929	Credit cycle 1 1954:3 to 58:1	Credit cycle 2 1958:2 to 60:4	Credit cycle 3 1961:1 to 67:1	Credit cycle 4 1967:2 to 70:3	Credit cycle 5 1970:4 to 75:1
Composition of financial flows	100%	100%	100%	100%	100%	100%
Directly held financial assets	63	23	17	5	15	1
Claims on financial intermediaries	37	77	83	95	85	99
Composition of "claims on financial intermediaries"	100%	100%	100%	100%	100%	100%
Currency and demand deposits	42	5	8	9	16	9
Savings deposits	29	51	47	56	47	63
Life insurance reserves	27	14	13	9	8	6
Pension fund reserves	3	30	32	26	29	22

three fourths of the *flows* of all net new household financial asset accumulation. During the late 1960s and early 1970s virtually all *net* household financial asset acquisitions took place in intermediaries. As intermediaries captured a larger and larger share of the growing flows of household financial savings, their growth in number, type, and assets under management was very rapid. As Table 3–4 suggests, they now account for most of the stock of outstanding financial assets held by households.

There have also been changes in the relative importance of different classes of financial institutions. In the early part of the century, demand deposits of commercial banks, the deposits of thrift associations, and the cash value insurance policy dominated household savings flows. By the decade of the 1950s, however, the relative flows into demand deposits at commercial banks had declined sharply, as had flows into life insurance reserves. Accumulations of savings deposits were more important, and most dramatically, flows to pension funds had come to account for about one third of the total flows of new financial savings. These changed financial savings patterns resulted in a slowing of commercial bank and life insurance company growth (relative to other financial institutions), a relatively faster growth for thrift institutions, and a very rapid growth in pension fund assets.[4]

As with any economic trend of such direction and importance, there are a large number of forces which have resulted in the changed composition of household financial savings. Savers themselves have changed. At the turn of the century, relatively few households had financial savings levels large enough to require more than currency or demand deposits. That small proportion of households with large financial savings chose to invest directly by financing homes or apartments with mortgages, and corporations with bonds or equities.

As the population and the economy grew, more households came to have significant amounts of savings to invest. Also, there was an increase in the number of businesses and households wishing to raise funds. Both these factors led to the development of financial institutions which created attractive savings outlets for households and convenient sources of funds for borrowers. The basic attractions of financial institutions (the pooling of risks, the expertise in risk evaluation, and the improved liquidity some of them offered) and the needs for life insurance and pension benefits also contributed to this growth.

The changing composition of borrowers during this period may have also contributed to the continued growth of intermediaries. At the end of World War II, the federal government was one of the largest debtors in the economy. Since that time, federal government financing demands have usually been moderate, and the private sector has demanded increased amounts of financing. Corporations have raised funds to finance plant and equipment and inventory. Households have raised funds for residential construction and the purchase of consumer durables. The required loans were relatively risky (at least relative to government securities), and much of the demand was long term in nature. Since household savers seem to prefer relatively safe and liquid or short-term assets, there was a mismatch between the needs and interests of borrowers and savers. Because of this mismatch, financial institutions have played a critically important role. Their abilities to evaluate risks, to reduce them through pooling, and to offer liabilities of shorter maturity and more liquidity than their assets, has enabled them to help bridge the gaps between the ultimate borrowers and lenders and facilitate both the saving and the investment process.

---

[4] Actually, in the 1960s, commercial banks began to capture an increasingly large fraction of household savings deposits. Despite the relative demise of demand deposits, therefore, commercial banks once again began to grow relatively quickly, acquiring a larger share of the total household deposits.

THE SHORT-RUN SENSITIVITY OF FINANCIAL ASSET FLOWS
TO INTEREST RATES

In addition to the gradual and persistent changes which have taken place in the financial behavior of households over the past decades, the short-run financial asset choices of households have been very sensitive to the prevailing structure of interest rates. Because the interest rates offered by most deposit institutions are limited by various regulatory ceilings, there are times when deposit institutions are unable to offer interest rates which are competitive with open-market securities.[5]

In response to these interest rate differentials, households shift the composition of their portfolios of financial assets. This causes very wide swings in the flow of new funds to deposit institutions. In 1966, 1969, 1973, and again in 1974, the flows of net new deposits plunged, each time in response to the widening spreads between open-market interest rates and the effective rates on consumer savings accounts. In these periods, the flow of household savings into open-market debt securities (including U.S. Treasury bills, commercial paper, corporate bonds, and state and local government bonds) soared, accounting for most of the loss of deposits (disintermediation) in deposit institutions.

The extreme sensitivity of deposit flows to interest rates has important implications for all deposit institutions but particularly for thrift institutions. As we have seen, deposit institutions have captured a greater and greater share of the increase in household financial assets. But the extreme variability of these deposit flows within a credit cycle has had wrenching effects on these institutions. These effects have an important impact on institutions' investment policies and hence on the cost and availability of funds in various markets, particularly the home mortgage market. At several places in this book we shall view these processes in more detail.

HOUSEHOLD CHOICES AS A PORTFOLIO
ADJUSTMENT PROCESS

The accumulation of household financial assets and liabilities is best viewed as a continual process of partial portfolio adjustments. Households enter each new time period endowed with a portfolio of existing assets and liabilities. In this time period, a host of economic and financial developments alter the relative values of assets, liabilities, incomes, and the prospective risks and returns from holding various combinations of assets and liabilities. In response to their changed condition and their new set of expectations, households formulate a new desired portfolio and

---

[5] These limitations will be discussed in detail in later chapters.

invest their funds in a way that moves their actual portfolio toward this desired portfolio. The current flows of assets and liabilities are thus indicative of the direction in which households have chosen to move, although households may not necessarily adjust their holdings all the way to their new desired levels.

The desired portfolios of households are affected by the changing rates of real economic growth and by inflation. During the unanticipated bursts of inflation that took place in 1968–1970 and 1973–1974, households curtailed their purchases and their borrowing and chose instead to build their net financial savings. There is no reason to believe that households will always respond to inflation in this way, however. Indeed, if inflationary expectations are raised high enough, and interest rates on financial claims do not respond, it is possible that households will believe that financial assets are an inferior investment whose value will be eroded and that borrowings are a cheap way of financing real assets that will retain their value.

Thus, households could respond to a burst in inflation by increasing their borrowings and by drawing on their financial savings and expanding their purchase of real assets. The response to unanticipated inflation is a complex matter, influenced as much by expected future inflation as it is by the financial effects of the current rates of inflation. This response, however, is a critical element in the behavior of the financial system when it is exposed to inflationary shocks.

In summary, household flows of both assets and liabilities are very sensitive to the cyclical fluctuations of financial conditions. These financial conditions, particularly interest rates, affect the rates of new household borrowing and the related rates at which households purchase real assets. This process is one of the important feedback linkages through which the effects of financial conditions impact the pace of real economic activity. In addition, there has been a set of interrelated secular trends in flows of assets, liabilities, and savings as the financial condition and financial behavior of households has evolved over time. These flows have had a substantial effect on the growth and development of different financial institutions and upon the financial markets.

APPENDIX
THE HOUSEHOLD SECTOR

DEMOGRAPHY OF SAVINGS AND WEALTH

The net savings for the aggregate household sector have been described in the previous section. But these savings, and their accumulation into wealth, are not distributed uniformly across all households. Numerous studies have attempted to investigate and analyze the demographic characteristics of savings and wealth.[6] Despite numerous difficulties in the data collected by these studies, several important features stand out—in particular the relationship of savings to income and age.

First of all, the average rate of savings is determined to a large extent by income. Lower income groups tend to save only a small fraction of their income. Higher income groups tend to save a much larger fraction of their income. Thus, savings are relatively concentrated in the higher income groups within our society.

Second, savings rates are also a function of age. As an impressionistic summary of the results of many studies, younger households earn relatively modest incomes on which they must support themselves and their children. Hence, they save only a modest fraction of their income. After middle age, however, as incomes continue to grow and the number of dependents is reduced, savings rates become relatively large. As wage earners near retirement, these savings rates begin to decline a little. After retirement, savings rates decline sharply as households draw down the wealth they have accumulated in prior years. The general character of the empirical results, while it has differed in detail from one study to another, is roughly congruent with the theory of the savings life cycle described earlier.[7]

Because wealth is the accumulation of savings, it, too, is dependent upon age and income. Tables 3A–1 through 3A–4 summarize some results of an earlier survey of wealth titled "The Survey of Financial Characteristics of Consumers," conducted by the Federal Reserve System in 1962 and 1963. Households, wealth, and income were defined in this survey as indicated by the notes to the tables. While there are data difficulties with any such survey, the principal features of the results presented here are consistent with the findings of most other such surveys. Table 3A–1 shows the distribution of wealth by age group in 1962. As expected, the average wealth of the youngest group was relatively modest. The average wealth of older groups increased, up to the 55–64 age group, and then declined somewhat for the 65 and over group. This is what we would expect from the life cycle models of saving and wealth.

Table 3A–2 shows the comparable distribution of wealth for different income groups. As expected, the average wealth increased as a function of income. Indeed, the wealth of U.S. households was concentrated such that a significant fraction of total wealth was held by a very small fraction of the households. Some later studies have attempted to analyze the time trends in this concentration of wealth. They suggest that, while the con-

---

[6] "Survey of Changes in Family Finances," Federal Reserve System, 1968; "Survey of Financial Characteristics of Consumers," Federal Reserve System, 1966.

[7] A. Ando and F. Modigliani, "The Life Cycle Hypothesis of Savings," *The American Economic Review* (March 1963).

Table 3A–1

Distribution of household wealth by age groups, 1962

Head of household age group*	Estimated percent of households	Estimated percent of wealth held†	Average wealth in group
Under 35	22	7	$ 6,300
35–44	21	16	16,100
45–54	21	22	22,600
55–64	18	28	32,500
65 and over	19	28	30,800

* Households: Consumer units, both families and unrelated individuals, as defined by the Bureau of the Census.

† Wealth: Includes automobiles (at market), home (at market), equity in business ventures, deposits, equity and debt securities, investment real estate, and other miscellaneous assets, less debt secured by any of these assets. Does not include investment in life insurance and/or retirement plan because of data deficiency.

Source: Data from *Survey of Financial Characteristics of Consumers,* Federal Reserve System, 1966.

Table 3A–2

Distribution of household wealth by income group, 1962

1962 income group*	Estimated percent of households†	Estimated percent of wealth‡	Approximate average wealth
0– 5,000	48	20	8,600
5,000–10,000	37	27	15,700
10,000–15,000	11	14	28,000
15,000–25,000	3	10	63,000
25,000–50,000	0.9	13	291,000
50,000 and over	0.3	15	

* Income group: Total money income from 1962, before tax.

† Households: see Table 3A–1.

‡ Wealth: see Table 3A–1.

centration of wealth did tend to decrease in the 1930s and during World War II, the fraction of wealth owned by the wealthiest 1 percent of the population has remained relatively constant in the postwar period.[8]

In addition, the composition of wealth among various real and financial assets tends to be a function of age and income. Table 3A–3 shows the composition of wealth by age groups. The younger age group appears to have relied relatively more upon real assets, automobiles and homes, and the equity in their own businesses (farms, proprietorships, partnerships,

[8] James D. Smith and Stephen Frandelin, "The Concentration of Personal Wealth, 1922–1969," *American Economic Association (May 1974).*

Table 3A–3

Composition of household wealth by age group, 1962

Head of household age group	Total wealth	Auto-mobile*	Own home†	Own business‡	Liquid assets§	Invest-ment assets‖	Miscel-laneous assets#
35–44	100%	5	31	23	10	22	9
45–54	100	4	33	23	11	26	3
55–64	100	2	25	20	13	38	2
65 and over	100	1	22	12	16	47	1

* Automobile: Estimate of market value, less debt secured by property.
† Own home: Estimate of market value, less mortgage secured by property.
‡ Own business: Equity in farm and nonfarm sole proprietorships, partnerships and closely held corporations.
§ Liquid assets: Deposits, savings and time deposits, U.S. savings bonds.
‖ Investment assets: Common and preferred stock (at market: 12/31/62), debt securities (at par), investment real estate.
Miscellaneous assets: Assets held in trust, loans to individuals, commodity contracts, and others.

and closely held corporations). Older age groups, on the other hand, tended to concentrate their wealth more in financial assets, to some extent in "liquid assets" (deposits and U.S. savings bonds), but primarily in "investment assets" (stock, debt securities, and some investment real estate).

Table 3A–4 shows the composition of wealth for different income groups. Low-income and middle-income groups appear to have relied relatively more upon real assets. Higher income groups relied much more upon investment assets, and to a lesser extent the equity interest in their own businesses. Other studies of the concentration of wealth, in particular financial assets, largely confirm these findings. The ownership of investment assets appears to be concentrated in a relatively small segment of U.S. households—more concentrated, for example, than total wealth or income.

Table 3A–4

Composition of household wealth by income group, 1962

1962 income group*	Total wealth	Auto-mobiles	Own home	Own busi-ness	Liquid assets	Invest-ment assets	Miscel-laneous assets
0– 5,000	100%	3	37	15	18	23	4
5,000– 10,000	100	4	36	14	14	26	5
10,000– 15,000	100	5	34	15	16	28	1
15,000– 25,000	100	3	24	16	14	37	6
25,000– 50,000	100	1	11	21	7	42	18
50,000–100,000	100	—	6	42	6	43	3
100,000 and over	100	—	5	17	3	69	6

* See Table 3A–3 for explanations of definitions.

Throughout this chapter we have examined the aggregate behavior of the household sector. But it is clear from the data presented here that there may also be important differences in the financial behavior of different segments of this household sector.

QUESTIONS

1. Consider the rates at which households have increased their holdings of real and financial assets. What are the long-run trends? The cyclical patterns? What factors seem to affect their issuance of liabilities?

2. Consider the "net saving" of households and its distribution among consumer durables, residential construction, net financial investment. What are the long-run trends? The cyclical patterns?

3. Consider the composition of households' increase in financial assets, that is, the rates at which they have chosen to add various kinds of financial promises to their portfolios. What kinds of financial assets do they appear to prefer? What has been their "financial strategy?" What have been the implications of this strategy for corporate financing?

4. What kinds of financial institutions have been successful at attracting household funds? Why?

REFERENCES

Consumer Spending and Monetary Policy: The Linkages. Proceedings of a Monetary Conference (Federal Reserve Bank of Boston, 1971).

Gramlich, Edward M. and Jaffee, D. M., eds. *Savings Deposits, Mortgages, and Housing.* Lexington, Massachusetts: D.C. Heath, 1973.

Kearl, James; Rosen, Kenneth; and Swan, Craig. "Relationships between the Mortgage Instruments, the Demand for Housing and Mortgage Credit: A Review of Empirical Studies." In *New Mortgage Designs for Stable Housing in an Inflationary Environment,* edited by D. Lessard and Franco Modigliani. Proceedings of a Conference (Federal Reserve Bank of Boston, 1975), pp. 93–109.

Mishkin, F. S. "What Depressed the Consumer? The Household Balance Sheet and The 1973–75 Recession," *Brookings Papers on Economic Activity,* vol. 1, (1977).

Modigliani, Franco. "The Life Cycle Hypothesis of Saving 20 Years Later." *Contemporary Issues in Economics,* edited by M. Parkin and A. R. Nobay. North Manchester, Ind.: Manchester University Press, 1975.

4

Financing demands
of the federal government

The federal government affects financial markets in many ways. As a result of the need to finance surpluses and deficits in the federal budget, it is a large and important primary demander of funds. In addition, the composition of its expenditures and the structure of its tax system play critical roles in the financial decisions of other actors in financial markets. The federal government also plays a large role as a financial intermediary. It uses its taxing and borrowing powers to raise funds that are subsequently distributed as direct loans to other primary sectors. In addition, it guarantees the borrowings of certain federal agencies and private sector borrowers.[1] In this chapter we discuss the expenditures, receipts, and budget of the federal government, and their relationships to financial markets.

FEDERAL GOVERNMENT FINANCING DEMANDS

The primary determinant of the financing demands of the federal government is its budget deficit or surplus. There are two features of the history of federal financing which stand out. First, as Figure 4–1 suggests, the volume of federal financing demands varies significantly at different times within the credit cycle. This cyclical variability was especially pronounced during the recession of 1975 when federal financing demands rose to an annual rate of 6 percent of GNP.

---

[1] The bulk of these federal loan guarantees and intermediary activities affect the residential mortgage market. They are discussed in Chapter 18.

Figure 4–1

External financing demands: Flows averaged over credit cycles (Expressed as percent of GNP)

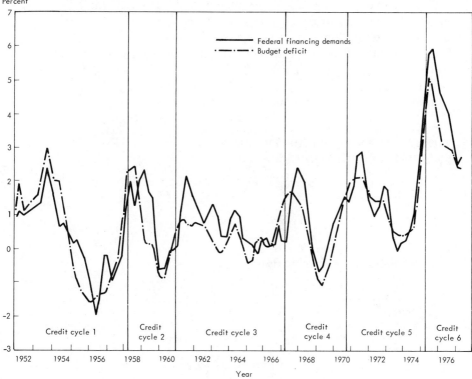

Table 4–1

External financing demands: flows averaged over credit cycles (Expressed as percent of GNP)

	Credit Cycle 1 1954:3 to 58:1	Credit Cycle 2 1958:2 to 60:4	Credit Cycle 3 1961:1 to 67:1	Credit Cycle 4 1967:2 to 70:3	Credit Cycle 5 1970:4 to 75:1
Federal government					
Outlays	17.7	19.0	19.1	20.7	21.1
Receipts	18.2	18.5	18.1	20.2	19.8
Deficit	−0.5	0.5	0.3	0.5	1.3
Compared to other demands for credit					
Federal financing*	−0.3	0.9	0.7	0.9	1.5
Business external financing	2.4	2.1	2.5	3.2	4.2
Household financing	3.9	3.8	3.8	3.2	4.5
State and local financing	1.1	1.1	1.0	1.1	1.2

* The federal financing is generally related to, but larger than, the federal deficit because of the net acquisitions of financial assets in the government sector as discussed later in this chapter.

The second important feature of federal financing has been its share in the total funds raised by all sectors. The data in Table 4–1 show that, in the credit cycles before 1970, the financing demands arising from the federal deficits and surpluses were small when compared to the financing demands of either the business or household sector.

In the 1970–1975 credit cycle, however, federal financing demands rose substantially, generating concern that the federal government's budget position was changing and that it might demand substantially increased amounts of financing on a continuing basis.

THE CHANGING COMPOSITION OF FEDERAL EXPENDITURES

The important components of federal expenditures are shown in the accompanying table.

	1979 fiscal year (billions of $)	
Purchases of goods and services	176.1	
Defense		108.1
Nondefense		63.5
Transfer payments	201.8	
Grants-in-aid to state and local governments	81.6	
Net interest paid	39.8	
Subsidies less current surplus of government enterprises	9.2	
Total budgeted federal expenditures	504.0	

While the overall level of federal spending has remained a relatively stable percentage of GNP, there has been a major shift in the composition of federal expenditures over the past 25 years. This shift has significant implications for the future level and variability of federal spending. As Figure 4–2 shows, defense purchases of goods and services have been a declining share of federal spending ever since the Korean conflict. There has been a corresponding rise in other components, especially grants-in-aid to states and domestic transfer payments. While this shift has been underway for over two decades, it has accelerated in recent years, as can be seen in Figure 4–3.

Spending for domestic transfer payments has expanded rapidly, primarily because of more beneficiaries and higher benefits under the Social Security insurance programs. Payments for medical care under the hospital and supplementary medical insurance programs (Medicare) have also expanded rapidly. At times, unemployment benefits have also been a significant factor in transfer payments. Transfers to persons accounted for

Figure 4–2
Distribution of federal sector expenditures by category

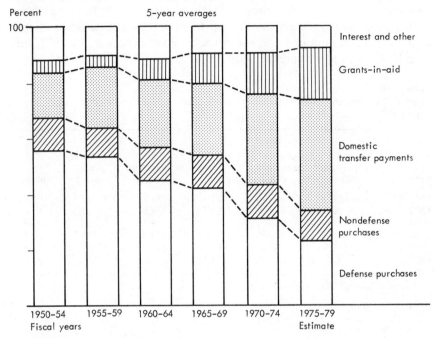

Figure 4–3
Composition of federal sector expenditures

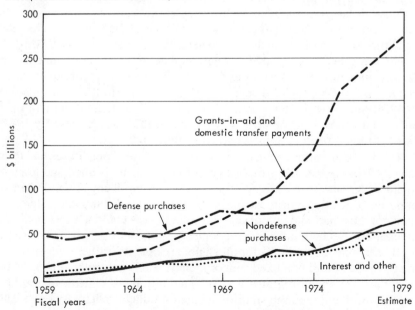

18 percent of federal spending in 1955, but grew to 40 percent in 1977. At least three fourths of the growth could be accounted for by new programs and expansions of existing ones, with the remaining growth arising from increases in the beneficiary population. In 1955, federal transfer payments to persons amounted to 4 percent of total personal income. By 1977, this figure had risen to 11 percent. (See Table 4–2.)

Table 4–2
Federal transfers and grants-in-aid as a proportion of personal income and state and local receipts

Year	Personal income	Federal transfers to persons	Percent	State and local government receipts	Federal grants-in-aid	Percent
1955	308.8	12.4	4.0	31.7	3.1	9.8
1960	399.7	21.6	5.4	49.9	6.5	13.0
1965	537.0	30.3	5.6	75.1	11.1	14.8
1970	801.3	61.3	7.7	134.9	24.4	18.1
1975	1,253.4	146.1	11.7	235.7	54.6	23.2
1977	1,536.1	169.4	11.0	294.5	67.6	23.0

Source: Economic Report of the President, 1978.

Grants-in-aid, programs designed to help state and local governments provide general public services, have also grown rapidly. General-purpose fiscal assistance has been provided in relatively small amounts under several programs for many years, but it became a major expenditure with the introduction of general revenue sharing in 1973. Such grants are generally available to operate state and local governments, to finance state or local transfer payments to the public, to retire debt, or to reduce taxes. Grants-in-aid accounted for 4.6 percent of federal spending in 1955, but grew to 16.0 percent in 1977. In 1955, federal grants-in-aid amounted to about 10 percent of total state and local receipts. By 1977, this figure had risen to 23 percent. (See Table 4–2.)

This transformation in the composition of federal expenditures had four major effects. First, the growth trend of domestic assistance and grants-in-aid programs posed a long-range budgetary problem of fundamental importance. Outlays for these purposes grew at a substantially faster rate than potential national output, and these increases could not be sustained indefinitely. Second, most federal domestic assistance programs created a legal entitlement to benefits for all eligible recipients, rather than specifying the expenditure of a fixed sum of money. Thus, controlling the growth of outlays for such programs was substantially more difficult than other expenditures and required statutory changes reducing eligibility or benefit levels. In 1967, such "open-ended" or "uncontrollable" programs amounted to about 36 percent of total federal outlays. By 1976, however, they had grown to about 59 percent of total federal outlays. Third, many federal assistance programs were indexed to the rate of inflation, and therefore substantial increases in the nominal level of outlays were outside immediate control. For example, about two thirds of the federal income security outlays ($156 billion in 1976) were tied to the rate of inflation. In addition, with medical costs experiencing very significant rates of price increase, health care benefits under entitlement programs increased rapidly. Finally, as income support payments became a more important federal function, the redistribution of income became a major objective of federal spending policy. This made expenditure control an increasingly complex and difficult political process, despite various improvements in the way Congress formally structured this process.

THE COMPOSITION OF FEDERAL RECEIPTS

The federal government collects taxes in four major categories (Figure 4–4). The largest category is individual income tax receipts. Contributions for social insurance constitute the second largest category of federal sector receipts. The rapid rise in the relative importance of these receipts, from 15.9 percent of the total in 1960 to 33 percent in 1977, has been

Figure 4–4
Distribution of federal sector receipts by category

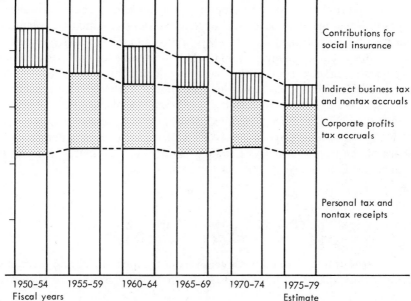

associated with the rapid rise in transfer payment expenditures for Social Security which were mentioned earlier.

Corporate profits tax accruals are another important source of federal receipts. The relative decline in corporate profits tax receipts, results mainly from three factors (1) a narrowing of the corporate profits tax base resulting from changes in the definition of corporate profits for tax purposes (largely increases in permissible depreciation allowances); (2) reductions in the effective tax rates on corporate profits resulting from statuatory rate reductions and provision for investment tax credits; and (3) in the 1970s, a decline in corporate profits relative to GNP.

The remaining sources of federal revenue are excise taxes, estate and gift taxes, customs duties, and miscellaneous receipts (the bulk of which are earnings of the Federal Reserve).

Inflation and federal tax receipts

Under current tax law, taxable income is not adjusted for inflation. As a result, during an inflationary period, individuals move from tax exempt into taxable brackets, and from lower into higher tax brackets, merely because their money incomes are rising although their real incomes are rising much less (or may even be declining). In addition, capital gains computed in dollar terms enter into the tax base, even though such nominal gains can represent very much smaller real gains (or possibly real losses). Thus, inflation raises personal taxes by a much larger percentage than nominal incomes, causing the average tax rate to rise and tax payments to increase in real terms.

Similar problems have developed in the corporate sector when two types of inflationary tax-raising effects arise from the standard accounting methods for computing business costs and profits. Depreciation expenses for tax purposes are computed on the basis of the historical cost of acquisition rather than on replacement cost. In addition, the cost of goods sold from inventory is sometimes valued at historic rather than replacement cost. These accounting procedures understate costs and hence overstate profits (see Chapter 2 for a detailed description of these effects).

Thus, the federal government's tax collections rise substantially as a share of both corporate and personal income as individuals and corporations are exposed to the effects of inflation.

FACTORS AFFECTING THE BALANCE IN THE FEDERAL BUDGET AND FEDERAL FINANCING DEMANDS

Two sets of forces affect the level of federal expenditures and taxes and thereby the balance in the budget. First, there are changes in the level of expenditures and in receipts which arise because of what the government itself chooses to do in terms of both expenditures levels and tax rates. Second, there are changes in expenditures and taxes which arise because of the effects the behavior of the economy has on these budget items. Because the actual volume of tax collections depends on the level of corporate and personal income, and because federal expenditures in areas such as unemployment compensation respond to movements in the level of economic activity, the pace of economic activity plays a large role in determining the balance in the federal budget. Changes in the budget position which arise from deliberate changes in the level of expenditures or tax rates are called *autonomous* changes, while changes which are the result of movements in the economy (in income and in unemployment rates) are called *induced*.

In an attempt to distinguish between the effects of these two different forces operating on the federal budget, analysts have developed three analytic or hypothetical notions: high employment expenditures, high employment receipts, and a high employment budget surplus or deficit. The concept of high employment expenditures is an estimate of those expenditures which would occur if the economy were operating at high levels of employment. Actual expenditures differ from high employment expenditures primarily because of the fluctuations in unemployment compensation and welfare payments.

Similarly, the concept of high employment receipts is an estimate of the revenue which the federal government would receive, given the existing structure of tax rates, if personal and corporate incomes were what they would be when the economy was operating at high levels of employment. Actual receipts are below this high employment level of receipts to the extent that actual levels of income are below the high employment level of income.

Thus, the actual balance in the budget is equal to the balance which would occur if the economy were at high employment plus the effects on spending levels and tax collections which arise from the fact that the economy is not operating at high employment. By using this methodology, movements in the actual budget surplus or deficit, and in Treasury financing demands, can be partitioned into two sources: autonomous changes in the high employment budget surplus or deficit, and induced deviations in the actual budget about this high employment budget which arise from fluctuations in the level of economic activity.

THE HISTORY OF BUDGET MANAGEMENT

Figure 4–5 shows the behavior of high employment expenditures as a fraction of actual GNP since 1952. Due in part to expenditures for the Korean conflict, high employment expenditures averaged between 20 and

Figure 4–5
Federal high employment receipts and expenditures (As percent of high employment GNP)

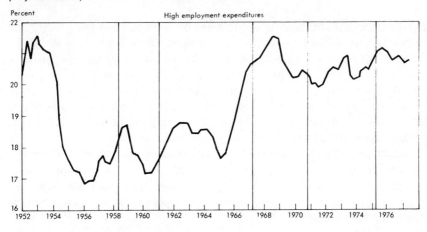

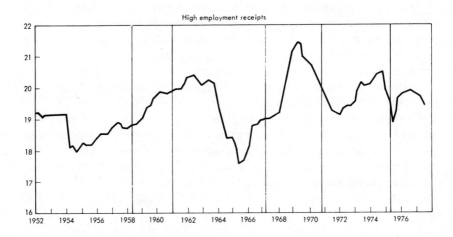

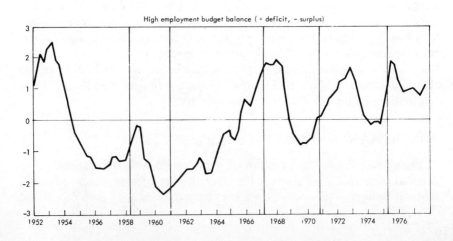

21 percent of GNP during 1952 and 1953. Between early 1965 and mid-1969, in part because of the Vietnam War, high employment expenditures rose from 17.5 percent to 21.4 percent of GNP. Thus, the two wars exerted significant upward pressure on federal expenditures. After each war, high employment expenditures fell substantially, although the decline in the 1950s was more pronounced than the decline after 1968. The dramatic growth in transfer payments and grants-in-aid during the late 1960s and early 1970s (sometimes referred to as the War on Poverty) kept high employment expenditures (relative to GNP) above their levels of the 1950s.

As can be seen in Figure 4–5, the level of federal receipts which the federal tax system would generate at high levels of employment has also varied as a percent of GNP. It showed less variability than did high employment expenditures during the 1950s and about as much variability in the 1960s and early 1970s.

Measured on this hypothetical basis, the federal budget was in surplus from the mid-1950s through the 1960s and in deficit during most of the period from mid-1965 through 1977. In early 1975, a temporary tax rebate designed to cushion the recession and stimulate an economic recovery resulted in a sharp fall in the level of high employment revenues relative to high employment GNP and a sharp rise in the high employment deficit.

Figure 4–6 shows the path of the actual and high employment budget deficit. The deficit in the actual budget has almost always been larger than the deficit in the high employment budget. In each of the periods when the economy experienced slow growth relative to its potential at high employment, for example, 1957–1958, 1960–1961, 1970–1971, and 1974–1976, the gap between the high employment budget surplus or deficit and the actual budget surplus or deficit widened considerably. The slower growth in corporate and personal incomes and the importance of income taxes in federal tax receipts resulted in significantly reduced revenue growth and a sharp increase in the size of the federal deficit. Also, expenditures on unemployment compensation increased during these periods, adding somewhat to the deficits. As the economy rebounded, after each of these recessions, however, tax collections rose rapidly and the recession-induced expenditures declined. As a result, the discrepancies between receipts and expenditures in the actual and in the high employment budget decreased substantially, and the actual deficit diminished significantly.

Thus, the sensitivity of the federal budget to the economy is responsible for much of the cyclical variability in federal financing demands. Recessions expand the deficit and financing demands sharply, and recoveries reduce these same financing demands. Changes in the level of the high employment budget balance have also made important contributions to federal financing demands, however. In the 1950s and early 1960s, the

Figure 4–6
Federal budget deficits as percent of high employment GNP (Smoothed data)

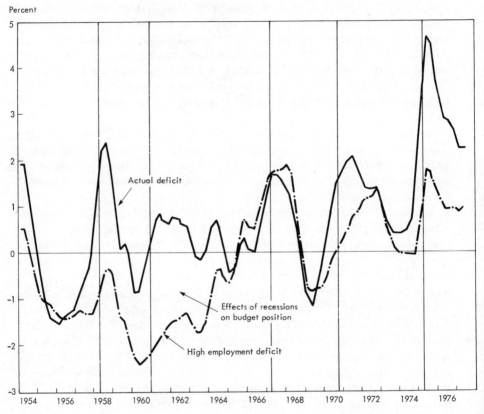

Percent

surpluses in the high employment budget kept the actual budget deficits at levels which were small on the average in relation to GNP. After 1964 or 1965, however, the deficits in the high employment budget added to federal financing demands.

By 1978, there were clear, and (to some) disturbing indications that federal financing demands would continue to be larger than they had been in the 1950s and early 1960s. First, the high employment budget was in deficit, not in surplus as had been the case earlier. Moreover, for the reasons discussed earlier in this chapter, it was proving increasingly difficult to limit the growth in expenditures. Furthermore, inflationary expectations and pressures were making it difficult to stimulate economic demand to levels which would generate high levels of employment without triggering the risk of unacceptable rates of inflation.

OTHER SOURCES OF TREASURY FINANCING DEMANDS

While the bulk of its financing demands arise from the effects of budget deficits and surpluses, the Treasury has several other sources of financial demands. The largest of these arises because the Treasury acts as a financial institution and raises funds in order to relend them to specific classes of borrowers. The U.S. government as a whole performs the role of a very large financial institution. It extends credit directly, and it guarantees the borrowings of a large and growing number of borrowers. Most of the funds raised for these purposes are channeled to the mortgage market and are raised by a set of federally sponsored credit agencies rather than by the Treasury itself.[2] Certain of these activities are lodged in the Treasury, however, and thereby add to the financing demands of the federal government or Treasury itself. Before the early 1970s, these lending activities caused only a small volume of financing requirements for the Treasury. In the three years 1974, 1975, and 1976, however, these lending activities totaled $34 billion and added significantly to the Treasury's financing demands during these years.[3]

In addition, the U.S. government owns (or partially owns) certain corporations and/or agencies whose activities are not part of the federal budget but who are nonetheless financed through the Treasury. Examples of such agencies are the Tennessee Valley Authority, the Postal Service, and the U.S. Railway Association. Much of the borrowing of these agencies is channeled through the Federal Financing Bank, which in turn borrows from the Treasury. Finally, the Treasury must finance its own cash position. Administering a budget with annual expenditures in the range of $400 billion and with irregular inflows and outflows requires a substantial working cash position. The Treasury's year-end cash balance averaged about $10 billion in the period 1973–1977.[4]

INDIRECT EFFECTS OF THE FEDERAL GOVERNMENT

In addition to the direct effects on financial markets arising from Treasury financing demands, the federal government affects financial markets in many other ways. Federal tax policy affects the investment choices of individuals and corporations. The personal income tax system allows interest expenses as deductions from taxable income, fostering the in-

---

[2] Chapter 18 contains a discussion of these agencies and their role in the mortgage market.

[3] These lending activities are spread widely throughout the economy. The Treasury buys home mortgages; it lends to farm businesses, unincorporated businesses, state and local governments, and even engages in a substantial volume of lending to foreign governments. See the *Treasury Bulletin* or the *Flow of Funds* for more detail.

[4] A detailed analysis of these elements of total federal financing is found in Special Analysis E of *Special Analyses, Budget of the U.S. Government* annual.

vestment in houses (or condominiums) financed with mortgages rather than the rental of apartments. It treats capital gains differently than either dividend or interest income and thus affects both investment decisions and corporate financial decisions. Federal corporate tax policy also affects business investment decisions through its definition of allowable depreciation charges and through investment tax credits.

Federal transfers to persons can also have a dramatic effect on financial markets. One such area of transfer spending whose impact on financial markets has been the subject of much discussion is the Social Security system. Prior to the introduction of Social Security, retirement income depended on savings accumulated during the working years. Since the introduction of Social Security, most retired persons have been guaranteed benefits at the age of 65. But this guaranteed retirement income may have affected personal savings behavior. To the extent that individuals are assured a certain minimum level of support after retirement, their need to save and accumulate wealth during their working years would seem to be reduced, and overall savings levels may be lowered.[5]

It has been estimated that the present value of the Social Security payments to be received by those potential pensioners in the workforce or retired at the end of 1971 was about $2.0 trillion. Households held an estimated $3.5 trillion in total household assets and $2.1 trillion in financial assets at that time (both figures excluding the effects of this Social Security "wealth"). Thus, this Social Security "wealth" could have a very large effect on savings choices. One study of these effects tentatively suggested that the wealth effect of Social Security reduced current savings from 30 to 50 percent.[6] Another study concluded the wealth effect was very significant but presented evidence that this effect was about balanced by the positive effect on savings which arose from the longer retirement periods induced by Social Security.[7]

While the empirical estimates of the effects of Social Security on savings flows (and thereby on capital markets) are as yet imprecise, it is clear that this type of federal transfer payment can exert a significant effect on individual saving behavior. As stated earlier, such transfer payments are the most rapidly growing part of federal expenditures. The more the federal government uses transfer programs to offer protection from all sorts

---

[5] The Social Security functions approximately on a pay-as-you-go basis. Payroll tax revenues from the working population are transmitted immediately to the elderly as retirement benefits. Thus, aside from a working balance of approximately seven months' payments, the Social Security system does not add to total savings.

[6] Martin Feldstein, "Social Security, Induced Retirement and Aggregate Capital Accumulation," *Journal of Political Economy* (December 1974), and Alicia H. Munnell, "The Impact of Social Security on Personal Savings," *National Tax Journal,* vol. 27, no. 4.

[7] The earned income limitations of Social Security provide a significant incentive to withdraw from the labor force at 65. If individuals have to save over a shorter working life for a longer retirement induced by the Social Security laws, then savings will be larger.

of contingencies such as disability, unemployment, and medical expenses, and from the expenses of retirement, the less individuals will have to save on their own to meet those needs.

SUMMARY

The federal government exerts major influences on financial markets. Deficits in its budget make it a primary demander of funds, and the primary source of these deficits in the past has been wars or economic recessions. In addition to being a net demander of funds and absorbing a part of the savings that the private sector generates, the federal government has a significant effect on the savings and investment decisions of every other sector. Thus, the federal government is not only a user of the private sector's saving, but a major factor determining the amount of private saving that actually takes place.

QUESTIONS

1. What have been the important trends in the size and composition of federal spending and taxes, and in the size of the deficits?
2. How might these trends affect private financial decisions?
3. What arguments can be presented in support of the position that the federal budget is "out of control?" What is the counterposition?
4. How does the budget react to recession and inflation?

REFERENCES

Blinder, Alan S. and Solow, Robert M. "Analytical Foundations of Fiscal Policy." In *The Economics of Public Finance,* edited by A. S. Blinder et al. Brookings Institution, 1974.

Feldstein, Martin S. "The Social Security Fund and National Capital Accumulation." In *Funding Pensions: Issues and Implications for Financial Markets,* Proceeding of a Conference. Federal Reserve Bank of Boston, 1976.

Stein, Herbert. *The Fiscal Revolution in America.* Chicago: University of Chicago Press, 1969.

The 1978 Budget, Setting National Priorities, Joseph A. Pechman, ed., (Brookings Institution, 1977).

Economic Report of the President. Annually.

5

Financing demands
of state and local governments

Another important primary financial sector is comprised of the state and local governments. Their net new issues of debt have averaged about 1.2 percent of GNP during the period 1954–1977. As Figure 5–1 demonstrates, their external financing has not fluctuated much, nor has it shown any pronounced cyclical pattern.

As these flows of new debt have accumulated, state and local government debt outstanding rose from 11 percent of GNP in 1954 to 15 percent of GNP in 1964 (see Table 5–1). By the end of 1977 it amounted to 14 percent of GNP.

Given the rapid growth in total budgets, however, debt outstanding has declined relative to total state and local receipts and has even declined relative to state and local receipts from their own sources (excluding federal grants-in-aid).

Most state and local obligations are general credit, or "full faith and credit," obligations of the issuing body. The promised payments of interest and principal for these obligations depend upon the general taxing power of the issuer rather than on any assets or prospective cash flows pledged as security. The other major group of state and local obligations is called revenue bonds. The full faith and credit of the issuing body is not pledged to support these revenue bonds. Instead, the payments of interest

Figure 5–1
External financing requirements of state and local governments (Expressed as percent of GNP)

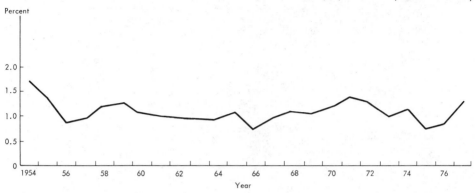

Table 5–1
State and local debt

	1954	1964	1977
State and local debt outstanding (billions)........	41	95	236
As percent of GNP	11	15	14
As percent of state and local receipts			
Total	141	137	80
Own sources	158	161	104

and principal are based upon specific revenues which arise from the sale of a public service, such as water, or are based on a lease with a public agency, such as a school district. Over the past 20 years, the importance of nonguaranteed issues has risen from about 24 percent to over 40 percent of total long debt issues of state and local governments (see Table 5–2). Nonguaranteed debt comprises a larger fraction of state debt than of local debt. The rise in revenue or nonguaranteed issues largely reflects a broadened concept of public services to include toll roads, transit facilities, utilities, and so forth.

State and local obligations are issued in a wide variety of maturities. Most issues are serial bonds, which mature at regular intervals over the life of the issue and carry original maturities ranging from 1 to 30 years or more. Some short-term municipal notes are also used to raise funds. While short-term debts have risen somewhat in importance over the past 20 years, they account for less than 10 percent of total debt.

Two sets of forces influence state and local debt issues: the level of expenditures on capital projects and the overall financial position of state and local governments.

Table 5–2

State and local government: composition of debt outstanding

	1973–74		
	Total	State	Local
Billions			
Total	206.6	65.3	141.3
Percent			
Total	100.0	100.0	100.0
Long-term debt	92.0	94.5	90.8
Full faith and credit	58.4	50.1	62.4
Nonguaranteed	41.6	49.9	37.6
Short-term debt..............	8.0	5.5	9.2

THE CONNECTION BETWEEN DEBT ISSUES AND CAPITAL OUTLAYS

Almost all state and local debt issues are raised in conjunction with specific capital projects. Debt is used to finance capital projects because, first, it allows the costs of the project to be paid for by taxpayers over the full lifetime of the project's benefits. This allows a more fair intertemporal matching of taxpayer costs with public benefits. Second, most states impose some type of limitation on the authority of the state legislature to borrow. These limitations often allow long-term borrowing only in conjunction with capital projects.[1]

As Table 5–3 demonstrates, long-term debt issues were used to raise an amount of funds equal to about 40 percent of state and local government gross fixed capital formation in the period 1958–1973. In addition, federal grants-in-aid for capital projects provided an amount of funds equal to 22 percent of the outlays. Most of the remainder was financed from current receipts.

The bulk of state and local capital expenditures are for highways, education, and sewer and water projects. Table 5–4 relates the volume of bonds which were issued with each of these stated purposes to the level of expenditure in each area. Debt issues were most important for education and for sewer and water facilities.

State and local government capital expenditures have been subject to a changing set of forces. Capital expenditures, in real terms, grew at a rather steady and rapid rate of 5.5 percent per year from 1958 to 1968 but

---

[1] In origin the limitations reflect reactions to periods of misdirected overborrowing. These periods of overborrowing occurred several times in American history. In the 1820s and 1830s states first borrowed extensively to build canals, highways, railroads and other "internal improvements." In the depression of 1837, much of this debt defaulted. After the Civil War, nine states' debt either defaulted or was repudiated. Defaults occurred again in the 1870s. By the mid-1930s about 10% of all municipal bonds were in default.

Table 5–3
Debt issues in relation to state and local
government expenditures on gross fixed
capital formation

	1958–1973
Long-term debt	40%
Federal aid*	22
All other†	38
Total	100%

* Consists of federal grants and loans.
 † Consists of tax and nontax accruals, short-term borrowing, and use of accumulated revenues.
  Source: Data taken from "State and Local Government Gross Fixed Capital Formation: 1958–1973," *Survey of Current Business* (October 1975).

Table 5–4
Debt issues by purpose in relation to all funds used to finance capital
outlays 1967–1973 (Percent)

Outlay	Federal aid	Long-term debt	All other	Total
Highways	41	17	42	100
Education	5	62	33	100
Sewer and water	12	72	16	100
All other	16	45	39	100

actually declined from 1968 to 1975 (see Table 5–5). They declined because the volume of highway projects decreased as the initial development of the highway system was completed. Capital expenditures on education decelerated as the number of children declined. In the latter period, the prices paid for the items included in state and local government capital outlays rose at very rapid rates, thereby making it difficult for many state and local governments to maintain their earlier pace of capital spending (in real terms).

Short-term borrowing

Only about 8 percent of the total state and local government debt at the end of 1975 was short-term debt (with an original maturity of less than one year). Not only was short-term debt relatively small, but it was also concentrated in a few issuers. As of 1975, the issues of the State of New

Table 5–5

Growth rates of gross fixed capital formation of state and local
governments (Percent)

	1958–1975	1958–1968	1968–1975
Nominal	6.9	7.5	6.2
Real	2.0	5.5	−2.5
Price	4.8	1.9	8.9

York and the City of New York amounted to about half of all the short-
term outstanding. State and local governments rely on three types of
short-term borrowing. Tax anticipation notes (TANs) are used to bridge
the gap between actual expenditures and anticipated tax receipts. In addition, housing authority notes (HANs) and bond anticipation notes (BANs)
are sometimes used as temporary sources of financing for capital projects,
particularly if credit market rates are high or are expected to fall.

Sensitivity to credit market conditions

Conditions in credit markets affect the volume of long-term debt issued
by state and local governments. In periods of tight credit, such as 1966
and 1969–1970, interest costs increase and state and local governments issue
fewer long-term bonds. A Federal Reserve study of state and local borrowing plans and realizations concluded, however, that only about one fifth of
the borrowing plans that were, in fact, postponed or canceled because of
high interest rates led to postponements or cancellations of capital spending
plans.[2] Many governments temporarily turned to alternative sources of
financing, such as floating short-term debt or liquid assets, rather than
change their capital spending plans, which usually involve extensive preparation.[3] Thus, while credit market conditions affect the timing of the issuance of long-term debts by state and local governments, they do not seem
to have had much effect on the pace of state and local capital expenditures
or on the eventual level of long-term state and local debt issues.

DEBT ISSUES IN THE OVERALL FINANCING OF STATE AND LOCAL GOVERNMENTS

While debt issues must often be legally authorized in connection with
capital outlays, they may not be necessary to finance capital outlays. The

---

[2] See John E. Petersen, "Response of State and Local Governments to Varying Credit
Conditions," *Federal Reserve Bulletin* (March 1971), pp. 209–32.

[3] See Paul Schneidermann, "State and Local Government Gross Fixed Capital Formation: 1958–73." *Survey of Current Business* (October 1975), p. 21.

proportion of debt financing used for capital projects depends in large part upon the ability of the state and local governments to finance their capital projects from current revenues. Thus, state and local debt issues are related not only to the specific expenditures for capital projects, but also to their more general need for both capital and operating funds.

From this more general perspective, the primary determinants of the external financing requirements of state and local governments are two: the need to finance budget deficits, and the need to finance their continually growing stocks of financial assets (mainly working or liquid asset balances). As can be seen in Figure 5–2, budget deficits were the larger

Figure 5–2

Composition of state and local government external financing: budget deficits and financial asset accumulations (Expressed as percent of GNP)

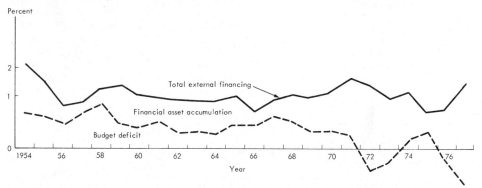

source of financing needs in the 1950s. During the 1960s, each source was of about equal importance. In the mid-1970s, however, state and local budgets were approximately in balance, and long-term debt issues were equal to the increases in the financial asset holdings of state and local governments.

State and local government receipts and expenditures

State and local government receipts and expenditures have grown from about 8 percent of GNP in 1955 to almost 16 percent of GNP in 1975. Several factors contributed to this expansion. While the total population rose by 31 percent over this period, the number of people living in urban areas, where supplies of government services are highest, grew by approximately 48 percent. The workload in traditional government services was increased by the growth in automobiles, amounts of solid waste, and crime. The postwar baby boom, in particular, created a surge in demand for education that moved from primary and secondary schools to colleges. Rising affluence enabled governments to establish higher levels of service in existing functions. Educational programs were improved, as were facilities in health, transportation, recreation, housing, and other fields. Finally, state and local governments expanded to new fields, such as manpower development and pollution control.

As Table 5–6 demonstrates, almost 90 percent of state and local expenditures are used for the purchase of goods and services, with em-

Table 5–6
State and local government expenditures and receipts, 1976

	Billions of $		Percent	
Expenditures				
Purchases of goods and services	231.2		88.7	
Compensation of employees		129.2		49.6
Services		41.7		16.0
Nondurable goods		21.3		8.2
Durable goods		7.3		2.8
Structures		31.7		12.2
Transfer payments to persons	25.9		9.9	
Net interest	−5.7		−2.2	
Subsidies less current surplus				
of government enterprises	−5.2		−2.0	
Net contribution to pension funds	14.5		5.6	
	260.7		100.0	
Receipts				
Indirect business taxes	127.1		48.0	
Sales taxes		57.3		21.6
Property taxes		57.6		21.8
Other		12.2		4.6
Personal taxes	49.6		18.7	
Corporate tax accruals	8.9		3.4	
Contribution for social insurance	18.1		6.8	
Federal grants-in-aid	61.0		23.0	
Total	264.7		100.0	
Surplus	3.9			

ployee compensation comprising about 50 percent of total expenditures. Increasing levels of employment and wages have contributed significantly to the growth in expenditures. Employment levels in state and local government grew at a compound annual rate of 4.8 percent from 1955 to 1975 compared with a 1.8 percent rate for private employment and a 1.2 percent rate for federal employment. During the period 1953 to 1973, the annual average earnings of state and local government employees rose at an annual rate of 4.5 percent. Under the pressure of increasing labor costs in their own sector, state and local governments turned increasingly to the private sector for the purchase of services. As a result, service purchases rose from 8.2 percent of expenditures in 1955 to 16.0 percent in 1976. In the face of this very rapid rate of increase in current outlays, the more moderate growth in capital outlays meant that capital expenditures (on structures) fell from 26.6 percent of expenditures in 1955 to 12.2 percent in 1976.

Transfer payments to persons, largely for unemployment, public assistance, and hospital and medical insurance payments, comprise about 10 percent of total expenditures. The amounts set aside in pension fund reserves to fund the employee pension liabilities assumed by state and local governments amount to about 5 percent of total expenditures. Since many state and local governments fund only a small fraction of their total pension liability, these amounts set aside for pension fund costs seriously understate the real expenses being incurred by state and local governments in this regard.[4]

Interest received on the financial assets held by state and local governments for their own operating purposes and interest earned on the assets in their pension funds exceeds interest payments made by state and local governments.[5]

Approximately one half of state and local receipts arise from indirect business taxes, largely sales and property taxes. While sales tax collections have remained a steady source of finance at about 22 percent of total sources, property taxes have fallen from about 33 percent of total sources in 1955 to about 22 percent in 1976. Taxes on personal income and such nontax charges as tuition and hospital and health charges comprise the bulk of personal tax receipts. This source of revenue has grown from 12.3 percent of total receipts in 1955 to 18.7 percent of total receipts in 1976. The most rapidly growing source of state and local receipts is the category of federal grants-in-aid. Between 1955 and 1965, these grants grew at a rate which averaged 13.6 percent per year. During the period 1965 to 1975, grants-in-aid grew at a 17 percent annual rate.[6] By 1975, federal grants-in-aid amounted to 23 percent of state and local receipts.

Inflation and state and local budgets

Inflation affects state and local receipts to about the same degree that it affects outlays. Sales tax receipts move roughly in proportion to the pace of inflation, as do their personal income tax systems, since they are primarily

---

[4] See, for example, Report of the Permanent Commission on Public Employee Pension and Retirement, State of New York, Executive Department, January 30, 1973; and David J. Ott, et al., *State Finances in the Last Half of the 1970s,* American Enterprise Institute for Public Policy Research, Washington, D.C., Domestic Affairs Study 29, April 1975.

[5] As of the end of 1976, state and local governments had $117 billion of time deposits and U.S. government securities. In addition, their retirement funds held $90 billion of bonds. At the same time the debt outstanding of state and local governments was $236 billion. During 1976, state and local governments received a total of $17.3 billion in interest payments; $9.9 billion on the assets held for operating purposes and $7.4 billion on their pension fund assets. During the same year, they paid $11.6 billion in interest on their debt outstanding. Net interest payments, therefore, amounted to *minus* $5.7 billion.

[6] See Chapter 4 for a discussion of the impact of these grants on the federal budget.

flat-rate taxes.[7] The property tax, which plays a large role in the financial affairs of the local governments, also moves in response to inflation, although with a lag, as this inflation is reflected in increased assessed values on property. On the outlay side, wage rates and labor costs also move with inflation.

The effects of recessions on state and local governments

Recessions have had a substantial impact on state and local budgets. While expenditure levels are not affected much by recessions, income and sales tax collections are slowed significantly. Figure 5–3 shows an estimate of the balance that would have existed in the combined budget of all state and local governments had the economy been operating at high employment throughout the period from 1958 to 1976. The sharp growth in federal revenue sharing, the broadening of state and local tax bases, and increasing restraints on spending caused the substantial high employment surplus of the mid-1970s. The economic recession of 1974–1976, however, kept the actual budget position of state and local governments from experiencing this movement into significant surplus.

The history of budget deficits

The state and local government sector experienced a deficit in every year from 1950 to 1971, but in 1972 that pattern changed dramatically, as Figure 5–3 demonstrates. In 1972 and 1973, large increases in personal income taxes and an especially large increase in federal grants-in-aid (mainly revenue-sharing grants) raised revenues above the sum of capital and current outlays, and state and local governments as a group experienced surpluses. Although the aggregate state and local surplus disappeared in the recession of 1974–1975, it reappeared in 1976 and 1977. If we assume the estimates of the high employment budget position in Figure 5–3 are correct, actual budget deficits are unlikely to generate large future financing needs until state and local spending programs are substantially increased or revenue bases substantially narrowed.

Financial asset accumulation

State and local governments also hold substantial amounts of financial assets ($169 billion at the end of 1977), approximately 80 percent of which are held in the form of demand and time deposits and U.S. government securities.

---

[7] This is in marked contrast to the progressive federal personal tax system which raises increasing amounts of revenue in response to inflation.

Figure 5–3
Budget balance of state and local governments (Expressed as percent of actual receipts)

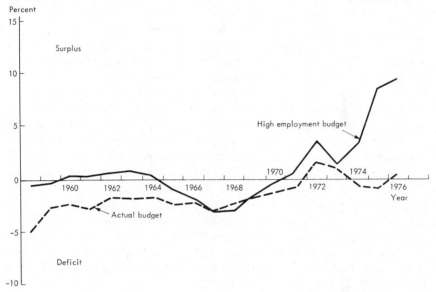

Between 1950 and 1970, the ratio of financial asset holdings to annual expenditures fell regularly from 0.76 to 0.52 (see Table 5–7). During this time, additions to liquid asset holdings required only modest amounts of funds. Beginning in 1972, however, state and local governments began to add significantly to their financial asset holdings. This use of funds came to be *the* primary determinant of state and local debt issues (see Figure 5–2). By the end of 1977, the ratio of total financial asset holdings to expenditures had risen to 0.62.

Table 5–7
State and local government holdings of financial assets in relation to annual expenditures

	Annual expenditures	Total financial assets	Assets/ expenditures
1950	23.2	17.7	0.76
1955	34.2	26.0	0.76
1960	52.0	33.1	0.64
1965	78.4	50.1	0.64
1970	138.6	71.9	0.52
1977 (est.)	274.4 (est.)	169.0 (est.)	0.62

The reason for this sharp rise in holdings of financial assets are not well understood. In part it may reflect the fact that financial asset balances had fallen too low in relation to annual expenditures. Also, since state and local government securities are exempt from federal income tax and U.S. Treasury securities are not, the interest rates which have to be paid by state and local governments are less than what they can earn on Treasury securities. This creates an incentive for state and local governments to issue debt and invest the proceeds in Treasury securities, even when there is no immediate need for the funds. In an attempt to give them flexibility with respect to the timing of their long-term debt issues, the Treasury allows state and local governments to borrow as much as three years in advance of some capital projects. There is also evidence that when interest rates fall from previously high levels, some governmental units which issued debt during these high rate periods issue additional debt and invest the proceeds in U.S. Treasury securities with maturities similar to their original debt issue. These interest rate "profits" are a tempting offset to the "losses" incurred by originally issuing the state and local securities during a period of high interest rates. Naturally, the U.S. Treasury limits this behavior whenever it can. Each of these activities, to the extent they occur, however, contributes to the size of the financial asset portfolios of state and local governments.

Net funds raised in financial markets

Whatever the reasons for the accumulations of financial assets, they grew to be approximately equal in amount to the volume of state and local debt issued in the 1970s. Taken as a group, state and local governments were recycling to other financial markets about as large a volume of funds as they were withdrawing from the state and local government securities market. As a result, the *net* financial pressure that state and local governments put on financial markets during the entire period, and especially in the 1970s, was very small. If we define net funds raised in financial markets as total debt issues sold minus the liquid financial assets accumulated, the net funds raised by the state and local sector rarely exceeded 1 percent of GNP and were about zero in the early 1970s (see Figure 5–4).

SUMMARY

State and local governments raise a considerable amount of funds through the sale of debt securities. Their financing needs have been rather stable over the postwar period and have averaged about 1.2 percent of GNP. In part, these debt issues are associated with capital projects. They allow the cost of these projects to be spread over the generations of users who benefit from them. The level of real expenditures on capital projects

Figure 5–4
State and local governments external financing requirements and net demands on financial
markets (Expressed as percent of GNP)

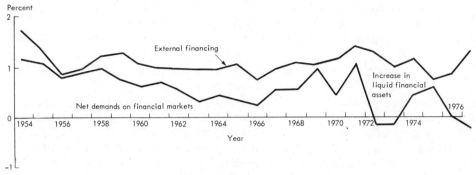

fell after the late 1960s, and because total outlays and receipts were growing quite rapidly, capital outlays came to represent a smaller fraction of
total expenditure or receipts.

Another factor affecting state and local debt issues is overall budget
position. Between 1950 and 1977, the budget of the state and local government sector has moved from a position of deficit to one of approximate
balance or modest surplus. This meant that by the mid-1970s, their own
revenues (and a rapidly growing volume of federal grants-in-aid) provided
approximately enough funds to finance both their current and capital outlays. As a result, the sector's nonfinancial transactions came to require
little, if any, external finance. Their recent external financing has instead
been matched approximately by their financial asset accumulation. In
essence, they have recently been raising a relatively steady flow of funds
in the markets for tax-exempt state and local government obligations, and
rechanneling these funds to other financial markets through their increased holdings of financial assets.

QUESTIONS

1. What are the determinants of the borrowing of state and local governments?
   How do these differ from the determinants of the federal government's
   borrowing?
2. Why do state and local governments hold liquid assets such as bank deposits
   and U.S. government securities?
3. What is the outlook for the volume of state and local borrowing?

REFERENCES

Financing State and Local Governments. Proceedings of the Monetary Conference, Federal Reserve Bank of Boston, 1970.

New York City's Fiscal Problem: Its Origins, Potential Repercussions, and Some Alternative Policy Responses, Background Paper No. 1, October 10, 1975, Congress of the United States, Congressional Budget Office, Washington, D.C.

Gramlich, Edward M. "State and Local Budgets the Day after It Rained: Why Is the Surplus So High," *Brookings Papers on Economic Activity*, vol. 1 (1978).

Maxwell, James A. and Aronson, J. Richard. *Financing State and Local Governments*, 3d ed., Brookings Institution, 1977.

Ott, David J.; Ott, Attiat F.; Maxwell, James A.; and Aronson, J. Richard. *State and Local Finances in the Last Half of the 1970's*, Washington: American Enterprise Institute for Public Policies Research, 1975.

Arthur F. Burns, Chairman, Board of Governors of the Federal Reserve System, before the Subcommittee on Economic Stabilization, Committee on Banking, Currency, and Housing, U.S. House of Representatives, October 23, 1975, in *Federal Reserve Bulletin* (November 1975), p. 736.

6

The impact of the rest of the world
on U.S. financial markets
and institutions

Financial markets and actors outside the United States affect United States financial markets and institutions in several ways. Nonresident borrowers and lenders create supplies and demands for funds in specific markets in the United States, and an understanding of the determinants of these flows of funds is important to an understanding of particular U.S. markets. Also, the sum of these financial transactions creates a net financial flow in U.S. financial markets, at times providing funds net and, at times, demanding funds net. Thus, transactions with the foreign sector affect the overall level of interest rates and the structure of interest rates in the different domestic markets.

The markets for financial assets denominated in dollars are not confined to the United States, however. There are also financial markets outside the United States in which dollar financial assets and liabilities are created and exchanged. The Eurodollar markets are the largest of these external dollar markets. Because many investors and borrowers can use either the internal or the external dollar markets, interest rates and credit flows in these internal and external dollar markets are closely related to each other. When analyzing certain financial markets in the United States, especially the markets for long-term and short-term corporate debt, we shall have to consider the effects of these external (Eurodollar) markets.

Finally, financial markets in currencies other than the U.S. dollar can affect the markets for dollar assets and liabilities. Since many investors have the option of investing or raising funds in any of several currencies, the interest rates and credit flows in the financial markets in these different currencies are related one to the other. In this chapter, and throughout the book, we shall concentrate attention on only the first two of these effects, that is, the direct effects of nonresident borrowing and lending in the U.S. markets and the indirect effects on financial markets in the United States which arise from transactions in the external dollar markets.

INTERNAL AND EXTERNAL MARKETS FOR DOLLAR DENOMINATED FINANCIAL CLAIMS

As noted above, the largest of the markets outside the United States in which dollar financial assets and liabilities are traded are the so-called Euromarkets. Figure 6–1 presents some examples of the investment alternatives open to foreign holders of dollar financial assets.

Whether transactions in dollar assets and liabilities take place in the internal or external dollar market depends in part on convenience, including the convenience of being geographically close to the borrower or to the source of the funds. However, differences in regulation and taxation are the primary reasons that transactions are conducted in the external dollar market. For instance, the interest rate which commercial banks can pay on the large certificates of deposit they offer in the United States has at times been regulated by the Federal Reserve Board. The interest rate which the foreign branches or subsidiaries of U.S. commercial banks can offer is not subject to these regulations. Also, U.S. commercial banks are required to hold noninterest bearing reserves against the deposits they raise in their domestic operations. No such reserve requirements exist for the deposits in their foreign branches. Thus, U.S. banks are induced to conduct some of their deposit-raising and lending activities in the external dollar market rather than in the internal market.

Different regulations in the internal and external markets affect more than commercial banks. Securities offered for sale in the public bond and

Figure 6–1
Examples of the alternative dollar denominated assets available to nonresident
holders of dollar assets

Held as claims against U.S. residents	Held as claims against nonresidents

With the transaction taking place
In the U.S.
 	
Purchases of:
  Deposits at U.S. banks
  Bonds or stocks of U.S. corporations
  U.S. government bonds
  Foreign direct investment in firms
    in the United States
	Purchases of:
	  Bonds issued by non-U.S. firms
	  Bonds issued by foreign governments

Outside the U.S.
 	
Purchases of:
  Bonds of U.S. corporations sold in
    Eurobond markets
  Special foreign issues of dollar
    denominated U.S. government
    bonds
	Purchases of:
	  Deposits at foreign branches of
	    U.S. banks
	  Deposits at foreign banks
	  Bonds of subsidiaries or foreign
	    branches of U.S. corporations
	  Bonds and stocks of foreign
	    corporations
	  Bonds of foreign governments

stock markets in the United States must be registered with the U.S. Securities and Exchange Commission and meet its requirements for adequate disclosure. No such regulation exists for dollar debts or equities sold outside the U.S. markets. When the benefits of this domestic regulation are not worth their costs to borrowers and lenders, transactions are diverted to the external market. On the other hand, the corporate bond market in the United States can absorb much larger issues than can the Eurodollar bond market, the major external dollar corporate bond market. Moreover, Eurodollar corporate bonds typically have a shorter maturity than do most American dollar corporate bonds. These facts induce many issuers of corporate bonds to transact in the internal rather than the external market for corporate bonds.

The taxation of investment income differs in the internal and external market as well. Foreign as well as domestic investors are often subject to income tax withholding when they invest in assets in the United States. While these withheld taxes are refunded when the asset holder demonstrates that no U.S. tax liability applies to the holdings, this fact must be demonstrated, and the refund comes some time after the withholding has occurred.

In addition, some nonresident investors seem to believe that the U.S. authorities might, under certain circumstances, block the transfer of, or expropriate, the funds of certain foreign investors. Since dollar claims on entities outside the United States would not be subject to the jurisdiction of the U.S. authorities, these investors prefer dollar claims in the external market rather than dollar claims on entities in the United States. Thus, for example, dollar deposits held in non-U.S. banks or even in the foreign branches of U.S. banks seem to be preferred by some foreign investors to dollar deposits in the home offices of U.S. banks.[1]

NONRESIDENT DEMAND FOR DOLLAR DENOMINATED FINANCIAL ASSETS AND LIABILITIES

The nonresident holders of dollar assets can be divided into two groups—private parties and official parties, or central banks. Private parties include nonresident individuals, corporations and commercial banks, and the foreign branches of U.S. commercial banks.

Private parties

Private nonresidents demand dollar denominated financial assets for transactions and investment or financing purposes. Because nonresidents purchase a large volume of U.S. exports which must be paid for in U.S. dollars, and because many internationally traded goods require payment in U.S. dollars, the transactions demand for U.S. dollars is substantial. The nonresident demand for dollar assets and liabilities for investment and financing purposes arises from several sources.

Nonresident borrowers and lenders are attracted to the markets for dollar assets because these markets are more liquid and have lower transaction costs than is true in markets in most other currencies. For much of the postwar period, the internal dollar markets were far more liquid (could handle a much larger volume of purchases and sales without a substantial movement in price) than were markets in most other currencies. This drew a substantial volume of nonresident funds to dollar assets. As the external market in short-term dollar assets (the Eurodollar market) developed great liquidity and low transaction costs, however, it drew some of this demand for dollar assets and liabilities away from the internal dollar market. The subsequent development of a Eurodollar bond market drew some of the transactions in these longer term securities out of the internal dollar market as well. Finally, as the internal markets of other countries

---

[1] This belief on the part of the Russians in the early 1950s is said to have been the origin of their practice of depositing their dollar holdings in British banks and the origin of the Eurodollar market.

reach a size where large transactions can be managed easily and at low cost, and as these national governments begin to allow residents and nonresidents to transact freely, the distinctive position of the U.S. dollar markets as the markets with the most liquidity and lowest transactions cost is being challenged. The growth of external markets in these other currencies accelerates this trend.

A second feature of the dollar which led to its use as an international currency was the fact that the banks which dominated the intermediation (deposit gathering and lending) in dollars were willing to charge a smaller spread between borrower cost and depositor return than were the banks that dominated the intermediation in other currencies. However, as the competition in international banking intensifies, these spreads are narrowing and the attractiveness to private nonresidents of borrowing and accepting bank deposits in other currencies is increasing. Indeed, since international banks now conduct a large volume of business in many currencies other than the currency of their ''home'' nation, the pricing behavior of a nation's banks no longer controls the pricing of the loans and deposits in its currency. The behavior of these international banks increases the attractiveness of dealing in currencies other than the dollar, and thereby lessens the dollar's distinctive position.

A third feature of the dollar which led to its use by nonresidents was that long-term investors in the internal dollar markets seem to require less of a premium over short-term interest rates than was the case in other currencies. Because of this fact, nonresident holders of short-term dollar assets could receive higher returns than available elsewhere—at the same time that nonresident borrowers of long-term funds had to pay lower rates than elsewhere. As more and more nonresidents attempt to take advantage of this situation, however, they tend to put downward pressure on short-term dollar rates and upward pressure on long-term dollar rates. This tends to bring the spread between short-term and long-term dollar rates in the United States more in line with this spread in other currencies and lessens this advantage of dollar markets.

Finally, the private nonresident demand for dollar assets depends in a major way on their expected return. The demand is strong only as long as the total expected return from dollar financial assets (the expected interest rate plus or minus the expected change in the value of the dollar) is commensurate with the total expected return from holding financial assets in any other currency.

For most of the period since World War II, the U.S. dollar held a special position, relative to all other currencies, which had an important effect on the nonresident demand for dollar financial assets. In 1944, the Articles of Agreement of the International Monetary Fund established the U.S. dollar as the central currency to which all other currencies had to relate themselves.[2] While the values of specific foreign currencies could change against the dollar, there was no expectation of either devaluation or revaluation of the U.S. dollar vis-a-vis all other currencies taken together. This implied that the international purchasing power of the U.S. dollar was supposed to behave as would the international purchasing power of a diversified portfolio of currency holdings. Thus, the U.S. dollar was a much safer store of international value than any other single currency. This made the U.S. dollar particularly attractive as a medium of exchange for international transactions. Furthermore, because it was the only currency which was not supposed to change in value relative to all other currencies taken together, it was an attractive currency in which to denominate international borrowing and lending.

Since 1970, however, the dollar has experienced several sharp declines relative to most indices of currencies (see Figure 6–2). This has to have reduced its attractiveness to nonresident asset holders (and to some resident asset holders as well). While this feature of the dollar has decreased its attractiveness, it is not clear which other currency or group of currencies offer better diversification against exchange rate changes. Thus, as long as the total expected return from dollar assets is commensurate with the total expected return from assets in other currencies, the private nonresident demand for dollars is likely to remain large.

Official parties (central banks)

The demand for assets on the part of foreign central banks arises in part from their need for reserves, which can be used to finance a temporary excess of imports over exports or as a store of value. The importance of the dollar as a transactions currency, the liquidity of dollar financial assets, and the attractiveness of the dollar as a relatively diversified store of value have caused dollar financial assets to be a most important element in these reserve holdings.

In addition, the foreign central banks' demand for dollars arises from their need or desire to affect the relative price of their currency. As we shall see, the volume of dollar assets outside the United States has grown each year. To the extent that the demand from nonresidents for dollar financial assets does not grow as fast as does the total of foreign dollar

---

[2] Under the agreement, often called the Bretton Woods Agreement, each country agreed to maintain the value of its currency within a narrow range around an official par value relative to the dollar. While any member country could propose a change in the par value of its currency relative to the U.S. dollar, it could do so only to correct a "fundamental disequilibrium" in its balance of payments. As its part of the agreement, the United States agreed to manage its affairs in a way which maintained that value of the U.S. dollar at its then-existing level relative to all other currencies taken as a whole. It agreed to allow other central banks to exchange their holdings of U.S. dollars for U.S. gold at the price of $35 per ounce of gold.

Figure 6–2
Movements in exchange rates*

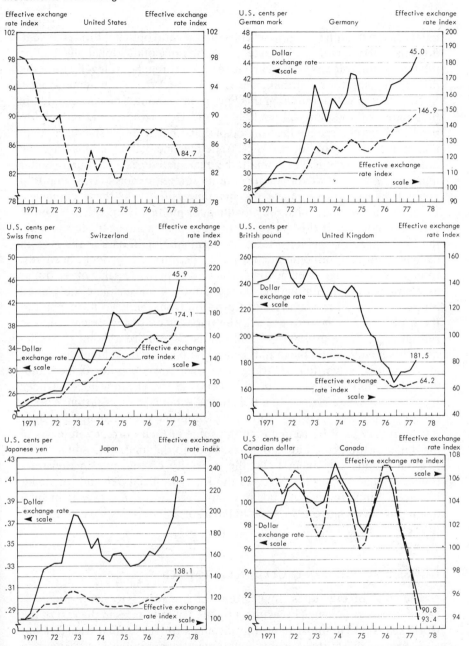

* Effective exchange rate changes are an indicator of the extent to which the external value of a country's currency has moved relative to other currencies. Effective exchange rate changes are computed as an index, combining the exchange rates between the currency in question and 20 other major currencies with weights derived from the International Monetary Fund's "Multilateral Exchange Rate Model." Each weight represents the model's estimate of the effect on the trade balance of the country in question of a change of 1 percent in the domestic currency price of one of the other currencies. The weights, therefore, take account of the size of trade flows as well as of the relevant price elasticities and the feedback effects of exchange rate changes on domestic costs and prices. The measure is expressed as an index based on the par values in May 1970.

Source: Jacques R. Artus and Rudolf R. Rhomberg, "A Multilateral Exchange Rate Model," *International Monetary Fund Staff Papers* (November 1973), pp. 591–611. Prepared by Federal Reserve Bank of St. Louis.

balances outstanding, foreign officials face several options. First, they can do nothing to offset the imbalance. If so, the price of the dollar will decline relative to the price of other currencies until it reaches a level where the private demand for dollar balances rises to meet the outstanding supply. Several forces will act to bring this equilibrium about. The depreciation in the value of the dollar will tend to expand U.S. exports and reduce imports and thereby reduce the volume of dollar balances outstanding. Also, the improved outlook for the U.S. trade balance could well increase the attractiveness (or at least eliminate the unattractiveness) of holding dollar financial assets. However, the decline in foreign exports (U.S. imports) could lead to a slower pace of economic activity in these countries. Foreign central banks might be unwilling, or politically unable, to tolerate this consequence. If this were so, foreign officials might try to maintain the existing set of exchange rates by accumulating dollars in the foreign exchange markets. Should such a policy be pursued for long, however, foreign officials might well become concerned about the value of the dollar assets they were accumulating. Such a policy would insulate the United States and the other countries of the world from the need to respond to the problems which were causing the imbalance. To the extent that the resolution of these problems would ultimately require a dollar depreciation, this policy would mean that central banks would accumulate dollars at overvalued rates, that is, trade their own currencies for dollars and, ultimately, their own goods for U.S. goods at too cheap a price.[3] Under the fixed exchange rate system which was established at Bretton Woods, central banks were *required* to buy or sell dollars in exchange for their own currency in order to maintain the value of their currency in terms of the dollar at the agreed-upon parities. Prior to the final breakdown of the Bretton Woods system in 1973, the necessity of engaging in these activities was an important factor in the foreign official demand for dollar balances. While foreign officials have not been *required* to engage in such dollar purchases since 1973, their holdings of dollar assets have continued to grow rapidly.

GROSS AND NET FINANCIAL INVESTMENT

The total of the funds flows from U.S. residents to nonresidents is called the gross financial investment by the United States in the rest of the world (ROW). The most important avenues for these fund transfers are U.S. foreign direct investment, government lending, purchase of foreign securities, and foreign lending by U.S. banks. Gross financial investment

---

[3] Foreign central bank purchases of dollars in exchange for local currency would also expand the reserve base of the local banking system. Unless the central bank took offsetting action, these increases in bank reserves would lead to expansion in the money supply and, ultimately, to an increased rate of inflation. This is another factor limiting their willingness to buy dollars to maintain their exchange rate.

by the United States in the rest of the world amounted annually to about 1 percent of GNP in the early 1960s. However, it increased substantially, to a rate of about 2.5 percent of GNP, in the mid-1970s (see Figure 6–3). The total of the funds flow into the U.S. financial system from nonresidents is called the gross financial investment by the ROW in the United States. These flows are comprised primarily of purchases of demand and time deposits, government securities, corporate bonds and stocks, as well as direct investments in business corporations and real estate. They amounted to about 0.5 percent of GNP in the early 1960s and fluctuated between 1 and 3 percent of GNP in the mid-1970s.

The difference between these two flows (gross financial investment by the United States in the ROW minus gross financial investment by the ROW in the United States) is called the *net financial investment* by the United States in the ROW sector. It is the measure of the net financing pressure put on U.S. financial markets by the transactions with the ROW. Net financial investment by the United States in the ROW sector is positive when U.S. residents extend more credit to nonresidents than nonresidents extend to residents of the United States. Net financial investment by the United States occurs whenever the United States experiences a surplus on its balance of payments on current account. That is, whenever the United States sells more goods and services abroad than it buys from abroad, it must accept claims (financial promises) from the ROW to repay at a later date. Thus, a current account surplus for the United States is matched by an equal amount of net financial investment by the United States in the ROW. A surplus in the U.S. current account balance implies the ROW sector is drawing funds out of U.S. financial markets on a net basis. Alternately, when the ROW sells more goods and services in the United States than it buys from the United States, the ROW must accept claims (financial promises) from the United States to repay at a later date. Thus, current account deficits in the U.S. balance of payments imply the ROW sector is providing funds to the U.S. financial markets on a net basis (and that the net financial investment by the United States in the ROW sector is negative).

The limits to the size of this net fund inflow or outflow are several. First, current account surpluses in the U.S. balance of payments lead to an increase in the demand for dollars relative to other currencies as nonresidents seek more dollars to pay for their imports from the United States than residents of the United States seek the foreign currencies necessary to pay for U.S. imports. This puts upward pressure on the value of the dollar, raises the cost of U.S. exports relative to the exports of other countries, and reduces the U.S. current account surplus. In addition, large current account surpluses imply high levels of production and employment in the United States. These tend to generate inflationary pressures in the United States. Ultimately, the rise in U.S. prices weakens the competitive position of U.S. exports and reduces the size of the U.S. surplus. Also, current

Figure 6–3

U.S. transactions with the rest of the world (ROW) (Annual amounts expressed as a percent of U.S. GNP)

A. Gross financial investment by the United States in the ROW

Composed of:

U.S. foreign direct investment
U.S. govt. lending abroad
Foreign security purchases by
    U.S. entities
U.S. bank lending abroad
Trade credit extended by U.S.
    firms
Unrecorded outflows

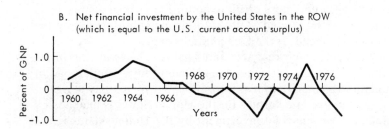

B. Net financial investment by the United States in the ROW
(which is equal to the U.S. current account surplus)

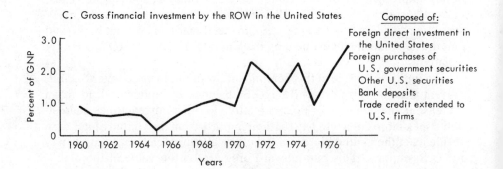

C. Gross financial investment by the ROW in the United States

Composed of:

Foreign direct investment in
    the United States
Foreign purchases of
    U.S. government securities
Other U.S. securities
Bank deposits
Trade credit extended to
    U.S. firms

account surpluses in the United States imply current account deficits in some other countries. These deficits give rise to forces in the deficit countries which add to the pressures limiting the U.S. surplus. The current account deficits lead to weakened levels of aggregate demand in these countries and to a relative decline in their rates of inflation. These factors stimulate their exports relative to their imports. Thus, imbalances in the current account (either surpluses or deficits) give rise to forces which tend to reduce the imbalances.

Dollar outflows and inflows

The transactions with nonresidents are often described as giving rise to "inflows" and "outflows" of dollars. For example, U.S. imports and U.S. direct investment abroad are referred to as a source of dollar outflows, as is U.S. bank lending abroad, or the purchase by U.S. investors of foreign securities. Similarly, U.S. exports and nonresident purchases of U.S. securities are often referred to as dollar inflows. Actually, there is no separate outflow and inflow of funds in these transactions. Every dollar outflow originating in a resident's purchase of foreign goods or financial assets must be matched by an equal dollar inflow as some nonresident takes possession of the dollar claim offered in payment by the resident. There is usually no direct connection between the dollar outflow and inflow, however. The nonresident who initially takes possession of the dollar claim may exchange it with other nonresidents, for example, with a foreign central bank in exchange for local currency, or to make a dollar payment. Ultimately, however, some nonresident must use the dollar claim to buy U.S. exports or to make a financial investment in the United States. Because the entities involved in the dollar outflow may be different from those engaging in the associated inflow, the inflow and outflow are often distinguished from each other. However, they are the two sides of the initial transaction, and the total of dollar "outflows" must equal the total of dollar "inflows."[4]

HISTORY OF NONRESIDENT TRANSACTIONS IN THE U.S. FINANCIAL MARKETS

1960–1965

Throughout the period from 1960 to 1965, gross outflows from the United States to the ROW amounted to about 1 percent of GNP annually.

---

[4] Another way to state these relationships is to note that the flow of funds accounting identity for international transactions requires that the volume of dollars which foreign entities obtain as a result of the gross financial investment by the United States in the ROW can be used for two purposes. Foreigners as a whole can use these dollars to buy U.S. goods or to buy financial assets in the United States. They have no further options.

Approximately one half of these outflows financed the U.S. current account balance of payments surpluses during those years. The other half was recycled to the United States in the form of financial investments by foreigners in the United States. The financial outflows were mainly long-term and somewhat risky in nature (U.S. government lending abroad and U.S. foreign direct investment abroad, primarily by U.S. corporations and their foreign subsidiaries). (See Table 6–1.) The financial inflows were invested primarily in very safe and short-term investments (bank deposits and short-term U.S. government securities). Thus, the international transactions in the internal dollar market were withdrawing substantial sums of funds from long-term financial markets in the United States and recycling part of these funds into short-term markets in the United States.

Table 6–1

Transactions between the United States and the ROW, selected periods 1960–1977 (Billions of $, cumulative flows)

	1960– 1965	1966– 1969	1970– 1971	1972– 1973	1974– 1976	1977
Dollar outflows						
U.S. foreign direct investment	12.8	12.6	8.8	6.4	12.3	5.0
U.S. government lending abroad	8.1	8.4	3.5	4.2	7.3	3.7
Foreign security purchases by U.S. entities	5.1	5.2	2.2	1.3	16.8	5.4
U.S. bank lending abroad	6.8	0.7	3.9	9.5	54.0	11.7
Short-term	4.4	−1.1	3.5	7.2	48.3	11.0
Long-term	2.4	1.8	0.4	2.3	5.7	0.7
Unrecorded outflows	4.9	0.7	10.0	4.7	−13.8	3.0
Other*	1.8	2.5	1.9	3.4	6.6	0.1
Total	39.6	30.1	30.3	29.5	83.1	28.8
Dollar inflows						
U.S. current account surplus	20.2	−0.4	−4.4	−9.8	5.1	−20.2
Accumulation of U.S. financial assets	19.2	30.6	34.7	39.0	78.0	49.0
By foreign official parties (central banks)	13.4	−0.7	38.6	17.1	31.4	37.2
Securities and bank deposits	7.4	0.7	33.8	16.9	35.9	37.4
U.S. gold and foreign exchange†	6.0	−1.4	4.8	0.2	−4.5	−0.2
By foreign private parties	5.7	31.3	−5.5	22.2	46.6	11.8
Short-term‡	4.5	18.0	−12.0	10.2	35.9	6.8
Long-term§	1.2	13.3	6.5	12.0	10.7	5.0
Special drawing rights	—	—	1.6	0.7	—	—
Total	39.4	30.2	30.3	29.2	83.1	28.8

* Mainly trade credit.
† Change in the U.S. official reserve assets, net.
‡ Increase in foreign holdings of U.S. government securities, short-term bank deposits, and short-term trade credit.
§ Foreign direct investment in the United States plus increase in holdings of other securities, long-term bank deposits, and long-term trade credit.
Source: U.S. International Transactions, Table 1, *Survey of Current Business.*

The forces behind these financial transactions were (and are) the subject of considerable disagreement. One analysis, originating mostly in Europe, implies that the United States was exploiting the demands for its currency which arose because of its special position in the international monetary system. It argues that the United States was forcing dollars on a world which was uninterested in holding them (given the existing interest rates in the United States and the outlook for the exchange rate of the dollar) but which was required to hold the dollars in order to maintain the existing pattern of exchange rates. Under this view, foreign central banks were required to hold dollar financial assets whose returns were insufficient at the same time that the United States was acquiring valuable claims on the real assets in these foreign countries.

The alternative analysis of the situation stresses the importance of two ideas. First, it is argued that there was a genuine demand for dollar assets on the part of the other nations of the world and that there is no evidence that their rate of accumulation of dollar assets was exceeding their demand for these assets. Also, it is argued that because long-term funds were more expensive in the financial markets of the rest of the world than they were in the United States, some nonresidents used the U.S. financial markets as cheaper and more convenient sources of long-term funds. Similarly, the inflows are said to reflect the attractiveness of the short-term dollar financial assets available in the U.S. financial markets. Rather than envision the United States as forcing overvalued dollars on an unwilling world, this view sees the United States as playing the role of an international financial intermediary—providing internationally attractive short-term assets and extending long-term credit (and direct foreign investment) to a world in need of it.[5]

In either case, by the mid-1960s, the dollar outflow from the United States continued at the steady rate of about 1 percent of GNP annually. In addition, the U.S. net export position failed to keep pace with the total dollar outflow. This resulted in increasing amounts of financial investment in the United States. The majority of this financial investment was short-term and was being accumulated by foreign central banks (not nonresident private parties). These transactions were reflected in the international balance sheet of the United States. As of the end of 1965, foreigners held $58.8 billion of financial claims on the United States. Of these, $32.4, or 55 percent were short-term, with foreign central banks holding $19.9 billion. On the other hand, the international assets held by the U.S. were mainly long-term assets. Official U.S. short-term balances amounted to only $4.8 billion and total short-term assets amounted to only $15.0 billion. The U.S. gold stock which, according to law was available to foreign officials

---

[5] This is analogous to the intermediation that takes place in the internal financial markets as, for example, thrift institutions accept the relatively short-term deposits of households and offer long-term mortgage credit to homeowners.

in exchange for dollars, was valued at $13.8 billion. This was smaller than the total stock of short-term dollar claims on U.S. entities held by foreign officials. Thus, nonresident holders of claims on U.S. residents held assets whose value and liquidity arose much more from the willingness of nonresidents to exchange these assets among themselves than it did from an ability to acquire international reserves such as gold or foreign currencies from the United States itself.[6] (See Table 6–2.)

Table 6–2
International investment position of the United States at year-end 1965 (Billions of $)

U.S. assets and investments abroad			Foreign assets and investments in the United States		
Short-term		15.0	Short-term		32.4
Private	10.2		By holder		
Official	4.8		Foreign central banks	19.9	
			Foreign commercial banks	7.4	
Long-term		90.2	Other private holders	5.0	
Private	70.9		By type		
Direct investment	49.3		Private obligations	18.2	
Portfolio investment	21.6		U.S. government obligations	14.2	
Official	20.3				
			Long-term		26.4
Gold stock		13.8	Direct investment	8.8	
			Portfolio investment	17.6	
Total		119.0	Total		58.8

Source: *Survey of Current Business*, September 1967.

As long as nonresident private parties felt sure that foreign officials would not permit the exchange rate of the dollar to decline, they had little reason for concern about this situation. These private parties could expect to sell their dollars to their central banks for local currency at the existing fixed exchange rates. Foreign officials, however, were concerned about the continuous growth in their dollar holdings relative to the U.S. holdings of gold and short-term assets. They continually pressured the United States to reduce the growth rate of these foreign dollar claims.

The United States responded to these concerns in two ways. It attempted to maintain relatively high short-term rates in the United States in order to make short-term dollar assets more attractive to nonresidents. At the same time, the Federal Reserve tried to offset the impact of this rise in short interest rates on the domestic economy by attempting to

---

[6] These nonresident holdings of dollars could also be used to acquire U.S. goods. However, any significant reduction of nonresident dollar holdings in this way would have required extraordinarily large U.S. current account surpluses.

lower long-term interest rates.[7] As the nonresident accumulation of dollar assets continued, however, the United States took additional actions to limit the size of the dollar outflows from the United States. In 1963, the U.S. government enacted the Interest Equalization Tax (IET) which added one percentage point, in effect, to the annual interest costs of nonresidents who borrowed at long-term in the United States.[8] As the nonresident demand for financing shifted from the U.S. securities markets to American banks, this IET was extended to the longer term loans of banks. In February 1965, voluntary programs were initiated to restrain capital flows by other financial institutions, mainly long-term lenders. Under a program administered by the Commerce Department, those American corporations that engaged in a large volume of foreign direct investment were asked to limit their net outflows. Commercial banks were asked to follow guidelines established by the Federal Reserve which suggested quantitative limits of short-term and long-term foreign lending.

These administrative and regulatory actions reduced the dollar out-flows from the United States. Limiting the growth of transactions in the internal dollar market, however, greatly stimulated the growth of the external dollar market. As the home offices of U.S. banks found them-selves unable to lend dollars raised in the United States to nonresidents, they shifted their international transactions to the external dollar market. By offering attractive interest rates on dollar deposits in their foreign branches, they induced nonresidents to hold a substantial volume of de-posits in these foreign branches. These funds were then used to meet the dollar loan demand which existed outside the United States. U.S. corpo-rations also shifted some of their borrowing to the external dollar markets. Enjoined from raising funds in the United States to finance their foreign operations, U.S. corporations and their subsidiaries increased their dollar borrowing from banks in the external market. They also sold dollar bonds in Europe to finance part of their foreign operations. Thus, even though the U.S. authorities were taking actions which reduced the volume of dollar outflows from the internal dollar market, the volume of dollar claims in the external market continued to grow rapidly.

1966–1969

During the four years 1966 through 1969, the gross dollar outflow from the United States remained a stable 1 percent of GNP. As had been true

---

[7] This policy was called "Operation Twist," and its effectiveness was the subject of much dispute. See, for instance, Chapters 8 and 9, and Franco Modigliani and Richard Sutch, "The Term Structure of Interest Rates: A Re-Examination of the Evidence," *Journal of Money, Credit and Banking,* vol. 1, no. 1 (February 1969), pp. 112–20.

[8] The security issues of Canada and investments in less-developed countries were exempted from this tax.

earlier, foreign direct investment and U.S. government lending accounted for about two thirds of the outflow (see Table 6–1). In those years, however, U.S. current account surplus began to turn negative. Unlike earlier years, then, the gross dollar outflow from the United States had to be entirely matched by foreign financial investment in the United States. Thus, while some foreigners raised a total of $30.1 billion in the United States during these four years, other foreigners invested a slightly larger sum—$30.6 billion—in U.S. financial assets.

There was a substantial shift in the composition of the foreign demand for investment in the United States during these years. While foreign central banks had been responsible for most of the ROW's investment in the United States in the 1960–1965 period, private foreign parties were responsible for all the increase in foreign claims on U.S. entities during the 1966–1969 period. Some of these private inflows arose from the purchase of demand and time deposits at U.S. commercial banks and from the direct investment by nonresidents in U.S. companies. Also, the sharp rise in stock prices in the United States in 1967 and 1968 drew about $4 billion of foreign funds into the U.S. stock market. However, the largest part of the inflow took place because of the actions of U.S. commercial banks and their foreign branches. In 1966 and especially in 1969, inflation accelerated in the United States and business financing demands grew sharply. The ability of U.S. banks to lend to business was limited by the Federal Reserve, which imposed limits on the interest rates banks could pay to attract time deposits in the internal dollar market. These limitations did not affect activities of the foreign branches of U.S. banks operating in the external dollar market. Nor did it affect the interest rate at which U.S. banks could borrow from their foreign branches. As a result, these foreign branches raised dollar deposits in the external dollar market and lent them to their home office for use in the internal dollar market.

During these four years, the demand for funds in the United States was large enough that borrowers in the United States were willing to pay interest rates that were high enough to induce private nonresidents to purchase enough dollar assets to recycle the entire dollar outflow that was taking place. While foreign officials' purchases of U.S. government securities had been the major mechanism for the reinvestment in the United States of the dollar outflows in the early 1960s, U.S. commercial banks were the major source of the reinvestment of the dollar outflows that took place in the years 1966–1969. They did so because their foreign branches were able to offer a very attractive investment vehicle to foreigners—the Eurodollar deposit.

During these years, the web of regulation affecting the dollar outflow from the United States (the volume of dollar funds raised by foreigners in the internal dollar market) continued to grow. In early 1968, the continued growth in U.S. foreign direct investment resulted in presidential action which transformed the previously existing voluntary direct investment program into a mandatory program with much lower levels of permitted capital outlays. At the same time, the Board of Governors of the Federal Reserve System issued new guidelines for foreign credits of all financial institutions, and the President gave the board the authority to make the guidelines mandatory if that proved necessary. This further reduction in the availability of dollar claims from transactions in the internal market resulted in the continued expansion of the growth of transactions in the external dollar market.

1970–1971

These two years saw a dramatic decline in the demand of private nonresidents for dollar claims on U.S. residents. The economic expansion in the United States which had led to the enlarged short-term credit demands of 1966, and especially of 1969, came to an end in 1970. Short-term interest rates in the United States fell sharply. Experiencing a sharp decline in business loan demand in the domestic market, U.S. banks were no longer willing to pay high interest rates to attract dollar deposits through their foreign branches. As a result, interest rates on Eurodollar deposits dropped sharply. In addition, the U.S. trade deficits of 1965–1969 became substantially larger. Private nonresidents began to recall their earlier concerns about the prospective value of the dollar. These concerns, the lowered interest rates, the increased stock of dollar assets which had been accumulated during 1966 through 1969, and the weak position of U.S. exports caused many private nonresidents to become concerned that the dollar was an over-valued currency. As a result, many private nonresidents exchanged their dollar assets for assets denominated in other currencies. In addition, some investors in the United States also became concerned about the value of dollar assets and sold them abroad in exchange for assets denominated in other currencies.

These very large sales of dollars and purchases of other currencies by private parties put downward pressure on the price of the dollar and correspondingly upward pressure on the prices of some foreign currencies, especially the German mark. Central banks in those countries attempted to resist the effect of the pressures on their exchange rates relative to the dollar by buying dollars and simultaneously selling their own currencies in the foreign exchange markets. These actions stabilized exchange rates somewhat in 1970 and early 1971 and allowed private investors to unload a part of their dollar holdings to the foreign central banks. By August 1971, however, the private and public pressure to convert dollars into other assets became overwhelming. On August 15, 1971, the United States suspended convertibility of the dollar, and its value in terms of several major currencies began to float. In December 1971, in the Smithsonian Agreement, a new set of "central rates," or parities were instituted, thereby restoring a revised system of fixed exchange rates. The dollar price of gold was raised 8 percent, and the band within which central banks agreed to maintain exchange rates was widened to 6.25 percent on either side of the parities agreed upon.

During these two years of turmoil in international financial markets, the volume of dollar outflows accelerated. U.S. foreign direct investment and government lending continued, and unidentified sources withdrew an extraordinarily large $10 billion from the United States in unrecorded outflows. Moreover, as the dollar showed signs of real weakness, private nonresidents reduced their existing holdings of deposits in U.S. banks, exchanging their dollars for other currencies at their respective central banks. Foreign central banks thereby acquired these dollar balances. As a result of the dollar outflow during the two years *and* the decrease in private nonresident holdings of dollar claims against the United States, foreign official (central bank) holdings of claims on the United States grew by $38.6 billion. Only $4.8 billion of this was taken in the form of U.S. gold or foreign exchange. Thus, $33.8 billion was invested by foreign officials in U.S. financial assets. Their holdings of U.S. bank deposits decreased by $2.2 billion and their holdings of U.S. government securities grew by $36.0 billion. The majority of their security purchases took the form of relatively short-term maturities.

Once again, transactions with the ROW were drawing substantial amounts of funds out of long-term markets in the United States and reinvesting them in short-term markets in the United States. In addition, funds were being withdrawn from some short-term markets in the United States (the reduction in nonresident holdings of deposits in U.S. banks) and reinvested in other short markets (the purchase of U.S. government securities by foreign officials).

1972–1973

The uncertainties in international financial markets continued into 1972 and 1973. The relative exchange rates agreed upon in the Smithsonian Agreement seemed inappropriate. Moreover, there was growing pressure to abandon fixed exchange rates in favor of a system which relied more on rates which moved as market forces directed them. In June of 1972, the British government decided to allow the pound to float. In January 1973, the Swiss allowed the franc to float. On February 12, 1973, renewed pressure on the dollar led the U.S. government to devalue the U.S. dollar by another 9 percent. On February 13, the Japanese yen and the Italian lira floated. In March, foreign exchange markets were so unsettled that governments closed exchange markets for two weeks. The major European countries agreed to try to keep their currencies relatively fixed with respect to each other but floating against the U.S. dollar. Finally, the markets were reopened.

During the years 1972 and 1973, the U.S. current account remained in deficit. As a result, the net effect of the transactions between entities in the United States and the ROW was a modest volume of net financial investment in the United States. The ROW continued to draw substantial amounts of long-term funds out of the United States (through foreign direct investment and government lending) and recycle them back into U.S. short-term markets. In spite of the uncertainties in international financial markets in general (and about the value of the dollar in particular) private nonresidents accumulated $22.2 billion, or slightly more than half of the total foreign investment in the United States (see Table 6–1).

1974–1976

The quadrupling of the price of oil in late 1973 caused dramatic changes in the current account balances of the nations of the world. It also had a substantial effect on both the internal and external markets for dollar claims. The major source of these imbalances was the OPEC trade surplus. There were many ways in which to finance these imbalances. At one extreme, the OPEC countries could accept payment for oil in the currency of each oil-consuming country and lend to each consuming country an amount equal to the difference between OPEC's sale of oil (and any other good or service) to them and OPEC's purchase of goods and services from them. At the other extreme, OPEC could refuse to accept financial promises from entities in all but a few countries. It could also require that these financial promises be denominated in a limited number of currencies. In this circumstance, the funds received by the favored consuming countries would have to be "recycled" to the other consuming countries. The central issue in these choices was the tradeoff between risk and expected return. Accepting financial claims from (that is, lending funds to) some of the consuming countries was clearly much more risky than lending to others.

OPEC's response to the recycling problem was very conservative, especially at the start. Rather than recycle the funds directly to each of the consuming countries, OPEC invested the bulk of its accumulation (about $55 billion in 1974 alone) in two currencies, the U.S. dollar and the British pound. Moreover, the majority of its financial asset accumulations were in the safest assets of the currency it chose. They were comprised mainly of bank deposits and government securities. Also, the bulk of the deposit holdings of dollars was accumulated in the Eurodollar market rather than as claims against the head offices of U.S. banks. Table 6–3 shows an estimate of the OPEC holdings of external assets as of mid-1977.

As a result of these portfolio decisions by OPEC investors, financial

Table 6–3
Estimated holdings of external assets by OPEC countries (Billions of $)

	Total holdings at June 1977	In the United States	In other countries
Net external assets (estimated)	141		
Identifiable investments	124		
Bank deposits			
Domestic currencies	14	9	5
Eurocurrencies	58	Primarily Eurodollars	
Treasury bills	6	6	1
Notes and bonds (primarily			
government securities.................	19	13	6
Equities	7	4	3
Direct loans	10	1	9
International organizations (IMF,			
World Bank, etc.)	9		

Source: *World Financial Markets,* November 1977, Morgan Guaranty Trust Company of New York.

markets and institutions in the United States and the United Kingdom, and the banks operating in the Eurocurrency markets, could engage in a large volume of secondary recycling. As individual institutions, of course, they would lend and invest only where the prospective return seemed commensurate with the risks. As a group, however, their recycling allowed the OPEC funds to find their way back to the consuming countries which incurred deficits that had to be financed.

The large U.S. banks which were active in international lending played an especially important role in this recycling. In January of 1974, the regulations that had limited foreign lending by the head offices of U.S. banks were lifted. The volume of foreign lending by the head offices of U.S. banks doubled (to $40 billion) in that year alone. By the end of 1976, their foreign lending attained a level of almost $75 billion. Thus, U.S. banks not only played a key role in this recycling, but did so in a way that much of the flow was channeled through their head offices (and thus, the U.S. financial system) and not just the external markets.[9]

---

[9] In principle, all of the foreign deposit gathering and foreign lending by U.S. banks in these years could have taken place in their foreign branches. If it had, none of these flows would have been recorded in the U.S. balance of payments statistics. Also, in principal, the head office of the U.S. banks could have directed their affiliates to channel all of their activities through the U.S. head offices. If so, the volume of gross inflows and outflows in the U.S. balance of payments would have included all these flows and would have been even larger than that which was recorded. While the decision of the banks to conduct a part of their foreign activities in their head offices rather than in their foreign branches is likely to have had very little effect on the banks or on financial markets in the United States, it did have a substantial effect on the size of the inflows and outflows recorded in the U.S. balance of payments statistics.

With bank lending growing substantially, gross financial outflows from the United States amounted to $83.1 billion during the three years from 1974 to 1976 (see Table 6–1). Since the U.S. current account experienced a surplus of $5.1 billion, gross financial investment in the United States totaled $78.0 billion.

In addition to affecting U.S. banks, the international flows during these years had a substantial effect on the securities markets in the United States (see Table 6–4). The U.S. government securities market received a

Table 6–4
International financial transactions, 1974–1977 (Billions of $)

	1974	1975	1976	1977
Purchases of foreign securities				
by U.S. residents	1.9	6.2	8.7	5.4
Common stocks	−0.2	—	0.3	0.4
Corporate and government bonds	2.1	6.2	8.4	5.0
Nonresident investment in the U.S.				
Official parties	11.0	7.0	17.9	37.4
Securities	5.2	9.1	17.0	36.3
U.S. government	4.9	7.0	14.9	34.3
Other*	0.3	2.1	2.2	2.0
Bank deposits	5.8	−2.2	0.9	1.1
Private nonresidents	22.6	7.3	16.6	11.9
Securities	0.8	5.0	4.4	3.5
U.S. government	0.5	2.5	3.1	0.6
Corporate bonds	0.1	−0.6	0.4	1.5
Corporate stock	0.2	3.1	0.9	1.4
Bank deposits	16.2	0.6	10.7	6.9
Foreign direct investment	3.7	1.4	2.2	1.5
Trade credit	1.8	0.2	−0.6	0.1

* Consists of investments in U.S. corporate stock and debt securities of private corporations and state and local governments.
Source: *Survey of Current Business,* U.S. International Transactions, Tables 7 and 9.

substantial inflow from foreign sources. Official parties accumulated $26.8 billion of government securities while private parties accumulated an additional $6.1 billion. During the same period, the ROW placed a substantial net demand on the U.S. corporate bond market. Nonresident bond issues in the U.S. markets totaled $16.7 billion, while nonresident purchases of U.S. corporate bonds totaled about zero. Also, nonresidents invested $4.2 billion in common stocks and $7.3 billion in the form of foreign direct investment in the United States. Since U.S. direct foreign investment in the ROW amounted to $12.3 billion over these three years, the net of these equity transactions (the $11.5 billion inflow and the $12.3 billion outflow) was a small net outflow from the United States.

Table 6–5
International investment position of the United States, year-end 1976
(Billions of $)

U.S. assets and investments abroad		Foreign assets and investments in the U.S.	
U.S. official reserve assets	18.7	Foreign official assets in the U.S.	106.3
U.S. government assets other than		U.S. government securities	73.6
official reserve assets	46.0	Other government liabilities	10.1
		Claims on U.S. banks	17.2
		Other	5.5
U.S. private assets	282.6		
Direct investment	137.2		
Foreign securities	44.6	Other foreign assets in U.S.	158.5
Bonds	35.1	Direct investment	30.2
Stocks	9.5	U.S. Securities	54.8
U.S. claims reported by		Bonds	11.9
U.S. banks	80.7	Stocks	42.9
Other	20.1	U.S. liabilities reported	
		by U.S. banks	60.5
		Other	13.0
Total	347.4	Total	264.8

Source: *Survey of Current Business*, October 1977.

As a result of these financial transactions, the international investment of the United States at the end of 1976 was as shown in Table 6–5.

1977–1978

During 1977 and 1978, the pattern of nonresident financial flows changed dramatically once again. In 1977, the United States experienced a current account deficit of $20.2 billion. This was the largest current account deficit (both absolutely and relative to GNP) of the postwar period. It gave rise to considerable concern about the value of the dollar. Between early 1977 and March 1978, the trade weighted value of the U.S. dollar declined by 7.0 percent (see Figure 6–3). The dollar's decline against the German mark and Japanese yen was much more pronounced.

The pace of dollar acquisition by foreign officials increased substantially. At $37.4 billion in 1977, it was even larger than their purchases of dollar assets during 1971, the year when the dollar experienced its first devaluation. Some of these purchases must have been intended to cushion the dollar's decline. At the same time, private nonresident accumulations slowed. A major reason was the U.S. banks reduced their pace of foreign lending from their head offices and, therefore, had less need to attract foreign deposits to their head offices. Nonresident purchases of corporate bonds and stocks and continued at about their earlier pace.

SUMMARY AND OUTLOOK

There are four phenomena which have had a dominant impact on the postwar history of foreign transactions in U.S. financial markets. The most important has been the problems which have arisen as the nations of the world have attempted to manage the values of their currencies. During the fixed exchange rate regime, adjustments or corrections in exchange rates were extremely difficult to make. It was difficult to obtain agreement on the existence of a need for a change, on the size of the change, and on how the change was to be brought about (that is, which currency or currencies should change in value). These problems were especially severe when the currency whose value had to be changed was the U.S. dollar. As a result of these difficulties in altering exchange rates, some central banks were required to buy large amounts of dollars to maintain the existing set of fixed exchange rates whenever the demand of other nonresidents for dollar assets was not sufficient to absorb all the dollars held by nonresidents. This problem emerged as a real one in the early 1960s, was submerged in 1966–1969, but reappeared with great force in 1970–1971. Ultimately, the fixed exchange rate system was abandoned, and it ceased to be a driving force in the foreign demand for dollar assets and liabilities.

Even in a world of floating exchange rates, however, governments often feel that the value of their currency is incorrectly assessed in the foreign exchange markets. As before, the problem is most severe when they feel their currency is misquoted relative to the U.S. dollar. Throughout the early 1970s, and especially in 1977 and 1978 as the U.S. dollar came under renewed pressure, several foreign governments purchased a very large volume of dollars in attempts to keep the value of their currencies from rising too far relative to the U.S. dollar and adversely affecting employment and economic growth in their own countries. This demand for dollar assets on the part of foreign central banks contributed to the substantial flows of funds into and out of the United States during these years. To the extent it was successful in propping up the U.S. dollar, it also added to the U.S. current account deficits. The attempts by foreign central banks to affect the value of their currencies with respect to the U.S. dollar are likely to continue to be a major factor in the nonresident demand for dollar assets and liabilities.

A second feature has been the ROW's use of the U.S. financial markets as a sort of financial institution. The dollar was perceived by private nonresidents as a "safer" or less volatile currency, and dollar markets were seen as more efficient. They were more liquid and had lower transactions costs, the intermediaries charged narrower spreads, and the premium of long-term rates over short-term rates was narrower. As the unique role of the U.S. dollar diminishes, as the internal financial markets of other countries become more efficient, and as the external markets in other currencies develop, these other currencies and markets are challenging the special attractiveness of the dollar markets. As world trade continues to expand and as the world becomes more economically interconnected, dollar financial markets are likely to command a decreasing share of these increasing international financial transactions.

The third major feature of the postwar history of foreign transactions in U.S. markets is the growth of the external market for dollar assets and liabilities. This occurred, in large part, because of the regulations which were imposed in the internal dollar market to deal with the problems of managing the value of the U.S. dollar relative to other currencies. The first of the domestic markets which developed an external market were the markets for bank deposits and bank loans, but an external market for longer term corporate bonds also exists. The developments in these external dollar markets will continue to affect U.S. financial markets in the years ahead.

The fourth event which had an important effect on U.S. financial markets and institutions was the emergence of OPEC as a major international investor. The rise in the price of oil left several of these OPEC countries with substantial sums to invest. It also gave rise to a substantial need for finance on the part of many other countries. The U.S. financial markets and institutions played a large role in the intermediation between the divergent interests of these two groups. Safety-conscious nonresident investors accumulated dollar bank deposits, U.S. government securities, U.S. corporate bonds and stocks in the U.S. markets, while nonresident borrowers raised funds in these markets in the form of bank loans and corporate and foreign government bonds.

As a consequence of these phenomena, nonresident borrowers and lenders have become important participants in our domestic dollar markets. Throughout the later chapters of this book, we will analyze their participation in each of the important financial markets in the United States. At times, their impact on specific markets has been quite large. However, their net effect or the net financing pressure associated with their transactions has been small when compared to the net demands of the U.S. government, the business sector, or the household sector. Whenever one group of nonresidents was investing large amounts of funds in one specific market or set of markets in the United States, it was usually true that a roughly similar amount of funds was being withdrawn by other nonresidents from another set of financial markets in the United States. By and large, the major effect of nonresidents has been to shuttle funds back and forth between different financial markets in the United States. While their activities have had an important effect on the flow of funds in certain markets, and have had some effect on the interest rates in these particular markets, they have had a much smaller effect on the overall supply or demand for funds and the overall level of yields when aggregated across all U.S. markets.

QUESTIONS

1. What factors led foreign central banks to hold over $100 billion of claims against the United States as of the end of 1976? Why was their accumulation so large in 1974–1977? What were the consequences of their accumulations on U.S. financial markets? What is the outlook for their future accumulation?

2. Table 6–3 presents an estimate of the external assets of OPEC countries as of 1977. How do you explain their decision to accumulate primarily dollar claims,

Table 6–6
Transactions with non-residents (Billions of $)

	1970	1971	1972	1973	1974	1975	1976	1977
Dollar outflows								
U.S. foreign direct investment ..	4.4	4.4	3.2	3.2	1.4	6.3	4.6	5.0
U.S. government lending abroad	1.6	1.9	1.6	2.6	−0.4	3.5	4.2	3.7
Foreign security purchases by U.S. entities	1.1	1.1	0.6	0.7	1.9	6.2	8.7	5.4
U.S. bank lending abroad	0.9	3.0	3.5	6.0	19.5	13.6	20.9	11.7
Short	1.1	2.4	2.2	5.0	18.3	11.2	18.8	11.0
Long	−0.2	0.6	1.3	1.0	1.2	2.4	2.1	0.7
Unrecorded outflows	0.2	9.8	2.0	2.7	1.6	−5.7	−9.8	3.0
Other	0.6	1.3	1.0	2.4	3.2	1.4	2.0	0.1
Nonbank short	—	1.1	0.8	2.0	2.7	1.0	2.0	0.4
Nonbank long	0.6	0.2	0.2	0.4	0.5	0.4	—	−0.3
Total	8.8	21.5	11.9	17.6	27.2	25.3	30.6	28.8
Dollar inflows								
U.S. current account surplus ...	−0.4	−4.0	−9.9	−0.4	−5.0	11.6	−1.4	−20.2
Accumulation of U.S. financial assets	9.3	25.4	21.8	18.2	32.2	13.7	32.1	49.0
Official parties	9.4	29.2	10.7	6.4	9.6	6.4	15.4	37.2
Securities and bank deposits	6.9	26.9	10.7	6.2	11.0	7.0	17.9	37.4
U.S. government securities	9.0	26.0	8.9	1.8	4.9	7.0	14.8	34.3
Bank deposits	−2.0	0.8	1.6	4.1	5.8	−2.2	0.9	1.1
Other	—	—	0.2	0.3	0.3	2.1	2.2	2.0
U.S. gold and foreign exchange	2.5	2.3	—	0.2	−1.4	−0.6	−2.5	−0.2
Private parties	−1.0	−4.5	10.4	11.8	22.6	7.3	16.7	11.8
Foreign direct investment in U.S.	1.0	−0.2	0.4	1.9	3.7	1.4	2.2	1.5
U.S. government securities	0.1	—	—	0.2	0.7	2.6	2.8	0.6
Other securities	2.2	2.3	4.5	4.0	0.4	2.5	1.3	2.9
Bank deposits	−6.3	−7.0	4.7	4.7	16.0	0.6	11.0	6.8
Short	−6.3	−0.7	4.6	4.5	16.0	0.9	10.8	6.4
Long	—	−0.3	0.1	0.2	—	−0.3	0.2	0.4
Trade credit	2.0	0.4	0.8	1.0	1.8	0.2	−0.6	0
Short	0.9	—	0.2	0.7	1.9	−0.1	0.3	0.4
Long	1.1	0.4	0.6	0.3	−0.1	0.3	−0.9	−0.4
SDRs	0.9	0.7	0.7					
Total	8.9	21.4	11.9	17.8	27.2	25.3	30.7	28.8

and claims on banks and government securities? What effect did those decisions have on financial institutions and markets in the United States?

3. Why are there external as well as internal markets for many financial assets and liabilities?

4. What is the outlook for the growth of the external dollar markets?

5. In what other currencies and what securities is it likely that large external markets will develop?

6. What are the effects of these external markets on the internal markets?

REFERENCES

Bell, Geoffrey. *The Eurodollar Market and the International Financial System.* New York–Ontario: John Wiley and Sons, 1973.

Kindelberger, Charles P. "Measuring Equilibrium in the Balance of Payments," *Journal of Political Economy* (November/December 1969), pp. 873–91.

Kouri, Pentti J. K. and de Macedo, Jorge Braga. "Exchange Rates and the International Adjustment Process," *Brookings Papers on Economic Activity,* vol. 1 (1978), pp. 111–58.

Mikesell, Raymond F. *The U.S. Balance of Payments and the International Role of the Dollar.* The American Enterprise Institute for Public Policy Research, 1970.

Mikesell, Raymond F. and Furth, J. Herbert. *Foreign Dollar Balances and the International Role of the Dollar.* National Bureau of Economic Research, 1974.

Willett, Thomas D. "The Oil-Transfer Problem and International Economic Stability." Essays in International Finance, No. 113, December 1975, International Finance Section, Department of Economics, Princeton University, Princeton, New Jersey.

7

Competition for funds among
the primary demanders

INTERACTION BETWEEN PRIVATE AND FEDERAL
    GOVERNMENT DEMANDS FOR FUNDS
COMPETITION FOR FUNDS BETWEEN BUSINESS AND
    HOUSEHOLDS
    Fund flows to the home mortgage market during periods of
    high interest rates
SUMMARY AND OUTLOOK

The previous chapters have discussed the determinants of the external financing demands of each of the separate primary sectors. This chapter analyzes the competition among these primary sectors for a limited supply of funds and previews later analyses of the linkages between the primary sectors' financial demands, interest rates, and the flow of funds through financial markets.

INTERACTION BETWEEN PRIVATE AND FEDERAL
GOVERNMENT DEMANDS FOR FUNDS

As we have seen, the primary sectors demanding funds within U.S. financial markets are business (nonfinancial corporate businesses), households, governments (both federal and state/local), and the international sector. The financing demands of state/local governments and the international sector have been relatively small and/or less volatile so that they have been relatively unimportant factors in the overall demand for funds. In comparison, business, households, and the federal government have been the important competitors for funds. Figure 7–1 shows the pattern of federal government financing, along with the volume of funds raised by the two private sectors—households and business. Throughout the period 1960–1976, the financing demands of the federal government and the private sectors were contracyclical. Enlarged federal financing demands coincided with reduced private sector financing and vice versa.

123

Figure 7–1
Federal government financing and the financing of the business and household sector, 1960–1977
(Expressed as percent of GNP)

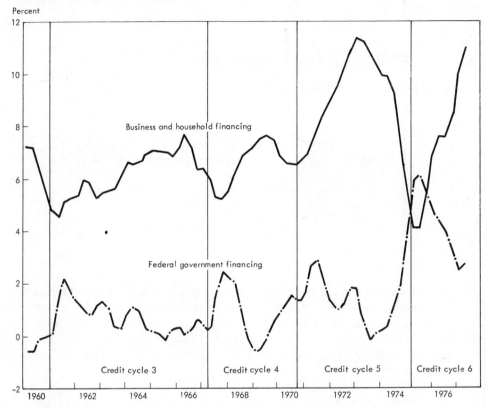

One possible interpretation of this contracyclical pattern is that the rising credit demands of the federal government have, on occasion, "crowded out" private financing. More precisely, this interpretation would suggest that as the credit demands of the federal government have risen, they have so increased interest rates that the private sectors found it difficult to justify their own investment and financing plans at the higher rates. On closer inspection, however, this interpretation does not appear to be consistent with the data.

Federal financing demands rose in 1961, 1967, 1970–1971, and 1974–1975. In each of these periods, the economy was in, or just emerging from, a recession. As explained in Chapter 4, the relative stability of federal expenditures, combined with the cyclical sensitivity of federal revenues, produces federal external financing demands which move counter to the cycles in the economy. Examining the behavior of interest rates at the times of enlarged Treasury financing demands, we find that short-term and long-term interest rates have fallen each time the Treasury's financing demands have expanded. Specifically, referring to Figure 7–2, we see that

Figure 7–2
Short-term and long-term interest rates, 1955–1977

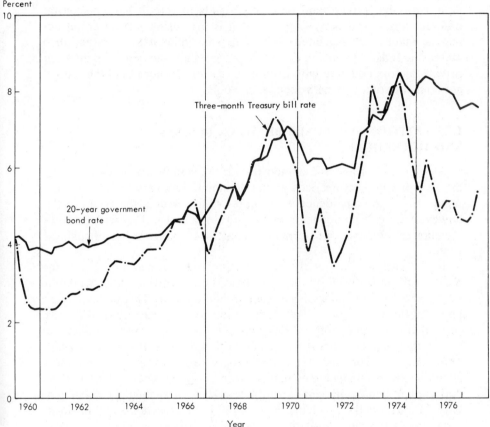

short-term rates fell significantly in 1960, in early 1967, in 1970, and again in 1975. Long-term interest rates fell at those times as well. On balance, this evidence suggests that federal financing demands have not been the source of the cyclical peaks in interest rates and have not "crowded out" private financing at these times. Rather they have expanded only when private credit demands were declining in response to a recession in real economic activity.

Moreover, whenever private credit demands did expand in each of the

economic expansions of the postwar period, federal financing requirements fell as federal tax receipts grew more rapidly than federal expenditures. Thus, at least in terms of cyclical patterns, the federal government has not appeared to be a major competitor for financing with the
private sectors. Of course, a positive interest rate, even in recessions,
implies that funds are not free and that this lack of competition between
the public and private sectors is always a matter of degree. However, the
data show that private and federal demands for credit have peaked at
different times, and they suggest that it is increasing private credit demands which are associated with increasing interest rates rather than
increasing federal financing demands. As we shall see next, the different
private sectors compete with each other for funds more than the federal
government competes with them as a whole.

COMPETITION FOR FUNDS BETWEEN BUSINESS
AND HOUSEHOLDS

As Figures 7–1 and 7–2 demonstrated, the sum of the funds raised by
the two private sectors rises as the economic recovery progresses and
moves in rough coincidence with interest rates. Within the credit cycle,
however, its two components move quite differently. Figure 7–3 shows
the different behavior of external financing for the household and business
sector.

In the early phases of the economic recovery (or credit cycle), the
volume of funds raised by the household sector grows rapidly, while the
volume of business financing remains relatively low. This behavior was
apparent during the early 1960s, when the economy was recovering from
the rather deep recession of 1960–1961. As Figure 7–3 shows, it was also
true in the early recovery periods of 1967–1968, 1971–1972, and in 1975–
1976. As the economic expansion progresses, however, the business
sector's external financing demands rise as inventory accumulation grows
and as plant and equipment expenditures grow faster than internally generated funds. As the financing demands of both households and business
grow and as the rate of inflation increases, short-term interest rates rise.
Ultimately, this rise in interest rates induces a sharp decline in the volume
of funds raised by households. However, the pace of business financing
continues to increase in spite of the increasing interest rates. Only when
the pace of economic activity slackens and a new recession ensues, do
business demands fall sharply. This general pattern of financial behavior
can be observed in each of the expansions since 1960, that is, in 1965, in
1969, and in 1973.

This behavior raises two questions. First, why does (and how can)
business continue to raise increasing amounts of external finance in spite
of the rise in interest rates? Second, why does the volume of funds raised
by households fall?

Figure 7–3
Financing of the household and business sectors, 1960–1977 (Expressed as percent of GNP)

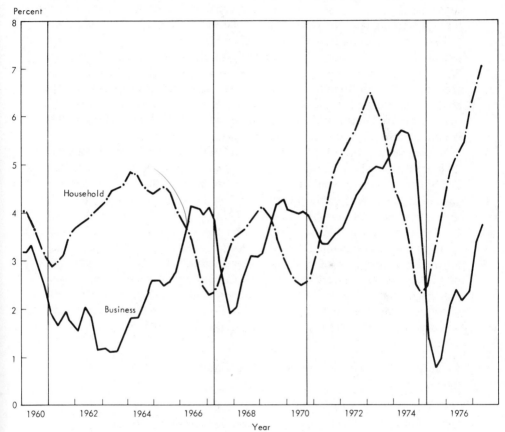

Chapter 2 suggested that in the short term the external financing demands of business corporations are relatively "insensitive" to interest
rates because of the dynamics of their investment needs. High interest
rates generally coincide with the peak levels of demand for businesses'
products and, hence, the peak needs for inventories, other working capital, and productive capacity. At these times, the increase in interest costs
generally appears to be a minor factor, at least compared to the forgone
income and loss of goodwill which would result from not meeting customers' demands. Furthermore, postponing investment (particularly in working capital) until a time of lower interest rates would be a most irrational
business policy. It would imply holding large amounts of working capital
when they were not needed and holding smaller amounts when they were
needed. For this reason, the financing demands associated with working
capital are not readily postponed. Much the same logic applies to plant

and equipment investment for businesses attempt to increase their productive capacity at those times when the demands for their products are greatest. Because of these factors, the peaks in the business sector's external financing tend to occur when economic activity is also at its peak.

Moreover, the markets through which businesses obtain finance, particularly with new debt, have evolved into effective channels for raising funds, particularly when economic activity is at its peak and interest rates are relatively high. In fact, as we shall see, high interest rates increase the ability of these markets to channel funds to business, albeit at relatively high costs. In Chapters 15 and 16, these markets, and their adaptation to large business financing demands, will be analyzed in detail.

In contrast, households' mortgage demands seem much more sensitive to interest rates. In our discussion of the external financing of households, in Chapter 3, two reasons for this behavior were advanced. First, mortgage interest costs are a very large factor in the total costs of purchasing a new home. Second, purchasing a new home is generally a decision which can be delayed until (hopefully) interest rates are lower. These factors seem to cause households to reduce their demand for mortgage market borrowing during periods of high interest rates. In addition, however, there are several factors which limit the supply of funds in the home mortgage market. Some of the more important features of this process affecting the home mortgage market will be previewed here, and a detailed analysis of these factors is taken up in later chapters.

Fund flows to the home mortgage market during periods of high interest rates

The primary sources of funds to the home mortgage market are thrift institutions, particularly saving and loan associations. Their ability to attract new funds has a major impact on the availability of home mortgage funds. Household savings deposits are the basic source of funds for thrift institutions, and households are attracted to these deposits because of their safety, liquidity, convenience, and return. Since most thrift institutions invest heavily in home mortgages and since (until recently) all home mortgages were fixed rate, relatively long-term contracts, thrift institutions' mortgage interest income responds slowly to changes in open-market interest rates. Thus, they are unable to quickly and substantially raise the interest rates they pay on their deposits, even if interest rates on open-market securities rise.

Furthermore, regulators have placed ceilings on the interest rates which both commercial banks and thrift institutions can pay on deposits. As a result of these regulations, household deposit rates at both commercial banks and thrift institutions are not allowed to change rapidly in response to open-market rates, even if they could. In contrast, however,

Figure 7–4

Interest rates, interest differentials, and household savings flows, 1960–1977

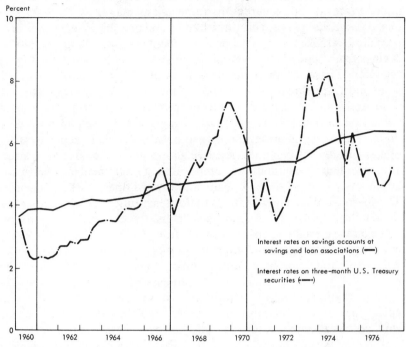

Interest rates on savings accounts at savings and loan associations (▬▬)

Interest rates on three-month U.S. Treasury securities (▬·▬·)

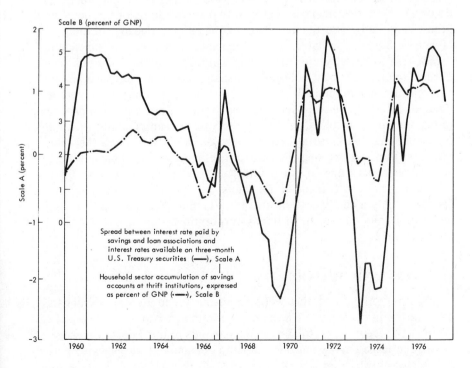

Spread between interest rate paid by savings and loan associations and interest rates available on three-month U.S. Treasury securities (▬▬), Scale A

Household sector accumulation of savings accounts at thrift institutions, expressed as percent of GNP (·▬·), Scale B interest rates on open-market instruments (such as U.S. Treasury securities, commercial paper, corporate bonds, and municipal securities) are not regulated. Households have become increasingly willing to shift their savings from deposits to open-market instruments in times of rising interest rates. These are the central features of the process which can limit home mortgage flow during periods of high or rising interest rates.

Figure 7–4 demonstrates that as open-market rates rise in an economic expansion in response to growing business and household demands for credit and rising inflation, the spread between savings deposit rates and open-market rates becomes negative and at times becomes very large. In response, households shift the composition of their financial asset accumulation away from savings deposits and toward open-market instruments. The sharply reduced flow of funds to thrift institutions significantly reduces their ability to extend home mortgage loans. Because of the features of the home mortgage instrument and other factors, alternative private lenders do not move in to supply the shortfall in mortgage funds. As a result, the volume of home mortgage funds available to households falls. As Figures 7–3 and 7–4 suggest, each of the elements of this process (the rise in open-market rates relative to rates on savings deposits, the shift in household financial asset acquisition patterns, and the downturn in mortgage lending) has taken place in each of the credit cycles since 1960.

The funds which households shift toward open-market instruments can be obtained by the business sector in two ways. Some of the household funds are directly invested in corporate obligations. Because of their preference for liquid and relatively safe financial assets, however, households' willingness to directly buy these corporate obligations is limited. Thus, during high rate periods, households usually purchase increased amounts of Treasury and municipal securities. At the same time, however, it is commercial banks who are selling these securities and using the proceeds to finance business loans. While interest rate regulations limit the ability of commercial banks to attract households directly through the sale of deposits, they cannot keep banks from selling some of their holdings of government securities to households and using these funds to finance business. As a result, commercial banks and the markets for government securities play a central role in the process that channels funds from the home mortgage market to business corporations during periods of high interest rates.

SUMMARY AND OUTLOOK

The three primary sectors whose demands for funds vary significantly over the credit cycle are the federal government, business, and household sectors. In recent years, the financing demands of the federal government have been large only when the financing demands of the private sectors have been small. Thus, the federal government has not tended to compete with the private sectors, at least at those times when the private sectors' demands for funds were large.

The real competition for funds has taken place between the business and the household sectors, whose financing demands have risen concurrently in each economic expansion and credit cycle of the postwar period. In each of these periods, household borrowing has turned down well before business borrowing. In part this has occurred because of the great differences in their respective sensitivities to interest rates. In part, however, it has occurred because of the structure of the home mortgage market itself and the vulnerability and regulations of the financial institutions that supply funds to this market. These problems with the home mortgage market have been a central concern of public policy throughout this period. This concern has generated a proliferation of responses, including among them: the creation of new federal agencies to assist the home mortgage market, more restrictive regulation of interest rates on household savings accounts, and recurrent proposals to more directly control businesses' access to funds.

As we shall see throughout the remainder of this book, the competition for funds between business and households, the attempts to limit this competition through regulation, and the attempts to change its nature through altering the securities and the institutions involved are all central features of the evolution of U.S. financial markets.

This competition has not been greatly influenced by large federal government financing demands, at least in recent times. However, this may not always be the case. The contracyclical nature of federal financing demands may not always continue. Indeed, many observers have been deeply concerned about the financial implications of the high-employment federal budget, which was in deficit so much of the time in the 1970s. Should that trend be continued, it is argued, the federal government's financing demands could remain relatively large, even as the economy expands and private financing demands grow. Should this occur, the nature of the competition for funds between the public and private sectors could change.

The nature of the competition for funds within the private sectors is changing as well. In recent years, business financial markets have evolved into particularly effective channels for raising relatively large amounts of external financing for business. There is every reason to believe that this evolution will continue. On the other hand, the capacity of the home mortgage market to deliver funds to households during the periods of high interest rates is also changing. This change could continue through further improvement in the flexibility of the mortgage market itself, through the assistance of regulation, or (more likely) through an expansion in the activities of several new federal agencies. As these changes continue to take place, the nature of the competition between households and business will continue to change.

Later chapters of this book examine, in detail, the structure of the competition for funds which has been previewed here.

QUESTIONS

1. What happens to the following items as the business sector's external financing needs rise in a cyclical expansion? Interest rates? The pattern of household financial asset acquisition? Fund flows in the home mortgage market?
2. What is the response of the federal government to these developments?
3. What are the consequences of all this behavior for the ability of corporations to raise funds? Home mortgage flows? Interest rates? The savings and loan associations that finance housing?
4. Suppose the federal government's budget position was such that at high levels of employment it experienced a deficit and needed substantial amounts of funds. How would this situation affect the financing capability of business firms and of households?

REFERENCES

Clauretie, Terrence M. "Interest Rates, the Business Demand for Funds, and the Residential Mortgage Market: A Sectoral Econometric Study," *The Journal of Finance,* vol. 28, no. 5 (December 1973), pp. 1313–26.

Gibson, William E. "Protecting Homebuilding from Restrictive Credit Conditions," *Brookings Papers on Economic Activity,* vol. 3 (1973), pp. 647–700.

Lessard, Donald and Modigliani, Franco. "Inflation and the Housing Market: Problems and Potential Solutions." In *New Mortgage Designs for Stable Housing in an Inflationary Environment,* Federal Reserve Bank of Boston, Conference Series No. 14.

Ways to Moderate Fluctuations in Housing Construction. Washington, D.C.: Board of Governors of the Federal Reserve System, 1972.

Housing and Monetary Policy. Federal Reserve Bank of Boston, Conference Series No. 4.

III

Equilibrium Forces in
Financial Markets

8

Inflation and interest rates

The relationship between interest rates and inflation is one of the most widely discussed of all financial relationships; for while there has been a clear correlation between interest rates and inflation, the exact reasons for the relationship remain troublesomely elusive. Figure 8–1 illustrates the recent time patterns of one measure of inflation and three interest rates: a very short-term rate (the federal funds rate), an intermediate-term rate, and a long-term rate. The recent correlation between inflation and interest rates, particularly short-term rates, is striking; but the longer run correlation is far from perfect. For example, in the 1950s this measure of inflation does not appear to be well-correlated with the levels of interest rates, particularly long-term rates. Moreover, in the years preceding the 1950s (not shown in Figure 8–1) the Federal Reserve "pegged" interest rates on short-term government securities at predetermined levels and through these actions influenced the levels of all other interest rates.[1] In those years, there was very little relationship between the levels of interest rates and inflation. In more recent years, as the Federal Reserve (the Fed) has

---

[1] We will discuss the Federal Reserve in considerable detail in a later chapter.

Figure 8–1

Interest rates and inflation

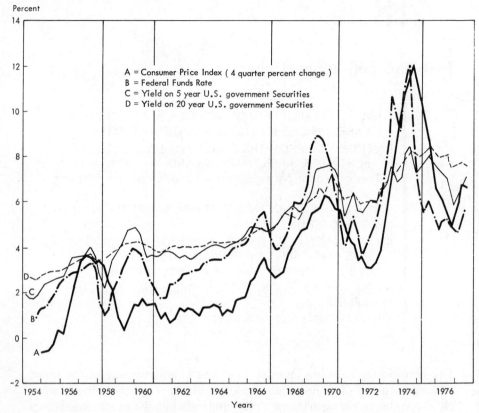

Percent

A = Consumer Price Index (4 quarter percent change)
B = Federal Funds Rate
C = Yield on 5 year U.S. government Securities
D = Yield on 20 year U.S. government Securities

Years

progressively backed away from "controlling" interest rates, and the free markets have taken over this function, interest rates have once again shown a closer correlation with inflation. In particular, short-term interest rates have been well-correlated with the rates of inflation (see Figure 8–2); and long-term interest rates have been well-correlated with the average inflation rate over the previous several years (see Figure 8–3).

Concentrating on this more recent period, we will first derive a basic equilibrium relationship between interest rates and inflation, based upon the concept of the financial markets' expectations of future inflation. Second, we will discuss how the forces of supply and demand can cause short-run departures from this basic equilibrium. Finally, we will investigate an extension of the basic equilibrium relationship, where the market's expectations of future inflation are assumed to incorporate all available information about the future course of inflation.

Figure 8-2

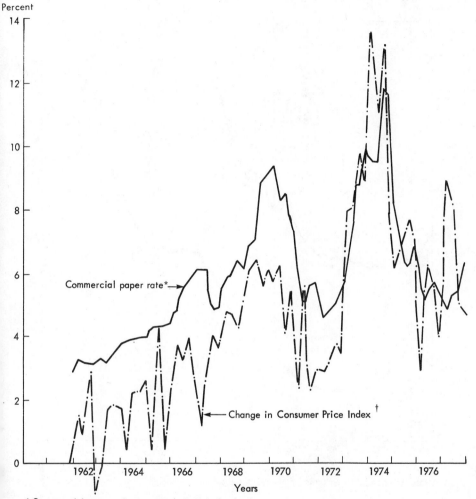

Percent

* Commercial paper rate measured at start of calendar quarters.
† Change in Consumer Price Index expressed at annual rate measured during calendar quarter.

THE BASIC EQUILIBRIUM RELATIONSHIP: INFLATIONARY EXPECTATIONS AND NOMINAL INTEREST RATES

To simply illustrate the basic equilibrium relationship, suppose that the markets for real assets and financial assets are interconnected by a number of potential investors who are constantly faced with two alternatives: owning "real" assets or owning financial assets. This choice is

Figure 8–3
Inflation and interest rates

Percent

* Rates of change in consumer prices over the previous five years.

diagrammed below, where some notation is also introduced, including the subscript *"t"* denoting "at some particular point in time:"

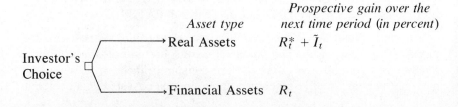

	Asset type	*Prospective gain over the next time period (in percent)*
Investor's Choice →	Real Assets	$R_t^* + \tilde{I}_t$
→	Financial Assets	R_t

R_i^* represents the real rate of return on real assets—the rate of return required by investors to hold real assets rather than use their funds for consumption. In this analysis, it is assumed to be a known amount. $\tilde{I}_t$ represents the uncertain (hence the $\sim$) inflation rate over the next time period. R_t represents the known return (the interest rate) from a bond that matures at the end of this same time period.

Consider a world with no inflation and, for the sake of simplicity, no risk. Investors could continuously choose between holding real assets and financial assets. Financial assets would have to be priced such that their return (R_t) was no higher and no lower than the return from real assets (R_i^*). If, initially, financial asset returns were higher, investors would buy more financial assets, driving their prices up and their future return down until their return was just equal to the return from real assets. If, initially, the financial asset returns were lower, the opposite would occur. Equilibrium could only be established when the two returns were equal.

Consider next a world with inflation. Because the financial assets are denominated in dollars and the real assets are not, their returns would be affected differently by inflation. In dollar terms, the value of the real asset would rise with inflation, augmenting its "real" return. The value of the financial asset would not rise with inflation, however, and its pricing would have to reflect that fact.

If the future pace of inflation were known for certain, investors would require the nominal return on financial assets to be equal to the sum of the known future inflation *plus* the real rate of interest. Since inflation is uncertain, however, investors would instead require that the return from the financial asset (the interest rate) be:

$$R_t \quad = \quad R_i^* \quad + \quad \text{Exp } \{\tilde{I}_t\} \tag{1}$$

$\underset{\text{Nominal Interest}}{}$	$\underset{\text{Real Rate}}{}$	$\underset{\text{Expectations of}}{}$
Nominal Interest Rate	Real Rate of Interest	Expectations of Inflation

where $\text{Exp } \{\tilde{I}_t\}$ is the market's expectation of the uncertain future inflation.[2] This relationship, first suggested by Irving Fisher and often bearing his name (the Fisher effect), has become one of the most important recurrent themes of financial theory.[3] While it was largely overlooked for several decades, it once again became the center of attention in the 1960s, no doubt in part because of the close correspondence between recent interest rates and inflation.

This relationship assumes that a sufficient number of financial participants will be willing, and able, to switch their holdings between financial

---

[2] This equilibrium relationship, like the others we will discuss here, will be strictly true only for markets which are dominated by rational profit-maximizing investors with negligible transactions costs.

[3] For his classic work, see Irving Fisher, "The Theory of Interest" (New York: MacMillan, 1930).

assets and real assets, conditional upon the relative "returns" available on these assets. The decisions of these investors cause the market to "price" financial assets, that is, determine their interest rate such that financial investors are just rewarded for foregoing consumption (the "real" rate of interest) and for expected inflation (the inflation premium). The Fisher effect is, therefore, really a model of how financial assets are priced—in particular how they are priced relative to real assets. In addition, however, if the real rate of interest is "known" (or varies slowly enough), the prevailing level of interest rates can be considered to be a forecast of future inflation because the nominal interest rate minus the "real rate" will just be the "market's expectation" of future inflation.

Unfortunately, however, it is not at all clear just which "inflation rate" is appropriate to the Fisher effect. Major components of the consumer price index—services, for example—are not storeable, nor are they tradeable; it is not at all clear that investors would really view them as an alternative to financial assets. Presumably the inflation rate on storeable commodities, for which convenient markets exist, is likely to be an inflation rate that is important in the pricing of financial assets, as are other broader price indices for real goods.

DIVERGENCES FROM THE EQUILIBRIUM RELATIONSHIP: FORCES OF SUPPLY AND DEMAND

The basic equilibrium relationship presented above is dependent upon the assumption that markets for real assets and financial assets are tightly interconnected by investors who freely transfer wealth between the two markets, according to the relative expected returns available from financial and real assets. But this assumption presents some difficulties.

First, most financial assets traded in the open financial markets are owned by financial intermediaries that do not hold real assets, nor are they structured to do so. One would be hard pressed to find many examples of financial intermediaries that continually consider the tradeoff between real goods and financial assets. While owners of the claims on financial institutions can be expected to reduce their holdings in institutions which invest without regard for the real returns they generate, this response is likely to be slow and not sufficient to assure a close and continual connection between the expected returns from real and financial assets.[4] Second, most of the holders of real assets do so because these real assets play an important role in consumption and/or business operations. Short-run changes in the demand for real assets arise more often from changing

---

[4] For example, if the expected returns from bonds do not offer a sufficient return relative to real assets, insurance companies may continue to buy bonds, but the attractiveness of the policies they offer to policyholders may be so eroded that eventually savers buy fewer policies and more real goods.

business needs and consumption patterns than from comparisons of the expected returns from real assets and financial assets. While the Fisher effect is an important factor affecting interest rates, there are legitimate doubts about whether there are enough smoothly functioning interconnections between the markets for real and financial assets to enforce the equilibrium in equation (1) at every moment of time.

If, in the short run, the markets for real assets and financial assets are partially segmented from each other, then the supply and demand for credit may well cause interest rates to diverge from their basic equilibrium relationship with the expected rate of inflation. In this case, changes in the nominal level of interest rates would reflect more than the changes in inflation expectations; they would reflect supply-demand imbalances as well.

The most important sources of supply and demand imbalances arise from the financing needs of the business sector. In each of the past credit cycles, as the economy has expanded, there has been a substantial increase in the credit demands of the business sector. Corporations tend to finance these needs initially through short-term borrowing, particularly bank loans. At the same time that businesses are seeking funds directly in the financial markets, commercial banks are increasing their efforts to obtain increased amounts of household savings and other forms of deposits in order to finance the increase in business borrowing at banks. Subsequently, as it becomes concerned about the pace of the expansion, the Federal Reserve attempts to curtail it by refusing to provide the increased reserves that banks need to supply the increased credit. Caught between expanding short-term credit demands and the restraining influence of the Fed, interest rates are driven up. As business financing needs continue and increased needs appear in the long-term markets, interest rates in these markets are forced up as well. Thus, because of the forces of supply and demand, credit flows and interest rates in the short-term markets (particularly the short-term markets for business borrowing) are forced up early in an expansion. Credit flows and interest rates in the long-term markets also respond, but with a lag.

The connection between inflation and the forces of supply and demand

As we have noted earlier, the supply and demand for funds in the different markets are intimately related to inflation. In each of the credit cycles, accelerating inflation has been a major cause of the enlarged external financing needs of business. Inflation has also played an important role in the Federal Reserve's decisions to restrict the flow of credit. Thus, increases in the actual rate of inflation can lead to two sets of forces causing interest rates to rise. First, actual inflation generates supply and demand pressures which increase interest rates. Second, actual inflation can lead to increased expectations of future inflation and a rise in nominal interest rates in order to keep financial assets offering nominal returns in line with the (increased) nominal returns expected from real assets.

Because each of these effects of inflation occur simultaneously and because both cause interest rates to rise, it has been difficult to determine their relative importance. That is, it has been difficult to tell how much interest rates are governed by the Fisher effect, the equilibrium force relating the expected returns from real and financial assets, and how much they are affected by changing patterns of supply and demand.

Because of these questions about the Fisher effect, numerous researchers, including Fisher himself, have attempted to empirically test its existence and importance. This question is of more than theoretical interest because its resolution is important to all those trying to forecast interest rates and inflation. If the Fisher effect is dominant, and the real rate of interest is constant or subject to only minor changes, forecasting nominal interest rates requires only a forecast of inflation, and changes in the level of nominal interest rates reflect changes in the market's forecast of inflation. If, on the other hand, forces of supply and demand exert an independent effect on interest rates, forecasting interest rates requires more than a forecast of inflation. It requires, in addition, a detailed understanding of the way in which inflation and other factors will affect the supply and demand for funds.

EMPIRICAL TESTS OF INTEREST RATES AND INFLATIONARY EXPECTATIONS

The principal problem in empirically testing for the existence of the Fisher effect is that, while interest rates are observable, inflationary expectations are not. Thus, appropriate and convenient proxies must be developed for the possible inflationary expectations of investors. The most common approach has been to define an "expectations model" which specifies ahead of time the inflationary expectations of the market, $\text{Exp}\{\tilde{I}\}$, as a function of past inflation rates. Assuming that the real rate of interest is constant, researchers have then tested the correlation between observed interest rates and the time-varying "inflationary expectations" specified by their model. The problem, however, is that these empirical tests are really joint tests of the relationship between interest rates and inflationary expectations (the Fisher effect) *and* the particular expectations model which is proposed. The tests could fail either because inflationary expectations do not explain a significant fraction of the variance of interest rates or because investors do not really formulate their inflationary expectations in the particular method prescribed by the model.[5]

---

[5] One exception to this is the work reported in David Pyle, "Observed Price Expectations and Interest Rates," *Review of Economics and Statistics* (August 1972), which suggests that nominal interest rates can be explained (in part) by the consensus inflationary expectations as determined by the answers to a survey questionnaire. This finding tends to support the Fisher effect, although such studies have their own attendant problems.

Many early tests, using data from periods before the 1960s, had only mixed success in searching for the Fisher effect, either because interest rates failed to reflect inflationary expectations or because the models of expectations were somehow inappropriate. Later tests, however, have been much more successful. Not surprisingly (Figures 8–1, 8–2, and 8–3) studies of the late 1950s, 1960s, and 1970s have uncovered strong relationships between inflation and interest rates. At the most simple level, such studies have suggested relatively straightforward rules-of-thumb for the recent behavior of long-term interest rates. For example, the long-term interest rate has equaled 3 percent plus the weighted average of inflation over the most recent five years (presumably the market's inflationary expectations). Indeed, Figure 8–3 can be interpreted as a direct empirical test of this simple proposition.

At a more complex level, a number of studies have combined their own particular version of an inflationary expectations model (defined as long-term weighted averages of past inflation rates) and other variables and have been able to explain a substantial fraction of the behavior of various interest rates.[6]

Most of these researchers have concluded that their results provide strong empirical confirmation of the existence of the Fisher effect. Thus, the basic equilibrium relationship we have described is consistent with the empirical data. On the other hand, variables representing the supply and demand for funds have also proven to be important in the determination of interest rates. Because of the empirical problems involved, these tests still leave considerable uncertainty about the exact importance of each of the two forces.

AN EXTENSION OF THE BASIC EQUILIBRIUM
RELATIONSHIP: THE HYPOTHESIS OF EFFICIENT MARKETS

It is possible to extend our model of the equilibrium relationship between the expected return on real and financial assets by restricting the

---

[6] In one study, Sargent combined a "loanable funds model" (a precisely specified variant of some supply and demand concepts) with a measure of inflationary expectations (a very long-term weighted average of past inflation rates) to explain the movement of both one-year and ten-year interest rates from 1902 to 1954. In another study, Yohe and Karnosky explained some of the more recent behavior (1952–1969) of both the commercial paper rate and a long-term bond rate, by using another version of inflationary expectations (again, defined as a weighted-average of past inflation rates). Similarly, in a third study, Feldstein and Eckstein explained the overwhelming majority of the recent fluctuations (1957–1969) of corporate bonds rates, using still another model for inflationary expectations (defined again over past inflation) and several other variables (notably, a measure of liquidity designed to capture the role of the supply and demand for money in interest rate determination). See T. J. Sargent, "Commodity Price Expectations and the Interest Rate," *Quarterly Journal of Economics* (February 1969), pp. 127–40; and W. P. Yohe, and D. S. Karnosky, "Interest Rates and Price Level Changes, 1952–1969," *Federal Reserve Bank of St. Louis Review* (December 1969); and Martin Feldstein and Otto Eckstein, "The Fundamental Determinants of the Interest Rate," *The Review of Economics and Statistics,* vol. 52 (November 1970), pp. 363–76.

possible ways in which the market's expectations are formed. In particular, we could make the *additional assumption* that investors have relatively costless access to all relevant information and that when they form their expectations, they do so in a way that uses the available information in an "optimal" way. The expectations which are formed in this way (optimally) have come to be known as "rational expectations."[7]

The implications of this additional assumption, or hypothesis, are far-reaching. It implies, first of all, that financial markets are "efficient markets" in the precise sense that financial assets prices have already considered, within their structure, all available information about future inflation.[8] It implies that the market's expectations of future inflation, which are incorporated into nominal interest rates, are the best possible forecast of future inflation rates (otherwise, the expectations so incorporated would not be optimal).

Empirical tests of the efficient markets hypothesis

The most direct empirical tests of the additional hypothesis of efficient markets (in this context) have examined the relative quality of the inflation forecasts imbedded within interest rates. Turning equation (1) around, and interpreting it as a forecast, we can write:

$$R_t \quad - \quad R_t^* \xrightarrow{\text{Forecasts}} \tilde{I}_t \qquad (2)$$

Nominal Interest Rate	Real Rate	Future Rate of Inflation

The hypothesis of efficient markets implies that this forecast is the best forecast of future inflation for it incorporates all available information about future inflation. Thus, the hypothesis can be tested by empirically evaluating this forecast relative to other possible forecasts. The first problem is, of course, that there are very few independent observations of the

---

[7] The concept of "rational expectations" was introduced and first discussed in John F. Muth, "Rational Expectations and the Theory of Price Movements," *Econometrica* (July 1961).

[8] For a more careful discussion of "efficient markets" and a review of the literature, see Eugene F. Fama, "Efficient Capital Markets; A Review of Theory and Empirical Work," *Journal of Finance,* vol. 25 (May 1970), pp. 303–417.

In its "weaker" form, the hypothesis of rational expectations assumes that market participants appropriately incorporate all available information within the time series of past inflation such that the market's expectations of future inflation are "optimal" (optimal, that is, with respect to arbitraging away the differences between the expected relative returns on real and financial assets). In its "stronger" form, the hypothesis of rational expectations assumes, in addition, that the market uses literally all of the available information (without restriction to any particular time series) in optimally forming its expectations. For example, not only does it incorporate all of the information within past inflation rates into market expectations, but any and all other available information as well.

forecasting ability of long-term interest rates. For example, there are only five non-overlapping 20-year periods in the past century, virtually the only period of reliable data, so that direct tests of the accuracy of long-term interest rates as forecasts of the long-term rate of inflation are not feasible. For this reason, empirical tests must be limited to tests of the accuracy with which short-term interest rates have forecasted inflation. Even with short-term interest rates there is a serious problem, however, for R_t^* (the real rate of interest) is unknown. Empirical tests of the accuracy with which short-term interest rates forecast inflation must rely either upon R_t^* being relatively constant or upon a model for estimating R_t^*.

Notwithstanding these empirical difficulties researchers have investigated the ability of short-term interest rates to forecast inflation rates. In one important study, Fama has shown that during 1953–1971, the observed nominal interest rates on one month U.S. Treasury bills explained approximately 30 percent of the variance of future one-month inflation, and the rates on six-month bills explained approximately 65 percent of the variance of future six-month inflation.[9]

Since Fama's data suggested that the real rate of interest on short-term security was relatively constant and about equal to zero over the period, he concluded that it was correct to interpret one-month interest rates as a forecast of the next month's rate of inflation. Unfortunately, these forecasts did not appear to be particularly valuable because forecasting future inflation with the short-term interest rate did not produce forecasts which were any better than a particularly naive procedure: that next period's inflation rate would be the same as this period's inflation rate. However, the inclusion of several other rather simple measures of the past time series of inflation did not measurably improve the future inflation forecast already contained in the Treasury bill rates.

This led Fama to conclude that all of the information inherent in past inflation rates which is relevant to a forecast of future inflation may well be contained within today's interest rates. To be more precise, he concluded that one cannot reject the hypothesis that today's short-term interest rate is set in such a way that it contains all the information about the future rate of inflation that is in the past rates of inflation. These findings were thus consistent with the Fisher effect and, even further, consistent with the hypothesis of efficient markets.

Later researchers have found reason to question some of Fama's conclusions. They have offered data suggesting that some of the information which past inflation rates contain about future inflation rates may not be contained in the current interest rate. Thus the market may not be totally efficient in the way in which it uses the past data on inflation to produce a

---

[9] See Eugene F. Fama, "Short-term Interest Rates as Predictors of Inflation," *The American Economic Review*, vol. 65 (June 1975), pp. 269–82.

forecast of future inflation. Also, there is some evidence that factors other than the expected rate of inflation enter into the relationship determining nominal interest rates, including factors which may plausibly be related to the supply and demand for funds.

The issues of the empirical validity of the efficient markets hypothesis and the Fisher effect appear to be very difficult questions. Their resolution depends upon a clearer understanding than we now have of how the real rate of interest varies over time, as well as how investors form their inflationary expectations.

A COMPLICATING FACTOR: INCOME TAXES AND THE FISHER EFFECT

In an environment with income taxes it is somewhat surprising that nominal interest rates seem to rise with inflation only about as much as the rate of inflation increases. Since the entire nominal interest rate is treated as income, the after-tax real rate of return on financial assets earning a nominal before-tax rate of return of R, is $[R\ (1 - T) - I]$, if T is the investors marginal tax rate and I is the rate of inflation. The fact that nominal interest rates seem to behave in a way that maintains before-tax real rates of interest relatively constant means that the after-tax real rates of interest have fallen substantially during the inflation of the 1970s. Also, real after-tax rates of interest are most likely negative for many investors. A Treasury bill yielding about 3 percent in a 3 percent inflation has a before-tax real return of about zero, and an after-tax real return of -1.5 percent to an investor who pays a 50-percent marginal tax rate. If, when the rate of inflation increases to 6 percent, the interest rate on Treasury bills increases to 6 percent, the real after-tax return for this investor falls to -3 percent. A long-term corporate bond yielding 9 percent when the long-run expectation of inflation is about 6 percent yields the same investor an after-tax real return of -1.5 percent [9 percent $(1 - 0.5) - 6$ percent].[10] The intersection of inflation and income taxes thus not only erodes the actual returns to investors, but complicates the more simple interpretation of the relationship between interest rates and inflation.

THE ALTERNATIVE VIEWS REVISITED

In this chapter, the ideas surrounding inflation and interest rates have been organized to separate and compare the alternative views about their interrelationships.

---

[10] For a discussion of this topic, see Martin Feldstein and Lawrence Summers, "Inflation, Tax Rules, and the Long-Term Interest Rate," *Brookings Papers on Economic Activity,* vol. 1 (1978), or Vita Tanzi, "Inflation and the Incidence of Income Taxes on Interest Income: Some Results for the United States, 1972–74," Staff Papers, International Monetary Fund, vol. 24, no. 2 (July 1977), p. 500.

We first derived a basic equilibrium relationship, the *Fisher effect,* which is based upon interconnected markets between which profit maximizing participants will freely move in search of expected returns. The dominant view of many economists (and included within many macroeconomic models), it emphasizes the equilibrium forces which keep the market's expected returns on real assets and financial assets roughly commensurate. (It makes no statement, however, about the market's ability to assess these expected returns, that is, to forecast future inflation.)

Second, we have discussed the possible divergences from this equilibrium which can occur because markets are segmented from one another in the short run, that is, because investors cannot or do not shift freely back and forth between real and financial assets in the short run. To the extent that this is true, inflation can affect interest rates through the *supply and demand for credit* rather than through inflationary expectations. This segmented markets view, which emphasizes the disequilibrium effects of inflation upon supply and demand for credit (rather than the equilibrium relationship between the expected return on real and financial assets) is the dominant view of most market practitioners.

Finally, we have examined an extension of the basic equilibrium relationship, using the additional hypothesis of *efficient markets.* The dominant view of many financial theorists, this perspective assumes the existence of the Fisher effect and makes the additional assumption that the collective efforts of many investors guarantee that the expectations of future inflation which are imbedded in the existing structure of interest rates use all available information optimally. This implies that these inflationary expectations are the "best" expectations in that they incorporate all that is known about future inflation.

The empirical validity of these different hypotheses has proven to be difficult to test. In recent years, however, the existence of the Fisher effect has been well-documented. As a result, explanations of interest rate movements have come to place less emphasis on supply and demand factors. However, much dispute still exists over the exact importance of supply and demand as opposed to equilibrium forces and over the accuracy of the forecasts on inflation which are implicit within nominal interest rates.

QUESTIONS

A. On the Fisher effect:
   1. How do proponents of the Fisher effect expect corporations to respond to discrepancies between short-term interest rates and their expectations for the rate of increase in the prices of the goods they hold in inventory?
   2. How are financial institutions supposed to react to long-term interest rates which seem low with respect to their expectations for the rate of inflation?

Figure 8–4

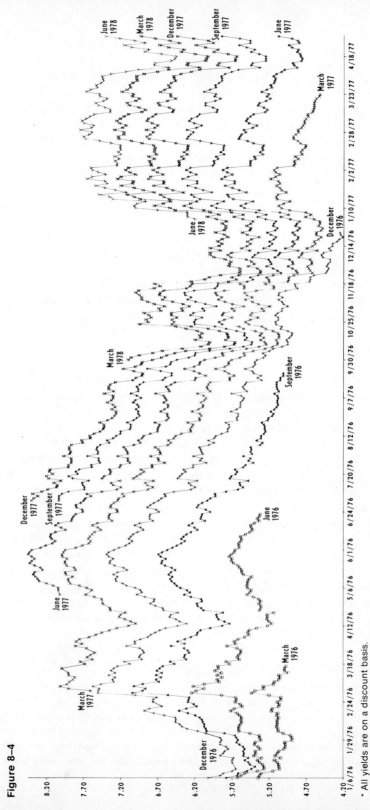

* All yields are on a discount basis.
Source: International Monetary Market Division.

3. How do the responses of these actors affect interest rates?
B. On the efficient markets hypothesis:
 1. What does the "weak" form of the efficient markets hypothesis say about the connection between the current short-term rate of interest, the market's outlook for inflation over the short term, and the past values of the rate of inflation?
 2. What does the "strong" form of the efficient markets hypothesis say about the current short-term interest rate as a predictor of the short-term rate of inflation?
C. On the accuracy of the short-term interest rate as a predictor of the rate of inflation:
 1. Figure 8–4 shows the yields on a number of Treasury bill futures contracts during 1976 and 1977. It shows, for example, that when the March 1977 T-bill was first offered in early March 1976, the market priced the contract so that the investor would receive the equivalent of 7.50 percent return when the bill was delivered in March 1977. Since the T-bill rate in March 1976 was about 5.0 percent, the market seemed to be forecasting a rise of 2.5 percentage points in the Treasury bill rate over the next 12 months.
   a. What happened to the price of the March 1977 T-bill future between March 1976 and March 1977?
   b. During the years 1976 and 1977, what was the "market" anticipating would happen to short-term interest rates in 1976 and 1977?
   c. Were those anticipations realized?
   d. What would an advocate of the "efficient market" position conclude from this?
   e. What might an advocate of an alternate hypothesis conclude?

REFERENCES

Feldstein, Martin and Summers, Laurence. "Inflation, Tax Rates, and the Long-Term Interest Rate," *Brookings Papers on Economic Activity,* vol. 1 (1978), pp. 61–110.

Friedman, Benjamin M. "Financial Flow Variables and the Short-Run Determination of Long-Term Interest Rates," *Journal of Political Economy,* vol. 85 (August 1977), pp. 661–89.

Nelson, Charles R. and Schwert, G. William. "Short-Term Interest Rates as Predictors of Inflation: On Testing the Hypothesis that the Real Rate of Interest Is Constant," *American Economic Review,* vol. 67, no. 3 (June 1977), pp. 478–86.

Sargent, Thomas J. "Interest Rates and Expected Inflation: A Selective Summary of Recent Research," *Explorations in Economic Research,* vol. 3 (Summer 1976), pp. 303–25.

9

The term structure of interest rates

Quite apart from their relationship with inflation, the interest rates on securities with different maturities are related to each other through the term structure of interest rates. For example, referring back to Figure 8–1, we see that the movements of short-term rates, intermediate-term rates and long-term rates were clearly correlated with each other.

The term structure of interest rates is often studied through yield curves. A set of actual yield curves for the U.S. Treasury securities market on several recent dates is shown in Figure 9–1. While these yield curves are generally pictured as smooth curves, they must in fact be interpolated through a number of discrete points, namely the prevailing interest rates on a collection of specific, hopefully representative, securities.

Observing these yield curves over time, market participants have noticed that more often than not, the yield curve is upward sloping (though at times it may be nearly flat, downward sloping, or take on more complex shapes). In the sections that follow, we will investigate an explanation of the changing shape of these yield curves, that is, a theory of the "term structure of interest rates."

Figure 9–1
Yield curves for U.S. Treasury securities

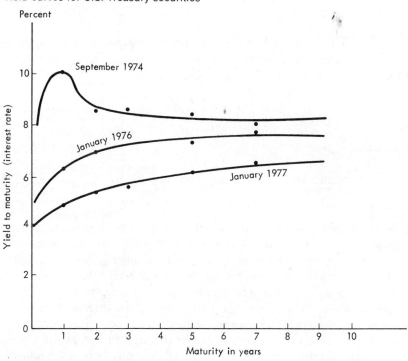

THE BASIC EQUILIBRIUM RELATIONSHIP: EXPECTATIONS OF FUTURE RATES

To develop a basic equilibrium relationship among interest rates in different maturity ranges, we will assume that these ranges are interconnected by borrowers and lenders who freely move among different maturities in search of greater expected returns or lower expected borrowing costs. Their actions tend to keep interest rates in equilibrium with one another such that financial assets with different maturities all yield the same expected returns.

To explicitly derive this relationship, we must unfortunately use some rather difficult notation, which is first summarized here. R will denote the known interest rates (yields) on securities today. r will denote the future uncertain interest rates on securities. The following subscript t will denote time; the preceding subscript τ will denote the maturity of a financial asset. In particular, then:

$_\tau R_t$ is the known interest rate at time t, on a security with maturity τ.
$_\tau \tilde{r}_{t+k}$ is the future (uncertain) interest rate which will prevail at time

$t + k$ (k periods into the future) on a security with maturity τ. Exp $\{_\tau \tilde{r}_{t+k}\}$ is the expected value at time t of the future uncertain rate, $_\tau \tilde{r}_{t+k}$.

To illustrate the basic relationship simply, suppose at least some investors are currently considering two alternatives: a one-year security and a two-year security.

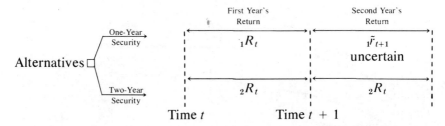

To make the two alternatives comparable, assume that the funds invested in the one-year security will be reinvested after the one year (time $t + 1$) in another one-year security, at the future uncertain one-year rate. Ignoring risk aversion for the moment, investors will select that strategy (the two-year security or two consecutive one-year securities) which offers the greatest expected return over the two years. If the interest rate on the two-year security is greater than the average of the one-year security and the expected rate on next year's one-year security, investors will choose the two-year security (and conversely). As they buy two-year securities (and sell one-year securities), the interest rate on two-year securities will be driven down (and the rate on one-year securities will be driven up) until the two alternative strategies offer equivalent returns. Ignoring the effects of compounding, we see that the equilibrium will occur when the two securities are priced such that:

$$_2R_t = \tfrac{1}{2}[_1R_t + \text{Exp } \{_1\tilde{r}_{t+1}\}]$$

That is, the equilibrium will occur when today's two-year rate is just equal to the average of today's one-year rate and the expected future one-year rate.

Consider compounding; the equilibrium occurs when the two securities are priced such that:

$$(1 + _2R_t)^2 = (1 + _1R_t)(1 + \text{Exp}\{_1\tilde{r}_{t+1}\})$$

or

$$_2R_t = [(1 + _1R_t)(1 + \text{Exp}\{_1\tilde{r}_{t+1}\})]^{1/2} - 1$$

That is, the equilibrium occurs when one plus today's two-year rate is equal to the geometric average of one plus today's one-year rate and one plus the expected one-year rate for next year.

Generalizing this argument, we see that a security which matures τ years from now can be compared to an alternative strategy of investing in a sequence of τ one-year securities. Investors will prefer that strategy which offers the greatest expected long-run returns and will be indifferent between the two strategies if (and only if) they offer the same expected long-run returns. In equilibrium, then, the expected returns on the τ-year security and the sequence of τ one-year securities should be related (considering the effects of compounding) by:

$$1 + {_\tau}R_t = [(1 + {_1}R_t)(1 + \text{Exp}\{{_1}\tilde{r}_{t+1}\})$$
$$(1 + \text{Exp}\{{_1}\tilde{r}_{t+2}\}) \ldots (1 + \text{Exp}\{{_1}\tilde{r}_{t+\tau-1}\})]^{1/\tau} \quad (1)$$

That is, one plus today's long-term rate should be just equal to the geometric average of one plus today's one-year rate and a series of expected future one-year rates. This is the basic relationship: Interest bearing securities of any given maturity are priced such that their current interest rate (their known yield to maturity) is just equivalent to the average expected returns from an alternative sequence of investments in short-term securities.[1] In this framework, the current interest rates on securities with various maturities are thus determined by a stream of expected future one-period interest rates, and through this relationship, they are determined relative to each other. The expected future one-period interest rates thus determine long-term interest rates and the shape of today's yield curve.

The forward rates imbedded in the yield curve

Given the data in the yield curve, $\{{_1}R_t, {_2}R_t, {_3}R_t, \text{etc.}\}$, it is possible to define an additional set of interest rates, called *forward interest rates*. These forward interest rates, denoted as ${_{t+\tau}}F_t$, are defined as of period t, and exist for each future period $t + \tau$. They are defined by the following equation:

$$(1 + {_{t+\tau}}F_t) = \frac{(1 + {_{\tau+1}}R_t)^{\tau+1}}{(1 + {_\tau}R_t)^\tau} \quad (2)$$

Note, for example, that the "three year ahead one-year forward rate," ${_{t+3}}F_t$, is a function of today's known three-year and four-year interest rates, ${_3}R_t$ and ${_4}R_t$.

As a numerical example of the connection between forward interest rates and yields to maturity, consider the data in Table 9–1. They show the yields to maturity which were quoted in the market for U.S. govern-

---

[1] Where, by average, we mean the geometric average in equation (1), which includes the effects of compounding. A reasonable approximation to (1), which ignores compounding, is that today's long-term rate is the simple or arithmetic average of the current short-term rate and the future expected short-term rates.

Table 9–1

Yields to maturity and forward interest rates of selected U.S. government securities, January 3, 1976

		Implied forward one-year interest rates			
Maturity	Observed yield to maturity (yield curve)	In 1977 $_{1977}F_{1976}$	In 1978 $_{1978}F_{1976}$	In 1979 $_{1979}F_{1976}$	In 1980 $_{1980}F_{1976}$
1 year $(_1R_{1976})$	6.31				
2 year $(_2R_{1976})$	6.69	7.07			
3 year $(_3R_{1976})$	7.00		7.62		
4 year $(_4R_{1976})$	7.25			8.00	
5 year $(_5R_{1976})$	7.38				7.90

ment securities on January 3, 1976. They also show the forward rates which were implied by this set of yields to maturity.[2]

Forward rates as expected future rates

If the relationship in equation (1) determines interest rates on long-term securities, the forward rates in equation (2) are equal to the expected future interest rates in equation (1). That is, if the equilibrium relationship by equation (1) holds, then:

$$_{t+\tau}F_t = \text{Exp}\{_1\tilde{r}_{t+\tau}\} \qquad (3)$$

This can be derived by substituting the expressions given by equation (1) for both $_{\tau+1}R_t$ and $_\tau R_t$ in equation (2).

Thus, if the equilibrium relationship holds, the forward interest rates can be considered to be forecasts of future one-period rates because they are the market's expectation of these future rates. Rather than summarize today's term structure of interest rates through the yield curve ($_1R_t$, $_2R_t$, $_3R_t$, . . . , $_\tau R_t$), we might instead summarize it through today's one-year rate and the sequence of one-year forward rates ($_1R_t$, $_{t+1}F_t$, $_{t+2}F_t$, . . . , $_{t+\tau-1}F_t$). This set of forward rates contains the same information as the yield curve but is more directly related to future expectations, the determinants of the yield curve.

Risk aversion and liquidity premiums

Thus far, we have assumed that borrowers and lenders seek to maximize the expected value of long-run income or return. In the pres-

---

[2] For example, $(1 + {}_{1977}F_{1976})$ is equal to

$$\frac{(1 + {}_2R_{1976})^2}{(1 + {}_1R_{1976})} \text{ or } \frac{(1 + 0.0669)^2}{(1 + 0.0631)} \text{ or } 1.0707.$$

ence of uncertainty, however, this may not be a sufficient description of their behavior.

For example, life insurance companies sell whole-life insurance contracts which promise a fixed nominal rate of return over the life of the contract. It is important for them to be reasonably sure of the long-run rate of return that their assets will generate. Because of this, they are likely to be willing to accept a somewhat lower long-run or average return from a long-term security (lower than they could expect from investing in a sequence of short-term investments) because the long-term security promises a long-term return with more certainty. Their preference for the long-term security would be reflected by a willingness to pay an "income stability premium" when buying long-term bonds. If life insurance companies were the dominant influence on today's interest rates, the forward rates from equation (2) could be underestimates of the expected future short-term rates.

Commercial banks, on the other hand, have short-term liabilities whose costs are changing continually with the level of short-term interest rates. They prefer short-term assets to long-term assets in order to reduce their risks. Indeed, banks may invest in short-term securities even though the long-run expected return from investing in a series of them is below the expected returns available on long-term securities. As a result, banks may demand an extra "liquidity premium" before they invest in longer term securities. If these banks were the dominant influences on today's interest rates, the forward rates in equation (2) could be an overestimate of the market's forecast of future short-term rates.

Some corporate borrowers may also have a preference for either short-term or long-term debt. To the extent they thought their income was relatively fixed, they would prefer to borrow long, that is, be willing to pay a larger expected amount over the life of the debt in return for the increased certainty about their actual interest costs. Conversely, to the extent they thought their interest paying capacity varied with the same forces affecting actual short-term interest rates, they would prefer to borrow short. Empirically, there seems to be a premium rate of interest which has to be paid to long-term investors in order to get them to accept the illiquidity of long-term investments.[3] This "liquidity premium" accounts in large part for the fact that yield curves, more often than not, are upward sloping.

Incorporating a "liquidity premium" into the development of the expectations model, we have

---

[3] Note that this conclusion relies upon an imbalance between the sources of supply and demand, with more borrowers desiring long-term funds than there are lenders who prefer long-term assets. In general, it is not clear (a priori) how large these liquidity premiums should be, for they depend in a detailed way on the size of this imbalance. In the next chapter, we will develop one possible specification of these liquidity premiums in the context of risks of holding period returns for different securities.

$$_{t+\tau}F_t = \text{Exp } \{_1\tilde{r}_{t+\tau}\} + L_\tau \tag{4}$$

where L_τ is just the liquidity premium required to hold securities with maturity τ. With this addition, the amended expectations model provides a basic equilibrium for the term structure of interest rates in a world of uncertainty. In particular, it suggests that the *equivalent* expected returns from financial assets of different maturity are equal, where by "equivalent" we mean the expected returns are adjusted to account for the decreased liquidity (increased risk) of longer term assets.

The existence of these liquidity premiums in the forward rates means, however, that forward rates cannot be used as *direct* measures of the market's expectations of future short-term rates.

DIVERGENCES FROM THE BASIC EQUILIBRIUM RELATIONSHIP: THE FORCES OF SUPPLY AND DEMAND

To develop this basic equilibrium relationship, we have assumed that the markets for financial assets with different maturities are interconnected by borrower/lenders who freely shift between maturities. But in the short run, this need not always be the case. If, in the short run, these markets are at least partially segmented from one another, then the forces of supply and demand for funds in specific maturity ranges may cause temporary divergences from the basic equilibrium relationship. In particular, short-term and long-term markets would be partially segmented from each other if borrowers and lenders required some significant premium to cause them to lend or invest outside their preferred maturity ranges.

For example, in the long-term market, a growing demand for long-term credit could drive long-term interest rates above their equilibrium levels until enough suppliers of long-term funds can be found. In the short-term market, a similar but separable process, complicated by the actions of the Federal Reserve, could affect short-term rates.

As an example of these divergences, it is tempting to conclude that a part of the force which caused short-term rates to be higher than long-term rates in 1974 (see Figure 9–1) was the very large volume of short-term business financing that occurred then (as businesses financed their burgeoning inventories and other short-term assets). Similarly, it is tempting to conclude that a factor causing short-term interest rates to be substantially lower than long-term rates in 1975 and 1976 was the absence of short-term business financing (as inventories were being drawn down and businesses were primarily financing with long-term debt).[4] Indeed, the changing maturity of businesses' external financing roughly corresponds with the changing shape of the yield curve, supporting the view that changing supply and demand forces may be partial determinants of the

---

[4] See Chapter 2, for a discussion of this pattern in the external financing of businesses.

yield curve. Many market practitioners believe that the changing shape of the yield curve is better explained by these supply and demand effects than by changes in the market's expectations of future rates.

These supply and demand effects must be temporary, however. If borrowers and lenders believe that supply and demand imbalances are driving interest rates away from their equilibrium relationship, they are induced to take actions which have the effect of reducing or eliminating these divergences. Suppose, for example, borrowers and lenders feel that the relationship between short-term and long-term interest rates is out of equilibrium due to, say, a rise in short rates caused by a surge in the demand for short-term funds. The rational behavior for borrowers is to shift a part of their borrowings out of the short market and into the long. Similarly, lenders have an incentive to shift a part of their funds to the short market. Thus, to the extent that supply and demand imbalances cause interest rates to depart from the equilibrium relationship, this pattern of interest rates itself induces changes in the supply and demand for funds. These changes force interest rates back toward their equilibrium relationship. Thus the departures from the basic equilibrium relationship due to the changing balance of supply and demand in each maturity range are self-eliminating and must be considered relatively small and/or short-run divergences, likely to be corrected in the long run by the equilibrium forces.

AN EXTENSION OF THE BASIC EQUILIBRIUM RELATIONSHIP: EFFICIENT MARKETS

The basic equilibrium relationship, the expectations theory of term structure, can be extended by adding the hypothesis of efficient markets. This additional assumption requires that borrowers and lenders, in forming their expectations, use the available information optimally.[5]

As in the previous chapter, the implications of this hypothesis are very fundamental. It implies that long-term markets are efficient in the precise sense that they use all available information in pricing long-term financial assets relative to short-term assets. This means that the forward rates imbedded in the yield curve are based upon the best possible current forecasts of future short-term rates.

Furthermore, with the assumption of efficient markets, it can be shown that today's forward rate for a specific future time interval is the best forecast of tomorrow's forward rate for that same time interval.

---

[5] In its "weak form," efficient markets requires that investors optimally use all the information imbedded within the time series of past interest rates when forming their expectations. In its "strong form," it requires that they use literally all the available information to form their expectations of future rates, and not just that information inherent in past interest rates.

Empirical studies of the term structure of interest rates

These theories of the term structure pose a number of important questions. First, to what extent can the changing term structure of today's interest rates be explained by changing market expectations, and to what extent can it be explained by supply-and-demand–induced divergences from these expectations? Second, to what extent do the expectations in the equilibrium structure incorporate all available information? Both of these questions have been investigated by an interrelated series of empirical tests.[6]

A number of studies, recognizing the existence of implied forecasts imbedded within forward rates, have tested the forecasting power of these forward rates. That is, from yield curves which were varying over time, they have computed a set of forward rates, which were varying over time, and they have tested whether these forward rates were actually good forecasters of future rates.[7]

The recent track record of forward rates as forecasters in the Treasury bill market is shown in Figure 9–2, which compares the actual six-month

Figure 9–2
The record of forward rates as forecasts of U.S. Treasury bill markets, six-month bills, 1966–1976*

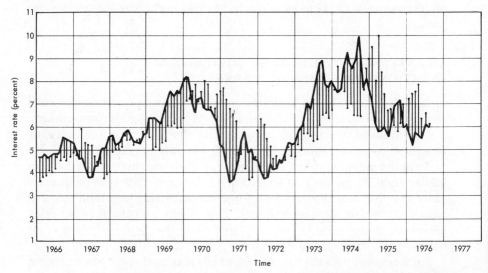

* The solid line is the actual yields on six-month Treasury bills as of the indicated time. The dots represent the forecasts of these rates that would have been made on the basis of the treasury yield curve six months previous.

---

[6] For a review of the early empirical work, see Lester G. Telser, "A Critique of Some Recent Empirical Research on the Explanation of the Term Structure of Interest Rates," *Journal of Political Economy* (August 1967), Supplement 75(4), pp. 546–61.

[7] Referring back to equation (4), we see that these tests require an assumption about the liquidity premia over time. In general, they usually assume that these liquidity premia are stationary over time. This assumption compromises the validity of the tests.

Treasury bill rate with the forward rate forecast based upon the six-month earlier yield curve (the technique assumes that the liquidity premium was constant at 0.24 percent, the average rate by which the forward rate exceeded the actual during this period). Impressionistically, the errors in the six-month forward rate look large.

Working with similar data on forward rates in different markets, researchers have carefully evaluated the forecasting ability of forward rates. As a group, they have found that forward rates offer little, if any, ability to forecast *changes* in interest rates. As an example, one recent study has concluded (using three-month ahead forward rates for three-month Treasury bills during 1961–1971) that forward rates have not been valuable forecasters of future changes in rates.[8] This study found that forward rates predict future interest rates no better than the naive prediction that future rates will be the same as today's rates. However, the study showed that several other plausible forecasting procedures also did no better than did forward rates.

Interpreting these empirical tests of forecasting ability is difficult. At first glance, it is troublesome that the forward rates inherent in yield curves do not seem to provide accurate forecasts of future interest rate changes (or at least forecasts that are more accurate than those produced by naive forecasting methods). On the other hand, the basic equilibrium relationship does not require that the markets' forecasts (that is, the forward rates) be accurate. Even the hypothesis of efficient markets does not require that the forward rates be good predictors in any absolute sense— only that they be the best in a relative sense. That is, the hypothesis of efficient markets requires only that forward rates include all the available information and thus be no worse than other potential forecasting methods. Thus, the empirical results (while they document the fact that forecasting the changes in interest rates is difficult) are not inconsistent with the basic equilibrium relationship or even with the hypothesis of efficient markets.

Other researchers have taken a quite different approach to testing the validity of the expectations theory. They have argued that the forecasting ability of forward rates is too strong an empirical test and that it is entirely possible that the market's expectations are determining the term structure of interest rates but that actual future rates do not turn out to correlate closely with the market's a priori expectations. They have argued instead that empirical tests should ascertain whether plausible models of expectations formation can explain the term structure of interest rates, quite apart from the eventual forecasting accuracy of these expectations.[9] These re-

---

[8] Michael J. Hamburger and Elliott Platt, "The Expectations Hypothesis and the Efficiency of the Treasury Bill Market," *Review of Economics and Statistics* (May 1975), pp. 190–97.

[9] See David Meiselman, *The Term Structure of Interest Rates* (Englewood Cliffs, N.J.: Prentice-Hall, 1962), for a pioneering study in this regard.

searchers have suggested particular models of the way in which investors might form their expectations of future rates (based upon past rates) and investigated whether forward rates, that is, the term structure of interest rates, could be explained by these models of expectations formation. These studies, however, have had to confront a most important dilemma. These empirical tests are joint tests of the expectations theory of the term structure of interest rates (equation 1 or 3) *and* the particular model of expectations formation that is proposed. If a particular test fails to explain the term structure of interest rates, it could imply *either* that the expectations theory of term structure is inadequate or that the particular model of expectations does not represent the true underlying method that the market used to form its expectations.[10] Interpreting the results of these studies, therefore, is also difficult. Nonetheless, they have demonstrated that the changing term structure of interest rates can be explained by, indeed replicated by, some fairly simple models of expectations formation which assume that expectations of future short-term rates are related to past interest rates. Moreover, these empirical tests have found that the variables they have used to measure the forces of supply and demand have not had much effect on interest rates.

For example, as a later version of this type of empirical test, Modigliani and Sutch (M & S) investigated the term structure of interest rates with a reasonably simple model.[11] They proposed that the market's expectations of future short-term interest rates were formed by a particular weighted-average of past short-term interest rates in the most recent 16 calendar quarters. Combining this model of expectations with some proxy measures of supply and demand forces, M & S were able to explain the vast majority of the relative behavior of long-term and short-term rates in the 1952–1966 period. Indeed, their specification of the market's expectations of future rates appeared to be the primary determinant of term structure, and the supply and demand variables contributed only a very small amount to the explanatory power of the full model. M & S believed these results confirmed the expectations theory of the term structure, the basic equilibrium relationship, and indicated that the shorter run supply and demand effects were relatively unimportant. In subsequent years, different variants of their term structure relationship became widely accepted

---

[10] One group of studies circumvented these difficulties by using future rate expectations gleaned from a survey of market participants, and it partially validated the expectations theory; see Burton G. Malkiel, and Edward J. Kane, "Expectations and Interest Rates: A Cross-Sectional Test of the Error-Learning Hypothesis," *Journal of Political Economy* (July–August 1968), 76(A), pp. 453–70.

[11] Franco Modigliani, and Richard Sutch, "Innovation in Interest Rate Policy," *American Economic Review* (May 1966), 56(2), pp. 178–97; and "Debt Management and the Term Structure of Interest Rates: An Empirical Analysis." *Journal of Political Economy* (August 1967), Supplement, pp. 569–89.

and incorporated within the large quantitative models used to understand and predict the U.S. economy.[12]

Thus, while the empirical tests of forward rates have demonstrated that they have not been particularly accurate or valuable forecasters of future interest rate changes, researchers have proposed plausible models of expectations formation which seem to explain the changing pattern of forward rates, and hence the term structure of interest rates. This evidence supports the basic form of the equilibrium relationship, namely that the market prices financial assets such that different maturities offer equivalent expected returns. Moreover, taken as a whole, the empirical tests suggest that the effects of supply and demand imbalances are relatively small and/or short-lived. The market's expectations of future short rates thus seem to play a very large role in the determination of long-term interest rates. However, the exact role of supply and demand versus expectations, and the usefulness of the forward rates as forecasters of future short-term rates, continue to be challenging areas for empirical research.

INFLATION AND THE TERM STRUCTURE OF INTEREST RATES: THE COMBINED THEORIES

Combining the equilibrium relationship between interest rates and inflation discussed in the previous chapter, and the term structure of interest rates discussed in this chapter, we can formulate an integrated equilibrium theory of interest rates. This basic equilibrium structure of interest rates can be derived by assuming that all markets are freely interconnected by the joint participation of rational profit-maximizing borrowers and lenders, whose actions constantly maintain an equilibrium between the expected returns from different assets: real assets, short-term financial assets, and long-term financial assets. This equilibrium requires a pricing structure for financial assets such that their returns are related to real assets through the market's expectations of future inflation, and the returns from short-term and long-term financial assets are related through the market's expectations of future short-term interest rates. These future

---

[12] These empirical results do, however, raise important questions about the hypothesis of efficient markets. If long-term rates are determined by expectations of future short-term rates, and these in turn are determined by past short-term rates, then past short-term rates may contain information about the future changes in relative long-term rates. However, if this is so, there may be relative profit opportunities available to long-term investors that have not been arbitraged away, even though investors had the information readily available to them in the form of past short-term rates. There is a potential conflict between this implication and the assumption of "efficient markets". For a discussion of this see; William Poole, "Rational Expectations in the Macro Model", Brookings Papers on Economic Activity, Vol. 2, 1976, pp. 463–505.

short-term rates will, in turn, be the market's future expectations of inflation in their respective future time periods. Thus, there is a mutually compatible linkage between our two equilibrium relationships. The expectations of inflation in the very next time period influence today's short-term rates directly, and the expectations of inflation rates in distant periods influence today's term structure of interest rates indirectly, through the expectations of future short rates.

Similarly, this integrated equilibrium theory can be extended by the additional hypothesis of efficient markets. This extension of the theory is based upon the additional assumption that borrowers and lenders use available information optimally, such that today's interest rates incorporate and reflect all available information about future inflation and interest rates. The best possible forecasts of future inflation and interest rates may thus be included within today's interest rates, however difficult they may be to extract (because of possibly time-varying real rates and liquidity premiums).

THE NOTION OF RANDOMNESS IN EFFICIENT MARKETS

One of the often-quoted implications of this extended efficient markets theory is that the future movements of interest rates are random. The word random in this connection has a very special meaning. In fact, this hypothesis does not suggest that future interest rate changes are "random" in the sense of haphazard or having no causal relationship with other variables. Rather it suggests they are predictable through the forward rates implied by the term structure. What is random in this hypothesis is not future interest rates but the errors in the forecasts of these future variables. These forecast errors are "random" because they are unrelated to the current state of knowledge (for if they were not, investors would have used this information to revise and improve their forecasting methods). Thus, efficient markets imply that real economic and financial forces cause inflation and interest rates to fluctuate but that the current term structure of interest rates reflects all that is knowable about these forces. At its most basic level, it is a hypothesis not of causal forces but of forecasting ability.

CONCLUDING COMMENTS

In this chapter and the previous chapter, we have observed that inflation, short-term interest rates, and long-term interest rates are related. Indeed, their fluctuations in recent years have been closely correlated as private market participants (as opposed to the Federal Reserve) have assumed an increasingly greater role in determining interest rates. We have also discussed possible short-run divergencies from these relationships. Finally, we have explored possible extensions of these relationships to markets which optimally use all available information.

Interestingly enough, the operational implications of these different perspectives are quite different. For example, let us examine the issue of forecasting. The basic equilibrium relationships imply that the market's forecast of future inflation and interest rates are imbedded within today's interest rates but make no statement about the quality of the market's forecasts (indeed, to the contrary, they distinctly hold open the possibility that these imbedded forecasts are not the best forecasts). In contrast, of course, to the extent that the forces of supply and demand cause short-run divergences from equilibrium, there is no necessary forecast of future inflation or future interest rates imbedded within today's interest rates. Borrowers, lenders, or arbitragers may feel free to profitably act upon their own forecasts. In further contrast, the additional hypothesis of efficient markets not only implies that there are forecasts of future inflation and interest rates imbedded within today's rates (however difficult they may be to extract), but that they are the best forecasts. Ironically enough, the proponents of this additional hypothesis believe that (1) the forecasts are not very good (the empirical results), (2) that they are the best (which is consistent with the theory), and (3) that they are not very useful (for, according to the hypothesis, they cannot be used to improve expected returns). Despite whatever similarities there may be in assumptions, therefore, it is clear that the operational implications of the basic equilibrium theories and their extensions (efficient markets) can be quite different.

QUESTIONS

A. On the theory:
  1. The chapter presents several different explanations of the yield curve. What are the assumptions upon which each theory is based? Which set of assumptions do you find more plausible?

B. On its use:
  1. Yield curves for U.S. Treasury securities as of four dates are shown below:

Yield curves

Maturity (years)	January 1975	January 1976	January 1977	January 1978
1	7.07	6.31	4.82	6.93
2	7.25	6.69	5.27	7.10
3	7.23	7.00	5.68	7.21
4	7.22	7.25	5.94	7.30
20	7.65	7.83	7.16	7.80

Compute the values for the missing entries in the following table:

Forward rate for one-year period ending in January of

	1976	1977	1978	1979	1980	1981	1982
As of							
January 1975	7.07*						
January 1976		6.31*					
January 1977			4.82*				
January 1978				6.93*			

* Actual one-year rates.

Assume that you believe markets are dominated by "expectations," that is, that the market prices of securities are determined largely by investors who invest their funds in those assets with the greatest expected returns (thus arbitraging away any significant differentials in the expected returns from different assets). Using the information incorporated in the above yield curves:

   a. What can you say about how the market's consensus forecast of inflation for the period January 1976 to January 1977 changed between January 1975 and January 1976?

   b. What can you say about how the market's consensus forecast of inflation for the period from January 1977 through January 1978 changed between January 1975 and January 1976 and between January 1976 and January 1977?

   c. What did the market in January 1978 seem to be saying about the likely rate of inflation between January 1978 and January 1979; between January 1978 and January 1980?

   d. How did the market's consensus forecast of the long-term rate of inflation change over these three years?

2. How would the existence of liquidity premiums or risk premiums limit the usefulness of the forward rates as measures of the markets forecast of future interest rates?

3. Suppose the equilibrium relationships hold and, in addition, that the forecasts they embody are "best."

   a. What does that mean for corporations considering the choice between short-term and long-term debt as a source of finance?

   b. What does it mean to investors in financial assets as they consider investing in short or long debts?

4. How would the answers to question 3 change if

   a. The equilibrium relationships held but the forecasts were "poor?"

   b. The forces of supply and demand for funds played a large role in determination of interest rates on securities of different maturities?

C. On the accuracy of the forecasts

   1. What do the data in Figure 9–3 lead you to conclude about the accuracy of the forecasts included in the term structure?

Figure 9–3
Yields on government securities—a five-year record

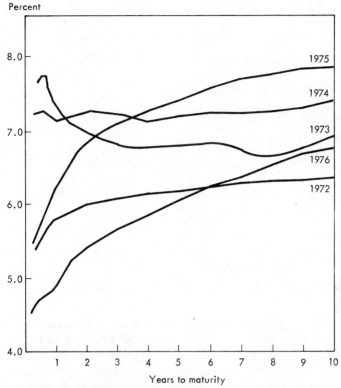

Note: Yield curves are as of each year-end. Treasury bill rates are included on a bond-equivalent basis.

REFERENCES

Fama, Eugene. "Forward Rates as Predictors of Future Spot Rates," *Journal of Financial Economics,* vol. 3 (1976) pp. 361–77.

Cornell, Bradford. "Monetary Policy, Inflation Forecasting and the Term Structure of Interest Rates," *The Journal of Finance,* vol. 33, no. 1 (March 1978), pp. 117–27.

Modigliani, Franco and Shiller, Robert J. "Inflation Rational Expectations and the Term Structure of Interest Rates," *Economica,* vol. 40 (February 1973), pp. 12–43.

Sargent, "Rational Expectations and the Term Structure of Interest Rates," *Journal of Money, Credit and Banking,* vol. 4, no. 1 (February 1972), pp. 74–97.

10

Risk and the structure
of equilibrium returns
for marketable securities

PRIOR PROBABILITY DISTRIBUTIONS FOR FUTURE UNCERTAIN
RETURNS
THE BASIC EQUILIBRIUM RELATIONSHIP: A THEORY OF RISK
PREMIUMS
A security's contribution to portfolio risk
A theory of risk premiums
AN EXTENSION OF THE BASIC EQUILIBRIUM RELATIONSHIP:
EFFICIENT MARKETS
VALIDITY AND USEFULNESS OF THE MODEL

Marketable securities are, by definition, securities which may be traded in secondary markets, where they are priced at levels which cause investors to be willing to buy and sell them. A relevant measure of investment performance for a marketable security (during a particular time period) is its holding period return, the sum of the current income from the security and its capital gain/loss measured as a percentage of its price at the beginning of the period. [1] For a corporate bond, for example, the holding period return in a particular time interval is the sum of the coupon income plus the change in price, expressed as a percent of the original price. In this chapter, we will derive an equilibrium relationship between the holding period returns for securities which have different risks.

The previous two chapters have already demonstrated the crucial element in such an equilibrium relationship: the concept of the market's expectations of the future. In this chapter, we will continue to derive our relationships in terms of expectations—in particular, expected holding period returns. Expectations are the elusive fabric that makes financial markets so interesting. Unfortunately expectations also make financial markets difficult to study, for while they may exist in the minds of investors, they are not observable in any direct sense.

---

[1] Actually, this is the relevant measure only for wealth-maximizing investors in markets with no transactions costs. We will be explicit about these assumptions shortly.

In the beginning of this book, in Figure 1–1, we observed the annual holding period returns from different assets. The average holding period returns were greater for those assets (like common stocks) where they had also been more volatile, and vice versa. After the fact (ex-post) then, the average long-run returns from different assets seem to have been related to the risks to which they have exposed investors. Before the fact (ex-ante), we should also anticipate that markets would price financial assets such that their expected returns compensate investors for their prospective risk. This chapter will derive a more precise statement of this ex-ante relationship.

PRIOR PROBABILITY DISTRIBUTIONS FOR FUTURE UNCERTAIN RETURNS

To develop an explicit theory of equilibrium structure, we must explicitly model the concept of risk. For potential investors, the future holding period returns from a particular security, or a portfolio of securities, are quite uncertain. Nonetheless, investors may be able to assess their prior probability distribution for future holding period returns, defined over all of the possible outcomes. These probability distributions do not involve "objective" probabilities (such as the observation that upon flipping a coin, the chances of a head are 50/50). Rather they involve "subjective" probabilities which are determined by the informed judgment of investors considering the relevant information.

A possible probability distribution for the next period's holding period returns for a particular security might look like the accompanying figure.[2]

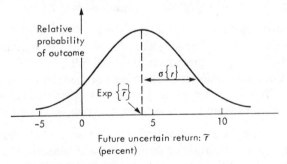

Future uncertain return: $\bar{r}$
(percent)

Important characteristics:
1. Expected Return: Exp $\{\bar{r}\}$
2. Uncertainty of Return: $\sigma\{\bar{r}\}$
3. Relationship, or correlation, with the return on other assets.

---

[2] For a discussion of subjective probabilities and their use, see Robert Schleifer, *Analysis of Decisions under Uncertainty* (New York: McGraw-Hill, 1969); or Howard Raiffa, *Decision Analysis* (Reading, Mass.: Addison-Wesley, 1968).

The relative probabilities indicate the relative likelihood of a particular outcome (return) actually occurring.[3] Two important characteristics of any particular distribution are the expected value of future returns, which we will denote as Exp $\{\bar{r}\}$ and the uncertainty of the future returns, which we will measure by the standard deviation, denoted $\sigma\{r\}$.[4] In addition, as we shall see, the correlation of a security's holding period returns with the holding period returns of all other securities will be important, particularly when that security is combined into what we shall call the "market portfolio." We will discuss this third characteristic in more detail shortly. Needless to say, these probability distributions, and their important characteristics, exist only in the minds of investors. They are not observable, yet they are one of the basic forces which lead to equilibrium in financial markets.

THE BASIC EQUILIBRIUM RELATIONSHIP: A THEORY OF RISK PREMIUMS

With the above distribution as background, an equilibrium structure for all marketable securities can be derived, with the following assumptions:

1. The markets for all securities are not segmented from each other, nor are there transactions costs for buying/selling securities, nor (for the sake of simplicity) are there differential tax rates.
2. Rational investors freely shift their portfolios among different securities, seeking greater expected returns and smaller risk (as measured by the expected value and standard deviation of their portfolios' return respectively).

In addition, two more important assumptions will be made:

3. All investors can borrow or lend (invest) at the "risk-free rate" over the next time period. For the sake of convenience, we can identify this risk-free asset as the short-term treasury bill.
4. All investors have uniform assessments of the future returns from each security; that is, their prior probability distributions for the next period's returns from each asset are uniform across all investors.

As the first step in the derivation, let us preview the general form an appropriate equilibrium relationship might take. Assume that each investor must choose, for the next time period, between holding the risk-free asset and holding a particular security. To identify it with a subscript, we will call it the jth security.

---

[3] They are, of course, restricted by the requirement that the total probability for all outcomes is 1.00; that is, there will be one and only one outcome in the next period.

[4] The standard deviation (σ) is defined such that, for a normal distribution, roughly two thirds of the relative probability falls within ± one standard deviation of the expected value.

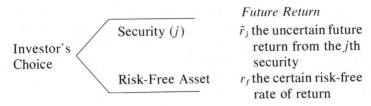

The prices of these two securities (the riskless asset and the *j*th security) will be in equilibrium if, and only if, investors are indifferent between holding the two assets. Introducing the concept of a risk premium for the *j*th security, investors will be indifferent between these two assets if, and only if, they are priced so that

$$E \{\tilde{r}_j\} = r_f + \text{Risk Premium}_j \qquad (1)$$

where the "risk premium" is a function of the uncertainty of the future return from the *j*th security. In equilibrium, each security should be priced relative to the risk-free asset, and all securities should be priced relative to each other through this relationship. Interpreting the time horizon to be a relatively short period (for example one year), the expected returns from all securities should be in (risk-adjusted) equilibrium with the known return from a one-year risk-free security (for example, a one-year treasury bill).

Given this general form for the relationship between expected return and risk, the question becomes: How can we specify the appropriate *risk premium* in this expectations relationship? We can preview the structure of these risk premiums through a few simple observations. Because all investors are assumed to be risk averse, they will hold diversified portfolios. In fact, because they are assumed to have identical assessments of the future returns from each risky security, it can be shown that all investors will hold identical portfolios of these securities.[5] Since all of the outstanding securities must be held by someone, and since all investors hold the same portfolio, each investor will hold a prorata share of all financial assets. We will call the portfolio consisting of a prorata share of each and every security the "market portfolio." Given this terminology, each investor will hold the market portfolio. This fact is critical to an understanding of the risk in a security, and to the determinants of the risk premium that is appropriate in equation (1).

Because each investor holds a security as a part of the market portfolio, the risk it represents to the investor is the increase in total uncertainty of the market portfolio which arises from its inclusion in the

---

[5] This is stricly true only if the risk-free asset exists, as we have assumed it does. It is possible to relax the assumption that all investors have uniform assessments of future returns, but the structure of the market equilibrium is then very complex, and the results are difficult to test empirically.

market portfolio. As we shall see, this risk is only a part of the total risk (or standard deviation of expected return) associated with the individual security itself. Indeed, one of the central ideas of the portfolio theory and the equilibrium pricing relationship we are developing is that only a certain part of the total uncertainty in a security is considered as risk by a holder of the market portfolio.

A security's contribution to portfolio risk

The returns from any security can be partioned into two parts—a part which is correlated with the return on all securities (as represented by the return on the above-mentioned market portfolio) and a part which is uncorrelated with the return on the market portfolio. That is, one can always write the following

$$\tilde{r}_j = \beta_j \cdot \tilde{r}_m + \tilde{\alpha}_j \tag{2}$$

where $\tilde{r}_j$ is the return on security j, and $\tilde{r}_m$ is the return on the market portfolio. The term $\beta_j \tilde{r}_m$ contains all the movement in $\tilde{r}_j$ which is correlated with $\tilde{r}_m$. This term is often called the market-related or systematic component of the security's return. The term $\tilde{\alpha}_j$ contains the movement in $\tilde{r}_j$ which arises from other factors which are uncorrelated with the return on the market portfolio. It is often called the nonsystematic component of the security's return.

It can be shown that the only part of the uncertainty in security j which matters, or accumulates, in the market portfolio is that part which is correlated with the market return itself.[6] Thus, if none of the uncertainty in a security's return is correlated with the return on the market, the addition of the security to the market portfolio results in no increase in the uncertainty of the portfolio.[7] That is, if β_j is equal to zero [in equation (2)], the security contributes no incremental risk to the market portfolio. Therefore, the security requires no risk premium from an investor holding the market portfolio. On the other hand, the larger the market-related portion of the uncertainty (the larger $\beta_j \cdot \tilde{r}_m$) the more the individual security adds to the risk of the market portfolio, and the larger must be its risk premium. Since $\tilde{r}_m$ is the same for all securities, the term β_j is the

---

[6] This proposition depends on the effects of the well-known process of diversification. As the number of securities in a portfolio becomes large, the risks which are unique or specific to any one security are diversified away. In the limit, as the number of securities becomes very large, these "specific risks" become very unimportant. The important risk that is left (for it cannot be diversified away) is the risk factor common to all securities in the portfolio—that is, the market risk for a market portfolio. The extent to which a given security augments this market risk is measured by the first term in equation (2). Fortunately for investors the risks inherent in the second term can be diversified away if they hold diversified portfolios.

[7] This is strictly true only if the number of securities (n) is infinitely large.

feature of the security which is proportional to the risk the security represents to a holder of the market portfolio. Thus β_j is a measure of the risk the security represents and will turn out to be the determinant of the risk premium it requires.

A theory of risk premiums

Thus far, we have collected a number of insights into the potential equilibrium structure of financial returns. We have seen that this equilibrium structure will have the expected value form of equation (1) and that the task is to develop a theory of risk premiums. We have observed that under the assumption of uniform assessments, each investor will hold the market portfolio, and that the risk premium which is relevant for each security should therefore be related to the contribution which this security would make to the total risk of the market portfolio. Finally, we have stated that the β in equation (2) is a measure which is proportional to this market-related risk.

We can now combine the above separate observations into a theory of risk premiums, by invoking one more of our assumptions—namely that all investors can borrow-lend at the riskless rate. Given this, each investor's portfolio can then be composed of two components, the risk-free asset and the market portfolio. All portfolios composed of different mixtures of these two components will have an expected return and a relative risk measure β which falls along the dotted line illustrated graphically in Figure 10–1, called the "market line."[8] The existence of this market line enables us to determine the relationship between the expected return and the β for any individual security (in equilibrium). It must also fall along this line.

To show this, consider the following investment choice (for investors who have a small amount of incremental funds to invest) which is deliber-

---

[8] Consider, for example, a composite portfolio composed of X percent in the "market portfolio" and $(1 - X)$ percent in the risk-free asset. The expected return of the composite portfolio will be:

$$\text{Exp } \{\tilde{r}_p\} = X \cdot \text{Exp } \{\tilde{r}_m\} + (1 - X) \cdot r_f$$

The β of the composite portfolio will be:

$$\beta_p = X \cdot (1) + (1 - X) \cdot 0 = X$$

Substituting the latter into the former, we get the relationship between the composite portfolios' expected return and β:

$$\text{Exp } \{\tilde{r}_p\} = r_f + \beta_p \cdot [\text{Exp } \{\tilde{r}_m\} - r_f]$$

But this is just the equation of a straight line in Figure 10–2. Therefore, the relationship between the expected return and risk of all possible composite portfolios formed from the risk-free asset and the market portfolio will fall along the "market line" in Figure 10–1.

Figure 10–1
Expected returns versus market-related risk for different portfolio combinations and securities

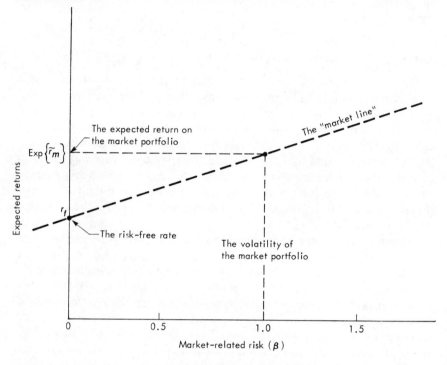

ately constructed to include two alternatives with the same market-related risk:

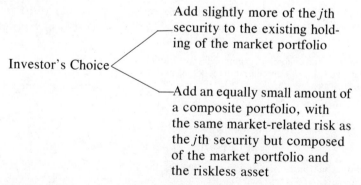

Investor's Choice

Add slightly more of the jth security to the existing holding of the market portfolio

Add an equally small amount of a composite portfolio, with the same market-related risk as the jth security but composed of the market portfolio and the riskless asset

Graphically, locate the jth security in Figure 10–1, where its expected return Exp $\{\tilde{r}_j\}$ is measured on the vertical axis and its market-related risk (β_j) is measured on the horizontal axis.[9]

[9] When Figure 10–1 is used to locate individual securities in this way, it is called a graph of the "security market line."

Suppose, for the sake of argument, that the investors' expected return for this security, Exp $\{\tilde{r}_j\}$, initially fell above the "market line" in Figure 10–1. This security would then be more attractive (have greater expected returns for the same contribution to portfolio risk) than a composite portfolio of the market portfolio and a risk-free asset. Investors would thus buy this security.

Their actions would tend to drive up the price of this security and therefore reduce its future expected returns. Investors would continue, until the expected return from security just fell along the dotted line in Figure 10–1, the "market line." Then, and only then, would investors be just indifferent between holding this security as a part of their portfolio and the alternative of adding a portfolio with equal systematic risk: adding a portfolio of comparable risk composed of the risk-free asset and the market portfolio. Then, and only then, would the expected returns from this security be in equilibrium with other securities.

Similarly, suppose for the sake of argument, that the expected return from this security fell below the market line. Investors would then sell this security, driving down its price, until its future expected return rose to the level of the market line. Only then would it be in equilibrium with other securities.

We know, therefore, that in equlibrium all possible securities should be priced such that their expected returns and their β's fall along the market line in Figure 10–1, which in that context we can call the "security market line."

$$\text{Exp}\{\tilde{r}_j\} \quad = \quad r_f \quad + \quad \beta_j[\text{Exp}\{\tilde{r}_m\} - r_f] \qquad (4)$$

Expected Return   Risk-Free   Risk Premium
                    Rate

This is the fundamental equation of the equilibrium structure of expected return and risk.

There is, in addition, a somewhat simpler form of this same expression. Suppose that we define "excess expected returns, (E_j)" to be, the expected returns from a security over and above the risk-free rate, that is:

$$E_j \quad = \quad \text{Exp}\{\tilde{r}_j\} \quad - \quad r_f \qquad (5)$$

Excess Expected   Expected   Risk-Free
Return   Return   Rate

Then, equation (4), together with the definition in equation (5), implies

$$E_j = \beta_j \cdot E_m \qquad (6)$$

That is, the excess expected return from a given security is, in equilibrium, equal to its index of market related risk, (β_j), times the excess expected return from the market.

By assuming that investors have uniform judgments about the future uncertain returns from each security, we have derived a particularly simple relationship which must hold in equilibrium: (1) The risk of a security should be measured by what we have called β, the sensitivity of its future return to the future returns from the overall market; (2) the expected returns from all risky securities should be related to their risk measures (β's); and (3) the risk premium, per unit of β, should be equal to the expected return on the market minus the risk-free rate.

AN EXTENSION OF THE BASIC EQUILIBRIUM RELATIONSHIP: EFFICIENT MARKETS

In the above derivation of an equilibrium relationship we assumed that all investors had uniform assessments of the future returns from each security. We assumed nothing, however, about the quality of these assessments; in particular, we assumed nothing about their relationship to the available information.

There is an extension of this equilibrium structure, however, which specifically addresses itself to this possibility. It is, as before (in the two previous chapters), the hypothesis of efficient markets. This hypothesis assumes, in addition to what has been assumed above, that investors (the market) use all of the available information optimally to form their assessments of the future. This implies that markets are "efficient" in the precise sense that all securities are priced to fully reflect all available information. In such markets, an investor can increase expected portfolio returns only by increasing market-related risk (as measured by β) but not by making superior estimates of the expected returns from an individual security or group of securities.

This extension is, on the one hand, simply a statement about the relationship between investors' expectations and the sources of information which can be incorporated into these expectations. It does nothing to change the fundamental relationship in equations (4) and/or (6). On the other hand, it is a very important and fundamental statement about the ways in which the prices of securities change over time. The hypothesis of efficient markets implies that the expectations in equations (4) and/or (6) are the best possible forecast of future security returns. The actual future holding period returns from any security will thus be composed of two distinct components: the forecastable components [the expected returns in equation (4) and (6)] and a perfectly random component, the errors in this forecast. According to the hypothesis, the sequential errors in these forecasts must, in fact, be random with respect to the current state of knowledge; otherwise investors would have included the estimated errors within their optimal assessments of expected returns. This property of efficient markets has led to the colloquial use of the term "random walk" to describe security price movements. But, as we pointed out in the previous chapter, this description can be misleading. The basic theory is not a theory of random causation, but of perfectly anticipated causation, of perfect equilibrium. It implies that security prices are driven by a host of underlying fundamental relationships, relationships which are understood by at least a sufficient number of investors to be reflected in the current price of securities. Because these fundamental forces are anticipated in *current* prices, however, only two things are left in *future* returns: the expected future returns determined by our basic equilibrium relationship and an unknown future return which will be determined by new information received in the next interval. Incorporating this last hypothesis, therefore, we have derived an abstract but general theory about not only the current prices of marketable securities, but the ways in which their future holding period returns (future prices) should behave over time. In particular, the actual future holding period returns from any security or group of securities should move randomly (with uncorrelated increments from one time period to the next) around the expected return in our basic equilibrium relationship.

VALIDITY AND USEFULNESS OF THE MODEL

There are many unrealistic aspects to the model which has been used to define risk and relate it to expected returns. We have assumed that investors have uniform assessments for all securities and thus hold the same portfolios. We know, however, that neither of these is really true.[10] Furthermore, we have assumed that investors can borrow and/or lend at the riskless rate, and we know that this is not strictly true. Nonetheless, the empirical evidence suggests that the rather simple risk-return relationship predicted by our theory may be useful. In particular, the difference between the returns which investors have earned on bonds and common stocks appears to be consistent with the theory. Moreover, many studies of the returns earned on different common stocks suggest that the basic equilibrium relationship is a useful approximation of the actual process generating returns in the equity market. We will discuss these empirical analyses of the behavior of investment returns in the bond and stock markets in Chapters 16 and 17, once we have developed a deeper understanding of the structure of these markets.

Finally, the model we have discussed is a model of the return of an individual security relative to the return on the market. It says nothing about this later quantity. We do know some things about the expected return from the market, however. We do know, for example, that the expected return from the market should exceed the risk-free rate because

---

[10] For a derivation of some more complex results when investors do not have uniform assessments, see John Linther, "The Aggregation of Investor's Diverse Judgements and Preferences in Purely Competitive Security Markets," *Journal of Financial and Quantitative Analysis* (December 1969), pp. 347–400.

we have assumed that investors are risk-averse, and by definition the market is riskier than the risk-free rate. The exact difference between the expected return from the market and the risk-free rate will depend, in general, on the "market price of risk," the tradeoff investors as a whole are willing to make between risk and expected return. This will depend, in general, on the risk aversions of all investors, and we have no theoretical tools to determine what these risk aversions *should* be. The historical "market price of risk" and the "excess expected return" from the market can, however, be empirically investigated, as we will do in a later chapter.

QUESTIONS

1. What are the assumptions behind the equilibrium relationship between risk and expected return? What are its implications? What is its relevance to investors?
2. Comment on the following: If most of society's wealth is held in investment units that hold relatively well-diversified portfolios, then investors who hold small amounts of wealth should also hold their wealth in diversified portfolios.
3. Venture capital investments are often thought of as risky investments. Suppose there is a lot of standard deviation in the returns from individual ventures but not much covariance between the returns on ventures and returns on the "market" portfolio. How much expected return would a holder of the market portfolio demand from a venture with a zero β but a large total standard deviation in its expected rate of return? How much expected return would be required by a small group of individuals which invested all its funds in a few such ventures? What would be the required rate of return from such a venture if it was held as a part of a venture capital mutual fund which was sold widely throughout the market place?
4. If the equilibrium relationship between risk and expected return holds, how could one forecast the return from a given portfolio of financial assets?
5. How might different mutual funds differ from each other?

REFERENCES

Lintner, John. "The Valuation of Risk Assets and the Selection of Risky Investments in Stock Portfolios and Capital Budgets," *Review of Economics and Statistics,* vol. 57 (February 1965), pp. 13–37.

Modigliani, Franco and Pogue, Gerald A. "An Introduction to Risk and Return," Parts I and II, *Financial Analysts Journal* (March/April 1974) and (May/June 1974).

Sharpe, William F. "Capital Asset Prices: A Theory of Market Equilibrium under Conditions of Risk," *Journal of Finance,* vol. 19 (September 1964), pp. 425–442.

11

Public versus private markets and the role of financial intermediaries

Financial markets serve as a conduit for the exchange of financial promises as the accompanying diagram illustrates:

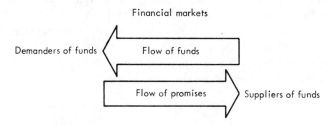

They provide a channel for the flow of today's funds, from suppliers to demanders of funds. In addition, they provide a channel for the equal and opposite flow, the flow of financial assets which promise patterns of future returns.

The other major function of financial markets is to price financial assets and liabilities correctly in the light of the alternatives available to investors and borrowers. In the previous chapters, we have analyzed equilibrium processes which affect the pricing of financial assets. We have derived equilibrium structures for the expected returns of financial assets versus inflation, the expected returns of short-term versus long-term interest-bearing assets, and the expected returns for all financial assets as a function of their contribution to the risk of a "market portfolio." Each of these derivations relied upon a common set of implicit assumptions about financial markets. In particular, they relied upon the assumption that relatively large numbers of suppliers and demanders of funds constantly interact in financial markets such that prices are determined by a competitive market clearing process.

In reality, there are a number of markets that seem to approximate this ideal—where large numbers of participants bid for securities in a process no one of them or group of them can easily control. The public markets for common stocks and U.S. Treasury securities, for example, seem to have these characteristics.

Interestingly enough, however, many financial markets are not "public" markets in the sense that financial asset prices are determined by the joint bidding of large numbers of buyers and sellers. In fact, most of the flows of new financing are transmitted through "private markets," where specific financial assets are structured and priced in a private negotiation between the potential borrower and potential lender. For example, the markets for business loans, privately placed corporate bonds, and home mortgages are all private markets in this sense. The lenders in these markets are generally financial intermediaries who subsequently hold the negotiated financial obligations of the borrower until maturity. For the most part, there are no secondary financial markets where these privately negotiated obligations can be later traded between different investors. In a number of important respects, then, these private financial markets are different than competitive public markets where prices are determined by the joint interaction of many supplier/demanders of funds. In this chapter we will explore the reasons for the existence of these private markets, the functions performed in these markets by financial institutions, and the factors affecting the pricing of the securities or, more accurately, the "private placements" in these private markets.

THE RISK AND RETURN FROM DIFFERENT SECURITIES

In the previous chapter, the risk of different securities was associated with their price movements relative to the market. We could go further, however, and analyze the determinants of this price volatility for different securities. For example, we could ask: Why are some securities' prices more volatile than others? Why are they riskier? Clearly, the character of the underlying economic activity being financed is an important determinant of risk. Economic endeavors with uncertain future returns are "riskier" than economic endeavors with certain future returns, and this uncertainty will be reflected in the price volatility of their securities over time. In addition, however, the way in which these economic endeavors are financed is important. In particular, the relative mix of different classes of security holders (financial structure) and their relative power (financial control) are both important determinants of risk.

To illustrate these risk determinants, consider a $1 million project with a future uncertain return which will be realized after one year (see accompanying diagram). At the most simple level, this underlying project can be financed with a mix of debt and equity securities. In one year, after the

returns are realized, the debt holders receive their promised return. The equity holders then receive the residual return after the debt holders are paid. Clearly, the equity holders bear relatively more of the project risk. In addition, however, the risk of both debt and equity investors is dependent upon the mix of debt and equity used to finance the project. As more debt securities are used to finance the project, the debt holders bear more of the economic risks of the underlying project. Hence, the financial structure of the project is an important determinant of the risk of the securities.

Equally important, though somewhat less obvious, is the issue of financial control. To illustrate, suppose that the above project was initially financed with equal amounts of debt and equity (0.5 million of each), and suppose the equity holders are the "management" of the economic project who control all of the relevant investment decisions. Suppose that after six months it becomes clear to the managers (equity holders) that the project will soon return only $0.5 million and no more. Upon obtaining the returns of $0.5 million, they will have two choices during the next six months: Repay the debt holders (leaving nothing for the equity holders), or gamble with the $0.5 million on some uncertain new venture. The management, operating in the best interests of the equity holders, will clearly gamble with the $0.5 million. They have nothing to lose and something to gain, even on what would appear (to other investors) to be a very poor and/or risky project. Indeed, the riskier the prospective project is, the better it may be for the equity holders, precisely because they currently have nothing to lose. Needless to say, this creates an important problem for the debt holders. The divergent interests of debt and equity holders can expose debt holders to serious risks. To control these risks, prospective debt holders generally attempt to fashion a series of protective devices which constrain the power of the managers (equity holders) and/or protect the interests of the debt holders. Sometimes these take the form of "covenants" in the debt agreements which limit the possible actions of the managers and perhaps transfer partial control to the debt holders under certain conditions. Sometimes they take the form of pledged security (real assets pledged to the debt holders in the event of financial default). Sometimes they take other forms. The art of devising such constraints and protections is one of the important elements of borrowing and lending. In this book, we will not delve deeply into these issues because they form an entire field of study themselves. For our purposes, however, it is important to observe that the risks of various securities are determined not only by the characteristics of the underlying economic enterprise and its financial structure, but also by the distribution of financial power and control among the debt and equity holders.

PUBLIC VERSUS PRIVATE MARKETS

From the perspective of security buyers and sellers, there are enormous advantages to public competitive markets where large numbers of potential suppliers and demanders of funds meet. The market clearing process caused by the continual interaction of these competitive financial participants helps to insure that the prices of securities traded in these markets will be affected and, in the extreme, precisely determined by the equilibrium processes we have examined in earlier chapters. From the perspective of potential security buyers (suppliers of funds), this is a very important characteristic. In a public competitive market, the potential security buyers can be confident of the markets' pricing mechanism. That is, they can be confident that they can purchase securities within these markets at a "fair" price, and sell them later at a "fair" price, where by "fair" we mean at a price determined by the underlying value of these securities to all other investors. In a competitive market, securities may still be very risky, but these securities will tend to be priced appropriately relative to their risk because of the equilibrium processes at work.

Similarly, sellers of securities (raisers of funds) benefit from public competitive securities markets. In competitive markets, the expected returns that corporations have to offer investors in order to obtain funds are set "fairly," where "fairly" means the expected returns from securities need only be commensurate with their risk (in particular, the risk they contribute to the market portfolio of all securities). Thus, the advantages of dealing in securities traded in active competitive public markets are substantial for both demanders and suppliers of funds.

Unfortunately, however, not all financial obligations can be actively traded in public markets. First of all, the prospective financial obligation must be represented by a relatively large number of standard homogeneous securities; otherwise they cannot be actively traded among a relatively large number of investors. Second, there must be a relatively wide dissemination of information about the underlying economic enterprise among potential investors (suppliers of funds); otherwise they would individually and collectively be reluctant to invest in the securities of an unknown and uncertain prospect.

In addition, there are some special factors which limit the trading of debt obligations in public markets. Recall, from the preceding section, that the interests of debt holders and equity holders can be divergent in a dynamic investment environment, and debt holders must therefore rely upon terms within the debt agreements to constrain the power of the equity holders and/or protect their own interests. From the debt holders' perspective, the problem is to devise a set of prior terms or conditions which will be stringent enough to adequately protect them in various future situations. From the debt issuers' perspective, the problem is to retain enough future flexibility within these terms and conditions to respond to new conditions as they arise. Unfortunately it can sometimes be very difficult to devise a set of standard terms/conditions whose future impact can be readily understood, that are restrictive enough for the prospective debt holders, and yet flexible enough for the prospective debt issuers.

On the basis of the above observations, we can predict the kinds of financial obligations which may normally be issued and traded in public markets and those which will generally be negotiated and issued in private markets. When the issuers (demanders of funds) are relatively small and relatively unknown, their obligations will often not be traded in public competitive markets. Furthermore, even when the issuers are large and well-known, their debt securities may not always be issued and traded in public markets. When it is difficult to protect prospective debt holders against unusual risks with relatively standard terms/conditions within the debt agreement or when there are clear advantages to tailoring a very special complex set of terms/conditions to the borrowers' needs, the debt securities are likely to be privately negotiated and privately issued, and they are not likely to be actively traded in public markets. Because of these difficulties, active public markets are most likely to exist for only the securities of relatively larger well-known enterprises and for only the equity and certain of the debt securities of these enterprises.

Looking to the financial markets, we observe that active public markets exist for securities like U.S. Treasury bonds, and the common stocks of well-known corporations. Relatively competitive, though less active, public markets also exist for the relatively standard bonds of large well-known corporations and for the common stocks of medium-size corporations. The bonds of even medium-size corporations, however, are generally not actively traded. These medium-size corporations, and often larger corporations with very specialized financing needs, generally finance through debt which is privately placed with financial institutions. Finally, both the debt and (often) the equity securities of small, poorly known corporations are often privately issued and generally not traded in anything resembling a public competitive market.

FUNCTION OF FINANCIAL INTERMEDIARIES—SUPPLIERS' POINT OF VIEW

Having examined some of the differences between public competitive markets and private markets, we can now discuss the role of financial intermediaries. From the perspective of the suppliers of funds, financial intermediaries provide an alternative channel for investing in financial obligations. As the accompanying diagram suggests, suppliers may chose to invest directly in the financial obligations of other primary sectors or channel their funds through intermediaries. The intermediaries can perform a number of potentially valuable services in this process, most of which are related to the risks of the financial obligations. Some of their more important general functions are listed below:

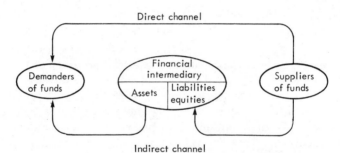

1. Risk management for individual financial assets
   a. Assessing the risk of individual financial obligations.
   b. Controlling the risks of debt obligations through special terms/conditions in debt agreements.
   c. Pricing financial obligations to compensate investors for risk.
2. Risk reduction through diversification
   a. Reducing the specific risk of individual assets by diversifying the portfolio.
3. Transformation of portfolio risk through the capital structure of the intermediary itself
   a. Risk reduction for liability holders by issuing equity capital which absorbs risks.
   b. Maturity transformation by mismatching the maturities of assets versus liabilities, for example, financing long-term assets with short-term liabilities.

Interestingly, suppliers of funds can, at least in theory, accomplish most of these functions themselves. In some cases, however, they can do so only at a substantial cost. The value of financial intermediaries is thus directly related to their *ability to perform these services at substantially lower costs* than would be possible otherwise.

Pursuing this line of argument more concretely, consider the functions of financial intermediaries in competitive public markets where large numbers of securities of different types are actively traded—for example, the markets for U.S. Treasury bonds, or common stocks, or the bonds of large well-known corporations. In these markets, individual suppliers of funds can, at some cost, perform most of the potential functions of financial intermediaries for themselves. They can assess the risks of actively traded financial obligations by observing their price volatility. They can rely upon the interactions of the many buyers and sellers to price the securities appropriately, relative to their risk. They can alter the riskiness of their own portfolios by chosing securities with differing characteristics. They can diversify their own portfolio by holding positions in a large number of securities, thus reducing their own portfolio risk. To be sure, financial intermediaries may still be able to perform these services more cheaply by taking advantage of the economies of scale inherent in pooling large numbers of suppliers. But the value-added of financial intermediaries is limited by the ability of suppliers to perform these same functions themselves.

In contrast, consider the private markets where financial obligations are privately issued and no later trading takes place. In these markets there is no readily available pricing mechanism for investors to rely upon. The risks inherent in different financial obligations must be carefully assessed and often controlled through negotiated provisions in debt agreements. The price of the obligations must then be negotiated between the parties and hopefully set so as to compensate the investors for the risks to which they are exposed. Because the financial obligations are not generally traded, it may be difficult for investors to adjust their portfolio positions when their own circumstances change. Because of the costs involved, it may be difficult and very expensive for all but the very largest investors to diversify their assets among large numbers of different private securities. Indeed, for all but the largest investors, the above functions may be prohibitively costly.

In sum, financial intermediaries which can pool the funds of large numbers of savers seem to be absolutely critical to the efficient functioning of private markets. They can develop the necessary expertise to assess, control, and price the risks of privately negotiated obligations. They can obtain the size necessary to provide adequate diversification. They can provide liquidity to an individual saver and yet hold relatively unmarketable financial assets. The value-added associated with their activities in private markets can be substantial because of the costs which would be incurred by suppliers of funds trying to accomplish these same functions for themselves.

FUNCTION OF FINANCIAL INTERMEDIARIES— DEMANDERS' POINT OF VIEW

Many demanders of funds (issuers of financial obligations) must continually choose between relying upon private or public markets for financing, as suggested by the accompanying diagram. There are, as we have

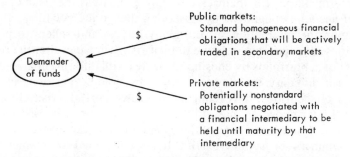

seen, considerable advantages to the competitive public markets. Within these public markets there are a wide variety of potential suppliers, both individual savers (who purchase securities directly) and financial intermediaries. This wide variety of potential suppliers not only enhances the variety of sources from which a borrower may obtain funds, but the constant interaction of these potential suppliers tends to keep the pricing process in equilibrium.

Unfortunately, there are also disadvantages to relying upon the public markets, particularly for debt financing. As we have discussed, debt securities that are traded in the public markets have a relatively standard set of terms and conditions, in part to protect the debt holders from risk. These terms and conditions may not be flexible enough, from the borrower's point of view, to allow them to respond to future contingencies. In the private markets, in contrast, a special set of terms and conditions can be tailored to the particular circumstances of the borrower. Furthermore, privately issued financial obligations that are held by a small number of large financial intermediaries (often one) can be much more easily renegotiated should the need to do so arise.

In addition, financial intermediaries in the private markets can help reduce the risks to which the borrower is exposed. In the public markets, the potential future borrowing costs can be uncertain right up until the time that the debt securities are actually issued. In fact, many medium-size borrowers are never really sure that the funds will actually be available in the public market at terms/conditions consistent with their needs. For example, in several recent episodes medium-size companies have been unable to issue conventional long-term debt securities in the public markets. Unfortunately, potential borrowers must often proceed with their own investment plans, even though the future costs and availability of public market funds are still uncertain. These uncertainties can expose potential public market borrowers to considerable risk. In contrast, the financial intermediaries operating in the private markets help to reduce these risks by offering various future commitments. As part of many private market borrowing agreements, the future availability of funds is guaranteed, subject to certain conditions, by the financial intermediary. For example, in the market for short-term business borrowing, commercial banks insure the future availability of funds by offering to provide lines of credit and more formal "revolving credit agreements." In addition, in many private market debt agreements, the financial intermediaries commit to the future cost of borrowed funds through various forward commitment procedures. Almost all mortgage market borrowing and most privately placed corporate debt obligations are negotiated with a forward commitment assuring the availability of the funds during a specific period of time and at a specified interest rate. By sharply reducing the uncertainties surrounding the future cost and/or availability of funds, financial intermediaries in the private markets reduce the potential borrowers' risk and permit more certain financial planning. In this way, financial intermediaries aid the potential demanders of funds as well as the potential suppliers of funds.

PRICING OF SECURITIES IN PRIVATE MARKETS

Because the securities in private market transactions are not subject to the pricing forces which arise from the active trading which takes place with public market securities, buyers and sellers of these securities cannot simply look to the market to establish "fair" terms for the transaction. The pricing of privately issued securities must rely upon other factors. First of all, the prospective lender (supplier of funds) must adequately understand and assess the fundamental risks of the economic enterprise. Generally there must be a set of specially designed terms/conditions to protect the interests of the debt holders. These terms/conditions and the price of the securities are the result of a sometimes lengthy negotiation between the parties, and the outcome of this negotiation can often be influenced by the relative bargaining strength of the parties.

Economic forces affect the pricing as well. First, public markets exert an important influence on the pricing of funds in the private markets because many of the borrowers in private markets have the alternative of raising funds in the public market as well. If the institutional lenders in private markets raise their lending rates too high relative to rates on public market securities, these prospective borrowers will finance in the public markets. Also, individual institutional lenders compete with each other to make private placements. This competition limits the premium that any one institution can charge relative to open market interest rates.

Market forces also affect the pricing of the nonmarket or private market liabilities issued by financial intermediaries. The savings deposit accounts of commercial banks and thrift institutions are an example of a private market liability. The interest rates which banks or thrift institutions pay are administered (i.e., set on a take-it-or-leave-it basis) and not established directly by a trading process. However, the level at which these interest rates are set depends to an increasing degree upon the interest rates available on short-term or intermediate-term securities traded in public markets. This arises in part because the brokerage firms which offer open-market securities to household savers are attempting to serve their needs more effectively. In addition, a number of new institutions (for example, money market mutual funds and bond mutual funds) have been established which give households greater access to these public market securities. As a result, more and more of the household investors who acquire savings deposits or the private market liabilities of intermediaries are doing so only as long as their returns are commensurate with the returns from open-market securities.

Thus the market pressure on the profit margins earned by financial intermediaries comes from two sides, the private markets in which they raise funds and the private markets in which they lend funds.

SUMMARY

There are substantial advantages to competitive public markets, where financial obligations are issued and actively traded among many different financial participants. In these markets, potential suppliers and demanders of funds can be confident that the current price of financial obligations reflects their approximate value to other investors. On the other hand, there are other competing advantages to private markets where financial obligations are privately negotiated with, issued to, and held to maturity by a limited group of investors. Small unknown enterprises must generally finance in these private markets. But even for large enterprises, there can sometimes be substantial advantages of enhanced flexibility and reduced risk in privately placed financial obligations, particularly debt obligations.

The functions of financial intermediaries center around the management of risk. From the perspective of funds suppliers, financial intermediaries can manage the risk of individual financial assets, diversify these risks within a portfolio, and transform these risks through the intermediaries' own capital structure. In public markets, financial intermediaries can provide a relatively inexpensive way for individual suppliers to accomplish these functions. While financial intermediaries can play a helpful role in public markets, their value-added is limited by the fact that suppliers can perform these same functions for themselves. In private markets, it is often prohibitively expensive for all but the largest suppliers of funds to perform these risk management functions for themselves. Financial intermediaries have thus come to dominate our private markets. They pool the resources of large numbers of suppliers so as to offer risk management, diversification, and maturity transformation to suppliers. In addition, they offer flexible risk-reducing borrowing arrangements for demanders of funds. Most importantly, they offer these services at costs which are substantially less than the costs that individual suppliers and demanders of funds would incur if they attempted to deal directly with each other. Not surprisingly, the financial intermediaries operating in private markets have come to be a very important part of our financial system. Indeed, in the recent years, the majority of the flows of funds through the financial systems has been channeled through private market intermediaries rather than through the public markets.

QUESTIONS

1. What characteristics of the issuer of the security and the security itself are necessary in order that a security be issued in the public security markets?
2. What benefits might a borrower obtain from a private transaction as opposed to a public issue?
3. What are the factors which limit the amount that a commercial bank can charge on its private or negotiated bank lending? How do these returns compare with the returns the bank can earn from the purchase of public market debts such as U.S. Treasury securities?
4. Why should a financial intermediary ever buy public market securities?

REFERENCES

Jensen, Michael C. and Mechling, William H. "Theory of the Firm: Managerial Behavior, Agency Costs and Ownership Structure," *Journal of Financial Economics,* vol. 3, no. 4 (October 1976), pp. 305–60.

Kin, E. Han; McConnell, John J.; and Greenwood, Paul R. "Capital Structure Rearrangements and Me-First Rules in an Efficient Capital Market, *Journal of Finance,* vol. 32, no. 3 (June 1977), pp. 789–810.

Leland, Hayne E. and Pyle, David H. "Informational Assymetries, Financial Intermediation," *American Economic Review,* vol. 32, no. 2 (May 1977), pp. 371–87.

Mandelker, Gershon and Raviv, Artur. "Investment Banking: An Economic Analysis of Optimal Underwriting Contracts," *American Economic Review,* vol. 32, no. 3 (June 1977), pp. 683–94.

12

Causal forces, equilibrium forces, and adaptation in financial markets

CAUSAL FORCES—SUPPLY AND DEMAND FOR FUNDS FROM
   PRIMARY SECTORS
EQUILIBRIUM FORCES
BARRIERS TO FULL EQUILIBRIUM
DISEQUILIBRIUM RETURNS AND INCENTIVE FOR CHANGE
MODES OF FINANCIAL ADAPTATION
WALL STREET'S INVESTMENT BANKERS IN THE ADAPTATION
   PROCESS
THE PROCESS OF ADAPTATION

Adaptation within financial markets results from the constant interaction of two types of forces: the supply and demand forces (discussed in Part II of this book) and the equilibrium forces (discussed in the immediately preceding four chapters). In the long run, the pattern of interest rates (expected returns) within financial markets is determined by the equilibrium forces. In the short run, however, the relative balance between these two types of forces can be influenced by a number of institutional practices and regulations which create barriers to the speedy and full achievement of equilibrium. The short-run interaction of these forces not only influences the time-varying structure of interest rates and credit flows, but it creates the incentives for change in the structure and behavior of financial institutions. Figure 12–1 presents a schematic diagram of this process.

   At any moment of time, the forces of supply and demand and equilibrium forces result in a set of actual interest rates or expected returns. To the extent that this actual structure of expected returns differs from the equilibrium structure of expected returns (because of institutional barriers), there will be incentives for borrowers, lenders, and financial intermediaries to change their behavior. While there are many practical limits to this process of change, adaptation does take place, and the pattern of actual interest rates and credit flows are changed. As long as actual interest rates

Figure 12-1
Adaptation in financial markets

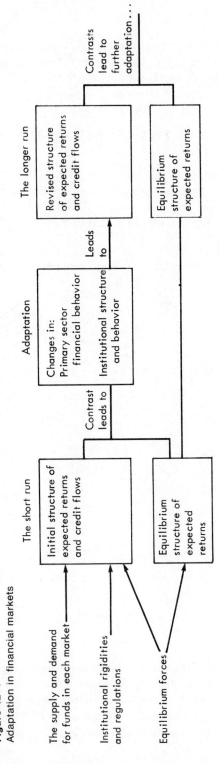

The short run

Initial structure of expected returns and credit flows

Equilibrium structure of expected returns

The supply and demand for funds in each market

Institutional rigidities and regulations

Equilibrium forces

Contrast leads to

Adaptation

Changes in:
Primary sector financial behavior

Institutional structure and behavior

Leads to

The longer run

Revised structure of expected returns and credit flows

Equilibrium structure of expected returns

Contrasts lead to further adaptation...

and credit flows deviate from the equilibrium set of rates and flows, adaptation continues to take place. This chapter presents an abstract overview of this process. In the financial market chapters that follow, we will describe this process more concretely in each separate market.

CAUSAL FORCES—SUPPLY AND DEMAND FOR FUNDS FROM PRIMARY SECTORS

The early chapters of this book analyzed the financial behavior of the primary sectors, which created the supplies and demands for funds in each of the financial markets. An overall view of some critical elements in this supply and demand are illustrated in Figure 12–2.

Figure 12–2
Some elements in the overall supply and demand for funds

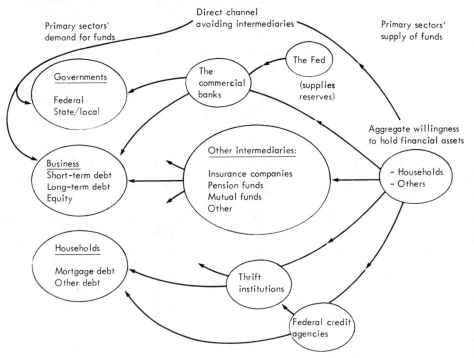

As the primary demanders of funds issue new securities, they expand the outstanding stock of financial assets, which must be eventually held by the ultimate suppliers, primarily households. Most of the flows of funds are actually transmitted through a set of financial intermediaries which purchase the original assets and, in turn, create the new financial assets actually held by suppliers. In the short run, the supply of money and credit can be influenced by the Federal Reserve's supply of reserves to the banking system. In the long run, however, the ability to finance the primary sectors' demands is determined by the aggregate willingness of savers to hold wealth in the form of financial assets. Within this perspective, the supply and demand for funds may influence the levels of interest rates. After the fact (ex post), of course, the supply and demand for funds are always equal because they are merely the opposite sides of the actual transactions.[1] Ex ante, however, supply and demand can be imbalanced at a particular level of interest rates. These imbalances, in one market or across all markets, are what we shall call the *causal forces* which can influence financial asset prices.

EQUILIBRIUM FORCES

In a world of idealized equilibrium within public markets, however, those causal forces would have no impact upon the *relative* prices of financial assets. The decisions of financial participants in these markets, and thus the flow of funds, would adapt quickly and completely to the potential imbalances, eliminating their potential impact upon relative interest rates and spreading their effects to other markets. In this world of idealized equilibrium, the prices of all financial assets would continuously be in equilibrium with each other through their risk-adjusted expected returns. In particular, the expected returns on different risky assets would be related to each other through the risk premium described in Chapter 10. The expected returns on long-term bonds would be in equilibrium with short-term bonds through their risk-adjusted expected returns, as evidenced by the term structure of interest rates. The (nominal) interest rates on all financial assets would continue to be in equilibrium with expected inflation.

BARRIERS TO FULL EQUILIBRIUM

There are a host of barriers to the equilibrium process, however, in both public and private markets. To begin with, there are transactions costs, which impede flows of funds into new financial assets even in the public markets. In their most simple role, these transaction costs may take the form of brokerage fees, or dealer spreads (between "bid" and "ask" prices), which levy a typically small, but nonetheless real, cost on portfolio changes. In a much broader sense, transactions costs can be

---

[1] This is one of the principal difficulties in empirical studies of financial markets for it is difficult to discern ex-ante imbalances in supply and demand from the ex-post flow of funds data.

defined to include the costs associated with the financial expertise and distribution systems in any investment organization. These costs are particularly important when a new form of investment activity is being planned, and they can be an important temporary barrier to the free flow of funds across markets.

In addition to transaction costs, there are a variety of nonequilibrium influences on interest rates that are particularly important in the private financial markets that are dominated by financial intermediaries. Perhaps the most important of these is the process of regulation because financial intermediaries are among the most intensively regulated of our economic enterprises. Recall that households are by far the largest single source of funds, and the market for household deposits is the most important channel through which households supply funds to the financial system. Interest rates in the household deposit market, however, are severely constrained by regulatory ceilings, and they are not necessarily free to adjust to the equilibrium forces of the market. In addition, other important financial institutions that compete for household funds (life insurance companies, for example) are heavily regulated, and this regulatory process is an important influence on the types of financial claims they are allowed to offer households. Even when financial intermediaries raise funds in relatively public markets, they are often regulated. For example, the ability of commercial banks to raise funds through large negotiable certificates of deposits (CDs) and/or various forms of open-market borrowing has been subject to several important regulatory constraints.

Regulatory and legal constraints also influence the interest rates on the debt instruments issued by the primary sectors. For example, state and local usury laws are an important influence on the markets for consumer credit and home mortgages. The rates on home mortgages are also influenced by various federal constraints, among them the interest rate ceilings on government-insured home mortgages. The interest rates on bank loans to business have been influenced on a number of recent occasions by a rather explicit form of federal "jawboning." Indeed, even the interest rates that the federal government itself can offer on long-term bonds are constrained by Congressionally established interest rate ceilings.

Quite apart from regulation, there are other nonequilibrium influences on interest rates within private markets, which originate in the financial intermediaries dominating these markets. In private markets, the financial institutions generally administer the interest rates that they charge, and these administered rates, while they are importantly affected by public market rates, are subject to other influences as well. The interest rate on bank loans, the "prime rate," is set by the commercial banks, and it does not precisely follow the movements in open-market rates. The interest rates on home mortgages, administered by the lending institutions, do not precisely follow open-market rates on long-term securities. Indeed, the deposit rates offered to households, even when they are substantially below regulatory ceilings and thus *not* subject to regulatory constraints, do not closely follow open-market interest rates. It is evident, then, that a host of regulatory constraints and institutional considerations can influence interest rates in private markets and keep them from converging immediately to the equilibrium structures that we have derived.

In addition to affecting interest rates, regulation and institutional considerations can also affect the potential flow of funds and raise barriers to the equilibrium process. Most financial intermediaries are constrained by regulations on the kinds of financial assets in which they may invest. This is particularly true of commercial banks and thrift institutions, the two largest classes of intermediaries. Many of these regulations exist to safeguard the interests of household savers, the suppliers of funds to the intermediaries. Other regulations have been used to influence the allocation of credit within the financial system. Relative to our equilibrium processes, these constraints act as substantial barriers to the free flow of funds across markets. In addition to regulation, the institutional considerations of private intermediaries can influence credit flows within their private markets. Most intermediaries have "preferred habitats" within the financial markets in which they prefer to lend in the short run—quite apart from regulatory constraints. The preferred maturity of their assets is generally influenced by the maturity of their liabilities. As we discussed in the previous chapter, they have often developed an expertise for assessing, controlling, and pricing the risks in certain kinds of loans, and this expertise is not necessarily transferable to other lending situations. In the short run, participating in new kinds of lending situations, where they may have little experience or expertise, can be either risky, or costly, or both.[2]

Finally, the equilibrium process within financial markets can be retarded by any large market participants who are not profit-maximizers. The Federal Reserve, for example, is not interested in maximizing the expected returns from its investments; nor is the U.S. Treasury necessarily driven to minimize its expected borrowing costs, although this may be one consideration. Moreover, because of public policy concerns, a group of federal credit intermediaries has been created to influence the supply of credit to particular sectors quite apart from the expected returns available to a private intermediary in the process. To the extent that a financial market is strongly influenced by one or more of these large actors, interest rates and credit flows within it may be deflected in the short run.

---

[2] In the longer run, of course, even institutions operating in private markets can and do change the character of their financial asset portfolios, as we shall see in subsequent chapters.

DISEQUILIBRIUM RETURNS AND INCENTIVE FOR CHANGE

Because of these transactions costs, regulatory constraints and barriers, and other influences (which some would call "market imperfections"), the actual structure of expected returns on different financial assets is not always equal to the basic equilibrium structure. This is especially true in private markets and more so in the short run. These departures of expected returns from the equilibrium structures are the driving force which provide the incentives for change in financial markets. In the world of idealized or total equilibrium, where all financial assets would be priced appropriately relative to one another, there would never be any incentive for change. There would be little to gain from altering the structure of financial assets or financial liabilities. In a world of partial equilibrium, however, there are opportunities to improve expected returns by adapting investment policies and financial structures to any perceived (albeit temporary) disequilibrium. In fact, the magnitude of the departure from equilibrium, that is, the extent to which the expected returns from a given asset diverge from the equilibrium structure, is directly proportional to the incentive for change.

It is important to realize, however, that these departures from equilibrium, like the concept of future expectations upon which they are based, may not in general be directly observable. There are some situations where these variables can be documented with some confidence. For example, the expected future returns on household savings deposits and short-term treasury bills, and the divergences between them, can be directly observed because they are both approximately risk-free assets.[3] With longer term and more risky financial assets, however, the expected future returns are never so clear. In later chapters, we will rely upon various proxy measures of relative expected returns, for example, the differing yields to maturity on financial assets of comparable maturity and risk. Often, though, we will never know for sure what the financial markets' expectations were, what the equilibrium structure should have been, and how great the past departures from equilibrium might have been. Even though departures from equilibrium may be difficult to observe directly, however, they will form one of the central links in our explanations of financial adaptation.

MODES OF FINANCIAL ADAPTATION

As long as a departure from equilibrium exists, the financial system will attempt to adapt to this departure, changing the prevailing structure of

---

[3] As we have seen, the divergence between these two is a reasonable measure of the incentives for disintermediation, and in empirical studies, it is well correlated with the magnitude of disintermediation that has actually taken place.

interest rates, flows of funds, and/or institutions. This adaptation takes place in many ways.

Consider a hypothetical primary market (either public or private) where one primary sector obtains funds from one or more financial intermediaries, who in turn raise funds from their own suppliers through a variety of channels. Suppose that the primary sector, to fund its new investment, attempts to issue a substantial amount of new securities/loans in this market. This surge in the demand for funds will presumably drive the market prices of the securities/loans down, and their expected future returns (interest rates) up. Suppose that various barriers to equilibrium keep the market from responding instantaneously to this change in relative expected returns.[4] What types of financial response are likely because of this departure from equilibrium?

The first, and most obvious, response is that the institutions currently active in this market may attempt to change their portfolio mix to include relatively more of this financial asset. There may be some limits to the speed with which they can accomplish this, particularly if their other assets are relatively unmarketable. The institutions currently active in the market may thus attempt to adapt in a second way by expanding their current sources of funds. They may be able to accomplish this by offering more attractive terms to their current suppliers of funds (usually, though not always, households). But there may be limits to their ability to quickly expand their current sources of funds, either because of regulatory constraints or institutional considerations. As an alternative, these institutions may be able to develop entirely new and different sources of funds, though again there may be some real limits to their ability to do this, particularly in a short period of time.

If the institutions that are active in the current market cannot adapt to supply the increased funds, other institutions may enter the market. Or, for that matter, household savers themselves may enter, if it is a public market, supplying the funds directly rather than through an intermediary. In either case, we shall refer to these new groups as the "swing investors," that is, the potential investors who are ordinarily not active in the market but who can be drawn into the market by increased relative returns. Failing these, it is entirely possible that rather perceptive entrepreneurs may develop an entirely new type of financial intermediary. This new type of intermediary may well be able to exploit the perceived increased returns without being constrained by existing regulatory constraints.

If the adaptation from the supply side is too slow, however, the de-

---

[4] Again, recall that any divergence will occur in relative expected (but uncertain) future returns, and it may not be quite so obvious as this simple example implies, either at the time or after the fact.

mander of funds can also adapt. The borrower may attempt to change the nature of the securities offered to induce new investors into the existing market, or the borrower may circumvent the existing market and obtain funds in another market whose channels of supply are less constricted by regulation and/or institutional problems. Conceivably, all of these adaptations could fail in the short run, and the demander of funds might just not be able to obtain funds at an expected cost commensurate with the equilibrium structure. This would be, however, an unstable state of affairs from which further adaptation was increasingly likely.

This entire process works in reverse too, of course. Suppose the primary demand for funds drops off sharply, or suppose that a large investor substantially enlarges the supply (perhaps an agency of the federal government, channeling funds to a particular sector). The expected future returns (interest rates) available in the market will then be lowered relative to other securities. The current institutional investors may then change their portfolio mix. If they are unable to do this (for regulatory reasons, for example) or are unwilling to do this, the returns that they are able to offer to their sources of funds will be affected. They must therefore either adapt themselves or eventually become a smaller and less successful part of the financial system.

As the adaptation within a particular market proceeds, it clearly affects other markets. A disequilibrium in one market affects other closely related markets relatively quickly and eventually all markets. Thus the effects of disequilibrium feed through the financial system, attenuating as they go, until the system is brought back into equilibrium again.

The various modes of adaptation have been described above in the approximate order of their potential speed. If, for example, the necessary adaptation can take place merely by currently active institutions expanding the rate at which they invest in this market, it is likely to proceed rapidly. This kind of short-run adaptation of expected return and flows is occurring constantly in the financial system. Where this kind of adaptation is possible, divergences of expected returns are not likely to persist for long at all. If, on the other hand, the adjustment must take place through other intermediaries (or direct suppliers) being drawn into the market, it may take somewhat longer. Finally, if the adaptation takes place through the development of entirely new intermediaries, or entirely new functions of existing intermediaries, it may take substantially longer.

WALL STREET'S INVESTMENT BANKERS IN THE ADAPTATION PROCESS

The rather loosely defined group of securities firms that are commonly referred to as Wall Street play an important role in this process. These firms are the agents (brokers) and dealers in the public markets and per-

form an important service in these markets. In their "investment banking" activities, they constantly search for opportunities in which they can
profit from bringing buyers and sellers together in various financial
transactions. These firms are all different from each other (indeed, particular firms can change dramatically over time), operating in different
"niches" of the financial markets. Perhaps the best general characterization of them is that they are relatively small groups of potential financing
agents with an entrepreneurial bent. They have only relatively modest
sums of capital themselves, and this limits their ability to serve as intermediaries in the same sense that commercial banks, thrift institutions, or
insurance companies can. But they have a very wide network of contacts
with the potential suppliers and demanders of funds, and these networks
allow them to locate profitable opportunities to bring suppliers and demanders together in mutually beneficial transactions. These Wall Street
firms are often among the first to sense departures from equilibrium that
provide the profitable opportunities for new transactions.

While acting in their own self-interest, these Wall Street firms provide a
valuable service to the financial system. In a sense, they "police" the
equilibrium structure of financial returns. In the short run, financial intermediaries in the private markets can raise the returns they require on
private financial obligations above an appropriate equilibrium structure.
But securities firms stand ready to bring potential suppliers and demanders of separate funds together outside the intermediaries, in the public
markets, should those returns be raised too far. Thus the public market for
commercial paper is a constant discipline on the private market for short-
term bank loans, and the public market for corporate bonds is a constant
discipline on the market for privately placed bonds. In addition, regulators
may attempt to deflect the returns or flows in certain financial markets to
accomplish public policy goals. But again, the Wall Street securities firms
stand ready to bring suppliers and demanders of funds together outside the
regulated market if returns diverge too far from their equilibrium structure.
The existence of these firms thus improves the responsiveness of public
markets, limits the potential pricing power of financial intermediaries,
limits the financial powers of regulators, and plays a key role in the
adaptability of the financial system.

THE PROCESS OF ADAPTATION

In this chapter we have constructed a perspective on financial adaptation and discussed this perspective in rather abstract terms. In the subsequent chapters (Chapters 15–20) we will review the adaptation of particular financial markets and observe each of the aspects of the process that we
have discussed here. As we have seen, one important set of forces influencing interest rates is the *causal forces*, the supply and demand for funds

which can cause interest rates (expected returns) to diverge from their equilibrium structure. In addition, however, there are the *equilibrium forces* which arise from the profit incentives for borrowers, lenders, and middlemen to adjust their financial activities according to the expected returns available in different markets. These equilibrium forces tend to drive the expected future returns on financial assets back into equilibrium. In the absence of any barriers, the equilibrium forces tend to dominate, and thus the expected returns in relatively competitive, unsegmented, public markets (with low transaction costs) tend to be in equilibrium with prospective risks. On the other hand, barriers to equilibrium can also exist, particularly in private markets, which cause at least short-run departures from these equilibrium structures. These departures are the basic incentives for financial change, both the short-run adaptation of financial flows and interest rates and the long-run adaptation of the financial system itself.

part IV

Commercial Banks
and the Federal Reserve

13

Commercial banks

The financial demands of the primary sectors are served by a large system of financial intermediaries. The commercial banks are the largest group of these intermediaries. The financial assets of the commercial banking system are almost as large as the assets of all other intermediaries combined. In contrast to most other intermediaries, banks serve the financial needs of all of the primary sectors. As Figure 13–1 suggests, not only do commercial banks accept deposits from all of the primary sectors, but they also help to meet the credit demands of each of those sectors. Commercial banks are by far the largest source of short-term financing for business corporations, and they extend intermediate-term credit to business as well. Commercial banks hold a significant fraction of the outstanding debt of the federal government, and they hold the largest fraction of the outstanding debt of state and local governments. They are an important source of mortgage financing and consumer debt for households. They sell a large volume of deposits to, and extend a large volume of credit to non-residents. Last, but not least, they serve as an important source of liquidity for other financial intermediaries.

Figure 13–1

Relationship of commercial banks to the primary financial sectors

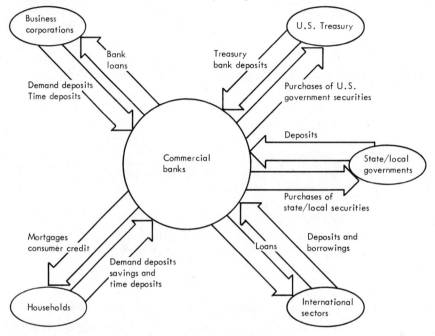

Commercial banks are also important because they alone issue demand deposits. Demand deposits, along with currency in circulation, are the means of payment for goods, services, and various financial transactions.

Because of their importance to the overall financial system and their unique role as the source of demand deposits, banks are subject to the authority of a number of regulatory bodies. The most important of these regulators is the Federal Reserve Board. Within this chapter we will refer from time to time to the regulations of the Federal Reserve Board and then explore its objectives and operations in more detail in the next chapter.

THE BALANCE SHEET OF A COMMERCIAL BANK

A balance sheet for a typical commercial bank, illustrating its primary assets and liabilities, is shown here.

The original source of most bank funds was demand deposits. The demand depositor, in exchange for today's funds, receives the promise of the commercial bank to repay those funds "upon demand" at any time. Hence, the name "demand deposits" and the liquidity of these funds. By

Commercial bank

Assets	Liabilities and net worth
Cash and bank balances	Demand deposits
Vault cash	
Reserves at Federal Reserve	Savings and time deposits
Other	Large certificates of deposit
	Other savings and time
Investments	deposits
U.S. government securities	
State/local government securities	Borrowings and other liabilities
Loans	Capital accounts
Loans to business	Long-term debt
Real estate mortgages	Equity
Consumer credit	
Miscellaneous loans	

law, the commercial bank cannot pay any interest on those deposits, although it can provide various services in exchange for demand deposit balances.

The second major source of bank funds is savings and time deposits. The savings accounts of individuals, for which banks pay a stipulated rate of interest, are one of the important types of these deposits. By law, individuals may be required to give "notice" before these funds can be withdrawn, although in practice they are generally withdrawn upon demand. Withdrawals cannot generally be used as a convenient form of payment to third parties, however, and hence these deposits are less "liquid" than demand deposits.[1] In addition, most banks offer a range of time deposit accounts to individuals, corporations, partnerships, and governments. These consumers leave funds with the bank for a specified period of time in exchange for a stipulated rate of interest. Finally, many large banks offer a particular form of time deposit, the large negotiable certificate of deposit (called CDs). These are deposits greater than $100,000 left with the bank for a short, specified period of time. The deposit is evidenced by a certificate which may be traded in the secondary markets. These CDs have become an important part of our financial system in recent years, and we will discuss them further in later sections. The

---

[1] In early 1978, the Federal Reserve proposed that commercial banks be authorized to allow certain depositors to automatically shift funds from savings accounts to demand deposits. This would make these savings accounts as liquid as demand deposits. Savings deposits so shifted would have to forfeit interest for the 30 days prior to their transfer into demand deposits, however. Commercial banks and savings institutions in several New England states are also allowed to issue to individuals a savings deposit against which depositors can write checks. Called "negotiable orders of withdrawal," or NOW accounts, these savings deposits offer the liquidity of demand deposits and pay an explicit rate of interest.

maximum interest rates that banks may offer on any of these time and savings deposits are regulated by various banking authorities.

To supplement their deposit sources of funds, banks have come to rely upon various short-term borrowings. Most of these borrowings come from other banks in the interbank markets, although some of them come from nonbank creditors.

Among the relatively smaller but more important segments of the balance sheet are the capital accounts. The capital accounts are composed largely of equity, the residual interests of the bank stockholders. This equity is sometimes supplemented by moderate amounts of long-term debt obligations within these capital accounts. The capital accounts serve as the cushion which protects creditors and uninsured depositors from the risk of loss due to risky assets.[2]

On the asset side of the category balance sheet, the safest and most liquid assets are found within the category "cash and bank balances." Banks retain a moderate amount of currency and coin on hand, called vault cash, to meet their operational needs. In addition, banks typically hold substantial amounts of other cash assets. Some of these assets are items in the process of collection, that is, cash that will be transferred between banks as checks in route are cleared through our check clearing system. Some of these assets are demand deposit balances with other banks. These are held both as an important source of liquidity and as a means of obtaining various services from these other banks.

The Federal Reserve Board requires that all banks that are members of the Federal Reserve System must keep reserves equal to a stated percentage of their deposits.[3] The reserve requirements differ according to the size of the bank. The reserve requirements applying to banks with large deposit bases are shown here.

Reserve requirements against

Net demand deposits	16¼%
Savings deposits	3%
Other time deposits	3–6%

One of the original purposes of these requirements was to guarantee that the banking system could meet unexpected deposit outflows. Today these reserves and reserve requirements serve as the focal point for the

---

[2] The Federal Deposit Insurance Corporation (FDIC) insures deposits up to $40,000, as do various state agencies. Almost all banks are insured by the FDIC or, in some cases, by these other state agencies.

[3] Other banks, called "nonmember" banks also generally have reserve requirements, but they are administered by state regulatory authorities and can be held in somewhat different forms.

process of monetary policy. They are discussed in more detail in the next chapter.

Loans are the largest class of assets held by commercial banks and the source of most of their profitability. For the banking system as a whole, loans to business are the largest and most important type of loans. These loans are generally short-term, periodically reviewed, credit arrangements with the principal business customers of the bank. To an increasing extent, banks have also been extending term loans to business. These are intermediate-term credit arrangements which finance a broad range of corporate financial needs. The second largest group of loans is real estate mortgages, mortgages on home residences for the household sector, and mortgages on large multifamily and commercial properties. In addition, an important group of loans are made to households for various purposes, and these are generally included within the category of consumer credit. Finally, banks hold a variety of miscellaneous loans, among them loans to security dealers, other banks, and other financial institutions.

The remaining class of assets is the investments held by commercial banks. These consist almost entirely of U.S. government securities and the tax-exempt securities of state and local governments. To some extent these securities serve as a source of liquidity that can be drawn down to meet unexpected deposit outflows or unexpectedly large loan demands. In addition, these securities earn a return while they are held, supplementing the income generating potential of the banks' loans. Thus the investment portfolio of a bank serves a dual purpose, liquidity and income. As we shall see, the management of this security portfolio is an important element in managing the overall assets and liabilities of the bank.

BANK ASSETS AND CREDIT DEMANDS
OF THE PRIMARY SECTORS

Throughout the past two decades there has been a continual evolution in the assets held by commercial banks. Table 13–1 documents some of the main features of this evolution. Throughout the period from 1954 to 1975, almost all of the major assets of the commercial banking system grew substantially, although at somewhat different rates. The dollar value of those assets is shown in the upper half of Table 13–1 and the assets as a percent of GNP are shown in the lower half.

In 1954 the largest component of bank assets was their investments, particularly their large holdings of U.S. government securities. But for most of the subsequent period, banks' holdings of U.S. government securities barely grew at all. However, the growth of all other investments and loans was particularly rapid. By 1975, the portfolios of banks had changed dramatically. Almost three quarters of all bank assets were held in various

Table 13–1
Assets measured at the times separating five recent credit cycles

	2d quarter 1954	1st quarter 1958	4th quarter 1960	1st quarter 1967	3d quarter 1970	1st quarter 1975
Holdings (in billions of $)						
Total selected loans and investments	$139.7	$163.6	$192.1	$311.1	$406.6	$677.8
Investments	78.7	77.1	80.9	107.8	132.5	193.5
U.S. government securities	66.6	62.6	63.3	64.4	66.8	93.9
State/local government securities	12.1	14.5	17.6	43.4	65.7	99.6
Selected loans	61.0	86.5	111.2	203.3	274.1	484.3
Business loans	26.2	37.7	46.8	86.1	123.6	186.4
Real estate mortgages	17.2	23.2	28.7	54.1	71.6	132.4
Consumer credit	10.8	15.4	20.6	38.0	53.6	89.9
Miscellaneous loans	6.8	10.2	15.1	25.1	25.3	75.6
As a percent of GNP						
Total selected loans and investments	38.8%	37.6%	38.2%	40.2%	41.2%	46.9%
Investments	21.9	17.8	16.1	13.9	13.4	13.4
U.S. government securities	18.5	14.5	12.6	8.3	6.8	6.5
State/local government securities	3.4	3.3	3.5	5.6	6.7	6.9
Selected loans	16.9	19.9	22.1	26.3	27.8	33.5
Business loans	7.3	8.7	9.3	11.1	12.5	12.9
Real estate mortgages	4.8	5.3	5.7	7.0	7.3	9.2
Consumer credit	3.0	3.5	4.1	4.9	5.4	6.2
Miscellaneous loans	1.9	2.3	3.0	3.2	2.6	5.2

kinds of loans, the investment portfolio had become much smaller in relative terms. Furthermore, the investment portfolios had become about equally distributed between U.S. government and state/local government securities instead of being dominated by U.S. government securities as they once had been.

The changing pattern of bank assets in these periods is a predictable response to the financial demands of the primary sectors. The sizeable holdings of U.S. government securities in the early 1950s had been accumulated during the years of World War II. Indeed the financing of the war effort was the principal function that the banking system provided during these war years. As we have seen, however, the financing demands of the U.S. government were moderate during the 1950s and 1960s, and the financial demands of other sectors, particularly household, business, and state and local governments grew rapidly during this same period. These financial demands were attractive lending and investment opportunities for the banks, and the assets of banks grew and evolved in response to these opportunities.

As we have seen, the external financing demands of the business sector have also been cyclical. Commercial banks, particularly large commercial banks, have been the most important source of the short-term component of this external business finance, and an important cyclical relationship has evolved between business corporations and large commercial banks. When the financing demands of business corporations have been moderate, banks have used their increased sources of funds to purchase increased investments, but in times of large corporate financial demands, when corporate loan demand has been particularly high, banks have channeled their funds to business loans and sharply curtailed their purchases of new investments.

Table 13–2 shows the net increase in bank assets during three years in

Table 13–2
Net increase in investments and loans by type (Billions of $)

	1971	1973	1975
Total selected loans and investments	48.2	81.3	26.2
Investments	19.8	4.3	31.9
U.S. government securities	7.0	−1.3	30.3
Municipal securities	12.8	5.6	1.6
Selected loans	28.4	77.0	−5.7
Business loans	5.9	34.0	−13.1
Mortgages	9.8	19.7	4.1
Consumer credit	6.7	10.6	2.9
Other loans	6.0	12.7	0.4

the 1970–1975 credit cycle. In 1971, a year of modest business financing demands, the increase in bank assets was moderate. It included an increase in investments and a moderate increase in loans. In 1973, however, business financing demands were much larger, and bank assets grew at almost double the rate of 1971. There was almost no increase in investments; however there was a striking increase in the rate at which loans were extended, from $5.9 billion in 1971 to $34.0 billion in 1973. In 1975, business sector financing demands plummeted and the financing demands of the U.S. government soared. The pattern of bank asset acquisition reflected this financing pattern.

STRUCTURE OF THE DOMESTIC BANKING SYSTEM

Thus far we have described the banking system as a whole, but among the nation's 15,000 banks there are enormous differences in terms of both size and function. On the one hand, there is a relatively small group of very large banks whose activities tend to dominate various aspects of the banking system. For example, the 50 largest banks hold somewhat more than 40 percent of all bank assets. On the other hand, there are a host of smaller banks, each of which has only a very modest asset position. Similarly, on the one hand, there is a relatively small group of "wholesale banks" whose customers are generally large corporations or institutions and whose deposits and other funds are raised in various nationwide financial markets. On the other hand, there are a host of "retail" banks whose customers are generally individuals or perhaps small corporations and whose deposits are drawn from their local market areas. In general, most wholesale banks are also large banks, and most small banks tend to be retail banks, but the correlation between these two attributes is far from perfect. Furthermore, there are other attributes which can be used to distinguish among banks. One somewhat subjective scheme for classifying banks divides them into four groups:

1. Large international money-center banks—There is a very small number (perhaps ten) of very large banks which tend to be headquartered in money-market cities (New York, and to a lesser extent, Chicago), which have a growing worldwide set of branches, subsidiaries, and affiliates and which serve a set of large multinational and domestic customers.
2. Dominant regional banks—There is a somewhat larger group of smaller but still sizeable banks which serve the needs of large corporations and other institutions within their regional area. They have an important and often dominant influence on their regional financial flows but are much less important on a nationwide and international scale than the large international money-center banks.
3. Important local banks—There is a still larger group of medium-sized banks which serve the needs of businesses, institutions, and households within their local area but are not active in either nationwide or international financial markets.
4. Small retail banks—These are a host of smaller retail banks which largely serve the needs of households and, to a lesser extent, small businesses and institutions within their immediate area.·

All of these banks can issue demand deposits, and all are subject to the same (or similar) sets of regulators and regulations. After this, however, their similarities end. These different groups of banks perform very different functions in the financial system. The large banks dominate the market for short-term business credit and through their international activities provide one of the important linkages between the United States and worldwide financial markets. The small retail banks, on the other hand, are (in the aggregate) important institutions in the markets for consumer credit and residential mortgages.

These classifications are neither complete nor particularly precise so that it is difficult to gather data for these four groups of banks. Table 13–3

Table 13–3
Relative composition of assets among different classes of commercial banks (As of June 30, 1977)

	Large banks in New York City and Chicago		Other large banks (Not NYC or Chicago)		All other member banks (not "large")	
Total loans and investments	100%		100%		100%	
Investments	25		26		34	
U.S. government securities		15		14		18
State/local government securities		10		12		16
Loans	75		74		66	
Commercial and industrial loans		39		27		17
Real estate loans		9		19		23
Loans to individuals		6		15		19
Other loans (primarily to other banks and financial institutions)		21		13		7

Source: Federal Reserve Bulletin (January 1978).

shows recent data on different banks' assets from the Federal Reserve System which provide some insight into their differential character. The series "large banks in New York and Chicago" is dominated by the small number of large money-center banks. These banks tend to have smaller holdings of investments, larger holdings of loans, and, in particular, large holdings of industrial and commercial loans. The series "large banks not in New York or Chicago" includes both what we have called dominant regional banks and some important local banks. The series "all other member banks" includes some important local banks but is dominated by the small retail banks. These banks have relatively large holdings of investments in general and U.S. government securities in particular, modest holdings of industrial and commercial loans, and sizeable holdings of both real estate mortgage loans and other loans to individuals, reflecting their retail orientation.

In part, these differences among banks are a natural outgrowth of our system of regulation. Banks cannot establish branches outside their own state. And in many states, even branching within the state is severely restricted or prohibited. Thus our banking system has developed in a legal environment which has insured the existence of a very large number of small local banking establishments. Some of the customers of banks have grown into large national and multinational corporations. These customers require large national and multinational banks to serve their financial needs. Thus from a largely fractured, varied local banking industry, a small number of large national and multinational banks have developed. The share of all banking services provided by these large banks has grown in recent years as our national banking system has consolidated and developed within its still predominantly local regulatory restrictions.

Correspondent banking

While there are these substantial differences among banks, they are all integrated into a banking system by their interrelationships with each other. Most important among these relationships are the correspondent banking ties which have developed among banks. Each small bank has at least one larger bank that serves as its correspondent, and most banks have several correspondents. In exchange for deposits and other forms of compensation, the larger correspondent bank provides various financial services to smaller banks. These services include bookkeeping, check clearing, information, and expertise. Also, correspondent relationships allow smaller banks to indirectly obtain funds from national markets and sometimes to share in the loans negotiated by larger banks in the national markets.

Interbank markets

Banks are also interconnected by the market for "federal funds." Federal funds are the reserves on deposit with the Federal Reserve System. To the extent that a bank has excess reserves on deposit with the Federal Reserve, it may choose to lend those reserves to another bank. A large and active market for these reserves, called the federal funds market, has developed in recent years. The federal funds market is essentially an interbank lending market, where the typical loan is very short term, normally one day. Indeed, the terminology federal funds market is misleading in so far as it implies a rather narrow function for this market. It is really *the* domestic interbank market. The annualized interest rate paid on these one-day interbank loans is called the federal funds rate. This interbank interest rate is one of the most closely watched and sensitive indicators of financial conditions within the banking system. Figure 13–2 shows the behavior of this interbank rate, along with the short-term Treasury bill rate.

The federal funds market allows the banking system to make much more efficient use of its reserves. Unexpected inflows and outflows of funds between banks can cause unexpected fluctuations in reserves for individual banks, though not necessarily for the system as a whole. By borrowing and lending short-term claims to these reserves, the individual

Figure 13–2

Fed funds rate and the interest rate on three-month Treasury bills

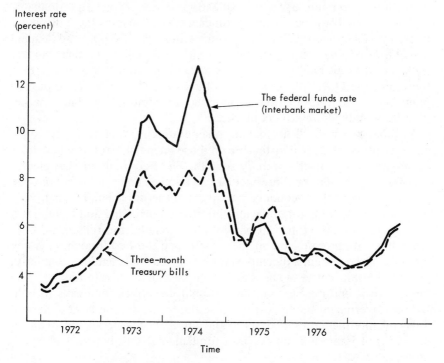

banks can continually adjust their reserves to compensate for unexpected flows.

More importantly, the federal funds market also provides an indirect mechanism for all banks to participate in credit agreements arranged with various borrowers. Small banks, participating through their larger correspondents, tend to be net lenders of federal funds. Large banks, participating directly in the market, tend to be net borrowers.[4] The small banks that are net lenders of federal funds participate in a series of persistent one-day loans to larger banks. The larger banks that are net borrowers of Fed funds finance their loan opportunities through a series of persistent one-day borrowings from smaller banks. This mechanism provides an additional attractive interbank outlet for funds for a smaller bank that has relatively plentiful deposits but relatively limited loan opportunities. It also provides an attractive interbank source of funds for larger banks that

---

[4] For example, in early 1977, the net federal funds borrowed by 46 of the largest banks fluctuated between $15 and $20 billion. These funds were, on balance, supplied by the smaller banks that constitute the remainder of the banking system.

may have better access to the more profitable loan opportunities. In this way, the interbank federal funds market tends to join rather disparate banks into a common effort to efficiently convert deposits into loanable and thus profitable funds. The Fed funds market also joins these disparate banks into an integrated banking system within which supply and demand conditions originating in one region (or even one bank) are quickly transmitted to all banks, large and small, throughout the country. Furthermore, the U.S. offices of foreign banks are also very active participants in the Fed funds market, integrating this domestic interbank market into the worldwide interbank markets.

In this book we will not devote a separate chapter to the Fed funds market for our focus will instead be on those financial markets which fund economic activity in the primary sectors. The Fed funds market merely transfers funds from one intermediary to another and thus is not *directly* involved in financing economic activity. On the other hand, it is a very important financial market because interbank borrowing and lending is a continuous alternative for all banks. For example, the relationship between the "prime rate" on business loans and the Fed funds rate is one measure of the marginal incentives for banks' business lending. Similarly, the relationship between the short-term Treasury bill rate and the Fed funds rate is one measure of the marginal incentives for banks to hold federal government securities. Because the banks are the largest class of financial intermediaries and serve the credit needs of all the financial sectors, the interbank market is a fundamental link between all these financial sectors.

Bank holding companies

The structure of our banking system has been altered substantially by the recent emergence of bank holding companies. A bank holding company is a nonbank corporate organization which serves as the parent company for at least one banking subsidiary and perhaps other nonbank subsidiaries. Bank holding companies have existed for some time, particularly in the form of multibank holding companies which consolidated the ownership of individual banks into one larger parent corporation. But, beginning in the 1960s, the trend toward *one-bank holding companies* vastly enlarged the importance of holding companies in our banking system. The one-bank holding company serves as a parent corporation for just one bank and usually several other nonbank subsidiaries. In the period 1965–1973, most large banks and many smaller banks formed one-bank holding companies. By 1977, more than two thirds of all bank deposits were in banks controlled by holding companies (as opposed to 8 percent in 1965).

These one-bank holding companies subsequently entered other financial service businesses through nonbank subsidiaries, either by acquiring existing companies, or by "de novo" originations of new activities. The subsidiaries of one-bank holding companies are now important factors within consumer finance, mortgage banking, leasing, and various other financial service industries. While these subsidiaries are generally small compared to the assets of their related banks, a number of them are still among the largest firms within their own industry.

In addition to serving as a vehicle for diversification, holding companies have also served as important sources of funds for their subsidiary banks. In several episodes in recent years, when the ability of the subsidiary banks to raise funds was constrained, holding companies were able to supply funds either directly or indirectly to their banks.

The diversification of banks into nonbank financial services and the development of new sources of funds are both of great concern to bank regulators. The Federal Reserve Board has thus been given rather broad powers to regulate bank holding companies as a part of their overall regulatory powers. As part of our study of the development of banks we will later return to examine the interactions between banks, bank holding companies, and the Federal Reserve Board.

INTERNATIONAL EXPANSION OF THE BANKING SYSTEM

Another important change in the structure of the U.S. banking system has been its increasing international activities. While a handful of U.S. banks have long been involved in various international activities, the great growth in most banks' overseas business has occurred since 1960. Much of this growth arises from their activity in the external dollar markets, although some of it arises from their operations in the internal and external markets for other currencies as well.

Most of the international expansion up until the mid-1970s was accomplished through a growing network of foreign branches. In 1964 there were only 11 U.S. banks with foreign branches. Between them, these banks had 181 overseas branches with total assets of $7 billion. By 1972, however, 108 U.S. banks had 627 overseas branches with assets of approximately $90 billion. Thus, a tenfold expansion of banks with overseas branches and their associated assets had taken place within a span of only eight years. In 1964, only 30 percent of the overseas assets of U.S. banks were held by their overseas branches, the remainder being held by the U.S. head office. By 1972, however, over 80 percent of all foreign assets were held by the overseas branches.

There were several reasons for this rapid pace of overseas expansion. First of all, there was a general increase in international trade, which had to be financed. Most of these trade transactions were denominated in U.S. dollars due to the dollar's special position as the largest of the freely convertible currencies and the one diversified international currency.

U.S. banks were in a better position to service this need than were banks whose primary dealings were in other currencies. In addition, throughout this period, U.S. multinational corporations were rapidly expanding their overseas operations, and U.S. banks followed this movement of their customers overseas. Once established overseas, U.S. banks competed aggressively to service the international and local needs of foreign customers as well. The sizeable foreign demand for dollar assets and liabilities to meet the demands of international investment and borrowing contributed to the growth of U.S. banking activities abroad.

While some of this foreign business had to take place in the foreign branches in order to provide the services required, large parts of this international business could have been serviced from the head offices of the U.S. banks. That is, much of this business could have taken place in the internal dollar market rather than in the external market. For a variety of regulatory and tax reasons, however, the U.S. banks chose to conduct the bulk of their transactions with foreigners in the external dollar market. These factors were discussed at some length in Chapter 6. In response to a growing concern about the level of and growth in short-term dollar claims against entities in the United States, the Federal Reserve developed the Voluntary Foreign Credit Restraint (VFCR) Program. This program subjected the foreign lending of domestic U.S. bank offices to fairly rigid guidelines. It brought the growth of foreign lending financed in the internal dollar market to a halt. These VFCR guidelines did not apply to the banks' operations in the external dollar market, however. In response, those U.S. banks with international customers and with the credit to raise substantial sums of dollar deposits in the external market substantially expanded their deposit raising and lending in the external dollar market. As a result, the number of banks with overseas branches and the deposits and loans of these branches grew enormously.

In addition to serving the financial demands of their international and foreign customers, the deposit-gathering abilities of these foreign branches proved to be a substantial advantage to the home offices of the U.S. banks in the late 1960s. In 1966 and again in 1969, domestic U.S. banks could not attract interest-sensitive funds in the internal dollar market because of the Federal Reserve Board's ceiling on allowable interest rates. However, the foreign branches of U.S. banks were not subject to these same ceilings and thus were able to attract funds in the external dollar market. The U.S. banks could then borrow the funds from their foreign branches, thereby supplying interest-sensitive funds to their domestic operations. These funds were of enormous benefit to the domestic lending activities of large commercial banks, allowing them to meet the demands of some of their domestic customers in these two very difficult periods. As more banks perceived the benefits of overseas branches in supplying funds to the head office, the growth of U.S. banks overseas was further accelerated.

In 1973, several factors changed. The sharp increase during late 1973 in the price of oil, and other factors, created enormous credit demands from foreign governments, particularly those of nonoil, less-developed countries. With the breakdown of the old monetary system and the devaluation and "floating" of the dollar's exchange rate, government constraints on dollar outflows were dismantled. The termination of the VFCR Program facilitated the recycling of the OPEC financial surpluses and the financing of the consuming countries' deficits. U.S. banks could then fund foreign lending with deposits raised in the internal dollar market. As a result, a part of the activity which had formerly taken place in the external market was shifted to the internal market. The home offices of the larger U.S. commercial banks as well as their foreign branches became actively involved in lending to entities outside the United States.

The international expansion of banks has been particularly rapid among the larger U.S. banks. Today, almost all of the major U.S. banks (the largest 20 banks) have significant operations overseas. For some of the largest U.S. banks, more than half of their deposits and, more importantly, more than half of their earnings are attributable to their foreign operations.

Some of the largest and most important international offices of these banks are based in London because of its traditional role as a center of finance, but in recent years, many smaller "shell" offices have been opened in the Bahamas and other previously obscure financial locations—generally as a device to avoid certain taxes.

Because of the differences in bank legislation in different countries, the overseas activities of U.S. banks have grown to be very diverse. They extend far beyond the more limited commercial banking functions performed within the United States. Most large banks, either through their overseas branches or subsidiares, have entered a wide variety of overseas financial service business including, for example, investment banking services from which the domestic offices of these same banks are clearly prohibited. The international growth of U.S. banks has thus also produced a continual diversification of the financial functions that these banks perform.

While large U.S. banks have been expanding their overseas activities very rapidly, foreign banks have also been entering the domestic U.S. banking markets. By 1977, there were about 200 offices of foreign banks within the United States with over $60 billion in assets (equal to about 12 percent of the assets held at the domestic offices of the large U.S. banks with whom these foreign banks compete). These U.S. offices of foreign banks have become active in financing international trade and transferring funds for international payments. In part, these offices have been funded by net advances from their overseas parents. They have also become particularly active in the domestic interbank market (the Fed funds market), borrowing and lending substantial sums. As the U.S. extensions of their parent banks, they have played an active role in arbitraging across the U.S. interbank market and the overseas dollar-dominated interbank markets (the Eurodollar markets). They have thus served as a channel through which financial conditions in other countries impact the U.S. financial markets, and vice versa.

By the latter half of the 1970s the increasing integration of worldwide banking systems had greatly altered the structure of U.S. banking. The largest U.S. banks had become truly multinational financial institutions, pursuing a diverse set of functions overseas. Banking within the United States was becoming affected by the increasing activities of foreign banks. Both of these trends contributed significantly to the growing integration of worldwide financial markets.

EVOLUTION OF BANKS' SOURCES OF FUNDS

The three principal sources of banks' funds are deposits, borrowed funds, and capital. As the banking system has evolved there have been important changes in each of these sources of funds.

Deposits as a source of funds

Deposits have always formed the largest proportion of bank funds, but the nature of these funds has changed dramatically in the past 20 years. In the 1950s, banks relied chiefly upon demand deposits for their deposit base. By law, banks cannot pay interest on demand deposits so banks compensated their depositors through various services. Households with demand deposits received the convenience and liquidity that their checking accounts offered as a payments mechanism. Corporations and other large depositors received not only the convenience but also other financial services. The demand deposit capability of banks was unique and separated banks from other financial intermediaries.

But by the 1970s the dominance of demand deposits had disappeared. Throughout the postwar period, demand deposits grew at a relatively modest rate, and their previous role of dominance was assumed instead by the fast-growing time and savings deposits. As Figure 13–3 demonstrates, by 1974 time and savings deposits had become about two thirds of all bank deposits. In retail banking, the real growth in consumer deposits came from the consumer savings and time deposits offered to small depositors. Similarly, in wholesale banking, the large negotiable certificates of deposit (CDs) accounted for most of the growth in large deposits. Throughout this period, both small and large depositors were becoming

Figure 13–3

Time and savings deposits as a percent of total deposits for all commercial banks

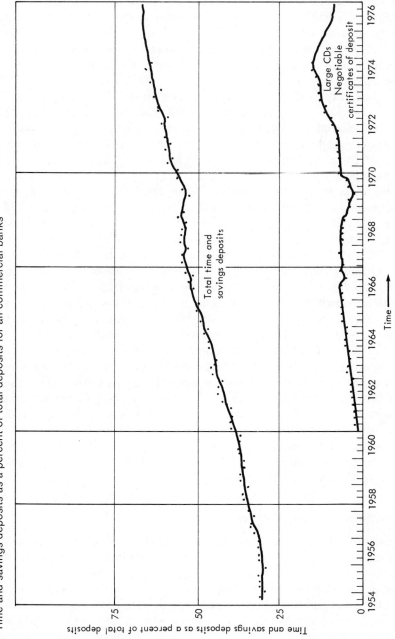

increasingly sophisticated in their approach to cash management. In addition, interest rates were rising throughout this period, increasing the penalty for holding funds in noninterest-bearing form. For both of these reasons, demand deposits were becoming less widely sought as a form in which to hold liquid assets. Banks therefore chose to compete actively for interest-bearing deposits to maintain their share of all intermediated funds.

The shift in deposit mix has been particularly important for the large money-center banks. In the early 1950s the overwhelming majority of their funds came from demand deposits, with time deposits and other sources accounting for only a small fraction of funds. The introduction of large CDs in 1961 provided them with an attractive financial instrument to retain those large deposits that were becoming interest-rate sensitive. By 1965, these large CDs had become an important, though still small, source of bank funds. But by the mid-1970s, these CDs had become one of the largest single sources of funds for many money-center banks, rivaling their total demand deposit balances from all customers.

This evolution from demand deposit banks to time deposit banks has important implications for the management of bank funds. As long as demand deposits dominated bank sources of funds, interest rates were not a determinant of competition among banks. Banks chose to compete, instead, on the long-term level of services they could provide customers. However, large certificates of deposits are purchased and sold in active, well-developed but more impersonal, financial markets, largely on the basis of interest rates. The funds attracted by large CDs are interest-sensitive funds, or "purchased monies" as some prefer to call them. In the old demand deposit world, a bank could obtain deposits chiefly by building and maintaining long-term customer relationships, but in the new world of interest-sensitive funds, a bank can generally obtain large time deposits from the national money markets if, and usually only if, it is willing to pay an appropriate rate for their use. Needless to say, this has had important effects on money-center banks.

Borrowing as a source of funds

Large CDs are not the only device for attracting interest-sensitive funds in today's banking system. As the underlying demands for bank loans have grown in both the household and corporate sectors, banks have responded by developing increasingly diverse channels through which they can borrow funds and relend them to their customers. Most of these borrowing channels have been developed first by the large money-center banks and then spread to the dominant regional banks.

As mentioned earlier, the interbank markets for federal funds have become one of the most important sources of borrowed funds. The large international money-center banks have also developed their overseas branch networks into a source of borrowed funds. Large banks have also periodically used the borrowing capabilities of their recently formed holding companies to raise funds. "Bank-related commercial paper," the short-term promissory notes of the holding companies, has been used to bring funds into the parent holding companies. Once borrowed by the holding companies, these funds can be used in a variety of indirect ways by the subsidiary banks. For example, the banks can sell their loans to the holding companies and thus free funds within the banks themselves.

Large banks have also developed a relatively active market for investments (or loans) sold under repurchase agreements (RPs). When an investment is sold "under an agreement to repurchase," the sellers commit themselves to repurchase the investment on a particular future date for a specified sum. The repurchase agreement makes the entire transaction functionally equivalent to collateralized borrowing, and it is recognized as borrowing by the financial reporting techniques that have evolved. The interest rate on this borrowing is implicitly determined by the difference between the sale price and the repurchase price for the security. Repurchase agreements have existed for some time as a complement to many money-market transactions. But in recent years, they have been developed into a very active short-term market, a market large banks have come to use as an important source of borrowed short-term funds.

Finally, banks that are members of the Federal Reserve System may also borrow from Federal Reserve banks. Indeed, at one time, this was one of the primary forms of borrowing for commercial banks. The interest rate on these borrowings is determined by the Federal Reserve System and is often substantially lower than open-market interest rates for other borrowings. The Federal Reserve, however, discourages persistent borrowing by any one bank. Most large banks prefer not to borrow from the Fed if any other sources are still available. Thus, borrowings from the Federal Reserve banks serve a somewhat different purpose than other borrowings we have discussed. They are a heavily regulated safety valve to be used only when necessary and even then only when approved by regulatory authorities rather than a large liquid market for interest-sensitive monies.

The emergence of interbank markets for federal funds, borrowing from overseas branches with access to the international money markets, commercial paper markets for one-bank holding companies, and repurchase agreement markets, when coupled with the emergence of the market for large certificates of deposit, have given the large commercial banks access to a wide variety of interest-sensitive funds or purchased monies.

Capital as a source of funds

Capital is the third and final major source of bank funds. Bank capital is subordinated to the interests of both depositors and other creditors; that is, in the event of liquidation the depositors and short-term lenders are repaid first from the proceeds of the bank's assets. Thus bank capital serves as a cushion to protect the uninsured depositors and other creditors from the risk of loss. The traditional and still dominant form of bank capital is equity. Most of this has been accumulated through the retained earnings of the banks, although from time to time it has been supplemented by new issues of equity securities. Since 1963, banks have been allowed to issue long-term debt securities to bolster their capital base. These issues of long-time debt grew rapidly in the early 1970s and became an important source of capital funds for large commercial banks, but they are still only a small fraction of the total capital of all U.S. banks.

Liability management as a source of liquidity

The newly developed availability of interest-sensitive deposits and borrowed funds have drastically altered the problems of bank liquidity. Banks had traditionally satisfied their short-term needs for liquidity by managing their assets. When the vast majority of their funds were provided by noninterest-bearing demand deposits, banks could not easily enlarge their deposit base toward the end of each credit cycle when their customers' demand for funds were the largest. Faced with expected or unexpected demands for credit in these periods, or unexpected deposit outflows, banks accommodated these needs by selling their short-term investments.

Short-term investments, primarily U.S. government securities, thus served as the principal source of bank liquidity. This liquidity was sometimes supplemented by borrowing from correspondent banks and borrowing from a Federal Reserve bank. But the job of liquidity management clearly revolved around the large portfolios of short-term securities, which provided a continuously available reservoir of liquidity to the banks.

The ability to attract interest-sensitive funds through either large CDs or borrowings has provided a new element of liquidity for the banks. Faced with enlarged credit demands, or unexpected demand deposit outflows, banks can now either sell short-term investments or purchase additional interest-sensitive funds. Their reliance upon traditional asset management as the source of liquidity has thus been reduced and replaced in part by a new emphasis on liability management for liquidity.

As we shall see later, however, banks' ability to attract these new funds through new liabilities is not without its limits. On the one hand, participants in the short-term markets may fear that over-reliance upon interest-sensitive liabilities can lead a bank to instability, and having become already heavily dependent upon purchased funds, a bank's ability to attract additional funds may be limited. More fundamentally, the Federal

Reserve System has a variety of regulatory tools through which it can control banks' access to various purchased funds. In particular, through what is called "Regulation Q," the Federal Reserve Board can control the interest rate that banks offer on all deposits, including large CDs. The ability to control interest rates offered in a rate-sensitive market is tantamount to controlling access to that market. Thus the Federal Reserve Board, in the final analysis, can choose to limit banks' ability to obtain various funds. For these reasons, liability management cannot be relied upon as the sole source of bank liquidity, but it has come to play an important and, at times, a dominant role in the management of bank liquidity in recent years.

ASSET AND LIABILITY MANAGEMENT IN THE BANKING SYSTEM

A commercial bank produces earnings for its shareholders by managing its asset and liability positions. The principal sources of a bank's revenues are the interest charges from its various assets, although these are supplemented by the gains and losses on securities and the fee income the bank receives from various services. The principal costs for a bank are the interest costs it pays for its deposits and other funds, although total expenses are of course determined in part by salaries, wages, and other supplementary operating expenses. The earnings stream produced by a commercial bank is principally determined by the difference between the stream of interest revenue from its assets and the stream of interest costs from its liabilities. The difference in these streams is critically dependent upon the "spread" or difference between the average yield from assets and its average cost of funds.

Earnings are only one of the objectives of a bank, however. In the long run, a bank must produce those earnings subject to the constraints that both the relative safety of its assets and the relative liquidity of its overall funds position are maintained. One of the challenges to bank management, therefore, is to manage the bank's asset and liability position in pursuit of earnings but to do so with a proper regard for the longer run safety and liquidity of the institution.

Evolution of asset and liability management

When commercial banks derived most of their deposit bases from relatively stable noninterest-bearing demand deposits, the job of asset and liability management was reasonably straightforward. The most stable of the deposits could be invested in longer term assets. The more volatile deposits could be invested in short-term assets. This would create a constant flow of earnings from the asset and liability mix. The pursuit of interest-sensitive funds from a variety of channels greatly complicated the problem, and enlarged the opportunities, for asset and liability management. Because they are borrowed for very short periods of time, the interest rates that must be offered to retain purchased funds are quite responsive to changes in open-market rates. These variable-rate liabilities produce streams of interest costs that are highly variable. In order to produce a stream of earnings that is reasonably stable in the presence of variable-rate liabilities, banks have progressively moved toward a portfolio of equally variable-rate assets. Bank loans to business, which form the dominant asset of large commercial banks, have been indexed to yield a return which varies with open-market rates. The prime rate, which is the basis of business loan pricing, has been effectively administered in such a way that it varies with open-market rates. Banks have thus been able to match the variable-rate nature of some of their liabilities with a correspondingly variable-rate set of business loans. This has made their earnings from these lending activities reasonably stable.

The emergence and development of these variable-rate asset structures has made large commercial banks a particularly effective set of competitors for funds. With a set of variable-rate assets, banks can be more assured that they will be able to compete for additional liabilities on an interest rate basis, at least in the absence of regulatory decisions to the contrary. With this assurance, variable-rate liabilities or purchased funds can be more heavily relied upon as a source of future liquidity. With their future liquidity more assured, banks are less dependent upon short-term investments as a source of liquidity. This reduces their need for investments in general and short-term investments in particular. It is not surprising, therefore, that the evolution of banks' dependence on interest-sensitive funds has coincided with a progression toward variable-rate assets, fewer investments, and investments of a somewhat longer term maturity.

In this context, the job of asset and liability management has become a more complex and increasingly more important role in the large commercial banks. These banks have evolved from relatively passive acceptors of deposits to relatively active competitors for funds and into active managers of their assets and liabilities. One of the important management tasks in these banks is to develop and maintain as large a stable low-cost deposit base as is possible, given the realities of the customer base. This stable deposit base must then be supplemented by a changing mix of interest-sensitive funds, purchased on the larger more impersonal open markets. Finally, these funds must be invested in a portfolio of assets whose risks and returns match the variable-rate profile of the existing liabilities and assure a continued ability to raise interest-sensitive funds without jeopardizing the earnings stream of the bank.

Figure 13-4
Bank capital/bank loans and bank capital/total bank assets for all commercial banks

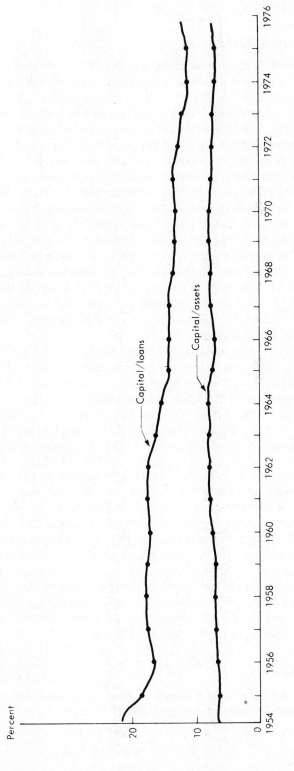

Percent

Bank capital as a constraint

As bank lending grew rapidly in the 1971–1974 period, the growth in overall assets and liabilities and particularly loans outpaced the growth of capital accounts. As these capital accounts became relatively smaller, an additional dimension to the overall problem of bank management became more clear. Figure 13–4 shows the time trend of bank capital accounts for all commercial banks as a percentage of total assets and as a percentage of loans (a proxy for those assets that may be risky). While there has been a moderate decline in the rates of bank capital to total assets, there has been a very steep decline in the ratio of bank capital to loans. Furthermore, the decline of equity capital relative to these measures has been even more severe because banks had issued long-term debt to supplement their equity capital during the period. In addition, the amount of equity capital from the holding company perspective was even smaller. Many banks, particularly the very large banks, had used the borrowing capacity of their parent one-bank holding companies to fund a part of the bank's equity position. Indeed, in 1977, despite some rebound in their capital position, the equity capital of the ten largest one-bank holding companies was still less than 4 percent of their total assets.

Recall from an earlier discussion that bank capital is the cushion that protects uninsured depositors and creditors from the loss of funds they provide to a bank. As the bank capital accounts become smaller relative to the risky assets of a bank, the perceived risk of large uninsured depositors and of the other creditors can increase. As this perceived risk increases, it may become more difficult for a bank to both retain its regular depositors and purchase additional interest-sensitive funds on the open market.

To preclude this chain of events, a bank must manage the growth of its total assets, and particularly its more risky loan assets, relative to the growth of its capital. While capital can be raised by new issues of long-term debt or capital, the majority of all capital has been added from retained earnings. The source of all retained earnings is the spread or average earnings on the portfolio of assets and liabilities. Thus a bank must not only manage the maturity and variable-rate character of its assets and liabilities, but also the average earnings from these assets and liabilities as well. The earnings are the principal source of capital account growth, and the growth of the capital accounts is the long-run constraint on the allowable growth rate of the bank.

QUESTIONS

1. How has the growth of commercial bank assets been related to the financing demands of each of the primary financial sectors?
2. How does the profitability of commercial banks depend on which primary

sector is demanding finance? How does it depend on the availability and cost of funds in the public markets?

3. What factors account for the differences in the balance sheets of local banks, regional banks, and international banks?
4. What factors give rise to the interbank markets? What are the effects of these markets on banks and on financial markets?
5. What are the determinants of the growth of the assets and liabilities of international banks?
6. What is the role of bank capital?

REFERENCES

Beebe, Jack. "A Perspective on Liability Management and Bank Risk." In "Real World Risk and Bank Risk," *Economic Review* (Winter 1977), Federal Reserve Bank of San Francisco.

Bowsher, Norman N. "Have Multibank Holding Companies Affected Commercial Bank Performance?" *Review,* vol. 60, no. 4, Federal Reserve Bank of St. Louis, April 1978.

Grubel, Herbert C. "A Theory of Multinational Banking," *Quarterly Review,* Banca Nazionale del Lavoro, No. 123, December 1977, pp. 349–64.

Lucas, Charles M. "Federal Funds and Repurchase Agreements," *Quarterly Review,* Federal Reserve Bank of New York, Summer 1977, pp. 33–48.

Rhoades, Stephen A. "Structure and Performance Studies in Banking: A Summary and Evaluation," *Staff Economic Studies (92),* Board of Governors of the Federal Reserve System, December 1977.

Taggart, Jr., Robert A. and Greenbaum, Stuart I. "Bank Capital and Public Regulation," *Journal of Money, Credit and Banking,* vol. 10, no. 2 (May 1978), pp. 158–69.

Willis, Parket B. *Federal Funds Market: Origin and Development.* Boston: Federal Reserve Bank, 1970.

14

The Federal Reserve, interest rates, and the flows of money and credit

Because of the central importance of money and commercial banks in our financial system, a complex set of regulations and regulatory authorities has evolved to protect, restrict, and control money and commercial banking activities. The most important of these regulatory authorities is the Federal Reserve (the Fed). The Federal Reserve is responsible for formulating and implementing policies to control the growth of money and credit.

In addition, the Federal Reserve controls other important aspects of member bank operations. For example, the Fed controls the interest rates that banks can offer on time and savings deposits and the terms upon which they can obtain other funds, many aspects of bank lending policies, and the restrictions which circumscribe the related businesses that bank holding companies can enter. Also, the Federal Reserve provides a number of important services, not only to commercial banks, but to the Treasury and the financial system as a whole. These include the collection and clearing of checks, the wire transfer of funds, the issuance of Federal Reserve notes, the handling of currency and coin, and serving as the principal fiscal agent of the U.S. government.

This chapter focuses on the Federal Reserve's activities in the area of monetary policy. In some later chapters we will also discuss some of its other regulatory powers.

There will be two aspects to our analysis of monetary policy. The first will deal with the Fed's control over member bank reserves and the impact of these changing reserves on the quantities of money, bank credit, and interest rates. This first aspect is rather straightforward, and its conclusions are not the subject of much dispute.

The second aspect of the analysis will describe the problems faced by the Fed as it formulates both objectives for monetary policy and operating procedures which are likely to be effective in achieving these objectives. This second aspect is much more complex and controversial. First, there is often considerable dispute over the relative importance of the different objectives of monetary policy. Equally important, however, there is considerable dispute over which actions the Federal Reserve should take to achieve any given set of objectives. Unfortunately, there are several competing models, or conceptual frameworks, of how the actions of the Federal Reserve affect the economy. Each of these models is supported by a respectable theoretical argument and a large body of empirical analysis. To add to the confusion, these different models often characterize an existing monetary policy in quite contradictory ways (one characterizing it as "expansive" and the other as "restrictive"). More importantly, the different models often call for policies which are in direct conflict with each other. This conflict has made the formulation of monetary policy very difficult and kept it at the center of much public and political dispute. This chapter will proceed with both of these two aspects of Fed policy, the first straightforward and the second complex, as we attempt to analyze the role of the Federal Reserve System in our financial markets.

THE STRUCTURE OF THE FEDERAL RESERVE SYSTEM

The Federal Reserve System can be thought of as a pyramidal regulatory structure, with the commercial banks that are its member banks on the lower level, the Federal Reserve district banks at the intermediate level, and the Federal Reserve Board at its upper level. While somewhat less than half of all commercial banks belong to the Federal Reserve System, these banks hold over three fourths of the assets and liabilities of all banks. Thus member banks of the Federal Reserve System control a substantial majority of the banking system's total funds. The 12 Federal Reserve district banks perform various central banking functions for the member banks within their respective geographic districts. Each Reserve bank serves as a "banker's bank" for its member banks, holding deposit balances for these banks and providing other services. Originally, each Reserve bank was to operate somewhat autonomously, tailoring its policies to the needs of its local district. Over time, as a national market for financial services was developed, the differences between the policies of the district banks have largely disappeared. Today, most of the important policies are established by the Federal Reserve Board, the centralized decision-making authority for the Federal Reserve System.

The Federal Reserve Board consists of seven members, each of whom is appointed by the President of the United States for a term of 14 years. The Federal Reserve Board oversees the operations of the district Reserve banks and initiates many of the important regulatory decisions that affect all member banks. Finally, the seven members of the Federal Reserve Board, the president of the Federal Reserve Bank of New York, and four of the other Reserve bank presidents (on a rotating basis) comprise the Federal Open Market Committee (FOMC). The FOMC is responsible for formulating the "open market operations" of the Federal Reserve, one of the central tools of monetary policy.

MEMBER BANK RESERVES AND THE FEDERAL RESERVE

The Federal Reserve requires that member banks hold reserves against their deposits. Through its control over these reserves, the Fed exercises its most important effect on banks and financial markets. While bank reserves may be held in the form of vault cash, most reserves are held as deposits with the Federal Reserve System. These deposits are assets of the member banks and deposit liabilities of the Federal Reserve. The consolidated balance sheets for the Federal Reserve banks and all member banks are shown in the accompanying table.

Federal Reserve Banks		All Member Banks	
Assets	*Liabilities*	*Assets*	*Liabilities*
Securities	Federal Reserve notes	Cash	Deposits
Loans to member banks	Deposit balances of member banks	Reserves on deposit with Federal Reserve	Borrowings from Federal Reserve
Other assets:	Other deposits:		
Gold certificates	U.S. Treasury	Securities	
Federal Reserve Float	Foreign		Capital
Foreign exchange	Capital	Loans	
Miscellaneous			

The member bank asset, "Reserves on Deposit with Federal Reserve," is equal to the Federal Reserve banks' liability, "Deposit Balances of Member Banks."

If a member bank experiences a temporary shortfall in its actual reserves, it can, with the permission of the Fed, borrow reserves from the Fed itself. This borrowing is accomplished through what is called the "discount window" of the Fed. The borrowings are more formally called "discounts and advances" because of their particular form. From the perspective of the Federal Reserve System, these discounts are best described as "Loans to Member Banks," and from the perspective of the member banks, they are best described as "Borrowings from the Federal Reserve." Thus, the Federal Reserve accomplishes its principal central bank function, that of a banker's bank, by both holding the deposits of, and intermittently making loans to, its member banks.

In addition, the Fed holds a variety of other assets and liabilities. Other depositors of the Fed are the U.S. Treasury and foreign central banks, for whom the Fed serves as agent in a number of financial transactions. The Fed also issues the Federal Reserve notes which, when distributed through the banks, form the bulk of our currency in circulation. These notes are simply the liabilities of the Federal Reserve System and are held by the general public for use as a medium of exchange.

The majority of the Fed's assets are held in the form of securities. These securities are composed primarily of securities of the U.S. Treasury. Like any investor, the Fed earns interest from the securities it owns and from its other loans. But unlike other investors, the Fed is a public institution and thus it turns back its overall "profits" to the U.S. Treasury after, of course, deducting its operating expenses. The Fed also holds a variety of other assets, including gold certificates and foreign exchange, which we will not describe in detail here.

Thus far, the Federal Reserve appears to be just another bank, although a bank only for other banks. It accepts deposits, makes loans, and holds securities like a commercial bank. But here the similarities end. For the Federal Reserve, through its various tools, can control not only its own assets and liabilities, but it can influence and, in the extreme, control the total assets and liabilities of its member banks.

THE IMPACT OF CHANGES IN BANK RESERVES

The Federal Reserve influences the reserve position of member banks through the use of three tools: reserve requirements, open-market operations, and discount window policy.

Open-market operations involve the purchase or sale of U.S. government securities by the Fed in the "open" market. Reserve requirements are the fraction of each type of their deposits which member banks must hold as reserves. Discount policy refers to the terms under which the Fed allows member banks to borrow from the Fed through the discount window.

Open-market operations are the most frequently used tool of monetary policy. For the purposes of illustrating the impact of these open-market operations, let us trace the effects of the Fed purchasing $1 million of Treasury bills in the open market. There will be three factors involved: the Fed, the commercial banks, and the securities firm from whom the Fed purchases the Treasury bills. Their starting balance sheets are shown in the accompanying table (M = millions).

Federal Reserve		The Banks		Securities Firm	
Securities	Federal	Reserves at	Customer	Bank	Borrowings
Loans to banks	Reserve	Fed ($20 M)	deposits	deposits	Net worth
Other	notes	Other	($100 M)	Securities	
	Deposit		Other	Other	
	balances				
	of member				
	banks				
	(20 M)				
	Other				

We shall assume, for the sake of simplicity, that the Fed has established reserve requirements of 20 percent against all deposits and that the banks hold these reserves entirely in the form of deposit balances at the Fed. We also assume that the required reserves of the banks are just equal to their actual reserves (see accompanying table):

Reserve Position Calculation for Banks

Deposits	$100 M
Required reserves (@20%)	20 M
Actual reserves	20 M
Excess reserves (Actual − required reserves)	0

In their current reserve position, the banks could not expand their deposits without encountering a deficit of reserves.

Suppose that the Fed purchases $1 million of Treasury securities from the securities firm. The Fed pays for these securities with a check drawn upon itself. The securities firm deposits this check with its local bank, and its deposit balances are thus increased by the $1 million. The receiving bank clears the check through the regular check-clearing process. As it arrives at the Fed, the receiving bank's deposit balances at the Fed are increased by the $1 million. The balance sheet changes from this set of transactions, which we shall call "Step One," are the following:

STEP ONE

Federal Reserve		**The Banks**		**Securities Firm**	

Securities
  + 1 M
Loans to banks
Other
	Federal
	  Reserve
	  notes
	Deposit
	  balances
	  of member
	  banks
	  (20 M
	  +1 M
	  = 21 M)
	Other
		Reserves on
		  deposit at
		  Fed (20 M
		  +1 M
		  = 21 M)
		Loans and
		  securities
			Deposits
			  (100 M
			  +1 M
			  = 101 M
			Other
				Bank
				  deposits
				  (+1 M)
				Securities
				  (−1 M)
				Other
					Borrowings
					Net worth

As a result of these events, the reserve position of the banks has been altered as follows:

Reserve Position Calculation for Banks

Deposits	$101 M
Required reserves (@ 20%)	20.2 M
Actual reserves	21.0 M
Excess reserves	0.8 M

The banks now have more reserves than they are required to hold against their deposits. They are therefore free to expand their deposits and assets accordingly. Let us assume that the banks, in the next step, decide to loan an incremental $4 million to their customers. The banks make these loans by augmenting their customers' deposit balances and recording the new $4 million of loans as an asset. During the second stage, the following transactions are thus recorded on the banks' balance sheets:

STEP TWO
The Banks

Reserves on deposit at Fed (21 M) Loans and securities (+4 M)	Deposits (101 M + 4 M = 105 M) Other

And the reserve position of the banks changes to:

Reserve Position Calculation for Banks

Deposits	$105 M
Required reserves (@ 20%)	21 M
Actual reserves	21 M
Excess reserves	0

232

Notice that the banks are now back in a reserve position similar to that which existed at the start. Their actual reserves are just equal to their required reserves, and their excess reserves are zero. For this whole series of transactions, the net changes for all participants are:

Federal Reserve		The Banks		Securities Firm	
Securities (+1 M) Loans to banks Other	Federal Reserve notes Deposit balances of member banks (20 M +1 M =21 M) Other	Reserves on deposit at Fed (20 M +1 M = 21 M) Loans and securities (+4 M)	Deposits (100 M +5 M = 105 M Other	Bank deposits (+1 M) Securities (−1 M)	

In addition, the public holds an additional $4 million in bank deposits as an asset and $4 million in additional bank loans as a liability.

By buying $1 million of securities the Federal Reserve has enabled the banking system to expand its deposits and assets by a total of $5 million.[1] Thus $5 million of "money" (the deposit balances) and $4 million of commercial bank credit have been created by this purchase of securities.

This whole process also works in reverse, as well. If the Federal Reserve *sells* $1 million of securities, let us say to a securities firm, the firm pays for these securities with a check drawn upon its bank. As this check clears through the system, the bank's deposit balances at the Fed are reduced by $1 million, leaving the bank short of reserves. In order to regain a satisfactory reserve position, the banking system ultimately has to reduce its deposits and loans, thus reducing the outstanding supplies of money and bank credit.

THE REACTION OF INDIVIDUAL BANKS TO RESERVE CHANGES

In the previous section, we examined the ways in which the Fed's open-market operations control the consolidated reserve position of the banking system. In this section, we will examine in more detail the possible reaction of an individual bank to reserve position changes.

[1] The overall expansion of deposits which takes place as the result of a given amount of open-market purchases of securities depends upon several factors. Most importantly, it depends upon the applicable reserve requirement percentages. Each dollar of reserves which remains in the banking system enables ($1/r$) dollars of deposits to be created, where r is the weighted average required reserve percentage. An expansion in the holdings of demand

Suppose that, as a result of the Fed's open-market operations, a large bank finds itself with a decline in demand deposits of $1 million and a fall in reserves of $1 million. For the sake of illustration, with 20 percent reserve requirements, the bank's balance sheet might be shown as in the accompanying table.

Bank (Initially)		**Bank (After 1 Million Open-Market Purchase)**	
Reserves on deposit at Fed Reserve ($4 M)	Deposits ($20 M)	Reserves on deposit at Fed Reserve ($3 M)	Deposits ($19 M)
Securities ($5 M)	Borrowings	Securities ($5 M)	Borrowings
Loans ($13 M)	Borrowings from Fed ($0)	Loans ($13 M)	Borrowings from Fed ($0)
	Fed funds borrowed from other banks ($0)		Fed funds borrowed from other banks ($0)
	Capital ($2 M)		Capital ($2 M)

Its reserve position after the open market purchase would be:

Reserve Position of the Bank

Deposits	$19.0 M
Required reserves (@ 20%)	3.8 M
Actual reserves	3.0 M
Excess reserves	−0.8 M

Faced with a reserve deficit of $0.8 million, the individual bank may choose to reestablish an acceptable reserve position by a number of possible actions, among them: (1) borrowing the needed reserves in the Fed funds market from another bank, or (2) borrowing the needed reserves from the Federal Reserve at the discount window, or finally (3) contracting its loans (or investments) and deposits. We shall trace each of these actions through to determine its effects on the individual bank, the collection of all banks, and the ability of the Federal Reserve to control the deposits and assets of the banks.

Generally, the first reaction of a bank with a reserve deficit is to borrow the needed reserves on a short-term basis in the interbank markets. By borrowing $0.8 million in the interbank Fed funds market, our bank can correct its reserve deficit in the short run. Indeed, by persistent interbank

---

deposits by the public is usually associated with an increase in currency holdings, however. These increased currency holdings withdraw demand deposits from the banks and remove reserves from the banking system. Thus, another important factor affecting the deposit expansion associated with open-market operations is the currency choice made by the public. Given the values of the different reserve requirement percentages, the mix of the different classes of deposits, and the behavior of currency holdings, the average multiplier relating open-market operations to deposit growth has been about 2.5.

borrowings, it could maintain its required reserve position for an extended period. These borrowings are a convenient and flexible method to obtain reserves, as long as there are other banks with sufficient quantities of excess reserves. But borrowings in the interbank Fed funds market clearly do not increase the total supply of reserves available to the commercial banking system. They merely redistribute the existing reserves among the individual banks. If the Federal Reserve persists in tightening the reserve position of all banks by selling securities, there will be fewer and fewer excess reserves available in the interbank markets, and the cost of borrowing them may rise commensurately. Thus, while the interbank markets provide a flexible and convenient method for an individual bank to manage its reserve balances, they do not allow the collection of all banks to increase their aggregate reserve balances.

The bank in deficit could also adjust its reserve position by borrowing reserves at the discount window of the Fed. This borrowing can be accomplished at the discount rate stipulated by the Federal Reserve. Indeed, because the Federal Reserve appears to be reluctant to raise its discount rate during times of rising open-market rates, this borrowing is often a way of obtaining the needed reserves at a bargain rate. Furthermore, borrowing from the Fed not only increases the reserves of the individual bank, but it similarly increases the reserves of the banking system as a whole because no off-setting reduction is made to the reserves of some other bank. Thus, while borrowing in the interbank market merely redistributes existing reserves among banks, borrowing at the Fed's discount window is a way of actually creating new reserves for the banking system.

The only difficulty with borrowing at the discount window is that the Federal Reserve considers this borrowing to be a privilege that they extend to banks and not a right. The Fed encourages banks to use this borrowing as a short-term temporary measure but discourages its use as a long-term source of funds. Thus any individual bank is reluctant to use this borrowing as much more than a temporary stop-gap measure. Some banks, particularly large banks, prefer not to use the discount window at all. What can result in a period of generally tight reserves is that a constantly changing group of banks borrow for short periods of time at the discount window. Thus, while no single bank remains in debt to the Fed for an extended period, the collection of all banks maintains a reasonably large amount of borrowed reserves. These borrowed reserves are then distributed among the individual banks through the interbank markets. The discount window can help the banking system to cushion the effects of a policy which restricts the growth in non-borrowed reserves.

If the two alternatives we have examined are judged undesirable, our deficit bank has little choice but to liquidate some of its loans (or investments) and deposits in order to restore balance between its required and actual reserves. By encouraging repayment of its existing loans and re-straining the extension of new loans, the bank can, over time, reduce its loans and deposits to levels consistent with its actual reserves. As the bank's loans and deposits are reduced, the aggregate supplies of bank credit and money are correspondingly reduced. This is the ultimate effect and the objective of the Fed's deliberate policy of reducing reserves.

The deficit bank could choose to restore a balance in its reserve posi-tion by selling $0.8 million of securities and depositing the funds at the Fed. While the original bank would now be in an acceptable reserve position, another bank would have to begin to adjust to a position of reduced deposits ($0.8 M), reduced reserves ($0.8 M), and a negative excess reserve position ($0.64 M). The adjustment alternatives open to this second bank would be identical to those faced by the original bank, and the requirement to adjust would be just as necessary. Whether the response to the initial reserve deficit is taken entirely by the first bank or partially shifted to other banks, the ultimate result of a reduction in re-serves is a decline in bank loans and/or investments and a decline in bank deposits.

The effects of reserve deficiencies within individual banks are spread rapidly throughout the financial system as these banks attempt to reestab-lish their required reserves. As banks attempt to borrow more reserves in the interbank markets, interest rates in these short-term markets are driven up. As banks attempt to sell securities in the open market, prices in these markets are driven down and interest rates up. As banks restrain their extensions of new loans, not only is the availability of credit affected, but the interest rates on new credit correspondingly rise. Thus, both the reduced availability of credit and increased interest rates spread the ef-fects of the reduced level of reserves throughout the banking system and to other segments of our financial markets.

These effects also work in reverse. As the Fed purchases securities, it expands the reserves of one or more individual banks. These individual banks have an incentive to purchase securities or extend loans and thereby to expand deposits. In these ways, an increase in the reserve positions of individual banks initially lowers short-term interest rates and results in conditions which lead to an expansion in the money supply and an increase in bank credit. The results of these effects are then transmitted throughout the financial system.

THE CHOICE AMONG THE POLICY TOOLS

Each of the three ways in which the Fed can affect member bank reserve positions has a somewhat different effect on the banks and finan-cial markets. The reserve requirement percentages in effect at any given time determine the total *required reserves* of the banking system. Because the Fed can alter these reserve requirements within the rather broad ranges determined by the Congress, the power to set reserve requirements is a potentially important tool of monetary policy.[2] But, in practice, the Fed has changed reserve requirements very infrequently in recent years. A sharp and sudden change in reserve requirements causes an equally sudden change in the liquidity position of all banks. Such a change could cause significant short-term adjustment problems in the banking system and throughout financial markets. Because of this, reserve requirements are considered to be a blunt instrument of monetary policy, a tool not "readily adaptable to short-run conditions." Perhaps more to the point, changes in reserve requirements have a direct affect on the profitability of member banks. Thus changes in reserve requirements impact the relative profit incentive for belonging to the Federal Reserve System or raise issues of equitable treatment between different classes of banks. For these reasons, the Fed has not chosen to exercise its authority to change required reserve percentages very frequently, preferring instead to conduct its monetary policy through the more flexible tools: open-market operations and discount window policy.

The most important tool for altering the reserve position of the banks is the open market operations of the Fed. The purchase and sale of securities can be used to vary the *non-borrowed reserves* that banks hold on deposit with the Fed. Open-market operations can be conducted on a continual basis, leading to gradual and controlled movements in bank reserves. Most open-market operations are conducted by purchasing and selling short-term Treasury bills because of the active trading in this market, but there is nothing that requires the operations to be carried out there. Indeed, in recent years, the longer term Treasury and Federal agency markets have been used intermittently by the Fed.

Finally, the Fed can influence the level of *borrowed reserves* through its third tool, discount window policy. By controlling the interest rate at which member banks borrow at the discount window, the Fed can control the incentive for such borrowing. A history of the discount rate at the New York Federal Reserve Bank is shown in Figure 14–1.[3] As this

---

[2] As of 1977, the legal ranges specified by the Congress were:

	Minimum	Maximum
Net demand deposits, reserve city banks	10%	22%
Net demand deposits, other banks	7	14
Time deposits	3	10

The Fed was free to specify any set of reserve requirements within these ranges.

[3] Actually, the discount rate changes are established by the district Reserve banks, and reviewed and approved by the Federal Reserve Board. Thus, for short periods of time, the discount rates at district Reserve banks can be somewhat different. Figure 14–1 shows the particular rate at the New York district office.

Figure 14–1
Discount rate and other short-term interest rates

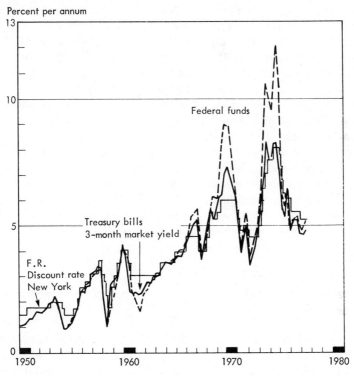

Percent per annum

figure suggests, the changes in the discount rate have tended to be correlated with but to lag open-market interest rates. Most of the discount rates changes, therefore, appear to be explained by the Fed's attempt to keep the cost of borrowing at the discount window in line with the changing costs of other methods of adjusting reserves. Notwithstanding their position as the most publicized and apparently newsworthy action of the Fed, these discount rate changes do not appear to be an aggressive tool of monetary policy. To some extent, the Fed's announcements of changes in the discount rate may be timed to signal changes in monetary policy or to deliver other messages to the financial markets. As such, these announcements may have an important effect on the expectations of financial market participants, and hence on developments in the markets. With this exception, however, the discount rate does not appear to be that important as an active instrument of monetary policy.

The Fed can, however, influence borrowings from the discount window in other ways. Recall that these borrowings are administered as a privilege and not as a right for member banks. The Fed can therefore exert various noninterest rate pressures on banks to curtail their borrowings. These pressures, along with the cost incentive implied by the current discount rate, can often be an important influence on the total borrowed reserves supplied to the banking system through the discount window. Furthermore, credit at the discount window can be made more available to particular financial institutions in difficulty, thus fulfilling the Fed's role as a lender of last resort to the banking system, without jeopardizing the objective of controlling overall bank reserves. The discount window policy can thus be used as a supplement to open-market operations in controlling the reserve position of the banks. In time of financial stress it can serve the needs of particular institutions and thus buttress confidence in the banking system as a whole.

Figure 14–2 is a diagrammatic summary of the tools of monetary policy. Each controls or influences a separate element of the bank reserve position. The required reserve percentages determine the *required reserves* that the banks must hold. The open-market operations can be used to control the *nonborrowed reserves* held by the banks. Discount window policy can be used to influence and in the extreme to control the amounts of banks' *borrowed reserves*.

Figure 14–2

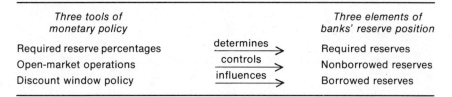

Three tools of monetary policy		Three elements of banks' reserve position
Required reserve percentages	determines →	Required reserves
Open-market operations	controls →	Nonborrowed reserves
Discount window policy	influences →	Borrowed reserves

MANAGING MONETARY POLICY

The ultimate objectives of monetary policy are to foster high levels of employment, economic growth, and price stability. However, these objectives cannot be affected directly by the Federal Reserve. Its primary control mechanism is its ability to alter member bank reserves. Thus the Fed needs to know the channels through which changes in bank reserves affect its ultimate objectives. This is an issue about which there is much dispute. One school of thought emphasizes the importance of interest rates in affecting economic activity. Another school emphasizes the importance of the aggregate amount of credit extended by the banks to the various primary sectors. A third school of thought, the monetarists, chooses instead to emphasize the importance of the quantity of money. These different views of the channel through which monetary policy affects the economy often lead to quite different interpretations of what the Fed *is* and *should be* doing. The Fed's uncertainty over the relative importance of these different channels makes the formulation of a monetary policy a very difficult task.

Interest rates and credit market conditions

The most "traditional perspective" of the channel through which the Federal Reserve can influence the economy emphasizes its effects upon interest rates and conditions throughout the credit markets. In this perspective on monetary policy, interest rates are a key intermediate target of Federal Reserve policy, for its is through interest rates that the Fed affects its ultimate objectives of employment, output, and the price levels. According to this view of the Federal Reserves' effects, interest rate movements are also a measure of the direction of the Fed's policy, lower interest rates signaling ease and higher rates signaling restraint.

According to this view, the Fed's control over interest rates arises from its ability to control the net free reserve position of the commercial banking system. As we have seen, the Fed determines the required reserves of its member banks by setting reserve requirement percentages against deposits, and the Fed controls the nonborrowed reserves of member banks by open-market operations. The difference between these two is called *net free reserves:*

nonborrowed reserves − required reserves = net free reserves.

Net free reserves are a measure of the pressure that the Fed is exerting upon the banking system. When net free reserves are large and positive, the banking system is encouraged to expand. The individual banks with excess reserves attempt to lend these funds in the interbank Fed funds market, driving interest rates down in these markets. They also attempt to purchase securities in the open market to earn a return on their otherwise excess reserves, again driving interest rates down in these securities markets. They may seek to expand their loans by offering less restrictive credit terms to potential borrowers.

Conversely, when the Fed chooses to contract nonborrowed reserves and/or perhaps raise reserve requirements, the net free reserves can become negative, indicating a net deficit reserve position for the banking system as a whole. The individual banks with deficit positions attempt to borrow in the interbank markets and also sell securities, thus driving up interest rates in these markets. In the short run, some banks have to borrow at the discount window of the Fed to reestablish their reserve balance. It is assumed that these banks borrow from the Fed reluctantly, heeding the Fed's counsel that such borrowing should only be a temporary measure. In the longer run, banks also begin to reduce their loans and deposits, in part by demanding more restrictive credit terms and higher interest rates on their loans. The banks directly impact interest rates and financial conditions in the interbank markets, the various securities markets in which they are active, and the market for bank loans. From these markets, the demand for funds and upward pressure on interest rates spread to other short-term markets and eventually throughout the financial system. To be sure, the banks are only one factor in these markets. As we have seen, the financial decisions of households, corporations, and governments are also important determinants of the general supply and demand for credit in these markets. However the banks are the only factor within these markets that the Fed can directly influence and control. The Fed, cognizant of the needs and financial condition of the primary sectors, attempts to control the banks in such a way that the desired conditions in financial markets are obtained.

Figure 14–3 is a schematic diagram of this first view of monetary pol-

Figure 14–3

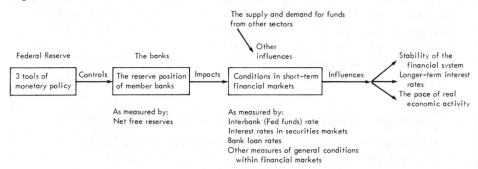

icy. The Fed, through its tools of monetary policy, controls the reserve position of its member banks. The Fed's effect on banks is best discerned by the level of *net free reserves,* a measure of the pressure exerted by the Fed on the banks' reserve position. The banks, in turn, affect interest rates and conditions in the short-term money markets. Some of the better measures of the severity of this impact are the level and stability of the Fed funds rate, the interest rates in the short-term securities market, and rates and conditions within the bank loan market. Finally, the level and movement of rates within these markets affect financial decision making, longer term interest rates, and through them, the pace of real economic activity generally.

The quantities of money and credit

The two other perspectives on monetary policy emphasize the importance of the aggregates of money and credit supplied by the banks. One chooses to emphasize the role of bank assets and accentuates the total amount of credit supplied by the banks. The other chooses to emphasize the role of bank liabilities, particularly demand deposits.

Aggregate bank credit. In this perspective on monetary policy, the growth of bank credit should be a key intermediate target of the Federal Reserve, for it is through its effects on bank credit that the Federal Reserve has its most important effects on spending activity within the primary sectors and, thus, on real economic activity and inflation. According to this view, the growth in bank credit is also an indication of the direction of monetary policy's direction—more rapid rates of growth in bank credit signifying ease and less rapid rates of growth signifying restraint.

The Fed's ability to influence the growth of bank credit arises from its ability to control the reserve position of the banks. As we have seen, the Federal Reserve can influence the level of member banks' borrowed reserves by its discount window policy. Furthermore, the Fed can control *nonborrowed reserves* through its open-market operations. The sum of borrowed reserves and nonborrowed reserves are just the *total reserves* of the member banks:

borrowed reserves + nonborrowed reserves = total reserves.

These *total reserves* can be both continually monitored and controlled by the Fed. Total reserves, whether borrowed or nonborrowed, form the basis from which the banks can expand their assets and liabilities. The total reserves supplied by the Fed are not the only influence on aggregate bank credit, however. Since different reserve requirements apply to different types of liabilities, the volume of bank liabilities that can be supported by a given amount of total reserves depends in part on the mix of different types of liabilities banks issue. This mix depends upon the preferences of the primary sectors for, say, time deposits versus demand deposits, and upon the actions taken by the banks to price these liabilities in ways which make them more or less attractive to the public. Thus the level of total reserves, the legal reserve requirements, and these preferences and pricing policies determine the total size of bank liabilities, the total size of bank assets, and, therefore, the aggregate amount of bank credit.

The quantity of bank credit is measured in a number of ways. On the one hand, the amounts of specific types of bank credit, for example, business loans, home mortgages, consumer credit, can be measured. On the other hand, the aggregate amounts of total bank credit can be measured, regardless of their mix, in order to monitor the total influence of the banks on the primary sectors. One such measure is the *credit proxy*. It measures the aggregate member bank deposits subject to reserve requirements. Because nondeposit sources of funds have been widely used by banks in recent years to supplement their deposits, this credit proxy has also been expanded to the *credit proxy adjusted,* which includes not only the member bank deposits, but bank-related commercial paper,

Eurodollar borrowings of U.S. banks, and certain other nondeposit sources as well. The *credit proxy adjusted,* while it actually measures bank liabilities, is used as a proxy for the measurement of total bank credit because of the necessary equality between banks' assets and liabilities.[4]

Figure 14–4 summarizes the monetary policy perspective based upon

Figure 14–4

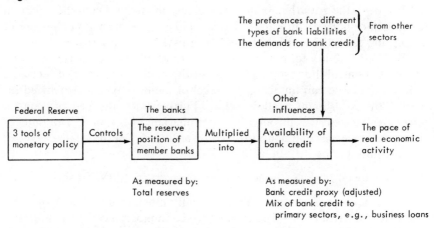

aggregate bank credit. The Fed, through its monetary policy tools, controls the reserve position of banks, as measured by the *total reserves* of member banks.[5] The banks, given the preferences of other sectors for bank liabilities, then expand these reserves into the total amount of bank liabilities. These additional liabilities support an equal increase in bank assets and thus add to the bank credit available to other sectors. The ways in which banks expand their reserves into available credit are best measured by the quantities of credit supplied to specific sectors and/or by the overall quantity of credit as measured by the *credit proxy (adjusted).*

The aggregate quantities of money. The third perspective on monetary policy, often called the "monetarist view," argues that the money supply should be the focus of the monetary authorities' attention. According to this view, the long-run rate of growth of *real* economic activity is deter-

---

[4] Also, the estimates of the credit proxy (adjusted) are available on a more prompt basis, and thus they provide a better means for short-term control than the direct measures of bank credit which are available only after a time lag.

[5] Actually, a variant of total reserves, reserves available to support private nonbank deposits (RPDs), is often used. The measure RPDs adjusts total reserves for the reserves required to back government and interbank deposits, on the grounds that these latter deposits and reserves are very volatile and that their movements do not exert any major effect on the economy. Their exclusion provides a measure of the reserve base with movements more indicative of the effect of reserve policy on the private economy.

mined by factors other than the rate of growth in the money supply (factors such as productivity and tax rates). The long-run growth in the money supply has its major effect on the economy through its effect on the rate of inflation. Higher average rates of growth in the money supply lead inevitably to higher average rates of inflation. Slower average rates of growth in the money supply give rise to (and are essential for) slower average rates of inflation. The monetarists do agree that, in the short run, changes in the rate of growth of the money supply can have some effect on the pace of real economic activity. However, they argue that the connection between short-run changes in the rate of growth of the money supply and changes in the growth rate of real economic activity are very variable and known imprecisely. The relationship is so poorly understood, say the monetarists, that little or no attempt should be made to use changes in the growth rate of the money supply to affect short-run changes in the growth rate of real economic activity. The monetarist perspective on monetary policy argues that the key intermediate target for monetary policy should be the rate of growth of the money supply and that the Federal Reserve should manage the growth in bank reserves so as to bring about a rather steady rate of growth in the money supply.

The monetarist prescription for monetary policy needs a definition for the term "money" to become operational. "Money" refers to the collection of all financial assets which can be readily and conveniently used as a medium of exchange. Currency in circulation is clearly money. The demand deposits of commercial banks are also money for they are generally accepted throughout our economy as a medium of exchange. After this, though, the definition of money becomes more elusive. There are a variety of financial assets which are relatively liquid and easily convertible into demand deposits and/or currency. While these assets are generally not used directly as a medium of exchange, they may be close enough to "money" to have a similar impact upon spending decisions. Hence, they are sometimes referred to as "near-monies." Three different formal definitions of money, called M_1, M_2, and M_3 have been used by monetary analysts. They are defined as:

M_1 = currency in circulation, plus private demand deposits (adjusted)[6].

M_2 = M_1 plus commercial bank time and savings deposits (excluding large negotiable CDs).

M_3 = M_2 plus deposits at mutual savings banks and savings and loan associations.

Of these three, M_1, the narrowly defined money supply, is the most commonly used definition of money. M_2 is also used frequently, in part be-

---

[6] Private demand deposits (adjusted) exclude government deposits, interbank deposits, and items in process of collection.

cause of its close correlation with various measures of economic activity. M_3 is the least often used, though it is reported and referred to from time to time by monetary analysts. In addition, the Federal Reserve and others have constructed other broader measures of money, each one of which has its particular advantages and disadvantages. Few of these are often used in general discussion of monetary policy, however, so that we shall restrict our attention to the more common definitions of money. In particular, our discussion of the Fed and the money supply will be developed in terms of M_1, though a comparable discussion would also apply to money as defined by M_2.

Just as the Fed directly controls only one of several influences on interest rates and the availability of credit, so the Fed controls only one of several influences on the supply of money. The Fed directly controls the reserve position of the banks through its control over their *total reserves*. The banks use a part of these reserves to support demand deposits, one of the components of M_1. But M_1 also includes currency in circulation, and this currency in circulation is not dependent upon bank reserves. In order to develop a more complete measure of the direct effects of the Fed, analysts have constructed a variable called the *monetary base*, which is the sum of total reserves and currency in circulation. The monetary base can be directly controlled by the Fed by observing the quantities of currency in circulation and adjusting banks' total reserves appropriately.

The Fed's control of the *monetary base* is only one of several influences on the money supply, however. Because of the changing public preferences for currency, demand deposits, time deposits, and other financial assets, a given size monetary base may be multiplied into a money supply of varying size. In more formal terms, we can define the relationship between the M_1 and the monetary base, B, to be:

$$M_1 = (\text{Multiplier}) \times (B)$$

Money supply   Monetary
base

While the Fed controls the monetary base, the *multiplier* is subject to a variety of influences, most of them beyond the control of the Fed. The Fed's job is to monitor the multiplier, its trend, and its probable fluctuations and control the monetary base in such a way that the desired rate of growth in the money supply is obtained.[7]

Figure 14–5 is a schematic summary of this final perspective on monetary policy. Through its control over the reserve position of member banks, the Fed controls the growth of the *monetary base*. Subject to the public's demand for currency, demand deposits, and time deposits, the monetary base is multiplied into the money supply.

---

[7] This is analogous to the link between total reserves and total bank credit.

Figure 14–5

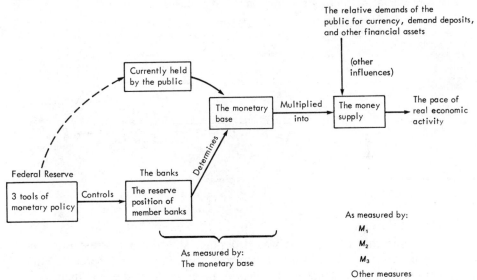

The three different perspectives of monetary policy presented here are essentially competing theories of the effects that the Fed has on economic activity. Each perspective begins with the assumption that the Fed, through its three tools of monetary policy, can control the reserve position of the banks. Each perspective assumes that one of the goals of the Fed is to impact aggregate economic activity, but there the similarities between these perspectives end. Each perspective has a different image of the process through which the banks impact the economy. Therefore each perspective emphasizes a different measure of the impact of the banks on the economy. The differences between these three perspectives are summarized in Figure 14–6.

Divergent movements in the indicators and the problems these pose

Because there are three different ways to interpret the direction of Federal Reserve policy (the direction of movements in interest rates, the rate of growth of money, or the rate of growth of bank credit), divergences among these three indicators can generate considerable difficulty both for the Federal Reserve and its observers. Unfortunately, at most critical junctures for monetary policy determination, the different indicators have moved in different directions.

For example, between the end of February and the beginning of July in 1974, as the economy was experiencing very rapid rates of inflation at the

Figure 14–6
A summary of three different perspectives on monetary policy

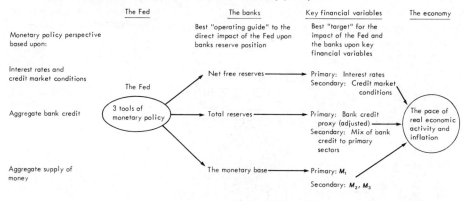

same time that real output was dropping, short-term interest rates as measured by the federal funds rate rose from 9.0 to 13.5 percent. Furthermore, member bank borrowings of reserves from the Fed increased from a level of just over $1 billion to over $3 billion, and free reserves declined from a negative $1 billion to a negative $3.2 billion. All these indicators seemed to suggest that the Fed was pursuing a relatively "tight" or "restrictive" monetary policy. On the other hand, over this same four-month period, the money supply grew at an annual rate of 8.5 percent. This was slightly larger than its 6.7 percent rate of growth in the previous 3 months and even further above its 5.8 percent rate of growth over the previous 12 months. Looked at by themselves, these developments in the money supply suggest a monetary policy of relative "ease." Moreover, during the four-month period, the bank credit proxy grew at an extraordinary annual rate of 20 percent. This compared with an 11 percent rate over the previous year. Whatever the signal from the movements in interest rates and member bank borrowings, these latter two indicators of Fed policy, the aggregates of money and credit, pointed towards moderate or perhaps even excessive ease.

As the year 1974 progressed and the depth of the recession became clear, the situation was reversed. Between early July of 1974 and early March of 1975, the federal funds rate fell from 13.5 percent to 5.5 percent. Member bank borrowings fell about $3 billion, and free reserves rose from a negative $3 billion to a positive $0.1 billion. To some, these movements suggested a considerable easing in monetary policy. Over the same period, however, the growth in the money supply fell to 2.5 percent. This represented a sharp reduction from its earlier pace of over 8 percent. The growth in bank credit as measured by the bank credit proxy dropped from its 20-percent range to between 5 percent and 6 percent. These sharply reduced growth rates for the aggregates suggested that monetary policy had become much more restrictive. As had been the case in early 1974, the different indicators implied quite different monetary policies. These disparate movements created considerable uncertainty over the exact role which monetary policy was playing.

These short-run divergences in the movements of interest rates and the aggregates arise from several factors. First, there are lags between the time the Fed takes its actions and the time they have their effect. Second, there are a myriad of technical factors which affect the money supply in the short run and introduce some volatility into its behavior. Most importantly, however, the divergences in the movements of interest rates and the aggregates arise from the constantly changing demands for money and credit within the private sector.

For example, the fluctuations in nominal GNP have an important impact upon the public's demands for money and credit. There are times, for example, in the expansionary phases of an economic cycle, when the growth in GNP leads to an upward shift in the demand for money (at the prevailing level of interest rates). In the face of this increased demand, the Fed can maintain stable interest rates only if it allows a more rapid increase in the growth of reserves, money, and bank credit. On the other hand, the Fed can attempt to maintain a slower and more orderly growth in these aggregates but only by accepting whatever upward movements in short-term rates this policy might imply. Unfortunately, it is not clear which of the indicators of Fed policy is the more correct or relevant measure of its effect upon economic activity. This uncertainty surrounding the exact importance of interest rates, money, and bank credit leaves most members of the Fed with a difficult choice.

The problem of choosing among the different indicators of Federal Reserve policy arises in recessions as well. As GNP begins to decline in the early phases of a recession, the net demand for money and bank credit falls (at the prevailing rates of interest). To stabilize money growth in the face of this shift in demand, the Fed would have to significantly increase the rate of growth of reserves. These actions would combine with the forces of the recession and drive interest rates down faster and further. This sharp decline in rates (which would be associated with a policy of stabilizing the rates of growth of the aggregates) might well be considered too extreme, either because it signaled too sharp a change in the direction of monetary policy (measured by the movement in interest rates) and/or because it could be inconsistent with an objective of maintaining orderly movements in financial markets. The alternative, of course, is to strive for more modest or controlled downward movements in interest rates, which could be accomplished by a sharply slower growth in reserves. Such a deceleration in the growth of reserves would imply a deceleration in the growth of the aggregates; and to those who measure the Fed's impact on the economy by its impact on the growth rate of the aggregates, such a policy would be restrictive at just the time the economy needed a stimulus.

Thus, given the interconnections between interest rates, the demand for money and bank credit, and changes in the level of GNP, the Fed has the option of managing reserves in a way to stabilize or control the movements in interest rates *or* the growth of the aggregates. It cannot independently control both. If it chooses to center its attention on managing interest rates, it must accept the consequences of this policy for the growth in the aggregates and vice versa.

Those who argue that the critical indicator of Fed policy is interest rate movements urge the Fed to control interest rates and to accept without much concern the associated movements in the aggregates. Those who see the Fed's policy as arising from its influence on the aggregates argue just the opposite. This is the fundamental dilemma when formulating monetary policy.

On this issue, the monetarists argue there is no alternative but to pursue a policy which attempts to stabilize the growth rate of money. The monetarists argue that any attempt to limit an increase in nominal interest rates by allowing bank reserves to grow somewhat more rapidly will not only fail, but will, in fact, have the opposite result. They argue that investors will interpret the rise in the growth rate of bank reserves as a precursor to an acceleration in the growth rate of the money supply and a subsequent rise in the rate of inflation. Anticipating an increase in the rate of inflation, investors will drive up the nominal level of interest rates until the nominal rate of return on financial assets is commensurate with the expected real rate of returns from real assets plus the (new, higher) expected rate of inflation. According to the monetarists, *lower* nominal rates of interest require lower rates of growth in money and not higher. Using the terminology of Chapter 8 the monetarists argue that the inflationary expectations (which arise from an acceleration in the rate of growth of bank reserves) have a larger effect in raising nominal interest rates than the increased supply of loanable funds has in lowering interest rates.

FORMULATION AND IMPLEMENTATION OF MONETARY POLICY

As we have seen, the most important of the Fed's monetary tools is its open-market operations. The Federal Open Market Committee (FOMC), the body which formulates open market policy, is thus the most important single forum within the Federal Reserve System. Indeed, while the other two tools are formally decided upon by other organizational units, in practice the policy for all three tools are coordinated within the FOMC.[8]

The FOMC meets at four-week intervals, or more often, to discuss and formulate monetary policy. The results of these meetings are published and distributed to the public, though with a considerable time lag. At the FOMC meetings, the first order of business is to review the financial and economic developments since the last meeting, paying particular attention to any divergences of economic activity or monetary policy from the course projected at the previous meeting. An important element of the discussions which follow concerns the appropriate objectives of current monetary policy. The Fed would generally like to guide monetary policy to foster growth in real output and incomes, with particular attention paid to various measures of unemployment. On the other hand, the Fed has also come to accept stable price levels as an important objective. In addition, the stability and health of financial institutions is an important intermediate objective, and the pace of economic activity in special sectors, such as housing, is often of considerable importance. The Fed may choose to try to maintain stability in financial markets and interest rates in order to assist the Treasury as it finances a large deficit. Finally, the various aspects of international economic activity, including balance of trade and payments, can be further considerations in monetary policy. While the FOMC would like to be responsive to all these needs and objectives, it is clear that the objectives can be conflicting. Indeed, the essence of the monetary policy dilemma is that these needs not only *can be,* but usually *are,* conflicting. The FOMC must thus carefully consider the current economic climate, its likely future development, and the pace at which the economic and financial system is likely to progress toward its multifaceted goals. Needless to say, different individuals may perceive a different relative importance for the hierarchy of monetary policy goals at any particular time, and different individuals might, therefore, prescribe very different directions for monetary policy based upon these objectives.

Even if all the members of the FOMC were agreed upon the relative importance of current objectives and the general directions for monetary policy, there is still considerable room for disagreement upon the appropriate *directive* to be formulated at the meeting. The FOMC merely formulates monetary policy; it does not implement that policy. Thus the FOMC must compile a reasonably explicit set of instructions, including appropriate "operating guidelines" and "targets" to the groups that implement that policy. As we have seen, there is relatively little agreement about the

---

[8] Formally, the District Reserve banks propose discount rate changes within their district, subject to the approval of the Federal Reserve Board. The Federal Reserve Board itself decides upon reserve requirement percentages.

linkages between banks' reserve positions (the quantities actually controlled by the Fed) and the pace of economic activity. Very different schools of thought emphasize different mechanisms for this linkage and thus prescribe very different methods for guiding monetary policy. Three individuals, all in basic agreement about the Fed's objectives and the broad directions of appropriate policy, could choose to present very different *targets* in the directives: the first emphasizing the need to control *net free reserves* and *interest rates* in pursuance of a certain policy, the second emphasizing the need to control banks' *total reserves* and aggregate *bank credit* in pursuance of the same policy, and the third emphasizing the need to control the *monetary base* and the *money supply,* again in pursuance of the very same policy. Clearly, the *operating guidelines* and/or the *targets* which the FOMC chooses to specify may be as important as the broad directions of monetary policy itself, and there is at least as much room for disagreement upon appropriate guidelines and targets for a monetary policy as there is upon the objectives and broad directions of that policy.

The open-market operations of the Fed are implemented by the manager of the System Open Market Account (SOMA). The SOMA, located with the Federal Reserve Bank of New York, actually buys and sells the securities which affect bank reserves. On the one hand, the SOMA endeavors to complete these transactions in a way that stabilizes the financial markets, the so-called defensive operations of the Fed. On the other hand, the manager of the SOMA also attempts to steadily move the financial system in conformance with the guidelines and toward the targets specified by the directive of the FOMC.

Evolution of the Federal Reserve's monetary policy

Throughout its history, the Federal Reserve's monetary policy has undergone constant change. The tools, objectives, theories, guidelines, and targets of monetary policy have all changed considerably. Indeed, the most important tool of monetary policy, open-market operations, was never deliberately planned and structured by the legislation which established the Federal Reserve. In some eras, the Fed has concentrated on one set of objectives, for example, financing the federal deficit at low interest rates, and in other times, it has focused on very different objectives, for example, fostering economic recovery. Most of the history of the Fed's evolution is beyond the scope of this book.[9] Suffice it to say that the Fed has developed and changed over the years in response to changing economic priorities and in response to an increasing understanding of the Fed's role and powers within our financial system.

---

[9] See, for example, M. Friedman and A. Schwartz, *A Monetary History of the United States* (National Bureau of Economic Research, Princeton University Press, 1963).

More germane to our immediate concern is the recent evolution of the Fed's interest in monetary targets. Throughout the 1950s and 1960s, the dominant image of the linkages between the Fed's monetary tools and real economic activity emphasized the importance of interest rates and money-market conditions. While the Fed itself rarely articulated these linkages in precise terms, it is clear that what we have called the "traditional perspective" held sway within the Fed itself. The Fed chose to focus on net free reserves as an indicator of the effects of monetary policy on the banks and on the level and direction of interest rates as a measure of the effects this policy had on the financial system. This policy perspective meant that the Fed would choose a rather narrow band within which it thought it would be appropriate to maintain short-term interest rates. The FOMC would instruct the manager of SOMA to manage bank reserve positions to maintain short-term interest rates within this range. The policy directive would remain in force until the FOMC felt that economic conditions had changed enough to warrant a change in the desired band within which short-term interest rates should fluctuate. As a result of this policy, some stability or inflexibility was introduced into the movements in short-term interest rates. Many market participants felt that a major element in any near-term forecast of the movements in short-term interest rates was a forecast of the Fed's view as to the appropriate trading range for short-term rates. According to this view, short-term rates would experience a major change only if the Fed found it necessary to cause or allow such a change. Forecasting short-term rates meant forecasting the Fed, and forecasting the Fed meant forecasting short-term rates.

In the 1960s, however, a formidable challenge to this traditional perspective of monetary policy arose from what we have described as the "monetarist school" of thought. This school accentuated the importance of the money supply in economic activity and argued that the Fed's concentration on interest rates had led it to follow quite inappropriate, in fact perverse, policies. Faced with this challenge, the Federal Reserve Board has attempted to discuss and formulate its procedures in light of the new and competing perspectives on monetary policy.[10] In addition, the U.S. Congress, the body to which the Federal Reserve is responsible, chose to interject itself more directly into the formulation of monetary policy than it had done before. In March 1975, Congress passed a resolution stating the "sense of Congress" that the Federal Reserve should "maintain long-run growth of monetary and credit aggregates commensurate with the economy's long-run potential to increase production. . . ."

---

[10] For example, a Committee on the Directive (a subcommittee of the FOMC) was formed in 1968 to examine and propose appropriate changes in the process of formulating monetary policy. See Sherman J. Maisel, *Managing the Dollar* (New York: Norton & Co., 1973).

The result of these discussions has led to a continued shift toward considering aggregates of money, credit, and reserves in what is often called an "eclectic approach" to monetary policy. Because the Fed now believes it does not completely understand the linkages between banks' reserve positions and economic activity, it chooses to establish a relatively broad range of guidelines and targets rather than focus attention on only one indicator. As a typical example, in a recent meeting, the FOMC: "concluded that growth in M_1 and M_2 over the January–February period at annual rates within ranges of tolerance of 3½ to 6½ percent and 7 to 10 percent, respectively, would be consistent with its longer run objectives for the *monetary aggregates.*"

Further "the members agreed that such growth rates would be likely to involve growth in [RPDs, a variant of *total reserves*] within a range of tolerance of 6¼ to 9¼ percent."

Still further "they also agreed that . . . the weekly average *federal funds rate* might be expected to vary in an orderly fashion within a range of 6½ to 7¼ percent, if necessary in the course of operations."

Thus, the FOMC chose to specify ranges of tolerance on a number of different financial variables, including aggregates of *money,* a measure of *total reserves,* and the *federal funds* rate itself. Presumably, the growth in the aggregates of money was the longer run goal, the growth in total reserves was more of an intermediate target, and the constraints on the federal funds rate were a way of avoiding undesirable instability in the money markets. In addition, since 1975, the Fed has been publicly announcing its growth targets for the monetary aggregates for the next year and updating these targets each calendar quarter. The Fed has thus been "going on the record" with its targets. Even though these are really moving targets, since they are updated quarterly, they are a standard against which the Fed's subsequent control of monetary growth can be measured. If the public's demand for money is so strong that short-term interest rates approach their upper bounds, the SOMA either has to increase total reserves faster than planned or allow interest rates to exceed their targets. If the growth rate of the money supply or of the reserve base approach their upper bounds, the SOMA might have to reduce their levels even though the open-market sales this would require might drive interest rates upward.

This evolution in the Fed's approach to the formulation of monetary policy has meant that the Fed has had to put less emphasis on attempts to maintain short-term rates within a desired trading range. Market participants can no longer always count on the Fed to attempt to stabilize rates and credit market conditions, as they did earlier. Forecasting the Fed now requires a forecast of its objectives for the growth of the aggregates as well as its concern for the level of interest rates. Frequently the Fed's attempts to control the growth of the aggregates can amplify rather than attenuate the swings in short-term interest rates arising in the private sector (or from abroad).

Furthermore, because the Fed now publicly announces its long-run growth rates for the monetary aggregates (M_1 and M_2), the private money markets themselves may tend to initiate interest rate swings. For example, suppose that the Fed has announced an M_1 growth target of between 7 percent to 10 percent for the next year, limits that are illustrated in the accompanying graph. Suppose, that because of the public's demand for

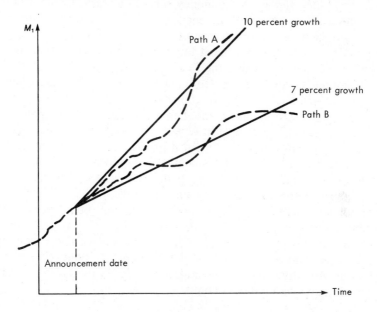

money, M_1 increases along a trajectory shown as Path A, which exceeds the publicly announced 10 percent upper growth limit. Private fixed-income investors will now surely expect the Fed to absorb reserves, steering future M_1 growth back into the target range but driving up interest rates in the process. In expectation of this Fed action, investors will tend to sell fixed-income securities, driving up their interest rates. Conversely, if the trajectory for M_1 proceeds below the lower limit (as in Path B), investors will tend to buy securities in anticipation of the Fed's actions, thus driving down interest rates. As long as the Fed publicly announces its targets, investors will attempt to anticipate the Fed's actions with respect to these targets, thus attempting to end-play the monetary authorities (who are driven by their own nonprofit-maximizing objectives in the money markets). This very process will be an important short-term determinant of the direction of interest rates as private investors compete to see who can outguess the Fed first. The end results of this process are several. First, the Fed, through its public announcements, can influence the market's expectations for future money supply growth and thus future inflation and economic activity. What the Fed "says" in its announcements becomes very important, as well as what it "does." Second, the Fed through its announcements tends to undermine its own independent ability to influence interest rates irrespective of the growth rates of the monetary aggregates. As the money supply approaches its upper limit, interest rates will tend to rise. The Fed can attempt to counteract this rise by open-market operations, but this would, in the long run, further increase the money supply. If the money supply increases further, interest rates will have a still further tendency to rise. The Fed may thus find it extremely difficult to control interest rates if private money market participants believe instead that it must target the money supply within predetermined ranges. Ironically, the Fed's only real alternative, if it wants to control interest rates independently, is to create considerable doubt as to whether it will really pursue its monetary aggregate targets.

The process of formulating and implementing monetary policy has undergone considerable change in recent years. The emergence of rapid rates of inflation has dramatized the distinction between real and nominal rates of interest as well as the connection between the long-run rates of growth in money and credit and the rate of inflation. As a result, the Fed's operating procedures have changed substantially. As the economic situation continues to change, the objectives of monetary policy are likely to continue to change. Furthermore, the process by which the Fed selects targets or intermediate objectives as it tries to achieve these objectives could change. The process of formulating monetary policy is still very much in its formative stages, and experimentation with new perspectives and new targets will doubtless continue.

QUESTIONS

1. In what ways is the balance sheet of the Federal Reserve System like that of a commercial bank? In what ways is it different?
2. Suppose the Federal Reserve bought a new computer and paid for it with a check drawn on itself. What would be the effects of this action on bank reserves, bank assets and liabilities, and on interest rates. Why does the Fed usually choose to buy (or sell) U.S. Treasury securities (rather than computers or other things) when it wishes to affect bank reserves?
3. Why do the monetarists think that attempts to limit a rise in interest rates by expanding bank reserves is doomed to failure? Or how can the monetarists believe that an "easy money" policy will lead to rising interest rates?
4. How has the Fed's conduct of monetary policy evolved in recent years?
5. Sherman Maisel, a former governor of the Federal Reserve System, has written that an important factor affecting the Fed's choice of monetary policy actions is

the belief on the part of some of the governors that "The Fed knows it knows not." What might he mean by that statement? How would such a belief affect the formulation of monetary policy?

REFERENCES

Blinder, Alan S. and Goldfeld, Stephen M. "New Measures of Fiscal and Monetary Policy, 1958–73," *The American Economic Review,* vol. 66, no. 5 (December 1976), pp. 780–96.

Fisher, Stanley. "Long-Term Contracts, Rational Expectations, and the Optimal Money Supply Rule," *Journal of Political Economy,* vol. 85, no. 1 (1977), pp. 191–206.

Mayer, Thomas. "The Structure and Operations of the Federal Reserve System: Some Needed Reforms." In *Financial Institutions and the Nation's Economy,* Compendium of Papers prepared for the FINE Study, Committee on Banking, Currency and Housing House of Representatives, 94th Cong., 2d sess., b. 2, p. 3, pp. 669–726.

Modigliani, Franco. "The Monetarist Controversy or Should We Forsake Stabilization Policies?" *The American Economic Review,* vol. 67, no. 2 (March 1977), pp. 1–19.

Poole, William. "Interpreting the Fed's Monetary Targets," *Brookings Papers on Economic Activity,* vol. 1 (1976), pp. 257–59.

Controlling Monetary Aggregates II: The Implementation. Conference Series No. 9, Federal Reserve Bank of Boston, 1972.

part **V**

The Principal Financial Markets

15

The market for short-term corporate debt

Business corporations' active demands for funds are a central feature of the supply and demand for funds throughout the financial system.[1] Corporate financial markets are an important set of interrelated markets, not only because they supply the necessary funds to the business sector, but also because behavior in these markets significantly affects all the other financial markets as well.

While corporations attract funds from a number of financial markets, short-term debt has played a particularly important role among their sources of external funds. The major forms of corporate short-term debt are summarized in Table 15–1.

Table 15–1
Short-term debt financing of nonfinancial business corporations
(Billions of $)

Form	Approximate outstandings as of 12/31/77
Loans from commercial banks (short-term)	$112
Loans from finance companies	45
Commercial paper	13

Bank loans are by far the largest source of short-term business debt. Finance companies are also an important source of supplementary lending, generally for smaller companies' working capital requirements. In addition, the largest corporations also use commercial paper, short-term unsecured promissory notes sold in the open market, to fund some of their short-term needs.[2]

Because bank loans are the dominant source of corporate short-term finance, their cost and availability play a pivotal role in corporate short-term markets. Unlike most external funds that are raised by the sale of securities (which may later trade in secondary markets), bank loans are negotiated privately between a corporation and its bankers. While the terms of each bank loan are tailored to the particular needs of a business, these terms have certain common characteristics. In particular, most bank loans are "priced" by setting their interest rates at some spread above the bank's *prime rate*, the interest rate reserved for the bank's most creditworthy borrowers. The prime rate itself tends to be an industrywide

---

[1] As usual, "business corporations" should be interpreted, more specifically, to mean nonfinancial business corporations. This category excludes firms that are essentially financial intermediaries, for example, banks and insurance companies.

[2] Augmenting these three important sources are a number of more specialized forms of short-term credit, notably: bankers acceptances, certain U.S. government loans, taxes payable, and for many individual firms, trade credit. From a macrofinancial perspective, however, each of these more specialized sources is less important than the three primary sources listed in Table 15–1, and they will not be analyzed here.

rate, with most banks quoting the same prime at any given time. Actually, the total costs of bank borrowing are more complex and vary according to several provisions of a loan agreement, particularly the compensating deposit balances that businesses are implicitly required to hold with the bank. Nonetheless, the prime rate is a readily observable proxy for the cost of short-term funds to most business borrowers.

In Figure 15–1, the recent history of the prime rate is compared to the

Figure 15–1
Short-term interest rates (Prime rate, and commercial paper rate)

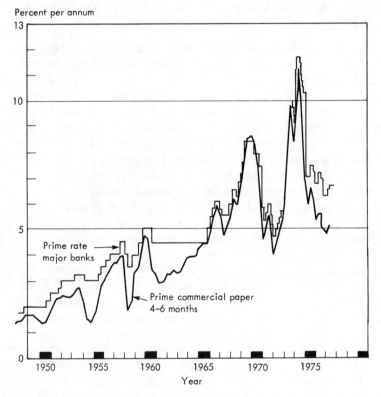

open-market commercial paper rate (the short-term interest rate that the most creditworthy borrowers pay in the open markets). The prime rate is, of course, not really a "market rate" because it is administered by the banks. Certain changes in the way banks have administered this rate are evident in Figure 15–1. In the earliest period, the prime rate appears to have been relatively unresponsive, or sticky, relative to open-market interest rates. The prime rate changed relatively infrequently. When it did change, it sometimes moved in relatively large increments. Furthermore, in times of lower interest rates, it did not fully reflect the decline in open-market rates.

More recently, however, the prime rate appears to have become much more responsive to open-market rates. Indeed, several large money-center banks have explicitly tied their quoted prime rate to open-market rates, specifically to the commercial paper rate.[3] Thus the cost of business loans has become more closely related to the market-determined costs of other short-term credit in the financial system.

SUPPLY AND DEMAND IN THE SHORT-TERM CORPORATE DEBT MARKET

The net new flows of short-term debt to business corporations are shown in Figure 15–2 and compared to the total new funds raised by these firms. The flows of new short-term debt are an important component of total new external funds, and their variability appears to account for most of the variability in total funds. Short-term debt is generally used by corporations to fund working capital needs, such as inventories. Indeed, the time patterns of new short-term debt appear to be closely related to the patterns of inventory accumulation. In addition, of course, short-term debt is used to fund other financial needs. Typically the new flows of short-term debt have tended to rise throughout the early and middle phases of each credit cycle, leading the expansion of other forms of business credit.

Figures 15–1 and 15–2 show that the recent increases in short-term business credit have coincided with increases in short-term interest rates. At the peak of short-term interest rates in 1966, and again in 1969, the new flows of business credit were constrained as the Federal Reserve was attempting to restrict the growth of money and credit. With the exception of these peaks, however, there has been a remarkable correspondence to the recent flows of short-term business debt and the time trace of short-term interest rates. In effect, businesses have been borrowing most when short-term interest rates were relatively high and borrowing least when rates were relatively low. To some extent, this may be caused by common underlying factors, in particular the pace of inflation (which increases interest rates and business financing needs). To some extent, it may also be caused by the direct impact of businesses' increased demands for funds upon interest rates in financial markets. Whatever the precise causal linkages, however, the flows of short-term business credit seem to be largely undeterred by the higher cost of short-term debt. This suggests

---

[3] See "The Prime Rate," *Business Conditions,* The Federal Reserve Bank of Chicago (April 1975).

Figure 15–2
External financing of nonfinancial corporations (Seasonally adjusted, smoothed annual rates as a percent of GNP)

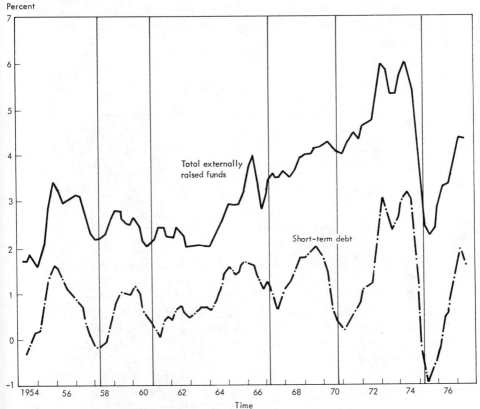

that the business demand for short-term credit is not particularly sensitive to the level of short-term interest rates.

LARGE COMMERCIAL BANKS AS SUPPLIERS OF SHORT-TERM CREDIT

While many commercial banks meet the demands of businesses in their local markets, a substantial fraction of the total short-term business credit flows through a limited number of large commercial banks.[4] The composi-

---

[4] For example, about 70 percent of all commercial and industrial loans are held by a limited group of only 160 large banks, out of a total of about 15,000 commercial banks in the United States.

tion of assets in a sample of such large banks is shown in Table 15–2. Supplying commercial and industrial loans (mostly loans to nonfinancial businesses) is one of the central functions of large banks. Generally the long-term relationships that have been established between a large bank and its corporate customers represent a major portion of the long-term profitability of the bank.

Table 15–2
Composition of assets in large banks (Loans and investments of large banks in New York City and Chicago as of 6/30/77)

Total loans and investments		100%
Investments		25
Selected loans		75
Commercial and industrial loans	39	
Real estate loans	9	
Loans to individuals	6	
Other loans (primarily to other		
banks and financial institutions)	21	

The large banks provide different types of loan arrangements for corporations which, for classification purposes, can be divided into lines of credit, revolving credit agreements, and term loans. Term loans are multiyear loan agreements and are generally considered to be intermediate-term rather than short-term financing. Both lines of credit and revolving credit agreements, however, are generally classified as short-term credit arrangements.

With a line of credit, the bank assures its customers that (if called upon) it will provide short-term funds up to some specified limit. The interest rate is generally set at some spread over the bank's prime rate and thus floats with the prime rate. The customer is generally required to keep certain compensating deposit balances with the banks as part of the line of credit. While these lines of credit do not appear to be legally binding, banks invariably attempt to stand behind the implied commitments, barring an altogether unforeseen and unmanageable change of circumstances. The lines of credit are, of course, periodically reviewed to make sure that they appropriately serve the interests of both the borrower and the bank.

A revolving credit agreement, on the other hand, is a written contractual agreement to provide short-term funds. It is binding upon the bank. The credit agreement provides the assurance of short-term funds, up to some specified limit, for a specified period of time, at an interest rate generally tied to the time-varying prime rate. The customer is often charged a commitment fee for this credit agreement in addition to the compensating deposit balances which are generally required by the agreement.

These lines of credit and revolving credit agreements are, in fact, remarkable agreements between a bank and its customers. The bank is essentially guaranteeing the availability of short-term funds, either implicitly or explicitly, to its customers. Business corporations enter into these agreements to insure that their expected, and for that matter unexpected, short-term needs can be met. The costs of this insurance are the compensating balance requirements and fees that are involved in the arrangements. Such an arrangement presupposes, of course, that the bank will be able to obtain the required funds should it be called upon to uphold a substantial fraction of its commitments. The aggregate availability of short-term business funds is determined, therefore, by the ability of large commercial banks to raise funds.

As Figure 15–2 demonstrated, the large banks have been successful at raising funds for their corporate customers because short-term loans to business have expanded sharply on several occasions in recent years, but the ability of large banks to raise funds has not been without its challenges. In particular, because banks are extensively regulated by the Federal Reserve (and other regulators), their ability to provide funds can be influenced and, in the limit, substantially restricted by a series of regulations. Throughout the 1960s and early 1970s, the sources of funds for large commercial banks continually evolved in response to a rapidly changing environment. This period spawned the growth of "liability management" as a source of large banks' funds, changing regulatory attitudes within the Federal Reserve System, and a series of "credit crunches" during which the needs of liability management within the large banks collided with the objectives of the Federal Reserve. We will trace the evolution of the relationship between large banks and the Federal Reserve and discuss its implications for the ability of business corporations to use the commercial banks as a channel for short-term funds.

The changing role of large banks in the competition for funds

Throughout the 1960s and early 1970s, the short-term financing demands of business grew very rapidly. During this same period, other credit demands within the private sectors were also expanding. The large banks were the focal point for many of these demands. Throughout the period the large banks strove to provide for the short-term financial needs of businesses and others by raising funds in various markets.

Unfortunately, during this same period, the traditional sources of most bank funds, demand deposits, were becoming less and less accessible. As corporations and others developed more sophisticated cash management techniques and interest rates rose, the supply of willing holders of demand deposits shrank compared to the supply of willing holders of interest-bearing assets. In response to these trends, large commercial banks developed new ways to compete for interest-bearing assets. By borrowing federal funds within the interbank markets, large banks were able to tap sources of funds from within the banking system, principally from smaller banks. By developing large negotiable certificates of deposit (CDs), large banks were also able to tap nonbank sources of interest-sensitive funds.[5] Furthermore, a variety of other borrowing channnels were employed by the banks. Table 15–3 shows the cumulative growth in these interest-

Table 15–3
Large negotiable CDs and other sources of funds outstanding at U.S. banks (Billions of $)

	1960	1966	1969	1974	1977
Large negotiable CDs	1.1	15.7	10.9	93.0	77.4
Federal funds purchased	0	0.9	3.8	9.8	26.0
Open-market paper..................	0	0	4.3	8.3	9.2
Liabilities to foreign affiliates	3.8	7.6	18.6	14.2	16.0

Source: *Flow of Funds.*

sensitive liabilities of large banks from 1960 to 1977. While demand deposits and consumer savings deposits had supplied the overwhelming majority of the funds in 1950, several new sources of interest-sensitive funds have become important since 1960. The largest single source of funds during this period was negotiable CDs. Because negotiable CDs have become so important to large banks and because they can be directly affected by Federal Reserve policy, this section will focus upon their role as a source of funds.

Negotiable CDs within the money markets

A substantial fraction of the negotiable CDs "sold" by large commercial banks are acquired by their normal customers, that is, the businesses (and other institutions) with whom they have maintained a long-term banking relationships. Thus a substantial part of the CD liabilities of the banks represents a continuing deposit relationship with their customers. In prior years, these deposits would have taken the form of demand deposits for which customers would have been compensated with various services, but because of the very large foregone income inherent in demand deposits when interest rates are high, these deposits have more and

---

[5] Large CDs are offered in denominations greater than $100,000, generally have a initial maturity between one month and one year, and can be traded in the secondary markets—hence the term "negotiable CDs."

more taken the form of interest-bearing CDs. The banks in turn have charged a fee for those services they used to provide in exchange for the demand deposits. Thus to some extent, the growth of the CD market and demise of demand deposits merely reflects a new pricing policy in the services of large banks, with explicit interest rates paid by the banks for deposits and explicit fees paid by the customers for bank services.

The ability of a large bank to expand its CDs in this way is limited, however, to the size of its normal customer base and often to its local region. But loan demand at many large banks has often outstripped the growth of the deposits that can be acquired from their natural customer base. When this has happened, large banks have relied upon the national CD market to raise additional interest-sensitive funds. Within the national CD market, the bank is selling its CDs, either directly or more commonly through dealers, to suppliers of funds with whom it probably does not have a continuing customer relationship. The national CD market is merely one segment of our domestic money markets where various suppliers place their funds in short-term, generally liquid, financial assets.

Within the domestic money markets there are a variety of financial assets available other than negotiable CDs, among them; U.S. Treasury bills, short-term notes of federal agencies, short-term notes of state/local governments (tax-exempts), commercial paper (short-term obligations of corporations), and others. In addition, the money markets of various nations have become effectively linked into a worldwide money market such that various short-term obligations of foreign borrowers also compete for funds in the domestic money markets.

To raise funds in the national money market, a commercial bank must offer CD rates that are fully competitive with not only the CDs of other large banks, but also other financial instruments as well. Even for the CDs sold directly to their long-term customers, large banks must be approximately competitive with open-market rates. Thus the evolution toward negotiable CDs has left large banks with a liability structure whose costs vary with open-market interest rates. The advantage of this evolution is, of course, that a bank can expand its liabilities and thus its assets by offering attractive rates on negotiable CDs. The disadvantage is that if, for some reason, banks will not or cannot offer competitive rates, the suppliers of funds will quickly turn to other more attractive short-term instruments.

The Federal Reserve and the control of bank liabilities

There are two major ways in which the Fed can influence the banks' use of CDs and other classes of time and savings deposits. First, it can alter the reserve requirements applicable to the different classes of deposits in order to influence the cost of these funds to the bank. Second, the

Fed, through its Regulation Q, can control the maximum interest rates that banks offer on various savings and time deposits. Throughout the early 1960s, the Fed used changes in Regulation Q ceilings as its primary tool to influence the banks' use of their money-market liabilities.

Regulation Q and the CD market

Figure 15–3 illustrates the history of Regulation Q limitations on large (greater than $100,000) CDs.[6] Since prime commercial paper is probably the closest competitor to negotiable CDs in the money markets (that is, the most similar financial asset), the open-market rates on prime commercial paper are also shown in Figure 15–3. The relationship between the Regulation Q ceilings and open-market interest rates is the principal determinant of the ability of large banks to compete for funds. In what follows, we will trace through the development of the CD markets by

Figure 15–3
Regulation Q ceilings on large CDs relative to a comparable open-market interest rate

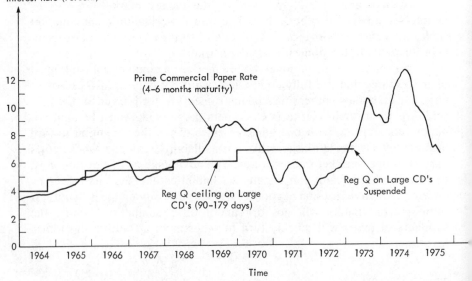

Interest Rate (Percent)

---

[6] Throughout the period, there were some differences between the interest rate ceilings as a function of the maturity of the CDs. Figure 15–3 shows the ceilings for CDs with a maturity of 90–179 days.

referring to the all-important interest rate spreads illustrated in Figure 15–3.

The initial phase of growth: 1961 to 1966. Negotiable CDs were the first developed in 1961 and used by large banks in the early years to secure deposits which otherwise might have been transferred to other interest-bearing assets. In these early years, the Federal Reserve deliberately raised Regulation Q ceilings on large CDs to encourage the growth of time deposits within the banks. The Federal Reserve wished to encourage the growth of bank credit to stimulate the economic expansion in those years, and the growing use of CDs appeared to be an attractive vehicle for financing this expansion. Slowly at first, and then with greater speed, the large banks expanded their use of negotiable CDs to attract additional funds. In the 1964 to early 1966 period, open-market interest rates generally trended upward. At several important junctures, the Federal Reserve Board raised Regulation Q to allow the banks to remain competitive with other short-term instruments (see Figure 15–3). The rapid growth in CDs contributed to a rapid growth in overall bank assets in this period.

Moreover there were important changes in the portfolio strategy of large banks because of the growth in large CDs. In the 1950s, the investment portfolios of large banks were concentrated in short-term and medium-term government securities. These investment portfolios were built up in times of low loan demand and served as a source of liquidity to be drawn down in times of higher loan demand. As CDs grew, however, it became clear that they could be used as a new source of liquidity to increase available funds in times of higher loan demand. Thus large banks came to rely upon their investment portfolios relatively less as a source of liquidity and relatively more as an actively managed source of income. Banks committed a relatively steady flow of new funds to their investment portfolios, altered the mix to include more tax-exempt obligations of state/local governments, and lengthened the average maturity of their portfolios. Essentially, large banks were becoming much more active intermediaries. Instead of just accepting demand deposits, making loans, and using their investment portfolios as liquidity buffers, they were now bidding for interest-sensitive time deposits, making loans, and more aggressively extending the maturity and mix of their investments in search of income. The natural result of these trends was that large banks became much less liquid in the traditional asset-oriented sense. Many observers did not consider this to be a serious problem, however, because large CDs and other borrowed funds had become an important incremental source of liquidity. As long as the Federal Reserve maintained the Regulation Q limits on CDs above open-market interest rates, as they had in the past, banks would be able to successfully bid for funds. Indeed, because of the increased exposure of banks, many observers felt that the Fed now had little choice but to keep the Regulation Q ceilings competitive with open-market rates.

The credit crunch of 1966. Throughout 1965 and early 1966, business loan demand at the large commercial banks intensified, inflation began to increase, and interest rates rose sharply. In the middle of 1966, open-market rates on competitive short-term instruments rose up through Regulation Q ceilings (see Figure 15–3). At that time, Regulation Q ceilings on CDs of $100,000 or more were not raised in line with market rates. This effectively eliminated the ability of the large banks to compete for interest-sensitive funds, and a rapid but short-lived runoff of large CDs soon followed. The large money-center banks were thus caught in a very difficult position. In the face of very high loan demand from their traditional customers, not only were they effectively unable to raise additional funds, but their existing liability base was eroding.

Furthermore, in the midst of this difficulty, the Federal Reserve attempted to directly influence business lending. An unusual letter that the Fed sent to bankers at the time was somewhat less than subtle in this regard: "A slower rate of business-loan expansion is in the interest of the entire banking system and of the economy as a whole. All banks should be aware of this consideration, whether or not they need to borrow from Federal Reserve."

In response to this situation, the large banks sold off large amounts of the investments they had previously accumulated and restricted the extensions of new loans. These actions exacerbated the already tight supply and demand conditions in security markets and the market for business loans. This was the first of the modern credit crunches, that is, the first credit crunch which occurred when large banks were generally dependent upon interest-sensitive funds. The quarterly flow of funds in the banking sector is shown in Table 15–4.

The credit crunch of 1969–1970. Following the credit crunch of 1966, short-term interest rates in the open markets receded below the Regulation Q ceilings (see Figure 15–3). The large banks were thus once again able to compete effectively for short-term funds. Banks responded by

Table 15–4
Increases in large CDs and selected bank assets (Annual rates in billions)

	1st Q 1966	2d Q 1966	3d Q 1966	4th Q 1966	1st Q 1967
Large CDs	4.6	3.6	−5.2	−5.3	14.6
Assets					
Loans to business	11.7	16.2	10.6	3.8	9.3
Investments	−3.0	8.6	−5.3	−3.6	29.5
U.S. government	−6.5	4.5	−8.6	−1.9	19.9
Municipals	3.5	4.1	3.3	−1.7	9.6

continuing to increase their reliance upon CDs. In early 1968, interest rates began to rise again, threatening the Regulation Q–controlled CD market. But the Federal Reserve raised the ceiling, thus continuing the ability of banks to bid for funds. By 1969, however, the expanding demands of the corporate and other sectors had driven short-term interest rates up to record levels. As part of the effort to slow the pace of economic activity, the Fed refused to raise the Regulation Q ceilings. The large banks were then unable to maintain competitive rates on their CDs, resulting in a potential credit crunch in the banking system which was much more severe than the experience of 1966. Figure 15–4 illustrates the magnitude of the change in CD volume within the banking system as maturing CDs were not renewed by depositors.

Figure 15–4
Growth in the outstanding stock of large Certificates of Deposit (1961–1977)

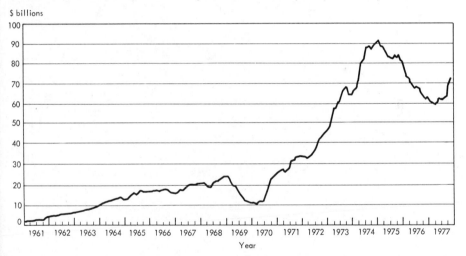

Source: Board of Governors of the Federal Reserve System.

This time, however, the large banks were better prepared for the effects of the credit crunch. Despite their inability to maintain CD balances, many large banks were able to effectively bid for interest-sensitive funds through other channels. For the first time, many large banks borrowed enormous sums from their overseas branches (located largely in London) because these branches were able to effectively bid for funds in the unregulated external or Eurodollar markets. In addition, the parent holding companies of these banks were able to bid for funds in the domestic commercial paper market. By selling loans to their holding companies, banks were able to relieve the pressure of the contracting CD market. Through these two innovative sources of funds, Eurodollar borrowings and bank holding company commercial paper, the large banks were able to at least partially compensate for the loss of CDs. Figures 15–5 and 15–6 display the rising importance of these new sources of funds in the 1969–1970 period.

Figure 15–5
Outstanding liabilities of U.S. banks to their overseas branches

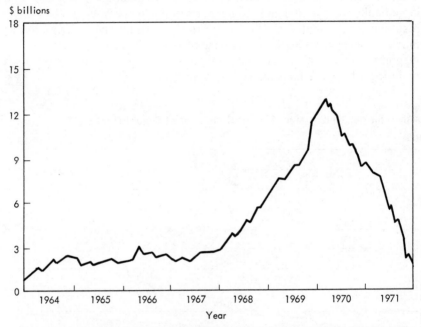

$ billions

Source: "A Macro-Economic Analysis of the Short-Term Commercial Bank Adjustment Process," Federal Reserve Bank of Boston, Research Report No. 55.

These were not the only alternative sources of funds used by large banks in these periods. The interbank federal funds market was relied upon to an increasing extent. In addition, in mid-1969, large banks began purchasing overnight funds from their corporate customers, paying the prevailing Fed funds rate on such funds. Furthermore, major banks began to enter into the sale of existing loans subject to a repurchase agreement, where nonbanks for the first time became the buyers. While this was equivalent to a loan or interest-bearing deposit from a nonbank, Regulation Q did not apply to these transactions. Finally, some banks issued small denomination capital notes, designed to be bought by household savers, which were not subject to either reserve requirements or Regulation Q ceilings.

Through the various new sources of funds, large banks were able to

Figure 15-6
Outstanding commercial paper liabilities issued by bank holding companies

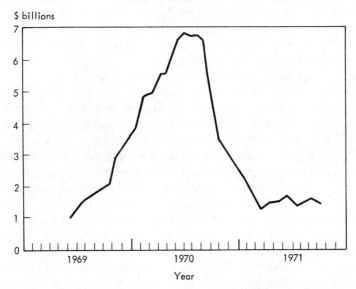

Source: "A Macro-Economic Analysis of the Short-Term Commercial Bank Adjustment Process," Federal Reserve Bank of Boston, Research Report No. 55.

cushion the effects of contracting CD volume. The increases in various bank assets in the 1969 period are shown in Table 15–5. Remarkably, in a period of very tight credit, the banks were able to continue financing much of the short-term demands of business. Additional studies have shown that the largest banks were particularly effective in expanding their business loans while the brunt of the contraction seemed to fall upon medium and small banks.

The Federal Reserve was, of course, aware of these continuing developments. In a sense, the growth of these alternative sources of funds

Table 15–5
Increases in large CDs and selected bank assets (Annual rates)

	4th Q 1968	1st Q 1969	2d Q 1969	3d Q 1969	4th Q 1969	1st Q 1970
Large CDs	4.8	−18.8	−14.0	−14.2	−3.3	5.3
Assets						
Loans to business	18.2	16.6	13.7	14.4	13.2	10.4
Investments	6.0	−14.9	−1.7	−11.6	−11.3	4.7
U.S. government	−6.5	−15.7	−5.2	−10.3	−9.2	0.8
Municipals	12.5	0.8	3.5	−1.3	−2.1	3.9

amounted to a circumvention of their policies. At the very least, this growth blunted their ability to control the aggregate amount of bank credit and its distribution to various sectors. Indeed, this ability was most blunted in the case of the largest banks, the suppliers of business credit that the Fed might most want to control. This time, however, the Fed deliberately chose not to directly influence business loans and did not repeat the "jawboning" contained in their 1966 letter to banks. Instead, the Fed moved to bring the alternative sources of funds within their existing regulatory powers. In the latter half of 1969, after Eurodollar borrowings had grown by almost $5 billion, the Fed amended Regulations D and M and applied 10-percent reserve requirements against any additional borrowings from overseas branches to raise the cost and curtail the additional use of these funds. In July of 1969, the Fed extended both reserve requirements and Regulation Q limits to overnight borrowing from corporations and to the sale and repurchase of existing loans. In 1970, the Fed applied marginal reserve requirements and Regulation Q to commercial paper issued by bank holding companies if the funds from this borrowing were used in any way to supply funds to the bank. As the Fed closed in on these new sources of funds, banks continued to search for other alternative sources. The Fed, for its part, attempted to close off, curtail, or otherwise regulate these sources of funds in a way that the major commercial banks were not immune from the effects of Regulation Q, but not so suddenly and dramatically as to create a disastrous contraction of the banking system. It did this by extending the range of its reserve requirements powers to many of the new liabilities banks were inventing and by raising these requirements to levels which significantly increased their cost to the banks.

In retrospect, the 1969–1970 period marked a turning point in liability management at the banks and liability regulation at the Fed. The major banks learned the effects of a dramatic runoff of CDs and sharpened their ability to compete for funds through other channels. The Fed gained an increased appreciation for the ability of the largest banks to quickly develop new sources of funds and began to shift away from Regulation Q and toward the use of additional reserve requirements which affected the costs rather than the availability of additional liabilities.

The period of growth: 1971–1973. In January of 1970, partly in response to the beginning of a recession, and partly in response to the occurrences in 1969, the Fed raised the Regulation Q ceilings on large CDs above the rates prevailing in money markets. In June of 1970, when the uncertainties precipitated by the collapse of the Penn Central Railroad generated sharply increased demands for bank credit, the Fed suspended Regulation Q ceilings on large CDs with maturities of less than 90 days. It did this to encourage the banks to respond to the financial stringencies emanating from the collapse. Because this measure was originally thought to be a temporary one, the ceilings on larger CDs maturing in more than 90 days was not changed.

As the recovery from the recession of 1970 ensued, the commercial banking system was once again given another opportunity to extend its reliance upon large CDs. Throughout 1971, 1972, and the first half of 1973, the Regulation Q ceilings that were still in effect were maintained well above the levels of open-market rates. Relative to previous recovery periods, the external financing demands of business remained fairly high. In these years, both large money-center banks and dominant regional banks aggressively expanded their operations both domestically and overseas. A large part of this expansion was financed in the CD market, and the reliance of banks upon interest-sensitive funds again expanded sharply (see Figure 15–4).

The high interest rate period of 1973–1974. As the credit cycle reached the peak of its expansion in 1973, the external demands of business and other sectors expanded rapidly. The expanding rate of inflation, coupled with these credit demands, drove short-term interest rates back up through the existing Regulation Q ceilings. In mid-1973, the Federal Reserve was once again presented with a crucial decision on Regulation Q ceilings. It could raise these ceilings on large CDs with maturity over 90 days and thereby expand the ability of large banks to compete for funds, or it could hold these Regulation Q ceilings down (and even reinstate interest rate limits on large CDs of less than 90 day maturity) and precipitate a replay of the credit crunches of 1966 and 1969–1970. The Fed chose to suspend Regulation Q ceilings on all maturities of large CDs. Consistent with its earlier moves, however, the Fed imposed a new 8-percent marginal reserve requirement on any further increases in large CDs and bank-related commercial paper. Later in 1973, the Fed raised this reserve requirement to 11 percent.

Thus, banks were free to compete for large CDs of any maturity, regardless of the level of open-market rates. Increased reserve requirements added to the effective cost of these funds however. The managements of large banks responded to this situation by vastly enlarging their dependence upon CDs and using these increasingly expensive funds to supply the credit needs of their customers. During 1973–1974, short-term interest rates moved to record heights, and yet throughout the period the banking system remained an effective competitor for funds (see Figures 15–3 and 15–4). During this period, the Fed evidently preferred to see if the new marginal reserve requirements against CDs, and the record high interest rates, would serve as an effective allocator of funds to credit demands rather than attempting to rely upon Regulation Q. The increase in CDs and various bank assets in this period are shown in Table 15–6.

Many individual companies experienced difficulties in negotiating new credit arrangements with the large banks during this period but only be-

Table 15–6
Increases in large CDs and selected bank assets (Annual rates)

	2d half 1972	1st half 1973	2d half 1973	1st half 1974	2d half 1974
Large CDs	17.4	30.2	9.8	31.8	25.7
Bank assets					
Loans to business	21.4	41.9	26.1	37.8	21.8
Investments	12.4	−0.2	8.8	10.7	2.1
U.S. government	6.6	−3.7	1.1	1.3	1.1
Municipals	5.8	3.5	7.7	9.4	1.0

cause of the already enormous increases in business credit. In the aggregate, the large banks remained effective suppliers of funds to business.

Late 1974: Problems in the CD market. The unprecedented growth of large CDs in the 1973–1974 period allowed the banking system to supply some of the enormous credit demands of that period, but it was not without its problems for some banks. As large banks grew in this period, they became more and more dependent upon "purchased funds," both large CDs and other borrowings; their capital bases, the cushions which protect large CD purchasers and other creditors, became smaller relative to the fast-growing size of the total assets. In 1974, there were several large banks that effectively failed: the Herstatt Bank in Germany and the Franklin National Bank in the United States. Because of the extended condition of many U.S. banks and these well-publicized bank failures, rumors began to circulate about the condition of various large banks. The rates paid by banks in the CD markets began to be disturbed. A handful of the very largest banks and other large banks with conservative images continued to be able to raise funds in the CD at rates consistent with their previous relationship to other money-market rates, but many of the large banks that had grown most rapidly in the preceding years and had fueled that growth with large CDs and other borrowed funds had more difficulty raising purchased funds. At best, a number of these large banks had to offer above-market rates to maintain their CD balances as tiers developed in the national CD market. In the extreme, some of these banks were simply unable to maintain the CDs they had raised in national money markets. They were forced to rely upon other, generally more costly, borrowed funds instead. The profit margins of some of these banks plummeted as the increased costs of purchased funds were translated into narrowing overall margins. Essentially, the perceived risk of the CDs had increased, either risk in the liquidity sense that banks might not be able to indefinitely roll-over their CDs in the national money markets, or risk in the sense that the capital of these banks could turn out to be too small relative to the riskiness of their assets.[7] In late 1974, while the banking system as a whole continued to expand its CDs, various segments of the banking system faced very different conditions. The very largest banks and certain other large banks continued to grow and expand their purchased funds and assets, but for many large banks, including some of the dominant regional banks that had grown so rapidly in 1971–1973, late 1974 was a most difficult period in the money markets and caused a severe contraction of both profits and growth. Late 1974 demonstrated the importance of perceived risk in the market for large CDs and highlighted the limits to the expansion of the banking system through a reliance on purchased funds.[8]

The respite from growth: 1975 and 1976. The corporate demand for short-term funds collapsed in 1975 and 1976, providing the banks with an adjustment period (see Figure 15–2). At the same time, however, loan losses on some of their outstanding loans grew, and the financial markets worried about the cumulative effects of ostensibly risky real estate loans, international loans, and New York City securities on the financial conditions of the large banks. During this time, the large banks contracted their open-market liabilities dramatically (particularly large CDs) as consumer savings deposits and other sources of funds expanded. Furthermore, the banks attempted to augment their capital bases by issuing new equity and capital notes and by expanding their profit margins on existing loans. These two responses helped to calm the fears of financial markets about the banks and to lay the foundation for future periods when the banks would be called upon once again to finance growing corporate loan demand.

The elements of competing for funds

The 1961–1974 period contains a fascinating series of episodes which serves to demonstrate the capacities which large banks must have in order to compete for funds. It became increasingly clear that in an environment of volatile interest rates and credit market conditions an effective competitor for interest-sensitive funds must satisfy certain conditions as to: (1) the return on its assets, (2) the regulation of allowable rates on its liabilities, and (3) the perceived risk of the institution.

Throughout the 1960s, large commercial banks strove to modify a significant portion of their asset structure such that the returns from these assets "floated" with open-market rates. These floating-rate returns enabled them to compete effectively with other money-market instruments

---

[7] While some of their business loans were perceived to be risky, the major attention was focused on other loans, in particular, real estate loans.

[8] For an account of the CD market in this period, see Dwight Crane, "Lessons from the 1974 CD Market," *Harvard Business Review* (November–December 1975).

even when rates were high. Large banks were successful at developing this asset structure, thus making them a potentially effective competitor for funds. But in 1966, and again in 1969–1970, the ability of large banks to compete for funds was severely limited by Regulation Q, the tool of the Federal Reserve. It became apparent that a continuing ability to compete for funds in a high interest period was conditional upon the support of regulators. It was equally apparent that the attitudes and objectives of regulators could change quickly when faced with unusual financial and economic circumstances. Finally, when Regulation Q was suspended in mid-1973, many large commercial banks and other money-market participants believed the final barrier to uninterrupted CD growth had been removed. In 1974, however, some segments of the banking system found that there was another limit, the market's perception of the risk inherent in their assets and thus their CDs. Thus the financial markets themselves emphasized that regulators were not the only barrier to CD growth. The reliance of banks upon purchased funds had to be carefully controlled and managed if they were to be effective competitors for funds during times of serious financial stringency.

The series of episodes also had considerable meaning for corporations as they assessed their own ability to raise funds from the financial system. Corporations have generally chosen to insure the future availability of their short-term funds by relying upon lines of credit and credit agreements with major banks. These remarkable arrangements presuppose the banks' ability to supply funds either from their stores of liquid investments (which have become less important) or by raising funds in the money markets (which had become more important). The large banks, for their part, have proven themselves to be successful and aggressive competitors for funds, supplying the bulk of short-term business demands even under stringent financial conditions. To be sure, there have been limitations to this ability in selected periods and at selected institutions, but the major commercial banks have successfully evolved such that they can continue to meet the financing demands of business.

The political factors. As we have seen, in 1973–1974 the Fed decided to suspend Regulation Q on large CDs and to instead accentuate the use of marginal requirements to control the growth in bank liabilities. In this way it allowed the rising costs of short-term credit to perform the task of constraining and allocating credit within the financial markets. There is no agreement that this produced a healthy financial climate during this difficult period. Some observers believe that the continued ability of banks to supply short-term credit encouraged and/or allowed business corporations to continue accumulating inventories and other assets in this period. It is claimed that this continued inventory accumulation both fueled the inflation of the period and eventually led to a sharper and deeper recession. Furthermore, some observers believe that by allowing banks to continue bidding for funds, short-term interest rates were driven to levels considerably higher than they might have been with an operative Regulation Q. These higher interest rates, it is believed, had adverse effects upon the allocation of credit to various economic sectors.

Indeed, the clear implication of the surprising ability of large corporations to raise substantial amounts of short-term funds is that other sectors are almost surely affected adversely. These adverse effects can encourage powerful political backlashes, particularly when they affect housing, state/local governments, small business, or other politically sensitive areas. In fact, pleas (and legislative proposals) for governmental systems of credit allocation have seemed to recur following each bout of enlarged business financing and high interest rates. In a sense, Regulation Q was a form (however unwieldy) of credit allocation because it attempted to indirectly control the lending ability of banks. Much more direct systems of mandatory credit allocation are often proposed however. They are almost invariably to be implemented through regulations on the banking system. Some of these would directly limit the percentage of different types of loans in a bank's portfolio. Others would after the profitability of specific types of assets by establishing different reserve requirements for different classes of assets. Still others would employ more informal influences (often jawboning) to affect the composition of bank lending, particularly to expand the supply of funds to politically sensitive sectors. Almost all of these credit allocation systems are proposed as assistance to sectors such as housing, state/local governments, small businesses, and so forth. Realistically, their objective is to restrict the ability of corporations (particularly large corporations) to obtain short-term funds from the banking system.

The recent history of bank regulation, including Regulation Q, raises serious questions about the effectiveness of these credit allocation systems. Credit allocation would have to contend with the basic facts that large corporations are active demanders of short-term funds, that large money-center banks are adaptable and resourceful agents for providing these funds, and ultimately that banks are not the only potential source of short-term business credit. As we have seen, the government can affect the supplies of business credit in the short run as, for example, in the credit crunch of 1966, but as the financial system becomes increasingly complex, adaptable, and international, a system of governmental credit controls is increasingly unlikely to be effective in the long run.[9]

THE COMMERCIAL PAPER MARKET AS AN ALTERNATIVE SOURCE OF SHORT-TERM DEBT FOR LARGE CORPORATIONS

While bank loans are the dominant source of short-term business credit, many large corporations also use the commercial paper market to

---

[9] See Edward J. Kane, "Good Intentions and Unintended Evil: The Case against Selective Credit Allocation," *Journal of Money, Banking, and Credit* (February 1977).

fund some of their short-term needs. As we have seen, the period from 1960 to 1975 was a time of substantial change within large banks. It was also a time of substantial change in the overall short-term financing patterns of large prime credit corporations.

Commercial paper as a money-market instrument

The commercial paper market provides a means for borrowers to obtain short-term funds from money-market investors without the direct services of the traditional intermediary, the commercial banks. Commercial paper refers to short-term, unsecured promissory notes issued by both financial and nonfinancial corporations. Traditionally, the commercial paper market has been divided into two segments: the directly placed market and the dealer-placed market.

Direct paper is sold directly to money-market investors by the issuing corporation through its own selling organization, supplemented by regional banks who may solicit orders. Dealer-placed paper is sold to investors through an investment banking or brokerage house. Direct issuers are primarily large finance companies that generally have a continuous need for money. Dealer-placed issuers, particularly nonfinancial corporations and smaller finance companies, have more specific borrowing requirements, both as to maturities and to amounts. Both directly placed and dealer-placed paper are usually tailored to investors' needs within the framework of each issuer's financial plans.

The primary requirement for borrowing in the money markets is that the borrower possesses an excellent credit standing. Since money-market lending is conducted on an unsecured and impersonal basis, financial strength and viability are necessary to insure minimal default risk and investor confidence. For this reason only large, financially strong corporations (sometimes referred to as prime credits) have usually been able to issue commercial paper. Credit ratings seem to be influential in assessing credit standing and determining whether a corporation will be able to sell commercial paper in the money markets.

While commercial paper notes are sold in a wide range of denominations, the dealer-placed notes of nonfinancial corporate issuers are generally available in denominations from $100,000 to $5,000,000. The exact times to maturity for commercial paper notes are primarily influenced by the needs of borrowers and the preferences of investors, but they generally have quite short maturities. The average maturity of outstanding dealer-placed paper is approximately 35 days. The upper limit on the time to maturity for commercial paper is 270 days.

While there is no secondary market for commercial paper, money market investors are not completely locked in during normal circumstances. Direct issuers will usually buy back their commercial paper notes on a rate-adjusted basis from a regular investor who faces an unexpected cash need. Some dealers maintain a limited secondary market for the commercial paper sold through them. Many dealers will attempt to arrange a resale for an investor with an unexpected cash need.

Another important aspect of commercial paper financing is the use of backup lines of credit. It is customary for a commercial paper issuer to secure a line of credit at a commercial bank. The backup line provides an additional measure of safety and liquidity to the borrowing corporation in the event that adverse money-market conditions and/or a temporary cash flow problem threaten the borrower's ability to redeem its notes at maturity. Although the granting of backup lines may facilitate corporate use of commercial paper financing (instead of bank debt), commercial bankers are willing to engage in this business for several reasons. First, because of competition among the banks, it is sensible for each individual bank to provide its prime-credit corporate customers with a high level of service including such services as backup lines. Furthermore, granting these backup lines may be viewed as a profitable business, for the bank can earn a return (compensating balances or commitment fees) without normally investing any assets.

Competition for funds in the money markets

The commercial paper market and the other money markets are closely related. Although there are many different borrowers in the money markets issuing a wide range of instruments, all borrowers compete for the supply of funds provided by money-market investors. Figure 15–7 displays the variety of instruments in the money markets. Except for certain institutional constraints, investors are free to supply funds to any of the competing money-market borrowers. It is sensible to assume that, within these institutional constraints, money-market investors are sensitive to both rate and risk differentials in choosing their portfolios of short-term investments. Table 15–7 documents the trends in the volume outstanding for some selected money-market obligations since 1960. The expanding volume of commercial paper during the period demonstrates the growing use of this short-term financing method.

Table 15–7
Outstanding volume of money-market obligations (In billions of dollars)

	1960	1965	1970	1977
U.S. Treasury short-term marketable securities (privately held)	$60	$68	$80	$161
Large negotiable CDs	—	16	26	77
Commercial paper	3	9	33	64

Figure 15–7
Compilation of money-market obligations

Money-market instrument	Issuer	Typical maturity	Comments
Fed funds	Bank	1 day	Basically overnight interbank loans, usually to satisfy reserve requirements
U.S. Treasury bills	U.S. Treasury	3–12 months	
Commercial paper	Large finance companies, NFCs, etc.	Less than 3 months	Unsecured promissory notes of private issuers.
Large negotiable CDs	Large banks	3–6 months	The most important source of "purchased money" for the banks
Bankers' acceptances	Bank guarantee of private credit	3 months	Used in foreign trade
Federal agency notes	Federally sponsored credit agencies, etc.	12 months or over	Short-term notes used to finance various government-related agencies
Eurodollar deposits	Overseas banks	1–6 months	Dollar deposits in banks outside the United States
Tax-exempt obligations (short-term)	State/local governments	Varies	Short-term financing for state/local needs

Demand for funds in the commercial paper market

Within the commercial paper market there are four major types of borrowers competing for funds: finance companies, nonfinancial corporations, the holding companies of large commercial banks, and the real estate investment trusts.

In the postwar period until 1966, the demand for funds by the large sales finance companies dominated the growth in commercial paper financing (even though nonfinancial corporations had been the predominant borrowers in the commercial paper market prior to World War II). During this early postwar period, many business corporations believed that commercial paper financing in the impersonal money markets was an unreliable source of funds, suitable for financing only very temporary needs. In addition, bank loans, for which terms could be adjusted, were considered a more flexible borrowing arrangement than commercial paper, for which rate and maturity were fixed when issued. Finally, it was believed that regular use of commercial paper financing would strain the all-important relationship between the borrowing corporation and its traditional supplier of funds, the commercial bank.

For these reasons, prior to 1966, the type of business corporation borrowing in the commercial paper market was generally limited to wholesalers, retailers, textile companies, meat packers, and other manufacturers who experienced a sharply seasonal pattern of sales. These businesses used commercial paper as a supplement to bank debt in order to meet peak financing needs for inventories and receivables.

In 1966, the restricted availability of loanable funds at commercial banks (due to the effect Regulation Q ceilings and additional qualitative controls imposed on commercial lending by the Federal Reserve) constrained bank credit. In order to alleviate this credit shortage, many corporations turned reluctantly to the commercial paper market to obtain short-term funds. These new borrowers included some steel companies, oil companies, railroads, and public utilities, among others. The commercial banks encouraged these corporations to borrow in the commercial paper market as a temporary supplement to bank loans during the period of monetary restraint and supported them with backup lines of credit.

After the 1966 credit crunch, the volume of commercial paper financing by nonfinancial corporations continued to expand at a rapid rate in spite of increased availability of loanable funds at the commercial banks, as illustrated in Table 15–8.

Table 15–8
Commercial paper financing by nonfinancial corporations (NFCs)

	1966	1967	1968	1969	1970
Outstanding commercial paper issued by NFCs (in billions)	$1.6	$3.0	$4.2	$5.4	$7.1
Numbers of borrowing NFCs	N.A.	275	345	488	454

Some corporations which experimented with commercial paper financing as a temporary expedient during the credit shortage continued to borrow regularly in the money markets. Furthermore, the Federal Reserve's attempts to constrain the flow of bank credit, through both rate ceilings and other devices, must have disturbed the confidence of corporate financial officers in the future ability of the banking system to provide funds at critical times. With this decreased confidence in the available supply of bank funds, it made more sense for corporations to develop diversified sources of short-term funds, and the commercial paper market figured prominently in their plans for developing alternative sources. Nonfinancial corporations benefited from having developed commercial paper financing as an alternative source of short-term funds when, once again, in 1969, monetary policy restricted the supply of loanable funds at commercial banks. By 1970, the commercial paper financing of nonfinancial corporations had become a significant factor in the demand for funds in the money markets.

The events of 1970

In 1970, there were two very important influences on the development of the commercial paper market. First, on June 21 of that year, the sixth largest nonfinancial corporation in the United States, the Pennsylvania Central Transportation Company, filed for bankruptcy and defaulted on $82 million of outstanding commercial paper notes. The immediate reaction of money-market investors was an increased perception of the riskiness of commercial paper. Investors responded by shifting funds to other money-market instruments and by investing in only very high-quality commercial paper. Some borrowing corporations, particularly those with cash flow problems, faced a severe liquidity shortage because they were suddenly unable to continue obtaining short-term funds directly from money-market investors. The actions of the Federal Reserve during June and July of 1970 enabled and encouraged the commercial banks to supply credit to corporations confronted with the financial difficulties of the paper market. These actions restored stability to the commercial paper market by the end of July and prevented the development of what might have been a major liquidity crisis.[10] Although the short-term effects were limited and controlled, the Penn Central default tended to limit the subsequent growth of the commercial paper market. More rigid concerns about credit quality, which had declined during the period of rapid growth, once again became important for many money-market investors and seemed to become a formidable barrier to entry for new potential borrowers. The emphasis on credit quality seemed to force weaker credits to withdraw from the market.

A second event which had an important effect on the commercial paper market was the apparent change which was taking place in the Federal Reserve's policies with respect to Regulation Q. Recall that nonfinancial corporations had expanded their borrowings in the commercial paper market when the interventions of monetary policy sought to limit the flow of short-term credit through the commercial banks. Thus, regulatory constraints on the normal bank channel of short-term credit flow enhanced the opportunity for commercial paper market to develop as a rate-competitive alternative to the intermediation of the commercial banks. In June 1970, the Federal Reserve suspended its rate ceilings on large negotiable CDs with maturities less than 90 days (initially, as part of the response to the Penn Central). Later in 1973, it suspended all rate ceilings on large CDs. Thus, the ability of commercial banks to compete for funds,

---

[10] See Sherman Maisel, "Managing the Dollar" (New York: Norton, 1975).

particularly in times of high interest rates, was restored. Presumably these actions should have once again increased the confidence of corporate borrowers in the available supply of bank funds and lessened the importance of the commercial paper market as an alternative source of short-term funds. Indeed the period of rapid growth in the number of nonfinancial corporations borrowing in the commercial paper market came to an end in 1970.

Allocation of short-term corporate borrowing between the two markets

Despite the lingering effects of the Penn Central default and the changing attitudes of the Federal Reserve, the commercial paper market has maintained itself as an active channel of short-term credit flows to prime-rated nonfinancial corporations and as a formidable competitor to bank loans. The number of commercial paper borrowers has decreased (due to the two factors described above), but the relative importance of commercial paper financing for the large prime-credit corporations has increased. A diagram representing corporate use of the commercial paper market is shown in Figure 15–8. The large corporate borrower can either use an intermediary (a large commercial bank) for short-term credit needs or rely upon the commercial paper market. In addition, many of the important suppliers of funds in the commercial paper market are also nonfinancial corporations. Thus the collection of large creditworthy nonfinancial corporations can either choose to finance each other (and other money-market participants) indirectly through an intermediary or directly through the more impersonal open markets.

Figure 15–8
Choices in the short-term markets

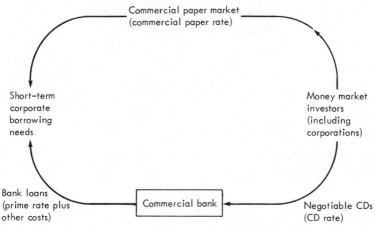

The choice between these two alternatives depends upon the perceived benefits and costs of the intermediary. The principal drawback of the commercial paper market is that potential investors may retreat in a time of financial stress and refuse to provide short-term funds. This could clearly have severe consequences for a borrower dependent only upon commercial paper. On the other hand, the banks have also encountered challenges to their ability to raise funds and thus provide credit, both from regulators and from the markets' concern about the risk of individual banks. For smaller corporate borrowers, the incremental ability of large banks to compete effectively for funds must be very valuable indeed, but as the corporate borrower becomes larger and more creditworthy, the incremental value of the intermediary becomes progressively smaller. The cost of using an intermediary are dependent upon the relationship between various interest rates, in particular the differential between the commercial paper rate, the prime rate, and the CD rate. Because the prime rate is an administered rate, the large banks can effectively control the relative pricing of their loans and thus the costs of using banks as an intermediary.

An examination of the patterns of short-term financing demonstrates the importance of rate differentials to the ultimate demanders and suppliers of short-term corporate credit. This rate sensitivity can be demonstrated by comparing a rate differential (in particular the differential between the prime rate and the rate on three-month CDs) with the percentage of their total short-term borrowings that nonfinancial corporations obtain from the commercial paper market. The prime rate is a convenient proxy for the cost of bank credit to the borrowing nonfinancial corporations.[11] The CD rate represents the return to money-market investors for lending to the bank. The differential between these two rates creates the incentive for commercial banks to act as intermediaries between ultimate demanders and suppliers and is the most important component of bank profitability. The (prime–CD rate) spread is also a measure of the incentive for the ultimate demanders and suppliers of the funds to use the direct commercial paper channel rather than the intermediated bank loan channel. By entering into credit arrangements in the commercial paper market without the risk protection of an intermediary, the borrower and the investor can share between themselves the profit margin of the intermediary. For these reasons, the (prime–CD rate) spread serves as an interesting measure of the rate sensitivity of the short-term financing decision.

The graph in Figure 15–9 illustrates the rate-sensitive behavior of nonfinancial corporations and money-market investors from 1971 to 1974.

---

[11] Actually, as we have seen, the total cost of bank borrowing also includes the required compensating balances and sometimes various fees.

Figure 15–9
The form of corporate short-term financing*

* Prime rate minus CD rate: Use solid line and left scale.
  Non-financial businesses: commercial paper as a percent of short-term debt outstanding: Use dotted line and right scale.

When the magnitude of the (prime–CD rate) differential was small, a greater percentage of short-term funds was channeled through the commercial banking system. However, as the banks attempted to improve their profitability by increasing this differential, nonfinancial corporations and money-market investors generally responded by diverting a larger percentage of their short-term credit flows through the commercial paper market. During 1973, the Committee on Interest and Dividends held bank lending rates below open-market rates. Nonfinancial corporations responded to the lower cost of bank credit and quickly replaced commercial paper borrowings with bank loans.

This analysis demonstrates the critical role of the commercial paper market in the flow of short-term credit to nonfinancial corporations. Commercial paper first became an important element in corporate financing when credit restraint limited the availability of funds from commercial banks. Since this introduction, the use of commercial paper by prime-credit nonfinancial corporations has evolved to a choice based more and more on the changing relative cost of bank debt and commercial paper financing as (within certain limits) prime credit corporations change their allocation of short-term funding needs between these two alternatives.

This development of the commercial paper market has had important implications for commercial banks. When the prime rate is held too high relative to open-market rates (in particular, the commercial paper rate), large prime-credit companies redirect their short-term borrowing away from the banks. The large commercial banks thus find it difficult to compete for the short-term borrowings of very large companies and yet maintain their desired margins on these loans. The commercial paper market has tended to limit the profitability of the intermediary function and reduce the market share of banks relative to all sources of short-term business credit.[12]

LINKAGES BETWEEN THE INTERNAL AND EXTERNAL DOLLAR MARKETS FOR BANK LOANS AND CDS

As we saw in Chapter 6, our domestic financial markets are now augmented by external markets for dollar-denominated financial assets and liabilities. The external markets for dollar CDs and dollar bank loans have grown to a very substantial size. The largest of the external markets is the Eurodollar market. Its growth is shown in Table 15–9. As the external markets have grown and the number of large U.S. banks and corporations participating there have grown, interest rates and credit flows in

Table 15–9
Relative size of the U.S. and Eurodollar markets (Billions of $ outstanding)

End of period	Eurodollar market (net size)	U.S. bank time deposits (excluding large CDs)	Large negotiable U.S. bank CDs	Commercial paper
1965	12	131	16	9
1970	46	206	26	33
1975	192	370	83	48

Sources: Morgan Guaranty Trust, *World Financial Markets*; U.S. Federal Reserve Board, *Flow of Funds*.

---

[12] In 1977, several commercial banks responded to the competitive pressures from the commercial paper market by offering corporations that borrowed funds in the commercial paper market a bank loan facility for 10- or 30-day credit at an interest rate only slightly above the banks' cost of funds, and well below the prime rate.

the internal and external markets have become highly integrated. First, interest rates on Eurodollar CDs have moved more in line with CD rates in the United States. Second, the pricing structure of bank loans in the Eurodollar market has affected the way bank loans are priced in the U.S. market.

Eurodollar and U.S. CD rates

There is a great deal of substituting between the CDs issued by U.S. banks in the internal market (U.S. CDs) and the CDs available in the external market (Eurodollar CDs). The liquidity of these two types of CDs is about the same, although Eurodollar CDs may be perceived as somewhat more risky.

Interest rates on U.S. and Eurodollar CDs are shown in Figures 15–10A and 15–10B. In 1966 and 1969, when Regulation Q limited the ability of U.S. banks to sell U.S. CDs, they used their foreign branches to raise Eurodollar CDs, and then borrowed these funds from their foreign branches. At that time, the Eurodollar CD market was relatively small. As the foreign branches attempted to sharply increase their outstanding CDs, the rates on Eurodollar CDs rose well above interest rates on U.S. CDs (in the secondary market). Indeed, in mid-1969, the Eurodollar CD rate rose almost 3 percentage points above the secondary market U.S. CD rate (and 5.3 percent above the 6.0 percent ceiling rate on new U.S. CDs).

In 1971, the spread between U.S. CDs and Eurodollar CDs widened once again at the same time the U.S. dollar came under substantial pressure in foreign exchange markets. This widened spread has generally been attributed to the greater relative sensitivity of the external markets to the impending plight of the dollar, in particular by a strong demand for Eurodollar loans (for conversion into Deutsche marks and other strong currencies) and a limited foreign supply of Eurodollar CDs (because of devaluation fears).[13]

In 1973 and 1974, when interest rates in the United States rose sharply, Eurodollar CD rates once again rose faster than U.S. CD rates. However, the differential expanded less than in the earlier high-rate periods. In part, this reflected the fact that the Federal Reserve did not maintain Regulation Q ceilings below open-market interest rates in 1973 and 1974 as it had done during those earlier periods. Because U.S. banks continued to be able to attract CDs in the internal market, they put less pressure on the external market. In part, however, these narrower differentials reflected the growth in the size of the Eurodollar CD market and the increased amount of substitution which took place between the two markets.

---

[13] This argument does not explain why U.S. residents (who had the alternative of acquiring U.S. CDs or Eurodollar CDs) did not shift enough funds to the Eurodollar CD market to keep these rate differentials from becoming so wide.

Figure 15–10A

Interest rates on three-month Eurodollar CDs and U.S. CDs

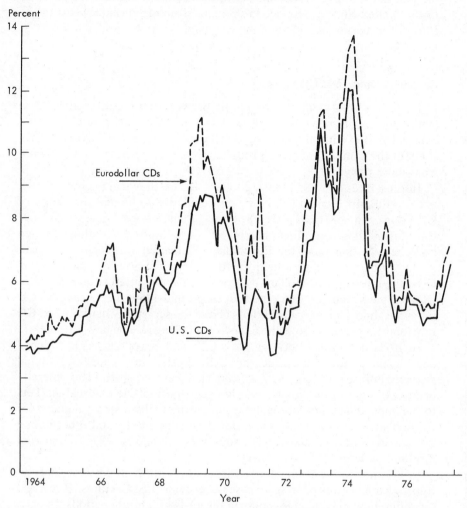

Percent

Year

In 1976 and 1977, the spread between interest rates on three-month CDs in the internal and external markets averaged less than 0.5 percentage point and fluctuated in a narrow range, suggesting the markets were becoming closely related to each other.

Terms on Eurodollar versus U.S. dollar bank lending

Bank lending to U.S. corporations in the Eurodollar market differs from most lending in the domestic market. The borrowers (among U.S.

Figure 15–10B
Spread between three-month Eurodollar CD rate and U.S. CD rates

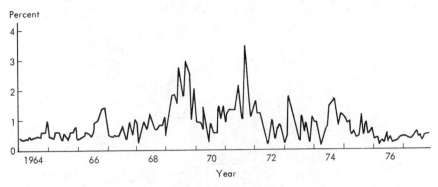

Percent

Year

corporations) are almost always large well-known corporations which have the alternatives of borrowing in the domestic loan market and possibly the domestic commercial paper market as well as the Eurodollar loan market. Also Eurodollar loans are usually individually arranged. Banks do not usually offer Eurodollar lines of credit under which they assure continuous availability of funds up to a predetermined limit. The Eurodollar loan market is a wholesale or "no-frills attached" market. In addition, banks have no legally imposed reserve requirements or deposit insurance fees. For all these reasons, lending costs in the Eurodollar bank loan market are lower than in the U.S. market.

Interest rates in the Eurodollar bank loan market float with open-market rates (as does the prime rate on U.S. bank loans). The Eurodollar borrowing rate is based on the London interbank offer rate (LIBO rate). The LIBO rate is analogous to the domestic federal funds rate for it measures the rate at which banks in the external market will lend dollars to each other.

Data published by the Morgan Guaranty Bank suggest that the spread between Eurodollar lending and Eurodollar CD rates has been declining since 1974 (see Figure 15–11). In 1976 and early 1977, however, U.S. banks chose to price loans in the domestic market well above the domestic CD rate. As a consequence, their spread in the external bank loan market was considerably narrower than their spread in the internal market. This pricing behavior in the external market may well have been a response to the competition in the internal market from the commercial paper market. By offering loans to their largest customers at lower spreads in the external market, the banks may have hoped to be able to retain that element of their business without having to reduce the interest rates they were charging the domestic firms which did not have the alter-

Figure 15–11
Eurodollar prime rate minus Eurodollar CD rate and U.S. prime rate
minus U.S. CD rate

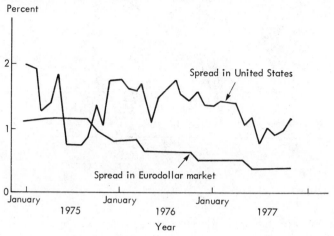

native of borrowing commercial paper in the domestic market.[14] There is
some evidence that, in response, some of the larger corporate borrowers
shifted their bank borrowing from the internal to the external market.

In sum, the external and internal markets for dollar CDs and dollar
bank loans are becoming more and more related to each other. U.S. banks
can now raise and lend funds in either the internal or external dollar
market. This enhances their flexibility and reduces their vulnerability to
regulations in the internal market. However, the largest corporations can
raise and lend funds in the external markets, too. This limits the banks'
freedom to price their loans in the domestic market. Thus the Eurodollar
market for loans, the domestic market for loans, and the domestic commercial paper market have become three separate and competitive channels for
raising short-term corporate debt.

SHORT-TERM CORPORATE DEBT AND THE
FINANCIAL SYSTEM: A SUMMARY

Nonfinancial business corporations are large active demanders of funds
with extremely variable short-term financing demands. For the most part,
their short-term funds are provided by the banking system where the large

---

[14] See "Bank Lending and Pricing: A Structural Change," Alan Gart, *Bankers' Magazine* (Spring 1977).

banks have developed a remarkably flexible and effective system for assuring the availability of short-term funds. The lines of credit and revolving credit agreements issued in the domestic market by these banks are commitments to provide short-term credit throughout various conditions in the financial markets. Banks have supported these commitments with an impressive record of obtaining funds. The external market for dollar CDs and dollar loans is an additional channel through which U.S. commercial banks provide U.S. business corporations with short-term financing. A key to the banks' ability to provide these funds is the fact that the borrowing demands of business corporations (compared to other potential borrowers) seem to be relatively insensitive to the costs of short-term funds.

The costs of short-term bank credit in the domestic market are usually tied to the prime rate. In the external market the interest rate on most loans floats with the London interbank offering rate. The large banks have progressively tied their domestic prime rates more closely to open-market rates (in particular the commercial paper rate) for at least three reasons:

1. First, by floating the returns from their assets with open-market rates, the banks can enhance their own ability to compete for interest-sensitive open-market funds while maintaining a relatively stable margin.
2. By managing the spread between the costs of bank loans and commercial paper, the banks can continue to compete for the borrowing demands of large creditworthy corporations.
3. By tying their pricing policies more closely to open-market rates, the banks are better able to defend themselves against political accusations that these pricing policies are arbitrary or unfair.

In addition to the negotiated or private market for short-term debt, there is also a public market for short-term debt, the commercial paper market. This market is an important financing alternative for large companies with very high credit ratings. In addition, its existence exerts a significant pressure on the pricing of bank loans and on the profitability of the commercial banks.

The adverse effects on the rest of the financial system of sharp increases in the volume of business borrowing often encourage powerful political backlashes. These include calls for additional systems of credit allocation. These credit allocation systems would attempt to restrict the ability of corporations, particularly large corporations, to obtain funds, and they would invariably be implemented through restrictions on the domestic branches of the banking system. However domestic commercial banks do not provide all the short-term credit to business. Large corporations have other sources of funds, among them the commercial paper market and the Eurodollar market, which they can use when the costs and/or availability of domestic bank credit are restricted. Their existence would pose substantial problems for regulators if they attempted to use the banks to control the flows of short-term credit to business.

QUESTIONS

1. If the Federal Reserve were to permanently remove the Regulation Q ceilings on CDs in excess of $100,000, what would be the limits to the volume of commercial bank lending to business?
2. What are the linkages between the commercial paper rate, the negotiable CD rate, and the prime rate?
   a. What spread among these rates determines the incentive for large corporations to finance through the banks rather than in the open markets?
   b. What spread among these rates determines the incentive for money market investors to lend to banks rather than directly to corporations in the money markets?
   c. What spread determines the profitability of the business lending of the banks?
3. How does the commercial paper market's existence weaken the Fed's ability to affect the total of business borrowing? How does the commercial paper market enhance the Federal Reserve's ability to control the share of business borrowing which flows through the commercial banks?
4. In what way does the Eurodollar market offer U.S. commercial banks options for product differentiation and market segmentation? What advantages could U.S. commercial banks obtain from such differentiation and segmentation? What are the limits on their ability to do this?

REFERENCES

"The Prime Rate," *Business Conditions,* Federal Reserve Bank of Chicago (April 1975), pp. 3–12.

"The Commercial Paper Market," *Federal Reserve Bulletin* (June 1977), Board of Governors of the Federal Reserve System, Washington, D.C.

Brimmer, Andrew F. "Multi-National Banks and the Management of Monetary Policy in the United States," *Journal of Finance,* vol. 28, no. 2 (May 1973), pp. 439–54.

Friedman, Benjamin M. "Regulation Q and the Commercial Loan Market in the 1960s," *Journal of Money, Credit and Banking,* vol. 7, no. 3 (1975), pp. 277–96.

Melton, William C. "The Market for Large Negotiable CDs," *Quarterly Review,* Federal Reserve Bank of New York (Winter 1977–78), pp. 22–34.

Hewson, John and Sakakibara, Eisuke. "The Effect of U.S. Controls on U.S. Commercial Bank Borrowing in the Euro-dollar Market," *The Journal of Finance,* vol. 30. no. 4 (September 1975), pp. 1101–10.

———. "A General Equilibrium Approach to the Eurodollar Market," *Journal of Money, Credit, and Banking,* vol. 8, no. 3, (August 1976), pp. 297–324.

16

The corporate bond market

THE PRIMARY BOND MARKET AS A SOURCE OF CORPORATE FUNDS

Corporate bonds are the dominant form of long-term corporate debt, although other forms play important supplementary roles (see Table 16–1). Commercial mortgages, for example, are important to real estate corporations in the financing of office buildings, shopping centers, and other commercial projects. Bank term loans are used as supplementary forms of intermediate-term finance by many companies. Special forms of tax-exempt financing are used to fund some industrial development projects and pollution control equipment. In addition, leasing arrangements are often used as substitutes for long-term financing. Despite these alternatives, the bond market is still the most important source of corporate long-term debt, accounting for more than the alternative sources combined.

Table 16–1

Outstanding long-term debt obligations of nonfinancial business corporations (In billions)

Debt form	Estimated outstanding as of 12/31/77
Corporate bonds.........................	$298
Commercial mortgages	147
Term loans from banks....................	75
Tax-exempt corporate obligations	13

The demand for funds

Nonfinancial corporations are the largest demanders of funds in the bond market, but they are not the only participants (see Table 16–2). In the early 1970s there was a substantial demand for long-term debt from financial intermediaries, mainly banks, real estate investment trusts, and

Table 16–2

The composition of demand in the corporate bond market (In billions of dollars)

	1971	1972	1973	1974	1975	1976	1977
Net increase in outstandings	$23.5	$18.4	$13.6	$23.9	$36.3	$37.0	$34.9
Nonfinancial business corps.	18.8	12.2	9.2	19.7	27.2	22.8	21.0
Financial institutions (including banks, finance companies, and REITs)	3.8	5.1	3.6	2.2	2.9	5.8	8.9
Foreign issues	0.9	1.0	1.0	2.1	6.2	8.4	5.0

finance companies. In addition, in some years a substantial number of foreign obligations are issued in the U.S. bond market, including a particularly large number of Canadian issues. Figure 16–1, taken from Chapter 2, shows the overall level of funds raised in financial markets by nonfinancial corporations and the portion of these funds raised in the form of long-term debt.[1] Long-term debt includes, for these purposes, funds raised through long-term corporate bonds and long-term corporate mortgages. From 1961 through 1974, the total funds raised by corporations in financial markets grew substantially even when expressed as a percent of GNP. As a part of that pattern, long-term debt financing increased as well. In addition, there was a clear cyclical pattern in the volume

---

[1] Both flows in Figure 16–1 have been divided by GNP to remove inflation and normalize them relative to the size of the overall financial and economic system.

of long-term debt financing. In the middle phases of each economic expansion, when total external financing needs were generally rising rapidly, long-term debt financing was typically decreasing. In these phases, corporations generally preferred to rely upon short-term debt as the principal component of their external financing. It was only in the very late phases of each economic or credit cycle and in the subsequent recession (when the total needs for funds was actually lower) that the pace of long-term debt financing expanded. In these periods, for example in 1970–1971 and 1975, nonfinancial corporations issued long-term debt to finance their current needs and to refund part of the short-term debt they had built up in early phases of the credit cycle.

Figure 16–1

Funds raised by nonfinancial business corporations (Seasonally adjusted, smoothed annual rates as a percent of GNP)

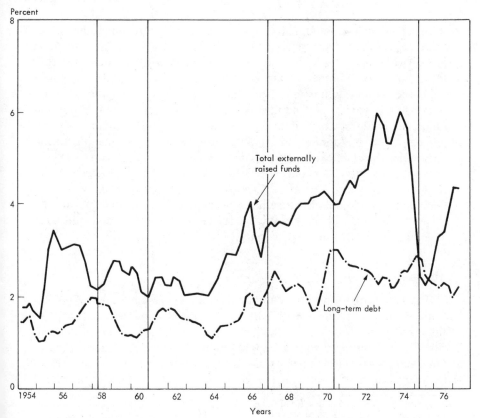

A more disaggregated description of the demand from nonfinancial corporations is shown in Table 16–3, which documents the gross offerings of corporate bonds by industry sector.[2] As Table 16–3 suggests, the demand for long-term debt from various regulated industries, specifically

Table 16–3
The composition of demand within nonfinancial corporations (Billions of dollars)

	1971	1972	1973	1974	1975	1976	1977
Gross cash offerings by sector*							
Utilities: electric, gas, water	7.6	6.4	5.6	8.9	9.7	8.3	8.3
Communication	4.2	3.7	3.5	3.7	3.5	2.8	3.1
Transportation	2.0	2.4	2.1	1.6	3.4	4.4	2.0
Manufacturing and mining	9.8	5.4	4.4	9.9	17.0	13.2	12.5

* Gross cash offerings before reductions to reflect cash retirements, conversions, calls, and other adjustments.
Source: Federal Reserve Bulletin.

transportation, communication, and public utility companies, has comprised a very large percentage of total demand in the corporate bond market. In many years, for example 1972 and 1973, the demand from these industries dominated the bond market. The demand from these regulated industries has also been relatively stable, reflecting the relatively steady capital expenditure demands and relatively stable internal funds generated by these industries. In contrast, the manufacturing and mining category (dominated by large capital-intensive manufacturing companies) has had extremely variable demand, ranging from a relatively small component of demand in 1973 to the dominant financing demand in peak financing years such as 1975. It is these long-term capital demands of manufacturing companies that have been primarily responsible for the extreme variability of bond financing, even though the regulated industries have accounted for the largest share of total bond financing.

The supply of funds

The long-term corporate bond market has a very broad range of institutional suppliers of funds (see Figure 16–2). This is in marked contrast with the market for residential mortgages, long-term federal government securities, and long-term state/local government securities. Each of these other long-term markets has its own set of institutional and/or tax-related factors which tend to inhibit the participation of long-term institutional

---

[2] Note that Table 16–2 described the *net* issuance of corporate bonds (after deductions for repayments, conversions, and so forth), whereas Table 16–3 describes the gross issuance of bonds.

Figure 16–2
Diagram of the supply and demand for funds in the corporate bond market

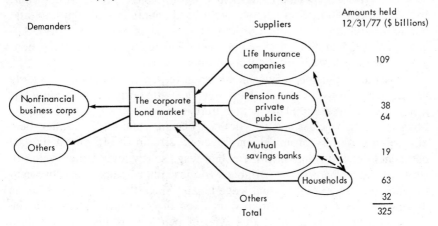

investors. Life insurance companies hold more than one third of the outstanding corporate bonds. Private and public pension funds also hold a third of the outstanding bonds. The remaining third is divided among households, mutual savings banks, and others, where "others" includes

Table 16–4
Net purchases of corporate and foreign bonds (Billions of dollars)

	1970	1971	1972	1973	1974	1975	1976	1977
Life insurance companies	1.5	5.5	7.0	5.9	4.0	9.1	16.9	18.3
Pension funds								
Private	2.1	−0.7	−0.8	2.1	4.7	2.8	1.3	5.3
Public......................	4.5	3.9	4.2	5.6	6.8	6.1	6.8	4.1
Mutual savings banks	1.2	3.9	2.1	−1.1	0.9	3.5	2.8	1.1
Households	9.5	8.3	4.4	1.3	4.7	8.2	4.0	1.5
Rest of the world	0.7	0.3	0.1	0.1	0.9	0.6	0.9	3.7
Others	3.9	2.2	1.4	−0.2	2.8	6.1	4.4	.9
Total	23.3	23.5	18.4	13.6	23.9	36.3	37.0	34.9

casualty insurance companies, mutual funds, broker-dealers, and foreign investors.[3] Table 16–4 shows the net flows of funds to the corporate bond market.

Private pension plans. Household savings is motivated by a number of goals, among them an adequate stock of wealth for retirement. In former years, individuals generally provided for their own retirement income,

---

[3] Here, as elsewhere, the category "households" includes not only individuals but the endowments of various educational, religious, and charitable institutions.

often from a stock of financial assets they held directly. More recently, however, various specific retirement programs have become important. In 1977, about 50 million persons were participants in major private and public pension and retirement programs (other than Social Security). Approximately 35 million of these persons were members of private non-governmental plans, mainly corporate pension plans.

The exact provisions of various corporate pension plans differ widely among corporate sponsors. Indeed, even a single corporation usually has a number of different plans with different terms. Many of these plans, however, can be classified as "defined benefit" plans. A "defined benefit" plan generally promises employees a stream of retirement income payments defined relative to their final wage/salary levels, their years of service, and perhaps other variables. In these plans, employee retirement benefits are "indexed" to final wage levels. Since these final wage levels depend upon the growth in real wages and the rate of inflation over the recipient's working lifetime, this type of pension promise represents a liability for the sponsoring corporation which has a very uncertain value.

The other major type of private pension plan is a "defined contribution" plan. In this type of plan, the employer contracts annually to contribute a specific sum which is invested in the employee's name. While the employer's future contributions are often related to the future salary of the employee, and are therefore uncertain, the employer accepts no responsibility for the investment returns which are realized on the funds invested. The uncertainty that this type of pension promise represents to its corporate sponsor is therefore much less than is the uncertainty associated with defined benefit plans.

In order to provide for these future liabilities, sponsoring corporations have established pension funds into which they make regular contributions. While employees sometimes provide some of the contributions themselves, the vast majority of contributions are made by the sponsoring company. The formula determining the appropriate annual contributions are complex, but generally they are constructed such that a rather steady stream of contributions is required from the sponsor. The contributions to the fund are tax-deductible for the corporation, and the investment returns within the fund are tax-exempt. The employee pays the appropriate individual income tax on the stream of benefits but only when they are distributed after retirement.

Private pension funds have grown at a very rapid rate in the postwar period, as Table 16–5 suggests. Their rapid growth has been fueled by demographic trends, by employees' desire for guaranteed retirement income, and by the substantial tax advantages of retirement saving in this particular form.

Private pension funds have been invested in a variety of assets, as is shown in Table 16–6. The long-term nature of pension plan liabilities

Table 16–5
Total financial assets in private pension
funds (In billions, with equities valued
at market)

1950	1960	1970	1976
$7	$38	$111	$176

suggests that only minimal liquidity is required in these funds, and not surprisingly, the bulk of the assets are long-term assets. Private pension funds have been relatively unregulated intermediaries and have thus been free to determine their own asset mix. Equities have been the major holding of most pension funds in recent years, although corporate bonds are also important.

Table 16–6
Private pension funds' estimated
portfolio holdings as of 12/31/75 (In
billions)

Corporate equities	$110
Corporate bonds	39
Other assets	27
Total assets	$176

The management of corporate pension funds was affected by the passage of the Employee Retirement Income Security Act of 1974 (called ERISA). This act required fuller coverage, vesting, and funding for some employee retirement plans. Furthermore, it extended the potential legal claims of pension beneficiaries beyond the pension funds' assets to the corporations themselves.[4] Finally, it required "prudent" investment policies for the funds, a prescription open to a wide range of judicial interpretations. The exact effects of ERISA are unclear, but it may encourage greater caution among corporate pension plan sponsors, both as to the benefits they extend to employees, and the investment policies of the pension funds standing behind these pension promises. At a minimum, ERISA will reinforce the view that pension liabilities have become ongoing financial obligations of corporations. To be sure, the legal standing of

---

[4] ERISA extends the claims to include up to 30 percent of the sponsoring company's net worth in the absence of "contingent liability" insurance. It is not clear whether this contingent liability insurance will be available and under what terms. For a duscussion of the impact of ERISA, see, J. L. Treynor, P. J. Regan, and W. L. Priest, *The Financial Reality of Pension Funding Under* ERISA (Homewood, Ill: Dow-Jones Irwin, 1976).

these pension liabilities is considerably different than more conventional liabilities like debt. Nonetheless, the fast-growing pension liabilities of most corporations have become an important consideration in their total financial structure.

Public pension funds. Most state and local governments also offer retirement plans to their employees with many of the same features for both beneficiaries and sponsors as in the private pension plans. These state and local retirement plans are funded by their respective governments, and the resulting pools of assets are generally called public pension funds. The rapid postwar growth of these public pension funds is recorded in Table 16–7.

Table 16–7
Total financial assets in public pension funds (In billions, with equities at market)

1950	1960	1970	1976
$5	$20	$60	$122

Public pension funds differ from private funds in several ways. In the public funds, it is much more common for the employees to provide a major fraction of the ongoing contributions. More important, the investment policies of public pension funds have been more strictly regulated. In particular, many state and local governments have not permitted investment of these funds in common stocks or other "risky" assets. In recent years, the investment restrictions for many of these funds have been eased considerably. However, their investment policies are still heavily regulated. Their asset composition is shown in Table 16–8. The

Table 16–8
Public pension funds' estimated portfolio holdings as of 12/31/76 (In billions)

Corporate bonds	$ 69
Corporate equities	30
Other assets	23
Total assets	$122

portfolio holding of public pension funds are dominated by corporate bonds. Corporate equities play a smaller role along with other assets such as mortgages.

Pension funds as suppliers of funds to the corporate bond market. As Figure 16–3 suggests, the flow of funds into public pension funds and thus

Figure 16–3
Public pension funds' investments in the bond market (Annual net flows)

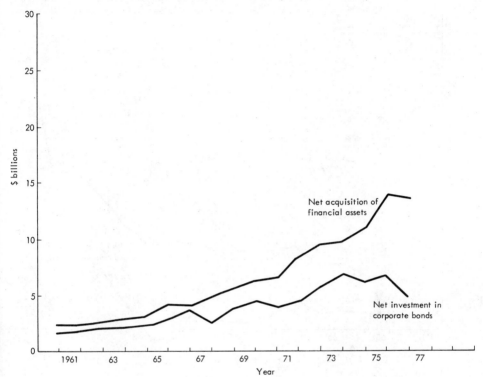

their "net acquisition of financial assets" has been growing rapidly. Public pension funds' net purchases of corporate bonds have also grown rapidly. To be sure, there have been several years, notably 1968, 1975, and 1977, when the flow of public pension fund monies into corporate bonds slackened a bit. By and large, however, public pension funds have become a steady, dependable, and important supplier of funds to the bond market.

In contrast, the participation of *private* pension funds in the corporate bond market has recently become much more variable (see Figure 16–4). In the early 1960s a relatively steady flow of funds was allocated to corporate bonds. By the 1970s, however, the investment strategies of private pension funds seemed to change sharply from year to year. In 1971 and 1972, despite sizeable inflows of funds, private pension funds were net "disinvestors" in the bond market. In these years they allocated more than 100 percent of their net inflows to the stock market, presumably in search of greater investment returns. During the stock market declines of

Figure 16–4
Private pension funds' investments in the bond market (Annual net flows)

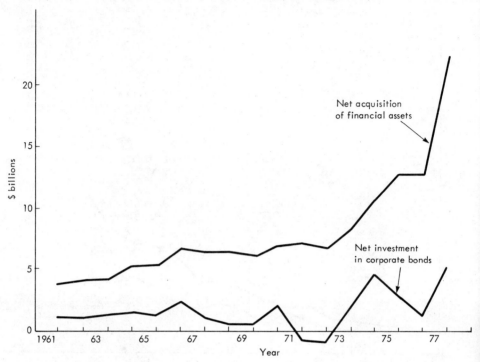

1973–1974 and 1977, however, private pension funds returned once again to the bond market, allocating sizeable fractions of their total flows of corporate bonds. Clearly the private pension funds are an important factor in the overall supply of funds to the bond market, although they have been a less stable source of supply than have the public pension plans.

Life insurance companies. Life insurance companies are involved in a number of different financial businesses, many of which result in an accumulation of financial assets. Traditionally the most important business of life insurance companies has been selling and administering whole-life insurance policies whose primary purpose is to insure individuals against an early death. In the course of providing this protection, however, the whole-life policy also includes a savings function. As the policy holder makes regular annual payments, a cash surrender value is accumulated, which may later be used for retirement wealth or other purposes. Thus, the life insurance company services its policy holders, both as a straightforward insurer and as a financial intermediary in the savings process. The steady contractual premiums from policy holders are invested in a pool of assets whose value accumulates over time. Various "reserves" are defined on the liability side of the balance sheet to provide for the future liabilities of the insurance policies. The liabilities accruing from the insuring and saving process are long-term and have, primarily, a fixed nominal value. Their size, in the aggregate, is predictable. Most of the funds are invested in long-term financial assets yielding relatively certain nominal returns.

Many of these insurance policies have an additional feature, "policy loans," which can have a major effect on the actual funds available for investment at any point in time. In many policies, policy holders can borrow against their cash surrender values at a known, fixed interest rate. In times of high interest rates, these policy loans can be a relatively inexpensive form of borrowing. In the high interest rate periods of 1966, 1969, and 1973–1974, policy loans expanded sharply. In essence, life insurance companies were "disintermediated" by their policy holders. At these times, the funds available for discretionary investment by the life insurance companies have been substantially reduced.

While whole-life policies are still a dominant component of insurance company business, their growth in recent years has failed to keep pace with other financial services. Many individuals are substituting term-life policies, which provide the same insurance function as whole-life policies, but no savings function.

Life insurance companies have also been active in a number of other financial service businesses. Life insurance companies sell a wide range of annuity contracts, both separately and as a part of other insuring arrangements. In exchange for a lump sum payment, annuities provide a continuous income stream to the holder. Closely related to these annuities are insured pension fund agreements under which a pension plan sponsor contracts with the insurance company to provide a continuous stream of specified retirement benefits to its employees. In addition, insurance companies have recently been selling various financial contracts, often to pension funds or other large investment pools, which guarantee a certain future sum in return for a current lump sum payment or stream of payments. In most states, life insurance companies are allowed to manage investment accounts for pension funds, separate from or without respect to the regulatory restraints imposed on their other businesses. All of these financial functions generate a pool of financial assets which must be invested to provide for the concomitant future financial liabilities. The growth in life insurance company assets is shown in Table 16–9. While the rate of growth of these assets has been considerably slower than pension funds, the assets of life insurance companies exceed the combined assets of private and public pension funds.

Table 16–9
Total financial assets of life insurance
companies (In billions)

1950	1960	1970	1976
$63	$116	$201	$311

Life insurance companies are heavily regulated by the states in which they operate, both as to the reserves required for various insurance functions and the investment policies for the underlying assets. These regulations, as well as the character of their liabilities, have tended to keep the investment policies of insurance companies relatively conservative, as suggested by the asset mix in Table 16–10. Life insurance companies have been a major investor in the corporate bond market and mortgage markets. In addition, policy loans and common stock are held as smaller elements of their portfolios.

Table 16–10
Life insurance companies estimated
portfolio holdings as of 12/31/76 (In
billions)

Mortgages on real estate	$ 92
Corporate bonds	122
Corporate stock	34
Policy loans	26
Other assets	37
Total assets	$311

Life insurance companies as suppliers of funds to the corporate bond market. As can be seen in Figure 16–5, the net acquisition of financial assets by life insurance companies has grown relatively smoothly because of the contractual nature of the insurance business. On the other hand, because of their low contractual interest rate, policy loans expanded sharply in periods of higher interest rates such as 1966, 1969–1970 and 1973–1974. Thus the flow of funds available for discretionary investment has been more irregular. Their net investment in corporate bonds has been even more irregular. One of the causes of this irregularity is the "forward commitment" process which is associated with the mortgage lending of life insurance companies. Funds for investment in real estate mortgages are committed forward for substantial lengths of time, often more than a year. These mortgage funds must be dispersed at the specified time, even if the total funds available for discretionary investment turn out to be less than was anticipated. Consequently, purchases of corporate bonds be-

Figure 16–5
Life insurance companies' investments in the bond market (Annual net flows)

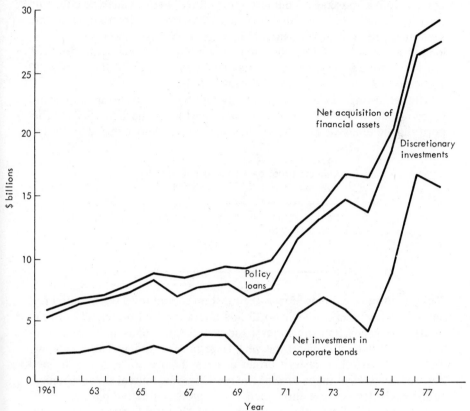

come one of the "swing factors" when the growth in discretionary investment funds falters at life insurance companies.[5]

The sizeable growth of corporate bond investments in 1975–1976 was caused by a number of factors, First, the net inflows to life insurance companies increased rapidly in this period. Partly because of ERISA (described earlier), life companies successfully attracted very large inflows from corporate pension funds under various guaranteed-rate contracts and other programs. Second, policy loans declined and released more funds for discretionary investment. Finally, the real estate mortgage funds dispersed by life companies were very small compared to earlier

---

[5] Actually, a large percentage of the corporate bond investment are also "committed forward." But the commitment periods are generally shorter. Also, some bonds are purchased without forward commitments, in the "spot" market. Hence, relatively speaking, bond purchases seem to be the swing factor.

years. The enormous problems of the real estate industry in these years (attributable to the overbuilding of the early 1970s) meant that relatively few attractive mortgage lending opportunities were available, either in commercial or large multifamily residential mortgages. In contrast, at the same time, there was a substantial increase in the demand for corporate long-term financing. Thus life companies redirected their cash flow toward corporate securities and thus substantially expanded the capability of the bond market to finance corporate needs.

Mutual savings banks. Mutual savings bank became an important source of funds to the corporate bond market in the late 1960s.[6] The portfolio holdings of mutual savings banks are shown in Table 16–11.

Table 16–11
Mutual savings banks' estimated portfolio
holdings as of 12/31/76 (In billions)

Mortgages on real estate	$ 82
Corporate bonds	20
Other	33
Total assets	$135

Clearly, corporate bonds are not the most important investment outlet for mutual savings banks. Their portfolios are comprised principally of real estate mortgages. On the other hand, corporate bonds have begun to attract the funds of some of the very large mutual savings banks in New York City and other eastern urban centers. Figure 16–6 shows the net flows of investment funds to financial markets from mutual savings banks. In the early 1960s these thrift institutions were not active purchasers of corporate bonds. Beginning in 1967, however, corporate bonds became an integral part of their investment strategy. Because of the tremendous cycles of disintermediation and reintermediation within thrift institutions, the total funds available for investment have been very cyclical. In the relatively low interest rate periods of 1967, 1971, and 1975, when mutual savings banks experienced strong inflows of funds and corporate bond demand was strong, corporate bonds were a major investment outlet. On the other hand, when higher interest rates substantially lowered the inflows of investable funds, in 1969 and 1973–1974, savings banks withdrew from the bond market.

Households. The other major class of investors in corporate bonds is households, primarily individuals. Households owned about $63 billion of corporate bonds at the end of 1977. This amounted to less than 3 percent

---

[6] Because mutual savings banks have their largest effect in the mortgage markets, a detailed analysis of their investment behavior is contained in Chapter 18, The Residential Mortgage Markets.

Figure 16–6
Mutual savings banks' investments in the bond market (Annual net flows)

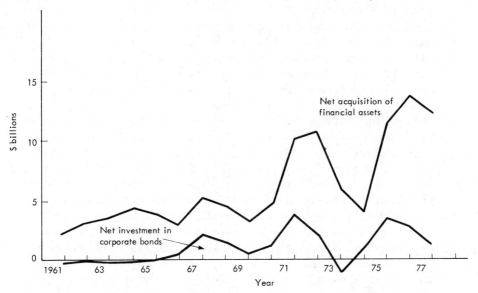

of households' financial assets. As a group, households owned a much larger amount of demand deposits, savings deposits, U.S. government securities, state/local government securities, and corporate equities. Even though corporate bonds were such a small percentage of the total financial assets of households, however, the net flow of funds from households into the bond market has at times been large relative to the volume of bond issues being sold (see Table 16–4). In periods of relatively low demand for corporate funds, households appear to purchase relatively few, if any, bonds. In periods of relatively large corporate demand, however, households become a major investor in bonds.

Interest rates on corporate bonds

The corporate demand for long-term funds displays wide cyclical fluctuations, rising in the latter stages of an economic expansion and reaching a maximum near, or just after, the peak in economic activity. The potential supply from the long-term institutional lenders who are active in the corporate bond market (pension funds and life insurance companies) is more stable. When the corporate demand for long-term funds is lower than the stable institutional supply, there is little if any upward pressure on corporate interest rates relative to other rates. As a group, corporations can satisfy their long-term funds needs without affecting corporate bond rates, and the traditional suppliers still have ample funds left over for their other investment alternatives. In contrast, periods like 1970–1971 and 1975–1976 have placed substantial pressures upon the corporate bond market. Prior to each of these periods, increasing inflation has led to expanded corporate financial needs, increased inflationary expectations, and higher nominal interest rates. During these periods, the enlarged corporate demand for long-term funds has exceeded the available institutional supply, thereby placing additional pressures upon the bond market.[7]

Figure 16–7 displays the behavior of three long-term interest rates in one of these periods, 1972–1976: the new long-term Aa utility bond rate (as a proxy for corporate bond rates), a (conventional) home mortgage rate, and a long-term U.S. government bond rate. The overall levels of all three of these long-term rates rose in 1974–1975, but each of the rates behaved somewhat differently. In 1974, the corporate bond rates rose most rapidly, opening up a wider spread between corporate rates and government rates and actually exceeding home mortgage rates for most of this same period. The large corporate demand for long-term funds drove corporate rates upward relative to other long term rates, enlarging the yield spread between corporate bonds and alternative long-term debts until enough incremental funds were supplied to satisfy the increased demand.[8]

As corporate bond rates rose relative to other rates in 1974, the additional suppliers that were attracted to the bond market were households. In 1975, they were households and mutual savings banks. Corporations have been able to raise substantial amounts of long-term funds during high-rate periods because they were willing to pay the high nominal rates and because of the willingness of these "swing investors" to invest in corporate bonds when their yields rose above the yields on other long-term debts.

Because the investors in the public bond market often discriminate against weaker credits, however, lower quality manufacturing companies

---

[7] This does not imply, of course, that corporations prefer to raise funds when rates are high. Indeed, as might be expected, just the opposite seems to be true. Other things equal, corporations prefer not to raise long-term funds when long-term rates are high. However, their total need for funds peaks near the times of high rates, and they seem to be less sensitive to high nominal rates than the other principal long-term borrowers. See Benjamin Friedman, "Financial Flow Variables and the Short-Run Determination of Long-Term Interest Rates," *The Journal of Political Economy,* vol. 85, no. 4 (1977).

[8] Supply and demand forces were not the only factors influencing corporate yield spreads in this period. In particular, possible increases in risk perceptions may have widened the yield spreads relative to government securities. A fuller discussion of these effects is delayed until later in this chapter. For an empirical analysis of some of these effects, see Ray C. Fair and Burton G. Malkiel, "The Determinants of Yield Differentials between Debt Instruments of the Same Maturity," *Journal of Money, Credit, and Banking* (November 1971), pp. 733–49; and Friedman, "Financial Flow Variables."

Figure 16–7
Comparative yields on long-term securities

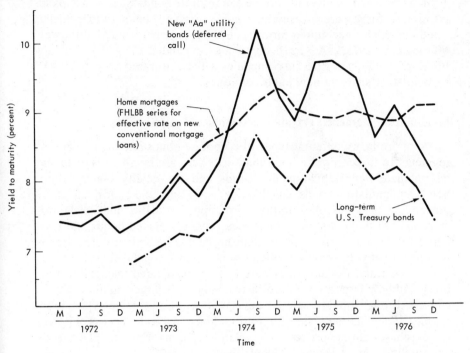

often experience special problems in obtaining large amounts of funds in the public markets. Indeed, while the corporate sector (in the aggregate) appears to be a relatively successful competitor for funds, this description does not always apply to the smaller and more risky (lower credit rating) companies. This is particularly true in times of increasing perceived risk in the economic environment and of large overall demands for funds. The composition (by credit rating) of publicly issued bonds is shown in Table 16–12. It demonstrates the sharp decline in the proportion of publicly

Table 16–12
Estimated composition of publicly offered straight corporate bonds—by credit rating

Credit rating	Average 1966–69	Average 1970–72	1973	1974	1975	1976
Aaa and Aa	48%	54%	61%	67%	57%	57%
A	21	33	29	29	36	28
Baa and below	25	10	5	6	7	14
Not rated	7	3	5	1	3	2

issued bonds with lower credit ratings in the early 1970s. During the years 1974–1975, when the overall volume of corporate bond issues was expanding rapidly, there were very few such publicly issued bonds. In 1974, higher rated companies accounted for an unusually large percentage of the new offerings. In 1975, ''A'' rated companies expanded their share of new offerings, but only in 1976 did companies with bonds rated lower than ''A'' recover their share of new public offerings.

Bond market segments: Private placements and public issues

There are many different types of corporate bonds and many different segments to the corporate bond market. There are long-term bonds and intermediate bonds, high-quality bonds and low-quality bonds, utility bonds and industrial bonds, callable bonds, sinking fund bonds, and many other types of bonds. Among the more important distinctions in the primary market is the distinction between privately placed bonds and publicly issued bonds. Private placements are highly illiquid corporate bonds sold to a relatively small number of purchasers through private negotiations. Generally, the purchasers are large sophisticated financial institutions. Publicly issued bonds are instead sold to a larger number of purchasers through a public sale, or underwriting. They are accompanied by a wider dissemination of investor information and a wider access of potential purchasers to the process. The relative volume of private placements and public issues is shown in Figure 16–8.

The markets for privately placed and publicly issued bonds are different in a number of respects, including, the suppliers of credit, the terms of the debt securities, and the demanders of credit. The life insurance industry typically supplies 90 percent of the private placements, and the ten largest insurance companies alone have typically accounted for 55 to 65 percent of this volume. In contrast, pension funds generally dominate the public issue market. Of course, individuals participate almost exclusively in the public issue market. The terms of the debt instruments are also different. In the public markets, the terms of the debt instruments reflect the prevailing norms and tend to be relatively standard. They vary relatively little from issue to issue and are rather inflexible in terms of any special needs of the issuer and/or investors. Conversely, the terms of a private placement can be extremely flexible. Special provisions are often created to meet particular financing problems of the borrower, and special protections are often included to meet the interests of the lender or lenders. In addition, private placements tend to have substantially shorter average lifetimes than publicly issued bonds, often because of a shorter final maturity (typically, 15 years instead of 25), and often through the use of more substantial cash sinking fund provisions which reduce the average life even further (typically, to 8–11 years).

Figure 16–8
Comparison of private placements and public issues (Annual net flows)

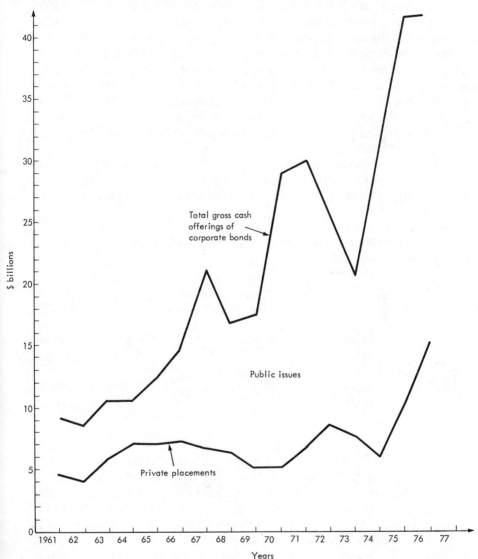

The differentiation in the corporate bond market between private placements and public issues is analogous to the segmentation that exists within corporate short-term markets. Private placements are in many ways longer term equivalents of bank loans. They are privately negotiated, specifically tailored debt financings, which are not traded on the open markets. (Indeed, shorter maturity private placements from insurance companies are very similar to term loans from banks.) Similarly, publicly issued bonds are the bond market equivalent of the short-term market instrument, open-market commercial paper. While the privately negotiated form of financing, bank loans, has dominated the short-term corporate market, the open-market form of bond financing, public issues, dominates the longer term bond market. Public utilities generally finance in the public markets, while manufacturing companies often finance in both the private and public markets. High-quality credits tend to finance in the public markets. Weaker credits, on the other hand, tend to finance through private placements, just as they relied upon bank loans in the short-term markets.[9]

Because of all these differences, the supply and demand characteristics in the privately placed and publicly issued markets can behave quite differently. Figure 16–9 shows the participants in the public and private

Figure 16–9
Diagram of market segmentation within the corporate bond market

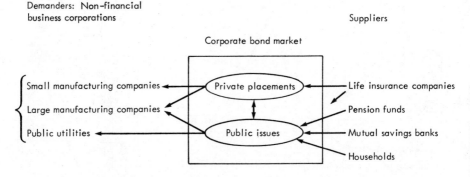

markets. Utilities tend to have a relatively steady demand for funds and tend to use the public markets. Thus there is a relatively steady flow of new public utility bonds in the public markets, punctuated by less frequent use of utility private placements when more unusual credit conditions prevail. Manufacturers, on the other hand, tend to have a very cyclical need for funds and use both public and private markets, depending upon the quality of the company and the available supplies of funds in the different markets. As Figure 16–8 suggests, the funds raised in the private placement market have been somewhat stable, while the funds

---

[9] There are, however, exceptions to these generalizations. For example, in 1975, the Sohio-BP Trans-Alaska Pipeline borrowed $1.75 billion in the private placement market, an all-time record. Because of the unique characteristics and risks of the "project financing," the private markets were better able to tailor a set of borrowing terms to its needs.

raised in the public markets have been more variable.[10] When the overall demand for funds is modest, the supply of private placements tends to be sufficient to meet much (if not all) of the manufacturing companies' needs for long-term funds. When the demand for funds soars, however, these manufacturing companies must attempt to raise funds in the public market. This component of bond financing (manufacturing companies in the public market) is the most variable of corporate bond flows.

The forward commitment process and the interest rates on private placements. Many private placements are arranged through forward commitments with life insurance companies. Recognizing the relative predictability of their future inflows, insurance companies will commit some of these future inflows to prescribed future private placements of long-term debt at prespecified interest rates. The borrower will have access to the "take-down" of this long-term debt over the period of the forward commitment, typically several months to one year. The insurance company bears the risk that long-term interest rates and/or their available funds will change significantly between the time of the commitment and the time that the funds are actually dispersed. In exchange for this service, insurance companies charge a commitment fee (often 0.5 percent of the principal) and an interest rate somewhat in excess of the current market rates at the time of the commitment. The interest rates on long-term private placements are thus really "administered" rates, much like bank loan rates. Like the bank's prime rate, however, they fluctuate with open-market rates (though with some lag) because of the close interconnection (on the demand side and on the supply side) between the various bond market segments. The potential competition offered by the availability of funds in the public markets tends to limit the rates that insurance companies can negotiate on these private placements.

One measure of the relative tightness of supply and demand conditions in the private placement market is the extent to which the life insurance companies, particularly the largest companies, have committed their expected fund flows forward. Once these companies have committed the largest fraction of their anticipated funds for the coming 12 months, the private placement market is considered to be relatively "tight." This is reflected in their reduced willingness to commit further funds except at effective interest rates that are relatively high compared to public markets. On the other hand, when these insurance companies have committed only a small fraction of their funds forward, they more aggressively seek further private placements at interest rates more comparable with open-market rates. The variations in the estimated forward-committed position can thus be used to monitor the relative supply and demand conditions in the private market.

---

[10] Except, of course, for the enormous increase in private placements in 1975–1976, fueled by the increased life insurance funds we have already discussed.

Adaptations of the corporate bond market

Institutions and individuals. One of the most interesting characteristics of a market is its ability to attract different groups of investors. In the early decades of this century, the corporate bond market was essentially a retail market, selling its securities through widespread distribution channels, largely to wealthy individuals. In the 1930s, however, the demand for long-term corporate funds fell sharply. Moreover, the personal income tax was becoming an important determinant of financial investment patterns. In the 1940s and 1950s, the large tax-exempt pension funds grew to be a major factor in our financial system. In response to these changes, the corporate bond market became an institutional market and remained so through the mid-1960s. The period 1961 through 1966 was typical of this institutional character. A relatively smooth and relatively small demand for corporate funds was met by the three long-term institutions: life insurance companies, public pension funds, and private pension funds. As Figures 16–3, 16–4, and 16–5 illustrated, the net new bond purchases of these three institutions were steady through this period, and they supplied almost the entire needs of the bond market.

This period of relative tranquility was disturbed beginning in 1967; and by 1970–1971 the bond market has drastically changed. The demand for corporate funds soared in 1970–1971 in response to the large external financing needs of both utilities and manufacturing companies. Even if the three steady institutional suppliers of funds had remained, they would not have been able to supply this increased demand. To make matters worse, the institutional suppliers also changed dramatically. The life insurance companies were disintermediated by their policy loans, and in 1969–1970 drastically reduced their heretofore steady supply of funds to the bond market (see Figure 16–5). Furthermore, around 1968, corporate pension funds began to reduce their purchases of corporate bonds. In 1971–1972, they actually began to disinvest in bonds, allocating more than 100 percent of their new funds to equities (see Figure 16–4). Thus two of the three large institutional suppliers of funds were no longer steady purchasers of bonds. Indeed, only the public pension funds remained to meet the vastly enlarged demand for funds. In response, relative interest rates were driven up until mutual savings banks became an important supplier to the bond market. More importantly, households once again became the largest net purchasers of new bonds. Attracted by relatively high interest rates and served by a revived network of stockbrokers turned bond salespeople, individuals stepped in to supply a surprisingly expanded volume of funds to the market. While institutions have returned to the bond market recently, individuals continue to be an important new source of funds in years of peak financing demands.

Convertible bonds. In the late 1960s and early 1970s, the corporate bond market adapted in other ways to the changing forces of supply and demand. Not only did the distribution channels change but the type of security itself changed. During the late 1960s and early 1970s, the equity market was a constant "threat" to the bond market's sources of supply. As we have seen, private pension funds became increasingly disenchanted with the bond market in those years, preferring instead the equity investments available in the stock market. In addition, both life insurance companies and public pension funds were allocating increasing fractions of their investible funds to equities. In response, the bond market revived what had been a relatively less well-known type of financing, the convertible bond. "Convertibles" were used, both in the privately placed and publicly issued market, to add an element of equity participation for the bond buyer.[11] These "convertibles" became a significant fraction of total bond financing for a number of years, as Figure 16–10 demonstrates. They helped to maintain the participation of major suppliers of funds during a period where their interest in straight long-term bonds was waning. With the disenchantment in equities (stemming from the market declines) of 1973–1974, convertibles became much less important. Indeed, by 1973–1975, they had become once again an almost negligible percentage of new public bond issues, and equity participation had similarly become very unimportant in the private placement markets.

Intermediate-term publicly issued bonds. Most corporate bonds, particularly most publicly issued bonds, have long-term maturities of 25 or 30 years.[12] Intermediate-term bonds (five to ten-year maturities) have also played an important role in the adaptations of the bond market. Because bonds are long-term fixed dollar contracts, the expected "real" value of their future payments is dependent upon the expected rate of future inflation. Furthermore, the current uncertainty about the future value of these payments is dependent upon the uncertainty of future inflation. As we have seen, the 1974–1975 period was characterized by important financial and economic crosscurrents, affecting both the possible rates of future economic activity and future inflation. In these years, traditional bond market investors were extremely concerned about the uncertainties of future inflation and its potential effects upon long-term fixed-rate bonds. At the same time, corporate demands for long-term funds expanded dramatically in this period, and one of the important "swing investors" who had to be attracted to the bond market was the household sector. As we have seen in earlier chapters, households appear to prefer short-term, more liquid financial assets (like time and savings deposits or short-term U.S. government securities) and require a premium to invest in longer

---

[11] In the private placement market, the equity participation is actually called an "equity kicker" rather than a "convertible," and it can take a variety of forms.

[12] Actually, these bonds are generally "callable" after five or ten years so that their expected maturity may be considerably less than their normal maturity. This will be discussed in more detail later.

Figure 16–10
Cash offerings of convertible bonds within the total bond market (Annual net flows)

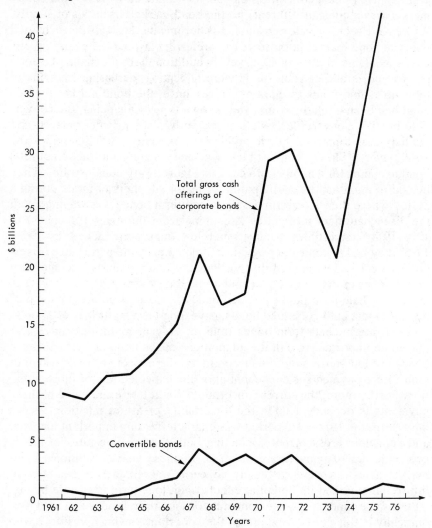

term securities. Caught between the increased need for long-term funds, the increased fears of uncertain inflation, and a shifting mix of investors, corporations adapted the maturity and terms of their bond offerings. As Table 16–13 suggests, intermediate-term maturities became a common feature of corporate bonds in 1974–1975. In fact, most of the very large increase in publicly issued corporate bonds in this period was attributable to the expansion in intermediate-term issues. In 1976, this surge of

Table 16–13
Maturity of publicly issued corporate bonds (Flows of funds in billions)

	1973	1974	1975	1976
Total publicly issued corporate bonds (gross new issues)	$13.3	$26.1	$32.7	$26.1
Long-term bonds	12.2	18.3	19.9	18.8
Intermediate-term bonds	1.1	7.8	12.8	7.3

intermediate-term issues receded. However, the ability of large corporations to adapt their bond maturities during this period played a key role in retaining some of their traditional investors and in attracting new investors to the bond market.

The bond market as a source of finance

As these episodes suggest, the bond market is an important and adaptable source of long-term funds. Large prime-credit corporations have raised large amounts of funds in the bond market at the times they were needed. They have been able to do so because long-term bonds have been generally well-suited to the investment needs of three large institutional investors, because the nature of long-term bond contracts has been adapted to the changing investment tastes of these investors, because the corporations have been willing to pay the higher rates necessary at times to attract new groups of "swing investors," and because of a flexible distribution system that has successfully attracted a changing mix of investor groups. Unfortunately, smaller (and riskier) companies have not always been able to finance through publicly issued bonds. Also because of the limited size of the private placement market, their overall ability to raise long-term funds has been occasionally constrained (particularly in times of enlarged perceived risks and large long-term financing needs). Nonetheless, from an aggregate perspective, the corporate bond market has adapted well to the needs of the corporate sector as a whole, supplying substantial flows of long-term funds.

PRICING IN THE SECONDARY MARKET FOR CORPORATE BONDS

Most of the trading in outstanding corporate bonds does not take place on any organized exchange, such as the New York Stock Exchange. Rather it is channeled through what has come to be called an over-the-counter (OTC) market, a group of dealer firms who sell (and buy) bonds to (from) investors. The liquidity of publicly issued corporate bonds can vary enormously from one issue to another. Dealer firms stand ready to make active markets in those large issues of prime-credit well-known firms which have wide appeal to various investor groups. Smaller issues, perhaps from firms with lower credit ratings, are not so widely traded. At the extreme, the market for them can be very illiquid indeed.[13]

The composition of outstanding corporate bonds

There are a wide variety of alternatives from which a potential investor in outstanding publicly issued corporate bonds may choose. Table 16–14

Table 16–14
Volume outstanding of publicly offered straight corporate bonds by industry and credit rating (Billions of dollars, as of December 31, 1977)*

Credit rating (Standard & Poor's)	Utili- ties	Indus- trials	Finance	Trans- portation	Total
AAA	31.4	12.4	8.1	2.5	54.3
AA	33.4	19.6	14.0	1.3	68.3
A	41.1	21.1	8.3	2.5	73.0
BBB	16.0	6.1	2.8	1.4	26.2
Other	0.9	7.2	1.8	3.6	13.5
Total	122.7	66.4	35.0	11.2	235.3

* Source: *The Anatomy of a Secondary Market in Corporate Bonds: Year-End, 1977 Update,* Salomon Brothers, 1978.

shows the composition of outstanding corporate bonds, classified by broad industry categories and credit ratings, as of the end of 1977. Utilities account for 52 percent of the outstanding corporate bonds. High-grade corporate bonds (rates AAA and AA) account for half of the market. Bonds rated A account for almost a third. Thus the largest segment of the secondary market for corporate bonds is the market for relatively creditworthy utility issues, with smaller amounts scattered through the other categories.

Unlike common stocks, a single issuer may have many different types of bonds outstanding, adding to the complexity of the secondary bond market. For example, there may be bonds outstanding with a relatively short time or with a long time to maturity. For a given maturity, there may be bonds outstanding with relative low coupons (probably issued some time ago, when interest rates were lower) and bonds outstanding with

---

[13] More precisely, a potential seller would have to make a substantive price concession to sell a large amount of these "illiquid" issues in a relatively short period of time.

higher coupons (probably issued more recently). Moreover, the particular details of different bond issues may vary because of call features, sinking funds, indentures, and other features.[14] Large companies who have actively financed in the bond market may have literally dozens of outstanding bonds (AT&T, for example), all with different maturities, coupons, call features, and so forth, all of which are competing alternatives for the bond investor.

Table 16–15 classifies the bonds outstanding in 1977 along two impor-

Table 16–15A
Volume outstanding of publicly offered straight corporate bonds by industry and coupon (As of December 31, 1977; billions of $)

Coupon (percent)	Utility	Industrial	Finance	Trans- portation	Total
Under 4	10.6	0.7	0.0	1.4	12.7
4–4.99	14.7	3.5	2.9	2.4	23.6
5–5.99	7.0	3.8	1.5	0.9	13.1
6–6.99	8.4	5.4	2.6	0.3˙	16.7
7–7.99	23.6	12.8	9.2	1.6	47.2
8–8.99	34.8	26.2	13.7	3.0	77.7
9–9.99	15.9	10.7	4.2	0.9	31.7
10 and above	7.6	3.4	0.9	0.8	12.7
Total	122.7	66.4	35.0	11.2	235.3

Table 16–15B
Volume outstanding of publicly offered straight corporate bonds by industry and final maturity (As of December 31, 1977; billions of $)

Final maturity	Utility	Industrial	Finance	Trans- portation	Total
1978	1.2	0.1	0.7	0.2	2.1
1979–82	11.0	4.6	8.2	1.3	25.1
1983–87	12.0	9.5	9.0	2.1	32.6
1988–97	26.5	23.0	9.0	4.1	62.6
1998–2007	56.1	29.1	8.1	2.7	96.0
2008 and later	16.0	0.1	*	0.8	16.8
Total	122.7	66.4	35.0	11.2	235.3

* Less than $50 million.
Source: *The Anatomy of a Secondary Market in Corporate Bonds: Year-End, 1977 Update*, Salomon Brothers.

---

[14] Most corporate bonds are callable, which means that the issuer may buy them back from the investors at prespecified prices at prespecified times, although most issues also now allow some initial call protection for the investor. Many issues also include "sinking funds," pursuant to which the issuer must continually retire the issue over time.

tant dimensions—final maturity and coupon. Almost one half of these bonds matured after 1998, the bulk of them carried coupons between 7 and 9 percent. In general, the shortest maturity bonds tended to have lower coupons and vice versa. The remarkable feature of Table 16–15 however, is the diversity of maturity-coupon combinations. They form a very broad matrix of alternative investments.

Increasingly, professional bond managers (for example, the investment managers representing some pension funds) have been attempting to improve their investment returns by taking advantage of this diversity. When these money managers expect rates to fall, they shift their holdings toward longer maturities. When they expect rates to rise, they shift their holdings toward shorter maturities. In addition, they shift their holdings among coupon rates, credit rating, and different individual issues in search of underpriced securities and therefore increased expected returns. The increasing trading activity of these bond investors has been an important factor in the increasing liquidity of the secondary bond market.

The variability of holding period returns for long-term corporate bonds

Holding period returns and yields to maturity. At any point in time, the yield to maturity of a bond is the discount rate which makes the discounted value of the future interest and principal repayments equal to the bond's current price. Considering a bond with price P, maturity τ, coupon C, and par value $1,000, the cash flows over its lifetime are:

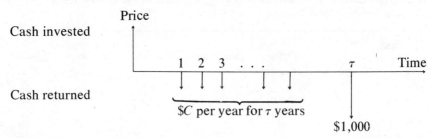

Algebraically, the yield to maturity, y, is the discount rate which solves the implicit equation:

$$P = \frac{C}{(1 + y)} + \frac{C}{(1 + y)^2} + \cdots + \frac{C}{(1 + y)^\tau} + \frac{1,000}{(1 + y)^\tau}$$

During a given period of time, the holding period return on a bond is comprised of the predictable income from the bond's coupon and the capital gain or loss which arises from any change in the price of the bond. Changes in yield to maturity are clearly related to holding period returns; in fact, they are inversely related. When the price of a bond increases, its yield to maturity falls and the investor receives a capital gain (and thus a relatively larger holding period return). When the price of a bond falls, its yield to maturity increases and the investor sustains a capital loss (and thus a smaller, perhaps negative, holding period return).

The empirical record for a composite index.   The long-run record of annual holding period returns from a composite index of long-term corporate bonds is shown in Figure 16–11 in the form of a histogram (a relative

Figure 16–11
A histogram of annual holding priced returns for high grade long-term corporate bonds, 1926–1976

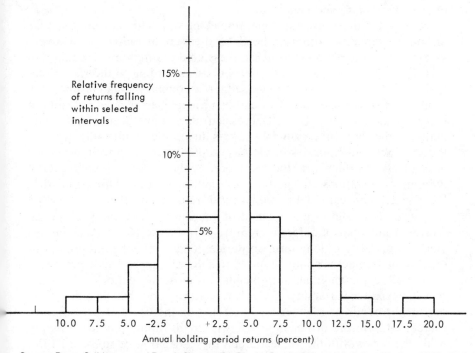

Source: Roger G. Ibbotson and Rex A. Sinquefield, *Stocks, Bonds, Bills, and Inflation: The Past (1926–1976) and the Future (1977–2000)*, The Financial Analysts Research Foundation, 1977.

frequency diagram). Over the 50 years from 1926 to 1976, the annual holding period returns clustered in the 2.5 to 5.0 percent per year range, although there were some years with much larger gains and losses. The arithmetic mean return (that is, the average annual return) was 4.2 percent. The standard deviation of returns, a measure of their variability, was 5.6 percent.[15] There is, of course, little reason to believe that the distribu-

---

[15] The standard deviation is defined such that roughly two thirds of the observations in a normal distribution should fall between ± one standard deviation of the mean. Thus, roughly two thirds of the observations fell between −1.4 percent and +9.8 percent.

tion of annual returns in long-term bonds should be stationary over time. Nonetheless, these long-run data provide an interesting benchmark against which to consider both recent returns and prospective future returns. The variability of these returns is also a quantitative measure of the risks to which bond investors were exposed during this 50-year period.

The variability of holding period returns for different corporate bonds. There are, as we have seen, many different types of corporate bonds outstanding. While the data in Figure 16–11 measure the past variability of returns for an index composed of many bonds, each type of bond has had its own unique price history. In particular, the different types of bonds have exposed investors to substantially different amounts of price variability and hence risk.

Perhaps the most obvious dimension along which to compare the risks of holding different corporate bonds is their credit rating. Subjectively assessed by various rating agencies, these credit ratings are an attempt to classify corporations, and thus their bonds, according to the risk of default. In the long run, of course, either a company defaults upon the promised payments of coupons and/or principal, or it does not, and in recent years (since the Great Depression) there have been very few defaults. In the short run, financial markets themselves continually evaluate the prospective default risk of various corporations and price their bonds accordingly. In the short run, therefore, as the underlying prospects of different corporations change through time, the prices of the bonds they have issued changes, and the holding period returns from their bonds vary.

Figure 16–12 shows one method of gauging the variability of annual returns from bonds of different credit risk. In Figure 16–12 the estimated yields to maturity of long-term corporate bonds with different credit ratings are plotted across time, inverted to show the approximate price variability of outstanding long-term bonds.[16] A close inspection of the figure reveals a greater variability of yields to maturity and thus holding period returns for bonds with lower credit ratings. In the Great Depression, for example, the prices of bonds with lower credit ratings slumped sharply while the bonds with the highest credit rating (Aaa) were stable. In 1974, for example, the price declines (yield increases) of bonds with lower credit ratings were significantly sharper than other bonds. As we might expect, the greater long-term default risks of bonds with lower credit ratings have been reflected in their greater short-term price variability. These riskier bonds have offered a greater yield to maturity to compensate for this risk.

Another important dimension along which to compare the price variability (and risks) of holding bonds is their maturity. The holding period

---

[16] For a very long-term bond, the percentage gain/loss in price is almost the inverse of the change in yield to maturity. Thus, the curve in Figure 16–12 can be thought of as a plot of price changes for outstanding long-term bonds.

Figure 16–12
Industrial bond yields by ratings (Monthly averages)

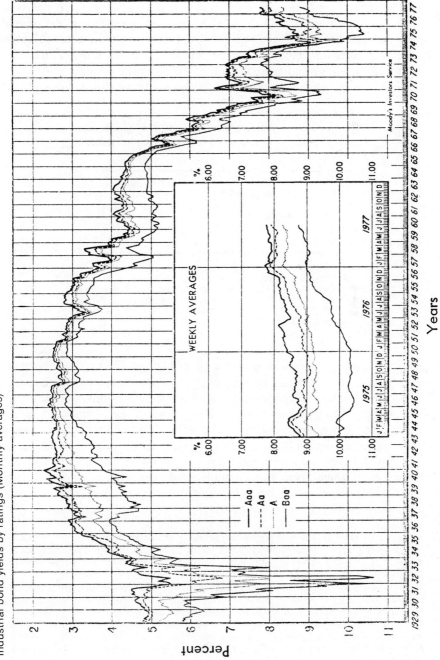

Source: *Moody's Industrial Manual,* 1977.

returns from long-term bonds have been more variable than those for very short-term securities. While the standard deviation of the annual holding period returns on long-term corporate bonds was 5.6 percent per year over the time period 1926–1976, the standard deviation of the annual holding period returns from a policy which continually invested in short-term U.S. Treasury bills was 2.1 percent per year. Moreover, this same effect can be observed over the entire spectrum of possible maturities. Table 16–16 shows the variability of annual holding period returns for the

Table 16–16
High-grade corporate bonds: the variability of annual holding period returns (1969–1976) measured relative to one-year risk-free rate*

Type of bond	Standard deviation of returns
Long-term bonds	9.0%
Intermediate (5–10 years) bonds	3.6%

* These data are taken from estimates of returns for different classes of bonds. See Salomon Brothers "1976 Annual Review of the Bond Market." The one-year risk-free rate is assumed to be the yield on one-year Treasury securities at the beginning of the year. Estimates of returns from intermediate bonds are not readily available for years before 1969.

long-term and intermediate-term bonds of high-grade corporate borrowers. The relative holding period returns for the long-term bonds have clearly been more variable than the intermediate bonds.[17] This is not surprising, of course, because relatively more of the actual cash distributions of the long-term bonds will be realized in the distant future when their value relative to other assets is substantially more uncertain.[18]

There are other dimensions along which the price variability of different bonds can be analyzed. For example, two outstanding bonds with the same credit rating and identical final maturities can have very different coupon rates. A lower coupon bond will have less of its total future value

---

[17] The standard deviation of the holding period returns from long-term corporate bonds during these years was substantially higher than the data in Figure 16–11 suggesting that the volatility of long-term bonds (in these years, at least) increased substantially relative to the past 50 years.

[18] Many analysts argue that a concept called "duration" is a better measure of the term of bonds than is their maturity. For a discussion of this idea, see Richard W. McEnally, "Duration as a Practical Tool for Bond Management," *Journal of Portfolio Management* (Summer 1977). The uncertainty is larger for cash flows in the distant future because, first, the probability of default increases, but more importantly, because the cumulative effects of uncertain inflation make the *real* value of the flows more uncertain the further they are in the future.

dependent upon its stream of coupon payments and more of its value dependent upon the final repayment of principal. Conversely, a higher coupon bond will have more of its value dependent upon the higher stream of coupon payments. For the same final maturity, a larger fraction of the cash flows from the low coupon bond will be realized in the more distant future when their value relative to other assets may be more uncertain. We would expect, therefore, that the current value of low coupon bonds (often called "deep discount" bonds) would be more uncertain and hence more variable over time. Other things being equal, this has indeed been the case.

Unfortunately, the relative values of bonds with different coupons is complicated by a complex variety of considerations surrounding the call provisions of bonds. Indeed, the call provisions, sinking fund provisions, and other complex features of bond contracts greatly complicate the simple observations we have made here. For example, suppose that a bond may be "called" by the corporation (that is, purchased from the investors) at a given price, say $105. This call provision provides an upper range beyond which the price of the bond is unlikely to increase. Investors would clearly be reluctant to pay much more than $105 for a bond that could be purchased ("called") from them, at any time, for only $105. The existence of a call provision thus tends to dampen the possible upward price movements of a bond, limiting the variability of its holding period returns, though in an asymmetric way. A more precise analysis of these call provision effects and the related effects of other complex parts of various bond agreements is beyond the scope of this book. For our purposes, it is clear that each outstanding issue of corporate bonds has its own unique characteristics—credit risk, maturity, coupon rate, call provisions, and so on. These characteristics all impact the variability of holding period returns and thus the risks of bond investing. As we have seen, all other things being equal, the price of an outstanding bond issue with greater credit risk, longer maturity, or lower coupon will tend to be more variable, and hence these bonds will be more risky.

The basic equilibrium relationship—corporate bonds and stocks

The above discussion has identified the risk of a bond with the variability of its price. As we showed in Chapter 10, a better measure of the risk of a security is the extent to which the individual security increases the overall portfolio risk for an investor. In this section, we use this concept of portfolio risk to examine the past holding period returns from corporate bonds relative to another class of assets—common stocks.

In Chapter 10, we derived a theory of financial asset pricing which stated that the expected returns of a risky security, should be proportional to the β of that security, where β was a measure the extent to which the security contributes to overall portfolio risk. Defining the "expected excess return" of a security to be its expected return minus the risk-free rate, the theory predicted that:

$$E_j = \beta_j E_m \tag{1}$$

That is, the theory predicted that all securities should be priced in equilibrium *relative* to one another such that their expected excess returns were just equal to their β times the expected excess returns of the market.

The basic risk-return relationship was derived in ex-ante terms; that is, it referred to the expectations for future security returns and prospective risks as they are assessed in the minds of investors. There is, of course, no direct way of observing these ex-ante expectations. Furthermore, in the short run, actual returns can depart substantially from expected returns, complicating any empirical test of the equilibrium relationship which is based upon data collected for short time periods. We can, however, observe long-run average returns from different types of securities, and compare them to their historical βs. These ex-post observations can be considered to be empirical benchmarks against which to compare the predictions of the equilibrium relationship.

In one such study, Sharpe estimated the average quarterly returns from three types of assets: corporate bonds, common stocks, and a "market portfolio" composed of both these bonds and stocks, during the years 1938–1971.[19] The annualized average excess returns for each of these security groups, and its β relative to the "market portfolio" are shown in Table 16–17. Interestingly enough, these long-run returns are approxi-

Table 16–17
A comparison of average excess returns and portfolio risk for corporate bonds and stocks (1938–1971)

Portfolio of securities	Annualized average excess returns	Estimated β relative to "market portfolio"
Corporate bonds............	4.3%	0.44
"Market portfolio" of bonds and stocks.........	8.5	1.00
Corporate stocks	9.2	1.14

---

[19] See William F. Sharpe, "Bonds versus Stocks: Capital Market Theory," *The Financial Analysts Journal* (November/December 1973). The quarterly returns for corporate bonds were estimated from the investment returns of a mutual fund portfolio of "medium-grade" corporate bonds. The common stock returns were estimated on the basis of the Dow-Jones Industrial Average. The "market portfolio" was assumed to consist of a mixture of those bonds and stocks, weighted according to the estimated market values of bonds (excluding U.S. Treasury bonds) and stocks listed on the New York Stock Exchange. The risk-free rate was assumed to be the rate on bankers acceptances. Needless to say, each of these was just an approximation to the returns from a more complete bond, stock, or market portfolio.

mately what we would have expected on the basis of the theoretical equilibrium relationship. Because the average *excess* returns for both bonds and stocks are greater than zero, we know that they both (on average) returned more than the risk-free asset, as we would have predicted they should in a world where investors are risk-averse. In addition, the average returns from stocks exceeded the average returns from bonds, as they should have, based upon their respective βs. Moreover, the ratio of the average long-run excess returns from stocks versus bonds was, roughly speaking, about the same as the ratio of their βs. This is exactly the ex-ante relationship that would have been predicted by the basic equilibrium theory, as quantified in equation (1).[20] In the very long run, the average relative returns from bonds and stocks have been consistent with the relative pricing predicted by the theoretical equilibrium structure.

Risk and the term structure of interest rates

In this chapter we have shown that long-term bonds are riskier than short-term bonds. That is, the holding period return from long-term bonds are more variable than for short-term bonds. More importantly, the holding period returns from long-term bonds have a higher degree of systematic risk than do the returns from short-term bonds. To compensate for this greater risk, investors demand a higher expected return from holding long-term bonds. In Chapter 9, this additional expected return from long-term bonds was called a liquidity premium. This chapter has demonstrated that these liquidity premiums can be seen as a rational response to the increased risk in holding long-term bonds.[21] Thus even if the market expected short-term interest rates to stay at their current levels, the yield curve should be upward sloping, reflecting the increased risks associated with longer term bonds. Not surprisingly, therefore, the yield curve for corporate bonds (and other bonds) does slope upward, on average. Even though long-term yields to maturity are less variable than short-term yields, the holding period returns from long-term bonds are more variable and have more systematic risk. The "usual" shape of the yield curve is upward sloping in order to compensate investors for this greater risk.

---

[20] While these empirical results are consistent with the theory, they are by no means a rigorous test. In particular, while they confirm a relationship between risk and average return, they are not a test of whether β is *the* appropriate measure of risk (as opposed to other potential measures). There is, however, an interesting byproduct of these tests. The long-run average excess returns earned on the "market portfolio" can be considered to be a benchmark for the expected return that investors require from all risk assets, the "market price of risk."

[21] This is strictly true, of course, only for those investors whose time horizons are consistent with the short holding periods we have examined.

The departures from equilibrium—the forces of supply and demand

While the equilibrium relationship between the expected returns from bonds and other securities may hold in the long run, the bond market is continually buffeted in the short run by the forces of supply and demand. In Chapter 9 it was shown that the relationship between long-term and short-term yields could be influenced by supply and demand if borrowers and investors have "preferred maturities" for their financing and investment. In addition, if the various markets for long-term debt are partially segmented from each other, these supply and demand effects can influence the levels of various long-term rates. In this chapter, it was argued that corporations can expand their ability to attract investors by driving up yields on long-term corporate bonds relative to other long-term debt obligations. Several researchers have studied this process and have concluded that supply and demand forces do influence the *relative* level of long-term corporate yields.[22] In addition, the forces of supply and demand may also affect relative yields and prices among the many various segments of the corporate bond market.

It is, of course, impossible to demonstrate that long-term bond yields were in equilibrium, or out of equilibrium, at any particular time. Because expected returns are unobservable, we just do not know for sure. The activities of most bond market participants, however, are deeply rooted in the perceived importance of supply and demand forces. While many issuers, investment bankers, and investors are willing to believe that bond prices and expected returns may be in equilibrium in the very long-run, they believe the forces of supply and demand cause a constantly changing set of yield spreads and expected returns for different securities in the short run. They believe these divergences from equilibrium offer the opportunities for creative financing decisions and astute investment decisions, the ends to which they strive.

The hypothesis of "efficient markets" in the bond market

In contrast, the hypothesis of efficient markets would deny the existence of these opportunities. The hypothesis of efficient market is based upon the assumption that investors are incorporating all available information into their expectations of future returns and is an extension of the equilibrium relationship. It implies that all corporate bonds should be appropriately priced relative to each other at all times through the risk-adjusted equilibrium relationship. Furthermore, corporate bonds should be appropriately priced relative to all other securities, for example, common stocks. Moreover it should be impossible for investors to improve

---

[22] Friedman, "Financial Flow Variables."

their risk-adjusted investment returns by actively buying/selling bonds because all relevant information about the future returns from bonds should have already been incorporated into their current price.

In a number of ways, the general thrust of this hypothesis is quite plausible. As we saw earlier, some investors in the household sector show a great willingness to move funds in and out of the corporate bond market if interest rates in that market move away from interest rates on other securities. There is also an active number of traders in the bond market who are increasingly willing to trade between the segments of the bond market in search of increased investment returns. These investors and traders embody the equilibrium forces which tend to force the expected returns from bonds back to their equilibrium structure. Moreover, the information most relevant to future bond price movements, economic data bearing upon future inflation and interest rate changes, is widely and quickly disseminated and repeatedly discussed throughout the financial community. It would not be surprising if, at that margin, active bond traders incorporated this information into their investment decisions and consequently into bond prices.

On the other hand, the extreme form of this hypothesis does seem implausible: namely, that each traded bond is precisely in equilibrium with every other bond at all times. In such a world, there would literally be no way to increase expected investment returns except by holding riskier bonds. The more practical question raised by the strong form of this hypothesis is: Do the increased transactions costs associated with trading marketable bonds outweigh the increased returns available? Unfortunately there is very little hard evidence on this question. Bond indexes, against which performance can be measured, have only recently been constructed, and as yet there are no publicly available studies on performance results. An empirical test of the strong form of this hypothesis awaits these results.

Ironically enough, the segmentation and imperfections of the secondary bond market sow the seeds of their own destruction. The more segmented these markets are, the more supply and demand forces will perturb market prices, forming opportunities for active traders; but the more traders attempt to exploit these opportunities, the more bond prices will be driven toward the basic equilibrium structure. The more astute these bond traders become in forecasting future prices (yields), the more prevailing bond prices will be described by the hypothesis of efficient markets. Ironically, in the world of an efficient bond market, the opportunities for bond trading would have disappeared. Despite the enormous complexity of the secondary bond market, therefore, more active bond trading will insure not only that markets are more liquid, but also that there are smaller rewards for active bond trading.

QUESTIONS

1. What do the institutions that buy corporate bonds seem to find attractive about them?
2. How are the corporate bond and home mortgage markets connected?
3. Why do some borrowers pay for forward commitments? Why do insurance companies offer them? What factors should affect the fees charged for forward commitments?
4. How should interest rates in the public issue and private placement markets be related to each other?
5. Analyze the changing terms of new bond issues in recent years. How would you explain these changes using supply and demand concepts, or expectations concepts?
6. Analyze the impact of inflation on the corporate bond market. How might it relate to some of the above phenomena?

REFERENCES

Bodie, Zvi and Friedman, Benjamin M. "Interest Rate Uncertainty and the Value of Bond Call Protection," *Journal of Political Economy,* vol. 86, no. 1 (1978), pp. 19–44.

Lindrall, John R. "New Issue Corporate Bonds, Seasoned Market Efficiency and Yield Spreads," *The Journal of Finance,* vol. 32, no. 4 (September 1977), pp. 1057–67.

Munnell, Alicia H. "Private Pensions and Saving: New Evidence," *Journal of Political Economy,* vol. 84, no. 5 (1976), pp. 1013–32.

Shapiro, Eli and Wolf, Charles R. *The Role of Private Placements in Corporate Finance.* Harvard University, Graduate School of Business Administration, 1972.

Treynor, Jack L., Regan, Patrick J., and Priest, William W. *The Financial Reality of Pension Funding Under ERISA,* (Homewood, Ill.: Dow-Jones Irwin, 1976).

Funding Pensions: Issues and Implications for Financial Markets. Conference Series No. 16, Federal Reserve Bank of Boston, 1976.

17

The corporate equity market

The market for corporate equities plays a unique role in the U.S. capital markets. The primary market for new equity securities provides a potentially important means for corporations to augment their equity capital, even though the actual flow of new equity capital through these markets is small compared to the flows of new credit in other financial markets. The value of outstanding equity securities is very large, and the secondary markets for trading these securities (the stock exchanges) are among the best-known and most closely followed of financial markets. They serve a very important function in our financial system—that of providing liquidity to a major share of our national wealth. This chapter deals with the equity market as a source of new funds for business and with the relationship between risk and the returns on common stock.[1]

A common stock is a claim on the residual income and/or value of the enterprise after the claims of creditors have been satisfied. Its value

---

[1] Common stock is the most important type of equity security. However, preferred stocks are also generally classified as equity securities. Convertible bonds, and other types of convertible securities, are a hybrid between common stock and bonds. Also, there are warrants and other special forms of securities, such as options, whose values are related to the value of an underlying equity security. While these other forms of equity and quasiequity securities may be an important element in a particular firm's financing decision, they are only of secondary importance in the equity market. This analysis will thus focus on common stock.

333

changes with changes in estimates of the future value or income-generating capacity of the enterprise. The existence of debt in corporate balance sheets means that changes in the expected future value of the underlying enterprises are magnified (or leveraged into even greater percentage changes in the expected future value of the residual equity claim). Thus, despite the rather smooth flow of dividend income which many corporations transmit to their shareholders, the level of stock prices has shown considerable variability. Figure 17–1 shows the value of the Standard & Poor's 500 Index, a reasonable proxy for the level of stock prices.[2]

Figure 17–1
The level of stock prices as measured by Standard and Poor's 500 Stock Index

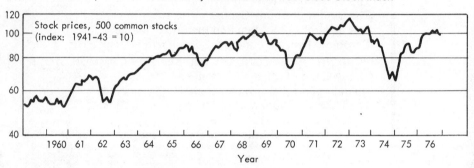

THE PRIMARY STOCK MARKET AS A SOURCE OF CORPORATE FUNDS

The demand for new equity capital

The issuers. The demand for new equity capital in U.S. markets has been dominated by domestic nonfinancial business corporations (see Table 17–1). Among these corporations, public utilities have been a particularly important demanders of funds, accounting for well over half of the gross new equity issues in the 1971–1975 period. Comparing Table 17–1 with other chapters, the total amount of equity capital raised is small relative to the volume of funds raised in other financial markets.

The dominant method of distributing new equity issues is an underwritten public offering, where a syndicate of investment bankers buys the issue from a corporations and distributes it to the investing public. There are other methods of distribution too. In particular, the rights offering is still an important form of equity distribution. In a rights offering, the

---

[2] Needless to say, many stocks are more volatile than this index and other stocks are less volatile, but Figure 17–1 is a reasonable proxy for the total returns from a well-diversified portfolio of common stock.

Table 17–1
The composition of demand for new equity capital (Billions of dollars)

	1971	1972	1973	1974	1975	1976	1977
Nonfinancial corporate business	11.4	10.9	7.9	4.1	9.9	10.5	3.7
Financial intermediaries	2.6	3.4	2.7	1.0	.2	1.7	1.4
Rest of the world	*	−0.4	−0.2	−0.2	0.1	*	.4
Total	13.7	13.8	10.4	4.8	10.2	12.2	5.5

corporation offers a new equity security (or debt, for that matter) to its existing shareholders on the basis of the prorata shares that they hold. In addition, equity securities are sometimes privately placed with institutional investors, although this is uncommon except for small companies and the preferred stock of larger companies. Finally, a number of corporations have begun issuing new equity directly to their shareholders through dividend reinvestment plans which allow investors to reinvest their dividends in newly issued stock of the company.

The timing of stock issues. The largest source of new equity capital for nonfinancial business corporations has been internally generated retained earnings. When the total need for funds has become very large relative to the volume of retained earnings, however, corporations have raised additional amounts of equity through the sale of new stock issues. Figure 17–2 displays the time pattern of corporate external financing. In the early and mid-1960s, the amount of net new equity issues was extremely small, at least for the nonfinancial corporate sector as a whole.[3] In the early 1970s, however, there were two surges in new equity financing, 1971–1972 and 1975–1976. Total corporate external financing needs were large throughout the 1970s and especially large in 1973–1974. However, the increased issuance of new stock occurred before (1971–1972) and after (1975–1976) the peak in external needs. Figure 17–1 provides some insight into this timing pattern. The years 1969 and 1970, and the years 1973 and 1974, were years of sharply falling stock prices, when most corporations would have had to sell common stock at prices considerably below their earlier highs. Even in the face of very large external financing needs, most companies were unwilling and/or unable to sell new equity issues in this environment. Only in periods like 1971–1972 and 1975–1976, when com-

---

[3] Actually, in the mid-1960s there was a very active new equity issue market, particularly for new companies. But most of these companies were small, and the aggregate value of their new equity issues was limited. Furthermore, equity was being retired by corporate acquisitions (funded by debt), and other forms of retirements, at a rapid rate. Thus the net rate of equity issuance for all corporations was very small.

Figure 17–2
Funds raised by nonfinancial business corporations (Seasonally adjusted, smoothed annual rates as a percent of GNP)

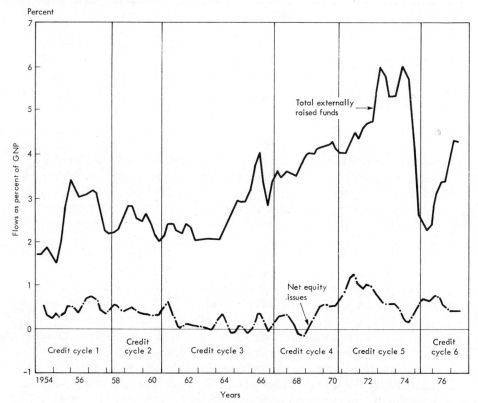

mon stock prices had recovered from their previous lows, did the pent-up perceived need for equity capital lead to new equity financing on a large scale.

Earlier, business corporations were portrayed as relatively pro-active demanders of funds, comparatively undeterred by the nominal cost of new external debt. This is certainly true of corporate short-term financing where the peak flows of new corporate short-term debt coincide with the peaks of short-term interest rates. It appears to be somewhat true of corporate long-term financing where business seems relatively insensitive to the cost of long-term funds (at least compared to other long-term borrowers, such as home mortgage borrowers). In the equity markets, however, businesses appear to be much more sensitive to financing costs. The long-term demands for equity capital are determined by the cumulative long-term external financing needs and the desire for a balanced capital structure. But the recent timing of new equity issues suggests that corporations are sensitive to the price at which common stock can be sold and thus the perceived cost of newly issued equity capital.

The supply of equity capital

The holders of common stock.   The largest holder of equities has been, and continues to be, households, primarily individuals (see Table 17–2).

Table 17–2
Holders of outstanding equity securities

Sector	Estimated value of equity holdings (Market value in $ billions) 12/31/76		Equity holdings as a percent of total financial assets held 12/31/76
Selected domestic financial institutions	$191		
Private pension funds		$110	63%
Public pension funds		30	25
Life insurance co.		34	11
Other insurance co.		17	19
Rest of the world	43		N.A.
Households–Total*	709		
Directly held		662	24
Held via mutual funds		47	2

* Households, as usual, is a residual, including individuals, various trust funds, and endowments. The individuals are the dominant component. It is estimated, for example, that foundations and endowments held slightly less than $40 billion of equities in 1975, and various personal and common bank trust funds held somewhat over $100 billion.
   Source: *Flow of Funds, Assets and Liabilities 1965–1976*, Federal Reserve Board, December 1977.

Equities accounted for almost 25 percent of the total value of households' financial assets in 1976. A number of financial intermediaries are also important holders of common stock. Private pension funds held nearly $110 billion of common stock in 1976. These holdings constituted the majority of their financial assets. The other intermediaries are less important equity investors, holding smaller amounts of equity securities in absolute terms and as a percentage of their total financial assets.

Individuals hold most of their common stock directly, but a small fraction is held through open-end investment companies, commonly called mutual funds. By investing in these funds, individuals (for a fee) can more easily obtain the benefits of diversification and professional management. Because these mutual funds are basically just another form for individual stock ownership, they will be classified under households rather than as a true financial intermediary.[4]

It is often tempting to imagine that individuals' common stock holdings are generally small, widely dispersed, and owned and managed by the average American. This, however, does not appear to be the case. Individuals' common stock holdings are concentrated in a relatively small fraction of the population. A study in 1971 by the Securities and Exchange Commission (SEC) showed that 87 percent of all individuals (the poorest 87 percent) owned less than 1 percent of the common stock. Similarly, the wealthiest 1 percent owned more than 80 percent of the common stock, and the wealthiest 0.1 percent owned more than 40 percent.[5] Thus most of the dollar volume of individuals' common stock holdings are concentrated into relatively large pools of funds. In addition, many of these pools of funds are professionally managed or professionally advised, in one form or another, often by the same group of professionals that manage various institutional portfolios.

The composition of the supply of new equity capital. A diagram of the primary market for new equity capital is shown in Figure 17–3. The recent

Figure 17–3
The supply and demand for new equity capital

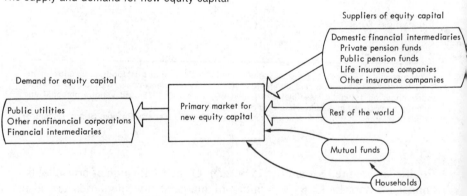

____

[4] The financial assets held by pension funds and life insurance companies are also held for the eventual benefit of individuals, of course, either pensioners or policy holders. In one sense, then, these intermediaries are also just middlemen for households. But both pension funds and life insurance companies generally make a defined-dollar or defined-benefit promise to their eventual beneficiaries rather than just conveying to them the risks and returns from their portfolio assets as is done by the mutual funds. To this extent, pension funds and insurance companies, unlike mutual funds, serve as true intermediaries, absorbing both risk and return as they hold one set of financial assets to fund the different set of financial promises they have made to their beneficiaries. For this reason they will be classified as intermediaries, distinct in their own right from individuals' holdings of common stock.

[5] See Institutional Investor Study Report of the SEC, Supplementary Volume I, 1971.

Figure 17–4
The balance of supply and demand for new equity capital (Annual net flows in $ billions)

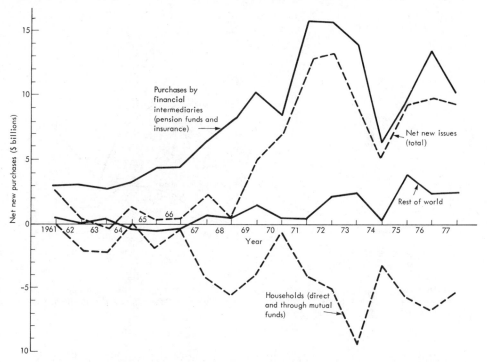

patterns of these net new purchases are shown in Figure 17–4, where the net new purchases of (1) domestic financial intermediaries, (2) households, and (3) foreign investors (the "rest of the world") combine to equal the net new issues of corporate equity. The outstanding feature of Figure 17–4 is the juxtaposition of financial intermediaries and households.

Throughout the period, the net new purchases of the domestic financial intermediaries have provided an important source of new equity funds. Beginning as moderate flows in the early 1960s and peaking in 1971–1972, the new purchases of these intermediaries have almost always exceeded the net new equity issues of corporations. Households, the most important owners of equities, have been substantial net sellers throughout the period.

The equity purchases of the larger intermediaries, the pension funds and life insurance companies, are examined in more detail in Figures 17–5 and 17–6. The equity purchases of public pension funds and life insurance companies were very small in the early 1960s, both in dollar terms and as a percentage of their funds for investment. This behavior arose in part from regulation and in part from the conservative tradition of these in-

Figure 17–5
The supply of new equity capital from three large financial intermediaries (Net flows in $ billions)*

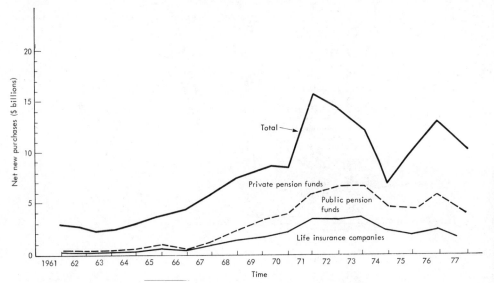

* The bottom line represents the purchases by life insurance companies. The middle line represents life insurance plus public pension funds. The top line represents life insurance plus public pension funds plus private pension plans (total).

stitutions.[6] During the 1960s, however, some of the regulations were relaxed and their investment behavior changed. For example, life insurance companies were allowed to manage pension fund monies as separate accounts—accounts separate from their life insurance activities and therefore not subject to the strict investment regulation in that business. As they expanded into this business their purchases of equities grew substantially.

The investments of private pension funds have followed a similar time pattern but with a higher average percentage in equity. As relatively unregulated institutions, private pension funds have always been free to invest heavily in common stocks. In the early 1960s, they allocated a relatively steady 50 percent of their fund inflows to common stock. This percentage increased, and in the 1971–1972 period, private pension funds were allocating more than 100 percent of their new inflows to equity. Lured by the attraction of greater expected returns, pension funds were net disinvestors in fixed-income securities in this period and instead concentrated their full attention on common stocks.

[6] A more complete description of these institutions can be found in Chapter 16.

Figure 17–6
Relative allocation of funds flows to equities in three large financial intermediaries

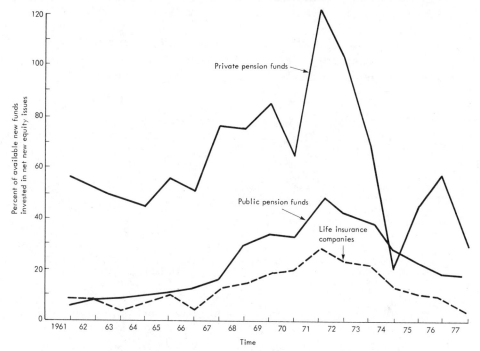

Pension funds (and life insurance companies managing pension funds through their separate accounts) were attracted to equities for several reasons. First, the funds realized that a large part of their pension liabilities would ultimately be affected by the rate of inflation. Therefore, they wanted an investment asset whose nominal returns might keep pace with inflation. While it was agreed that all financial assets should be priced to reflect the expected rate of inflation, it was felt that equities offered the best hedge against unexpected inflation. It was argued that inflation would raise the value of the real assets owned by corporations. Since the terms of their debt were fixed in nominal terms, any increase in the value of real assets which was associated with an inflation rate faster than the expected rate would flow directly to equity holders. This belief implied equities could be an especially attractive investment for pension funds to own.

Second, most pension funds anticipated a rather prolonged period of growth in assets during which cash inflows were expected to exceed outflows. Because of this, pension funds were unlikely to have to liquidate a major part of their asset holdings in order to meet outflows in the near term. To many, this meant that pension funds could be less concerned about any year-to-year variability in the market value of their assets. This ability to look more to the long-run value of their assets was thought to put pension funds in a better position to bear the risks which equities represent.

Finally, equities had a history of returning a great deal more than had long-term or short-term bonds. Table 17–5 shows the returns that investors experienced on stocks and bonds over one particular long interval.

Table 17–5
Total annual returns from bills, bonds, and common stocks, 1926–1976

	Geometric mean	Arithmetic mean	Standard deviation
Common stocks (S & P 500 stock index)	9.2%	11.6%	22.4%
Long-term corporate bonds.................	4.1	4.2	5.6
Long-term government bonds	3.4	3.5	5.8
Treasury bills	2.4	2.4	2.1
Consumer price index	2.3	2.4	4.8

Source: Roger Ibbotson and Rex Sinquefield, *Stocks, Bonds, Bills, and Inflation: The Past (1926–1976) and The Future (1977–2000),* The Financial Analysts Research Foundation, 1977.

The intermediaries' enchantment with common stocks came to a sudden halt, however, in the 1973–1974 period. In these years a drastic decrease in the flow of net equity purchases coincided with the sudden plunge in equity values (see Figure 17–1). As always, it is most difficult to sort out cause and effect. Some observers argue that the plunge in equity values was caused by the reluctance of these intermediaries to invest in stocks in 1973 and particularly in 1974. On the other hand, the sharp decrease in stock purchases may well have been as much an effect of the plunging equity prices as the cause.

Turning to households, as shown in Figure 17–4, we find strikingly different behavior. First, households have been consistent net sellers of common stocks. Of course, because corporations retain a large fraction of their earnings after tax, all equity investors are continually (re)investing additional funds in corporate equities.[7] Household investors seem to have felt, however, that the amount they wished to invest in equity investments each year was less than the earnings that corporations retained in their name. Thus they have been modest net sellers of equities in each year since 1960.

Second, the time pattern of households' net sales of equity have also been very different from that of the institutional holders. If we compare

---

[7] As shall be explained in some detail later in this chapter, the tax system makes it advantageous for equity investors to have corporations raise equity through the retention of earnings rather than through the sale of new stock.

Figure 17–4 with the earlier Figure 17–1, households seem to reduce their rate of selling equities during times when stock prices are depressed. Particularly in 1970 and 1974, years of low equity prices, households' net liquidations of common stock were reduced substantially. Conversely, in years of higher equity prices, for example, 1968 and 1972–1973, households were very active net sellers of equity. Recall that in some other markets, notably corporate debt markets, households were identified as one of the important "swing investors" who could be drawn in by relatively attractive yields to supply some of the capital demanded. These data suggest that households play a similar role in the equities market. When stock prices have plunged (and yields have risen) households have substantially slowed their rate of net selling, lifting from the primary equities market one of its substantial selling pressures. In this regard, households have behaved quite differently than either domestic intermediaries or foreign investors. Had households continued their heavy rates of net selling in 1970 and 1974, the ability of corporations to issue net new equity would have been substantially impaired. The apparent price and/or yield sensitivity of household investors seems to serve as one of the important counterbalancing forces in the time patterns of supply and demand.

Foreign investors also play a role in the U.S. equity market, albeit a less important role than either domestic individuals or intermediaries. In the 1960s, the net purchases/sales of equities by foreign investors were small. In the 1970s period, however, foreign investors became more active purchasers. As was discussed in Chapter 6, private nonresident investors were accumulating substantial dollar balances during these years. Much of these funds was placed either in federal government securities or bank deposits because of the liquidity and low risk of these assets. By 1975, however, foreign investors seemed to be more optimistic about the prospects for U.S. equities, and a small but growing flow of funds was channeled into the purchase of U.S. common stocks. Indeed, in 1975, the net new purchases of common stocks by foreign investors were almost one half of the net new issues of stock by U.S. corporations (see Figure 17–4). Foreign investment had thus become a reasonably important contributor of equity funds and an important factor in the ability of U.S. corporations to raise new equity capital.

The federal tax system and the equity market

The structure of the federal tax system has very important influences on the patterns of equity financing. At the corporate level, neither dividends nor retained earnings are deductible as expenses when computing the income on which corporate taxes are levied. Interest payments are deductible expenses however. At the shareholder level, dividend receipts are taxed as income while any appreciation in the value of the security is taxed as a capital gain.[8] Taxes on capital gains are deferred until the capital gain is actually realized. The capital gains tax rate is equal to the individual income tax rate but is levied on only one half of the capital gain.

The differential treatment of interest and equity payments at the corporate level has affected the desired mix of debt and equity in business capital structures. Corporations have clearly been induced to use larger amounts of debt relative to equity. In addition, the differential treatment of dividend and capital gain at the shareholder level has created an important incentive for corporations to retain their earnings rather than pay dividends to shareholders. Without this incentive to retain earnings, many corporations would undoubtedly pay out a much larger stream of dividends. A large part of these dividend payments would likely be returned to corporations through a much enlarged volume of new equity issues. Thus the small flows of new equity issues (relative to the other source of equity, retained earnings) that are actually observed are attributable in large part to the federal tax system. Changing the tax system could have a substantial effect on the debt-equity decision and on the decision to distribute dividends.

In addition, the tax system has been a primary force behind the growth of one of the institutions which supplies much of the new equity capital to business, the corporate pension funds. A corporation may deduct contributions to its pension fund as an expense (and thus pay no taxes on this portion of its cash flow), even though its employees do not pay any taxes on the pension contribution. Furthermore, as they accumulate in the fund, the contributions earn a tax-free return. Only when the employee ultimately receives the retirement income is a personal income tax levied. The tax-exempt nature of pension funds has created a powerful incentive for individuals to save through the form of accrued pension benefits, funded by their employers, rather than direct individual ownership of financial assets. The resulting shifts of retirement savings to pension funds has been a major determinant of the changing supply of equity funds.

Corporate pension funds, a consolidated perspective

Thus far corporate pension funds have been considered to be just one more institutional supplier of funds to the primary equity market. Because of the special relationship between a corporate pension fund and its sponsoring corporation, however, there is another, considerably different,

---

[8] The practice is often called the "double taxation" of dividends. In fact, corporate after-tax income is taxed twice at the shareholder level whether the corporation chooses to pay dividends or retain the earnings. When retained, however, the tax is deferred and at a lower effective rate.

image of their overall role in the supply and demand for equity. Corporate pension funds have been formed by corporations as vehicles to accumulate the assets necessary to meet their pension liabilities. In many corporate pension plans, the corporation promises to pay a defined pension benefit, for example, 85 percent of the average salary earned by the worker during the last five years of work. This payment must be made regardless of the investment performance of the assets held by the pension fund. That is, the corporation is liable for any difference between the assets and the liabilities of the pension fund. Accordingly, corporate pension funds may be consolidated with the corporations themselves for analytical purposes and considered as part of the "extended" corporate sector. Viewing the supply and demand data in the equity market from this perspective, we see that the major purchaser of corporate equity has been the corporate sector itself, and the amount of equity capital issued to entities outside the corporate sector has been very small indeed. As Table 17–6 suggests, the consolidated corporate sector (corporations plus their

Table 17–6
Private pension plan purchases versus net new corporate equity issues (Average annual rates in billions)

	1961– 1965	1966– 1970	1971– 1975	1976– 1977
Net new equity issues	$1.1	$3.4	$10.7	$8.9
Equity purchases of private pension funds (net)	$2.4	$4.6	$ 5.9	$5.9
Percent purchased by private pension funds	218%	130%	55%	66%

pension funds) was a consistent net buyer, not a net seller, of equity throughout the 1960s. And even in the early 1970s, a period of ostensibly active equity sales, more than half of equity issues were bought by private pension funds. In fact, throughout the whole 15-year period, only a very small amount of net new equity was absorbed by parties outside the consolidated corporate sector. Even when we considered corporate pension funds to be an entity separate from the corporate sector, the size of the market for new equity capital appeared to be limited, but from this different consolidated perspective, it appears to be very limited indeed, particularly relative to the size of other financial markets.[9]

---

[9] Of course, funding a corporation's pension fund with a diversified portfolio of other companies' common stocks does serve some purpose. The process does remove much of the specific risk that a corporation will be unable to meet its pension obligations. In addition, the funding of the pension fund does reduce the corporate tax liability.

PRICING IN THE SECONDARY MARKET FOR
COMMON STOCK

The secondary market is particularly important for common stocks because these equity securities are outstanding in perpetuity, and investors need a secondary market which will allow them to realize the current value of their shares. At the end of 1976, the estimated market value of outstanding common stock was greater than $1 trillion, making it the largest single class of outstanding financial obligations. For most of these shares, there was a relatively active secondary market, allowing even large investors to buy and sell substantial volumes of common stock very close to the current market price.

Unlike corporate bonds, most common stock trading takes place on organized stock exchanges: the New York Stock Exchange (the largest), the American Stock Exchange, and various small regional exchanges. In most transactions on these exchanges, various brokers act as agents for their customers, securing for them the best available price through a form of auction process on the "floor" of the exchanges. In a smaller number of large transactions, the brokers act as dealers, buying and selling from their own inventories to facilitate market trading. Some common stock trading also takes place off the exchanges, in the over-the-counter (OTC) market where securities firms also generally act as dealers.

Because most common stock trading takes place on organized exchanges, the role of these exchanges in the secondary market is critical. In recent years, trading on the New York Stock Exchange (NYSE) has averaged about 15 to 20 percent of the outstanding number of shares listed on that exchange. There has been a long-term change in the composition of this trading as it has come to be dominated by institutions. In the early 1960s, institutions accounted for only about one third of the trading on the NYSE, but in the mid-1970s, they accounted for about two thirds. The shift toward institutional trading has proceeded more rapidly than the shift toward institutional ownership because the institutions have become more active and aggressive common stock traders. Of course, some of the institutional trades take place in relatively large "blocks" of stock. The shift toward serving these large sophisticated institutional investors with large buy/sell orders has been responsible for many changes in the secondary market structure, among them the growth in the 1960s of brokers specializing in institutional research, the growth of securities firms capable of assembling large trades, and the more recent demise of fixed commission rates in favor of a system of negotiated commissions within which volume discounts can be flexibly priced. The separate exchanges and secondary markets for common stock are currently evolving toward a "central marketplace," and institutional trading will continue to be an important determinant of this evolution.

The valuation problem for common stocks

Most (though not all) companies have only one type of common stock outstanding, but among all the securities that this book will discuss, common stocks pose a uniquely difficult valuation problem. For fixed-income securities, the future stream of cash payments is clearly specified. There may be some doubt, of course, that a corporation (or other borrower) will be able to meet these payments, leading to the problem of default risk. Disregarding this default risk, however, the lender or bond investor knows exactly what cash flows to anticipate from the borrower. With common stocks, of course, the investor does not know what future stream of payments to expect. Indeed, for most stocks, the stream of future payments is very uncertain.

Holding period returns for common stocks

Over any specified time horizon, the holding period return from a common stock is the sum of its dividend plus its capital appreciation, expressed as a percent of its original value. Figure 1–1 showed a histogram of annual returns for an index of common stocks from 1926–1976. The average (arithmetic mean) return of the index in these years was 11.6 percent, while the standard deviation was 22.4 percent, illustrating the variability of the returns.

The basic equilibrium relationship among stocks: Risk-adjusted expected returns

In Chapter 10, we devised a basic equilibrium relationship for all securities which suggested that they should be priced such that their expected future returns are directly related to their risk (where risk is measured by their contribution to the risk of an overall portfolio). In particular, defining "excess returns" to be a security's return relative to the risk-free rate, we showed that the expected excess return for any security should be related to the expected excess returns for the market in a quite simple fashion, namely:[10]

$$E_j \quad = \quad \beta_j \quad\quad E_m \tag{1}$$

E_j	β_j	E_m
Expected excess return for jth security	"Volatility" of jth security	Expected excess return of the market

As we showed in Chapter 10, β is the appropriate measure of the incremental risk that a security contributes to a well-diversified portfolio. In Chapter 16, we showed that this simple relationship seems to be consis-

---

[10] In this expression, β_j (which we shall also call volatility) is a measure of the "sensitivity" of the security's price movements to the price movements of the overall market. See Chapter 10 for further details.

tent with the observed long-run returns from bonds relative to common stocks. In this chapter, we will examine the relevance of this relationship for the relative pricing of different common stocks. To do this, we will define the "market" to be a market-weighted portfolio of all common stocks (but no bonds or other securities) and then examine the price movements of each common stock relative to this "market."[11]

We can measure the past sensitivity of an individual stock's returns to market returns and thus obtain an estimate of the underlying β of each stock. It has been found that the βs determined by empirical procedures explain, on average, about 30 percent of the variation in a typical individual stock's monthly returns. The other 70 percent is thus independent of the "market" and dependent only upon each individual stock's specific price movements. Thus it is important to diversify common stock portfolios to reduce this specific risk, for as equation (1) suggests, only market-related risk (β) leads to greater expected returns.

The relationship described in equation (1) refers to the ex-ante expected returns and βs, those that exist (before the fact) in the minds of investors. As always, there is no direct way of measuring these expectations to see if common stock's expected returns are really in equilibrium. Nor can we rely upon past data drawn from relatively short time periods to verify equation (1), for in the short-run, stock prices are so variable that actual price movements can diverge substantially from expectations. We can, however, investigate the very *long-run average returns* from different common stocks. If investors make no systematic errors over time in estimating stock returns, the long-run average returns should approximate their ex-ante expected returns.

A large number of empirical studies have been devoted to testing equation (1) (the basic equilibrium relationship) within the stock market. Generally speaking, the risk-free rate has been approximated by the rate on short-term Treasury bills. Using this proxy, the long-run average returns from different common stocks, and portfolios of common stocks, have been compared to their observed volatilities (βs), measured relative to an index representing the overall stock market.[12] Results from one of these studies are shown in Figure 17–7 which plots the average excess monthly returns (over and above the risk-free rate) during 1931–1965 for ten common stock portfolios which were continuously updated to provide different levels of

---

[11] The Standard & Poor's 500 Stock Index, for example, is a reasonable proxy for a market-weighted portfolio of all common stocks.

[12] See the empirical results presented in (1) Miller, Merton, and M. Scholes, "Rates of Return in Relation to Risk: A Re-Examination of Recent Findings," in *Studies in the Theory of Capital Markets,* ed. Michael Jensen (New York: Praeger, 1972) and (2) Friend, Irwin, and M. Blume, "Risk and the Long-Run Rate of Return on NYSE Common Stocks," Working Paper No. 18–72, Wharton School of Commerce and Finance, Rodney L. White Center for Financial Research.

Figure 17–7
Relationship between risk and returns on common stocks*

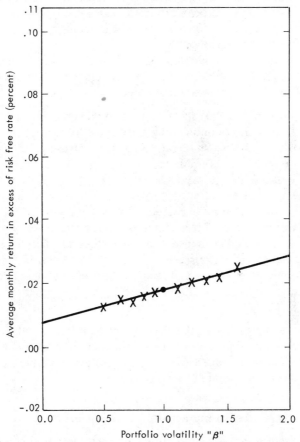

* Average monthly returns versus β for the 35-year period 1931–1965 for ten portfolios.

Source: Fischer, Black, Michael C. Jensen, and Myron S. Scholes, "The Capital Asset Pricing Model: Some Empirical Tests," in *Studies in the Theory of Capital Markets,* ed. Michael Jensen, (New York: Praeger, 1972), pp. 79–121.

volatility. Clearly the average long-run returns were greater for common stock portfolios with higher volatilities. Furthermore, the relationship appears to be described reasonably well by a straight line, which is the relationship that is predicted by equation (1) above. Unfortunately, the straight line does not pass through the origin of Figure 17–7, suggesting that it has a somewhat different slope than the predicted line.[13] This suggests

---

[13] Equation (1) predicts that the straight line should have a slope such that when β equals zero, the average excess returns are zero. Extrapolating the straight line in Figure 17–7 to zero, however, the excess returns are still positive (though small).

that, in the 1931–1965 period, low β stocks (low-risk stocks) actually returned somewhat more than would be predicted by the basic equilibrium relationship, and high β stocks returned commensurately less. With this exception, however, these long-run empirical data are consistent with the basic equilibrium relationship.

The other studies of long-run risks and returns from common stocks have produced comparable findings. The conclusions from these studies, somewhat roughly summarized, have been:

1. Higher long-run average returns have in fact been associated with more volatile (higher β) common stock portfolios, as predicted.
2. The relationship between average long-run returns and β has appeared to be a straight line, as predicted.
3. The slope of the line, however, is less than predicted. Lower β stocks have yielded greater average returns, and higher β stocks have yielded smaller average returns than predicted by the theory.
4. While β has been correlated with average returns, it is not clear that it is the best (or the only) measure of risk. Other alternative measures of risk also appear to be correlated with average returns, and it is extremely difficult to make statistical judgments about whether β has been better correlated with average returns than other potential risk measures.

In short, several aspects of the theoretical equilibrium relationship are consistent with the long-run empirical evidence, although distinguishing between the risk premium based upon β and alternative measures of risk is a controversy still clouded by statistical problems.

The hypothesis of efficient markets in the stock market

While the evidence presented above suggests that the average returns from different common stocks are in risk-adjusted equilibrium in the very long run, it says nothing about the short run. Indeed, most market practitioners believe that stock prices are driven in the short run by the forces of supply and demand, and speculation. Recent tests of the efficient market hypothesis raise serious questions, however, about whether common stock prices really do depart very far from our equilibrium condition. As we discussed in Chapters 8 through 10, the efficient markets hypothesis is based upon the assumption that investors continuously evaluate all available information such that the price of a security continuously incorporates all information about its future value. In the world of this hypothesis, there are no departures from equilibrium, and the expected returns from all stocks are described by equation (1) at all times. Otherwise, it is assumed, investors pursuing greater expected returns would surely reestablish the equilibrium as they served their own best interests. In fact, of course, transactions costs (for example, brokerage fees) impede investors from taking advantage of very small disturbances from equilibrium. The operational version of the efficient markets hypothesis assumes, therefore, that the expected returns from different stocks are held within a band around the equilibrium structure, a band whose width is determined by transactions costs. The efficient markets hypothesis implies that supply, demand, and speculative forces do not drive stock prices away from equilibrium to any appreciable extent and investors cannot improve their risk-adjusted expected returns by actively trading back and forth between different common stocks.

In earlier chapters, we advanced two forms of the hypothesis of efficient markets: the weak form and the strong form. In its weak form, the hypothesis implies that all the information in the time series of past stock price movements has been incorporated by the market into its current expectations such that investors will not be able to increase their expected holding period returns [above that predicted by equation (1)] by decision rules based upon past price data. This implication is in direct conflict with many of the techniques of so-called technical analysis, which analyzes past stock price movements. A number of researchers have rigorously tested various decision rules based upon past price information and (almost) uniformly concluded that these decision rules did not provide increased risk-adjusted returns after considering transactions costs.[14] In its weak form the hypothesis has thus been found to be quite consistent with the data.

In its stronger form, the efficient markets hypothesis states that literally all information has been incorporated into current market expectations. Therefore, decision rules based upon other relevant information, corporate earnings for example, have also been extensively tested.[15] These empirical tests also seem unable to identify any decision rules which consistently provide greater risk-adjusted expected returns.

Furthermore, a number of researchers have analyzed the investment performance of institutional investment managers, particularly the managers of mutual funds, to see if they have been able to consistently realize greater risk-adjusted average returns.[16] These studies have suggested that mutual funds managers (and other institutional investment managers) as a group have had great difficulty producing above-average returns. Indeed, the average returns seem to be about what equation (1) would predict

---

[14] See Paul Cootner, (ed.), *The Random Character of Stock Market Prices* (MIT Press, 1964) and Richard Brealey, *An Introduction to Risk and Return from Common Stocks* (MIT Press, 1969).

[15] See Brealey, *Common Stocks*.

[16] See Jensen, Michael, "The Performance of Mutual Funds in the Period: 1945–1967," *Journal of Finance,* May 1968, and a more complete discussion in Jensen, Michael C., Capital Markets: Theory and evidence," *Bell Journal of Economics and Management Science,* Autumn 1972 vol. 3, No 2, p. 357–398.

after the costs of active management are taken into account. Moreover, within the group of all investment managers, the evidence is consistent with the proposition that there is not a subset of managers that consistently outperforms the group, although this is a much more difficult proposition to test.

While this is still a subject of much dispute, the empirical evidence seems to provide considerable support for the hypothesis of efficient markets. In so doing, it raises serious questions about the importance of potential departures from equilibrium caused either by supply and demand or speculative influences. The long-run average returns from different common stocks appear to be related to their incremental portfolio risk through the basic equilibrium condition, and it appears to be very difficult for investors to improve their returns by exploiting short-run departures from this equilibrium. At the very least, the management and transactions costs associated with trading different common stocks appear to be large enough to erode the potential increased returns available to most investors. Thus the empirical evidence suggests that the basic equilibrium relationship is a useful approximation to the pricing process for common stocks and describes the *relative* performance investors may expect from stocks with different risks.

QUESTIONS

1. Why have individuals been net sellers of equity and institutions net buyers? What could induce individuals to change their behavior and become substantial net purchasers of equity?
2. There have been many proposals to change the way that the income of corporations is taxed by the federal government.
   a. What would be the effects on the new issue equity market of the integration of the personal and corporate income taxes, that is, an abolition of the income tax at the corporate level, an imputation of the income earned by corporations to the shareholders, and the inclusion of that income as taxable income in the personal income tax?
   b. How would a tax-exempt institutional holder of equities feel about integrating the corporate and personal income tax?
3. How would you expect each of the following groups to feel about integration of the corporate and personal tax system, increasing the investment tax credit, accelerating depreciation, and lowering the corporate tax rate? An investment banker who engages in a large volume of underwriting? A retail broker for a large brokerage firm? The treasurer of A T & T? An economist concerned with the problems of capital formation?
4. What does it mean to the other holders of common stock that corporate pension funds hold a large amount of common stock? Or that corporations have promised to pay a large volume of pensions in the future?

5. If the stock and bond markets are efficient, is it true that all mutual funds are identical? If not, what are the dimensions of the different products that different mutual funds could offer?

REFERENCES

Institutional Investor Study Report of the Securities and Exchange Commission. U.S. Government Printing Office, 1971.

Brealey, Richard A., *An Introduction to Risk and Return from Common Stocks,* (MIT Press, 1969).

———, *Security Prices in a Competitive Market* (MIT Press, 1971).

Fama, Eugene F., "Efficient Capital Markets: A Review of Theory and Empirical Work", *Journal of Finance,* XXV, No. 2 (May, 1970), pp. 383–417.

Friend, Irwin and Blume, Marshall. "The Demand for Risky Assets," *The American Economic Review* (December 1975).

Jensen, Michael, ed., *Studies in the Theory of Capital Markets* (New York: Praeger, 1972).

Lorie, James and Brealey, Richard, eds., *Modern Developments in Investment Management: A Book of Readings* (New York: Praeger, 1972).

Lorie, James H. and Hamilton, Mary T., *The Stock Market, Theories and Evidence* (Homewood, Illinois, Irwin, 1973)

Pogue, Gerald A. and Modigliani, Franco. "An Introduction to Risk and Return," Parts I and II, *Financial Analysts Journal* (March/April 1974), and (May/June 1974).

Schlarbaum, Gary G.; Lewellen, Wilbur; and Lease, Ronald C. "Realized Returns of Common Stock Investments: The Experience of Individual Investors," *The Journal of Business,* vol. 51, no. 2 (April 1978), pp. 299–326.

Sharpe, William F., *Investments* (Prentice-Hall, 1978).

18

The residential mortgage markets

The residential mortgage markets are among our largest and most important financial markets. As the data in Table 18–1 suggest, more funds are raised in those markets over a typical credit cycle than in any other long-term market in the United States. In addition, the mortgage markets are very complex, involving a variety of special institutions and market mechanisms. Because of this complexity, this chapter starts with a description of two important background factors: the structure of the mortgage markets, and the institutions of the mortgage market, including their competition for funds in the household deposit market. It then analyzes the behavior of the supply and demand for mortgage funds and the interest rates on mortgages. The final section of the chapter analyzes the effectiveness of the many federal government activities in the mortgage market.

354

Table 18–1
Relative size of long-term primary markets, average
annual flows in 1971–1975 (Billions of dollars)

Residential mortgages	$47	
Home mortgages (1–4 family)		$39
Multifamily residential mortgages		8
Commercial mortgages	14	
Corporate bonds.........................	18	
Corporate equities	9	
State/local government securities	17	

STRUCTURE OF THE MORTGAGE MARKETS

Residential mortgages are debt instruments backed by the specific collateral of residential real estate. While there are other types of mortgages (specifically, commercial mortgages and farm mortgages), nearly three fourths of all mortgage debt in the United States is backed by residential property. Most residential mortgages have relatively long nominal maturities, generally 25 to 30 years. Because they are scheduled to be repaid in equal monthly installments of interest and amortization, however, the effective maturity of the loan is considerably shorter than its nominal maturity. The fact that they are often prepaid or refinanced ahead of schedule shortens their average maturity even more.

Residential mortgages are traditionally catagorized as home mortgages (the mortgages secured by one to four family dwellings) or multifamily residential mortgages (the mortgages secured by dwellings intended for more than four families). The borrower for a "home mortgage" is almost invariably the individual homeowner. The borrower for a multifamily mortgage can be an individual, partnership, or corporation for whom the dwelling serves primarily as a source of income.

Importance of local financial institutions

The development of the home mortgage markets has been dependent upon several special features of home mortgage debt. Relative to other financial securities, home mortgages are small, potentially long-term loans, often with nonstandard terms, backed by heterogenous (indeed unique) pieces of local real estate. Their potential specific risks can thus be considerable and, more importantly, difficult to evaluate without very detailed knowledge about the borrower, the mortgaged property, and the local real estate market. For these reasons a specialization of tasks has developed in the mortgage market. The tasks of originating and servicing a mortgage loan are often distinguished from the task of providing the funds to permanently finance the loan. Almost all of the origination and servicing of mortgage loans is done by firms with a specialized knowledge of a region or local area. The permanent financing for these mortgage loans may be provided by local firms, but it may also be obtained through a number of channels which tap the national markets for funds.

The mortgage market relies heavily on funds which are committed in advance of the actual mortgage takedown. The home mortgage is generally so large a fraction of the funds used to purchase a home that the availability of funds at a prespecified rate is often a precondition of the purchase itself. For example, most home purchase/sale agreements are preceded by a commitment from the lender to the borrower for a specific loan at a prespecified rate. Similarly, before embarking upon the construction of a large-scale single-family housing development, a builder often seeks a commitment from a potential lender to provide prearranged mortgage financing to the eventual home buyers. The fact that home mortgage loans are small, heterogenous, and potentially risky loans and the fact that they generally require a forward commitment of funds means that the existence of local financial intermediaries is crucial to the functioning of the market.

Mortgage insurance and mortgage bankers

Because the specific terms and provisions of mortgages differ from locale to locale and from mortgage to mortgage, it has been difficult to develop a "secondary" market in which to sell mortgages.

In 1934, the Federal Housing Administration (FHA) began to insure approved home mortgage loans made by private lenders. In later years, the Veterans' Administration (VA) began a similar program of guaranteeing approved home mortgage loans to veterans. These government mortgage insurance programs provided an element of fungibility to residential mortgages. They gave the mortgage investor an assured standard of quality and protection against credit losses. Essentially, they transformed home mortgages from small heterogenous, potentially risky investments into small homogeneous safer investments.

In response to these government insurance programs, a new group of institutions developed, the mortgage companies (sometimes called mortgage bankers or mortgage brokers). These mortgage companies originate mortgages not for their own portfolios but for sale to other investors. They are financed typically with interim bank loans and only small amounts of equity funds. These mortgage companies depend on permanent or long-term mortgage investors who issue "forward commitments" (that is, commitments to purchase, on delivery by the seller, a specified amount of mortgages within a certain period of time). These commitments, by serving as the assurance of a takeout of the interim commercial bank borrowings, enhance the mortgage companies' access to bank financing.

Private mortgage insurers developed in the 1960s to provide insurance in the conventional (that is, nongovernment insured) home mortgage market.[1] Private mortgage insurers seem to be able to coexist (indeed, to compete successfully) with federal insurance programs because of their relative freedom from constraints, their responsiveness to the market's needs, and their willingness to insure various nonstandard mortgages. This private mortgage insurance has provided a similar (though less complete) set of market advantages to privately insured conventional mortgages. Using private mortgage insurance, local lenders in regions of high mortgage demand may originate privately insured conventional mortgage loans and resell them to institutions in locations with a relative surplus of funds.

Origination and financing of home mortgages

Table 18–2 shows the relative importance of the institutions that originate and permanently finance home (one to four family) mortgages. Al-

Table 18–2
Originations and holdings of home (one to four family residential) mortgages

Lender group	Originations Yearly average 1970–1976		Holdings December 31, 1976	
	Billions of $	Per-cent	Billions of $	Per-cent
Private sector..........................	69.8	96.9	411.4	84.0
Savings and loan associations	35.8	49.7	235.5	51.7
Commercial banks	15.6	21.7	77.5	15.8
Mortgage companies.................	12.8	17.8	4.2	0.9
Mutual saving banks	4.5	6.2	52.4	10.7
Life insurance companies	0.4	0.5	15.5	3.2
Others	0.7	1.0	8.4	1.7
Federal sector	2.2	3.1	78.5	16.0
Federal credit agencies	2.2	3.1	36.6	7.5
Federally sponsored pools	0.0	0.0	41.9	8.6

This data is taken from "The Secondary Market for Home Mortgages," *Monthly Review*, Federal Reserve Bank of Kansas City (September–October 1977).

most all home mortgages are originated by private financial institutions. Savings and loan associations are the largest originator, though commercial banks and mortgage companies also engage in a significant volume of origination. Almost all of the mortgages originated by mortgage companies, and some of the commercial bank originations, are sold to other

---

[1] Actually, private mortgage guaranty insurance companies had existed before, but because of wholesale failures, they had been legislated from existence in the Great Depression. Beginning in 1957, the states began to once again permit such private mortgage insurers.

institutions. Some institutions, such as mutual savings banks, provide the permanent finance for a larger volume of mortgages than they originate.

Private financial institutions also account for the bulk of the permanent funds in the home mortgage market. A number of federal agencies have come to play an important and rapidly growing role in providing permanent financing to the home mortgage market, however. It is to an analysis of the behavior of these private and public intermediaries that we turn next.

THE INSTITUTIONS OF THE HOME MORTGAGE MARKET

Private financial institutions

The private financial institutions that provide the bulk of the permanent finance to the home mortgage market are the savings and loan associations, the mutual savings banks, and the commercial banks. Savings and loan associations and mutual savings banks are commonly called thrift institutions to distinguish them from commercial banks.

Savings and loan associations (S & Ls) attract funds from households by offering time and savings deposits.[2] Until the mid-1960s, the vast majority of these deposits were held in regular passbook savings accounts. Subsequently, time deposits with a wide range of maturities have come to assume an equally important place in the liability structure of S & Ls. Because of their specialized role (by law) as mortgage lenders, the investment side of most S & Ls is relatively simple. A small liquidity reserve is held (usually in federal government securities), and the remaining funds are invested in long-term mortgages, principally fixed-rate, single-family home mortgages (as shown in Table 18–3).

Mutual savings banks (MSBs) are state-chartered mutual associations, which also attract funds from individuals by offering time and savings

Table 18–3
Savings and loan associations, estimated assets as of 12/31/77 (In billions)

U.S. government securities	$ 33	
Mortgages	381	
Home mortgages		$308
Multifamily residential		33
Other mortgages		40
Other assets	45	
Total	459	

---

[2] While there are various legal and technical differences between federally chartered S & Ls and state-chartered S & Ls, and between S & Ls organized as corporations and those organized as mutual associations, we will ignore most of these differences, focusing instead upon their similarities.

deposits. Most of the mutual savings banks are located in the northeastern region of the country. While S & Ls dominate the thrift institution industry in other parts of the country, MSBs dominate the industry in the Northeast, particularly in the urban centers. Although the liability structure of mutual savings banks is very similar to S & Ls, there are important differences in the investment policies of the two types of institutions. MSBs generally have considerably more flexibility in the types of assets they can acquire. In addition to liquidity reserves (usually U.S. government securities) and home mortgages, MSBs are permitted to invest in a variety of commercial mortgages, corporate bonds, and small amounts of corporate stock (see Table 18–4).[3] Moreover, since many of the largest

Table 18–4
Mutual savings banks, estimated assets as
of 12/31/77 (In billions)

U.S. government securities	$ 17	
Total mortgages	88	
Home mortgages		$58
Multifamily residential		15
Other mortgages		15
Corporate bonds	21	
Other	21	
Total	147	

MSBs are located in relatively dense urban areas with limited opportunities for single-family home ownership, these institutions have invested a much larger fraction of their total residential mortgage portfolio in large multifamily residential mortgages.

The deposits in almost all mutual savings banks, S & Ls, and commercial banks are insured by various federal and state deposit insurance programs up to a limit of $40,000.[4]

Relative to commercial banks, thrift institutions are clearly a more specialized form of institution. While commercial banks obtain their funds through demand deposits, time and savings deposits, and other more recently developed liabilities, thrift institutions are almost completely dependent upon time and savings deposits. Commercial banks derive their deposits from a wide variety of depositors, including business, government, and households. Thrift institutions are almost totally dependent upon households as a source of deposits. While commercial banks hold a variety of different forms of assets, thrift institutions are relatively special-

---

[3] The role played by mutual savings banks in the corporate bond market was discussed in Chapter 16.

[4] Principally the Federal Deposit Insurance Corporation (FDIC) and the Federal Savings and Loan Insurance Corporation (FSLIC).

ized investors in long-term mostly fixed-rate residential mortgages (with the exception of some of the large urban MSBs described above). It would be somewhat misleading, however, to rely completely upon these sweeping characterizations. As described earlier, there are enormous differences between the different groups of commercial banks, ranging from the large international money center banks to the local retail banks. In addition, there are also enormous differences among thrift institutions—for example, among the large mutual savings banks, the large savings and loan associations in California, and the smaller thrift institutions throughout the country. Furthermore, deposit institutions are evolving in such a way that the difference between thrifts and retail commercial banks are becoming blurred. Nonetheless, in the following analysis of the changing competition for household deposits, we shall concentrate on the differences between thrift institutions and banks.

Competition for household deposits

Asset structure and the ability to compete for savings deposits. The ability to attract a stable and growing deposit base in the household savings market is critically important to both retail banks and thrift institutions. Competitive deposit rates are an important way in which intermediaries seek to attract deposit flows, and asset structures are an important determinant of the ability of institutions to keep their deposit rates competitive.

The assets of most commercial banks consist primarily of loans to corporate businesses and investments in government and municipal securities. The yields earned by commercial loans, the largest component of the asset portfolios, generally fluctuate with the banks' prime rate, which itself varies with changes in market interest rates. In addition, a substantial portion of the securities are short-term investments which amortize quickly, providing funds for reinvestment at current market rates. These short-term and floating-rate assets enable commercial banks to continue to compete for deposits during periods of rising interest rates without suffering a substantial decline in their profitability.

The long-term mortgage portfolios of thrift institutions differ considerably from the assets of commercial banks. Unlike a commercial loan, a mortgage is generally a fixed-rate instrument whose return does not adjust to subsequent changes in the market rate of interest. In addition, the amortization process implies that a mortgage portfolio will generate funds for reinvestment at a relatively slow rate and, therefore, will require a considerably longer time to adjust its average yield to a change in the overall level of market interest rates.[5]

---

[5] A number of savings and loan associations (and other mortgage lenders) in California have begun to offer "variable rate mortgages" rather than fixed-rate mortgages, and this practice will surely spread. Thrift institutions as a whole, however, will continue to have long-term fixed-rate mortgages for some time to come.

During periods of rising interest rates, this less flexible asset structure forces thrifts into the dilemma of choosing between stable profit margins and stable deposit flows. On the one hand, thrifts could adopt the strategy of maintaining profitability by keeping deposit rates in line with the average yield of their portfolio. In times of rising market interest rates, however, this policy would cause them to offer uncompetitive deposit rates. On the other hand, they could offer competitive deposit rates during periods of escalating interest rates, thus maintaining deposit flows. However, this policy would erode the earnings generated by their slowly adjusting fixed-rate portfolios and, in the extreme, endanger their solvency.

A comparison of asset structures suggests that commercial banks, with their more flexible asset portfolios, are better positioned to compete for household savings in times of rapidly changing and particularly rising interest rates. Indeed, in the absence of deposit rate regulation, they might quickly dominate the household savings deposit market during such a period.

Regulation of household deposit rates.   Interest rate regulations have become an active instrument of regulatory policy, substantially impacting deposit flows at intermediaries. They have been used to protect deposits at thrifts and thus to preserve the household savings market as a source of low-cost funds for financing residential mortgages. Three separate federal agencies share responsibility for administering rate control policies. Through Regulation Q, the Federal Reserve Board (FRB) determines the maximum deposit rates that member commercial banks may offer. The Federal Home Loan Bank Board (FHLBB) exercises similar authority over member savings and loan associations. Finally, the Federal Deposit Insurance Corporation (FDIC) is responsible for regulating the deposit rates of mutual savings banks and insured commercial banks that are not members of the Federal Reserve System. By law, these three agencies must coordinate their rate control policies.

As interest rates have risen in recent years, regulators have been periodically forced to reassess their rate ceilings and raise them in order to keep returns on at least some types of consumer deposits comparable with yields available in the open markets. These increases in rate ceilings occurred in 1970, and again in 1973, when the rates of interest on open-market instruments were at or near their cyclical peaks. Table 18–5 shows the rate ceilings which prevailed from 1973 through 1977.

In revising rate ceilings, the regulators have sought to encourage the growing segmentation of the household savings market. Rate ceilings have encouraged financial intermediaries to offer both highly liquid passbook accounts (at lower rates) and a range of fixed-maturity time deposits (at higher rates). This multitier rate policy has permitted financial intermediaries to attract rate-sensitive funds with time deposits while still drawing a substantial portion of their funds from lower cost passbook accounts. In addition, the minimum term features of time deposits have

Table 18–5
Ceilings on deposit rates (Deposits less than $100,000)

Maturity/type	Thrift institutions		Commercial banks	
	Nominal rate	(Effective annual yield, %)*	Nominal rate	(Effective annual yield, %)*
Passbook savings	5¼	(5.47)	5	(5.20)
Time certificates (less than $100,000)				
90 days–1 year	5¾	(6.00)	5½	(5.73)
1–2½ years	6½	(6.81)	6	(6.27)
2½ or more years	6¾	(7.08)	6½	(6.81)
Minimum denomination of $1,000				
4–6 years	7½	(7.90)	7¼	(7.63)
6 years or more	7¾	(8.17)	7½	(7.90)

* Using daily compounding, deposit institutions have been able to raise the effective annual yields on their deposits above the "nominal rates" incorporated in the regulation.

extended the effective maturity of deposits and enhanced the stability of the deposit base at financial intermediaries.

The revision of interest rate ceilings in 1970 had standardized a deposit rate differential favoring thrifts over banks by 0.5 percent for most deposit classes. The changes in 1973 reduced this differential to 0.25 percent for most deposit classes. Even so, the deposit rate ceilings incorporated an incentive for savers to maintain their deposits at thrift institutions.

Competition between banks and thrifts. The competition between banks and thrifts is clearly dependent upon the regulatory environment. Return and risk criteria—which typically dominate financial decisionmaking—are generally less important factors in the market for household deposits. Deposit rate ceilings, as we have seen, limit the returns that an individual depositor can be offered by competing deposit institutions. Federal deposit insurance eliminates any risk of loss for household savers. Thus public policies severely constrain the flexibility of financial intermediaries to compete for household savings on the basis of rate and risk differentials.

Within this regulated framework, other factors (such as services, convenience, and customer relationships) assume an influential role in the competition among financial intermediaries.[6] In addition to savings and time deposits, commercial banks offer demand deposits (checking ac-

---

[6] Competition on the basis of nonrate factors is also limited by the regulations of state banking authorities. These state agencies define the range of services which different types of financial intermediaries are permitted to offer individual savers.

counts) which provide individual depositors with a convenient means of making third-party payments. Also, banks offer a variety of other services including credit cards, cash advances, and consumer loans. Within regulatory constraints, many commercial banks have attempted to develop into multiservice "one-stop" financial centers. In most states, however, thrift institutions have been unable to offer the variety of services available at commercial banks. In most states, thrift institutions still cannot offer third-party payment accounts such as checking accounts. Their ability to extend consumer credit is more limited (although both of these restrictions are changing). Thrifts have had to rely more upon the interest rate differentials built into ceiling rates (and upon their long-term association in the consumer's mind with household savings and mortgage borrowing) as their principal advantage in competing for the deposits of individuals.

Trends in the household savings market.   The net flows of household financial savings have grown substantially. In addition, these flows have increasingly taken the form of deposits, enhancing the importance of the household deposit market as a source of funds for financial intermediaries (see a discussion of these trends in Chapter 3). During the 1950s, thrift institutions captured most of the growth in the household deposit market. Figure 18–1, which depicts the thrifts' share of the total household time and savings deposit market, illustrates this trend. Strong demand for mortgage credit and the relatively high mortgage yields enabled thrifts to pay attractive rates to depositors. In addition, prior to 1961, commercial banks were not aggressive competitors for household time and savings deposits, relying instead upon demand deposits from a variety of sectors to finance their asset growth.

In the 1960s, however, this competitive relationship began to change. Corporate loan demand and other credit needs began to expand. With rising interest rates, the banks' depositors began to economize on their noninterest bearing demand deposits. Thus demand deposit growth was no longer sufficient to fund the commercial banks' needs. In response the large commercial banks developed large CDs and other new forms of liabilities to capture an increasing portion of their funds from the open-money markets.[7] In addition, all commercial banks began to be much more active competitors in the household savings deposit market. With their inherently flexible asset structures, commercial banks were well-positioned to compete for households' deposits during the periods of rising interest rates in the 1960s and early 1970s. Figure 18–1 shows the commercial paper rate, which can be used as a proxy for all short-term open market interest rates during this period. While regulatory rate ceilings constrained direct rate competition during most of this period, banks

---

[7] This behavior was analyzed in Chapter 15.

Figure 18–1
Trends in the competition for household deposits

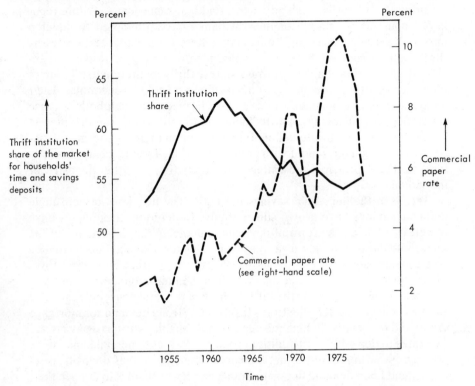

successfully attracted funds through their marketing emphasis on nonrate factors: a wider range of financial services, consumer convenience, and active promotional programs. The enlarged commercial banks' market share is reflected in its complement—the dwindling thrifts' share. Because of the overall expansion of the household deposit market, thrift institutions continued to grow during these years although they were attracting a smaller share of this rapidly expanding market.

Disintermediation. Superimposed upon these longer run trends have been the disruptions of deposit flows caused by periods of especially high interest rates, the by now familiar process of disintermediation.

A detailed analysis of this process can be made by focusing on the years 1973 and 1974, when inflation and corporate credit demands caused an extended period of high interest rates. Figure 18–2 illustrates the course of the relevant interest rates: the rate on large CDs (an open-market rate, since Regulation Q ceilings on large CDs were not effective during the period), the maximum rate that could be offered by thrifts on

Figure 18–2
Comparison of rate ceilings in the household deposit market with open-market interest rates

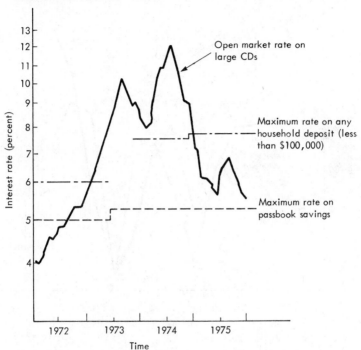

any type of household time or saving deposit less than $100,000, and the maximum rate that could be offered on ordinary passbook savings accounts by thrifts.[8] The resulting quarterly increases in household deposits (net deposit inflows *plus* interest credited to deposit accounts) are shown in Figure 18–3.[9] The household deposit inflows into both commercial banks and thrift institutions were disrupted by disintermediation, but the process seems to have been more severe at thrifts. In the low interest rate periods in late 1972 and early 1975, thrift institutions obtained greater

---

[8] The "maximum rate on any type of household time or saving deposit" generally applied to a longer term time deposit. Until July 1973, commercial bank ceilings were ½ percent below the thrift ceilings in Figure 18–2; after July 1973 they were ¼ percent below these ceilings.

[9] For commercial banks, Figure 18–3 plots the increase in time deposits other than large CDs. While these deposits are sold to more than households, households purchase the bulk of these deposits. There were approximately $340 and $320 billion of comparable deposit balances in thrifts and commercial banks, respectively, in the latter half of 1974. A rough estimate of the "interest credited" portion of the deposit increases in Figure 18–3 is therefore about $17–20 billion at annualized rates. The net deposit inflows can be gauged by subtracting this estimate from the deposit increases of Figure 18–3.

Figure 18–3

Net household time and savings deposit increases in commercial banks and thrift institutions (Quarterly flows at seasonally adjusted annual rates)

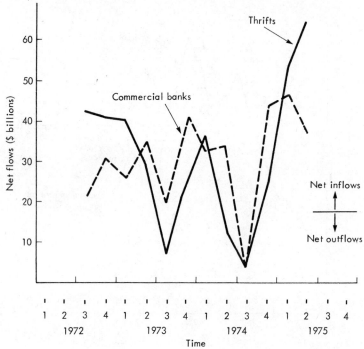

deposit inflows than the banks. Throughout most of the high-rate periods in 1973 and 1974, however, thrifts were unable to maintain this advantage. Indeed, in these high-rate periods, thrifts generally had smaller inflows (or greater outflows) than the banks. This pattern could be predicted, of course, on the basis of rate sensitive consumer behavior. In low-rate periods, rate-sensitive consumers tend to prefer deposits over lower rate open-market instruments. In particular, they prefer thrift institution deposits, because of the ¼ to ½ percent competitive differential. In high-rate periods, however, these same rate-sensitive consumers tend to move toward open-market securities, causing disintermediation at all deposit institutions and greater disintermediation at the thrifts.

A more detailed analysis of Figure 18–2 and 18–3 reveals some other key differences between commercial banks and thrifts. In mid-1973, the sharp decline in household deposit inflows (that accompanied the rapid escalation of interest rates) induced the regulators to revise their rate ceilings. In addition to raising almost all deposit rate ceilings, the new regulations (issued in early July of 1973) did away with any rate ceiling on medium-size long-term household time deposits (at least $1,000, with a maturity of four or more years). In response, deposit institutions offered a variety of innovative long-term household deposits, including some with floating rates, called "wild-card accounts." These wild-card accounts were issued by banks and thrifts to compete with similar securities available in the open markets. During the third quarter of 1973, when disintermediation pressures were most intense, banks (with their floating-rate asset portfolios) extensively used this flexible pricing power and maintained deposit inflows at an annual rate of almost $20 billion. Thrifts, however, constrained by their long-term fixed-rate assets, lacked the earning power to pay the competitive rates, and their deposits inflows shrank to an annual rate of only $7 billion in the third quarter. By late 1973, political and regulatory concern brought an end to the wild-card powers of depository institutions and rate ceilings were once again established for all deposits less than $100,000. This brief experiment with unregulated household deposit rates had clearly demonstrated the competitive advantages of the banks, particularly the large banks, in a period of high interest rates and large corporate credit demands. Looking back upon 1973, the banks had managed to maintain their household deposit inflows with relatively few problems. The thrift institutions, however, had experienced severe disintermediation.

After a brief respite in early 1974, short-term interest rates again began to rise (Figure 18–2). Open-market rates soared above the deposit rate ceilings in the second quarter of 1974 and peaked in the third quarter at unprecedented levels. This time the deposit rate ceilings for household deposits were neither abandoned nor changed by the regulators. As a consequence, rate-sensitive household deposits flowed out of both banks and thrift institutions in a period of severe disintermediation.

The destination of these rate-sensitive deposits was an important feature of the competition for funds. As usual, most of the disintermediating funds could be traced to government securities (federal and state/local securities) and other open-market alternatives. It appears, though, that large commercial banks were also able to capture some of these flows. First, during the summer of 1974, the holding companies of large commercial banks sold almost $1.4 billion of small-denomination floating-rate notes to household savers. Because these notes were sold through their holding companies, they were not subject to deposit rate regulations. In addition, the money-market mutual funds (mutual funds investing in money-market obligations) became another attractive investment outlet for households. These money-market mutual funds sold shares to individuals in amounts as low as $5,000 and invested the funds primarily in the large-denomination CDs of the major commercial banks, thus providing a new unregulated channel connecting household savers with the large, rate-competitive commercial banks. These creative financing strategies and new channels for the large commercial banks intensified the disintermediation problems of thrift institutions and smaller banks, which lacked the means to compete for interest-sensitive funds in the national money markets. While the summer of 1973 had demonstrated the problems of removing deposit rate ceilings in a period of high interest rates, the summer of 1974 demonstrated the problems of attempting to maintain these ceilings. These two episodes are very reminiscent of the Fed's use of Regulation Q to control the issuance of large CDs by large commercial banks in 1966, 1969, and 1973–1974. During times of high interest rates, the large commercial banks (aided by other organizations, like money-market mutual funds) have seemed to be remarkably adept at formulating innovative circumventions of deposit rate ceilings.

In sum, the regulatory rate ceilings that have built a series of interest rate barriers in the household deposit market to protect the specialized position of thrifts seem to be increasingly less effective. As households become more experienced and adept at moving to various unregulated alternatives in the future, and as the investment alternatives available to do so increase, the prospective effectiveness of these rate ceilings will be even further diminished. The process of disintermediation is likely to reoccur, therefore, and perhaps at even greater rates, in future periods of high interest rates.

Federal credit agencies

An adequate supply of housing has been an important national goal for some time, and the housing lobby has been a formidable political force. The perceived relationship between the residential mortgage market (particularly for single-family homes) and housing has kept the mortgage market a matter of continuing political concern, and the recent sharp bouts with disintermediation have, of course, heightened that concern. Interestingly enough, Congress has not responded by encouraging thrift institutions to change their asset structure (the crux of the problem), presumably for fear this would detract from the overall supply of mortgage credit. Congress has, however, enacted a wide variety of different housing programs which have a pervasive effect on the mortgage and housing markets. Key elements in these programs in the mortgage market are activities of the Federal Home Loan Bank System, the federally sponsored credit intermediaries, and federally sponsored mortgage pools.

The Federal Home Loan Bank System. The Federal Home Loan Bank System consists of 12 regional Federal Home Loan banks and a governing Federal Home Loan Bank Board in Washington, D.C. Nominally a regulatory system, it has become at least as important as a supporter of the S & Ls. The regional Home Loan banks are owned by the savings and loan associations that are their members. They provide a number of services.

The most important of these are the loans (generally called advances) they provide to their member savings and loan associations. These loans may be for the specific purpose of meeting an unexpected withdrawal of funds or more generally to enhance the ability of the savings and loans to make mortgage loans. The maturity of these advances range from 30 days to ten years, and their terms are specified by the Home Loan banks. These advances are funded primarily by selling Federal Home Loan Bank System securities, the consolidated obligations of the regional Home Loan banks. These securities are sold in the federal agency securities market and allow the Home Loan banks to borrow at relatively attractive open-market rates and thus offer relatively attractive rates on their advances to member institutions.[10] Their advances have become a very active instrument of policy in the mortgage markets. Primarily they supply funds to the savings and loans during periods of disintermediation and are repaid in times of easier credit.

Federally sponsored credit intermediaries. The federally sponsored credit intermediaries involved in the mortgage market include the Federal National Mortgage Association (FNMA), the Federal Home Loan Mortgage Corporation (FHLMC), and various farm credit agencies.

The Federal National Mortgage Association (FNMA) is the largest of the federally sponsored credit intermediaries. Begun in 1938, FNMA (nicknamed "Fannie Mae") was transformed into a private corporation in 1968. It was organized to provide assistance to the home mortgage market by purchasing home mortgages insured by the FHA. The original concept was that by alternatively buying and selling these mortgages, FNMA would improve both the liquidity and stability of the "secondary" mortgage market. As things have developed, however, FNMA has provided several different, but related, functions. FNMA has provided (by auction) forward commitments to purchase FHA-insured home mortgages from mortgage companies.[11] The auctions of FNMA's commitments are a key part of the mortgage origination process. Even if the mortgage originators who purchase these commitments at auction eventually sell their mortgages to other permanent lenders (instead of delivering them to FNMA, pursuant to its commitment), the existence of these commitments assures the mortgage companies of access to the interim bank lending so important to their operations.

When and if FNMA is called upon to purchase these mortgages, it supplies funds directly to the home mortgage market. In recent years, it has purchased relatively large amounts of government-insured mortgages, particularly in times of relatively high interest rates. Essentially, FNMA

---

[10] The federal agency securities market is described in Chapter 19.

[11] Since 1972, FNMA has also issued commitments to purchase and purchased conventional home mortgages, but this has been a less important part of their activities.

has become a very large permanent mortgage lender by virtue of its assured source of low-cost funding in the federal agency securities market.[12]

The Federal Home Loan Mortgage Corporation, FHLMC, nicknamed Freddie Mac, was established in 1970 as an agency of the federal government to provide support for the conventional portion of the mortgage market. FHLMC buys conventional mortgages, mainly from savings and loan associations. The agency then sells some of the mortgages by creating pools and selling shares or participations in the pools. During the 1970–1976 period, FHLMC purchases averaged $1.1 billion per year, while sales averaged $0.4 billion. Sales exceeded purchases for the first time in 1976. Most of these transactions were in conventional mortgages, although FHLMC has bought small amounts of FHA and VA loans.

While these two federal credit agencies are in many ways unique, they have some common features which lead to their general classification as federally sponsored credit intermediaries (FSCIs). Each of them operates as a financial intermediary, raising funds in one segment of the financial markets and disbursing these funds in the mortgage market. Each of them is privately owned, but each of them is also constrained to pursue the public policy goals that led to its charter. Each is subject to some form of federal supervision to insure that its operations are consistent with public policy. They are quasigovernment agencies and quasiprivate intermediaries which straddle the boundaries between the private and public sectors. Indeed FNMA has evolved in recent years from a purely governmental agency to a private company whose common stock is held by private shareholders.

In return for the close supervision and regulation of the federal government, and their dedication to particular public policy goals, these FSCIs can raise funds on particularly favorable terms in the financial markets. Instead of accepting deposits, these intermediaries sell their debt securities in the open markets. Given their implicit federal backing, the FSCIs can borrow in these markets at interest rates below the best rated corporate securities and only moderately above the rates on U.S. Treasury securities. Because of this special ability to raise low-cost funds and unencumbered by any interest rate ceilings, the FSCIs can be a successful group of financial intermediaries and a potentially powerful means to influence the allocation of credit within the financial system.

Federally sponsored mortgage pools. Mortgage pools are created by setting aside a package of mortgages and issuing securities that represent shares in the pooled mortgages. Federally sponsored pools are pools for which a government agency guarantees payment of the principal and

---

[12] FNMA may become more active on the selling side of the market in the future. The agency has plans for new programs that call for buying and then selling participations in mortgages. The programs are to involve conventional mortgages and could increase FNMA's participation in the conventional sector.

interest on the securities of the pool. There are a number of federal programs which sponsor pools. The most important one is the GNMA pass-through program, which began in 1970.[13] Under this program, pools are formed and securities issued by GNMA-approved private originators. Upon formation of the pools, GNMA guarantees the payment of interest and principal on the securities of the pool. The private creators assume responsibility for servicing the mortgages, but the holders of the securities are the owners of the mortgages. All payments on the mortgages, including prepayments, are passed through monthly (less servicing and guarantee fees) from the mortgages to the holders of the securities—hence the term "pass-through securities." On December 31, 1976, there was $29.6 billion of outstanding GNMA pass-throughs backed by one to four family federally insured mortgages.

Having examined some of the special features of the mortgage security and the participants in the markets supplying funds to the mortgage market, we are now in a position to explore the dynamics of the mortgage market.

DYNAMICS OF THE SUPPLY AND DEMAND FOR RESIDENTIAL MORTGAGE FUNDS

Demand for funds

The demand for residential mortgage funds is related to the underlying demand for housing. Housing for these new households can take many forms, among them single-family homes, mobile homes, condominiums, or rented apartments. Housing is probably the largest single expense for most households, and a prospective move to a more desirable form of housing is an important decision and one that can often be postponed. The choice between the various forms of housing can be quite sensitive to a household's current and prospective financial condition. While the long-run demand for housing is determined by long-run demographic trends, short-run housing decisions seem to be very sensitive to the relationship between anticipated household income, housing costs, and the financing costs of home mortgages. Not surprisingly, therefore, there have been substantial short-run cyclical fluctuations in the pace of housing demands over the economic cycle.

---

[13] The Government National Mortgage Association, GNMA or Ginnie Mae, was established in 1968 to take over certain functions formerly performed by FNMA. GNMA buys home mortgages partly to support the housing market during periods of credit stringency but mainly to help finance housing for low-income families. GNMA may buy mortgages from originators at above-market prices and then sell the mortgages to FNMA or other investors at market prices, absorbing the difference as a housing subsidy. Alternatively, GNMA may simply guarantee the payments of a mortgage pool.

New residential construction. The most common measure of new residential construction is "housing starts," shown in Figure 18–4. Housing starts have been particularly variable, falling sharply in years of higher interest rates like 1966, 1969, and 1973–1974.

The bottom panel of Figure 18–4 displays the recent trends in the composition of new residential construction. In the 1950s and early 1960s, new housing starts were dominated by single-family homes. Multifamily units grew relatively rapidly in the late 1960s, however, and in the early 1970s they became an extremely important component of new housing. The reasons behind this shift toward multifamily dwellings were complex. To some extent it mirrored the shift toward increasingly urban living and changing lifestyles. It was stimulated by a wide variety of government subsidies and special financing arrangements for low-income and middle-income urban housing. The growing use of condominiums as second homes in vacation areas was also a factor. In retrospect, however, the real estate developers (and real estate lenders) overbuilt; in 1974, as vacancy rates soared, new multifamily construction dropped precipitiously. It remained depressed for several years despite substantial lowered interest rates and revived single-family home construction.

Other demands for mortgage financing. While the purchase of newly built homes and apartments are one important factor in mortgage demand, new mortgage credit can be used for other purposes too, such as to finance the purchase of existing homes or to finance general household purposes. As a relatively mobile population moves from one locale to another, and as different age groups move through the existing housing stock, there is a continual turnover of existing homes from one owner to the next. Indeed, most housing purchases involve an existing home, not a newly constructed home. Many of these existing home purchases are financed with new residential mortgages. If there were no inflation in home values, this turnover of the existing housing stock should cause no increase in outstanding mortgage credit (assuming a constant loan-to-value ratio for mortgage credit). In recent years, however, there has been a substantial increase in the value of existing homes, and this has caused a substantial demand for net new mortgage credit.[14]

While it is true that homes serve as the security for mortgage debt, there is nothing that requires new mortgage credit to be used to finance housing purchases. Financial resources are quite fungible. Once provided, they can be used for a variety of purposes. The rapid increase in the value of existing homes has allowed some homeowners to refinance their current homes, take out a second mortgage on their current homes,

---

[14] In essence, all existing home owners have been incurring substantially more debt to finance the same existing housing stock. Those households who (typically, later in life) move to a smaller home or apartment are thus realizing capital gains which can be used to finance other needs.

Figure 18–4
New residential construction as measured by housing starts (Seasonally adjusted)

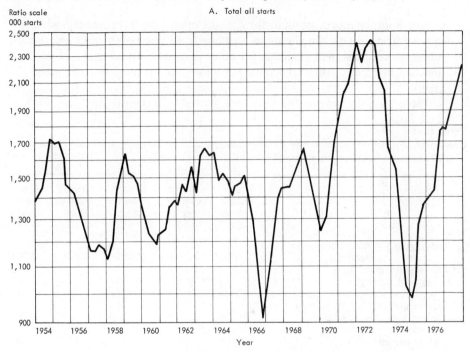

A. Total all starts

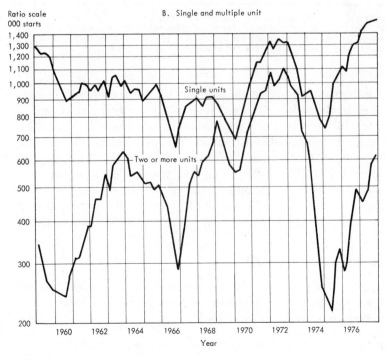

B. Single and multiple unit

Source: U.S. Department of Commerce.

or use a larger mortgage than they might otherwise have needed when moving from one existing home to another. In all three of these cases, the mortgage credit is then available for other purposes, for example, education, automobiles, other consumer purchases, or investment in financial assets.[15]

Table 18–6 documents the long-term increase in the net flows of new

Table 18–6

New home mortgage credit and new residential construction (Data are flows as a percent of GNP averaged over five recent credit cycles)

	Credit cycle 1 1954:3 to 58:1	Credit cycle 2 1958:2 to 60:4	Credit cycle 3 1961:1 to 67:1	Credit cycle 4 1967:2 to 70:3	Credit cycle 5 1970:4 to 75:1
1. Net increase in home mortgage credit (of households)	2.54%	2.28%	2.17%	1.55%	2.74%
2. Net investment in new residential construction (by households)*	3.79	3.04	1.96	1.32	1.82
3. Increased mortgage credit as a percent of investment in residential construction (1 as percent of 2)	67	75	111	117	151

* Net investment is the gross purchases of new homes by households, minus an imputed capital consumption allowance to cover the costs of actual depreciation and obsolescence in the housing stock.

† As noted before, home mortgage refers to debt secured by one to four family residential dwellings. When more than four families, a mortgage is classified as a multifamily mortgage.

home mortgages relative to the net amount of single-family home construction. In the 1950s, the total amount of new home mortgage credit amounted to between two thirds and three quarters of household net investment in residential construction. This relationship changed dramatically by the 1970s, however, when the net new flows of mortgage credit greatly exceeded the net residential investment. This changing relationship suggests that a substantial fraction of the net increase in home mortgage credit in the 1970s was used to finance the increased costs of existing homes and/or to provide for other household financial needs.

Supply of home mortgage funds

A diagram showing the principal actors in the supply and demand for new home mortgage funds is shown in Figure 18–5. Their flows of funds to the market are shown in Figure 18–6.

---

[15] For a discussion of this topic, see "Household Borrowing in the Recovery," *Federal Reserve Bulletin*, March 1978.

Figure 18–5
Diagram of supply channels for the primary market for home mortgages

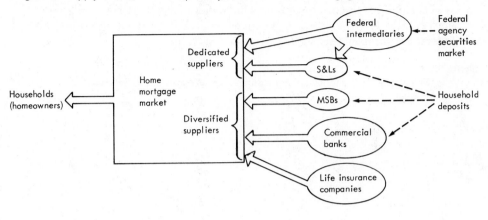

Figure 18–6
Composition of supply in the home mortgage market (Billions of dollars)

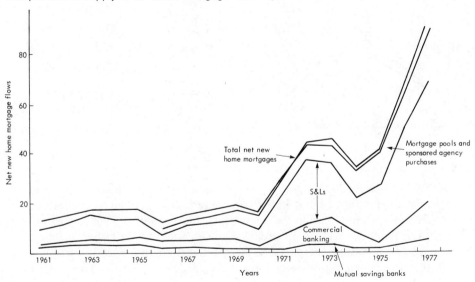

In the early 1960s, the bulk of the funds came from the dedicated supplier, the S & Ls. Three private institutions with a wider array of investment alternatives, mutual savings banks, commercial banks, and life insurance companies, also invested funds in the home mortgage market. By the late 1960s, however, life insurance companies had become net sellers of home mortgages.[16] Also the MSBs began to invest a smaller fraction of their total available fund flows in home mortgages (see Figure 18–7). The most important change which took place in the home mortgage market after 1965 was the sharp expansion in scale of the activities of the federal credit agencies.

Figure 18–7
Mutual savings banks' net acquisitions of residential mortgages and other assets (Billions of dollars)

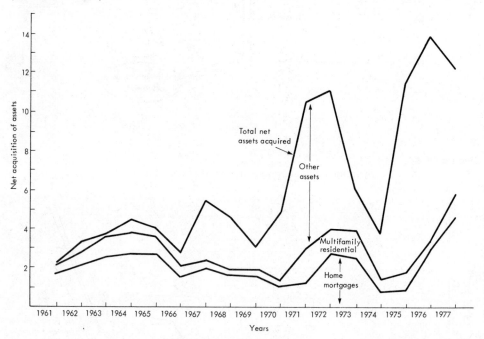

The disintermediation which took place in 1966 and 1969–1970 brought forth a substantial increase in the volume of funds supplied by the federal credit agencies involved in the home mortgage market. In 1969, for example, the federally sponsored credit agencies bought $3.8 billion of home mortgages, and the Federal Home Loan Bank Board advanced $4.0 billion to the S & Ls to supplement their reduced deposit inflows (see Figure 18–8). This federal assistance amounted to over 40 percent of the net increase in new home mortgages that year. Even after open-market interest rates declined in 1971 and 1972, and savings flows to S & Ls rebounded, the volume of federal assistance to the home mortgage market

---

[16] Actually, most of these home mortgages were not really sold, in part because of their illiquidity. As the old mortgages were amortized, they were not replaced by new mortgages, and thus life insurance companies were net disinvestors.

Figure 18–8
Home mortgage market funds supplied directly or indirectly from federal agencies: New Mortgage purchases by FSCIs, GNMA mortgage pools, and FHLB advances to S & Ls

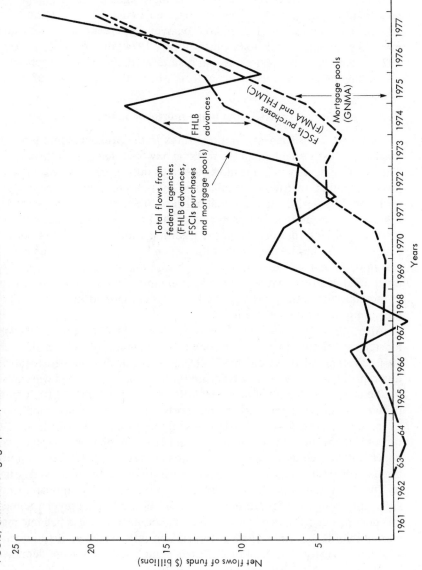

remained substantial. Then, during the high interest rate period of 1974, the role of the federal agencies increased further as they tried to limit the effects of the disintermediation at the thrift institutions on the home mortgage market. Direct purchases of home mortgages by government agencies, federally insured mortgage pools, and Federal Home Loan Board advances amounted to $17.6 billion, or over 50 percent of the new home mortgage lending which took place during 1974. In the third quarter of 1974 (the peak in interest rates and disintermediation), 85 percent of the net home mortgage credit came from these three sources of federal financing.

Behavior of interest rates in the home mortgage markets

As Figure 18–9 suggests, interest rates in the primary home mortgage market are less variable than the rates on newly issued corporate bonds.[17] This relative rigidity in home mortgage rates may be caused by state usury laws and other restrictive regulations, by nonrate changes in mortgage terms, and by various institutional barriers to abrupt rate changes.[18] This rigidity in rates adds to the problems of the home mortgage market. During times of high interest rates, the traditional mortgage lenders not only experience disintermediation, but the rise in home mortgage rates lags the rise in open-market rates. In these high-rate times, therefore, even those diversified lenders that are not experiencing disintermediation are not attracted to the home mortgage market. This compounds the cyclicality in the supply of mortgage credit.

Also, there has been a long-run decline in the spread of home mortgages relative to corporate bonds (see Figure 18–10). In the early 1960s the spread between these alternative securities helped to attract diversified lenders to the mortgage market. In part, the spread was caused by the lack of marketability, the default risk, and the rather large administrative costs associated with home mortgage lending. Since then, however, this spread has been dramatically reduced. Indeed, from 1969 through 1975, the rates on home mortgages in the primary markets were approximately equal to the interest rates on newly issued Aaa corporate bonds. To some extent this decline is attributable to the observed "rigidity" of home mortgage rates, although six years would appear to be a sufficiently long time for mortgage rates to adjust to higher levels. Some of this decline occurred because conventional home mortgages became more marketable as a result of the growth of private mortgage insurance. In addition, investors' perceptions of their default risk may have decreased

---

[17] It is difficult to accurately measure the costs of home mortgage credit because of the nonstandard features of mortgage loans: changing loan-to-value ratios, fees and special charges, prepayment penalties, and other technical factors. Thus the yield spreads between home mortgages and other long-term securities must be interpreted with caution.

[18] For a discussion of the rigidity, and its possible causes, see Jack M. Guttentag and Morris Beck, *New Series on Home Mortgage Yields Since 1951* (New York: National Bureau of Economic Research, 1970).

Figure 18–9
Yields on home and multifamily mortgages versus AAA corporate bonds (Quarterly observations based upon reported average rate for the final month in each calendar quarter)

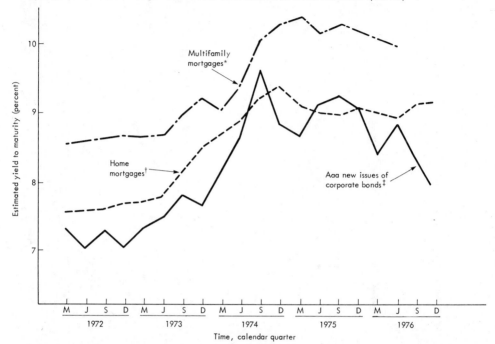

* As reported by American Council of Life Insurance for new commitments on U.S. income-producing property mortgages (residential *and* nonresidential).
† As reported by FHLBB for effective rate (reflecting fees and charges) on conventional mortgages for new homes in primary market (weighted averages of sample survey).
‡ As reported by the Federal Reserve Bulletin.

due to relatively favorable default experience in the postwar period. Finally, the rather large supplies of mortgage funds from federal credit agencies is likely to have depressed these spreads.

As a result of these declining yield spreads, the lenders with investment alternatives outside the mortgage market (life insurance companies and mutual savings banks) reduced their participation in the home mortgage market. Thus the growing dependence of the mortgage market on captive lenders, the S & Ls and the federal credit agencies, has been a direct result of these changes in yield spreads. The evolution of the structure of the supply of funds in the home mortgage market is thus both a cause and an effect of the changing relative behavior of home mortgage rates.

Multifamily mortgage markets

Unlike single family homes, most multifamily properties are large income-producing properties. The mortgages used to finance these prop-

Figure 18–10

Yields and yield spreads in the mortgage markets: average annual yields reported for home mortgages and multifamily mortgages relative to corporate bonds

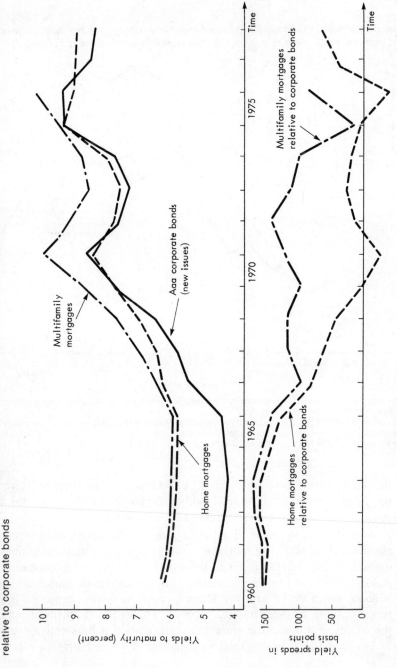

erties are privately negotiated placements of secured debt where the income producing capability of the project is the primary (and often the only) security behind the debt. In these respects, the market for multifamily mortgages is more like the market for commercial mortgages (on large income-producing nonresidential property) than the home mortgage market. The principal lenders of mortgages on multifamily properties are insurance companies, mutual savings banks, and savings and loan association. In many ways, this is a nationwide market, less dependent upon the local deposit institutions and more dependent upon larger more distant financial intermediaries who have a variety of investment opportunities in different markets and different regions of the country. The terms and conditions of each multifamily mortgage are tailored to the particular multifamily project so that it is difficult to identify standard multifamily mortgage terms. Because of the heterogeniety of the mortgage terms and the risks of each of the underlying properties, there is no secondary market for multifamily mortgages, despite the nationwide character of the primary market.

The development of large multifamily projects can take a considerable time and involve a number of risks. The permanent lender generally does not finance the project until it is complete and ready to be rented. In the interim, the developer must rely upon construction financing from banks, real estate investment trusts, or other specialized lenders. There are thus two types of financing, the permanent mortgage loan and the construction loan, which are critical to the success of a project. Generally speaking, however, the interim construction loan is obtained only after the permanent financing has been firmly committed by the lender.[19] The data and analysis presented here refer primarily to the permanent financing of the property.

Supply and demand for funds.   The principal holders of outstanding multifamily mortgages are shown in Table 18–7. The mainstays of the multifamily market have been large thrift institutions (both S & Ls and MSBs) and large life insurance companies.

The flows of funds from these suppliers are shown in Figure 18–11. In the 1960s, the supply of funds was dominated by the three classes of large financial intermediaries, though other suppliers (primarily federal intermediaries and commercial banks) have become more important. The patterns of supply contrast sharply with the home mortgage market. Life insurance companies and mutual savings banks have remained important suppliers of funds over most of the period. In the 1971–1972 period there was an enormous burst of new multifamily mortgage financing, primarily

---

[19] Although many interim lenders departed from this practice in the multifamily boom of the early 1970s. Unfortunately, many of them became de-facto permanent lenders when difficulties developed.

Table 18–7

Principal holders of outstanding multifamily residential mortgages, estimated holdings as of year-end, 1977 (In billions)

Total outstanding	Multifamily mortgages held	Percent of total assets held
Private intermediaries	$67	
Savings and loan associations	33	7%
Mutual savings banks	15	14
Life insurance companies	19	6
Federal intermediaries (FSCI's plus GNMA pools)	10	

Figure 18–11

Supply of funds to the multifamily residential mortgage market (Net flows of funds in billions of dollars)

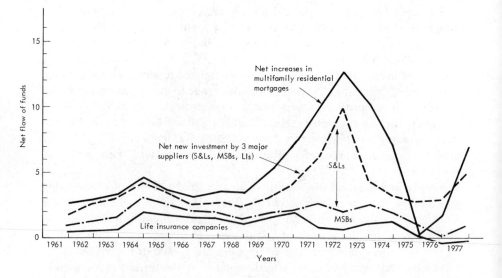

by the S & Ls and other lenders (commercial banks, real estate investment trusts, and federal intermediaries). This burst of funds was the financial vehicle accompanying the burst of multifamily housing starts shown earlier in Figure 18–4. Following the collapse in multifamily housing starts in 1973–1974, this flow of new financing collapsed in 1975–1976 as the problems of the multifamily housing industry became more clear. Many observers have argued that the easy availability of attractive financing in very large amounts was partly responsible for the boom and the ensuing bust.

With the exception of this financing peak around 1972, the flows of funds into multifamily mortgages have been less cyclical than the home mortgage market. Contrasting Figures 18–11 and 18–6, for example, we see that the adverse effects of the disintermediation of 1966 and 1969–1970 on the multifamily market are much less evident. Also, while home mortgage lending rebounded sharply in each of the subsequent lower rate periods (1967, 1971, and 1975), the multifamily mortgage market did not. On balance, the process of disintermediation appears to be a much less important feature of this market.

The reasons for this reduced vulnerability to disintermediation are partly attributable to the different mix of suppliers in the multifamily market. Life insurance companies, which are less exposed to disintermediation than thrift institutions, have been a major factor in this market, unlike the home mortgage market. Also, there are greater time lags in the process of constructing, and thus financing, multifamily dwellings. The funds dispersed in a given year have generally been committed earlier, often before the problem of higher interest rates and disintermediation became clear. Finally, the reduced exposure of the multifamily market to higher interest rates is partially attributable to the behavior of interest rates on multifamily mortgages.

The behavior of interest rates in the multifamily mortgage market. As with home mortgage rates, it is difficult to accurately describe the changes in multifamily mortgage rates because of the nonstandard factors of these mortgages and the paucity of data available. Nonetheless, Figures 18–9 and 18–10 attempt to portray the changing behavior of these rates. Figure 18–9 suggests that the interest rates on new multifamily mortgage commitments (and other mortgages on nonresidential income-producing properties) may be more responsive to changes in open-market rates than home mortgages. This may help to explain the decreased vulnerability of multifamily mortgages to disintermediation because their more responsive rates keep multifamily mortgages more attractive to diversified lenders in high interest rate times.[20]

More importantly, with the exception of the sharp increases in corporate rates in 1974, multifamily mortgage rates better maintained their yield spreads relative to corporate rates (Figure 18–10). Unlike the home mortgage markets, therefore, the multifamily market has retained its basic attractiveness to diversified lenders, and not surprisingly, the life insurance companies and mutual savings banks have maintained their participation in this market. Once again, therefore, the behavior of mortgage market rates explain some features of the recent evolution of these mar-

---

[20] Since life insurance companies are active in both the multifamily residential and privately placed corporate markets, their investment choices should tend to keep these markets in rough equilibrium.

kets. Furthermore, it highlights some of the basic differences in the behavior of the home mortgage market and the multifamily mortgage market.

GOVERNMENT PROGRAMS AND THE EVOLUTION OF THE HOME MORTGAGE MARKETS

Evaluating the federal programs

Nowhere else in the private financial markets are government programs so numerous, or their effects so important, as in the home mortgage market. This presence reflects a continuing political consensus that housing in general and mortgage markets in particular are appropriate areas of public concern. The government has attempted to achieve three objectives: to insure that mortgage funds are available in all regions of the country, to reduce the cyclical shortage of mortgage credit, and to increase the average amount of mortgage credit available and reduce its cost in order to increase the size of the housing stock. Unfortunately some of these objectives have proven to be difficult to achieve. In the financial markets, home mortgage borrowers must compete with other borrowers for funds. Business corporations are active and relatively interest-insensitive demanders of funds. The federal government itself is also an important and interest-insensitive borrower. Household borrowers, on the other hand, appear to be very sensitive to the nominal cost of mortgage funds. A number of the problems of the mortgage markets are related to this basic fact.

As we have seen, the federal government has formulated a variety of programs and regulations to deal with the home mortgage market, among them federal insurance programs, deposit rate regulations, subsidies, and federal credit agencies. An evaluation of the effectiveness of these activities must distinguish between the three different policy objectives (see Table 18–8). At the most modest level, there are the geographical imbalances which can occur because of the difficulties in moving mortgage funds freely from one region of the country to another. The federal government has established programs which enhance these flows, for example, mortgage insurance programs, and FNMA forward-commitment procedures for new mortgage originators. As a result, there now exist a variety of channels which allow mortgages which are originated in regions of high demand to be permanently financed with funds drawn from savers in other low-demand regions. Coupled with federal insurance programs and private initiatives, these federal activities have clearly helped to develop a more geographically efficient mortgage market.

In contrast, the cyclical shortages of mortgage funds have occurred because funds have been able to flow "too freely" out of the mortgage market to other markets when interest rates in these other markets are

Table 18–8

	Objective 1	Objective 2	Objective 3
Objective	Diminish geographic imbalances in the mortgage market	Diminish the cyclical shortages of mortgage credit	Increase mortgage availability and reduce mortgage costs in order to enhance the long-run housing stock.
Underlying problems . .	The inability of mortgage funds to flow freely from one region to another	The ability of mortgage funds to flow freely to other financial markets in times of high interest rates	The ability of funds to flow freely among markets and the competition for real resources from other sectors and other household needs
Attempted solution	Provide federal mechanisms to encourage and enhance the free flow of funds to regions of high mortgage demands, such as federal mortgage insurance and the auctioning of FNMA mortgage commitments	Devise regulations to restrict the movement of interest-sensitive funds and provide federally supported intermediaries to rechannel funds back to the mortgage market (in times of high interest rates)	Maintain (or increase) the barriers to the long-run movement of funds out of the mortgage market and supply additional funds from the long-run activities of the federal intermediaries.

higher. The government's response to this problem has been to attempt to curb this free flow of funds. This has proven to be an immensely more difficult task. The first step was Regulation Q and the other deposit rate ceilings. These were designed to help keep the deposit funds at the mort- gage lenders by building protective deposit rate barriers between thrifts and the commercial banks. Unfortunately, in response, interest-sensitive funds have flowed out of both types of deposit institutions and into open-market or unregulated investments. The second step has been the cyclical activities of the federal credit intermediaries. They borrow funds in the open-market and "pump" these funds back into the deposit institu- tions and into mortgage market in times of high interest rates. However, there are some leakages of funds from this "pumping system." For exam- ple, as the federal intermediaries raise funds in the agency securities market, they tend to drive up open-market rates and exacerbate the disin- termediation that caused the problem in the first place. The results of several studies suggest that the federal intermediaries were probably able to provide a limited amount of temporary support to the mortgage market in these times of disintermediation.[21] It is clear, however, that the gross flow of funds from the federal intermediaries (Figure 18–8, for example) substantially overstate their net impact. Despite these activities, the pace of housing starts has collapsed during each period of high interest rates. At best, the cyclical activities of the federal credit intermediaries seem to have been a limited success.

At a more ambitious level, there is the question of whether the federal credit agencies have expanded the supplies of mortgage credit in the long run. At first glance, they appear to have been very effective in supplying funds to the mortgage market. Over the 1971–1975 period, they supplied over 25 percent of the total home mortgage funds.[22] In addition, as we have seen, the average yield spread between home mortgages and other securities has declined, suggesting that these federally supported suppliers of mortgage funds may have helped to effectively lower the relative cost of home mortgage debt.[23] A first reading of the evidence seems to suggest that these federal flows of credit have successfully in- creased the average flows of funds in the mortgage market and, by impli- cation, the housing industry.

Nonetheless, a number of observers have argued that these activities have had little effect on either the cost and availability of funds. They

---

[21] See Dwight M. Jaffee, "An Econometric Model of the Mortgage Market," E. M. Gramlich and D. M. Jaffee, *Savings Deposits, Mortgages, and Residential Construction* (Lexington: Health-Lexington, 1972), chap. 5.

[22] For arguments in this regard, see Harris C. Friedman, "Secondary Market Behavior and Analysis," *FHLBB Journal* (May 1970), pp. 6–12.

[23] See Timothy Q. Cook, "The Residential Mortgage Market in Recent Years," *Economic Review of the Federal Reserve Bank of Richmond* (September–October 1974).

argue that even if the federal credit agencies are successful in providing new funds to the mortgage market and in reducing the level of mortgage interest rates, they may well be driving discretionary lenders to other markets. As we have seen, the discretionary lenders (MSBs, commercial banks, and life insurance companies) have not been investing in home mortgage in high-rate periods. Furthermore, the life insurance companies seem to have abandoned the home mortgage market altogether, and the MSBs may well be close behind. The mortgage funds that the federal intermediaries have been supplying (either cyclically or on average) may simply be displacing private investors, leaving only the S & Ls and the federal intermediaries themselves as captive suppliers of funds. It can be argued that these federal intermediaries are really the competitors of private intermediaries and unfair competitors at that for they use the credit of the federal government to finance themselves with low-cost funds. Some observers have argued that these agencies are driving the diversified lenders out of the home mortgage market, weakening the position of the private intermediaries that remain, and turning the home mortgage market into the ward of the federal government. One econometric study suggested that every dollar FNMA supplied to the mortgage market has been offset within several years by an equal withdrawal of private mortgage funds.[24] Thus, both a cursory examination of the flow of funds data and a more careful econometric study raise serious questions about the long-run impact of the federal intermediaries. Indeed, it would be surprising if the long-run impacts were considerable, for it would imply a long-run segmentation of the home mortgage markets from other financial markets.[25]

Finally there is the question of whether in the long run the federal intermediaries have successfully stimulated the housing industry itself and augmented the nation's stock of housing. This is, however, the least plausible proposition and the most difficult to document. It relies upon not only a long-run segmentation of financial markets, but on a firm linkage between the flows of mortgage credit and the volume of new housing investment. However, new housing is only one possible use of new mortgage credit. It can also be used to finance the turnover of the existing housing stock or other household needs. The mortgage funds supplied by federal intermediaries could easily be used for these other purposes and thus not influence the housing industry itself. These funds could indeed by just providing a financial "windfall" in the form of more plentiful, lower cost funds to anyone fortunate enough to own a home (which is required as collateral for this special form of subsidized financing). It is difficult to

---

[24] Jaffe, "Econometric Model."

[25] It is easier to believe that markets are segmented in the short run, or for a limited period of time, than that they are segmented in the long run.

demonstrate on the basis of the record that the federal credit agencies have had any important long-run influence on the housing industry itself. Indeed, one study concludes that the new investment in housing appears to be relatively unaffected by the federal government's credit programs.[26]

The effectiveness of these different federal programs provides some important guidelines for all government credit programs. When the perceived problem is that funds cannot flow freely to finance real economic demands because of various market barriers, the government does seem to be able to play an important role. By devising programs to reduce these barriers, perhaps through the creation of new channels, the government can effectively enhance the free flow of funds. When the real problem is that funds are flowing too freely (from politically sensitive markets to other markets that offer more attractive returns), the effectiveness of government programs is much more limited. To some extent, the federal government can attempt to support the politically sensitive markets in the short run by creating and/or taking advantage of various short-run partial segmentations in the financial markets. In the long run, however, the barriers necessary to make these programs work are very difficult to sustain.

The changing character of the mortgage market

Given the continuing concern over an adequate supply of housing, federal programs designed to expand the long-run supply of housing are likely to continue being developed. These programs are likely to continue attempts to expand the supply of mortgage finance in the hopes of stimulating housing either through the existing federal credit intermediaries or through entirely new channels. One proposal which is periodically introduced in Congress is an expanded set of credit controls for private intermediaries. It would require that all thrift institutions, banks, and/or other intermediaries hold residential mortgages as a specified percentage of their overall portfolios. This proposal would (at least, in the short run) enhance the effectiveness of federally supported mortgage supplies by closing off one of the leakages, namely the exit of the currently diversified lenders from the market. Other proposals to influence the flow of home mortgage credit suggest the use of incentives such as reduced taxes or reduced reserve requirements against preferred assets rather than mandatory controls to accomplish these same goals.

These potential programs give rise to serious questions about their equity, feasibility, and effectiveness. In addition, it is most likely that one of their long-run effects would be to weaken the competitive position of

---

[26] See Allan H. Meltzer, "Credit Availability and Economic Decisions: Some Evidence from the Mortgage and Housing Markets," *Journal of Finance,* vol. 39 (June 1974), pp. 763–79.

those intermediaries whose asset portfolios were controlled. Barring a system of controls for all of the possible financial channels, the controlled intermediaries would become less successful and less competitively viable, perhaps necessitating a net set of protective measures to sustain their position. In the light of our analysis of the mortgage markets, the ultimate effects of such policies seem very questionable. Efforts to stimulate the long-run supply of housing are probably better directed toward encouraging (through direct subsidies, tax incentives, and so forth) residential construction itself rather than further attempts to affect the cost and availability of home mortgage funds.

There are also a number of proposals directed at the cyclical problems of thrift institutions and the mortgage markets. The current government approach relies upon barriers to deposit flows (rate ceilings) and specialized federal intermediaries to rechannel the disintermediating funds back to the mortgage markets. An alternate public policy would be to attempt to strengthen the competitive position of the thrift institutions by changing their asset structures. One possible alternative would be to encourage deposit institutions to offer variable rate mortgages (VRMs), whose returns would vary with the overall level of interest rates.[27] By accumulating a substantial portfolio of these floating-rate mortgages, the thrifts could improve their ability to compete for funds in high-rate times and thus strike at the basic cause of disintermediation. Indeed, since 1976, a number of S & Ls (particularly in California) have been lending through floating-rate mortgages. The thrift institutions could also be allowed to diversify into consumer credit and other short-term loans. These short-term loans would provide a sizeable cash flow from amortization, which would enhance their ability to weather a period of disintermediation. There have also been some experiments in this direction in several regions of the country.

A number of federal commissions and other organizations have examined the cyclical problems of the mortgage market.[28] Each of them has recommended long-term solutions along these lines. They proposed that thrifts be encouraged to diversify their assets and experiment with variable rate mortgages. They also proposed a strengthening of the thrifts' ability to compete for funds, in part by removing the barriers (such as rate ceilings) in the household deposit market. Unfortunately both variable-rate mortgages and diversified assets imply some (initial) withdrawal from

---

[27] For various analysis of these VRMs, see *New Mortgage Designs for Stable Housing in an Inflationary Environment,* Federal Reserve Bank of Boston Conference Series, No. 14, January 1975, and "Financial Intermediaries and Variable Rate Mortgages," George G. Kaufman, Research Working Paper No. 16, Federal Home Loan Bank Board, August 1977.

[28] For example, the Commission on Money and Credit in the early 1960s, the Hunt Commission in the early 1970s, the Financial Institutions and the Nation's Economy (FINE) Study in 1975.

the housing inspired goal of dedicated long-term fixed-rate mortgage lenders. Furthermore, the proposed new institutional structures threaten the vested interest of some of the existing intermediaries. As a result, Congress has been unable to move in these directions despite the obvious difficulties experienced in recent credit crunches.

However, the current institutional structure is probably not a stable structure, and future bouts with disintermediation will continue to emphasize the need for institutional change. The institutions themselves, and the "technology" of the household deposit market, also seem to be developing a momentum of their own. Electronic funds transfers systems (EFTS) probably represent the future technology of the household financial services markets. They will bring major competitive changes in the household deposit market. In some states thrift institutions and commercial banks are moving toward more flexible asset structures and a wider variety of deposit-based services which will improve their competitive position in the market.[29] Sometimes these new services have been encouraged by regulatory changes. More often they have occurred as the result of circumventions (or contraventions) of existing regulations. Out of this changing technology and competition, however, a new household savings market is developing.

Also, an aspect of the mortgage market which has been at the heart of its cyclical problems, the grossly mismatched structure of long-term fixed rate mortgages financed with short-term deposits, has changed substantially. An early step in this process came when the federal credit intermediaries began to provide long-term funds to the mortgage market and to the S & Ls. A much more important step occurred as the banks and thrift institutions began to aggressively market longer term savings accounts. For example, while passbook savings accounts amounted to 88 percent of all savings accounts at S & Ls in 1966, they amounted to only 43 percent of all their savings accounts in 1976. Almost all of the roughly $150 billion increase in S & L deposits over this ten-year period came from these longer term accounts. As a result, the average maturity of their deposits increased dramatically. In 1977, several private financial institutions adopted additional ways to use the long-term markets to finance home mortgages. Some savings institutions issued long-term fixed-rate bonds collateralized by existing mortgage loans. Following the lead of the GNMA pass-through certificates on pools of federally insured home mortgages, several private institutions created pass-through certificates to finance pools of privately insured conventional home mortgages. These "mortgage backed bonds" and mortgage "pass-through certificates" resulted in home mortgages being financed with funds whose maturities and

---

[29] For example, the "NOW" accounts (essentially checking accounts) offered by thrifts in New England, various other third party payment accounts offered by thrifts in other states, etc.

interest rates were identical to or which closely matched the maturity and interest rates on the home mortgages themselves. On balance the mismatch in the assets and liabilities in these institutions was reduced. Out of this changing structure, the mortgage markets may well be developing their own ways to survive when interest rates increase.

Cyclicality of housing revisited

Throughout our discussions, we have implicitly assumed that the extreme cyclicality of the housing industry (see Figure 18–4) is undesirable. This assumption, however, deserves to be challenged. In many ways the cyclicality of housing may serve as an important and useful balance wheel for the economy. As we have seen, some other components of spending tend to be cyclical, particularly business investment in inventory and fixed assets. It would be highly undesirable for all economic sectors to fluctuate coincidentally, magnifying their individual cycles into one large economy wide pattern for expansions and recessions.

Fortunately the financial system tends to prevent this by converting housing into a contracyclical industry. The inflation and the demands for business finance that accompany the latter phases of an expansion drive up interest rates and crowd out the more interest-sensitive expenditures on housing. While housing expenditures collapse in the expansion, they generally lead the economy out of a recession in the ensuing period of lower interest rates. In fact, because new housing is often a postponable household purchase, it is in many ways ideally suited to play such a contracyclical role. Furthermore, households may even profit from playing such a contracyclical role. As we have seen, corporations tend to borrow heavily when rates are highest. Households tend to borrow least when rates are highest. It is not obvious that households would be better off if they also borrowed more when rates are high, even though that is the presumption behind many attempts to smooth out the cyclicality in home mortgage flows.

On the other hand, the severe fluctuations in housing may increase its average cost. The boom or bust cycles make it difficult for builders to plan, to retain a skilled labor force, and to smooth out the production process for housing. This cyclicality may be responsible for some of the longer term cost increases in housing that have been experienced.

Nonetheless, while there are reasons for attempting to reduce the severity of the cycles in housing construction, it would probably not be in the best interests of our economy to eliminate these cycles altogether. The mortgage markets compete primarily with the corporate financial markets, and residential construction is the competitor of corporate investment. Both cannot operate simultaneously at high rates without overheating the economy. The patterns of rising interest rates, the wrenching effects of disintermediation and thrift institutions, and the resulting fluctuations in mortgage funds have all played important roles in channeling funds to corporate investment and smoothing out the fluctuations in the economy wide levels of economic activity. Efforts to solve the problems of the mortgage markets must take account of its relationship to these other sectors.

QUESTIONS

1. In early 1978, open-market interest rates began to rise above the interest rates paid by commercial banks and thrift institutions on consumer savings deposits. As a result, the federal regulatory authorities authorized the issuance of six-month saving certificates which paid a rate of interest equal to the six-month Treasury bill rate at the time the deposit was originated. The minimum denomination was $10,000.
   a. How attractive would you expect these deposits to be to a savings and loan association? To a commercial bank?
   b. What other alternatives were open to the regulatory authorities and the federal credit agencies? Which of these alternatives might S & Ls have preferred?
2. How might the growth of money-market mutual funds (that is, funds which invest in short-term marketable securities and offer their owners the opportunity of writing checks against their shares) affect savings and loan associations and the home mortgage market?
3. How has the home mortgage market been changed by the growth of GNMA pass through mortgage certificates? How does this contrast with the effects which variable rate mortgages have on the home mortgage market?
4. How is home mortgage market related to the other markets in which consumers can borrow?

REFERENCES

"The Residential Mortgage Market in Recent Years: Structural Changes, Sectoral Behavior, and the Cost and Availability of Mortgage Credit," *Economic Review,* Federal Reserve Bank of Richmond, September/October 1974, pp. 3–18.

New Mortgage Designs for Stable Housing in an Inflationary Environment. Conference Series, No. 14, Federal Reserve Bank of Boston, 1975.

Symposium on the FINE Study, *Journal of Money, Credit and Banking,* vol. 9, no. 4 (November 1977), pp. 605–61.

Brady, Eugene. "An Econometric Analysis of the U.S. Residential Housing Market." In National Housing Models, edited by R. Bruce Ricks, Lexington, Massachusetts: D.C. Heath & Co. 1973.

Jaffee, Dwight M. "An Econometric Model of the Mortgage Market." In *Savings Deposits, Mortgages, and Housing,* edited by E. M. Gramlich and D. M. Jaffee. Lexington, Massachusetts: D. C. Health, 1973, pp. 139–208.

Kane, Edward J. "Good Intentions and Unintended Evil: The Case Against Selective Credit Allocation," *Journal of Money Credit and Banking,* vol. 9, no. 1 (February 1977), pt. 1, pp. 55–69.

19

Markets for U.S. government securities

The external financing demands of the U.S. Treasury, which arise primarily from the federal deficit, are financed by issuing new Treasury securities. The great majority of these Treasury securities are short-term, publicly issued, marketable obligations. They are almost completely risk-free and highly liquid. Together these securities comprise a huge reservoir of safe, short-term, marketable securities which transmit many important financial forces and which interact with most of the other important segments of the financial system.

In addition to the Treasury, various federal agencies issue their own special form of "federal agency debt." Furthermore, various federally sponsored credit intermediaries issue their own debt. At the end of this chapter the federal agency securities market will be discussed. In the beginning, however, the analysis concentrates on Treasury securities, the direct and explicit obligations of the U.S. Treasury itself.

Figure 19–1
Federal debt relative to other debt obligations*

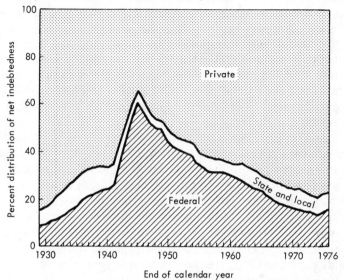

End of calendar year

* Federal net indebtedness is the federal debt held by the public (including the Federal Reserve System). Private net indebtedness includes the debt of the government-sponsored enterprises which are federally established and chartered but privately owned.

Table 19–1
Compositions of the outstanding federal debt by holder and by type
(As of December 1977)

	Outstanding ($ billions)
Total gross federal debt (U.S. Treasury securities)	718.9
By holder	
Held by U.S. government agencies and trust funds	155.1
Held by Federal Reserve banks and private investors . . .	563.8
Held by Federal Reserve	102.5
Held by private investors	461.3
By type*	
Marketable	459.9
Bills	161.1
Notes	251.8
Bonds	47.0
Nonmarketable	255.3
Savings bonds and notes	77.0
Foreign issues	22.2
Held by trust funds	139.8
Other	16.3

* Excludes $3.7 billion of noninterest bearing debt.
Source: *Federal Reserve Bulletin.*

The magnitude of the outstanding federal debt relative to private indebtedness is shown in Figure 19–1. Following World War II, the size of the federal debt dominated our financial system because of the massive federal financing during that war. Indeed, at one time, nearly two out of every three dollars of privately held debt were obligations of the federal government. To a considerable extent, Treasury markets *were* the financial system, and Treasury securities were *the* standard of value. By the 1970s, however, the federal debt had become a much smaller fraction of outstanding financial assets, and the importance of Treasury markets had been commensurately reduced.

There are several important distinctions which must be made when analyzing federal government securities. First, not all of the outstanding federal debt is really "net indebtedness" of the federal government. In fact, a good deal of the U.S. Treasury debt is actually held by accounts of the federal government itself (see Table 19–1). In a sense, the government owes itself these funds, and they amount, for all practical purposes, to nothing more than bookkeeping entries within the internal accounts of the government. While it is officially counted as part of the gross federal debt, this fraction of the U.S. Treasury debt will be excluded from further discussion and data presented here.

A variety of definitions and terms are used to distinguish various forms of Treasury debt. While most Treasury securities are marketable, there are two major forms of nonmarketable debt: U.S. Savings Bonds sold to households (about $77.0 billion outstanding at the end of 1977), and special nonmarketable Treasury issues held by certain foreign central banks (about $22 billion outstanding in 1977). Thus the "marketable debt" is somewhat smaller (about $460 billion outstanding in 1977) than the total Treasury debt. The terms "bills" and "coupon issues" are commonly used terminology for various forms of marketable Treasury debt. Treasury bills (T-bills) are short-term obligations with an original maturity of one year or less. They are issued on a discount basis with no attached coupons. Coupon issues, on the other hand, have an initial maturity of more than one year, and the investor earns a current income from the attached coupons. The two types of coupon issues are Treasury notes (initial maturity of one to ten years) and Treasury bonds (initial maturity of over ten years).

Perhaps the most important feature of the marketable Treasury debt is its concentration in relatively short maturity instruments. In recent years, almost 50 percent of the privately held marketable Treasury debt has been in securities with maturities of less than one year and over 75 percent in securities with maturities of less than three years. Relative to business enterprises (and for that matter, any other primary sector, the U.S. Treasury has very little long-term marketable debt outstanding.

The secondary market in which Treasury securities are traded is dominated by a relatively small number of dealers located primarily in New

York.[1] The average trading volume in Treasury securities has approached $15 billion a day, dwarfing the volume of corporate debt trading and exceeding by several times even the trading activity in corporate equities. The large inventories which dealers hold and the large volume of trading make Treasury securities, especially the shorter maturity issues, the most liquid of all securities (see Table 19–2).

Table 19–2
U.S. government securities dealers' transactions and inventories—
1977 (Average of daily figures, in billions of dollars)

	Volume of transactions	Amounts held in inventories
Total	$10.8	$5.2
By maturity		
Bills.....................	6.7	4.8
Other in one year	.2	.1
1–5 years	2.3	.1
5–10 years	1.1	.1
Over 10 years	.4	.1

Source: *Federal Reserve Bulletin.*

The recent yields to maturity of three-month Treasury bills trading in these secondary markets are shown in Figure 19–2 and are compared to the yields on two other important short-term obligations: commercial paper and large negotiable CDs. In general, the yields of Treasury securities have been lower. Furthermore, in times of sharply rising short-term yields (1966, 1969, and 1973), Treasury yields have not risen as fast, nor as far, as other obligations' yields. Treasury bill yields and the associated holding period returns are less volatile than comparable private investments. In terms of both market volatility and perceived credit risk, Treasury bills are among the safest financial assets available. This safety of Treasury securities, coupled with the extremely active and liquid market in which they are traded, makes them a uniquely attractive financial asset. Unfortunately, the counterpart of this attractiveness is their rather modest yields. Indeed the "real" (inflation-adjusted) holding period returns from very short-term Treasury bills over an extended period of time (1926–1976) has averaged just about zero.[2] It appears, therefore, that investors have been willing to accept a less-than-generous real return in exchange for the relative liquidity and safety that Treasury bills offer.

---

[1] For an analysis of the behavior of these dealers, see "The Dealer Market for United States Government Securities," The Federal Reserve Bank of New York, *Quarterly Review* (Winter 1977–1978), pp. 35–47.

[2] Roger Ibbottson and Rex Sinquefield, "Stocks, Bonds, Bills, and Inflation: The Past (1926–1976) and the Future (1977–2000)": The Financial Analysts Research Foundation, 1977. Actually the real returns averaged 0.1 percent per year.

Figure 19–2
Short-term yield: Three-month Treasury bills, commercial paper, and certificates of deposit

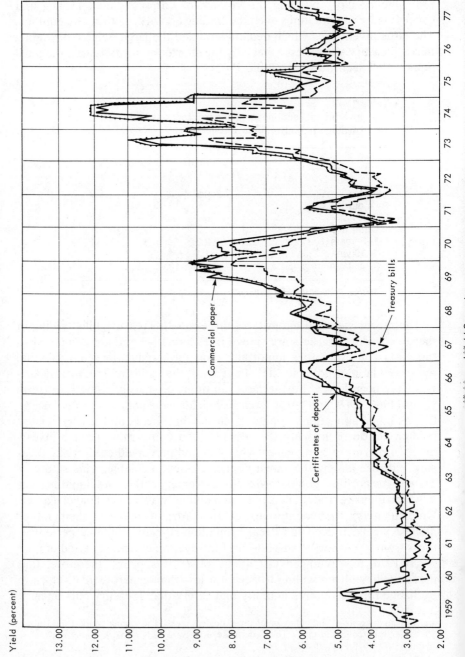

THE SUPPLY AND DEMAND FOR TREASURY SECURITIES

The demand for funds

Figure 19–3 documents the recent history of federal borrowing as a fraction of GNP. The Treasury's demands have been variable. Its de-

Figure 19–3
Federal financing requirements and the federal budget deficit (Expressed as percent of high employment GNP)

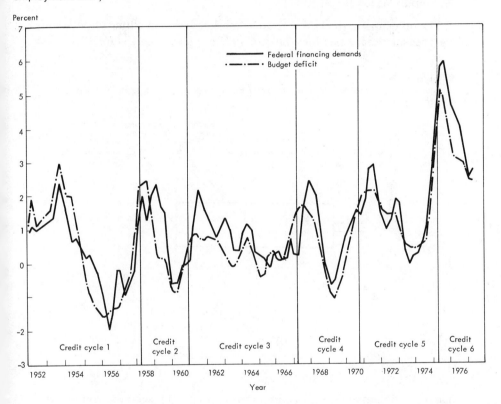

mands, when averaged over the credit cycles of the 1950s and 1960s were relatively modest.[3] Indeed, for most of the period from the 1950s through 1974, the U.S. Treasury market was basically a secondary market. To be sure, during this time period the Treasury was continually involved in huge financings, to "roll-over" its existing debt, but the net *new* Trea-

---

[3] As Chapter 4 demonstrated, federal financing demands in all but one of the recent cycles have *averaged* less than the financing demands of either business, households, or state/local governments.

sury financing was small relative to the roll-over of existing debt, small relative to the trading activity in government securities and small relative to the credit demands of other primary sectors. The recessions during those years, however, spawned periodic bursts of net new Treasury financing. For example, in 1975, the Treasury's new financing demands grew substantially as the U.S. economy suffered a severe recession, and Treasury financing became a major force in U.S. financial markets.

The supply of funds

The investors in the U.S. Treasury market and the volume of outstanding Treasury securities they held in 1977 are shown in Figure 19–4. The

Figure 19–4
Investors in the U.S. Treasury security market (With holdings as of the end of 1977)

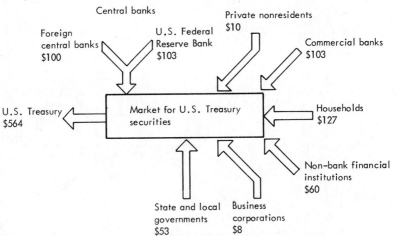

Source: Federal Reserve Flow of Funds and Survey of Current Business.

market is dominated by three important groups: households, commercial banks, and central banks (both the Federal Reserve and foreign central banks). Other groups such as business corporations, state/local governments, and nonbank financial institutions play a smaller role. The recent annual net supply of funds from the investor groups is shown in Table 19–3.

Central banks as suppliers. Central banks have been important suppliers of funds to the Treasury market. The U.S. Federal Reserve System purchases Treasuries through its open-market operations in accordance with the course set by overall monetary policy. The Federal Reserve could theoretically choose to implement its open-market opera-

Table 19–3
Composition of the supply of funds to the market for U.S. Treasury securities (Net flows, in $ billions)

	1967	1968	1969	1970	1971	1972	1973	1974	1975	1976	1977
Net increase in marketable outstandings	8.9	9.8	-1.2	12.6	23.7	11.0	5.2	9.0	81.8	64.5	52.9
Net purchases by											
Central banks											
Federal reserve	4.8	3.8	4.2	5.0	8.1	-0.3	8.6	2.0	7.4	9.1	5.8
Foreign	2.1	-0.5	-2.0	9.3	26.3	8.4	0.2	3.7	8.1	11.6	31.5
Private domestic parties	2.0	6.5	-3.4	-1.7	-10.7	2.9	-3.6	3.3	66.3	43.8	15.6
Commercial banks	6.5	2.1	-9.7	6.9	3.1	2.4	-8.8	-2.6	28.8	18.2	-2.1
Other financial institutions (nonbank)	-2.4	0.5	-3.9	—	-4.2	0.3	-3.6	-1.4	14.1	16.5	14.4
Business corporations	-2.4	0.3	1.7	2.6	2.8	-2.6	-5.3	2.1	6.2	8.1	-5.7
Households	0.2	4.2	6.1	-13.3	-10.5	-0.1	12.8	6.8	12.9	-7.9	-4.8
State and local government general fund		-0.5	3.1	0.9	-1.3	4.1	1.4	-1.9	2.8	7.4	17.2
Other	-0.1	-0.1	-0.6	1.1	-0.5	-1.2	*	0.4	1.5	1.5	-3.5

* Less than $50 million.

tions in almost any market, but the Fed wants to remain flexible enough to buy and/or sell substantial amounts of assets in a short period of time. The bulk of its operations are therefore concentrated in the Treasury market because it is the largest and most liquid of secondary markets. While the Federal Reserve is an important investor in the Treasury market, it is not an interest rate-sensitive investor. Its supply of funds to the Treasury market is not directly sensitive to the structure of prevailing yields but is instead determined by the overall goals of monetary policy.

Foreign central banks are the most important group of foreign investors who hold Treasury securities. Their holdings of U.S. Treasury securities were modest in size before 1969. They grew rapidly in the 1970s however. As was shown in Chapter 6, there is a large and rapidly growing volume of dollar claims on U.S. entities held by investors outside the United States. In 1971, when there was great concern that the dollar would devalue, there was a sharp decline in the private foreign demand for dollar assets and, as a result, a sharp increase in foreign central banks' holdings of dollars. In that year, foreign central banks accumulated $26.3 billion of Treasury securities and became an important feature of the Treasury market (see Table 19–3).[4] These purchases were largely the result of their attempts to support the value of the U.S. dollar relative to the values of their own currencies.

In 1976 and 1977, foreign central banks' accumulation of U.S. Treasury securities grew sharply once again. During these two years, the total volume of foreign dollar claims on the United States rose by $81 billion as the United States experienced a current account deficit and as the gross dollar outflows from U.S. gross financial investment abroad continued. While private foreign parties accumulated some of these additional dollar claims on the United States, foreign central banks accumulated over $52 billion, primarily in Treasury securities. As a result of these large purchases of U.S. Treasury securities, foreign central banks held $70 billion or about 14 percent of the net Treasury debt outstanding at the end of 1977 (see Figure 19–4).

As was the case with the U.S. Federal Reserve, the supply of funds to the Treasury market from foreign central banks does not depend primarily on the level of interest rates prevailing in the Treasury market. It arises from their desire to reduce the variations in the value of their currencies and from their need to hold dollar assets as a result of the special role of the dollar as an international currency.

Private domestic investors. From the early 1960s, up through 1974, private domestic investors *as a group* did not provide a large volume of financing to the Treasury market. During this period, the Treasury market

---

[4] Note that these foreign official inflows to the Treasury market were *not*, however, net inflows to the U.S. financial system because the offsetting effect was the liquidation of U.S. liabilities to foreign *private* investors (primarily, bank deposits).

acted as a channel for fund flows from the household sector to the business sector during cyclical peaks in domestic financing demands. In 1969, and again in 1973–1974, overall business financing demands were large. Short-term business financing demands were particularly large, and interest rates were rising rapidly. Examining the behavior of domestic investors during these years, (see Table 19–3), commercial banks liquidated substantial holdings of Treasuries in 1969 and 1973 to meet the increased business loan demand (and the partial run-off in CDs in 1969). In addition, other financial institutions also sold Treasuries in those years, particularly the thrift institutions that were experiencing heavy deposit outflows. Business corporations also sold Treasury securities in 1973 as they converted some of their liquid asset balances to inventories and other real assets. All three of these investors (banks, thrifts, and businesses) hold Treasury securities because they are a safe liquid form in which to invest financial assets, pending the use of these funds in a period of unusually large credit demands. The combined selling pressure of these three groups of private investors in times of high interest rates means that a significant number of other private investors has to be found for Treasury securities (even though the Treasury itself may have very modest financing needs). In these times, the Treasury market adapts to the supply and demand pressures by attracting a new class of investors.

Table 19–3 clearly identifies households as the major "swing investors." They purchased unusually large amounts of Treasuries in these years. Households are attracted to open-market instruments in high-rate times and in particular to Treasury securities.[5] The ability to attract this interest-sensitive group of investors is the crucial link in the supply and demand forces which operate within the Treasury market.

This entire process works in reverse as interest rates drop. In 1970 and again in 1975, business short-term financing needs fell sharply, and commercial banks (with little loan demand) rebuilt their government security portfolios. Other financial institutions also stopped liquidating Treasuries and in 1975 purchased substantial new amounts of these securities. Conversely, households also changed their behavior. In 1970 and 1971 when interest rates fell, households liquidated a total of $23.8 billion of the (by then) "low-yield" short-term Treasuries.

In 1975–76, however, a new set of pressures asserted themselves. As Table 19–3 showed, the Treasury's demand for new funds in these two years totaled $146 billion, an enormous increase over previous periods. Even with the substantial purchase of short-term Treasury securities by

---

[5] The total household supply of funds to the Treasury market seems to have two distinct components: a noninterest sensitive component and an interest-sensitive component. On the one hand, households have recently purchased a small but relatively steady amount (about 14 billion in 1972–1977) of net new (nonmarketable) U.S. savings bonds. On the other hand and more importantly, households' purchases of *marketable* Treasuries have swung sharply back and forth from heavy purchases to substantial liquidations in response to interest rates.

commercial banks, by other financial institutions, and by business corporations, this volume of new Treasury securities was difficult to place. Therefore the Treasury expanded its long-term financing and placed several long-term issues with households. In 1975–1976, households substantially reduced their holdings of short-term Treasury securities (as in similar past periods), but their purchases of long-term securities continued until late in 1976 when the Treasury's need for funds lessened somewhat. On balance, they actually supplied funds to the Treasury market in 1975. In 1976, however, their net supply of funds became negative as is more typical of low interest rate periods. In these years, as in earlier periods, the interest-sensitive household sector continued to play the role of the major "swing investor" that allowed the Treasury market to adapt to rapidly changing supply and demand forces.

The Treasury market as a conduit for financial forces

The Treasury market can be depicted as a large reservoir of safe, highly marketable, primarily short-term financial assets. Because of these unique characteristics, it serves as a conduit for many important financial forces. As we have seen, the fiscal policy of the federal government, which determines the federal deficit, is financed in the Treasury market. The monetary policy of the Federal Reserve is implemented in the Treasury market. The foreign exchange rate policies of other countries impact the Treasury market (through their central banks' holdings of Treasuries). Commercial banks, thrift institutions, and business corporations use the Treasury market for their liquid-asset buffers. Interestingly, the transactions of most of these large participants are not very interest-sensitive. A major class of interest-sensitive investors appears to be households. They have proved to be the key to the market's ability to adapt to cyclical changes in the demand for Treasury securities on the part of the existing holders.

YIELD SPREADS BETWEEN THE TREASURY MARKET AND OTHER MARKETS

Figure 19–2 displayed the yield on Treasury bills and two other market obligations: large CDs (the obligations of banks) and commercial paper (the obligations of prime credit business corporations and others). The yields of large CDs and commercial paper have generally been very similar because of the many interlinkages between banks, business corporations, and the short-term markets.[6] However, the yields on these two corporate securities have sometimes risen substantially above Treasury yields. The recent history of the yield spreads between corporate obligations and the Treasury obligations are shown in Figure 19–5.

Because of the equilibrium forces at work in financial markets, we

---

[6] See the discussion in Chapter 15 for further details.

Figure 19-5
Yield spreads of three-month commercial paper and certificates of deposit from Treasury bills

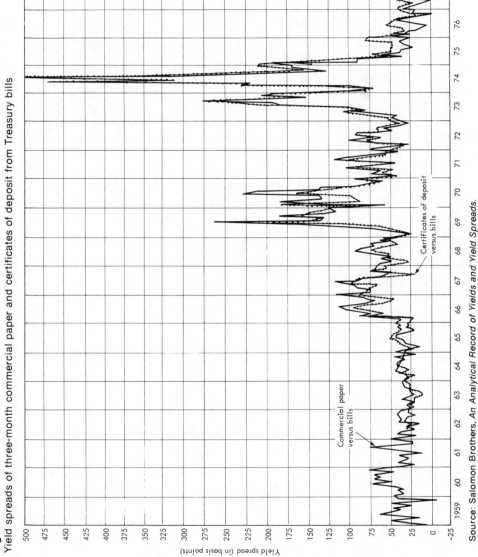

Source: Salomon Brothers, *An Analytical Record of Yields and Yield Spreads.*

would expect the yields of short-term Treasury securities and corporate market obligations to be in continuous equilibrium with each other. If, however, the corporate short-term markets are partially segmented from the Treasury market, then the different forces of supply and demand in the Treasury and the corporate markets could perturb yield spreads from their equilibrium structure. As Chapter 15 demonstrated, large CDs have generally been used by the large commercial banks in order to fund business loan demand. In addition, much of the commercial paper is sold by large nonfinancial corporations to fund their short-term needs directly in the money markets. In both cases (CDs and commercial paper), a significant fraction of the demand for funds can be attributed to the external financial demands of business. The demand for funds in the corporate money markets relative to the Treasury market can be measured, therefore, by comparing the financial demands of the business sector with the financial demands of the Treasury.

A measure of this relative demand pressure, the difference between corporate external financing demands and government demands, is shown in Figure 19–6.[7] Comparing Figure 19–6 with the yield spreads between private short-term rates and Treasury bill rates (Figure 19–5), we see that the proposed measure of relative demand pressure correlates well with

Figure 19–6
Relative demand pressures: non-financial business corporations net external financing minus U.S government net external financing (Net difference between these flows as a percent of GNP)

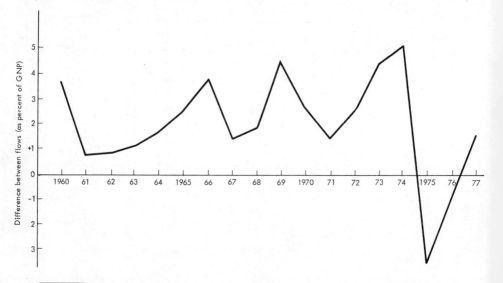

---

[7] Businesses' financial needs have peaked in expansion, whereas the Treasury's needs have peaked in recessions. To a large extent, this contracyclicality has been a natural function of counterbalancing economic forces, although it can be altered by the deliberate fiscal policy decisions of the government.

the yield spreads between short-term interest rates on Treasury and corporate securities. Specifically, the corporate sector was demanding relatively more external financing than the federal government in 1960, 1966, 1969, and 1973–1974. These were also the years when yield spreads between private short-term rates and Treasury bills widened appreciably. Similarly, in 1961, 1967, 1970–1971, and 1975–1976 the relative demand from corporations declined and federal government financing expanded sharply. These were also the years when the yield spreads declined substantially. This correlation suggests that relative supply and demand pressures have been one of the forces causing yield spreads between corporate markets and Treasury markets to change over time.

These effects have been studied by researchers in long-term markets as well. Fair and Malkiel, for example, concluded that the yield spreads between long-term corporate bonds and long-term Treasury bonds were influenced by the relative outstanding amounts of these securities and hence by the relative demands for funds from these different primary sectors.[8]

Supply and demand pressures are not the only factors which determine yield spreads however. The perceived credit risks of various obligations also affect their yields. Because Treasury bills have minimal default risk, the changing yield spreads in Figure 19–5 are also a function of the changing perceived risk of large banks and large prime-credit corporations. In 1966, 1969, and 1973–1974, the economy was reaching a cyclical peak. To the extent that perceptive investors were forecasting ensuing recessions, they might rationally have increased their risk perceptions of large banks and corporations at these times. At the same time that yield spread between corporate money-market obligations and Treasury obligations widened, equity prices were plunging. The coincidence of these events is consistent with the view that the increasing default risks of corporate money-market obligations was causing the yield spreads between Treasury and corporate securities to widen.

Unfortunately it is rather difficult to empirically determine the relative importance of these two effects: the forces of supply and demand on the one hand and the increasing risks of default on the other. Both forces have undoubtedly contributed significantly to changing yield spreads.

Observed yield spreads in the summer of 1974 and the adaptability of the financial system

The summer of 1974 was a particularly wrenching financial episode in the money markets and was an interesting opportunity to observe the adaptability of the financial system. The corporate demand for short-term

---

[8] See Ray C. Fair, and Burton G. Malkiel, "The Determination of Yield Differentials between Debt Instruments of the Same Maturity," *Journal of Money, Banking and Credit* (November 1971), pp. 733–49.

funds was extremely large—larger than it had ever been before. The federal government, in contrast, had minimal net financing demands at that time. A large U.S. bank (the Franklin National) experienced severe financial difficulties and, for all practical purposes, failed. While even large depositors did not suffer losses at this bank, the risk perceptions of many money-market investors increased nevertheless. Because of the late 1973 oil price increases, large amounts of dollars also suddenly flowed to oil-producing countries, who shunned the corporate money markets and chose instead to invest a large fraction of those dollars in short-term Treasury securities. For all these reasons, the yield spreads between corporate obligations and Treasuries increased to unprecedented levels in the summer of 1974. At their peak, these yield spreads reached 5 percent. While the increased credit risks of the corporate borrowers were surely a partial cause of the large yield spreads, it is difficult to believe they were the only cause. In retrospect it appears that supply and demand forces were responsible for a substantial part of those yield spreads.

Despite the enormous corporate demand for funds, it is surprising that yield spreads could open this wide. Most of these markets seem to be reasonably well interconnected by the arbitraging activities of various investors. There were, however, a number of important market segmentations during this period which help to explain what occurred. A principal source of incremental funds during this period was the household savings flowing out of deposit institutions. Yet it was difficult for the corporate sector to access these funds directly or even indirectly through the banks. Recall that for the first time, the Federal Reserve had abandoned Regulation Q on large CDs, leaving commercial banks free to compete vigorously for funds in the open-money markets. Regulation Q still applied to deposits less than $100,000 so that commercial banks could not price their retail deposits to attract households (relative to the open market rates). Large CDs and commercial paper were both sold in denominations so large (at least $100,000) that most households could not buy them. On the other hand, Treasury securities were available to households in denominations as low as $1,000, and households flocked to these securities. In addition, one of the indirect linkages between these markets had dissipated because by the middle of 1974 the large commercial banks had already liquidated almost all of their "free" Treasury securities. Most of those remaining had to be pledged against various deposit accounts. Thus banks could not fund additional loan demand from security sales. Rather they had to fund loan demand by issuing more and more CDs and commercial paper—driving up yields in the private markets. As a result, the unusually large demand for funds from corporations and the supply of funds from households were partially segmented from one another— driving corporate rates up and driving yield spreads from a more normal equilibrium relationship.

These unusual forces were not sustainable in the long run, however. The wide yield spreads between corporate obligations and Treasuries soon set into motion a rapid process of financial adaptation. First, because short-term Treasuries were no longer attractive on a yield basis with other market obligations, funds from several traditional Treasury investors flowed into short-term obligations other than Treasuries (federal agencies, municipals, commercial paper, and so on). Second, these yield spreads spawned a series of financial innovations to attract investors to new instruments. Money market funds, mutual funds that invest primarily in short-term corporate obligations (CDs and commercial paper), developed quickly in this period. Because of the very large yield spreads, mutual fund management companies could invest in large CDs and commercial paper, subtract a management fee equal to ½ percent of the assets managed, and still compete very effectively vis-a-vis Treasury securities for household savings flows. In the latter half of 1974, market funds grew from almost nothing to a size of $2.5 billion. Large commercial banks and other security issuers also took advantage of the yield spreads to create innovative financial obligations. One-bank holding companies issued a series of floating-rate notes whose returns "floated" at 1 percent above the Treasury bill rates. These notes were sold in denominations of $1,000 and could be traded on the New York Stock Exchange, which made them very attractive to households. Indeed some thrift institutions and an industrial corporation also issued floating-rate notes tied to the Treasury bill rate in this period.

Through a variety of channels, some old and some new, the flows of funds in the financial markets reacted to the very large yield spreads. In the process, they operated as a set of countervailing forces which tended to reestablish narrower spreads in a new equilibrium. Indeed, within a matter of several months, yield spreads between corporate and Treasury short-term debts had narrowed to levels consistent with earlier periods.

Thus the summer of 1974 in the short-term markets provides an interesting illustration of financial adaptation.[9] A number of large and wrenching financial shocks, coupled with a partial segmentation between markets, opened historically wide yield spreads in the short-term markets. But a series of countervailing flows and financial innovations were spawned by these spreads, and these equilibrium processes soon reestablished a more normal relationship among short-term obligations. The adaptation and innovation of financial intermediaries (and even the primary sectors themselves) seem to have been a powerful set of forces driving the prevailing yields in financial markets back toward a more normal equilibrium.

---

[9] See Chapter 12 for a more abstract discussion of this type of financial adaptation.

FEDERAL DEBT MANAGEMENT

Like private borrowers, the U.S. Treasury must manage both the composition of its outstanding debt and its net new money raising activities. In particular, the Treasury must be concerned with three aspects of federal debt management: (1) the average maturity of the outstanding federal debt, (2) the cyclical timing of new long-term federal financing, and (3) the special features of federal debt which make it attractive to different investors, particularly households. With respect to each of these three factors, the Treasury considers a number of different objectives, including both its own narrow interest in sound, efficient financing, and its more general effects upon the overall financial and economic system.

Average maturity of the federal debt

The single most important influence on the average maturity of the federal debt in the past two decades has been a legislative constraint—the bond interest rate ceiling. The statutory restriction on the interest rates that may be offered on Treasury *bonds* originated with the Liberty Bond acts of 1917 and 1918, which established an interest rate limit of 4¼ percent.[10] This limit did not cause too much controversy for many years for government bond yields in the secondary markets rarely rose above the ceiling. Since 1965, however, bond yields have generally exceeded the ceiling, and the Treasury has generally been unable to sell long-term bonds.[11] As a result the average maturity of the debt has significantly shortened. The average maturity of the federal debt decreased from ten years in 1947, to five years at the end of 1965, to about two and one half years at the end of 1976. In early 1976, about one half of the total publicly held debt had a maturity under one year. While most of these issues were regular Treasury bills which could be rolled over with little difficulty or market impact, the enormous volume of refinancing requirements meant the Treasury was persistently in the market. When, as in 1975 and 1976, the Treasury began to have very substantial *new* money requirements in addition to these refinancing needs, Treasury financing activities became very large indeed.

Viewed strictly from the Treasury's own perspective, the appropriate average maturity involves a trade-off between financing costs and financing flexibility similar to the trade-offs faced by private borrowers. Because

---

[10] Note that the ceiling applies only to "bonds," not to shorter term Treasury bills or notes.

[11] Two alternations of the legal rate ceilings have been enacted by Congress. Treasury notes, which are not subject to the interest rate ceiling, have been redefined to include maturities up to ten years (instead of the earlier five years), thus enabling the Treasury to finance somewhat longer term without interest rate restrictions. In addition, the Treasury has been granted exemptions to issue up to $30 billion of long-term bonds that were not subject to the interest rate ceilings.

the yield curve slopes upward (on average) reflecting the existence of liquidity premia, financing with the shortest maturities should lead to the lowest average financing costs (over a credit cycle), although these costs could be variable within the cycle. On the other hand, the shortest maturities create an almost constant refinancing problem and limit the flexibility the Treasury would obtain from an appropriately planned set of longer dated issues whose initial issuance and refinancing could be better timed to market conditions.

Because the Treasury is a public agency, however, it has to consider more than its own interests. It has to consider the effects of its financing decisions on the other financial sectors. If, for example, short-term and long-term markets are partially segmented from each other, and supply and demand forces do drive interest rates away from their equilibrium relationship, the issuance of substantial amounts of long-term Treasury securities could drive up long-term interest rates and thereby inhibit the long-term financing of other sectors (corporations and households in particular). In this circumstance, the most important effects of federal financing may be its impact on other sectors rather than its effects on the financing costs and flexibility of the Treasury itself. On the other hand, if the equilibrium forces dominate, the Treasury's choice of the maturity of its debt issues would not affect the term structure of interest rates. Most of the studies which have examined the effects of the federal debt maturity upon the term structure of interest rates have concluded that the maturity of the federal debt has had relatively little impact upon this term structure.[12] As a result of these studies, many economists and academicians believe that the short-term and long-term Treasury markets are efficiently interconnected markets and therefore that the average maturity of the federal debt has little effect on the structure of interest rates. Unfortunately, however, the interpretation of these empirical studies is fraught with difficulties. Most market practitioners continue to believe that the Treasury's financing patterns do affect the term structure of interest rates, and they are concerned about the effects which any significant amount of long-term financing by the federal government would have on interest rates throughout the long-term debt markets.[13]

Cyclical patterns of federal debt management

Given any target average maturity for its debt, it is often argued that the Treasury should manage the *cyclical timing* of its long-term issues in an

---

[12] See Chapter 9 and Franco Modigliani and Richard Sutch, "Debt Management and the Term Structure of Interest Rates: Am Empirical Analysis of Recent Experience," *Journal of Political Economy* (August 1967), pp. 569–89.

[13] For a further analysis of the issues involved in Federal debt management see W. D. Nordhaus and H. C. Wallich, "Alternatives for Debt Management," *Issues in Federal Debt Management*, Federal Reserve Bank of Boston, 1973.

attempt to pursue two objectives. First, the Treasury could attempt to time its long-term issues to minimize its own financing costs, financing long-term in the later phases of recessions and in the early phases of expansions when long-term interest rates are lowest.

Alternatively the Treasury could choose to sell its long-term debt in ways which would improve economic stability. This is often called an "anticyclical" debt management policy. In order to pursue this objective, it is argued that the Treasury should finance with short-term debt in the later phases of a recession to minimize the upward pressure on long-term interest rates and thus encourage economic activity. Then in the later phases of an economic expansion, the Treasury should finance long-term—increasing long-term interest rates and slowing the rate of expansion. The cyclical timing of its financing would thus tend to cushion economic cycles and smooth the pace of economic activity.

Whether either of those policies would be effective depends, once again, upon the importance of the basic equilibrium relationship in determining the term structure of interest rates. If markets are segmented such that the Treasury's financings can perturb the term structure of interest rates from its equilibrium relationship, then the Treasury's potential ability to aid economic stabilization is important, suggesting that an anticyclical debt management policy may be appropriate. If, however, the term structure of interest rates is held in equilibrium by investors' expectations of future returns, then the Treasury is unable to use such a policy to bring about anticyclical movements in interest rates. Moreover, if the Treasury market is efficient in the sense that the market's current expectations about future interest rates incorporate the best forecast of these rates, then there is no way for the Treasury to concentrate its issuance of long-term debt at periods of abnormally "low" long-term rates. On the contrary, the market will always charge the U.S. Treasury an "appropriate" rate for long-term financing today which incorporates and reflects what can be known about the costs of long-term financing tomorrow. The different perspectives on interest rate determination that we have discussed in this book lead to strikingly different operational implications for the Treasury, just as they do for most private sector financing policies.

Marketing Treasury debt to households

A final aspect of federal debt management is the tailoring of the terms of federal debt issues to suit potential investor groups—most importantly, to suit households. Households hold federal debt issues in two forms, nonmarketable U.S. savings bonds and marketable Treasury issues. Savings bonds are sold through a variety of special distribution channels (employer-sponsored payroll savings plans, for example) in denominations as small as $25. They were a central feature of the war financing effort during World War II. Their interest rates have generally been below market rates, and their attractiveness has thus been limited. Nonetheless, there has been a small but steady increase in savings bonds, bringing the total outstanding to $77 billion in 1977. Households also buy marketable Treasury issues, particularly in times of relatively high interest rates. The attractiveness of these securities can be influenced by a number of factors, including the method used to sell them and the minimum denomination.

By tailoring debt securities and distribution channels to meet the needs of household savers, the Treasury could improve its own ability to finance. However, such Treasury securities would most likely be very competitive with time and savings deposits. The more successful the Treasury is in attracting household savers, the fewer funds will be available for thrift institutions to channel into the home mortgage market. This problem is particularly severe, of course, during periods of high interest rates and disintermediation.

If the existing markets for households savings were not segmented and households already shifted freely between various financial alternatives, then improving the attractiveness of the Treasury's offerings to households would not have very much of an effect. But as we have seen the markets for household funds are segmented by numerous barriers, such as interest rate ceilings on deposits, and large minimum denominations for Treasury securities. Increasing the attractiveness of the federal securities to household savers is likely to affect the pattern of financial flows and the allocation of credit. Thus, the Treasury is torn between two conflicting objectives: enhancing its own ability to finance through the sale of its debt to households and protecting the home mortgage market from the inevitable effects of this policy.

Once again the more segmented the markets are, the more important federal debt management is and the more important it is for the Treasury to consider the broader spectrum of objectives in managing the federal debt.

THE MARKET FOR FEDERAL AGENCY SECURITIES

The fastest growing financial market in the United States has been the federal agency securities market. Starting from almost nothing in the 1950s, it has become a major part of our financial system with about $130 billion of securities outstanding in 1977. The classification "federal agency securities" includes the securities of a number of government-sponsored enterprises and the mortgage pool securities backed by the Government National Mortgage Association (GNMA).[14]

---

[14] Until 1974, a large number of additional federal agencies sold their own debt in the federal agency market. At that time, the Federal Financing Bank (FFB) was established to coordinate agency borrowing and to reduce the cost to the government of some of their borrowing activities. The FFB purchases the debt issues of these agencies and indirectly finances these purchases through the issuance of Treasury securities. The financing requirements of the FFB have added significantly to the Treasury's overall financing.

As can be seen in Table 19–4, the federal agency securities market is dominated by the securities of government-sponsored enterprises active in two markets: the residential mortgage market and the market for farm credit.

Table 19–4
Outstanding federal agency securities (Outstandings in billions 12/31/76)

			$ Billions
Mortgage market related	79.7		
Federally sponsored credit intermediaries		49.1	
Federal Home Loan banks			16.8
Federal Home Loan Mortgage Corporation (FHLMC)			1.7
Federal National Mortgage Association (FHMA)			30.6
GNMA-guaranteed mortgage pool securities		30.6	
Farm credit related	31.9		
Federal land banks		17.1	
Other farm credit		14.8	
Other	0.4		
Total	112.0		

Source: Federal Reserve Bulletin.

Each type of federal agency security is unique in some ways. Most of them are issued under authority of an act of Congress, exempt from SEC registration, and "backstopped" by an authority to borrow from the Treasury. A few are backed by the "full faith and credit of the United States." Regardless of their particular terms, all of these federal agency securities are believed to carry at least the *implicit* backing of the federal government. As such, they are considered to be relatively risk-free assets, safer than all but the securities of the U.S. Treasury itself. Not surprisingly, the federal agency securities tend to be priced to yield slightly more than Treasury securities and considerably less than most corporate market rates. The relationship between federal agency and comparable Treasury and corporate yields for several time periods is shown in the accompanying table.

Relative yields to maturity for outstanding Treasury, federal agency, and corporate securities (Yields for seven-year securities)

	12/30/75	12/30/76	12/30/77
U.S. Treasury	7.60%	6.45%	7.66%
Federal agency securities	7.70	6.60	7.80
Aa utility bonds	8.20	7.35	8.23

The relationship between the yields on particular federal agency securities and other securities also seems to be influenced in the short run by the forces of relative supply and demand. For example, in 1974–1975, a substantial volume of issues of a new type of federal agency security— "GNMA pass-throughs"—were issued to help support the home mortgage market. These securities were relatively unfamiliar to most investors. The surge in supply of these securities drove their yields substantially above yields on Treasury securities and even above yields on some corporate sector securities. In time, however, investors were attracted to these new securities by their generous yields (and low risk), and they became an important part of some investors' portfolios. By 1976, the yields on these securities receded to a more normal level—somewhat above Treasury yields but below corporate sector yields.

At one time households were the dominant investor in federal agency securities. More recently, financial institutions have become the most important investors. For investors, these federal agency securities serve the same portfolio objectives as Treasury securities. They are not as liquid nor as risk-free as Treasury securities, but then they yield a somewhat higher return. They are "near-Treasury" securities from the investor's point of view.

Cyclical pattern of agency financing

The net annual increase in federal agency securities and mortgage pools are shown in Figure 19–7 along with the net financing demands of the Treasury. Federal agency financing has increased during the times when the Treasury's demands have been falling. Indeed the large financing demands of the federal agencies seem to coincide with the large financing demands in the corporate sector. This is not surprising since the most important of the federal agencies are designed to protect the mortgage market during just those times when corporate demands are large. Thus, while federal agency securities and Treasury securities are similar, their roles within the financial system are different. Federal agency financing, the smaller of the two federal government financing components, may well have the greater effect on corporate credit markets. The more effectively these federal agencies support the residential mortgage markets, the more they compete with business corporations' ability to finance their periodically large external financing demands.

Problems and issues surrounding federally sponsored credit agencies

The federally sponsored credit agencies and their financing in the federal agency market raise a number of important issues. The organizational form and legal status of these powerful credit allocators is peculiar. Sev-

Figure 19–7
Two components of net new federal government financing

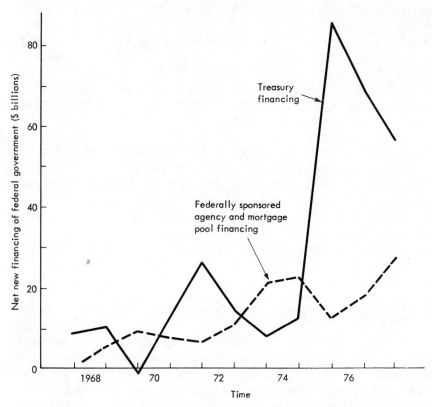

eral of them are shareholder-owned and thus should presumably operate
in the best interests of their shareholders. On the other hand, they must
also operate pursuant to the goals of their public charters. These two sets
of objectives can often conflict. Moreover, the transactions of these enterprises are not included within the federal budget and their debt is not
considered to be part of the federal debt. These facts tend to shelter them
from the more complete control that Congress exercises with most public
programs. A number of critics argue that they are powerful, fast-growing,
relatively uncontrolled instruments of public policy with conflicting public
and private objectives and with a dubious ability to accomplish their
long-run public objectives.[15] Whatever their dangers, however, they remain a useful way for the federal government to allocate credit toward certain "socially desirable" sectors without affecting the federal budget

---

[15] See "Federal Agency Financing," The Morgan Guaranty Survey, August 1974, and
MacLaury, Bruce K., "Federal Credit Programs—The Issues They Raise," *Issues in Federal Debt Management,* Federal Reserve Bank of Boston, June 1973.

or forcing private financial institutions to change their investment portfolios. As such, they are likely to continue their growth and expand the relative importance of the federal agency market within the financial system.

SUMMARY

U.S Treasury securities are a large pool of safe, marketable, primarily short-term securities which are attractive to certain investors because of their safety and liquidity. Because of these special features, the U.S. Treasury market serves as a conduit through which many important financial forces are transmitted—among them the financing needs of the federal government, the monetary policy of the Federal Reserve, the exchange rate policies of foreign central banks, and the indirect channeling of household funds to business corporations during periodic credit crunches.

Because of its interconnections with other markets, interest rates in the U.S. Treasury market have generally fluctuated with other market interest rates. The yield spreads between U.S. Treasury securities and open-market corporate securities (large CDs and commercial paper, for example) seem to have been determined both by the risk perceptions of investors and, in the short-run, by the forces of supply and demand. Abnormally large yield spreads between these markets, caused by the forces of supply and demand, have quickly spawned a process of financial adaptation, however, which has reestablished more normal yield spreads.

Because of the importance of the U.S. Treasury market, the federal government is continually faced with the problems of managing the federal debt, including its average maturity, the cyclical timing of new long-term financing, and the attractiveness of particular securities to household investors. If all markets were efficiently interconnected and the basic equilibrium processes were the sole determinants of interest rates, then the Treasury could finance without affecting relative interest rates. But to the extent that its supply and demand for funds affects interest rates, it must consider the impact of these rates upon private financing. In the future, however, the more important impact upon private financing may come from federal agency securities whose characteristics are similar to U.S. Treasury securities. One of the fastest growing segments of our financial markets, the federal agencies which issue these securities have been created to cushion the mortgage market (and other markets which provide funds to "socially desirable" activities) from the impacts of higher interest rates and large corporate financing demands. As a result, large federal agency financing demands coincide with, and compete with, corporate financing more than does their larger but contracyclical counterpart, the financing needs of the U.S. Treasury itself.

QUESTIONS

1. Using the interest rate data in Figure 19–2 and the flow of funds data in Table 19–3, answer the following questions:

   a. What supply and demand factors might have caused the increase in interest rates in 1969 and 1973?

   b. What supply and demand factors might have caused the reduction in rates in 1967 and 1970?

   c. What factors prevented an increase in rates in 1971 even though the volume of new issues grew substantially?

   d. What factors prevented a rise in interest rates in 1975 and 1976?

2. Suppose at the extreme that the Congress entirely removed the now anachronistic 4¼ percent interest ceiling on U.S. Government bonds, and in response the Treasury began to raise a substantial amount of funds over the next few years through issuing a long-term marketable U.S. Treasury bonds (say, $30–35 billion per year of issues with maturities of 15 to 30 years).

   a. What would be the direct effects of this new long-term financing method on financial flows? Who will buy the long-term securities? What other changes will be set in motion?

   b. What would the likely effects of such a policy be on interest rates?

   c. How might such a policy affect spending in the economy?

   d. As a commercial banker, what would you think of this proposal?

   e. As an investment banker, what would you think of this proposal?

   f. As a believer in efficient markets, what would you think?

   g. As a person representing the "public interest," would you allow the Treasury to issue a significant amount of long-term debt or would you confine their financing to short-term debt?

3. Suppose the Treasury was allowed to sell a sizeable amount of 5–10 year floating-rate non-marketable U.S. Savings Certificates in small denominations (say of $500 or $1,000), whose yields fluctuated with the open-market yields on marketable U.S. Treasury Securities.

   a. Who could be expected to buy these certificates? What other financing flows would be affected?

   b. How would large banks, small banks, and thrifts be affected?

   c. What role might the Federal Agencies play in all this?

   d. What might be its effects on interest rates?

   e. On economic activity?

4. How are the fortunes of the different financial institutions dependent on the spreads between the interest rates on the securities issued by the Treasury and by private entities?

5. What determines the size and profitability of the money market or liquid asset mutual funds?

6. In what ways do the debt issues of the Treasury compete with businesses as they try to raise funds? How does this compare with the effects of federal agency borrowing on business' ability to raise funds?

REFERENCES

Banks, Lois. "The Market for Agency Securities," *Quarterly Review,* Federal Reserve Bank of New York, vol. 3, no. 1 (Spring 1978).

Garbade, Kenneth D. and Hunt, Joseph F. "Risk Premiums on Federal Agency Debt," vol. 33, no. 1 *Journal of Finance* (March 1978), pp. 105–16.

Garbade, Kenneth and Silber, William L. "Price Dispersion in the Government Securities Market," *Journal of Political Economy,* vol. 84, no. 4 (1976, pt. 1, pp. 721–40.

Lang, Richard W. and Rasche, Robert H. "Debt Management Policy and the Price Elasticity of Demand for U.S. Government Notes and Bonds," *Monthly Review,* Federal Reserve Bank of St. Louis, September 1977, pp. 8–22.

McCordy, Christopher J. "The Dealer Market for United States Government Securities," *Quarterly Review,* Federal Reserve Bank of New York, Winter 1977–78, pp. 35–47.

Joint Treasury—Federal Reserve Study of the U.S. Government Securities Market. New York: Board of Governors of the Federal Reserve System, 1969.

Issues in Federal Debt Management. Conference Series No. 10, Federal Reserve Bank of Boston, 1973.

20

The market for tax-exempt securities

SUPPLY AND DEMAND IN THE MUNICIPALS MARKET
The Demand for Funds
The Supply of Funds
The Dynamics of the Municipals Market
Changes in Investor Behavior
EFFECTIVENESS OF TAX-EXEMPTION FOR REDUCING STATE
AND LOCAL BORROWING COSTS
Proposals for the tax-exempt market
Tax exemptions and public policy

Tax-exempt securities are the fixed-income obligations of state/local governments. Their tax exemption arises because of the special legal relationship which exists between the states and the federal government, and has served as a kind of tax subsidy to reduce the borrowing costs of these governments. The market for tax-exempt securities has come to be called the "municipals market," although it includes the obligations of not only municipal but state governments as well as a number of other affiliated agencies and projects.

The municipals market is very diverse and consists of a number of different submarkets. There is a market for obligations of large well-known prime-credit state and local government obligations. These securities are generally distributed in the primary market by nationwide underwriting syndicates. They later trade in relatively active secondary markets where dealers stand ready to buy/sell reasonable amounts of securities, and price quotations are continuously available. Equally as important, however, are the obligations of an extremely large number of smaller and less well-known governments (and their agencies). For example, in 1975 alone, there were over 8,000 new municipal issues, only a small fraction of which were obligations of well-known state or city governments. The great majority of these municipal obligations are issued in what are essentially regional primary markets. After issuance, these secu-

420

rities are not actively traded in any secondary market, and price quotations for most of them are not available on a regular basis.[1]

Tax-exempt securities are most often issued in the form of "serial bonds," where a single financing is spread across a wide spectrum of bonds with different maturities. Thus the municipals market contains bonds with a wide variety of maturities. The municipals market is a relatively unregulated market with comparatively few restrictions on municipal security dealers and comparatively undeveloped norms for financial disclosure by issuers.

SUPPLY AND DEMAND IN THE MUNICIPALS MARKET

The demand for funds

As Chapter 5 demonstrated, the net new issues of state/local government obligations have been relatively constant (as a percent of GNP) in recent years. Figure 20–1 shows the recent composition of demand in the municipals market measured in dollar terms. The great majority of the new flows of tax-exempt securities have been the obligations of state/local governments, both general obligation bonds and revenue bonds.[2] Beginning in 1971–1972, however, the tax-exempt bonds used by business corporations to fund their pollution control expenditures have become a growing fraction of the total.[3] The bottom line in Figure 20–1 shows the net new issues of short-term notes by state/local governments. In 1969 and 1974, when interest rates peaked, state/local governments issued a relatively large fraction of these short-term notes. In 1972 and 1975–1976, when interest rates were lower, they relied more upon long-term financing. Evidently state/local governments do attempt to time their long-term financing vis-a-vis interest rate movements.

The supply of funds

The attractiveness of municipal securities to potential suppliers of funds is dependent in part upon their tax brackets. Table 20–1 lists a number of potential suppliers and their respective tax brackets.

---

[1] In 1975 another group of distinct "submarkets" appeared for the obligations of New York City (and some other state/local governments in financial difficulty). Because of the financial risks, these obligations were not issued or traded in anything resembling a true market but were purchased as part of a political/economic compromise between the various local governments, financial institutions, and others involved. The markets for the obligations of even large well-known governments can thus become essentially local affairs, particularly in a time of financial stringency.

[2] See Chapter 5 for a description of the composition of these bonds.

[3] Technically these pollution control bonds and other small industrial development bonds are the securities of the local government in whose jurisdiction the facilities are built. In reality, however, the business corporation guarantees these obligations, and investors consider them to be tax-exempt corporate securities.

Figure 20–1
Composition of demand within tax-exempt markets, net new issues of tax-exempt securities

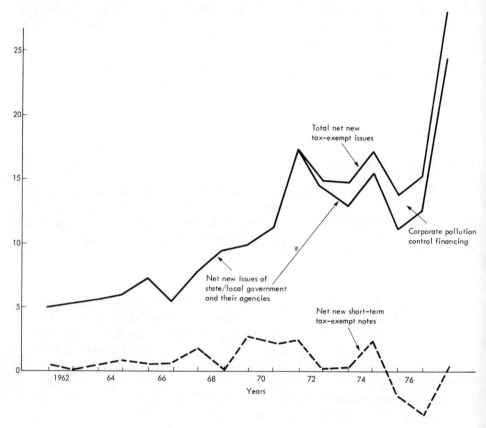

Among financial intermediaries, only casualty insurance companies and commercial banks have relatively high marginal tax brackets. The principal long-term institutional investors. pension funds and life insurance companies, have either relatively low or zero marginal tax rates. The

Table 20–1
Approximate marginal federal tax brackets for various potential investors

Financial intermediaries	Tax bracket (percent)
Pension funds	0
Most thrift institutions	<20
Most life insurance companies	20
Casualty insurance companies	48
Commercial banks	48
Others: individuals	0–70

other group of potential suppliers, high-income individuals, have relatively high tax brackets. Not surprisingly, therefore, the major investors in tax-exempt securities are high-income individuals, commercial banks, and casualty insurance companies. Figure 20–2 depicts these suppliers and their ownership of outstanding municipals as of 1977.

Figure 20–2
Principal actors in the market for tax-exempt securities, holdings as of 1977 (Billions of dollars)

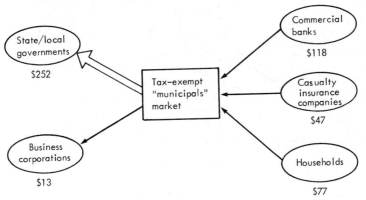

Commercial banks are the most important owner of municipal securities. Indeed from 1960 through 1971 they were the dominant supplier of funds, purchasing about two thirds of all the net new municipals issued during that time period. The remaining supply of funds in these years was divided between casualty insurance companies and individuals. Because of the character of their liabilities, commercial banks have generally preferred to purchase shorter term municipals, whereas the capital projects being financed by state/local governments are primarily long-term projects. Fortunately, individuals and casualty insurance companies have tended to purchase relatively longer term securities, thereby helping to relieve the potential mismatch of maturity needs between state/local governments and commercial banks.

The dynamics of the municipals market

Interest rates within the tax-exempt market are naturally lower than in the taxable fixed-income markets, but they tend to follow the same general fluctuations. The top panel of Figure 20–3 displays the clear similarity in the recent fluctuations of tax-exempt and taxable yields. In the short-term market (one year or less) the ratio of tax-exempt to taxable (Treasury) yields can fluctuate, but it generally has stayed in a range of 0.50 to

Figure 20–3
Comparison of tax-exempt and taxable yields

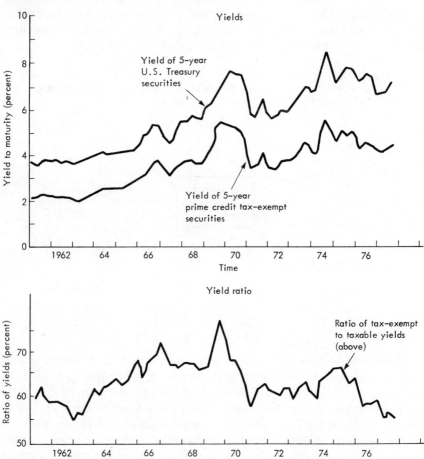

0.55. This is, of course, about what one would expect; for in this range the two markets offer approximately equal after-tax returns to investors in the 48-percent marginal tax bracket. For intermediate and longer term maturities, yields can move somewhat more disparately, causing a wider fluctuation in the range of yield ratios. As the bottom panel of Figure 20–3 shows, the ratio of five-year tax-exempt to taxable yields has fluctuated recently between 0.55 and 0.70. Moreover, these changing yield ratios have a cyclical character which is related to the cyclical financial processes we have already explored in early chapters.

Figure 20–4 shows the overall supply of funds to the municipals market

Figure 20–4
Composition of supply within tax-exempt markets, net new purchases of tax-exempt securities

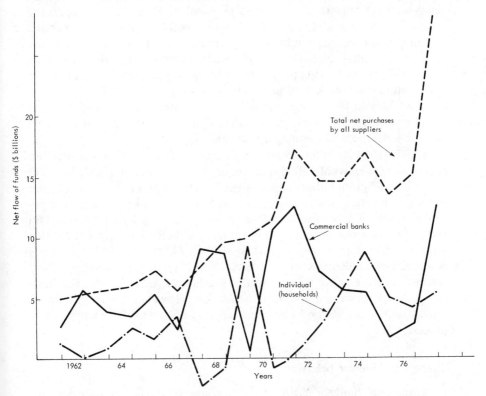

and the particular contribution of commercial banks and individuals. While commercial banks supplied the majority of the funds in this market from 1960 to 1971, there was considerable year-to-year variability in their purchases.

The demands for corporate financing and the Federal Reserve have a major effect upon the willingness of commercial banks to supply funds to the municipals market. In the credit crunches of 1966 and 1969, for example, the Federal Reserve used Regulation Q to cut off the large banks' sources of funds just when business loan demand was very high. In response, the banks funded loans in part by selling off their investments. They sold Treasury securities and, to a lesser extent, municipal securities. The Treasury markets were generally liquid enough (and Treasury securities were attractive enough to a wide spectrum of potential purchasers) that the selling pressure of the banks could be accommodated without too large a change in interest rates. But the municipal markets, dependent as they were upon the buying power of the banks, had greater difficulties. The levels of tax-exempt yields were driven up both absolutely and relative to taxable yields as the market attempted to attract some new purchasers. As the bottom panel of Figure 20–3 shows, the tax-exempt taxable yield ratio (for five-year securities) was driven above 0.70 in each of these credit crunches, providing a very attractive after-tax yield for potential investors in high tax brackets. Figure 20–4 identifies individuals as the "swing investors" who have provided the adaptability in the municipals markets. Individuals stepped into the market in each of these periods to fill the vacuum left by the banks. In 1967 and 1970, as banks reentered the municipals market and yield ratios fell, individuals became net sellers of municipal securities.

In 1973–1974, as interest rates and credit demands rose sharply, the events were somewhat different however. The elimination of Regulation Q eased the difficulties that banks might have encountered in funding the enormous business loan demand of this period. The banks were not required to sell off municipal securities as they had been during parts of 1966 and 1969. As a consequence, the *relative* yields for municipal securities were not driven to as high levels in 1973–1974.[4] To be sure, the banks purchases of municipals were reduced in this period, the yields on tax-exempt securities rose relative to the yields on taxable bonds, and individual investors were drawn into the market. However, the severe financial difficulties of 1966 and 1969 were largely avoided as the relative yields suggest.

Changes in investor behavior

Commercial banks. Prior to 1975, whenever business loan demand was weak, commercial banks were the dominant supplier of funds, purchasing an amount about equal to the net new issues of securities. In 1975–1976, however, when business loan demand fell sharply, the banks did not enlarge their participation in the municipals market. In fact, the banks' purchases of new municipals in these years actually decreased from their levels during the 1973–1974 period of high interest rates and strong loan demand. This change in behavior gave rise to concern that the interest which commercial banks had shown in the municipals market might be permanently reduced and that other investors would have to be found to meet the demands of the market. In part the banks were not purchasing municipals because of a concern for their reduced capital and

---

[4] In fact, the pressures that Regulation Q had earlier induced in the municipals market may well have been partially responsible for the Fed's decision to abandon this tool. By cutting off the larger bank's source of funds in a time of high loan demand, Regulation Q seemed to transfer a good deal of the financial pressure to the municipal market. By eliminating Regulation Q, the pressure upon the banks and thus the municipals market were eased in part by transferring it to other parts of the financial system.

the need to restore their depleted holdings of more liquid Treasury securities. Given a surplus of funds, they prefered to reduce their outstanding CD liabilities and augment their liquidity by buying Treasury securities rather than buying municipals. Table 20–2 shows an additional reason for this behavior.

Table 20–2
Federal income taxes paid by commercial banks (1970–1975)

	1970	1971	1972	1973	1974	1975
Ratio of federal income taxes to gross income	0.23	0.20	0.18	0.15	0.15	0.14

Throughout the 1970s, commercial banks had been reducing their federal income taxes relative to their before-tax income. This trend was particularly discernible at the very large banks. Through their holding companies the large banks were becoming actively involved in leasing activities which provided substantial tax shelters for the earnings of the subsidiary banks. In addition, the foreign tax credits (obtained for the taxes paid abroad on their foreign income) reduced their domestic tax burdens. Consequently the need for tax-exempt income from municipal securities decreased. From 1972–1976, commercial banks purchased only 30 percent of the net new tax-exempt securities, down from 68 percent in the previous decade.

In 1977, however, bank purchases of municipal securities increased substantially, and the banks reasserted themselves as a major supplier of funds to this market.

Households.   The municipals market has always been an important outlet for the investment funds of those households who pay high marginal income tax rates. The inflation of the 1970s, by rapidly increasing nominal income, pushed more households into the tax brackets where tax-exempt income became attractive and thereby increased their interest in this market. There are some important obstacles to individuals' continued participation in this market relative to other fixed income markets however. Relative high minimum purchase requirements make it difficult for investors to hold a diversified portfolio of municipals. In addition there are many securities from small relatively unknown issuers with limited financial disclosure, with no active secondary markets, and with no readily available price quotations. Furthermore, the details of the securities themselves are not well-suited to the less than wealthy investor.[5]

---

[5] For example, the securities are not "registered" and therefore require continual coupon clipping and continual monitoring to obtain the income.

As a partial response to these problems, legislation was passed in 1976 which enabled the sale of mutual funds which invested in municipal bonds. Within a few months of this legislation's passage, many different municipal bond funds were founded, and they began to attract individual investors. While they charged a variety of fees for their service, they could (by pooling many individual investors' funds) surmount many of the difficulties mentioned above. These mutual funds will undoubtedly play an important role in attracting household funds into the municipal market. They are likely to be especially important to the market as it tries to adapt to periods of strong credit demands.

EFFECTIVENESS OF TAX-EXEMPTION FOR REDUCING STATE AND LOCAL BORROWING COSTS

From the federal government's perspective there are a variety of ways to influence the financial system, among them credit allocation, federally sponsored credit intermediaries, and the federal tax system.

The tax system influences financial flows in several ways. First, it affects the institutions in which households hold their savings. For example, the contributions to pension funds and the investment income earned by pension funds are not treated as taxable income until the pensions are drawn down. This preferential tax treatment creates a substantial incentive for households to allocate their savings to pensions. Second, the tax system also affects the investment decisions of the different financial institutions. Pension funds pay no taxes, and thrift institutions and life insurance companies pay tax at reduced rates. The third major effect of the tax system on financial flows arises from the federal government's attempts to reduce the financing costs of certain preferred borrowers. It does this in many ways, for example, by exempting the interest on state and local securities from federal income tax, by allowing especially generous depreciation allowances when computing the taxable income from certain investments in housing, or by treating the dividend and capital gains from common stocks differently for tax purposes.

Unfortunately the intersection of these tax preferences can have undesirable side effects. First, because many investors and investing institutions are partially or totally exempt from tax, they have no interest in tax-exempt securities. As a result the market for tax-exempt securities is narrowed. Also, to the extent that more and more types of investments are given preferential tax treatment, there is increased competition among these tax-sheltered investments for the funds of tax-paying savers and financial institutions. The growing use of tax-exempt and/or tax-sheltered investments has given rise to considerable concern over the efficiency and fairness of these tax subsidies.

Table 20–3 shows the recent relationships between financing costs in the tax-exempt market and a comparable taxable market.

Table 20–3
Typical recent ratios for yields on prime tax-exempt securities
to comparable taxable securities

Yields on	Ratio
Short-term prime tax-exempt securities	0.50 to 0.55 of yields on Treasury securities
Intermediate prime tax-exempt securities	0.58 to 0.70 of yields on Treasury securities
Long-term prime tax-exempt securities	0.65 to 0.75 of yields on prime long-term corporate bonds

Short-term municipal securities yield about the same after-tax return as taxable securities for an investor in the 48-percent marginal tax bracket. This arises because commercial banks, who pay a marginal tax rate of 48 percent, dominate the short-term segment of the tax-exempt market. They have been an important enough force in the short-term market to drive the banks' returns on short-term municipals down to the bank's after-tax return on Treasury issues. In the long-term tax-exempt markets, however, state/local governments have had to offer much higher after-tax yields relative to taxable securities.

The observed ratios of long-term yields raise serious questions about the "efficiency" of the tax exemption for state/local government obligations. From the perspective of a wealthy individual in the 70-percent marginal tax bracket, tax-exempt securities need only offer 30 percent of taxable securities' yields to allow a comparable after-tax return. Instead they have yielded about 60 percent in the intermediate maturity ranges and about 70 percent in the longer maturities (Table 20–3). When wealthy households invest in long-term tax-exempt bonds instead of long-term taxable bonds, the Treasury loses tax revenues equal to the marginal tax rate of the household, and the state/local governments save only 30 percent to 40 percent over the taxable yields. Thus only a part of the tax loss to the Treasury results in a savings to the state and local government. The remainder allows high tax bracket individuals to increase their after-tax returns substantially. Opponents of the tax exemption have noted that this seems to be an extremely inefficient form of tax incentive. Moreover, they have argued, it is an inequitable tax incentive, providing "windfall profits'' to wealthy investors, tax losses for the U.S. Treasury, and nothing for the low-income individual.[6]

Proposals for the tax-exempt market

A number of proposals have been offered to deal with the problems in the tax-exempt market. Under one proposal, a federal "Urban Development Bank" would be formed which would lend funds to state/local governments at reduced (subsidized) rates, financing itself in the taxable bond market (probably the federal agency securities market). Instead of issuing tax-exempt securities, a substantial fraction of whose tax benefits are captured by wealthy investors, state/local governments would borrow directly from this "Bank," capturing all of the federal subsidy themselves.

Under a second proposal, state/local governments would receive a direct federal interest subsidy on new types of taxable securities that they issue. Some versions of this proposal would continuously offer state/local governments two options: issuing traditional tax-exempt bonds or issuing a new type of taxable bond with a direct interest subsidy. Presumably the interest subsidy would be set high enough to induce a substantial fraction of all state/local government borrowing into the taxable markets. In these markets, it is argued, state/local governments could have greater access to a wider variety of investors from whom they are now cut off (pension funds, life insurance companies, and so forth); they could reduce their dependence upon the cyclically constricted banking industry, and the "value" of their tax exemption would be replaced by the more direct and more efficient federal subsidy.

Despite the obvious advantage of these proposals, they have thus far not been enacted. Indeed they have generally been opposed by many state/local government officials who fear the long-run loss of their fiscal autonomy to the federal government. Under either of these proposals, the relatively hidden "tax incentives" of the current system would be replaced by a more visible and explicit system of subsidies to state/local governments, subsidies whose future could be altered (it is feared) at the discretion of the federal government.

Tax exemptions and public policy

In the long run, many of the tax incentives enacted by the federal government compete with each other. For the household investor, for

---

[6] This should not be surprising of course. We can imagine a larger market where "tax-exemptions" are traded, and these tax-exemptions will have the greatest value to taxpayers in the highest brackets. Those who are taxed the most will inevitably reap much of the benefit of various "tax incentives."

example, there are tax benefits for owning real estate and common stocks. The tax exemption for municipal securities must compete with the tax benefits of these other assets. Similarly, from the commercial banks' perspective, the tax exemption of municipal securities must compete with the tax benefits of leasing arrangements and other activities.

In a hypothetical world where there were no other tax benefits, the enactment of a tax exemption for a particular class of securities would be enormously valuable.[7] As more and more tax benefits for different assets exist, however, the addition of one more tax exemption becomes less valuable. This explains, in part, why the ratios of long-term tax-exempt yields approximate 70 percent of taxable yields. Tax-exempt securities must compete with these other tax benefit programs, not just with fully taxable securities. For these reasons there is a limit to the government's aggregate ability to influence borrowing costs with tax exemptions.

In earlier chapters we observed some of the real limitations of the government's ability to influence the financial system through other means. Credit allocation systems seemed to be only temporarily effective (at best) because of the private markets' process of financial adaptation. Federally sponsored credit intermediaries had a similar set of limitations. The potential for using tax policy to influence financing costs seems much more promising, though it too has its limitations. The interaction of tax exemptions for borrowers and intermediaries can severely limit the potential market for tax-exempt securities and create dysfunctional results. In addition, the total effects of all tax benefits and exemptions are limited by their tendency to compete with each other for directing the investment flows of limited numbers of taxpayers. The problems of the tax-exempt municipals market are an excellent example of these inherent difficulties.

QUESTIONS

1. What are the "problems" in the municipal securities market?
2. How would these problems be affected by:
    a. The introduction of an optional taxable security where the federal government paid 30 percent of the interest?
    b. The establishment of a federal agency which purchased tax-exempt bonds and financed their purchases through the sale of taxable federal securities (the operating deficit of this agency would also be subsidized by the federal government)?
    c. Who would be in favor of each of these proposals? Who would be opposed?
    d. How would each of these proposals affect other financial markets?

---

[7] Valuable, that is, from the perspective of public policy in that it would allow the issuer of these securities to finance at significantly lower rates.

REFERENCES

Financing State and Local Governments. Conference Series No. 3, Federal Reserve Bank of Boston, 1970.

Alternatives to Tax-Exempt State and Local Bonds. Hearings before the Committee Ways and Means, House of Representatives, 94th Cong., 2 sess., January 21, 22, 23, 1976.

Fortune, Peter. "Tax-Exemption of State and Local Interest Payments: An Economic Analysis of the Issues and an Alternative," *New England Economic Review,* Federal Reserve Bank of Boston, May/June 1973, pp. 3–20.

Hendershott, Patric H. and Koch, Timothy W. "An Empirical Analysis of the Market for Tax-Exempt Securities: Estimates and Forecasts," Monograph 1977–4, Monograph Series in Finance and Economics, New York University, Graduate School of Business Administration, Center for the Study of Financial Institutions.

Kimball, Ralph C. "Commercial Banks, Tax Avoidance, and the Market for State and Local Debt Since 1970," *New England Economic Review.* January/February 1977, Federal Reserve Bank of Boston.

Rosenbloom, Richard H. "A Review of the Municipal Bond Market," *Economic Review,* Federal Reserve Bank of Richmond, March/April, 1977, pp. 10–19.

21

An overview
of the financial system

This book has attempted to explain the functions, the participants, and the forces at work in U.S. financial markets. The earlier chapters in this part of the book have dealt in considerable detail with the institutional structure of these markets and their historical development. This chapter presents a brief recapitulation of the major concepts which have been discussed.

Financial markets perform two critical functions. First, they are the channels for the flows of funds between the demanders and suppliers of funds. They allow both consumption and investment in the real economy to be financed with external funds; and they allow wealth to be accumulated in a way that it contributes to and shares in the rewards of real investment. Securities play a major role in this process. In the simplest of terms, they are the explicit contracts between suppliers and demanders of funds, and thus the vehicles used to raise or lend the funds. Securities also serve a more subtle function, however. They are used to divide or allocate the risks inherent in real investments in ways that are responsive to the needs of both the borrowers and the lenders of the funds.

The second important function of financial markets is to establish "fair" prices for securities, by continually assessing the risks in specific securities and establishing the expected rates of return that these securities must offer. This pricing process plays a crucial role in a free market economy, for it serves to allocate capital to relatively more productive forms of real investment.

A system of financial markets can perform these functions relatively more effectively if it satisfies a number of criteria. The markets should be cost-effective in the sense that the risk inherent in specific securities can be assessed and priced, and funds can be raised, with only minimal costs. Financial markets should also contain a collection of different types of securities that is heterogenous enough to span the needs of borrowers and financial asset holders. Financial markets should also continuously price these securities in a way that accurately reflects the risks they add to the "market portfolio" of all securities. Such a system of financial markets not only provides savers with a convenient mechanism for accumulating wealth, but it assures them that their stores of wealth will generate expected returns commensurate with the risks that they bear. Such a system of financial markets not only provides real investors with a variety of channels from which to raise funds, but it assures them that the cost of these funds will be commensurate with the incremental risks they are asking suppliers of funds to bear. In addition, for separable investment projects in the real economy, such a system provides prospective real investors with a market-generated estimate of the expected returns that these projects should offer if they are to be a desirable relative use of the economy's savings.

There are two types of securities in financial markets: publicly marketable securities, and privately placed or negotiated securities. When the issuer of the security is well known, and when the terms of the contract are relatively standard and easily enforceable, the security is often issued and later traded in public markets. When information about the issuer is not widely disseminated, or when standard contract terms do not provide enough safety to the lenders or flexibility to the borrowers, private securities or negotiated financings are generally necessary. Private securities are used by business firms (bank loans and privately placed long-term debt) and by households (home mortgages). Many business firms also raise funds in public markets (commercial paper, corporate bonds, and stocks). Almost all government debt (both federal and state and local) is raised in public markets.

Financial institutions are an integral and important part of the financial system. By pooling the supply of funds from many savers, they can accomplish some of the functions of financial markets (assessing risks, pricing them, etc.) in more cost-effective ways. In particular, by holding large pools of different securities, they can provide a cost-effective form of diversification for savers. By maintaining different types of assets and liabilities, they can transform the risk-return combinations otherwise available to savers, thus providing additional types of financial contracts which are better tailored to the needs of savers. In the markets for privately negotiated securities, these are particularly important institutional functions, for savers generally cannot accomplish these things for themselves in a cost-effective way. By negotiating, structuring, and purchasing private non-marketable contracts, financial institutions essentially substitute their internal processes for most of the functions of a public financial market. They serve as a channel for funds flows. They help create a range of private securities adapted to the needs of borrowers. They issue a variety of securities which help to divide and allocate risk in different forms for different suppliers of funds. And they assess and price the risks that these privately-placed securities entail. Because financial institutions can accomplish these functions with substantially smaller costs than savers would experience directly, they have grown to completely dominate the markets for privately placed securities.

There are two types of forces which operate in financial markets: equilibrium and disequilibrium forces. These two types of forces operate at a number of different levels within the financial system. They affect the financing demands of each of the primary sectors, they affect the pricing of the securities in each of the public markets, and they affect the processes and pricing of privately-placed contracts. In the early chapters of this book, we observed these disequilibrium and equilibrium forces in each of the primary sectors. For example, in the short run, the investment plans of business firms can dramatically exceed the internal funds provided by their profitability. Such a discrepancy is what gave rise to the enormous business financing demands experienced in 1973–1974. On the other hand, relatively high levels of investment outlays will persist in the long run only if their prospective profitability is actually realized. This necessary long-run connection between profitability and investment is the equilibrium force that keeps the volume of business financing demands from staying very high, or very low, for long periods of time. Similarly, in the case of the federal government, disequilibrium forces can arise from changes in the pace of economic activity and inflation. These have a dramatic destabilizing effect on the balance in the federal budget in the short run. In the longer run, however, the belief that the federal budget should be approximately balanced at high levels of employment is a strong political force keeping the financing needs of the federal government from becoming too large.

More importantly, equilibrium and disequilibrium forces affect the pricing of securities in the public financial markets. The causal or disequilibrium forces are the *forces of the supply and demand for funds* in each market, or maturity segment of a market. At any moment of time, these forces affect each market or segment differently and tend to drive the expected returns (interest rates) in these markets apart. However, there is also a set of *equilibrium forces* affecting the expected returns on all the securities. These forces tend to keep the expected returns on different securities close to a risk-adjusted equilibrium relationship which is largely, if not completely, independent of the current balance of the supply and demand for funds in each market segment. These equilibrium forces arise from the trade-offs made by borrowers and lenders as they consider real versus financial assets, and financial assets and liabilities of different maturities or different risks.

The empirical behavior of security prices within public markets suggests that the equilibrium forces are quite powerful, and play the major role in determining security prices and returns. This is especially true for those public markets where there are many participants, financial information is available and widespread, transactions costs are low, and the volume of trading is large (e.g., corporate equities and U.S. government bonds). Even in some public markets, however, there is evidence that the returns in some maturity ranges, or groups of secu_ities, can be temporarily pushed away from their equilibrium relationships if a large and sudden shift in demand or supply occurs. For example, some of the short-run variations in yield spreads within public fixed-income markets can be explained by these forces of supply and demand.

Due to their nonmarketable character, the pricing of privately-negotiated securities is not subject to the direct effects of the equilibrium forces at work in the public security markets. For example, the prime rate on business loans can diverge from comparable public market rates, as can the rates on home mortgages. And, because of regulation, deposit rates do not generally vary with open market rates. However, there are still a great many market forces limiting the interest rates that financial institutions can charge on their loans and offer on their nonmarketable liabilities. The most important arise because some borrowers have access to both public and privately-negotiated markets, and because many suppliers of funds have the alternative of acquiring marketable securities as well as the nonmarketable liabilities of the intermediaries. In addition to the competition from the securities available in the public markets, the rates which any one financial intermediary or group of intermediaries offer are also subject to the competitive actions of other intermediaries. As a result, the equilibrium forces within public markets can quickly spread to markets for privately negotiated securities, and their effects are very evident in the pricing of these securities.

Sometimes, however, because of the constraints of regulation and various institutional barriers, market segments within the private markets can be effectively segmented or disconnected from the equilibrium of public markets. When this happens, the forces of supply and demand become the principal determinant of the flow of funds and the pricing of securities. But in the long run, this is an unstable condition, because of the relative profit opportunities that are sure to be implied by any divergence between private and public market prices. In the long run, the character of markets and institutions themselves will change to arbitrage away these opportunities. Indeed, in the long run, the adaptation and evolution of the financial system itself can be best explained by its attempt to continually reestablish a consistent set of equilibrium prices throughout the markets for both public and privately-placed securities.

Cases

1. Paul Guthrie

Paul Guthrie, the owner of a small business in Gary, Indiana, carefully studied the financial pages of the *Chicago Tribune*. The steady rise in interest rates to record levels during the summer of 1974 had attracted Guthrie's attention. In late July, when the minimum term on his $10,000 time deposit at the Northern Savings and Loan expired, Guthrie intended to place these funds in an investment with a more attractive yield. While he was eager to take advantage of the higher returns available in the financial markets, Guthrie was still concerned about the safety of his investment. In addition, although he also maintained considerable funds in checking and regular savings accounts and could foresee no anticipated need for this $10,000 during the next several years, Guthrie still wanted the money to be a cushion in case of unexpected events which might affect his family or his business. Therefore, he was interested in an investment that would provide him with access to these funds in a reasonable period of time, should the need arise.

At first, Guthrie had wanted to invest in government securities. The Treasury recently announced plans for an August issue of 33-month Treasury notes carrying a coupon rate of 9 percent. Paul realized that his knowledge of financial markets was limited and that the responsibilities of managing his own business would give him little time to oversee his investment. Because of the safety of government securities and their attractive yield over the life of the investment, Paul initially believed that these Treasury notes might be the appropriate investment for him.

During his search for information on government securities, Guthrie uncovered other investment opportunities available to the individual saver in late July of 1974. James Halsted, a LaSalle Street stockbroker, suggested that Guthrie carefully evaluate an innovative debt issue of Citicorp, the holding company of a large commercial bank located in New York City. Halsted stated that the Citicorp notes had many features that thrifty individuals might consider very attractive. He advised Mr. Guthrie to examine the prospectus and to decide if the Citicorp notes were consistent with his investment objectives. (See excerpts from the Prospectus in Appendix A.)

Paul carefully read the prospectus several times but still had not resolved some of his questions. The floating rate feature of the Citicorp notes was very attractive to Guthrie. The inflation problem deeply troubled him both as a businessman and as a saver. He believed that a security whose return adjusted with changing interest rates might offer substantial advantages in this inflationary environment.

The Citicorp notes promised a return of at least 9.7 percent for the next ten months. Afterwards, the return would float at 100 basis points (or 1 percent) above the Treasury bill rate. On a return basis it seemed likely that the Citicorp notes might be preferable to an investment in Treasury notes, at least during the initial ten-month period when the Citicorp rate was fixed at 9.7 percent.

The Citicorp notes also seemed to meet Guthrie's objective of maintaining access to his funds if unforeseen contingencies should occur. Every six months after an initial two-year period, an investor could choose to redeem his notes at par value plus accrued interest. Guthrie particularly liked this redemption privilege which his broker had referred to as a "put." He also noted that the Citicorp issue would be traded on the New York Stock Exchange, which would provide another means of liquidating his holdings should the need arise.

Considering these factors, Guthrie believed that the Citicorp notes were likely to give him both a high yield and some liquidity. But his concern with the safety of his funds continued to trouble him. By temperament Paul was a practical businessman with little patience for the dry technicalities of finance. The distinction between Citicorp and its bank eluded him. He knew that the difference meant that his funds would not be a deposit in the strict legal sense, and thus they would not be protected by FDIC insurance. But, for all practical purposes, he thought the notes

Table 1
Interest rates during 1974

	Current rates: July 19, 1974	Earlier rates	
		March 30, 1974	December 31, 1973
Short term			
Federal funds (overnight)	12.35%	9.79%	9.50%
U.S. Treasury bills (three months)	7.83	8.30	7.45
Prime commercial paper (three months)	11.75	9.35	9.15
Prime certificates of deposit (three months)	12.00	9.75	9.10
Prime certificates of deposit (six months)	11.40	9.30	8.40
Intermediates (5 to 7 years)			
U.S. Treasury notes (five years)	8.40	7.59	6.77
Corporate Aa	9.75	8.35	7.50
Banks AAA	9.80	8.18	7.45
Long term			
Corporate Aa	10.00	8.75	8.10
Banks AAA	10.23	8.83	8.14

might really just be deposits with a higher rate. He wondered what additional considerations were implied by the differences between Citicorp and Citibank. For example, he wondered why Citicorp and/or Citibank thought they needed the funds, why they would do with the funds, and how this might affect the ultimate safety of the notes.

Finally, in response to an advertisement, he had requested promotional material from the Dreyfus Liquid Asset Fund (see Appendix B). The Fund was a "money-market fund," another new investment alternative available to individual savers like Guthrie. By investing directly in corporate commercial paper and bank certificates of deposit, the Dreyfus Fund seemed to offer investors both a redemption privilege and returns as high as 11 percent. Paul found the additional return very tempting, as it was comparable with the highest rates then available (see Table 1).

PROSPECTUS

$650,000,000

Floating Rate Notes Due 1989
Repayable Semi-Annually at Par Commencing June 1, 1976
at the Option of the Holder

Interest on the Notes is payable semi-annually on June 1 and December 1, commencing December 1, 1974, at the rate through November 30, 1974 of 9.70% per annum and at the rate from December 1, 1974 through May 31, 1975 equal to the higher of 9.70% per annum or the rate established as described below. The rate per annum for each semi-annual period subsequent to May 31, 1975 (and for the period from December 1, 1974 through May 31, 1975, to the extent provided above) will be 1% above the "interest yield equivalent" of the average of the weekly per annum discount rates for three-month U.S. Treasury bills, as reported by the Federal Reserve Bank of New York during the 21 days immediately preceding the twentieth day of May or November, as the case may be, prior to the semi-annual period for which the interest rate on the Notes is being determined. The interest rate payable on the Notes for each semi-annual period will be determined before the beginning of such period. See "Description of Floating Interest Rate" and "Description of Notes—Floating Interest Rate".

Except under certain limited circumstances, the Notes may not be redeemed at the option of Citicorp prior to June 1, 1984 and will be redeemable on and after such date at their principal amount plus accrued interest. The Notes will be repayable on any June 1 or December 1, commencing June 1, 1976, at the option of the holders thereof at 100% of their principal amount together with interest payable to the date of repayment. The holders of the Notes will be required to exercise such option before the interest rate on the Notes can be determined for the subsequent semi-annual period. See "Description of Notes—Redemption", "—Special Redemption" and "—Repayment at Option of Holder".

Application will be made to list the Notes on the New York Stock Exchange

THESE SECURITIES HAVE NOT BEEN APPROVED OR DISAPPROVED BY THE SECURITIES AND EXCHANGE COMMISSION NOR HAS THE COMMISSION PASSED UPON THE ACCURACY OR ADEQUACY OF THIS PROSPECTUS. ANY REPRESENTATION TO THE CONTRARY IS A CRIMINAL OFFENSE.

	Price to Public(1)	*Underwriting Discounts and Commissions(2)*	*Proceeds to Citicorp(1)(3)*
Per Note	100%	1%	99%
Total	$650,000,000	$6,500,000	$643,500,000

(1) Plus accrued interest from July 31, 1974, if any.
(2) See "Underwriting" for indemnification arrangements with the several Underwriters.
(3) Before deduction of expenses payable by Citicorp estimated at $850,000.

THESE NOTES ARE UNSECURED DEBT OBLIGATIONS OF CITICORP, ARE NOT LEGALLY ENFORCEABLE OBLIGATIONS OF ANY BANK AND ARE NOT INSURED BY THE FEDERAL DEPOSIT INSURANCE CORPORATION.

The Notes are offered by the several Underwriters for delivery on or about July 31, 1974, when, as and if issued by Citicorp and accepted by the Underwriters and subject to their right to reject orders in whole or in part. The Notes will be issued in fully registered form only in denominations of $1,000 and integral multiples thereof. The minimum principal amount of the Notes which may be purchased initially is $5,000.

The First Boston Corporation

Goldman, Sachs & Co.

Merrill Lynch, Pierce, Fenner & Smith
Incorporated

The date of this Prospectus is July 24, 1974.

APPENDIX A (*continued*)

PROSPECTUS SUMMARY

Citicorp .... Citicorp (the issuer), a bank holding company organized in 1967.

Citibank .... First National City Bank ("Citibank"), Citicorp's principal subsidiary. As of March 31, 1974 it was the second largest commercial bank in the world in terms of total assets and total deposits and at such date, together with its subsidiaries, had total assets of $45.8 billion and total deposits of $36.7 billion.

Other Subsidiaries .... Companies of Citicorp provide a wide range of financially related services throughout the United States and the world, including mortgage banking, consumer finance, credit card services, management consulting, equipment leasing, factoring, realty appraisal and advisory services, payments mechanism research, travel services and the sale of travelers checks. These companies do not have assets, revenues or income material in amount compared to Citibank. See Note 21 of Notes to the Financial Statements.

Securities

    Amount $650,000,000

    Maturity .... June 1, 1989

Use of Proceeds .... It is expected that the net proceeds from the sale of the Notes offered hereby will be applied to the repayment at maturity of a like principal amount of commercial paper issued by Citicorp to finance the activities of Citicorp's non-bank subsidiaries.

SELECTED FINANCIAL DATA

	Year Ended December 31,			Three Months Ended March 31,	
	1971	1972	1973	1973	1974
Consolidated Revenues and Earnings:			(In Thousands)	(Unaudited)	(Unaudited)
Operating Revenue	$1,788,584	$1,954,750	$3,091,638	$600,987	$1,008,507
Income before Securities Gains (Losses)	168,198	201,801	254,820	58,157	73,180
Net Income	169,073	201,844	252,019	58,182	73,203
Ratio of Income to Fixed Charges:					
Parent Company Only	6.9	.8	.6	.6	.7
Consolidated:					
Excluding Interest on Deposits	3.3	3.3	2.2	2.9	2.1
Including Interest on Deposits	1.3	1.3	1.2	1.3	1.2

	Year Ended December 31,			Three Months Ended March 31, 1974
	1971	1972	1973	
Consolidated Statement of Condition (Averages):			(In Millions)	
Loans	$16,404	$19,207	$23,869	$27,348
Investment Securities	3,004	3,032	3,067	3,404
Deposits	21,995	24,518	29,961	34,708
Stockholders' Equity	1,289	1,465	1,704	1,769

The above summary is qualified in its entirety by the detailed information and financial statements appearing elsewhere in this Prospectus.

IN CONNECTION WITH THIS OFFERING, THE UNDERWRITERS MAY OVER-ALLOT OR EFFECT TRANSACTIONS WHICH STABILIZE OR MAINTAIN THE MARKET PRICE OF THE NOTES OFFERED HEREBY AND CITICORP'S 6⅝% NOTES DUE NOVEMBER 15, 1979 AND ITS 6⅝% NOTES DUE NOVEMBER 15, 1980 AT LEVELS ABOVE THOSE WHICH MIGHT OTHERWISE PREVAIL IN THE OPEN MARKET. SUCH TRANSACTIONS MAY BE EFFECTED ON THE NEW YORK STOCK EXCHANGE OR IN THE OVER-THE-COUNTER MARKET. SUCH STABILIZING, IF COMMENCED, MAY BE DISCONTINUED AT ANY TIME.

APPENDIX A (*continued*)

CITICORP

Citicorp (formerly named First National City Corporation) is a holding company incorporated under the laws of Delaware on December 4, 1967. Pursuant to a plan of reorganization effective October 31, 1968, Citicorp became the sole shareholder of First National City Bank ("Citibank") except for directors' qualifying shares.

Citibank is a commercial bank offering a wide range of banking services to its customers in the New York City metropolitan area, throughout the nation and around the world. As of March 31, 1974, it was the second largest commercial bank in the world in terms of total assets and total deposits and at such date, together with its subsidiaries, had total assets of $45.8 billion, total deposits of $36.7 billion and total loans of $28.1 billion. Citibank has more than 230 branches in New York City and the adjoining counties of Nassau and Westchester and with its affiliates has approximately 1,100 offices in some 95 countries.

The principal asset of Citicorp is its shareholding in Citibank. However, the reorganization of Citibank in 1968, which resulted in the acquisition of Citibank's shares by Citicorp, was designed to create a holding company which could offer a broad range of financially oriented services. In addition to commercial banking and trust services, Citicorp's subsidiaries are engaged in mortgage banking, consumer finance, credit card services, management consulting, equipment leasing, factoring, realty appraisal and advisory services, payments mechanism research, travel services and the sale of travelers checks. These subsidiaries other than Citibank do not have assets, revenues or income material in amount compared to those of Citibank. See "Business—Related Services and Activities" and "—Supervision and Regulation" and Note 21 of Notes to the Financial Statements.

Citicorp is a legal entity separate and distinct from its bank and non-bank affiliates. Investors should be aware that the Notes offered hereby do not represent obligations of such bank or non-bank affiliates and are not insured by any agency of the U. S. Government. Investors should also be aware of the various legal limitations on the extent to which bank subsidiaries of Citicorp can finance or otherwise supply funds to Citicorp or various of its affiliates. In particular, subsidiary banks of Citicorp in which deposits are insured by the Federal Deposit Insurance Corporation are subject to certain restrictions imposed by Federal law on any extensions of credit to Citicorp or, with certain exceptions, other affiliates, on investments in stock or other securities thereof and on the taking of such securities as collateral for loans to borrowers. Such restrictions prevent Citicorp or such other affiliates from borrowing from such subsidiary banks unless such loans are secured by U. S. Treasury or other specified obligations. Further, such secured loans by any such subsidiary bank are limited in amount as to Citicorp or to any other such affiliate to 10% of such bank's capital and surplus and as to Citicorp and all such affiliates to an aggregate of 20% of such bank's capital and surplus. See "Business—Dividends of Citibank" for a description of certain limitations on the payment of dividends by subsidiary banks.

The principal office of Citicorp is located at 399 Park Avenue, New York, New York 10022; telephone number (212) 559-1000.

USE OF PROCEEDS

The net proceeds from the sale of the Notes offered hereby are expected to be applied to the repayment at maturity of a like principal amount of commercial paper issued by Citicorp. While Citicorp has in the past issued commercial paper chiefly to finance the activities of its non-bank subsidiaries, it has also invested proceeds of its commercial paper in loan participations purchased from Citibank. However, only commercial paper utilized to finance the activities of Citicorp's non-bank subsidiaries, including Advance Mortgage Corporation, Citicorp Leasing, Inc., Citicorp Leasing International, Inc., Citicorp Credit Services, Inc. and Nationwide Financial Services Corporation, will be repaid from the net proceeds of the Notes. See "Business—Related Services and Activities". Such non-bank subsidiaries have used the proceeds of commercial paper to fund current transactions in their businesses. See "Capitalization—Commercial Paper". Citicorp expects to continue issuing commercial paper to repay outstanding commercial paper as it matures and to finance expansion of the activities of its subsidiaries, including Citibank. With the anticipated continued growth of Citibank and other Citicorp subsidiaries, Citicorp also expects that it will engage recurrently in the future in additional financings in character and amount to be determined as the need arises.

APPENDIX A (*continued*)

Commercial Paper

Citicorp, the parent company, incurs short-term indebtedness by issuing commercial paper. During 1973 the average amount of commercial paper outstanding was $700 million, the highest month-end balance was $943 million and the amount outstanding on December 31, 1973 was $909 million. During the six-month period ended June 30, 1974 the average amount of such paper outstanding was $1.1 billion and on June 30, 1974 $1.4 billion was outstanding. The increase of approximately $500 million in commercial paper outstanding between December 31, 1973 and June 30, 1974 reflects growth in the activities of Citicorp's subsidiaries. Of the increase, $115 million (23% of the increase) was utilized by Advance Mortgage Corporation, primarily to carry an increased inventory of mortgages. A further $223 million (45% of the increase) was utilized to finance short-term consumer loans, including approximately $170,000,000 of credit card receivables purchased from Citibank by Citicorp Credit Services, Inc. in May 1974. The commercial paper outstanding on June 30, 1974 had an approximate average rate of 11.30% and a weighted average maturity of under 30 days. See Note 3 of Notes to the Financial Statements.

As of June 30, 1974 Citicorp held demand loans to non-bank subsidiaries totaling $1,230 million which were funded with the proceeds of commercial paper, and which were used by such subsidiaries for current transactions in their businesses, as follows:

Subsidiaries	Use of Proceeds by Subsidiaries	Amount of Loans
		(In Millions)
Advance Mortgage Corporation	Carrying mortgage portfolio	$ 430
Leasing Subsidiaries	Carrying lease portfolio	240
Credit Card Financing Subsidiaries	Carrying credit card receivables	182
Nationwide Financial Services Corporation	Carrying consumer loan portfolio	92
All other non-bank subsidiaries	Other current transactions	286
		$1,230

It is expected that the net proceeds from the sale of the Notes offered hereby will be applied to the repayment at maturity of a like principal amount of commercial paper utilized by Citicorp to fund such demand loans. See "Use of Proceeds". At June 30, 1974 Citicorp also held loans or participations in loans aggregating $171 million which were purchased from Citibank with the proceeds of commercial paper and with funds available from other sources.

Repayment and Redemption Sources

Commencing June 1, 1976 and semi-annually thereafter any holder may request Citicorp to repay the principal amount of his Notes together with interest to the date of repayment and, under certain circumstances, Citicorp will be required to redeem all of the Notes at their principal amount plus accrued interest to the date of redemption. See "Description of Notes—Repayment at Option of Holder" and "—Special Redemption". Citicorp currently has outstanding approximately $1.4 billion of commercial paper, $225 million of long-term debt and $27 million of convertible debentures. In addition, Citicorp has available lines of credit from unaffiliated banks. Depending upon prevailing market conditions, the principal amount of Notes presented from time to time for repayment or required to be redeemed and other factors which cannot be predicted at this time, Citicorp would expect to use one or a combination of the sources of funds of the type described above or such other sources as might then be appropriate and available to obtain the funds required for such repayments or redemptions. Citicorp does not anticipate that the cash needs to meet such repayment requests or redemption requirements will adversely affect its liquidity or capital resources.

446

DESCRIPTION OF FLOATING INTEREST RATE

Interest on the Notes offered hereby is payable semi-annually on June 1 and December 1, commencing December 1, 1974, at the rate through November 30, 1974 of 9.70% per annum and at the rate from December 1, 1974 through May 31, 1975 equal to the higher of 9.70% per annum or the rate established under the formula set forth below. Except as provided below, the rate per annum for each semi-annual period subsequent to May 31, 1975 will be equal to 1% above the "interest yield equivalent" of the arithmetic average of the weekly per annum discount rates for three-month U. S. Treasury bills, as reported by the Federal Reserve Bank of New York during the 21 days immediately preceding the twentieth day of May or November, as the case may be, prior to the semi-annual period for which the interest rate on the Notes is being determined. The interest yield equivalent of such arithmetic average of such U. S. Treasury bill rates will be rounded to the nearest five hundredths of a percentage point. The interest rate payable on the Notes for each semi-annual period will be determined before the beginning of such period.

The following chart sets forth for the periods indicated: (1) the monthly average per annum rates for three-month U.S. Treasury bills as reported on a discount basis by the Federal Reserve System and (2) the pro-forma per annum interest rates which would have been paid on the Notes offered hereby if they had been outstanding from January 1, 1964. As may be seen from the chart, the U.S. Treasury bill rate has varied widely over the period in question and is near its historic high for such period. Accordingly, there is no assurance that this rate will not decline from its present level. Such rates will continue to vary in the future and as a result the rates of interest payable on the Notes offered hereby will also vary.

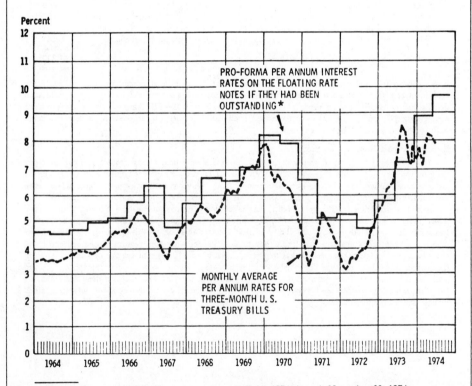

* Actual interest rate of 9.70% per annum from July 31, 1974 through November 30, 1974.

APPENDIX A (*continued*)

BUSINESS

The principal asset of Citicorp is its shareholding in Citibank. However, the reorganization of Citibank in 1968, which resulted in the acquisition of Citibank's shares by Citicorp, was designed to create a holding company which could offer a broad range of financially oriented services. In addition to commercial banking and trust services, Citicorp's subsidiaries are engaged in mortgage banking, consumer finance, credit card services, management consulting, equipment leasing, factoring, realty appraisal and advisory services, payments mechanism research, travel services and the sale of travelers checks. These subsidiaries other than Citibank do not have assets, revenues or income material in amount compared to those of Citibank.

Significant Statistics

The following tables indicate significant statistics of Citicorp (Consolidated):

	1969	1970	1971	1972	1973	Three Months Ended March 31, 1974
Average Loans			(In Millions)			
In Domestic Offices						
Commercial and Industrial	$ 5,532	$ 6,118	$ 5,771	$ 5,814	$ 7,235	$ 7,732
Mortgage and Real Estate	948	1,019	1,192	1,587	2,003	2,291
Loans to Financial Institutions	461	518	508	692	1,199	1,316
Loans for Purchasing or Carrying Securities	288	310	583	863	669	876
Other Loans	1,606	1,698	1,823	1,995	2,419	2,890
Total in Domestic Offices	$ 8,835	$ 9,663	$ 9,877	$10,951	$13,525	$15,105
In Overseas Offices	3,215	4,434	6,527	8,256	10,344	12,243
Total Loans	$12,050	$14,097	$16,404	$19,207	$23,869	$27,348
Federal Funds Sold	226	363	137	103	90	112
Total Loans (Including Federal Funds Sold)	$12,276	$14,460	$16,541	$19,310	$23,959	$27,460
Average Maturity of Loans (excluding Residential Mortgages and Consumer Loans)						
In Domestic Offices* (In Months)	24	23	21	25	26	27
Average Investment Securities						
U. S. Treasury and Federal Agencies ...	$ 1,119	$ 1,267	$ 1,544	$ 1,378	$ 1,315	$ 1,413
State and Municipal	1,080	930	812	974	929	1,053
Other	349	448	648	680	823	938
Total Investment Securities ...	$ 2,548	$ 2,645	$ 3,004	$ 3,032	$ 3,067	$ 3,404
Average Trading Account Securities ..	$ 242	$ 283	$ 290	$ 264	$ 416	$ 701
Average Deposits						
In Domestic Offices						
Demand Deposits	$ 6,435	$ 6,617	$ 6,631	$ 6,586	$ 7,372	$ 8,122
Savings Deposits	1,378	1,318	1,473	1,550	1,511	1,458
Negotiable Certificates of Deposit ..	796	1,045	2,633	3,179	4,429	5,533
Other Time Deposits	1,608	1,672	1,626	1,726	1,920	2,103
Total in Domestic Offices	$10,217	$10,652	$12,363	$13,041	$15,232	$17,216
In Overseas Offices	6,183	7,901	9,632	11,477	14,729	17,492
Total Deposits	$16,400	$18,553	$21,995	$24,518	$29,961	$34,708

* Average maturity of loans in overseas offices at year-end 1973 was 10 months.

APPENDIX A (*continued*)

	1969	1970	1971	1972	1973	Three Months Ended March 31, 1974
			(In Millions)			
Demand Deposits in Domestic Offices ...	$ 6,435	$ 6,617	$ 6,631	$ 6,586	$ 7,372	$ 8,122
Items in Process of Collection	(1,753)	(1,761)	(1,798)	(1,630)	(2,104)	(2,593)
Applicable Reserves	(819)	(850)	(845)	(867)	(929)	(976)
Net Demand Deposits in Domestic Offices After Applicable Reserves	$ 3,863	$ 4,006	$ 3,988	$ 4,089	$ 4,339	$ 4,553
Return on Stockholders' Equity						
Income before Securities Gains (Losses)	$ 133	$ 145	$ 168	$ 202	$ 255	$ 270*
Average Stockholders' Equity	$ 1,172	$ 1,216	$ 1,289	$ 1,465	$ 1,704	$ 1,769*
Percentage Return on Average Stockholders' Equity	11.3%	11.9%	13.0%	13.8%	15.0%	15.3%*
Average Earning Rates in Domestic Offices (Taxable Equivalent Basis)						
Loans:						
Commercial and Industrial Loans ..	7.44%	7.90%	6.36%	5.98%	8.62%	9.81%
Total Loans (Including Federal Funds Sold)	7.75%	8.05%	6.80%	6.47%	8.64%	9.59%
Investment Securities:						
U.S. Treasury and Federal Agencies	5.74%	6.27%	5.80%	5.74%	6.28%	6.78%
State and Municipal	8.69%	8.52%	8.45%	7.92%	8.53%	8.68%
Total Loans (Including Federal Funds Sold) and Investment Securities	7.62%	7.89%	6.78%	6.48%	8.40%	9.23%
Average Rates Paid in Domestic Offices						
Negotiable Certificates of Deposit	6.65%	7.92%	5.58%	5.17%	8.11%	8.97%
Savings Deposits	3.94%	4.39%	4.43%	4.36%	4.46%	4.39%
Other Time Deposits	5.22%	5.86%	4.55%	4.25%	5.84%	6.37%
Commercial Paper	8.45%	8.50%	5.52%	4.52%	8.58%	9.08%
Other Borrowed Money (Excluding Long Term Notes)	7.84%	7.00%	4.66%	4.38%	8.77%	8.92%
4% and 6⅝% Long Term Notes	4.00%	4.00%	4.00%	4.82%	5.87%	6.27%
Total Interest-Bearing Funds	5.56%	6.33%	4.92%	4.65%	7.31%	7.96%
Net Loan Losses (In Thousands)						
In Domestic Offices	$11,171	$44,839	$36,320	$25,417	$50,130	$ 5,131
In Overseas Offices	272	4,045	10,371	12,954	26,152	2,214
Total Net Loan Losses	$11,443	$48,884	$46,691	$38,371	$76,582	$ 7,345

* Twelve months ended March 31, 1974.

APPENDIX A (*continued*)

--- --- ---

Dividends of Citibank

National banks are subject to regulation by the Comptroller of the Currency. The approval of the Comptroller of the Currency is required if the total of all dividends declared by a national bank in any calendar year exceeds the bank's net profits (as defined) for that year combined with its retained net profits for the preceding two calendar years. Under this formula, as of June 30, 1974, Citibank can declare dividends in 1974 without approval of the Comptroller of the Currency of approximately $650,000,000 plus an additional amount equal to Citibank's net profits for 1974 subsequent to June 30, 1974 and up to the date of any such dividend declaration. The Comptroller of the Currency also has authority under the Financial Institutions Supervisory Act to prohibit a national bank from engaging in what in his opinion constitutes an unsafe or unsound practice in conducting its business. The payment of dividends could, depending upon the financial condition of the national bank, be such an unsafe or unsound practice.

During the years 1969 through 1971 dividends declared by Citibank payable to Citicorp exceeded the dividends declared by Citicorp payable to its shareholders as follows:

Dividends Declared By:	1969	1970	1971	Total
		(In Thousands)		
Citibank	$86,170	$152,725	$160,000	$398,895
Citicorp	62,292	68,531	72,227	203,050
Excess	$23,878	$ 84,194	$ 87,773	$195,845

The dividends paid by Citibank were used by Citicorp, in part, to acquire and expand the activities of several subsidiaries, principally Advance Mortgage Corporation (1970) and Cresap, McCormick and Paget Inc. (1970), and to establish and develop several companies, including Citicorp Leasing International, Inc. (1969), Transaction Technology Inc. (1969) and Citibank (Suffolk), National Association (1971). Additionally, during 1971 Citicorp repurchased 3,085,200 shares of its Common Stock at a cost of $55,508,000. Since 1971 Citibank has declared no dividends to Citicorp while Citicorp has declared dividends payable to its shareholders as follows:

1972	1973	Six Months Ended June 30, 1974	Total
	(In Thousands)		
$75,271	$86,417	$49,147	$210,835

Thus, in the period from January 1, 1969 through June 30, 1974 Citicorp's dividends to its stockholders exceeded Citibank's dividends to Citicorp by $14,990,000. It should be noted that Citicorp assumed responsibility for payment of interest on the 4% Convertible Capital Notes Due 1990 issued by Citibank in 1965. Since January 1, 1969 through June 30, 1974 these interest payments by Citicorp have totaled $37,300,000 without reimbursement from Citibank. Since January 1, 1972 Citicorp has issued $225,000,000 of long term debt of which $125,000,000 was invested in the Capital Stock of Citibank. Citibank has declared no dividends to Citicorp since 1971 because, in the judgment of Citicorp's management, the expansion of Citibank's assets and deposits made it desirable to increase the capital of Citibank. From January 1, 1972 through June 30, 1974 the capital accounts of Citibank increased by about $730,000,000. Future dividend policies of Citibank cannot be determined at this time. In the determination of the dividend policies of Citicorp, its Board of Directors considers the earnings of Citibank available for the payment of dividends to Citicorp. Citicorp would anticipate that a portion of such earnings would be paid to it as dividends if such payment were required as a source of funds to pay Citicorp dividends in the future.

--- ---

APPENDIX A (*continued*)

CITICORP

(Parent Company Only)

STATEMENT OF CONDITION
(In Thousands)

	December 31, 1973	March 31, 1974 (Unaudited)
Assets		
Cash on Deposit with Subsidiary Banks:		
Demand	$ 9,115	$ 8,008
Loans (Note 19)	194,595	127,195
Due from Subsidiaries Arising from Tax Benefit Accrued..................	39,313	43,342
Advances to Subsidiaries Other Than Banks............................	958,793	1,108,625
Investments in Subsidiaries:		
First National City Bank..	1,985,963	2,069,162
Other	122,826	124,659
Other Assets	27,162	25,404
Total	$3,337,767	$3,506,395
Liabilities		
Commercial Paper Outstanding (Note 3)	$ 908,947	$1,000,665
Accrued Expenses and Other Liabilities................................	326,882	339,198
Provision for Dividend Declared.......................................	21,954	24,518
6⅜% Notes Due 1979 (Note 4)	100,000	100,000
6⅜% Notes Due 1980 (Note 4)	125,000	125,000
4% Convertible Capital Notes Due 1990 (Note 5)	38,343	33,099

Stockholders' Equity

Preferred Stock (without par)................................ 10,000,000 shares authorized but unissued	$ —		$ —	
Common Stock ($4.00 par) (Note 7) .... Issued Shares: 124,952,697 in 1973 / 125,575,489 in 1974	499,811		502,302	
Surplus (Note 7)	678,264		687,450	
Undivided Profits (including $581,375 and $663,044, respectively, attributable to undistributed income of bank subsidiaries and $758 and $2,769, respectively, attributable to undistributed income of subsidiaries other than banks)	592,039		647,566	
Unallocated Reserve for Contingencies........................	100,000		100,000	
	$1,870,114		$1,937,318	
Common Stock in Treasury, at Cost (Note 7) .... 2,987,122 shares in 1973 / 2,983,206 shares in 1974	53,473	1,816,641	53,403	1,883,915
Total		$3,337,767		$3,506,395

Accounting policies and explanatory notes on pages 37-52 form an integral part of the financial statements.

APPENDIX A (*continued*)

CITICORP
And Subsidiaries

CONSOLIDATED STATEMENT OF CONDITION
(In Thousands)

	December 31, 1973	March 31, 1974 (Unaudited)
Assets		
Cash and Due from Banks	$ 8,740,511	$10,484,458
Investment Securities (Notes 2 and 16):		
U. S. Treasury and Federal Agencies	1,363,832	1,532,287
State and Municipal	997,299	986,745
Other	903,435	1,005,306
Trading Account Securities	772,530	518,136
Loans	27,615,643	29,025,397
Federal Funds Sold and Securities Purchased Under Agreements to Resell..	355,657	61,392
Customers' Acceptance Liability	851,288	1,090,911
Premises and Equipment	341,834	382,824
Direct Lease Financing	442,946	484,310
Other Assets	1,634,243	1,753,799
Total	$44,019,218	$47,325,565
Liabilities		
Demand Deposits in Domestic Offices	$ 9,054,384	$ 8,486,358
Time Deposits in Domestic Offices	8,898,806	9,164,103
Deposits in Overseas Offices	16,989,177	18,980,503
Total Deposits	$34,942,367	$36,630,964
Federal Funds Purchased and Securities Sold Under Agreements to Repurchase	1,789,687	2,835,522
Commercial Paper Outstanding (Note 3)	903,997	994,865
Other Funds Borrowed	1,374,399	1,350,523
Acceptances Outstanding	883,896	1,145,251
Accrued Taxes and Other Expenses (Note 12)	782,684	867,606
Provision for Dividend Declared	21,954	24,518
Other Liabilities (Note 9)	678,936	669,650
Unearned Income	251,369	351,945
6⅝% Notes Due 1979 (Note 4)	100,000	100,000
6⅝% Notes Due 1980 (Note 4)	125,000	125,000
4% Convertible Capital Notes Due 1990 (Note 5)	38,343	33,099
Reserves		
Reserve for Possible Losses on Loans (Note 6)	309,945	312,707
Stockholders' Equity		
Preferred Stock (without par)	$ —	$ —
10,000,000 shares authorized but unissued		
Common Stock ($4.00 par) (Note 7)	499,811	502,302
Issued Shares: 124,952,697 in 1973		
125,575,489 in 1974		
Surplus (Note 7)	678,264	687,450
Undivided Profits	592,039	647,566
Unallocated Reserve for Contingencies	100,000	100,000
	$1,870,114	$1,937,318
Common Stock in Treasury, at Cost (Note 7)	53,473 1,816,641	53,403 1,883,915
2,987,122 shares in 1973		
2,983,206 shares in 1974		
Total	$44,019,218	$47,325,565

Accounting policies and explanatory notes on pages 37-52 form an integral part of the financial statements.

APPENDIX A (*continued*)

CITICORP
(Parent Company Only)

STATEMENT OF CHANGES IN FINANCIAL POSITION
(In Thousands)

	Year Ended December 31,					Three Months Ended March 31,	
	1969	1970	1971	1972	1973	1973 (Unaudited)	1974 (Unaudited)
Funds Provided							
Net Income	$121,608	$140,618	$169,073	$201,844	$252,019	$ 58,182	$ 73,203
Deduct Equity in Undistributed Net Income of Subsidiaries	40,470	(15,936)	14,030	202,074	266,762	60,431	76,838
Funds Derived from Operations	$ 81,138	$156,554	$155,043	$ (230)	$(14,743)	$ (2,249)	$ (3,635)
Increase in:							
Funds Borrowed Net of Funds Sold	1,649	438,877	—	74,251	515,317	85,877	91,718
Accrued Expenses and Other Liabilities	1,209	90,538	88,133	76,789	69,761	11,732	12,316
Decrease in:							
Loans	—	—	233,350	—	27,159	25,660	67,400
Investments in and Advances to Subsidiaries	44,969	—	—	—	—	—	—
Cash on Deposit with Subsidiary Banks	—	—	—	—	46,909	—	1,107
Issuance of 6⅝% Notes Due 1979 and 1980 (Note 4)	—	—	—	225,000	—	—	—
Other (net)	—	—	—	8,554	—	10,992	13,638
Total	$128,965	$685,969	$476,526	$384,364	$644,403	$132,012	$182,544
Funds Used							
Cash Dividends Declared	$ 62,292	$ 68,531	$ 72,227	$ 75,271	$ 86,417	$ 21,237	$ 24,518
Acquisition of Treasury Stock	—	4,070	55,508	—	—	—	—
Increase in:							
Loans	—	438,500	—	16,604	—	—	—
Investments in and Advances to Subsidiaries	—	150,760	223,458	245,755	554,191	109,168	158,026
Cash on Deposit with Subsidiary Banks	4,681	1,968	2,404	46,734	—	1,607	—
Decrease in Funds Borrowed Net of Funds Sold	—	—	121,147	—	—	—	—
Other (net)	61,992	22,140	1,782	—	3,795	—	—
Total	$128,965	$685,969	$476,526	$384,364	$644,403	$132,012	$182,544

Accounting policies and explanatory notes on pages 37-52 form an integral part of the financial statements.

APPENDIX A (*concluded*)

CITICORP

And Subsidiaries

CONSOLIDATED STATEMENT OF CHANGES IN FINANCIAL POSITION
(In Thousands)

	Year Ended December 31,					Three Months Ended March 31,	
	1969	1970	1971	1972	1973	1973 (Unaudited)	1974 (Unaudited)
Funds Provided							
Net Income	$ 121,608	$ 140,618	$ 169,073	$ 201,844	$ 252,019	$ 58,182	$ 73,203
Increase in:							
Deposits	2,498,953	1,870,816	3,247,295	3,444,422	7,237,871	873,279	1,688,597
Funds Borrowed Net of Funds Sold	343,504	532,674	224,936	1,047,123	1,051,022	417,577	1,407,092
Decrease in:							
Securities	170,037	—	418,435	—	—	—	—
Cash and Due from Banks	—	4,072	—	—	—	—	—
Issuance of 6⅞% Notes Due 1979 and 1980 (Note 4)	—	—	—	225,000	—	—	—
Other (net)	—	—	241,971	94,653	—	—	55,695
Total	$3,134,102	$2,548,180	$4,301,710	$5,013,042	$8,540,912	$1,349,038	$3,224,587
Funds Used							
Cash Dividends Declared	$ 62,292	$ 68,531	$ 72,227	$ 75,271	$ 86,417	$ 21,237	$ 24,518
Increase in:							
Loans	1,809,927	1,777,130	3,436,254	3,062,050	6,099,844	963,209	1,409,754
Securities	—	677,452	—	232,385	601,374	753	5,378
Cash and Due from Banks	964,995	—	763,611	1,612,443	1,495,776	80,787	1,743,947
Premises and Equipment	41,688	23,413	29,618	30,893	39,558	3,025	40,990
Other (net)	255,200	1,654	—	—	217,943	280,027	—
Total	$3,134,102	$2,548,180	$4,301,710	$5,013,042	$8,540,912	$1,349,038	$3,224,587

Accounting policies and explanatory notes on pages 37-52 form an integral part of the financial statements.

APPENDIX B
EXCERPTS FROM PROMOTIONAL MATERIAL

DREYFUS
Liquid Assets, Inc.
600 Madison Avenue New York N.Y. 10022

CALL (800) 223-5525
IN NEW YORK (212) 935-8500

Dear Friend:

There are a great many ways idle cash can be put to work. For example, on May 15th of this year, these were typical rates of return:

Savings Bank	5-1/4% (Regular Account)
Savings & Loan	5-3/4% (90 Day Withdrawal)
Treasury Bills	8%
Savings Bank, 4-Year Certificate	7.5% (To yield 7.9% over 4 years)
Prime Commercial Paper	11-1/8%
Certificates of Deposit	11-1/8%
Bankers Acceptances	11%

Obviously, the opportunity to receive the better returns on cash investments is available. But we both know that not everyone can take advantage of this opportunity.

Why? To purchase some money market instruments the minimum amounts are too high, or your money must be tied up 30-60-90 days or even years. And the money market changes quickly – it can be confusing or present too many mechanical problems for busy people.

Dreyfus Liquid Assets, Inc. was formed to meet these problems – and it was formed for the person responsible for corporate money as well as the individual investor. The Dreyfus Corporation, managers of $2 billion, is behind this idea, and The Bank of New York is custodian and transfer agent.

Dreyfus Liquid Assets, Inc. is something you should know about – it's something you should take the time to find out about.

The enclosed prospectus explains Dreyfus Liquid Assets, Inc. in detail.

The Question and Answer booklet should answer most of your questions.

And our toll-free number, 800-223-5525 (call collect on 212-935-8500 if you live in New York state), will connect you with a Dreyfus expert who can answer any other questions.

Once you are prepared, the enclosed application form will enable you to put your cash to work to seek maximum yield.

Sincerely,

Jerome S. Hardy
Chairman

JSH/mg

APPENDIX B (*continued*)

What is Dreyfus Liquid Assets and how does it work?

Dreyfus Liquid Assets, Inc. is a new opportunity that allows the smaller investor to receive nearly the same high yields in the money market that large investors have enjoyed for so long. Large investors have received higher yields in the past by being able to afford $100,000 certificates of deposit or other large denomination money market instruments. Now people who can't or don't want to put up such sums can also take advantage of attractive money market rates.

1 / What are money market instruments; and why have they been so attractive?

There is nothing mysterious about money market instruments. They are just short term obligations of banks, corporations, and the U.S Government, that these institutions sell to meet any immediate cash needs they may have. For example, a CD is sold to the public by a bank to increase the level of deposits they can then lend out. Commercial paper is an IOU issued to the public by corporations and financial institutions to finance short term business needs. Both of these kinds of instruments are usually sold only in large denominations, such as $100,000 but more often in $1,000,000 units. As a result the general public is not too familiar with them, and has not had ready access to them.

The chart enclosed with your initial mailing shows if you did have access to CD's over the years the rate of return on your money would usually be much greater than in any regular savings account. For banks and corporations, in order to attract the short term money they need, have frequently found it necessary to pay higher rates of interest —while regular savings accounts are limited by rules and regulations which fix their interest rates.

2 / But if all money market instruments are some form of debt, how can you be sure they are safe?

Some money market instruments are, of course, safer than others and an investor has to check carefully before buying. That is one of the risks in going alone into the money market; a high yielding "piece of paper" may be the weakest from the viewpoint of safety.

Dreyfus Liquid Assets is very conservative in its approach to the money market. As stated in our prospectus, we will invest only in:
(a) Issues guaranteed by the Government of the United States or its agencies;
(b) Certificates of Deposit and Bankers Acceptances issued by banks that have assets over $1 billion; and
(c) Corporate commercial paper rated Prime-1 by Moody's or A-1 by Standard and Poor's.

In addition to holding to these standards, we must remain quite diversified for your protection—no more than 5% of our assets can be invested in the commercial paper of any one company or more than 15% in the obligations of any single bank. We do not believe that this conservative approach appreciably alters the yields our investors receive, but we do believe it creates a safer and more liquid portfolio for you.

3 / If I wanted to, however, couldn't I go to the money market myself and receive these yields?

Of course, if you had enough money on hand, you were convinced of your own expertise (not only to choose what to buy, but when to buy), and you knew when to move from one instrument to another for highest yield.

In addition, direct purchase by individual investors entails the added burdens of bookkeeping, safeguarding securities, diversifying maturity dates, research and redirecting investments—all of which Dreyfus Liquid Assets provides as part of its service.

4 / Who is behind Dreyfus Liquid Assets?

The organization and administrative responsibilities of Dreyfus Liquid Assets are in the hands of a group of officers and directors who are well known in the financial community. This investment company was created by The Dreyfus Corporation, managers of approximately $2 billion for more than 500,000 investors. The Dreyfus Corporation, listed on the New York Stock Exchange and for over twenty years one of the most reputable investment firms in the country, will direct the investment decisions of Dreyfus Liquid Assets.

All money market investments owned by Dreyfus Liquid Assets are held by The Bank of New York, with total assets in excess of $2,300,000,000, and all money transactions must pass through them. Further information on The Dreyfus Corporation and the people responsible for Dreyfus Liquid Assets may be found in the Prospectus.

5 / Who may invest in Dreyfus Liquid Assets and in what amounts?

Any investor who can make an initial minimum investment of $5,000 can participate in Dreyfus Liquid Assets. Subsequent investments can be made in amounts of $1,000 or more. There is never a sales charge for investing—and there is never a charge for withdrawing your investment.

6 / What happens if for business or personal reasons I need some or all of my invested cash back—on very short notice?

When you fill out your application you will notice that in the second box you can check whether you want the "Expedited Redemption Payments." If you choose this service, it will be possible for you to wire redemption requests to The Bank of New York and they will automatically wire the amount of money you wish to withdraw to your commercial bank account. And, in most instances, your bank account will be credited one business day after The Bank of New York has received your telegram. The Prospectus contains all the details on this special service, and we suggest that you read those instructions carefully to make sure that your specific needs can be met.

7 / What is the total cost for all these services?

As we mentioned before, there is no charge to invest your money, and no charge to withdraw it.

Dreyfus Liquid Assets, however, does have business expenses, but at no time can these expenses exceed 1% of the assets of this investment company in any calendar year. And that includes the ½ of 1% charged by The Dreyfus Corporation to manage your investment. If in any full year expenses do exceed 1%, The Dreyfus Corporation bears those excess costs. On the other hand, if expenses prove to be lower, you will realize the benefit.

8 / If I wish to invest—what do I do?

On the following pages there is an Application and Order Form. You will also find instructions on how to complete the application.

9 / Can I wire Funds from my bank account?

If you have an account with a commercial bank that is a member of the Federal Reserve System, or one having a correspondent bank in New York City, you may request your bank to transmit immediate available funds by wire to The Bank of New York, Attn: Mutual Funds Department "D"/Dreyfus Liquid Assets for purchase of shares in your name. Your address should also be included. Information for remitting funds in this manner may be obtained from your bank.

For information relating to the timing of investments made under this procedure please refer to the section "Purchase of Shares" in the Prospectus

If you have any unanswered questions, we urge you to call us toll free at 800-223-5525 (If you live in New York State call collect 212-935-5700.) (In 212 Area call 935-5700.)

APPENDIX B (*continued*)

Dreyfus Liquid Assets, Inc. Statement of Assets and Liabilities June 30, 1974

ASSETS

Investments in securities, at market value—see statement $144,125,452

	Cost	Market Value	
U.S. Government agencies	$ 2,868,952	$ 2,866,887	
Negotiable bank certificates of deposit	133,475,000	133,295,484	
Bankers acceptances	5,573,695	5,569,014	
Commercial paper	2,394,743	2,394,067	
	$144,312,390		
Cash in bank			1,405,416
Interest receivable			1,159,874
Other assets			19,376
			146,710,118

LIABILITIES

Due to The Dreyfus Corporation for management fee	$ 46,249	
Payable for Common Stock redeemed	286,018	
Accrued expenses and taxes	33,588	365,855

NET ASSETS at market, applicable to 14,661,136 outstanding shares of $1 par value Common Stock, equivalent to $9.98 per share (50,000,000 shares authorized) $146,344,263

Statement of Operations for the period from September 6, 1973 (date of incorporation) to June 30, 1974 (Note A)

INVESTMENT INCOME:

Interest income—Note A(2)		$ 1,674,461
Expenses:		
Management fee—Note B	$ 77,327	
Registration fee	31,803	
Custodian, transfer and dividend disbursing agent's fees	25,934	
Legal and auditing fees	3,000	
State and local taxes	2,298	
Prospectus and stockholders' reports	20,225	
Directors' fees—Note B	4,687	
Miscellaneous	1,603	
Total expenses		166,877
NET INVESTMENT INCOME—Note A(3)		$ 1,507,584

REALIZED AND UNREALIZED (LOSS) ON INVESTMENTS:

Realized (loss) from securities transactions—Notes A(2) and C:		
Proceeds from sales	$ 40,160,370	
Cost of securities sold	40,162,145	
Net realized (loss), identified cost basis—same on the basis of average cost—Note A(3)		($1,775)
Unrealized (depreciation) of investments for the period—Note A(4)		(186,938)
NET REALIZED AND UNREALIZED (LOSS) ON INVESTMENTS		($188,713)

The accompanying notes are an integral part of these statements.

APPENDIX B (*continued*)

Dreyfus Liquid Assets, Inc. Statement of Changes in Net Assets
for the period from September 6, 1973 (date of incorporation) to June 30, 1974 (Note A)

FROM INVESTMENT ACTIVITIES:

		Shares	
Net investment income		$ 1,507,584	
Dividends to stockholders ($.368 per share)		(1,507,584)	–
Net realized (loss) from securities transactions, identified cost basis—same on the basis of average cost			($1,775)
Unrealized (depreciation) of investments for the period			(186,938)
(Decrease) in net assets derived from investment activities, after dividends of $1,507,584			(188,713)

FROM CAPITAL SHARE TRANSACTIONS—Note B:

	Shares	
Received on issuances:		
Initial offering to Manager	70,000	700,000
Shares sold	15,284,728	152,760,880
Reinvestment of income dividends	149,530	1,494,422
Exchanges	907,091	9,069,388
Total	16,411,349	164,024,690
Paid on (redemptions):		
Shares redeemed	(1,716,035)	(17,150,084)
Exchanges	(34,178)	(341,630)
Total	(1,750,213)	(17,491,714)
Net increase in net assets derived from capital share transactions	14,661,136	146,532,976
NET ASSETS at end of period		$146,344,263

The accompanying notes are an integral part of this statement.

APPENDIX B (*concluded*)

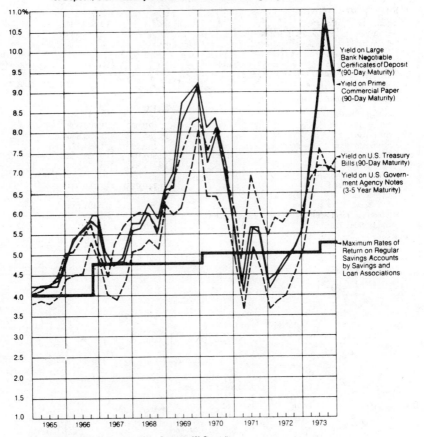

HISTORICAL YIELDS
Savings Accounts, Prime Commercial Paper, Negotiable Certificates of Deposit, U.S. Treasury Bills and U.S. Government Agency Notes.

This chart covers the period from January, 1965 to December, 1973. The results shown should not be considered a representation of the yield to be achieved from an investment made in the Company. In addition, the chart does not represent all of the money market instruments permitted for purchase by the Company.

Sources: Salomon Bros ; Federal Home Loan Bank Board Journal

2. The Manhattan Mutual Bank

Henry Pleasants stared intently at the Deposit Flow Statement of the Manhattan Mutual Bank for the first seven months of 1974 (see Exhibit 1). Three times within the last ten years, Pleasants, the chairman of the bank, had observed the effect of volatile interest rate movements on the cash flow of the Manhattan Mutual. However, he could scarcely believe the rise in interest rates that had developed in 1974. Short-term interest rates were approaching the 12 percent level, while some mortgage rates had already exceeded 9 percent (see Exhibit 2). Individual savers, who typically maintained sizable deposits at the Manhattan Mutual Bank, withdrew $221 million during the first seven and a half months of 1974, presumably to buy investments at these very high short-term rates. These substantial withdrawals had sharply reduced the prospective liquidity of the Bank.

Early in the morning of August 17, Pleasants met with Edwin Forbes and Gerald Sterling in order to consider alternative courses of action which would alleviate, at least temporarily, the stress of the recent cash outflows. Discussion centered around the proposal to borrow approximately $50 million dollars with an innovative type of financing, the floating rate notes. The purpose of the notes was to increase the cash position of the bank. The notes were tentatively scheduled for public offering on August 20, but the bank had to give the approval of its investment bankers by late this afternoon.

At the meeting Forbes had argued cogently that the notes were a necessary step because of the pressing liquidity needs of the bank during this period of high interest rates. In addition, he believed that the high level of interest rates, accompanied by large volumes of withdrawals, could continue for the foreseeable future. He felt that it was extremely important for the Manhattan Mutual Bank to borrow from the capital markets now in order to preserve other sources of funds and to maintain some degree of financial flexibility for dealing with future contingencies.

Sterling, a generally cautious man, advised against the floating-rates notes. Although he was quite uncertain about the future course of interest rates, Sterling agreed that they could remain very high. Nevertheless, he argued that it was unwise to undertake this unusual form of financing at a time when the Manhattan Mutual Bank was under considerable pressure.

He believed that the bank should continue to use its current sources of contingency funds—bank borrowing and the sale of assets—to the fullest extent before experimenting with new methods.

Before coming to a decision, Pleasants wanted to evaluate the impact of each alternative in terms of securing additional liquidity and in terms of the current and future viability of the Manhattan Mutual Bank. He realized that it was important to consider the role of his mutual savings bank as a competitive financial intermediary in the current economic environment. In addition, he had to evaluate each proposed alternative in relation to the current asset and liability structure of the bank and its future opportunities for growth.

THE BUSINESS OF THE MANHATTAN MUTUAL BANK

The Manhattan Mutual Bank was the fifth largest mutual savings bank in the nation with assets of $2.8 billion and deposits of $2.55 billion.[1] It was chartered by New York State and located in New York City. The bank operated 14 branches within the city and 1 in Westchester County. Table 1 presents summary data on major classes of the bank's assets and liabilities during recent years.

Table 1
Summary of recent growth for year ending December 31 ($ millions)

	1969	1970	1971	1972	1973	June 30, 1974
Assets	$2,036	$2,103	$2,414	$2,756	$2,860	$2,836
Deposits	1,830	1,891	2,205	2,519	2,612	2,551
Mortgage loans*	1,712	1,748	1,906	1,975	2,007	2,011
Net worth	155	158	161	171	186	190
Number of savings accounts	489,000	501,000	519,000	519,000	575,000	562,000

* Mortgage loans net of unearned discount.

The growth of the Manhattan Mutual Bank was characterized both by the development of new investment strategies and by an attempt to segment the savings market by offering individual savers an assortment of deposit accounts varying in terms of liquidity and return. The most recent balance sheet, shown in Exhibit 3, indicates the asset and liability structure which had resulted from these developments.

---

[1] See Appendix A for a description of the mutual saving bank industry and Appendix B for a description of the competition for savings deposits, particularly in the New York City region.

Mortgage loans represented the largest category of investment assets held by the Manhattan Mutual Bank. The bank had provided long-term financing for various types of real estate including family homes, apartment buildings, and nonresidential commercial properties. The mortgage portfolio as of June 30, 1974, consisted of 62,471 mortgages with a book value of $2,042,765,000. The portfolio included both conventional mortgages and mortgages backed by government insurance or a government guarantee. (Government-backed mortgages are considered less risky investments because the U.S. government guarantees the payment of principal and interest in case of default by the borrower. The credit worthiness of a conventional mortgage depends on the income-generating ability of the apartment house or other commercial property, or on the earning power of the homeowner.) Because of their different risk characteristics, conventional mortgages generally provided a more attractive yield than government-backed mortgages. Exhibit 4 indicates the distribution of funds invested in different types of properties and in various classes of mortgages. Exhibit 5 compares recent yields on commercial mortgages, government-backed home mortgages, and on Baa corporate bonds.

In the two decades following World War II, the bank had responded to the favorable yields on, and high demand for, housing credit and channelled its investible funds into financing mortgages on one-to-four family homes. The bank's urban location in the densely populated New York City area limited its opportunities or originate its own local home mortgages. However, the growth of a nationwide secondary market in government-backed, out-of-state home mortgages provided the bank with a means of purchasing a considerable volume of such mortgages. (Because of the standardization of credit quality inherent in government-backed mortgages, they became acceptable for purchase and sale arrangements in the "secondary" market. Mortgages that were not government-backed, generally called "conventional" mortgages, were not bought and sold because of their heterogeneity and the difficulties of judging credit quality.) The yields on government-backed mortgages then varied from 4 to 6 percent and were generally above the yields on other long-term instruments such as corporate bonds. Their favorable yields and their relatively less risky character made government-backed mortgages a seemingly attractive investment outlet for the Manhattan Mutual Bank during this period. Investment policies of the 1950s and early 1960s accounted for most of the bank's sizeable investment in government-backed home mortgages. As of June 30, 1974, the bank held 57,851 government-backed mortgages on one-to-four family homes; the book value of these mortgages was $591,932,000.

In recent years, however, the changing structure of conventional mortgage yields and the overall level of market interest rates had caused substantial changes in the bank's investment policies. In its mortgage investments, the bank channeled a growing volume of its investible funds into financing multifamily and commercial mortgages (see Exhibit 6). This type of mortgage financing was typically a high unit-value loan on an office building, apartment complex, or a retail store, secured by the future income-generating capacity of the property. As of June 30, 1974, the bank held 129 mortgages on office buildings; 87 of these were located in New York State. The book value of these mortgages was $504,790,000. In addition, the bank's mortgage portfolio also included 473 mortgages on apartment buildings, valued at $404,355,000, and 175 mortgages on store buildings, valued at $173,400,000. Although the Manhattan Mutual had tended to concentrate its investment in income-producing properties in its own metropolitan area, it also provided a considerable amount of financing for similar projects outside of the New York City area.

Investment securities were the other major asset held by the Manhattan Mutual Bank. Within its regulatory constraints, the bank had the authority to invest in a wide spectrum of securities including government, federal agency, municipal and corporate debt instruments, as well as corporate equities. In recent years the rising yields on securities had made them an attractive investment opportunity for the bank. Exhibit 6 shows the growing importance of the securities portfolio in the investment strategy of the Manhattan Mutual Bank. The book value of the securities portfolio had grown from $288 million at the beginning of 1969 to almost $671 million by June 30, 1974. Exhibit 7 shows the book value and market value of the bank's investment in each class of securities as of June 30, 1974. The recent escalation in interest rates had adversely affected the market value of the securities portfolio. A description of the maturity structure of the portfolio is also presented in Exhibit 7. The heavy concentration in long-term instruments indicates that most of the short-term investments originally held for liquidity had already been sold to meet deposit outflows. Most of the securities remaining in the portfolio were originally purchased for investment rather than liquidity purposes.

The Manhattan Mutual had sought to finance its changing investment strategy with a well-managed deposit policy. Statutes limited the bank to accepting deposits from individuals and nonprofit organizations; the savings of individuals represented over 95 percent of the bank's total deposits. The deposit rate ceilings of the Federal Deposit Insurance Corporation exerted a considerable influence upon the ability of the Manhattan Mutual Bank to compete for the savings of individuals. For example, from 1970 to 1973, savings banks were allowed to pay 5.75 percent on time deposits with a maturity from one to two years, and 6.00 percent on time deposits maturing within two to five years. The Manhattan Mutual Bank had followed a policy of actively promoting these time deposits among individuals as a competitive move to increase its volume of deposits. In adopting this policy, the bank also believed that the minimum term requirements of the new time deposits would lengthen the maturity and enhance the stability of its deposit base.

In July of 1973, the FDIC revised its regulations concerning the maximum allowable rates payable on savings and time deposits because of a considerable rise in the overall level of market rates of interest. The current rate ceilings are shown in Exhibit 11. To a certain extent, the liberalization of these rate ceilings had enabled the Manhattan Mutual Bank to maintain deposit volume in spite of the rising interest rates of 1973 and 1974. Exhibit 8 indicates the changing distribution of deposits.

The performance of the Manhattan Mutual Bank during this period of change in its investment strategy and deposit policy is summarized by the data in Table 2. The table compares the return on assets with the cost of funds for the Manhattan Mutual.

Table 2
Asset yield versus cost of funds

	Year ended December 31					Six months ended June 30, 1974
	1969	1970	1971	1972	1973	
Rate earned on average daily investment	5.77%	5.90%	6.15%	6.52%	6.84%	6.97%
Rate paid on average daily deposits	4.96	5.07	5.18	5.32	5.53	5.85
Differential	0.81	0.83	0.97	1.20	1.31	1.12

The differential between its asset yield and its cost of funds is an indication of the bank's ability to maintain desired reserves and to pay competitive interest rates on deposits. The Condensed Income Statements (Exhibit 9) and the Cash Flow Analysis (Exhibit 10) provide a detailed description of the profitability of the bank's assets and the variability of its deposit flows during the last five years.

THE EVENTS OF 1973 AND 1974

In assessing the developments of the last two years, Pleasants realized that the Manhattan Mutual Bank and the U.S. economy confronted a set of difficult and highly unpredictable conditions. In the aftermath of the oil embargo, the economy was experiencing the longest and the most intense period of inflationary pressures since the end of World War II. Consumer prices in 1974 were rising at an annual rate of 12 percent, while wholesale prices had increased 26 percent on an annual basis. The bulge in prices following the end of wage and price controls and a rising worldwide demand for industrial materials and farm products further contributed to the sharp increases in the general price level. In addition, the combined shocks of high inflation rates and energy shortages could threaten to move the economy into a recession of undetermined magnitude.

These unsettled economic conditions placed considerable pressures on financial markets and institutions. The movements in interest rates and their effects on the deposit flows of the Manhattan Mutual and on the competition for the savings of individuals particularly troubled Pleasants. He remembered the conditions of the last cyclical peak of interest rates, in 1969, and the problems the high rates caused.

Pleasants was even more keenly aware of the substantial pressures confronting the Manhattan Mutual Bank since 1973. The steady rise in interest rates had adversely affected the bank's cash position and its ability to maintain and expand its deposit base and asset portfolio.[1] In the first half of 1973, when interest rates on savings and time accounts were competitive with open-market yields, the bank experienced a cash inflow of $32 million in new deposit money and a total growth of $101 million in its deposit base including the crediting of interest on deposits. (See Table 3.) However, in the last six months of the year, higher market interest rates encouraged savers to withdraw $83 million from the Manhattan Mutual, causing the deposit base to shrink to $2,611.5 million after crediting interest on deposits (Table 3). On an annual basis, withdrawals totaled $51 million in 1973.

Table 3
Changes in the deposit base ($ thousands)

Balance, January 1, 1973	$2,519,456
Interest credited to deposits, 1H, 73	68,827
New deposits, 1H, 73	31,895
Balance, July 1, 1973	$2,620,178
Interest credited to deposits, 2H, 73	74,328
Withdrawals, 2H, 73	(82,991)
Balance, January 1, 1974	$2,611,515
Interest credited to deposits, 1H, 74	75,484
Withdrawals, 1H, 74	(135,604)
Balance, July 1, 1974	$2,551,395

Pleasants realized that the bank had limited the cash outflow to $51 million only because it was able to offer higher yielding time certificates to its depositors. Indeed, throughout 1973, the Manhattan Mutual Bank made extensive use of its longer dated time deposit powers in order to compete for individual savings and to maintain its volume of deposits (see

---

[1] See Exhibit 2, for a plot of recent interest rate movements.

Exhibit 8). However, the long-term implications of these changes in deposit rates and their effect on the bank's cost and structure of deposits greatly troubled Pleasants.

The pressures on the Manhattan Mutual Bank from unfavorable interest rate movements and deposit outflows intensified throughout 1974. In the first six months of the year, the bank experienced a cash outflow of $136 million due to withdrawals (see Table 3). Savers also continued to shift their deposits into higher yielding time certificates. In July, withdrawals reached a record volume of $63 million, and another $22 million was withdrawn during the first 16 days of August.

Several factors aggravated the particular cash flow problems of the Manhattan Mutual in 1974. First, a substantial percentage of the time deposits that were obtained during the bank's promotional campaigns of the early 70s reached maturity in 1974. At maturity, many savers shifted these funds into time deposits with still higher yields, or into investment opportunities in the open market where even more favorable returns were available. Pleasants attributed the relatively more severe cash flow problems of Manhattan Mutual (see Exhibit 1) to the greater percentage of these maturing time deposits that were in their deposit mix.

The competition from other types of financial intermediaries also became especially intense in 1974. In July, Citicorp, the holding company of the First National City Bank, issued $650 million in floating rate notes. The terms of this large issue were very attractive to individuals, whose savings were the primary source of deposits to thrift institutions, such as the Manhattan Mutual. Since Citicorp was a holding company rather than a bank, its notes were exempt from interest rate ceilings and reserve requirements. Therefore, Citicorp was able to offer investors a rate of return higher than the yield on deposits at commercial or mutual banks. The yield of the Citicorp notes was fixed at 9.7 percent until December 1974. From December 1974 to June 1974, the notes would pay the higher of 9.7 percent or 1 percent above the Treasury bill rate. Afterwards, the yield on the notes was set to float at 1 percent above the Treasury bill rate. The notes were sold in denominations of $1,000 with an initial minimum purchase order of $5,000. The issue was listed on the New York Stock Exchange in order to provide a secondary market. In addition to a higher yield, a small denomination size, and a secondary market, the Citicorp issue carried an unusual redemption feature which increased the liquidity of the notes and enhanced their attractiveness to individuals. After an initial two-year period, Citicorp gave investors the semiannual option of redeeming their notes at par value plus accrued interest. By combining a high yield with this redemption option, Citicorp offered individuals an instrument that provided both a better return and greater liquidity than time deposits.

The reaction of investors and of competing bank holding companies demonstrated the attractiveness of the Citicorp notes. Investors quickly oversubscribed the issue, and the notes were essentially sold out soon after the initial announcement. The Chase Manhattan Corporation, another bank holding company, followed with a $200 million issue of floating rate notes. Two other large bank holding companies and one major industrial company—Standard Oil of Indiana—announced plans for similar issues. In August 1974, approximately $1.4 billion was raised in the capital markets through issues of floating rate notes. Many leaders of the savings bank industry believed that the floating rate notes of bank holding companies violated the spirit of Regulation Q which determined interest rate ceilings for depository institutions.

In addition to the floating rate notes of bank holding companies, other open-market borrowers also issued debt instruments that increased the competition for the savings of individuals. In early August, the U.S. Treasury issued 8.5 percent intermediate-term notes in denominations as low as $1,000, although the minimum denomination size in the past was usually $10,000. These Treasury notes were very popular among individual savers, especially those interest-sensitive savers in urban financial centers. Because of their yield, liquidity, and safety, the notes were more attractive than savings deposits to many individuals. In early August 1974, the Treasury issued $4 billion in notes with maturities of 33 months and six years.

The money-market funds (open-end investment companies) became another attractive means for individuals to invest in the high returns available in the money markets during 1974. Individuals with as little as $5,000 could invest in the shares of these money-market funds. The liberal redemption policies of the funds provided the individual investor with substantial liquidity. By investing primarily in commercial paper and negotiable certificates of deposit yielding as much as 12.5 percent during this high-rate period, the money-market funds were able to provide individuals with returns substantially above the ceiling rates on savings bank deposits. Within the last 18 months, the assets of these money-market funds grew to almost $500 million dollars. Their rapid growth represented increased competition for individual savings.

On August 18, 1974, the cash flow problem was the most pressing concern confronting the chairman. During this long period of rate advances, the alternative sources available to the Manhattan Mutual Bank for obtaining cash had dwindled. However, if the Manhattan Mutual was to avoid the problems of illiquidity, it was necessary for Pleasants to provide the bank with additional cash in order both to fund withdrawals and to finance its forward commitments. In addition, the high level of interest rates and the rapid rate of inflation disturbed the chairman because these factors erode the value of financial assets including the purchasing power of depositors' savings and the market value of the bank's investment assets.

FINANCIAL RESOURCES AND ALTERNATIVES

The chairman concluded that the Manhattan Mutual Bank had three principal alternatives for obtaining additional liquidity. He wanted to evaluate the viability of each alternative separately and then to consider the sequencing of possible combinations of the three alternatives.

The floating rate notes were an innovative financing proposal modeled in part after the highly successful Citicorp issue. The bank planned to sell the notes in denominations as low as $1,000 through a large nationwide syndicate of brokerage firms assembled by their investment bankers. The notes would presumably be sold to individuals interested in higher yielding instruments. These notes were not considered deposits of the bank and would not be insured by the FDIC. As direct, unsecured obligations of the Manhattan Mutual, the notes were subordinate, with respect to principal and interest payments, to the bank's obligations to its depositors and all other creditors.

The proposed yield on the Manhattan Mutual issue would initially be fixed at 10 percent until May 31, 1975. From June 1, 1975 to February 29, 1976, the notes would pay the higher of 10 percent or 1.25 percent above the Treasury bill rate. After February 29, 1976 until maturity, the interest rate would be set at the higher of 8 percent or 1.25 percent above the Treasury bill rate.[2] The notes would mature in 1981 and contained no call options or redemption privileges. The notes would be listed and traded on the New York Stock Exchange so that investors could have some liquidity via the secondary market.

Although the bank would prefer to float a substantial issue of these notes, their investment banker had recently informed them that the market outlook for these floating rate notes was becoming clouded. While the original plan was to issue up to $100 million of these notes, the investment bankers thought that $50 million, or perhaps as low as $40 million, was all the market could now safely digest.

As an alternative to issuing floating rate notes, the Manhattan Mutual Bank could borrow from its commercial banks. The Manhattan Mutual maintained two different types of credit arrangements with commercial banks. First, the Manhattan Mutual had line of credit arrangements with two commercial banks which could provide total borrowings of $40 million under their current agreements. These loans were to be secured by U.S. government or corporate securities. The Manhattan Mutual could borrow on these lines of credit at the prevailing prime rate. As of June 30, 1974, no borrowings on these lines had been outstanding. Since then, however, the Manhattan Mutual had been forced to both draw down its liquid assets and utilize these lines of credit to meet the recent deposit

---

[2] The bank had originally resisted the "floor" of 8 percent on these notes. Their investment bankers had convinced them, however, that if the notes were to be successfully sold, they would need either the unusual redemption feature of the Citicorp notes, or a "floor" on the interest rate of 8 percent.

outflows. If the need arose, Manhattan Mutual could probably obtain somewhat larger lines of credit, although the limits and/or costs of this were not clear.

The other borrowing arrangements of the Manhattan Mutual Bank were mortgage-warehousing agreements with eight commercial banks. Under the warehousing agreements, the commercial banks would, on request, purchase and temporarily hold certain mortgages. The Manhattan Mutual would then repurchase the mortgage loans from the warehousing commercial bank within 12 months of the original closing, at the same price initially paid by the commercial bank. The Manhattan Mutual received the interest payments on the warehoused mortgages and paid the commercial bank the prevailing prime rate for the warehousing services. In August of 1974, prime was set at 12 percent. The Manhattan Mutual could warehouse up to $141 million of mortgage loans under these agreements. Currently, the bank had warehoused mortgage loans totaling over $60 million; these warehoused mortgages had to be repurchased by the end of 1974.

The final alternative available to the Manhattan Mutual was to continue selling its investment securities or mortgage loans in the secondary markets. Given reasonable time, a substantial fraction of the investment securities could probably be sold to other investors (indeed, even some of the mortgages might be sold, although the market for these was much less liquid). Unfortunately, though, since the bank had acquired most of its remaining portfolio of securities and mortgage loans when the overall level of interest rates was lower, the sale of these financial assets during this current period of historically higher interest rates could generate a considerable book ''loss'' and weaken the book value of the bank's reserves and surplus. While the bank had adequate reserves now, the bank's regulators would conceivably become concerned if they were seriously depleted in this way.[3] The reduction in the book value of these capital accounts could be the factor constraining the use of this option as a financing alternative. Exhibit 12 exemplifies the effect of a change in interest rates on market value of a fixed-rate investment.

THE DECISION

Pleasants' review of the prospects and alternatives of the Manhattan Mutual Bank was almost complete. Based on the experience of the past

---

[3] The bank's current net worth was over 7 percent of deposits. It was unclear what the implications of a lower net worth would be, but there were two specific regulations. New York Bank Law required prior approval of the state Superintendent of Banks before a savings bank could credit its savings accounts with interest (formally, dividends) which would reduce its net worth below 5 percent of deposits. Furthermore, FDIC regulations required regional office referral to Washington of such matters as new branch applications for banks whose ratio of net worth to assets fell below 6 percent of deposits.

seven and a half months, Pleasants guessed that deposit outflows for the remaining four and a half months of 1974 could be severe if interest rates remained unchanged. He also noted that the bank was required to fund its forward mortgage commitments including the repurchase of $62.4 million of warehoused mortgages. Table 4 shows the bank's obligation under its forward commitments for 1974, 1975, and 1976.

Table 4
Forward mortgage commitments

1974 (remainder)........	$ 65,300,000
1975	88,900,000
1976	8,500,000
Total	$162,700,000

Pleasants recalled the arguments advanced by others at their meeting earlier today. Forbes forecasted continued unfavorable deposit flows and financial market conditions, and he had no way of knowing if or when interest rates would recede. He emphasized that the bank must maintain some degree of flexibility. He advised the chairman to proceed with the floating rate issue while access to the capital markets was still available and to preserve the bank's other sources of liquidity for future contingencies.

Sterling was not so sure that short-term rates would remain high. The federal funds rate had receded a little recently, although it was not clear that other short rates would follow. He believed that the floating rate note issue could have harmful long-run effects on the bank, that the notes might not be well received by investors. He urged Pleasants to devise an alternative plan to obtain cash through bank borrowings and the sale of securities.

Henry Pleasants knew that he had to resolve these conflicting arguments sometime today.

APPENDIX A

THE MUTUAL SAVINGS BANK INDUSTRY

The traditional functions of the mutual savings banks have been to encourage thrift and to provide a safe depository for the savings of individuals. The savings bank industry invests the savings of individuals in a variety of securities and mortgages in order to pay depositors a reasonable return on their funds.

Savings banks are mutual organizations. In principle, a savings bank is "owned" by its depositors and managed in their interests by professional managers whose performance is overseen by a self-perpetuating board of trustees. All "earnings" on assets (after paying for operation expenses and providing for reserves that are required by law or judged necessary by management) accrue in theory to the benefit of deposit holders.[1]

At the end of 1973, there were 482 mutual savings banks in the United States with assets of $107 billion—deposits of $96 billion and reserves of $8 billion. Although savings banks have existed since the early 1800s, they are located in only 17 states which provide charters for organizations of this type. These 17 states are concentrated primarily in the Northeast where the earliest mutual savings banks in the United States originated. In 1973, 384 savings banks holding 90.3 percent of total savings bank assets and 65.5 percent of total deposits were located in five northeastern states. Although mutual savings banks are located in a limited number of states, the larger banks carry on their investment and lending activities in national markets, especially in the bond and secondary mortgage markets.

All mutual savings banks are regulated by the banking authorities of the state in which they are chartered. State banking authorities set requirements for reserve accounts, require an annual audit by an outside trustee, and control other operating aspects such as the number of branches and types of services that saving banks are allowed to provide. In order to protect deposits and enhance the stability of the savings banks, state authorities regulate the type and quality of assets in which savings banks are permitted to invest, and set maximum limits on the amounts of some types of investment. In most states mutual savings banks are permitted to invest in mortgages and in a range of securities including debt instruments and equities. However, many state banking authorities prescribe a "buy list" of allowable securities.

Most mutual savings banks also belong to the Federal Deposit Insurance Corporation (FDIC) and must abide by its regulations. As of August 1974, the FDIC insured deposits at savings banks up to a maximum of $20,000. The FDIC also regulates the maximum allowable rates which savings banks can pay depositors on their various types of time and savings deposits.

Savings banks are financial intermediaries which obtain funds by providing individuals with highly liquid savings accounts and a return consistent with liquidity. In the past, the large number of savings accounts usually created a stable deposit base, despite fluctuations in individual account balances. The overall stability of this low-cost deposit base enabled mutual savings banks to invest the funds obtained from very liquid

---

[1] Actually, these funds are paid out to depositors only in the form of interest on their deposits, and there are regulatory ceilings on allowable deposit rates. Additional "earnings" are accumulated in the various reserve and surplus accounts of the banks, presumably accruing to the eventual benefit of current and future depositors.

savings accounts in long-term, high-yielding investments such as mortgages and securities. By combining a stable deposit base with a strategy of investing in long-term assets, savings banks have generally been able to generate returns which cover their operating expenses and the cost of funds.

APPENDIX B

THE COMPETITION FOR THE SAVINGS OF INDIVIDUALS

Savings and time deposits at financial intermediaries have been a major channel which directs the savings of individuals into productive investments. In 1973, savings and time deposits represented 27.6 percent of the financial assets held by individuals. Since the end of World War II, the growth in savings and time deposits has generally exceeded the increase in other types of financial assets. On a nationwide basis, three financial intermediaries—savings banks, savings and loan associations, and commercial banks—are the traditional competitors for the savings and time deposits of individuals. These three institutions differ in their organization, their geographic distribution, and their investment and deposit powers.

In the New York City area, the large mutual savings banks and large commercial banks dominated the competition for individual savings. Until 1973, regulatory ceilings allowed mutual savings banks to offer deposit rates that were 0.5 percent higher than rates on similar deposits at commercial banks; at that time, the differential was reduced to 0.25 percent. Exhibit 11 shows the existing regulatory ceilings on deposit rates for mutual savings banks and commercial banks. Because of this rate differential and their traditional image of stability, savings banks had maintained a dominant share of the savings market in the New York area.

Since the early 60s, the large commercial banks of New York City—Citibank, Chase, Manufacturers Hanover, Bankers' Trust and Chemical Bank—had intensified the competition for the savings of individuals. These large commercial banks are among the central intermediaries of the financial and economic system, and they have viewed the household savings market as a large potential source of relatively low-cost funds. Despite the unfavorable deposit rate regulations, these commercial banks had been able to compete for savings by providing individuals with a wide range of financial services, including free checking accounts, credit cards and consumer loans. In addition, the large commercial banks competed by maintaining an extensive network of branch offices which substantially outnumbered the branches of mutual savings banks, and which are designed to provide convenience and a high service level to individuals.

With the upward trend in interest rates, financial intermediaries as a group had also confronted increased competition for individual savings from open-market instruments. The rise in the overall level of interest rates and the increased financial sophistication of savers had made deposit flows at financial intermediaries more sensitive to conditions in the financial markets. This increased financial sophistication was especially evident among individual savers living in the urban financial centers of the Northeast, such as New York City.

Open-market instruments can become particularly effective competitors for individual savings during periods when yields in the capital markets rise above the regulatory ceilings on savings and time deposits. Three periods of high market interest rates, occurring in 1966, in 1969–1970, and again in 1973, caused the disintermediation (the substantial outflow of deposits from financial intermediaries), which created severe liquidity problems for many depository institutions.

Exhibit 1
Statement of gross deposit outflows

	In millions of dollars	As a percent of deposits: beginning of period
January 1, 1974 to June 30, 1974		
Manhattan Mutual Bank	$136	5.2%
All other savings banks in NYC	554	1.5
All savings banks in NYC	$690	1.7
Month of July, 1974		
Manhattan Mutual Bank	63	2.5
All other savings banks in NYC	480	1.3
All savings banks in NYC	$543	1.3

Note: On a national basis, all mutual savings banks experienced a deposit outflow of $502 million during the first six months of 1974; in the month of July, all mutual savings banks experienced a deposit outflow of $733 million.

Exhibit 2
Short-term interest rates

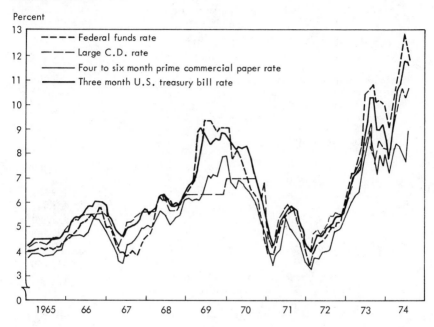

Exhibit 3

MANHATTAN MUTUAL BANK
Statement of Financial Condition
June 30, 1974
(in thousands)

Assets

Cash and due from banks	$ 1,888
One-day loans to banks	58,000
Investment securities	
U.S. government obligations	76,462
State and municipal obligations	94,630
Other debt obligations	364,310
Corporate stocks	135,178
	670,580
Mortgage loans on real estate	
Conventional	1,298,829
FHA	457,932
VA	286,004
	2,042,765
Less: Unearned discount	32,116
	2,010,649
Other loans (Less unearned discount of $1,518,000	
at December 31, 1973 and $1,773,000, at June 30, 1974	19,390
Bank premises and equipment.............................	28,448
Accrued interest receivable	22,827
Other assets	24,211
	$2,835,993

Liabilities and net worth

Due to depositors	$2,551,395
Other deposits	24,937
Borrowed funds	62,402
Other liabilities	7,291
Net worth	
Surplus Fund	50,612
Contingency Surplus Fund	64,550
General Reserve	2,272
Undivided profits	72,534
Total net worth	189,968
	$2,835,993

Exhibit 4
Distribution of funds invested in different types of mortgages as of June 30, 1974 (percent)

	New York State	Adjoining states	Other states	Total
Residential properties: One-to-four family homes				
Government-backed mortgages	3.0	0.9	25.1	29.0
Conventional mortgages	1.5	0.3	0.5	2.3
Home mortgages	4.5	1.2	25.6	31.3
Multifamily residential properties				
Government-backed mortgages	4.3	0.6	2.5	7.4
Conventional mortgages	8.7	3.5	7.6	19.8
Multifamily mortgages	13.0	4.1	10.1	27.2
Commercial properties				
Office buildings	16.9	3.1	4.8	24.8
Store buildings	1.4	4.0	3.0	8.4
All other properties	4.2	2.7	1.4	8.3
Commercial mortgages	22.5	9.8	9.2	41.5
Distribution by geographical area	40.0	15.1	44.9	100.0

476

Exhibit 5

Yields on long-term investments

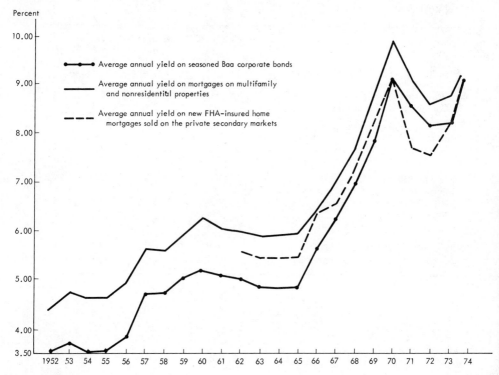

Exhibit 6

Recent investment strategy: Increase and (decrease) in investment ($ thousands)

| | Year ended December 31 | | | | First six months of 1974 |
	1970	1971	1972	1973	
Investment securities	1,913	148,407	230,199	39,858	(22,465)
Mortgages					
Residential properties:					
Government-backed (primarily single-family home mortgages)	(56,694)	(85,113)	(87,669)	(32,069)	(35,722)
Conventional (primarily large multifamily apartment complexes)	44,105	106,078	(9,321)	(45,429)	25,210
Commercial properties	47,320	87,479	173,059	111,386	11,478
Change in investment assets	36,644	256,851	306,268	73,746	(21,499)

Exhibit 7

A. Securities portfolio of the Manhattan Mutual Bank, June 30, 1974
(Dollar amounts in thousands)

	Book value	Percent of total assets at book value	Market value
Bonds			
U.S. Treasury	$ 51,000	1.8%	$ 44,075
Federal agencies	4,600	0.2	4,238
U.S. guaranteed	25,462	0.9	22,754
State and municipal	94,630	3.3	84,034
Corporates			
Railroad	6,160	0.2	4,889
Public utility	281,815	9.9	248,214
Industrial	42,665	1.5	36,514
World Bank	3,994	0.1	3,802
Canadian	25,076	0.9	21,409
Total bonds	$535,402	18.8%	$469,929
Stocks			
Common	54,196	1.9	58,333
Preferred	80,982	2.9	52,864
Total stocks	$135,178	4.8%	$111,197
Total securities portfolio	$670,580	23.6%	$581,126

B. Maturity distribution of debt securities based on face amount, June 30, 1974
(Dollar amounts in thousands)

	U.S. government obligations	State and municipal	Other securities	Total
Within one year	$ 105	—	$ 1,163	$ 1,268
One to five years	27,189	—	5,796	32,985
Five to ten years	28,702	$ 100	32,136	60,938
After ten years	26,101	105,892	345,026	477,019
Total	$82,097	$105,992	$384,121	$572,210

Exhibit 8
Distribution of deposits

Type of account and nominal interest rate	December 31					June 30, 1974
	1969	1970	1971	1972	1973	
Conventional accounts						
4.75%	1.2%	—	—	—	—	—
5.00	98.8	84.0%	74.3%	67.1%	—	—
5.25	—	—	—	—	57.1%	56.1%
Time accounts						
5.00%	—	—	—	—	—	—
5.25	—	0.1	0.1	0.2	—	—
5.75	—	2.0	1.6	1.9	1.6	0.6
6.00	—	13.5	23.0	28.6	23.1	15.5
6.50	—	—	—	—	2.9	5.7
6.75	—	—	—	—	4.2	5.3
7.00	—	—	—	—	1.2	1.2
Above 7.00	—	—	—	—	8.3	14.3
Other	—	0.4	1.0	2.2	1.6	1.3
Total ...	100%	100%	100%	100%	100%	100%
Total deposits (in thousands)	$1,829,857	$1,891,492	$2,205,148	$2,519,456	$2,611,515	$2,551,395

Exhibit 9

MANHATTAN MUTUAL BANK
Condensed Income Statements
($ thousands)

| | Year ended December 31 | | | | | Six months ending June 30 | |
	1969	1970	1971	1972	1973	1973	1974
Income from interest and fees	$118,058	$119,336	$139,082	$169,219	$190,187	$92,772	$95,655
Other income	1,520	1,688	2,468	4,012	3,342	1,772	1,438
Operating income	$119,578	$121,024	$141,550	$173,231	$193,529	$94,544	$97,093
Dividends and interest to depositors	(91,356)	(92,801)	(107,144)	(128,293)	(143,155)	(68,827)	(75,484)
Operating expenses	(18,928)	(20,495)	(22,877)	(25,000)	(29,762)	(14,931)	(16,704)
Income before federal taxes, securities gains (losses) and extraordinary items	$ 9,294	$ 7,728	$ 11,529	$ 19,938	$ 20,612	$10,786	$ 4,905
Federal taxes	(2,951)	(2,286)	(3,549)	(6,199)	(4,398)	(2,561)	471
Securities gains (losses) net of tax	(3,035)	(2,252)	(4,456)	(4,974)	(1,638)	101	(1,102)
Extraordinary credits (tax carry-forwards)	149	208	—	960	168	168	—
Net income	$ 3,457	$ 3,398	$ 3,434	$ 9,725	$ 14,744	$ 8,494	$ 4,274

Exhibit 10

MANHATTAN MUTUAL BANK
Cash Flow Analysis
Sources and (Uses)
($ thousands)

	Year ended December 31				
	1969	*1970*	*1971*	*1972*	*1973*
Amortization	$104,657	$ 90,008	$ 96,387	$135,526	$156,153
Operating income	119,578	121,024	141,550	173,231	193,529
	$224,235	$211,032	$237,937	$308,757	$349,682
Operating expense	(18,928)	(20,495)	(22,877)	(25,000)	(29,762)
Taxes and the effect of noncash items	(9,962)	(8,253)	(12,623)	(16,732)	(15,762)
Funds provided by operations after tax	$195,345	$182,284	$202,437	$267,025	$304,158
Net changes in miscellaneous assets and liabilities	6,941	2,403	(8,671)	14,000	(5,560)
Gross cash flow before deposit flows and investment	$202,286	$184,687	$193,766	$281,025	$298,598
Deposits, withdrawals	(103,774)	(31,165)	206,512	186,015	(51,096)
Cash flow before reinvestment and new investment	$ 98,512	$153,522	$400,278	$467,040	$247,502
Gross investment	(102,299)	(125,797)	(419,191)	(443,010)	(226,556)
Net change in cash	$(3,787)	$ 27,725	$(18,913)	$ 24,030	$ 20,946

Note: Gross investment includes primarily investment in mortgages and securities.

Exhibit 11
Ceiling rates on savings and time deposits: New regulations effective July 1973

	Commercial banks (percent)	*Thrift institutions (percent)*
Regular savings accounts	5.00	5.25
Time deposits		
90-day to 1-year maturity	5.50	5.75
1 to 2½ years	6.00	6.50
More than 2½ years	6.50	6.75
Minimum denomination of $1,000:		
4 years or more*	7.25	7.50

* As revised, November 1973.

Exhibit 12
Market value of a fixed-rate financial asset for a range of market rates of interest*

Maturity (years)	Market value at prevailing market rate of interest				
	6 percent	7 percent	8 percent	9 percent	10 percent
5	$1,042	$1,000	$960	$918	$886
10	$1,073	$1,000	$932	$871	$815
20	$1,114	$1,000	$901	$817	$744

* Assumptions: Face value of the financial asset is $1,000. Coupon rate is 7 percent. Principal is repaid at maturity.

3. Gotham Savings Bank

On the afternoon of April 12, 1976, James Munson, the chairman of the Gotham Savings Bank, leaned back in his chair and considered the current position of his institution. Following the depressing experience of 1974, the most recent 15 months had been a welcome and encouraging period. Deposit inflows at Gotham had been very strong, just as they had been for all deposit institutions. Because of those inflows, the bank not only had a growing deposit base, but a relatively liquid position.

While these developments were very encouraging, a new set of issues was beginning to trouble Munson. Several weeks before, he had read a recent speech by the president of the Federal Home Loan Bank of San Francisco, focusing on some concerns in the savings and loan industry. (Excerpts from this speech are shown in Exhibit 1.) He was wondering about the relevance of these concerns for his institution and for mutual savings banks in general. Shortly thereafter, the treasurer of Gotham Savings had suggested that it was time to consider adjusting some of Gotham's deposit rates. In response, Munson had called a meeting of the Senior Management Committee for the morning of April 13 to consider this possibility. This afternoon, April 12, Munson wanted to gather his own thoughts in preparation for the meeting.

THE GOTHAM SAVINGS BANK

The Gotham Savings Bank was one of the oldest and largest of the mutual savings banks in New York City. Throughout its history, it had enjoyed an excellent relationship with its depositors and a reputation as a sound and well-managed institution. A recent balance sheet and statement of net operating earnings for Gotham Savings are shown in Exhibits 2 and 3. Some further information on the deposits and assets of Gotham Savings are shown in Exhibit 4.

RECENT COMPETITION FOR DEPOSITS

Like other deposit institutions, Gotham Savings offered both the conventional savings account and a range of possible time deposits to its prospective depositors. The existing regulatory ceilings for deposit rates

482

of both commercial banks and thrift institutions are shown in Table 1, including both the nominal ceiling and the corresponding "effective annual yield" which could be obtained using daily compounding.

Table 1
Ceilings on deposit rates (Deposits less than $100,000)

Maturity/type	Mutual savings banks		Commercial banks	
	Nominal rate	(Effective annual yield)	Nominal rate	(Effective annual yield)
Passbook savings	5¼	(5.47%)	5	(5.20%)
Time certificates (less than $100,000)				
90 days to 1 year	5¾	(6.00)	5½	(5.73)
1 to 2½ years	6½	(6.81)	6	(6.27)
2½ or more years	6¾	(7.08)	6½	(6.81)
Minimum denomination of $1,000				
4–6 years	7½	(7.90)	7¼	(7.63)
6 years or more	7¾	(8.17)	7½	(7.90)

Gotham Savings was currently offering the maximum rate on all these accounts, including the advantage of daily compounding, which gave their depositors the highest available "effective annual yields." Indeed, most of the other mutual savings banks in New York were also continuing to offer these rates. In recent weeks, however, one of the largest savings banks in New York had begun to back away from the highest of these yields. In particular, this savings bank was offered only 6¾% (or 7.08 effective annual yield) on all time deposits with a maturity of 2½ years or more, for their highest available rate.

OPEN-MARKET RATES AND DEPOSIT INFLOWS

The recent decline in open-market rates shown in Exhibit 5 was probably beginning to motivate more than one savings institution to at least consider lowering its rates. As open-market rates had fallen over the recent 18 months, the deposit rates of savings institutions had become more than competitive with various open market alternatives. The current structure of interest rates is shown in Exhibit 6. James Munson wondered if savings institutions might have possibly become "too rate-competitive" now. The rather strong savings inflows at Gotham Savings, and throughout the thrift industry, had been led by the inflows into conventional (passbook) savings accounts, a rather surprising development in view of recent years' experience. Indeed, fully 50 percent of the total net inflows in the most recent year had been in savings accounts. For the first quarter of 1976, the net deposit inflows (excluding interest credited) at Gotham had been $118 million, of which slightly more than half was accounted for by the net inflows into passbook savings accounts. Recent gross savings inflows into the various maturities of time certificates at Gotham Savings are shown in Table 2.

Table 2
Gross inflows (new accounts and renewals) into various time certificates for the three months ending March 1976 (Certificates less than $100,000)

Nominal rates	Millions of $	Percent of total
5.75	$ 40.8	20%
6.50	71.4	35
6.75	20.4	10
7.50	38.7	19
7.75	32.6	16
	$203.9	100%

The staff of Gotham Savings believed that a surprisingly large proportion (perhaps somewhat more than half) of the dollar inflows into the 90-day 5.75 percent accounts were in deposits over $50,000. Munson was both pleased with the prospect of this deposit growth but somewhat concerned over how stable it might be. He wondered how the character of these inflows should affect Gotham's investment policy, particularly if they turned out to be less stable funds. While Munson had learned not to put much faith in the interest rate forecasts of economists, these forecasts were currently predicting that long-term interest rates might continue to decline for a while. Later in the year, however, both short-term and long-term rates might rise somewhat with the expanding economy.

COSTS AND MARGINS

One of the more difficult problems in setting deposit rates was estimating the various costs of deposit services. From within Gotham's total costs, it was possible to estimate that at least 22 basis points, attributable directly to state and city taxes and FDIC assessments, applied to each dollar of deposits. Thus, the minimum variable cost of each new deposit dollar was at least the effective annual yield to the depositor, plus 22 basis points. After this, though, the cost allocation problem became extremely difficult. Most of the remaining costs were attributable to the operations of the branches and to general overhead in the institution's head office. The majority of these costs appeared to be fixed, at least in the short run. The savings accounts generally had a higher rate of deposit, withdrawal, and other transaction activity associated with them. Thus, to the extent that Gotham attempted to allocate costs, presumably more of these costs should be attributed to savings accounts than to the less transaction-oriented time certificates. Furthermore, small accounts tended to have almost as many transactions as large accounts so that the effective costs per deposit dollar for the smaller accounts were substantially higher. Roughly speaking, the 80 percent of the Gotham's accounts that were the smallest accounted for only about 20 percent of the total deposit dollars, and almost surely accounted for at least half of the operating costs. It was not clear, however, exactly how to allocate operating costs. Indeed, Munson was not sure it really would make sense to allocate these costs at all, given the relatively fixed nature of a savings bank's operations.

Similarly, it was not clear how to determine the appropriate average investment rate for new funds. In recent years, the Gotham Savings had been investing largely in commercial and multifamily residential mortgages, and corporate bonds. In the portfolio, however, there were still some relatively low-yielding home mortgages that had been purchased many years ago. The income from this mix of assets is shown in Exhibit 3.

Most recently, many of the new deposit inflows had been invested in government securities, to rebuild liquidity, and in longer term corporate bonds for investment income. In addition, the bank had recently been investing some funds in GNMA "pass-through" securities, essentially mortgage-backed government insured securities. Because of the recession and difficulties in real estate markets, almost no money had been directly invested in mortgages recently. As the economy recovered, however, the Gotham Savings Bank hoped to be able to invest a reasonable percentage of its available funds in the relatively high rate commercial and multi-family mortgages.

It was tempting to use a relatively simple proxy, like the new Aa ultility rate for corporate bonds (which now stood at 8.60 percent) for the incremental rate at which long-term funds could be currently invested. One of the difficulties with such a long-term rate, however, was the prospective volatility of some of the new deposit inflows. To the extent that some of these funds might not be stable, they should presumably be invested in intermediate or probably even short-term securities. And, of course, the obtainable yields in these markets were considerably lower than long-term yields, as shown in Exhibit 6.

THE REACTION OF COMPETING INSTITUTIONS

One of the crucial aspects of a potential change in deposit rates would be the reaction of other institutions. As mentioned earlier, one of New York's savings banks had already reduced some of its deposit rates. And the commercial banks had also been altering some of their rates (with the prime rate stuck in the 6¾ percent range, and loan demand continuing to be very weak, it was not clear that commercial banks would want to aggressively compete for consumer savings). In particular, one large money-center bank with an extensive retail branch system in the New York City area had lowered its passbook rate below the applicable ceilings and suspended daily compounding on most of its accounts. Munson had requested a survey of the prevailing deposit rates in the New York metropolitan area, the important findings of which are shown in Exhibit 7.

If the Gotham Savings Bank lowered some of its deposit rates and other institutions followed, James Munson believed they might all be better off. But he was concerned whether all of these institutions would follow. If most other institutions didn't follow, Mr. Munson was concerned both about losing deposits, and about damaging the bank's reputation for providing competitive deposit rates.

On several occasions in recent years, another large savings bank in New York had lowered its deposit rates, perhaps prematurely as it turned out, and few other institutions followed. As open-market rates turned around and headed higher, this savings bank again rejoined the industry norms. Munson wondered if they had lost some of their market share and their consumer franchise in the process. He wondered, even if it was obvious that deposit rates were too high, whether the Gotham Savings should try to be the last bank to lower rates. That way, they could always claim to have offered the highest rates in New York. In short, he wondered whether he should strive to be a price leader, or a price follower, in deposit rates.

THE MARKET FOR HOUSEHOLD DEPOSITS IN NEW YORK CITY

In the New York City area, the largest mutual savings banks and large commercial banks dominated the competition for individual savings. Since the early 60s, the large commercial banks of New York City—Citibank, Chase, Manufacturers Hanover, Bankers' Trust and Chemical Bank—had intensified the competition for the savings of individuals. These large commercial banks were among the central intermediaries of the financial and economic system, and they viewed the household savings market as a large potential source of relatively low-cost funds. Despite the unfavorable deposit rate regulations, these commercial banks had been able to compete for savings by providing individuals with a wide range of financial services, including free checking accounts, credit cards, and consumer loans. In addition, the large commercial banks competed by maintaining an extensive network of branch offices which were designed to provide convenience and a high service level to individuals.

The mutual savings banks, in contrast, had a limited number of retail branches. Gotham, for example, had only 11 well-located branches, compared to over 100 branches for some of the largest commercial banks. Furthermore, the mutual savings banks offered a much more limited set of services, confined primarily to passbook savings accounts, time certificates, and certain other minor services. They had no checking accounts, no credit cards, and no consumer loans. The chief competitive advantage of the savings banks was their higher deposit rates. Until 1973, regulatory ceilings had allowed mutual savings banks to offer deposit rates that were 0.5 percent higher than the comparable commercial bank deposit rates. In 1973, the differential was reduced to 0.25 percent for most types of deposits. Nonetheless, mutual savings banks had retained an enviable market share. The vast majority of household deposit dollars was kept in the form of savings or time deposit (where they earned interest) rather than demand deposits. Furthermore, most of these savings and time deposits were still held in mutual savings banks, not in commercial banks. Various marketing studies had indicated that, relative to commercial banks, the customers of mutual savings banks tended to be older, have a higher average income, and hold greater average deposit balances.

LONG-RUN CONSIDERATIONS

Many observers predicted that the market for consumer deposits would become increasingly more competitive in the future. Nationwide, the differences between commercial banks and thrift institutions were beginning to blur, as each moved more aggressively into some of the traditional functions of other financial intermediaries. Within New England, thrift institutions could offer "NOW" accounts, essentially interest-bearing checking accounts, and this was expected to spread to other areas. Nationwide, many consumer deposit institutions were offering more and better services for their depositers. Within the New York City area, the largest commercial banks were now investing substantial sums into the development of various consumer-oriented EFTS systems (electronic funds transfer systems) that most experts believed would become the technological basis of future retail banking. The New York City savings banks, including Gotham, had been actively lobbying for a bill which would permit them to offer checking accounts. Commercial bankers opposed this bill, unless it also permitted the commercial banks to offer the same rates on all deposits as thrift institutions, removing the current ¼ percent differential. While it was difficult to predict exactly when or if many of these changes would occur, most observers predicted a rapid future pace of increasing competition and change for New York City retail deposit institutions.

ALTERNATIVES

If Gotham Savings were to lower some deposit rates, there were several alternatives to consider. On the one hand, they could lower rates on the longest maturity of time certificates, the nominal 7½ and 7¾ certificates for these were the highest rates offered and barely earned an "adequate return," even when invested long term. On the other hand, it was not clear that these longer term certificates were the most "out-of-line" with their open-market equivalents. Furthermore, Munson was concerned about some of the large sums that seemed to be moving into the 90-day 5¾ percent deposits, and wondered if these should be discouraged by lower rates. Finally, from a marketing point of view, some of the funds in regular savings accounts were probably the least interest-sensitive. He wondered if Gotham could minimize possible deposit losses by lowering rates on these accounts rather than tampering with the rates on what he judged to be the more interest-sensitive time certificates.

In the past, Gotham Savings had adjusted its deposit rates by explicitly changing the nominal rate within the customary maturity ranges (these ranges stemmed from the maturity ranges specified in regulatory ceilings). But this was, of course, not the only means for altering the effective deposit rates. One of Munson's key subordinates had been arguing recently that there were more subtle, and thus better, methods for adjusting rates. He had proposed in a recent memorandum that rates should be adjusted by altering the form of compounding (from daily to monthly, quarterly, and so forth) and by shifting the maturity ranges associated with each of the posted nominal rates. Thus, Gotham could continue to post the same nominal rates, apparently without change, and yet significantly reprice its deposits.

Furthermore, he argued, Gotham Savings should explore and eventually use some of the sophisticated pricing policies pioneered by the commercial banks, such as minimum balances and fees, to change its effective cost of funds. In the past, these suggestions had not been too warmly received by other senior officers in the bank. They believed that the more subtle deposit changes and pricing policies would surely confuse their customers and probably confuse their own "new accounts consultants" who served potential new customers. In addition, they believed that a more complex pricing structure for deposits would be more difficult for other savings banks and institutions to understand and follow, and thus dilute the opportunities for price leadership within the market. While Munson was sympathetic with these concerns, he wondered if now was the time to more fully consider some of these other alternatives.

PREPARING FOR THE MEETING

James Munson wanted to discuss these decisions within the Senior Management Committee, but he knew that he should think about the possible directions he would prefer. Before the next morning's meeting, therefore, he wanted to consider a range of issues. In the long run, what would be most important to the bank: today's deposit growth, market position, income, or reserves? What deposit rate structure would make sense for Gotham Savings relative to the open market, to investment opportunities, and to other deposit insitutions? In the sense of both strategy and tactics, was now an appropriate time for the Gotham Savings Bank to adjust its deposit rates? And, if so, how should this be done?

Exhibit 1

Excerpts from an Address at the California
Savings and Loan League Management Conference
by Dr. Maurice Mann, President
Federal Home Loan Bank of San Francisco
March 1976

A cursory glance at the news about the savings and loan industry in March 1976 would undoubtedly lead an observer to conclude that S & Ls have seldom been in better financial shape. Savings inflows were at high levels in 1975 and have been tremendous in early 1976. Liquidity is high and still rising, and S & L borrowings from the FHL banks and other sources of funds are significantly below levels of a year or two ago. Furthermore, mortgage loan deliquencies have not generally been a problem during the recent period.

Despite all of this, S & Ls do not have reason to be complacent.

I doubt that anyone in this audience would disagree that, during recent years, the savings and loan industry has faced increasingly intense competition for consumer savings. Not only have commercial banks become much more aggressive competitors for savings deposits, but credit unions also have become a more formidable factor. In addition, investment outlets such as money-market mutual funds have attracted large consumer dollars.

At the same time that these sources of competition were developing strength, consumers also became increasingly sophisticated in money matters, quickly learning how to shift investments among alternative instruments in order to maximize returns without sacrificing safety and liquidity beyond reasonable limits. Certainly the trend toward more vigorous competition for liabilities will intensify in the future, tending to raise the cost of such funds.

Moreover, as S & Ls and other restructured depository institutions further diversify assets in order to serve all of the financial needs of consumers, gross rates of return on such investments, on balance, will tend to be reduced. In brief, spreads will narrow further and S & Ls will need to rely upon increased asset turnover to maintain or raise earnings.

In taking on expanded powers and assets and liabilities, S & Ls will need to focus more attention on the bottom line of the income statement and on

Exhibit 1 (continued)

the equity portion of the balance sheet. The days are gone when we can afford the luxury of preoccupation with savings or asset growth, simply for the sake of growth.

In the past, the growth syndrome seemed to work because earnings and net worth generally took care of themselves. But in the future, with increased competition and new untried powers for S & Ls, the road to success will concentrate on earnings and net worth, with growth becoming—at best—a residual.

Let me cite a few numbers that may be a bit surprising—if not disturbing. As you know, a basic measure of the capital adequacy of depository institutions compares total capital or net worth with the total assets of an institution. What has been the recent trend of capital adequacy for banks and S & Ls, according to this measure?

From the end of 1968 through 1975, the capital adequacy of commercial banks remained in a narrow band around 7 percent. In contrast, the same measure for all savings and loan associations declined steadily, from a high of 7.2 percent at the close of 1968 to a low of 5.9 percent at the end of 1975.

These numbers suggest that S & Ls should shift their objectives from growth for the sake of growth, to net income and net worth—particularly when it is remembered that the numbers are a reflection of the maturation of the industry and its competitive environment.

Obviously, to improve earnings, there are some things that could—and perhaps should—be done. For one thing, you could stop daily compounding of interest on savings; you could also discontinue paying interest from the first of the month on deposits received by the tenth; and you can end premium give-aways, and even charge fees for some of the services that are provided free to savers.

These suggestions may sound like heresy to some of you, but they certainly are worth considering—and worth doing—even if they fail to provide a miracle cure for the malady of a shrinking capital base relative to assets.

Related to this question are the cost implications of the industry's fight to retain Regulation Q, a fight that, on some grounds, is understandable. Of particular significance is the impact of Regulation Q on your modus operandi and the bottom line. When interest rates on investments that compete with savings fall below Regulation Q ceilings, S & Ls continue to pay above-market interest rates; in other words, the ceilings become a floor on rates.

At the same time, however—and what has happened in 1976 illustrates my point precisely—the rates you charge on mortgages decline in step with market rates. Thus, the greatest volume of lending by S & Ls tends to occur when current returns on newly acquired assets are declining and/or are relatively low, but rates paid on liabilities are above the market.

But what happens when rates are high and/or rising above Regulation Q limits? Ceilings prevent S & Ls from attracting deposits when current market rates on mortgages are also high or rising. As a result, S & Ls are forced to cut back lending volume when opportunities exist to lock in relatively

Exhibit 1 (*concluded*)

high mortgage yields at a fixed rate for long periods of time. The introduction of variable mortgages represents some relief, but it would appear to be a cumbersome and politically troublesome attempt to circumvent the situation of adverse yield selection by S & Ls.

In this regard, one could argue that the removal of Regulation Q would be a more powerful and, in the long run, more beneficial approach, particularly if it were accompanied by other major structural changes. As part of a complete package of restructuring proposals, the elimination of Q has much in its favor. And, pending the elimination of interest-rate ceilings on deposits, there is nothing in the law or regulations preventing S & Ls from lowering rates paid on savings when market rates decline below those seemingly cemented into Regulation Q.

I know that some of you would prefer that the regulators would make this decision for you and lower the permissible ceiling. Speaking only for myself, I believe this to be an undesirable approach in that it totally intrudes on the prerogatives of management.

As a postscript to my comments on Regulation Q, is it a surprise to anyone in this audience that savings flows have poured into S & Ls in record volumes during early 1976—when market rates are well below the ceilings? What is the cost of carrying excess liquidity at levels not seen in several years? At the beginning of my talk I commented that, in early 1976, the S & Ls have seldom been in better financial shape. To this statement I added that, nonetheless, S & Ls should not be complacent.

Exhibit 2

GOTHAM SAVINGS BANK
Statement of Condition
December 31, 1975
(In thousands)

Assets

Cash and due from banks	
Plus: One-day loans to banks	$ 96,436
Investment securities	
U.S. government obligations	180,140
State and municipal obligations	81,783
Other debt obligations	438,590
Corporate stocks	125,788
Mortgage loans on real estate	
Less: Unearned discount	2,195,759
Other loans	
Less: Unearned discount	19,280
Bank premises and equipment	32,542
Accrued Interest Receivable	24,118
Other assets	26,460
	$3,220,898

Liabilities and Net Worth

Due to depositors	$2,955,430
Other deposits	26,935
Borrowed funds	19,972
Other liabilities	10,860
Net worth	
Surplus fund	55,619
Contingency surplus fund	70,022
General reserve	2,476
Undivided profits	79,584
	$3,220,898

Exhibit 3

1975 operating data as a percent of average deposits

Income		7.74%
Total expenses (excluding interest)		1.18
Employee compensation and benefits		0.45
Advertising		0.09
Occupancy		0.18
Other expenses		0.46
Net before interest and taxes		6.56
Depositors' interest	6.06	
Taxes		
Federal	—	
State/local	0.17	
Net operating earnings		0.33

Exhibit 4

December 31, 1975

Approximate distribution of deposits
  Conventional accounts (5.25 percent rate)
    passbook savings 55.9%
  Time accounts
    5.75 to 6.75 (nominal rate) 23.9
    7.00 and over (nominal rate) 18.8
    Other 1.4

                                                    100.0%

Effective rate on average deposits in 1975 .... 6.06
Approximate distribution of investments
    (at book value)
  U.S. government obligations 6.1
  State and municipal obligations 2.7
  Corporate bonds 13.4
  Other bonds 1.0
  Corporate stock 4.1
  Mortgage loans
    Residential—insured or guaranteed* 26.8
    Residential—conventional† 15.4
    Commercial‡ 29.8

                                                    100%

* One-to-four family residential mortgages, government-insured, most of which were purchased many years ago.

† Mostly multifamily residential mortgages on apartment buildings, although a small number of one-to-four family mortgages are also included.

‡ Mortgages on income producing properties such as office buildings, shopping centers, and so forth.

Exhibit 5

Money-market and long-term interest rates (Monthly averages of daily figures)

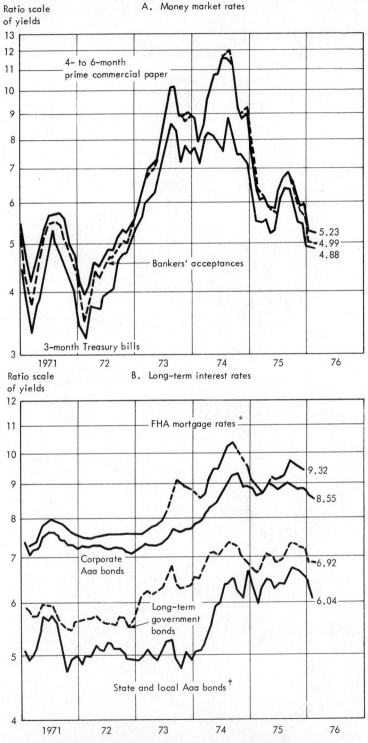

Ratio scale
of yields

A. Money market rates

4- to 6-month
prime commercial paper

5.23
4.99
4.88

Bankers' acceptances

3-month Treasury bills

1971   72   73   74   75   76

Ratio scale
of yields

B. Long-term interest rates

FHA mortgage rates *

9.32

8.55

Corporate
Aaa bonds

6.92

Long-term
government
bonds

6.04

State and local Aaa bonds †

1971   72   73   74   75   76

Latest data plotted: February. Prepared by Federal Reserve Bank of St. Louis.

* FHA 30-year mortgages. Dashed lines indicate data not available.
† Monthly averages of Thursday figures. Latest data plotted: FHA—December;
others—February. Prepared by Federal Reserve Bank of St. Louis.

Exhibit 6
Current interest rates (April 12, 1976)

Maturity	Treasury bills/notes	Federal agencies	Negotiable CDs (Prime)
One month	4.80%		4.95%
3 months	4.88		5.10
1 year	5.86	5.95%	
3 years	6.80	6.95	
5 years	7.20	7.35	
Intermediate maturities			
7-year Treasury notes		7.34%	
7-year federal agency notes		7.65	
Medium-term Aa utility bonds		8.10	
GNMA pass-thru (7¼%)		8.14	
Long-term securities			
20-year federal agency		8.00%	
New long-term "Aaa" utility		8.38	
New long-term "Aa" utility		8.60	
New long-term "A" utility		8.90	
Mortgage rate on income-producing properties (office buildings, apartments, etc.)		Varies with property (in vicinity of 9% or better)	

Exhibit 7
Excerpts from a brief market survey of rates offered on certificates (April 1976, NYC)

	Paying maximum effective rates allowed	Comments
Savings banks		
Savings bank A	Yes	
Savings bank B	Yes	
Savings bank C	No	6¾ percent is highest nominal rate offered
Savings bank D	Yes	
Savings bank E	Yes	
Savings bank F	Yes	
Commercial banks		
Commercial bank A	Yes	
Commercial bank B	Yes	
Commercial bank C	No	Less than maximum compounding lowers effective rates. And, 7¼ percent is highest nominal rate offered
Commercial bank D	Yes	
Commercial bank E	No	Less than maximum compounding lowers effective rate. Passbook savings rate is below ceiling

4. E. I. Du Pont de Nemours & Company-1976

In May 1976, Roger Brookes, Financial Vice President of Du Pont, was formulating a framework to evaluate alternative debt refundings. Over the last several years, Du Pont had accumulated $550 million in short-term debt. While some of this debt was held in foreign currencies for exchange rate protection, fully $400 million had been raised in the U.S. commercial paper market and from U.S. banks. The commercial paper rate was now a low 5 to 5½ percent, but Brookes knew it had been as high as 12 percent within the last two years, and he felt uncomfortable holding so much debt with an average maturity of only 20 days. With long-term rates now relatively low (8 to 8½ percent), he felt it was a good time to refund some of the short-term debt. Preliminary investigation had narrowed the refunding options to either ten-year intermediate term notes or 30-year long-term debentures.

THE COMPANY

E. I. Du Pont de Nemours and Company, one of the oldest American companies, had been founded in 1802 by E. I. Du Pont as a gunpowder manufacturer. It had long since diversified its operations into most phases of the chemical industry and was now the largest chemical company in the United States and the 33d largest industrial company (by sales) in the world. Du Pont had some 1,700 product lines, almost all of which were sold to other manufacturers rather than directly to consumers. The products ranged from chemical commodities to proprietary products, such as Dacron® and Teflon®, which had been created by Du Pont's extensive R & D effort ($336 million in 1975).

Du Pont had always been considered one of *the* AAA rated manufacturing companies, of which there were only six in 1976. For many years Du Pont had had virtually no debt, and in the early 1970s, debt was still only 10 percent of capitalization.

496

CURRENT FINANCIAL SITUATION

In 1974–75, however, a combination of events had caused Du Pont to experience a large need for external financing (see Exhibits 1–5 for financial statements). The recession had caused a decline in unit sales, although dollar sales had risen due to price increases. Raw material and energy costs, both affected by the drastic increase in petroleum costs, had risen faster than prices, causing net income to drop from 10 percent of sales in 1973 to 4 percent of sales in 1975. The cost of a large capital investment program, planned and begun before 1974, had increased more than 50 percent as construction costs skyrocketed. Working capital, primarily inventory, had increased $600 million in 1974, due in large measure to the increases in raw material costs.

Management had responded quickly to the large cash need, switching to LIFO inventory accounting to decrease taxable income, and cutting the common stock dividend from $5.75 per share in 1973 to $4.25 per share in 1975. Still, in 1974, Du Pont had been obliged to issue their first public long-term debt since the 1920s, a $500 million issue consisting of $350 million in 8.45 percent, 30-year debentures and $150 million in 8 percent, 7-year notes. At the time this had been the largest public debt issue ever undertaken by an industrial company.

The cash need had continued through 1975, and Du Pont had responded by increasing its short-term debt to the current $550 million level. (See exhibits 3, 4, and 5.) Though still AAA rated, Du Pont's debt ratio had increased to 27 percent of capitalization, and fixed-charge coverage had dropped to 4.6 times from 32 times in 1973. Du Pont maintained over $1 billion of bank credit lines, largely unused, to back up its commercial paper borrowings and to insure financial flexibility.

While profits had improved dramatically in the first three months of 1976, Brookes thought it unlikely that the debt acquired in 1974 and 1975 would be retired within the foreseeable future. The chemical industry had become very competitive, and other companies were approaching Du Pont in size and technology. It appeared that the projected levels of retained earnings alone might not be sufficient to finance the growth that Du Pont was planning, especially because capital expenditures were expected to continue at the $1 billion level for the next two years. Thus, he expected the debt to be a part of Du Pont's capital structure for the foreseeable future, although he doubted that another debt issue would be required for at least the next five years.

INTEREST RATES

Du Pont's board of directors had authorized a $400 million debt issue, up to $200 million of which could be in 10-year notes and the balance in

30-year debentures. This was in line with what the company's investment bankers felt the market could absorb without a large increase in yield.

The current yield curves, for both U.S. Treasury and federal agency securities are shown in Exhibit 6. Brookes believed, on the basis of current market conditions, that a Du Pont 30-year AAA callable debenture could be sold with a yield in the vicinity of 8½ percent. On the other hand, a ten-year note could be sold for considerably less. He had received various estimates of the cost savings for the ten-year notes, ranging from 50 to 80 basis points, depending upon the market conditions at the time of the offering.

Brookes believed that future interest rates, particularly future intermediate and long-term rates, would be dependent upon the future course of inflation. As usual, though, the financial and economic system seemed to be buffeted by various crosscurrents, which made inflation very difficult to predict. The current concensus of "experts" seemed to center around an expected inflation rate of 5 to 6 percent for the foreseeable future, though some forecasters were predicting considerably less, and some considerably more. Brookes felt that as long as the concensus predictions remained at these levels, long-term interest rates might not drop much lower and, in fact, might drift back up to their 1974–1975 levels (see Exhibit 7). Thus he felt that this was a good time to refund the short-term debt with an intermediate or long-term issue.

THE CHOICE

It had been decided that Du Pont would proceed with the entire $400 million of new debt, issuing either $400 million of the 8.5 percent (estimated yield) 30-year debentures, or a combination of the debentures and up to $200 million of the less costly 10 year notes. Du Pont's investment bankers seemed to believe that the market could probably absorb up to $300 million of the long-term debentures without a perceptible increase in yield. On the other hand, a $400 million long-term issue might require an increase in yield (over 8½ percent) to be successfully sold. As always, though, it was difficult to be precise about these market effects.

The 30-year debentures would be structured with a sinking fund requirement starting in 1987, while the notes would have no sinking fund. The debentures would be callable by the company at any time, at declining premiums over par value, but they could not be refunded with money borrowed at less than 8.5 percent before 1986. The notes would not be callable until 1983, when they would be callable at par. (See Exhibit 8 for a complete description of call and sinking fund provisions.) These were essentially the "standard" provisions for long-term debentures and intermediate notes of industrial companies, and virtually all recent industrial issues contained similar provisions. Du Pont's investment bankers had invariably advised them to offer "standard" provisions on their debt securities for the markets reacted adversely to unconventional public debt issues.

Brookes considered these provisions relatively favorable to Du Pont, giving them, for example, a three-year "window" within which to refinance the ten-year notes and a five-year window at par for the debentures. This helped to maintain financial flexibility, which he considered a key goal of Du Pont's financial policy. He wondered which combination of the notes and bonds would maximize his long-run financial flexibility, and how much Du Pont, as one of the largest most creditworthy companies, should be willing to pay for this maximum flexibility. He wondered, additionally, what the expected long-run financing costs would be for the two different alternatives, given varying assumptions about the course of future interest rates.

Brookes had already reviewed the capital structure of other chemical companies (see Exhibits 9 and 10). He noted that, even after this debt issue, Du Pont would still be among the more conservatively financed industrial companies, and he believed there was no chance that this debt issue would alter Du Pont's AAA rating. He felt that the choice between issuing all long-term debt, and a package of intermediate and long-term debt, should depend in part on the outlook for future interest rates and the expected financing costs of the two alternatives. He soon expected a report from his investment bankers on the current market conditions and, in particular, more precise estimates of the probable financing costs of the two alternative in today's markets. In preparation for his meeting with the investment bankers, he wanted to formulate an appropriate framework for choosing between his various alternatives.

Exhibit 1

E. I. DU PONT DE NEMOURS & COMPANY
Consolidated Balance Sheet
(Millions of dollars)

	December 31, 1975	March 31, 1976 (Unaudited)
Assets		
Current Assets		
Cash and marketable securities	$ 139	$ 163
Accounts and notes receivable	1,163	1,289
Inventories	1,221	1,238
Prepaid expenses	51	57
Total Current Assets	$2,574	$2,747
Plants and properties	$8,585	$8,779
Less: Accumulated depreciation and obsolescence	4,993	5,096
Other assets		
Investment in nonconsolidated affiliates—at equity in net assets	$ 103	$ 99
Goodwill, patents, and trademarks	56	55
Other assets and investments	100	100
Total other assets	$ 259	$ 254
Total	$6,425	$6,685
Liabilities and stockholders' equity		
Current Liabilities		
Accounts payable	$ 400	$ 403
Short-term borrowings	540	552
Income taxes	171	261
Other accrued liabilities	187	225
Total current liabilities	$1,298	$1,441
Long-term borrowings	889	915
Deferred income taxes	126	127
Deferred investment tax credit	152	149
Other liabilities	42	39
Minority interests in consolidated subsidiaries	83	85
Stockholders' equity	3,835	3,930
Total	$6,425	$6,685

Exhibit 2

Consolidated Income Statement

	Years ended December 31					Three months ended March 31, (unaudited)	
	1971	*1972*	*1973*	*1974*	*1975*	*1975*	*1976*
Sales	$4,371	$4,948	$5,964	$6,910	$7,222	$1,597	$2,098
Other income	53	49	72	67	57	13	15
Total	$4,424	$4,997	$6,036	$6,977	$7,279	$1,610	$2,113
Cost of goods sold and other operating charges	$2,867	$3,262	$3,879	$5,052	$5,410	$1,220	$1,486
Selling, general and administrative expenses	489	520	595	675	709	183	192
Depreciation and obsolescence ...	399	418	450	506	580	141	153
Interest on borrowings	18	24	35	62	126	29	30
Total	$3,772	$4,224	$4,959	$6,295	$6,825	$1,153	$1,862
Earnings before income taxes and minority interests	$ 652	$ 774	$1,077	$ 682	$ 453	$ 36	$ 251
Provision for income taxes	289	353	481	267	177	13	112
Earnings before minority interests	$ 363	$ 421	$ 597	$ 415	$ 277	$ 23	$ 140
Minority interests in earnings of consolidated subsidiaries	7	7	11	11	5	2	2
Net income	$ 357	$ 415	$ 586	$ 404	$ 272	$ 19	$ 138
Dividends on preferred stock	10	10	10	10	10	3	3
Amount earned on common stock	$ 347	$ 405	$ 576	$ 394	$ 262	$ 19	$ 135
Earnings per share of common stock	$ 7.33	$ 8.50	$12.04	$ 8.20	$ 5.43	$ .39	$ 2.80
Dividends per share of common stock	$ 5.00	$ 5.45	$ 5.75	$ 5.50	$ 4.25	$ 1.25	$ 1.00
Ratio of earnings to fixed charges	18.2	18.3	19.2	8.6	3.9	2.0	7.7

Exhibit 3

Selected cash flow items (Millions of dollars)

	1971	1972	1973	1974	1975	First three months 1975	1976
Net income	$357	$415	$ 586	$ 404	$ 272	$ 21	$138
Plus noncash charges	422	446	495	545	601	128	155
Funds from operations	$779	$861	$1,081	$ 949	$ 873	$149	$293
Less							
Capital expenditures	472	553	771	1,008	1,036	286	248
Dividends......................	247	269	285	274	215	63	51
Increase (decrease) in working capital, excluding short-term debt	36	110	54	599	(78)	116	13
Cash surplus/(external financing need)	$ 24	$(71)	$(29)	$(932)	$(300)	$(366)	$(19)

Exhibit 4

Recent external financing of the company (Millions of dollars)

	1971	1972	1973	1974	1975	First three months 1975	1976
Equity (in compensation plans)	$21	$20	$19	$ 29	$ 26	$ 25	$ 8
Debt (net of redemptions)							
Short-term	(14)	44	48	152	220	361	12
Long-term	74	5	9	544	95	1	26
Total external financing	$60	$49	$57	$696	$315	$362	$38

Exhibit 5

Capitalization of the firm (Millions of dollars)

	End of the calendar year 1971	1972	1973	1974	1975	3/31/76
Short-term debt....................	$ 78	$ 118	$ 169	$ 321	$ 540	$ 552
Long-term debt	236	241	250	793	889	915
Total debt	$ 314	$ 359	$ 419	$1,114	$1,429	$1,467
Equity	3,095	3,268	3,594	3,753	3,835	3,930
Total debt and equity	3,109	3,627	4,013	4,867	5,264	5,397
Ratios						
Debt/total capital	9%	10%	10%	23%	27%	27%
Short-term debt/total debt	25	33	40	29	38	38

Exhibit 6
Yields to maturity as of May 13, 1976

U.S. Treasury securities	
3 months bills	5.20%
1-year bills	6.25
2-year coupons	6.92
3-year coupons	7.20
5-year coupons	7.48
7-year coupons	7.69
20-year coupons	8.08
30-year coupons	8.15
Federal Agency securities	
1-year	6.45%
3-year	7.35
5-year	7.70
7-year	7.85
10-year	8.00
20-year	8.30

Exhibit 7
Corporate bond yields by ratings

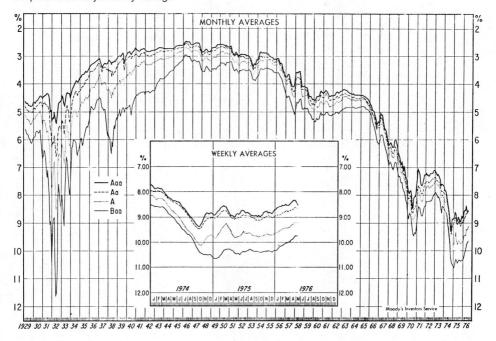

Exhibit 8
Terms of proposed debt issues

10-year notes
No sinking fund.
May be called at par after seven years.

30-year bonds
Sinking Fund: Starting after ten years, there would be a mandatory annual sinking fund payment of 3.95 percent.* Each year Du Pont would repurchase 3.95 percent of the par value of the bonds, either at par via a random drawing held by the trustee bank, or in the open market, at the company's option. The company also would have the option of increasing the sinking fund repurchase by up to another 3.95 percent per year. This optional increase could be counted as fulfilling any future year's sinking fund obligation.

Call provisions: May not be called for the purpose of refunding at less than 8.5 percent for ten years. Otherwise, may be called at any time at the following percentage of face value:

Year	Percentage	Year	Percentage	Year	Percentage
1976	108.50%	1986	105.10%	1996	101.70%
1977	108.16	1987	104.76	1997	101.36
1978	107.82	1988	104.42	1998	101.02
1979	107.48	1989	104.08	1999	100.68
1980	107.14	1990	103.74	2000	100.34
1981	106.80	1991	103.40	2001	100.00
1982	106.46	1992	103.06	2002	100.00
1983	106.12	1993	102.72	2003	100.00
1984	105.78	1994	102.38	2004	100.00
1985	105.44	1995	102.04	2005	100.00

* The 3.95 percent would be just enough to retire 75 percent of the bond issue in the 19 years of the sinking fund.

Exhibit 9

Comparative capitalization of some chemical companies as of fiscal year-end 1975

	As percent of total capitalization*			Short-term debt as percent of total debt
	Long-term debt	Equity (book value)	Deferred tax liabilities	
Allied Chemical	34%	57%	10%	3%
Dow Chemical	36	57	6	18
Du Pont	17	75	5	38
Monsanto	29	65	4	9
Union Carbide	28	61	6	14
Celanese Corp.	31	45	7	13

* In this table, total capitalization excludes short-term debt. The components may not add to 100 percent because of minority interests in consolidated subsidiaries.

Exhibit 10

Terms of outstanding debt issues of some chemical companies as of May 1976 (Includes only U.S. listed issues)

	Outstanding ($ millions)	Coupon	Maturity	Earliest call date*	Earliest call price	Sinking fund
Allied Chemical	122	5.2%	1991		103.3	Yes
	100	7⅞	1996	1981	103.5	Yes
	89	6.6	1993	1978	103.3	Yes
	75	9	2000	1985	104.1	Yes
	3	3.5	1978		100	Yes
	2	4	1978		100.25	Yes
	75	8⅜	1983	1981	100	No
Dow Chemical	61	4.35	1988		101.65	Yes
	88	6.7	1998		104.3	Yes
	92	7.75	1999	1979	104.25	Yes
	143	8⅞	2000	1980	104.9	Yes
	144	8.9	2000	1980	105.1	Yes
	100	7.4	2002	1982	104.4	Yes
	100	7⅝	2003	1983	104.6	Yes
	225	8.5	2005	1985	105.1	Yes
	200	8.5	2006	1986	105.1	Yes
Du Pont	350	8.45	2004	1984	105	Yes
	150	8.0	1981	1980	100	No
Monsanto	100	8.0	1985	1982	100	No
	175	8.5	2000	1985	104	Yes
	150	9⅛	2000	1980	104.4	Yes
Union Carbide	250	5.3	1997	1977	103	Yes
	300	8.5	2005	1985	105.1	Yes
Celanese Corp.	21	3.5	1976		100	Yes

* Blank means callable now. Date is when issue may be refunded at a lower rate.

5. The General Manufacturing Company

In late March 1976, William Paulson was considering some policy issues concerning General Manufacturing's pension fund. Paulson was the manager of Employment Benefit Plans at General Manufacturing. As such, he was responsible for various aspects of their pension and profit-sharing programs. He was currently considering whether fixed income investments should play a larger role within pension funds such as General's; and if so, whether marketable bonds or the new "guaranteed investment contracts" were more desirable as a form of fixed income investment.

General Manufacturing was a large producer of capital equipment (see Exhibit 1 for a set of recent financial statements). Most of General's employees were covered by one of several pension plans. In addition, General maintained several profit-sharing programs for selected groups of employees. The details of the several pension plans differed somewhat, but they were largely "defined benefit plans," where the retirement benefits were to be set for employees upon retirement at some computed percentage of their final salary.[1]

The expected future liabilities of these pension plans were funded by annual contributions from General to the pension fund. The actuaries estimated the expected future benefits to be paid under the plans, subject to various assumptions about life expectancy, and so forth. By discounting these back to the present (using an assumed "actuarial rate" of 6 percent), the actuaries compiled the present value of the expected future benefits. The annual contributions by General to the pension fund were then determined by comparing the current value of the pension fund to the present value of the future expected benefits, although the computation was performed in such a way that General's annual pension contributions

---

[1] Accordingly, the future benefits to be paid to already retired employees in the plan were fixed and could be determined on an actuarial basis, based on their expected lifetime. The future benefits to be paid to employees currently working at General were, however, much more difficult to project. While one could compute the annual benefits employees would receive if they retired today, the benefits they would actually receive depended on their salary increases before retirement as well as whatever changes might be made in the pension plan between now and then.

were smoothed over time.[2] As with all qualified pension plans, the pension expenses attributable to the plans were tax deductible, and the investment returns within the fund were tax exempt.

The current market value of the pension fund was $170 million. Approximately 70 percent of the fund was invested in common stock and the remainder in bonds. Four outside investment managers were retained to manage the accounts, three for the equities and one for the fixed income securities.

Several recent events had combined to make Paulson wonder about the relatively heavy investment of the pension fund in common stock. The drastic stock market decline of 1973–1974, when the value of the broad-based stock market averages had tumbled 45 percent, had heightened his concerns about the volatility of common stock. Furthermore, the recent pension fund reform act (ERISA) had applied the "prudent man" standard to pension funds for the first time. While the judicial interpretations of the new law were still unclear, ERISA seemed to have reinforced the trend toward more diversified and conservative investment policies. In particular, many corporations seemed to be switching back toward a heavier emphasis on fixed income securities in their pension funds.

Observing these trends, William Paulson wondered if fixed income securities should play a larger role in General's pension fund. Currently, rather attractive yields were still available in the bond market, as shown in Exhibit 3. These yields substantially exceeded the assumed actuarial rate of return used in the computation of General's pension funding requirements (6 percent). Paulson recalled that Trans Union, a smaller midwestern firm, had switched to an "all bonds" strategy several years before. Excerpts from a recent speech by the treasurer of Trans Union are shown in Exhibit 4, describing some of the advantages of this strategy.

In addition, another fixed income alternative had recently become popular among corporate pension funds—the "guaranteed investment contracts (GICs)" that were being marketed by large insurance companies. There were many forms of GICs, and they varied substantially

---

[2] Actually, the computation of pension plan expenses and pension fund contributions was quite complex, and the details are not particularly relevant to the decisions considered here. Basically, the size of the contributions could be affected by, among other things, the choice of an actuarial rate, and the recent investment results within the fund. By assuming a high actuarial (discount) rate, the present value of the expected future benefits could be reduced, and thus the current cash contributions (and accrued pension expense) of General could be reduced and vice versa. Any recent increases in the market value of the pension fund could also decrease the required cash contributions (and accrued pension expense) and vice versa, although the fund's value was averaged over the past several years for the purposes of this calculation to "smooth out" the effect of the market's volatility on the required contributions. The pension expense accrued by General was an accounting entry to reflect these, and other, factors in an appropriate change to current income. The cash contributions to the pension fund were theoretically a separate financial decision for General could choose to "fund" these pension expenses or not, subject to some limitations. As a practical matter, General had chosen to fund most recent pension expenses.

from one life insurance company to another. The most common form guaranteed a specified return, compounded annually, for a specified time, at the end of which the interest and principal would be returned. Paulson believed he could currently obtain a ten-year GIC plan from a major insurer at a guaranteed rate of 9 percent. The insurance company would retain the funds for ten years, and the guaranteed rate extended even to the reinvestment of returns. At the end of ten years, General would receive a lump sum return of all principal, income and reinvested proceeds. Exhibit 5 describes the growing popularity of these GICs among pension funds. Exhibit 6 describes the recent decision of a major corporation to move the majority of their pension funds into GICs.

William Paulson was intrigued by some of the very attractive features, particularly the guaranteed return, offered by these contracts. But he wondered whether they were superior to bonds. He read with interest an analysis of GICs undertaken by a bond management firm (Exhibit 7), which concluded, perhaps not surprisingly, that these plans compared unfavorably to bonds. Because any funds that General might contribute to a GIC would become "pooled" with other funds, and the general undivided portfolio of the insurance company would stand behind both the guaranteed contract and all other liabilities, the financial condition of the insurance company was important. Paulson would, of course, deal only with very large, well-known insurance companies with excellent reputations.

Having perused some of the available information, Paulson settled back to ponder the issues. He did not want to be deflected by an attempt to take advantage of short-run financial timing. As a matter of long-run policy, however, he wondered whether fixed income securities should be a larger component of pension funds like General's. And in particular, he wondered if GICs or marketable bonds were the best form of fixed income securities for General's pension fund.

Exhibit 1

A. Data from recent financial statements: Balance sheet items as of December 31, 1975
(Millions of dollars)
Net Working Capital: $220
(Current Assets Minus Current Liabilities)

Fixed assets	$315	Long-term debt	$171
Other	10	Stockholders equity	374
Total	$545	Total	$545

B. Sales and income data (Millions of dollars)

	1967	1968	1969	1970	1971	1972	1973	1974	1975
Sales	$625	683	712	828	949	961	1,043	1,221	1,473
Operating income	79	63	41	44	61	65	65	93	103
Net income (after depreciation and taxes) . . .	32	24	11	14	20	24	22	35	38

Exhibit 2
Information on pension plan expenses and the underlying pension fund

Employees and pension expenses	General manufacturing	Median of sample of 40 large U.S. firms
Number of employees	36,280	
1975 pension expense	$27.4 million	
As a percent of pretax profits	36%	23%
Per employee	$755	$886
Average annual growth rate of pension expense (1970–1975)	21%	15%
Dollar amounts (in millions)		
Pension fund, total assets at market value	$170	
Unfunded past service costs*	$108	

* Literally, the difference between the actuarial value of the pension assets and the present value of the future pension benefits that the company expects to pay out, under the plans. These unfunded past service costs stem from changes in the company's pension plans. At the time that certain benefits are enacted or improved, employees obtain future pension benefits from their past service with the company. The company "funds" these past service costs over time, effectively amortizing them with enlarged annual contributions over a period of 20 to 30 years.

Exhibit 3

Current yields in the bond markets, March 1976

New issues: utility bonds	
Long-term (NR-5 year) Aaa	8.65%
Long-term (NR-5 year) Aa	8.85
Long-term (NR-5 year) A	9.15
Medium-term Aa	8.20
New issues: industrial bonds	
Long-term (NR-10 year) Aa	8.45
Medium-term Aa	7.95
Seasoned issues: utility bonds	
Long-term deep discount (4¼%) Aa	8.17
Current coupon (8⅞%) Aa	8.79
Federal agency bonds	
7 year	7.75
10 year	7.90
20 year	8.10

Note: NR denotes nonredeemable for the time period specified.

Exhibit 4

Bonds useful in meeting predetermined, realistic, bold investment goals

by Paul J. Johnson*

Since mid-1971, the Trans Union pension fund has been invested entirely in bonds, A-rated or better, in the 15-year to 30-year range. The move from equities to fixed income securities has given us much more reasonable certainty that we will fulfill our obligation to shareholders, thus reducing pension fund drains on current income each year.

I would like to discuss how we begin with setting realistic objectives in terms of what we know we can reasonably attain. Then I will outline the disciplines we follow to insure that these objectives are met. Then I will show how fixed income securities can be an alternative worth considering in today's nerve-wrecking investment climate.

During the past three and one half years we have picked up some of our own refined techniques in bond management, but I think it's important to emphasize that we didn't ignore our basic principle. We set reasonable investment goals in mind.

I often hear the common misconception that stringent goal-setting is best suited for a limited number of situations—things like a government pension plan or a university expansion trust.

These "obvious" examples are only obvious because the goal is built in, as in the case of a university that has $4 million now and knows it will need $5 million three years hence.

---

* Mr. Johnson is treasurer of the Trans Union Corp., with responsibility for the firm's $15 million pension fund. These are excerpts from his talk, January 25, 1975, at the New School for Social Research in New York.

Exhibit 4 (continued)

But what about the investment manager with $10 million now? Should he work under the assumption that he'd like to have "as much as possible" three years hence? I think not. Such a view may in fact result in less growth than would have been possible with reasonable, defined goals. Such helter-skelter activity also defies measurement.

First, let's discuss the example of Trans Union's all-bond pension fund.

We begin first with what has been called an "ambitious" actuarial assumption of 7 percent. This was at a time when the average level of 5.3 percent, up from 5.2 percent one year ago. Incidentally, this 7 percent actuarial assumption gives us a pension expense 30 percent lower than it might be with an average 5.3 percent assumption.

Obviously, with current interest rates, we've been surpassing our 7 percent annual growth goal. This is icing on the cake; the important point is that we've managed to achieve a goal we reasonably expected to achieve, based on a far more inclement bond climate.

This seems to suggest that many other actuarial assumptions are set inordinately low. It was the Greenwich Research Associates' 1974 annual executive report on large corporate pension funds—that put average actuarial assumptions at 5.3 percent. But that same report revealed that executives really expect future returns of 8.9 percent, up from 7.7 percent.

The report comments: "With actual returns so frequently below expectations, perhaps the time has come for a careful review by corporate executives of why their actual returns have been disappointing and whether their long-term expectations are realistic."

While the report properly questions the discrepancy between actual and expected returns, it slights the apparently larger discrepancy between actual rate of return an original actuarial assumption.

Historical data suggest that equities have given a return in the 8.5 to 9 percent range and that would suggest an actuarial assumption of like figures. The problem with using such rates is that this average is achieved erratically, if at all.

Obviously, using a high actuarial assumption and then failing to achieve it will result in additional charges against income, usually in periods when such charges can least be swallowed. Such a risk is usually not acceptable; thus the lower actuarial assumption.

But should the discrepancy be so wide? Furthermore, what's the difference if your actuarial assumption is low, as long as your actual rate of return is good?

At Trans Union, we think the difference is this: Instead of using actuarial assumptions as a deflated benchmark against which to measure inflated expectations, we manage it as if it were another cost center.

When a corporation sets a low actuarial assumption, the charges against income are greater than they otherwise might be. The company presumably pays this price in the hope that at some future date, it can reduce pension expenses against current income because of "better than expected" performance. But what are the ramifications of this? Let's take a closer look.

Let's say a corporation is earning in excess of its actuarial assumption. They

Exhibit 4 (continued)

have already incurred higher charges against income than necessary. The money naturally has gone into the pension fund, where let's say it can earn 8 percent. Perhaps, because of the higher actual return, the company can reduce pension pay-in by $100 during year four. But what happens to that $100? After 50 percent taxes, the corporation has $4 from its 8 percent return.

Trans Union's higher—yet reasonable—actuarial assumption, on the other hand, allows us to keep that $100 working in our business, which means that we can earn 12 percent to 13 percent after taxes.

By retaining the $100 we end up with $50 after taxes, and roughly $6 income at 12 percent. Furthermore, it's $6 today, not $4 at some future date. In addition, our net income is higher; our pension expense lower.

The cumulative compounding effect is startling. Our retention of funds within the business reflects on income as shown here.

This situation, we feel, is more consistent with our obligations to shareholders. If that income was earned in a given period, it should appear as income during that period—not at some point in the future, namely year four. It should not be an undeserved bonus to future shareholders, who are not necessarily today's.

Looking at this example in the "cost center" light, we can do better by using the money ourselves in our business, and the key to maximizing profits in this manner is a realistic actuarial assumption.

The need for a reasonable actuarial assumption is recognized in the Pension Reform Act of 1974, which calls for "all most liabilities, rates of interest and other factors" under a pension plan to be determined on the basis of actuarial assumptions and methods which in the aggregate are reasonable. The act calls for consideration of the experience of the plan and reasonable expectations in arriving at the rate.

Let's take an example in the reality of present market conditions. Assume you are investing $1 million over 20 years with an actuarial assumption of 5.3 percent. This implies an aggregate of $2,809,101 in 20 years. A 9 percent bond net you $45,000 semiannually for 40 periods, or total coupons of $1,800,000. Add the original principal and you have $2,800,000, or only $9,101 short of the $2,809,101 needed to fulfill the actuarial assumption of 5.3 percent.

It doesn't take a bond-booster like myself to suggest that the 5.3 percent assumption is ridiculous. The reinvestment rate required on coupon income to achieve this goal is less than 0.06 of 1 percent.

I strongly suggest that although the excessively timid actuarial assumption is commonplace, it is useless as an investment standard. And if it is a bad measurement of the investment manager's skill, his problem is compounded by measurement devices that are inconsistent with his objectives.

The Greenwich Research Associates report I cited earlier says that although corporate executives consider themselves quite familiar with money managers, when asked to identify which specific investment skills money managers have, they very frequently say they are not sure.

The result, I feel, is that for lack of a viable long-term measuring device corporate executives view even long-term performance with the more familiar short-term yardsticks. The A. G. Becker performance evaluation studies come out quarterly, and perhaps if an investment manager doesn't match average growth

Exhibit 4 (*continued*)

after a year or two, he's fired. Such yardsticks may be appropriate to short-term goals, but somehow they creep into even long-term situations.

If you tell someone he's been hired to play baseball and you tackle him the first time he suits up, he's certainly going to be confused. If he comes back again the next day and gets tackled again, he should see the light. If he doesn't come back on the third day dressed to play football, he's got no one to blame but himself.

So he plays football, but he really isn't sure why. And when it comes to keeping score, while the coach may be happy with the number of touchdowns he's scored, it becomes difficult to determine how this reflects on his batting average.

Another mistake in long-term performance evaluations as I see it is the use of relative comparisons—the market did "this" and we did "this," without thinking back to consider "what you were about" in the first place.

At Trans Union, we have developed our own measuring device—we call it R3, which keeps us constantly aware not only of "what we're about," but what we have to do at any point in time to achieve it. It also reminds us that chasing the short-term rainbow is not only unrelated to our real goals, it can and does jeopardize them.

Just as a similar device would help the trustee of a university gauge progress in a building fund or help the individual determine whether or not he had enough money to send children to college three and five years hence, R3 keeps in touch with our goals.

Simply stated, R3 represents the required reinvestment rate at which the cash flow in our all-bond pension fund must be reinvested if we are to realize an over-all goal of 7 percent over the next 20 years.

It's the best measurement device we know and the only one we need consider in managing our fund. And its use is not limited to pension fund management or even bond management. In fact, right now, I'm thinking of applying it to an equity fund.

Obviously, getting a 7 percent bond is no trick these days, but total rate of return is another question. As in any investment of this type, the critical factor is the rate at which we can reinvest coupon interest, then the interest from that interest, and so on, ad infinitum.

If we buy an instrument with a yield to maturity that matches our goals, we still have to match that rate on all reinvestments of interest on that security. If the reinvestment rate drops, total return drops accordingly and vice versa.

The area of uncertainty then is this reinvestment rate, and that's what R3 focuses on, telling us at any point in time where we stand in relation to our goal.

So given a known coupon rate, a maturity date and our own 20-year horizon, our portfolio managers have the required reinvestment rate, R3, to run against. His job is first of all to meet it, and then to reduce it as much as possible. He always knows what he's fighting, if you will, rather than running toward a goal that does not become apparent until the race is over, if at all.

So when our investment manager faces a choice between a 90-day 12 percent note and a long-term 10 percent bond, he will almost always take the latter, because it will meet his goals and also eliminate the reinvestment risk to both principal and coupon interest 90 days hence.

Exhibit 4 (*continued*)

As I said, part of his job is to reduce R3 as much as possible, so the risk must be calculated within the framework of our goals. The 12 percent note is a risk he needn't take, and a risk we don't want him to take. The risk is too great.

Similarly, if the same investment manager has an 8 percent 20-year par bond and has a chance to trade it for a bond of like quality and maturity with an 8.05 coupon, he'll do it, simply to increase cash flow from $40 to $40.25 every six months. Whether the nominal price is 90, 60, or 110, he's better off with the second bond. The market price is irrelevant.

In fact, market price is not even a factor in calculating R-3, which is concerned only with the flow of cash from a given issue, which by definition is fixed.

Market rates do play a role in our management of long-term bonds, although that role may seem reversed by some standards. If market prices increase, interest rates will generally drop. But if market prices drop, interest rates will generally rise.

Since the total return from a fixed income security depends partially on the reinvestment rate we can obtain, a drop in market prices—accompanied by a rise in interest rates—implies a higher reinvestment rate. Therefore, the total realized return on a bond will likely be greater than the original yield to maturity.

In this situation, then, the typical understanding of a bond price is upside down. A reduction in market value improves investment return, while an increase in market value reduces total return.

But what about investments for a shorter time horizon? History would seem to suggest that equities could do better, but do they? Again let's look at the real world. Take a five-year time horizon for example. Even if the Dow Jones average is back up to 1200 in three years, who can say where it will be in five years—that point in time when you have to come back to cash.

Now, in 1975, I'm sure it is little comfort to those steeped in equities to check the numbers and see that the Dow Jones average had hit 1051 back in January 1972. Again it's a matter of goals. Can you afford the risk that equities will be in a position to meet your goals at that certain point in time that you have to come back to cash?

Furthermore, I agree with the notion that we should be skeptical about predictions of high returns from common stock price appreciation at all times. If goals are realistic they can be achieved with minimal dependence on forecasts.

A study of stock prices beginning in 1871 shows how misleading a fixation with the two Great Bull Markets can be. The first, 1926–1929, was unbelievably steep—but to its participants, unbelievably short lived. The second, from the early 1940s to the late 1960s, became so habit-forming that its demise seemed almost as incredible as that of the first.

Of course there have been other periods of rising prices, but I think sometimes we view the second Great Bull Market as the norm and not a phenomenon that has occurred only twice in more than 100 years.

On the contrary, it may be wishful thinking to suppose that the recent debacle is only a brief respite in a continuing common stock upsurge.

Another possible objection to a fixed income portfolio is current inflation since stocks have traditionally been suggested as a hedge against this. But recent history

Exhibit 4 (concluded)

suggests that this too is an illusion. Over the inflationary long haul, stock prices have not gone up as rapidly as the increase in other commodities.

What about bonds in periods of inflation? I feel they do provide a hedge—however modest. Inflation can put rockets on interest rates. And in the case of a pension fund, inflation's erosion of purchasing power is minimized. Our commitment is in terms of dollars, not what those dollars will buy.

An 8 percent bond bought at maturity offers a compound yield of 4.8 percent without reinvestment. The interest reinvested at 10 percent—up because of inflation—should bring total yield to the area of 9¼ percent. Surely this is a better hedge against inflation than stocks.

But what about the reverse situation? What if inflation subsidies and market rates fall to 6 percent or lower? Well, I expect we'd be back into equities with at least some of the new money. But frankly, I don't foresee this in the near future.

Anyway, we'd be back in the same equity boat with most other fund managers, certainly no worse off for our years of meeting goals and getting a good night's sleep. And most certainly we would be reexamining our goals.

We would have enjoyed a reasonably high actuarial assumption with a very real improvement to earnings per share, an improvement maintained with consistency and safety not available with a portfolio of equities. But in today's situation it provides a hedge against inflation, and it permits the portfolio manager to concentrate on the long-term goals.

Using this philosophy, we see that the performance of Trans Union's pension fund, as an example, has been very good. Based on the advantage of hindsight it looks even better, yielding a return far superior to our former equity portfolio. But from a corporate viewpoint, the all-bond fund was a good move simply because it met our goal. While it looks better with the Dow Jones at 600, it would look just as good if the average were over 1000.

In conclusion, I realize that not all the examples I discussed have universal application. But I hope I have emphasized that bonds are a viable investment alternative in a wide range of situations. And finally I hope I have shown that the money manager who measures his performance in terms of how well he has met predetermined, realistic but bold objectives will sleep better nights and enjoy his days more than the manager who worries too much about market fads and panaceas.

Source: Reprinted from *The Money Manager*, February 1975. Reproduced by permission.

Exhibit 5

The growing appeal of the insurance company guaranteed—return contract
by Sandra Kazinetz

After years of watching investment counselors and banks run circles around them with glamorous new products for pension funds, the nation's insurance companies have lately found themselves with a product that, in these times, looks pretty glamorous itself: the guaranteed return contract. "When you consider that for the past two years, we've been in a lousy economic market," says one bank trust officer begrudgingly, "and until recently in a lousy stock market, too—not to mention the complications of the new pension law—it's perfectly logical to see why there's a trend for investing in these contracts."

Unlike the venerable insured pension fund, in which the company pays its money to the insurance company, which guarantees to pay the pensions and the company never sees the money again, these contracts simply guarantee a certain return on a company's assets for a given number of years. Then, when time is up, the company gets the money back. Historically, such contracts have appealed primarily to thrift and profit-sharing plans.

During the last 18 months, though, pension funds have begun to look at the contracts as a way to lessen risk and to be sure of meeting their actuarial assumptions. And while the contracts were originally designed for smaller funds, "it is the Fortune 500-type company that has shown the most interest," according to R. W. McLaughlin, a vice president at the Travelers Insurance Co.

BOND SUBSTITUTE

Typically considered by the pension funds that buy them as a part of their fixed income portfolios, the guaranteed return contracts, individually negotiated, usually run for a period of 5 to 10 years—although some insurers, such as Metropolitan Life, offer contracts of up to 20 years, and the Travelers will sign one for as short a period as 3 years. Should the fund, perhaps believing in the recent rally, want to get out of the contract, it can do so; "escape hatches" are written into them, usually allowing the client to get out at market value of the assets invested.

In addition, the guaranteed rates are quite healthy. During the last six months of 1974, for instance, they generally averaged 8.5 to 9.5 percent, net of management fee, depending on the market environment (Chicago-based Continental Assurance, at one point last year, wrote a five-year contract for 10.1 percent). Finally, by law, each contract must include an option to purchase an annuity.

You can't get much safer than that. But, can you do better?

Many pension officers don't feel you can. "Although our other outside managers say they can beat 9 percent," says one pension officer whose fund has committed 8 percent of its $160 million pool to a five-year contract, "they don't."

Scott Snead, director of pension investments at Champion International, feels the same way. In 1973, his fund took that option of buying an annuity on existing retired and salaried lives with 25 percent of its $100 million fund. "Before we made the decision, however, we asked several investment managers to set up a hypothetical fixed income portfolio," he says. "But the return they came up with

Exhibit 5 (continued)

was only slightly higher than what the insurance company offered, and the managers could not guarantee it—whereas the insurance company plan offered us no risk whatsoever."

Inland Steel is another company that sees considerable appeal in these contracts. "For a portion of our fixed income assets, the locked-in return we obtained compares favorably with our 6 percent actuarial assumption and with the 9.3 percent historical rate of return from the equity market," says treasurer Robert Greenenbaum, whose pension fund recently placed 10 percent, or $25 million, of its assets with Equitable Life in a ten-year, 9 percent contract. At the end of the contract, that $25 million will grow to $59 million.

OPPORTUNITY COST?

There is a certain disadvantage, of course, in that the pension fund gives up the potential gains that could result from an equity market turnaround. But boosters point out that having a portion of their funds' money in the contracts actually offers *more* flexibility in managing the rest of the assets. At the same time, however, these officers, such as Park Davidson, assistant vice president at Burlington Industries (which has put 5 percent of a $40 million profit-sharing fund into a guaranteed account for five years), say they do not intend to place a disproportionate amount of their assets into the contracts. "We've been seriously considering allocating additional profit-sharing and even pension money," says Davidson. "But I don't believe any one portion will amount to more than 5 percent of assets." Beric Christiansen, pensions and benefits manager at General Mills (which has two contracts: one with Equitable and one with John Hancock—both paying 9.5 percent), agrees: "We would not want to lock up our fund *totally* in this type of commitment, and I don't know who would," he says. "It'd be like investing all your assets in one bond."

But that's just fine with the people who market the contracts. "Precisely because there is a certain inflexibility, we have some reservations about using this type of contract for a large portion of a pension fund's assets," says Thomas E. Baxter, assistant vice president at Equitable. The insurance company, therefore, pushes the small-percentage idea—and in doing so has opened a very broad market.

There are competitors of the insurance companies, of course, which sneer at the contracts. One investment counselor calls the growing interest in them a "short-lived triumph for all those conservative 'I-told-you-so's' in corporate management." But such attitudes could well change if the insurance industry's predictions of sales reaching $1 billion by the end of this year turn out to be true. Indeed, at least one major New York bank is already investigating the possibility of offering its own guaranteed return contract to pension funds. And a trust officer at a New England bank, which is also pondering such a step, says: "We're looking into it from a business and legislative point of view. If this checks out, we feel that, done with enough size, there's no conceptual reason why banks can't offer it, too."

It's still too early to tell, however, what will happen when current contracts expire, since the phenomenon is a relatively recent one and none have yet done so.

Exhibit 5 *(concluded)*

Aetna, in fact, has already announced its intention of limiting the number of contracts it writes as interest rates come down. But until some economist's predictive powers are potent enough to guarantee what the Dow will close at or what the level of interest rates will be, say, eight years from now, a great many corporate signatures could be appearing on the bottom line of a great many guaranteed-return contracts.

Source: *Institutional Investor*, April 1975. Reproduced by permission.

Exhibit 6

Crown Zellerbach goes guaranteed; four money management firms terminated
by Julie Rohrer

San Francisco—In what is probably the biggest corporate pension fund management shakeout since the passage of ERISA, Crown Zellerbach Corp. is moving two thirds of its pension fund assets (about $150 million total) into fixed return investment contracts with insurance companies. The remaining portion of the assets will go into equities with "one or two major investment management institutions."

The insurance companies signed by the large forest products company are The Travelers, Prudential, and Mutual Life Insurance Co. of New York.

They are offering rates that range from 8¾ to 9½ over various time periods of up to ten years.

Being terminated in the CZ rearrangement are four highly regarded independent money management firms: Boston's Battery–march Financial Management, New York's BEA Associates, Houston's Fayez Sarofim & Co., and San Francisco's Rosenberg Capital Management.

Bankers Trust in New York will continue to run a bond account for the firm.

No decision has been reached on who the new equity managers will be, according to Charles LaFollette, senior vice president for finance at Crown Zellerbach and a member of the company's investment committee. However, they will probably be major banks or the investment divisions of large insurance companies, he told *Pensions & Investments*.

Frank Russell Co. is consulting on the selection of the new equity managers and was expected to come up with recommendations by the end of last week.

Russell did not participate in the final recommendations or decision on moving much of the fund into guaranteed-return contracts.

"As you know, ERISA took over in January (1975) and because of the uncertainty of the interpretation of fiscal prudence we chose to be reasonably conservative for the next year or two," Mr. LaFollette told this magazine. The move, he added, may not be permanent.

"We had a strategy which we created a few years ago in which we signed with a number of equity accounts and have already gotten the gains (there will be)," he said.

Too, he added, "there will be additional funding going into the fund in the

Exhibit 6 (_continued_)

future and we can, if we choose, put these funds into different kinds of investments.''

Mr. LaFollette also observed that Crown Zellerbach has clearly placed fiduciary responsibility for management of the fund on the company's board of directors, which works with the firm's investment committee.

Members of the investment committee, set up last December, include, in addition to Mr. LaFollette, Bill Parkinson, vice president industrial relations, and Harry Flewderman, vice president and general counsel for the corporation.

According to a source at one of the terminated firms, the naming of Crown Zellerbach's board as fiduciaries may have indirectly led to the shakeout of the company's fund.

''At least one member of the board,'' said this source, ''is known to have worried considerably about potential liabilities under ERISA and put a lot of pressure on others to take a very conservative approach to investment management of the fund.''

Source: _Pensions & Investments,_ March 15, 1976. Reproduced by permission.

Exhibit 7

The guaranteed investment contract: An analysis
by Madeline W. Einhorn

The waning of the growth stock syndrome of the 1960s and the exceptional interest rates of the 1970s have impelled many trust administrators to reconsider the risk relationships of different asset classes. Volatility of the equity market has created a more dubious environment asset classes. Volatility of the equity market has created a more dubious environment for those employee benefit plans which have been largely equity-oriented, and in the light of a changing financial environment many trust administrators and fund managers are seeking an alternative to equities.

While volatility of both the equity and bond markets has increased in the past five years, the relationship of the two has remained relatively constant. Throughout the period one standard deviation of total return in the equity market, as measured by the leading equity indices, has been approximately two and one quarter times one standard deviation of the total return of the bond market, as measured by the bond market indices. Stated another way, the measure of risk or the degree of dispersion from the anticipated return is more than twice as great for equities, and the ''confidence level'' one can have for realizing the return from equities is less than one half that for bonds.

Following a period of prolonged high inflation, the most savage decline in the equity market in recent history, and severe deterioration in the market prices of fixed income securities, and with the passage in 1974 of the Employee Retirement Income Security Act (ERISA), many insurance companies began to intensify their efforts to sell guaranteed investment contracts (GIC). These contracts promise a fixed rate of return annually and repayment of the principal upon maturity of the contract. They have attracted widespread attention because they appear to offer

Exhibit 7 *(continued)*

100 percent protection against market risk. And it is believed, on the basis of present views of the probable future interpretation of the provisions of ERISA, that a corporate official who is a named fiduciary to an employee benefit plan, in choosing the GIC as the investment vehicle for the plan, would avoid any potential future personal liability.

Similarly, under the provisions of ERISA a fiduciary to the plan ought not to be personally liable if, after careful investigation and sound analysis, he chooses a qualified investment management organization of good reputation—whether bank, investment counselor, or insurance company—which has demonstrated a capacity to supervise investments with the professional competence to meet the plan's requirements. Assuming that the funding provisions of the plan are reasonably related to the plan's forecast needs, that honest and competent management of the investments is provided by the investment manager, and that the fiduciary exercises diligent oversight, in our view, no personal liability would attach to a plan fiduciary for this choice even if the investments fell short of plan requirements.

COMPARED WITH A CORPORATE DEBENTURE

Although the GIC must be regarded as a fixed income investment, there are several characteristics which distinguish the contract from other types of fixed income investments. The GIC "guarantee" is similar in some ways to any corporation's promise of the payment of interest and principal on its unsecured debentures. Both "guarantee" payment of a stated rate of interest and repayment of principal at maturity. What "guarantees" the corporate debenture is essentially the general assets, earning power, and creditworthiness of the corporation in contrast to the specific, segregated assets which constitute the specific security for a railroad equipment trust certificate, a mortgage bond, or a debt issue whose repayment is assured by funds held as collateral or in escrow.

There is no separate identification of assets in the general account of an insurance company for any individual contract or group of contracts bearing a guaranteed rate of interest. Rather, the back-up credit for a GIC is a large undivided portfolio of primarily fixed income investments value at the insurance company's amortized cost, not at market value, which must be shared pro rata with all other contract and policyholders. The surplus account of the insurance company, measured at market value, is the protective buffer for the future claims of those covered by the various lines of insurance written (e.g., individual line, group line, GIC, accident, and health). It remains to be seen—and it is not now clear—how much the surplus account could be penetrated to meet obligations of one class of policyholders or contract holders to the detriment of other obligations. If the financial environment were such that there was a sustained drop in long-term interest rates lasting for, say, 15 years, such as that witnessed in the period 1932–1945, the return on general account assets could reflect a negative spread against the guaranteed contracts which had been put out at a higher rate, especially those which provide for reinvestment of interest. Although the putting out of the GICs and the purchase of the opposing investment vehicles may occur simultaneously, once on the books there is no separate identification of assets to contracts within the general account.

We regard a GIC as a nontradeable debenture of an insurance company, yet

Exhibit 7 (continued)

substantive elements found in the indenture covering a publicly issued corporate debenture are in many cases absent or significantly weaker in the contract. Since assets are not separately identifiable to the contract, the purchase of a GIC involves the purchase of a contract the performance of which is dependent upon the adequacy of the asset coverage provided by the insurance company's general account, which consists of assets carried and valued at amortized cost, not at their market value, at the date of the GIC purchase. The profile of a typical life insurance company portfolio shows a large segment of corporate private placement bonds, a large segment of mortgages, some municipal bonds, some U.S. Treasury issues, and relatively small holdings of common stocks. The larger life insurance companies show particularly heavy concentration in corporate private placement debt and mortgages which, judging from the yield ascribed to these holdings in the annual reports, have suffered a decline in imputed market value of up to 30 percent of cost. Of course, it should be recognized that the new cash flowing to the insurance company through GIC sales will tend to shore up the value of the assets available to satisfy prior policy and contract holders' claims, since new dollars are augmenting eroded asset values, and all policy and contract holders' claims are to be satisfied out of these assets.

It may never be necessary for the insurance company to liquidate in the securities markets the financial instruments which are the insurance company's assets. We believe it is improbable that all or most contract holders ever would want to withdraw their funds at the same time. While improbable under normal conditions, massive liquidations could well be forced upon insurance companies in a straitened economic environment, and the GIC holder may find that there would be insufficient value realized for the satisfaction of all the claims of all policy and contract holders.

How can this risk be evaluated? We have found that not enough information is available for evaluation purposes. Is it prudent to purchase a debenture where it is not possible to calculate asset coverage and/or earnings coverage? Surely, a fiduciary contemplating the purchase of a publicly issued A-rated or Aa-rated debenture would examine the trend of the issuer's fixed charge coverage and would scrutinize the balance sheet to determine the quality and magnitude of the issuer's assets. This is not possible with a GIC.

VARIATION IN GIC TERMS

Terms offered by the GIC are subject to negotiation and are as varied as there are contract issuers. However, the basic contract commonly provides for a fixed maturity generally ranging from 3 to 20 years and a fixed rate of interest compounded *annually*. At a 9 percent coupon level annual compounding is equivalent to a difference of approximately 20 basis points in yield; the semiannual bond equivalent yield would be 8.80 percent. Certain of the contracts provide for reinvestment of interest at the stated rate of the GIC, and in a market with declining interest rates this might be viewed as an advantage, but it would certainly be offset by inability to realize capital gains on asset value. In a market with rising interest rates this provision would be a distinct disadvantage because there would be no opportunity to capture higher coupons.

A disturbing aspect of the issuance of the guaranteed investment contracts is

522

Exhibit 7 (continued)

their lack of uniformity. Insurance companies differ from each other in the contract terms they offer, and this is appropriate, as also would be the case among different corporate issuers of debentures. In the sale of guaranteed investment contracts, however, not only do the contract terms vary from one insurance company to another, but the terms offered by the same insurance company at the same time to different prospective GIC purchasers are materially different depending upon the total amount of the purchase, the identity of the purchaser, and perhaps other factors as well. By comparison, if one of the Bell System companies were to issue $300 million of debentures, every buyer—whether for $5,000, $500,000, $5 million, or $50 million—would be entitled to exactly the same terms as every other buyer.

Furthermore, when corporate debentures are publicly issued, either through competitive bidding or negotiated underwriting, the issuer must meet Securities and Exchange Commission requirements for reporting and certification with respect to the magnitude and condition of assets, earnings, pending lawsuits, and, just as importantly, must agree to specified indenture covenants which might concern mergers, acquisitions, and defined financial restrictions. The GIC holder is not afforded SEC protection, as the insurance companies are under the jurisdiction of the individual state insurance commissions whose strength and strictness of surveillance and regulation vary widely.

THE GIC AS PART OF PRUDENT INVESTMENT POLICY

Questions have arisen as to whether a plan fiduciary choosing a GIC need be concerned with the principle of diversification. Good diversification has always been a tenet of trusteeship responsibility and now is codified as a standard of prudent investment policy by ERISA. A fund holding different types of investments is less subject to specific risks deriving from any one of them. The guidelines given to asset managers with respect to particular funds under management typically require that certain quality levels be maintained in the portfolio; that securities held be limited to those of sizable corporations; and, among other requirements, that the investment in any one credit be limited to no more than 5 percent of the total fund.

Fiduciaries electing a GIC have generally committed an amount to the contract that exceeds the percentage of portfolio which prudent management would place in any one corporate issue. And, while it appears likely that this would not be deemed to be a violation of ERISA's diversification provision, it is well to remember that, although it may not be probable, an insurance company may suffer from mismanagement, financial risk, or market risk, or a combination of these, and that there is no lender of last resort for insurance companies. In such circumstances the size and diversification of the underlying portfolio in which all contract holders share might not be sufficient to recover plan assets.

DO INSURANCE PRINCIPLES APPLY TO THE GIC?

It is not only with regard to the terms of the offering and the lack of governmental supervision that the insurance companies selling the GIC are in a

Exhibit 7 (continued)

twilight zone—a larger and more diffuse area of imprecision lies in the concept of the contract itself. The insurance business has a singular purpose: the transference of risk. For many years insurance companies have been profitable because they have successfully spread the risks they were paid to insure against, and they have been able to do this because there are reliable methods of predicting incidence of risk. For example, mortality tables and epidemiological studies make it possible to insure mortality risk intelligently and profitably. Casualty risk is somewhat more difficult to quantify. Yet even catastrophe risk can be spread. Farmers require financial protection against crop damage from hailstorms, and insurance companies, using the records of occurrences of hailstorms in past years, sell this insurance on the basis of wide geographical dispersion, insuring farms here and there from Texas to Montana (and not every farm in any one country), knowing that over so large an area hailstorms will not occur everywhere at any one time.

The kinds of risks that are insurable, the kinds that insurance companies have been able to transfer successfully from the individual insured to the pool of insureds, are specific risks the incidence of which is forecastable, like mortality or hailstorms. Such risks are, in the terms used by insurance actuaries, "poolable" because they occur randomly in large populations. The event insured against will not simultaneously affect all or any very large portion of the insureds. In contrast, systemic risk such as that of fluctuations in securities markets, which are determined by aggregate economic and political conditions, are not poolable.

When an insurance company sells a GIC it purportedly is providing insurance both on the yield return and on market fluctuations affecting the principal amount invested in the contract. Insurance companies claim that the size and diversification of their own large underlying portfolios of financial instruments will constitute protection to the GIC holders against significant interest rate changes and market risk. But we know that diversification ties us more closely to market risk, and we know that all market assets are simultaneously exposed to risk. Thus, highly diversified equity portfolios do not tend toward risklessness; truly, the degree of market risk remaining in a perfectly diversified equity portfolio can be quite substantial.

Under state insurance department requirements, the sale of a GIC requires the setting up of a reserve, at a present value discount, against the future liability of all payments connected with the contract. In practice, upon the sale of a GIC an asset (either the dollars committed to the contract or the investments purchased with that dollar commitment) is created on the insurance company's balance sheet; correspondingly, a reserve for the liability is set up at the same time. This reserve may entail a different discount rate from that which is in the contract. Higher present value discount rates are more favorable to an insurance company than lower ones, and these discount rates are subject to intense lobbying at the state level. If a GIC were put out at 9 percent, a reserve established at a discount rate of 8½ percent would require a smaller transfer from surplus than a reserve at 7½ percent. In New York State a lower discount rate is used to establish a reserve for those guaranteed contracts which provide for reinvestment of interest. The higher the present value discount rate used in setting up the reserve, the weaker is the coverage for the contract.

Under the GIC, investment risk is the only, and indeed the entire, risk that is

Exhibit 7 (concluded)

assumed by the insurance company. Because investment risk is a function of future securities market risk, which cannot be quantified or forecast or made to fall upon only some of the insureds and not the rest, and since all securities markets may be affected materially and simultaneously by the same or related occurrences, we do not believe that it is possible to set up a true "insurance reserve" to reflect the GIC liability.[1] And where there is no true insurance reserve, there can be no true insurance guarantee.

The strong case for a high quality bond portfolio as an alternative to the GIC rests on several premises:

1. Investment expectations should have the potential of fulfillment on the upside as well as on the downside. There is no potential for capital gains in a guaranteed contract, only the potential for detriment or capital loss.
2. The sacrifice of liquidity and flexibility for the lock-up situation of a private placement should command a commensurate premium, which the guaranteed contract does not provide.
3. The guaranteed contract is not insurance. It is a security without separate specific asset protection and with uncertain governmental supervision.
4. Insurance principles, which are concerned with the transference of risk, are not and cannot be completely applied to market risk, which is noninsurable.

Today's financial environment makes necessary a full commitment to quality in investing. We feel this commitment can better be met with a high-rated marketable bond portfolio which provides diversification, flexibility, and liquidity while yielding equivalent or potentially larger returns than a guaranteed investment contract.

Source: Reproduced by permission from BEA Associates, Inc., 366 Madison Avenue, New York, New York 10017.

---

[1] As an indication of the magnitude of interest rate changes which may occur in a 21-year period, it should be noted that the net rate of interest earned on invested funds for all U.S. life insurance companies in 1925 was 5.11 percent; in 1945, it was 3.11 percent. Source: Institute of Life Insurance, *The Life Insurance Fact Book*.

6. American Telephone and Telegraph Company-1975

In January 1975, the financial vice president of the American Telephone and Telegraph Company (AT&T) was considering recommending an important change in the company's Dividend Reinvestment and Stock Purchase Plan (DRISPP). The plan currently allowed AT&T shareholders to automatically reinvest their dividends and/or additional cash into the company's stock at the market price as of the dividend payment date. This plan had become an important part of AT&T's new financial programs. The financial vice president was now considering offering a discount from current market price for shares purchased under the DRISPP in order to attract even more shareholders into the plan.

The DRISPP had started in 1969 (see Exhibit 1 for a history of the DRISPP) under the management of a commercial bank which charged shareholders a small fee for the purchase of shares on the open market (fractional shares were accumulated so that the entire dividend could be reinvested). In late 1972, shareholders were given the option of investing up to $3,000 new cash per quarter, per shareholder, in addition to their dividends. In 1973, AT&T took over management of the plan and eliminated the service charge so that shareholders could reinvest free of all transaction costs. At the same time, the plan was changed so that new stock, rather than stock purchased in the open market, was issued to participants. This meant that the DRISPP had become a source of new equity capital for AT&T. The DRISPP plan had grown rapidly since its inception; and in a few short years, it had become a prominent part of AT&T's financing plans.

THE COMPANY

The Bell System, as AT&T and its subsidiaries are known, provided local telephone service to over 80 percent of the telephones in the United States via its operating subsidiaries such as the New England Telephone and Telegraph Company. It provided interstate and international telephone service via the Long Lines Department of AT&T. It had its own

R&D facility in Bell Telephone Laboratories, one of the most famous research labs in the world, and its own manufacturing arm in Western Electric, itself large enough to be one of the biggest industrial companies in the United States.

The total investment to provide this service was $74 billion (book value), making AT&T the world's largest company. Most of this investment, $65 billion, was in the telephone plant (see Exhibits 2, 3, and 4 for financial statements). In 1974, AT&T required almost $3.00 in total assets to produce $1.00 in revenue, indicating the capital intensity of its business relative to the average manufacturing company, which required only $0.60 in assets to produce $1.00 in revenue (see Exhibit 5 for some comparative statistics of AT&T).

AT&T's revenues, which derived from data transmission and other services as well as voice communication, had grown at an 11.5 percent annual rate over the last five years (see Exhibit 5). This growth, combined with rapid technological change requiring investment in new facilities such as computerized Electronic Switching Systems, had led to large capital expenditures, averaging $8.2 billion in the last five years, and almost $10 billion in 1974 alone. Despite profits averaging $2.6 billion over the last five years, the internal funds generated by AT&T had been inadequate to meet these investment needs, and large amounts of external capital had been raised, averaging $4 billion per year (see Exhibit 4), or about $1 billion every 90 days. Most of this financing had been in the form of debt, and AT&T's debt was now 49.8 percent of their total capitalization.

AT&T management was strongly committed to maintaining its common stock dividend, which had not been lowered since 1885. Even in the depths of the depression, when earnings had fallen to under $6.00 per share for three consecutive years, the dividend was maintained at $9.00 per share. The 1974 dividend was $3.24 (the stock had split since the $9 dividend), or 61 percent of the $5.28 earnings per share.

REGULATION

The prices charged for telephone service were regulated by a number of regulatory agencies: the Federal Communication Commission set interstate rates, and each state had its own agency to set intrastate rates. While the regulatory process was complicated and political, it was generally agreed that AT&T should be allowed to earn a "fair return on investment" to compensate the suppliers of capital and to attract the large amounts of new capital that were required.

A "fair rate of return" was of course quite difficult to define, but it was generally determined, or at least rationalized, relative to a computation of AT&T's weighted average cost of capital, assuming a reasonable debt/

èquity ratio. The investment base against which this rate of return was applied was the "rate base." The rate base included that investment deemed necessary for the provision of telephone service, generally at cost, depreciated according to the regulatory authorities' allowable schedules. AT&T prepared its financial reports such that there was a reasonable correspondence between this rate base and the book value reported on AT&T's financial statements.

Because of the lengthy and complex procedures required by the regulatory agencies, there was a time delay between AT&T's request for a rate increase and its approval. This "regulatory lag" was an important consideration in a period of rapidly increasing costs.

COMPETITION

The Bell System had traditionally been granted a monopoly on telephone service in its local service areas. Although there were over 1,600 independent (non-Bell) telephone companies in the United States, they serviced collectively less than 20 percent of the telephones, and served nonoverlapping geographic areas. AT&T's Long Lines Department handled the interstate transmission of calls, even if they originated with an independent company, and the revenues were split according to negotiated "separations agreements."

In the last several years, however, the FCC had allowed direct competition in certain areas of AT&T's business, especially in the provision of station equipment (telephones, computer terminals, office switchboards) that was connected to AT&T's system, and the long distance transmission of messages via microwave stations and communications satellites. While these areas represented only a small part of AT&T's revenues, the regulatory climate seemed to point to more competition in the future.

PAST SOURCES OF EQUITY CAPITAL

AT&T had used several methods of obtaining equity capital in the past.

1. *Shareholder rights.* AT&T was currently obligated to offer all new equity issues to existing shareholders in the form of preemptive rights. Each shareholder, for each share that he held, was given a "right" to purchase a given number of new shares at a stated price. In order to induce participation, of course, the price was below the prevailing or expected market value of the security.

There were some interesting advantages to rights offerings, and they had been used frequently in the past for various types of equity securities. But this type of distribution could be quite cumbersome, too. With many small shareholders, the minimum size of a reasonable rights offering seemed to be very large, probably substantially greater than a billion dollars.[1]

2. *Warrants.* There were warrants outstanding for the purchase of 31.3 million new shares at $52 per share, exercisable through May 15, 1975. If exercised, they would bring $1.6 billion of new equity into AT&T. With AT&T currently selling at $44 (see Exhibit 6), it seemed unlikely that they would be exercised. The warrants were originally isssued in 1970 and included as a "sweetener" with debentures sold to existing shareholders.

3. *Convertible preferred.* There were outstanding 27.4 million preferred shares convertible into 28.8 million common shares. They were callable at a premium until July 31, 1976, and thereafter at their stated value of $50.

4. *DRISPP.* AT&T raised $185 million in new equity during 1974 by selling 4 million shares at market value to existing shareholders through the DRISPP (see Exhibit 1).

FUTURE FINANCIAL POLICIES

Concerned over the rising levels of debt in their capital structure and the possible implications of this debt, AT&T management had decided to attempt to lower their debt ratio over the next several years. They believed an appropriate goal might be a 45 percent debt to total capitalization by 1980, although they realized that this could change as circumstances demanded.

Management was as strongly committed as ever to continuing the common share dividend. The implicit dividend policy might be described as: at the very least, maintain the cash value of the dividend; raise the dividend with increasing earnings; and endeavor to raise the dividend with inflation. (The chairman, John D. de Butts, said, "AT&T management explicitly recognizes its obligation to commit its energies to maintaining the integrity of its common share dividend in the face of inflation."[2]

Because of the lack of flexibility entailed in preemptive rights, and because direct underwriting was felt to be more efficient in some ways than a rights offering, AT&T management had decided to ask the shareholders to waive preemptive rights at the 1975 annual meeting. They believed there would be no problem in obtaining shareholder approval, based on the experience of several other large firms that had waived preemptive rights in the past few years.

Capital expenditures for the next few years were expected to stay at

---

[1] To be fair to small shareholders, a rights offering had to offer them some reasonable value which would make it worth their time and trouble to either exercise, or sell, their rights. A minimum size rights offering of equity might be 1 new share for each 20 shares held. Since AT&T had almost 560 million shares outstanding, this would be a 28 million share offering. At a price of $45 per share, this would imply a stock offering of $1.26 billion. This would be a massive size for a single public stock issue.

[2] 1974 Annual Report of American Telephone and Telegraph Company.

about the 1974 level, as AT&T responded to continuing growth in demand and technological change.

FUTURE EQUITY FINANCING

The capital expenditures and financial policies described above were expected to produce a demand for external equity financing over the next several years which loomed rather large compard to the past amounts of equity capital raised by all U.S. corporations (see Exhibit 7).

To raise this equity capital, AT&T had a number of options:

1. *Underwriting.* If, as expected, preemptive rights were waived by the shareholders, underwriting syndicates could be used to sell new equity issues to the public. Future underwritings might offer the advantages of a wider distribution of the stock.
2. *Rights offerings.* Even with the waiver of preemptive rights, AT&T could use a rights offering as a way of raising equity. The rights could be transferable or not, and exercisable at any discount from market that seemed appropriate.
3. *Warrants.* While the current $1.6 billion worth of warrants seemed unlikely to be exercised, AT&T had made this type of financing more ''respectable,'' and it could be used again. The present warrants had been attached to debentures sold to existing shareholders, but there were other ways that they could be used.
4. *Convertibles.* Convertibles had been used in the past and could be used again. Convertible preferred and convertible debentures probably appealed to different markets and seemed to combine some of the features of both debt and equity.
5. *DRISPP.* Management felt that their current shareholders could continue to be a significant source of new equity, despite the elimination of preemptive rights, especially if the appeal of the DRISPP were enhanced through a discount from the current market price.

From among these options, AT&T wanted to choose the most desirable long-term mix of equity sources. The costs associated with a number of these possible options are described in Exhibit 8.

One of the clear problems in choosing the best mix of equity financings was the diversity of the current 3 million shareholders. AT&T had many small shareholders. Indeed 31 percent of the shareholders each held 20 shares of stock or less, and collectively held about 1½ percent of the outstanding stock. Moreover, about two thirds of the shareholders each held less than 100 shares, and collectively held less than 10 percent of the outstanding stock. But many large institutions held AT&T stock also. And the equity financing plans would have to be formulated with this diverse shareholder base in mind.

Exhibit 1
History of Dividend Reinvestment and Stock Purchase Plan

Quarter	Dividend paid	Shares purchased (thousands)	Price	Total dollars (millions)	Cash— added portion (millions)	Percent cash— added
1969						
3d	$0.60	155	$54.43	$ 8.4		
4th	0.60	170	50.87	8.7		
				$ 17.1		
1970						
1st	0.65	193	49.90	9.6		
2d	0.65	204	49.78	10.1		
3d	0.65	221	44.31	9.9		
4th	0.65	224	44.35	9.9		
				$ 39.5		
1971						
1st	0.65	196	51.09	10.0		
2d	0.65	202	49.84	10.1		
3d	0.65	223	45.52	10.3		
4th	0.65	230	44.33	10.2		
				$ 40.6		
1972						
1st	0.65	220	46.94	10.3		
2d	0.65	242	43.38	10.5		
3d	0.65	343	41.96	14.4	NA†	
4th	0.70	367	47.91	17.5	NA	
				$ 52.7		
1973						
1st	0.70	333	53.61	17.9	NA	
2d	0.70	351	51.07	17.9	NA	
3d	0.70*	740	50.94	37.7	$13.7	36
4th	0.70	804	51.69	41.6	16.2	39
				$115.1		
1974						
1st	0.77	849	49.81	42.3	14.4	34
2d	0.77	787	49.44	38.9	14.7	38
3d	0.77	1,019	46.38	47.2	19.8	42
4th	0.85	1,383	40.56	56.1	18.5	33
				$184.5		

* First quarter under AT&T management.
† Not Available: Portion represented by cash-added feature not readily available.

Exhibit 2

AMERICAN TELEPHONE AND TELEGRAPH COMPANY—1975
Summary Consolidated Balance Sheets
($ billions)

	12/31/74	12/31/73
Assets		
Cash and cash equivalents	$ 1.12	$ 1.06
Other current assets	3.74	3.50
Current assets	$ 4.86	$ 4.56
Deferred charges	0.69	0.61
Investments	3.57	3.31
Telephone plant (net)	64.93	58.57
	$74.05	$67.05
Liabilities and capital		
Current liabilities	$ 4.43	$ 4.23
Deferred credits (mostly deferred taxes)	4.72	3.23
Debt (all maturities)	32.31	28.37
Equity		
Preferred	3.00	2.98
Common (559.8 million shares)	28.76	27.42
Minority interest	0.83	0.82
	$32.59	$31.22
	74.05	67.05
Debt/Debt + Equity)	49.8%	47.6%

Exhibit 3

AMERICAN TELEPHONE AND TELEGRAPH COMPANY—1975
Summary Consolidated Income Statement
($ billions)

	1974	1973	1972	1971	1970
Revenues					
Local service	$12.81	$11.42	$10.36	$ 9.14	$ 8.46
Toll service	12.46	11.28	9.77	8.63	7.87
Other	0.90	0.83	0.78	0.67	0.63
	$26.17	$23.53	$20.91	$18.44	$16.96
Operating expenses	16.72	15.00	13.52	12.07	10.87
Net operating revenues	$ 9.46	$ 8.53	$ 7.39	$ 6.37	$ 6.09
Interest expense	2.06	1.73	1.50	1.29	1.00
Tax expense	4.77	4.35	3.81	3.31	3.26
Other income (includes Western Electric)	0.54	0.50	0.45	0.43	0.36
Net income	$ 3.17	$ 2.95	$ 2.53	$ 2.20	$ 2.19
Per share					
Net income	5.28	5.07	4.34	3.92	3.99
Dividends	3.24	2.87	2.70	2.60	2.60

Exhibit 4

AMERICAN TELEPHONE AND TELEGRAPH COMPANY—1975
Summary Consolidated Cash Flow
($ billions)

	1974	1973	1972	1971	1970
From operations					
Net income	$3.17	$2.95	$2.53	$2.20	$2.19
Add noncash expenses					
Depreciation	3.69	3.33	3.04	2.76	2.53
Deferred taxes	1.26	0.87	0.65	0.42	0.08
Investment tax credit—net	0.26	0.23	0.23	0.05	0.02
Deduct noncash income	0.34	0.34	0.35	0.34	0.29
Cash from operations	8.04	7.04	6.10	5.09	4.53
Subtract					
Capital expenditures	9.82	9.08	8.08	7.21	6.93
Increase in working capital*	0.09	(0.33)	0.25	0.09	0.16
Dividends paid (including preferred)	2.04	1.78	1.63	1.49	1.43
Cash surplus (external financing need)	(3.91)	(3.49)	(3.86)	(3.70)	(3.99)
External financing					
Debt (net)	3.94	2.35	3.19	2.38	4.59
Equity (including preferred)	0.22	1.06	0.85	1.38	0.01
	$4.16	$3.41	$4.04	$3.76	$4.60

* Excluding short-term debt.

Exhibit 5

Comparative statistics (percent)

Compounded growth rate (1970–1974)	
Revenue	11.5%
Earnings	9.7
Earnings per share	7.3
Revenue/total assets	35.3
Earnings/total assets	4.3
Earnings/equity (book value)	9.7
Earnings/equity (market value)*	12.0
Debt/total capitalization (book value)	49.8
Common dividend payment ratio	61.4
Compounded growth rates (1970–1974), as reported by the U.S. Department of Commerce	
GNP	9.4
Corporate profits	9.0

* Average of high and low stock prices for fourth quarter, 1974.

Exhibit 6
AT&T market price and book value 1964–1974

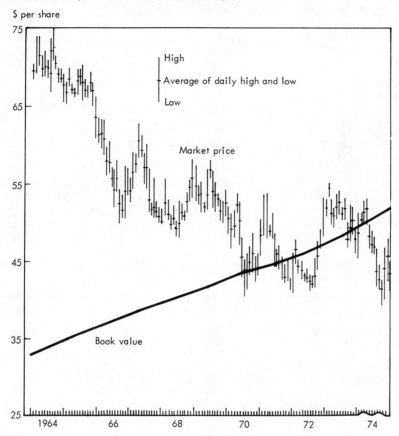

Exhibit 7

Supply and demand for all new equity capital in the domestic market

A. Net new issues and net purchases of corporate equities ($ billions)*

	Average annual flow 1961–1968	1969	1970	1971	1972	1973	1974
Net new issues	$0.9	$ 4.4	$ 6.3	$12.7	$12.1	$ 8.9	$5.3
Net purchases							
Savings banks	0.1	0.2	0.3	0.5	0.6	0.4	0.2
Life insurance companies	0.6	1.7	2.0	3.6	3.5	3.6	2.2
Private pension funds	3.1	5.4	4.6	8.9	7.1	5.3	2.3
Public pension funds	0.5	1.8	2.1	3.2	3.5	3.9	3.5
Fire and casualty insurance companies	0.3	1.0	1.0	2.5	3.0	2.2	−1.4
Mutual funds	1.3	1.7	1.2	0.4	−1.8	−2.3	−0.5
Total domestic institutions	$5.9	$11.8	$11.2	$19.1	$15.9	$13.1	$6.3
Foreign purchases	0.3	1.6	0.7	0.8	2.3	2.8	0.4
Individuals	−5.3	−9.4	−5.7	−7.3	−6.2	−7.3	−1.6

B. Net new purchases as percentage of net new inflow of funds to major institutional investors in stocks

	1967	1968	1969	1970	1971	1972	1973	1974
Life insurance companies	12%	14%	18%	20%	28%	23%	22%	13%
Private pension funds	75	73	86	65	122	104	69	21
Public pension funds	16	30	34	33	49	42	41	29
Fire and casualty insurance companies	15	26	35	18	38	38	39	−27
Mutual funds	125	60	65	70	67	†	†	†

Source: Federal Reserve Flow of Funds tables.

* Includes equities issued by nonfinancial corporate business, and various financial institutions (for example, banks, insurance companies) but not shares of mutual funds or REITs.

† Net outflow, or insignificant inflow.

Exhibit 8

Cost estimates for various equity alternatives

DIVIDEND REINVESTMENT PLAN

The costs of administering the dividend reinvestment program were thought to be about $4 to $5 per year per participating stockholder. In addition, if the dividends were reinvested at a discount in the future, the company would not receive their full market value. For example, with a 5 percent discount at the current market price of $44, the company would receive net proceeds of only $41.80 per share from the DRISPP.

Exhibit 8 (continued)

UNDERWRITTEN ISSUES

The prospective cost of underwriting an equity issue varied with the size of the issue and certain other factors, probably in the 4 to 5 percent range. In addition, there could be some downward pressure on the stock price during the offering period, although this was very difficult to estimate. The net proceeds to the company might be as in the accompanying table.

Assumed current market price	$44.00
Costs of underwriting	1.75
Offering period price pressure	2.00 (?)
Net proceeds to AT&T	$40.25

RIGHTS OFFERINGS

The administrative costs of past rights offerings had averaged somewhat less than the prospective costs of an underwritten issue, but a substantial discount from the market value was needed with this option. For example, with a right to purchase 1 new share of stock for each 20 shares held, the discount from the current market price of $44 might be $8. This would allow for a market decline of $3 during the rights offering period, and yet give a value of $5 to the rights held by a small (20 shares) shareholder. The net proceeds to the company might be as in the accompanying table.

Assumed current market price	$44.00
Administrative costs	0.75
Minimum desired value of rights to purchase one share	5.00
Allowance for price decline during offering period	3.00
Net proceeds to AT&T	$35.25

THE DECISION

The immediate decision for the financial vice president was whether or not to recommend a discount from the current market price for shares purchased by existing stockholders through the DRISPP. He felt that a discount would surely increase participation in the plan, but he wasn't sure either how large a discount was needed or how large an increase it would generate. He knew that there were costs to raising capital through other methods and felt that these costs could be given to the current shareholders in the form of a discount.

Some of the questions he had to answer were Should there be a discount? If so, how much? Should it apply to the $3,000 cash added, or just to reinvest dividends?

He felt that this decision had to be made in the larger context of an overall strategy for raising equity capital. From among AT&T's available options, he wanted to choose the best overall strategy, considering among other things:

536

Exhibit 8 (concluded)

1. The cost of the company for raising capital.
2. The effect of the current stock price.
3. The dilution effect on existing shareholders, especially where shares must be sold below book value.
4. The degree of control by management as to the timing, pricing, and size of the offering.
5. The overall costs and benefits of the alternative options for various shareholder groups.
6. The overall impact on the securities industry of the company raising large amounts of equity directly.

7. The Hanover Management Company

In October 1972, Arthur Sutter, the executive vice president of the Hanover Management Company, was reviewing his organization's investment policies and controls. Hanover was one of the larger mutual fund complexes within the United States, with assets of over $1.3 billion under management. Over the last several years, the management of Hanover had developed a set of policies designed to direct, review, and control the investment process within their several mutual funds. Sutter wanted to evaluate this set of policies, and he particularly wanted to evaluate the set of volatility measurements that Hanover used to monitor and review the risk levels of their funds. He was concerned about whether these volatility measurements served as an adequate set of guidelines for controlling the riskiness of the assets under management.

THE HISTORY OF HANOVER

The Hanover Management Company traced its origins back to the establishment of the Hanover Fund in the late 1930s by James Lattimore. Started primarily as an investment vehicle for some of Lattimore's friends and associates, the fund invested in both corporate bonds and equities. Though the investment performance of the fund was adequate in its early years, it labored along in relative obscurity until the early 1950s. Buoyed by the rise in stock market prices, the fund began to attract large inflows of savings dollars in the first half of the 1950s. By 1955, it had reached a total size of $80 million, and Lattimore had assembled a small staff of investment professionals to help him manage the fund.

In that same year, 1955, James Lattimore launched a new fund, the Hanover Equity Fund. This new fund was designed to be a more aggressive fund, investing primarily in common stocks. Investments were to be chosen on the basis of the long-term growth of the capital and the income from these stocks. Over the next several years, both of these funds attracted sizable inflows of investors' capital, and Lattimore enlarged the staff of investment professionals and formed The Hanover Management Company.

In 1958, Lattimore and his associates formed the next in a series of funds, the Hanover Growth Fund. With the exception of the market break of 1962, the Growth Fund performed adequately through its early years, as did the two earlier funds. Relatively steady sales of the funds throughout the early 1960s increased their already substantial size, and by 1966, the Hanover Management Company was managing about $700 million, distributed approximately equally among its three funds.

In late 1967, encouraged by the impressive growth of the performance funds, Hanover launched the Ranger Fund, the next of its major equity funds. The Ranger Fund invested primarily in the more speculative issues of growth corporations, hoping to obtain more rapid capital growth. The Ranger Fund could also employ leverage in the pursuit of capital gains, thereby increasing both the possible returns and risks from its investment policies. This fund was offered successfully, and was followed shortly thereafter by a similar speculative fund, the Ventura Fund, and several special purpose funds which completed the Hanover complex of equity funds.

Throughout the 1960s, Hanover also had entered other investment management areas. For example, two income funds investing primarily in corporate bonds and preferred stock (The Hanover Surety—1, and the Hanover Surety—2) had been started. Though these funds had enjoyed only modest investor acceptance during the 1960s, the stock market decline of 1970 and concurrent high bond yields had lead to a resurgence of demand for income funds in 1971 and 1972. By late 1972, these two funds together totaled $80 million in assets, the largest percentage of which was still invested in corporate bonds and preferred stock. A compilation of the major Hanover mutual funds, their investment objectives, and their size as of September 1972 is shown in Exhibit 1.

INVESTMENT PERFORMANCE

Throughout a substantial part of their history, the various Hanover funds had achieved investment performance which was at least comparable with other investment management organizations. The performance of several of their more aggressive funds had been marred by the market decline of 1969–1970, as had the record of many mutual fund managers. Since the market bottom in June 1970, however, the Hanover funds had tended to concentrate their assets in the growth areas of the equity markets, and their performance records had been excellent. The recent investment performance of their four largest equity funds is shown in Exhibit 2, as measured by the net asset value per share adjusted for dividends and capital gains distributions. In the fall of 1972, a substantial percentage of their funds' assets continued to be concentrated in the high-growth sectors of the market, though the fund managers were beginning to have some doubts about the continued attractiveness of these sectors. The equity holdings of their four largest funds as of September 30, 1972, are shown in Exhibits 3A to 3D.

THE ORGANIZATION

As the assets under management had grown during the 1950s, James Lattimore had realized the need to replace his highly personal style of money management with the skill of an investment organization. Through at least 1958, however, the firm was still rather tightly controlled by a committee composed of Lattimore and two close associates. As the number of funds proliferated, though, the need for decentralization became obvious; and throughout the 1960s, more and more of the investment decision-making was delegated to the individual portfolio managers associated with each fund. By 1968 and 1969, like most of the mutual fund industry, Hanover had developed an investment organization where almost all of the investment decisions were being made by the relatively independent portfolio managers at the head of each fund, with fairly limited direction or control from the central organization. Some of the problems with this system had become clear in the steep market decline of 1969 and 1970. Subsequently, though Hanover retained a good deal of the authority and responsibility at the fund manager level, a set of procedures and organizational features were designed to serve as both monitors and controls on the fund managers. Exhibit 4 shows the current organization chart of Hanover, though in actual operation Hanover, like most mutual fund managers, tried to maintain a highly interactive and participatory style by minimizing the importance of formal organizational structure. The decision-making process for the mutual funds was still focused around the fund managers who were both responsible and accountable for the investment decisions in their funds. They were responsible for following, on a regular and consistent basis, each of the stocks held in their fund. There was a meeting each morning where attendance was encouraged but not mandatory for all investment personnel, including both fund managers and analysts. At this meeting, a fund manager would describe any new stocks that he planned to purchase that day, and these would be discussed by his fellow fund managers and the appropriate analysts. The fund manager retained the authority to buy or sell, but if his plans stimulated active disapproval from his peers at these morning meetings, he would often revise them accordingly.

Each fund manager was responsible for the investment performance of his fund as measured chiefly against his "competitive group." The competitive group was a collection of funds managed by other competing investment advisors which were judged to be similar in terms of objectives, size, and the image with which the funds were sold by broker-dealers to the public. The exact choice of funds for each competitive group was made by the senior officers of the firm, in consultation with the fund manager involved and could be altered once a year if problems arose. Using these competitive groups as the universe of funds against each Hanover fund was to be compared, performance was then periodically measured. In particular, on every Monday a series of "pink sheets" was distributed throughout the organization which measured the percentage increase of each fund in each group for the most recent week, the most recent two months, and for the year to date. Funds within each competitive group were ranked and listed in order of performance for the year to date, and a fund's position on its respective list was considered the primary measure for monitoring investment performance. A set of these sheets for the four largest funds (as of October 3) is shown in Exhibits 5A to 5D.

At the end of each year, the fund manager received an annual bonus which was determined by his position on the final list. If a fund ranked in the bottom quarter of the list, no bonus was given. Positions on the list above the bottom resulted in a stepwise-increasing bonus which became a substantial fraction of salary for the top position.

A group of the senior officers of the firm, called the Investment Strategy Committee (ISC), met periodically to discuss and review the investment strategy for the firm as a whole. The asterisks in Exhibit 4 show the composition of the ISC. Every quarter, this committee, with all of the portfolio managers in the organization, would discuss the broad direction of investment policy. Outside economists participated in the initial discussions of the economy and the capital markets. The committee in conjunction with the individual portfolio managers would attempt to reach a set of general projections for the economy and the stock market, and decide upon an appropriate investment posture for the firm. In addition, various individual sectors of the economy were discussed in greater depth and the outlook for particular industries was argued. As chairman of this committee, Arthur Sutter reported its discussions to the organization as a whole through a written summary, which enunciated a recommended strategy for the firm in terms of both the kinds of securities to be considered, and appropriate risk levels to be maintained. For example, the summary might recommend that "above average," "average," or "below average risk levels" seemed appropriate, where risk levels quite naturally translated into the volatility measures which will be described later.

This same committee (ISC) also reviewed the strategy and performance of each fund. At various intervals, each fund manager reported in depth on his fund, its holdings, its performance, and his investment strategy. Individual stocks and industry groups were reviewed and discussed, including earnings performance and forecasts. At these sessions, each fund manager presented and defended his planned investment strategy, including the anticipated fund "risk levels" for the coming months.

As chairman of the Investment Strategy Committee and executive vice president of the firm since 1970, Arthur Sutter was responsible for reviewing the overall performance of the funds. He viewed his position as an extension of the ISC and felt responsible for translating the general policies of the ISC into implementable guidelines for the firm. In addition, the recommended policies of the quarterly ISC meetings had to be continually updated and reinterpreted in terms of the most recent changes in the equity markets, a task he undertook with discussion and guidance from the other senior personnel. Sutter regularly consulted with each of the fund managers, reviewing the fund's recent performance, and suggesting and discussing any changes in its investment posture that seemed appropriate in view of market developments. In addition, Arthur Sutter was the chief administrator for the investment division of the management company, and he was responsible for establishing a general set of information and control systems to aid him in that job.

THE INVESTMENT PHILOSOPHY

Arthur Sutter's investment philosophy tended to both mirror and in part influence the investment philosophy of the firm. He believed first and foremost that a fund must concentrate its investment resources in particular industries and stocks in order to attain above-average performance. "Owning a crosssection of American industry" was to him the surest route to mediocre performance and to be avoided by professional money managers who believed they could produce superior investment returns. Sutter believed that "your best 20 investment ideas are better than the next 20, which are better than the next 20, which should be better in turn than a crosssection of American industry." Thus, the key to success was to analyze industries and companies thoroughly, select the very best of your investment ideas, and concentrate your funds in this relatively small group of situations. Secondly, he believed that growth in earnings per share was the basic underlying force behind investment appreciation, and thus the focal point for fundamental analysis. The organization as a whole tended to confirm and support these views. For example, Exhibit 3 demonstrates that the $345 million Equity Fund was concentrated in 30 positions, a relatively small number of situations for sizeable fund; and similarly the Ranger Fund was invested in only 24 issues. All of the Hanover funds tended to select stocks with relatively high earnings growth rates, though as one might infer from Exhibit 3, this was more pronounced with the more speculative funds. Sutter believed that this concentration in what proved to be high growth areas was an important factor in Hanover's successful investment performance in recent years.

EVOLUTION OF THE VOLATILITY MEASURES

One of the principal tools used to monitor and control the risk levels of the various funds was a system of volatility or "beta" measurements which had been developed by Frank Dowling, the head of the Computer Investment Research Department.

In early 1966, Dowling had graduated with a Ph.D. from the Operations Research Department of a major midwestern university. He had remained on the faculty of that university for several years, and had become interested in the application of management science techniques to problems in the investment business. In mid-1968 he had joined the Hanover Management Company as the head of the newly created Computer Investment Research Department. His mandate was to explore the use of quantitative techniques and computers to both the day-to-day operations of Hanover and to possible systems for predicting price movements in the equities markets.

Because he was familiar with the basic concepts of the capital asset pricing models that had been described in the academic literature, one of Frank Dowling's first projects was to compute and analyze the volatilities or betas of the various Hanover funds. Frank Dowling had experimented with a number of different methods of computing these volatility measurements. There were several "beta services" available from brokerage firms that used several years of weekly or monthly price data for each stock listed on a major exchange to develop estimates of individual stock betas. The weighted average of these betas for all stocks in the portfolio (weighted, that is, by their dollar amounts in the portfolio) would give an estimate for the beta of the equity portion of Hanover's funds. Unfortunately, "betas" were not generally available for the warrants, bonds, and convertible issues that formed a sizeable portion of several of Hanover's funds. Furthermore, it was impossible to get a continuously updated listed of the holdings of competitive funds to compute their volatilities. Because of these factors, Frank Dowling chose a system for estimating volatility that ignored the individual betas for particular securities and instead was derived from daily net asset value changes for a fund as a whole. Basically, his beta system worked like this for a given fund: The daily net percentage change of the fund was divided by the daily percentage change of the stock market as a whole (as measured by the NYSE Composite), to yield a daily estimate of beta.

$$\beta = \frac{\Delta(f)}{\Delta(\text{NYSE})}$$

These daily estimates were then smoothed and adjusted in various ways to remove misleading statistical noise. The time series of recent daily estimates of beta was then combined into an "exponentially weighted average," where the most recent days received the largest weights, and succeedingly earlier days received exponentially decreasing weights until there was an effective weight of zero for the estimates of the distant past. The quantitive details of this method are explained in Exhibit 6. Basically, the method yields an estimate of the portfolio beta which is dependent upon recent daily net asset value changes, and which is continuously updatable on a daily basis. A number of empirical experiments were conducted which studied the ability of these exponentially weighted beta estimates to predict the market-related movements of a fund over the future three months. Dowling found that the best predictions were obtained when the exponential weights "tailed off" rather slowly, such that effectively half of the composite beta estimate was dependent upon the most recent three months of daily price changes. Unfortunately if the weights "tailed off" this slowly, the beta estimate in the actual monitoring system would be very slow to respond to known near term changes in the underlying portfolio composition. Dowling realized that fund managers would need a volatility system which responded more quickly to their portfolio changes. He therefore adjusted the actual weights for the real-time system so that effectively one half the weight was dependent upon only the most recent five weeks of data, sacrificing some predictive ability in order to construct a more responsive system.

In the late fall of 1969, a monitoring system based upon the above betas was begun. In the monitoring system, a set of volatility measures or betas was calculated daily not only for Hanover's funds, but for all funds in the "competitive groups." These volatility measurements were reported on the weekly "pink sheets" (see Exhibit 5). Though these early monitors of volatility were widely circulated throughout the firm, they had little immediate impact upon the investment policies of the fund managers or senior officers of the firm.

Throughout 1969 and the first half of 1970, the general stock market decline took a heavy toll on the performance of Hanover's aggressive funds. In this period, Arthur Sutter had been promoted to executive vice president of the manager company and charged with the responsibility of monitoring the overall investment posture of the firm. Upon accepting this position in the early part of 1970, Sutter tried to analyze some of Hanover's recent problems, and in June had enlisted the cooperation of Frank Dowling in the Computer Department. Dowling presented an analysis of the volatility levels of the funds during the 1968–1970 period which demonstrated that the severe declines during the bear market of 1969 and early 1970 were entirely consistent with the high volatilities of the funds. Throughout the first part of 1970 several of the aggressive fund managers had continued to hold on to stocks which had already suffered severe declines, presumably in the belief that the worst must be over, at least for these stocks. In retrospect, however, these stocks had continued to decline with the market until the bottom was reached in the early summer, as might have been predicted on the basis of their volatilities.

As a by-product of these studies, Arthur Sutter, Frank Dowling, and the rest of the organization became convinced that volatilities should be used more to help monitor and control the risk levels of Hanover's funds. In particular, they designed a way that the volatility measurements might be used within the organization in response to changing market conditions and forecasts to monitor the risk levels of Hanover's funds relative to other competitive funds.

An informal system for adjusting and monitoring the fund's volatilities through various phases of the market cycle began in the early fall of 1970. The ISC and the individual fund managers had discussed the outlook for the economy and capital markets and concluded that an optimistic fore-cast for the stock market seemed appropriate. However, some of the individual fund managers at Hanover had been badly burned by the effects of the market decline and were still rather cautiously investing in cash and stable stocks. The volatilities of most funds, including Hanover's had been dropping sharply at the time the market bottomed out in June and had remained fairly modest relative to their previous levels. The ISC and Arthur Sutter decided that, in view of their market forecast, Hanover's funds should be postured with higher-than-average risk levels, that is, higher volatilities than the average of their respective competitive groups. The fund managers were thus encouraged to raise their volatilities by placing money in more aggressive issues.

In the fall of 1970, the funds thus began to move into more aggressive stocks, including some of the issues that had dropped precipitously in the market decline. Noting that the individual stock betas in the computer peripherals industry were very high, the managers of two of the aggres-sive funds invested heavily in this group, including Memorex, Telex, and several others. To their dismay, as the stock market indices rose, these computer peripheral issues sunk to successive new lows. Later in the year, the two aggressive funds bailed out of these issues, realizing sub-stantial losses which significantly impeded their already rather poor per-formance in 1970. Left rather disgusted and frustrated with this concept of volatilities which had prompted them to purchase computer peripherals, some of the fund managers were highly skeptical of the new beta system. They nonetheless maintained relatively high portfolio volatilities at the urging of Arthur Sutter and continued to invest in higher growth rate stocks.

Throughout the prolonged bull market from the fall of 1970 to the spring of 1972, fund managers were urged to keep their fund betas high relative to their competitive group. Many of the fund managers had also decided that the somewhat uncertain inflationary environment demanded that they invest in companies with a very strong competitive position in high growth sectors of the economy with little to lose from government controls or union demands, for example, IBM, Xerox, Polaroid, Avon Products, McDonald's, Merck, and similar companies. This combined strategy resulted in impressive investment performance through the various phases of the bull market.

The important variables that Arthur Sutter and the fund managers monitored were the performance and volatility relative to the other funds in a competitive group. This raw data was compiled into "performance charts," as shown in Exhibits 7A to 7D, which gave a pictorial time history of these variables. At the top of this chart, the weekly performance (percent change in net asset value) of a fund and its performance relative to the average of funds in its competitive group were graphed. At the bottom of this chart, the time series of beta estimates was plotted to monitor volatility. These "performance charts" were widely distributed throughout the organization and provided one of the principal tools for observing investment performance.

MONITORING AND CONTROLLING THE RISK LEVELS OF THE FUNDS

The events of mid-1972 lent some insight into the operational use of the volatility measures. Throughout May of 1972, the senior investment personnel (working in part through the ISC) and the fund managers began to become less optimistic about the outlook for the equity markets. Though there was some divergence of opinion on the future progress of the stock market, in general they believed a neutral or perhaps somewhat pessimistic projection was appropriate for the next six months. Accordingly, the ISC decided that Hanover funds should maintain "average risk levels" rather than the more aggressive posture several funds had been maintaining.

In practice, "average risk levels" translated into a rule-of-thumb for the volatilities of the mutual funds; in particular, the volatility of a fund should equal the average of its competitive group ±10 percent. In the investment advisory area, "average risk levels" meant the volatilities should be around the middle of their historical range, which generally fluctuated between 0.8 and 1.25. These rules-of-thumb were used only as guidelines, and money managers theoretically were permitted to set their own volatility levels, using the Investment Strategy Committee only as an advisor. In practice, though, Arthur Sutter tended to monitor the volatility of the various funds and advisory accounts rather closely. For example, Arthur Sutter once rather abruptly recalled one of the money managers from the middle of a long-delayed vacation and asked him to explain why his volatility was so high. The fund managers thus felt some pressure to conform to the guidelines whether they agreed with the ISC or not.

Consequently, in late May and June of 1972, most of the fund managers began a deliberate effort to scale down their volatilities, particularly those fund managers who had been "running fairly high betas" in the early part of 1972. The results of this effort are illustrated by the "performance charts" in Exhibit 7. While the volatility of the more conservative Hanover Fund remained about the same, the volatilities of the Equity, Growth, and Ranger funds dropped substantially in the summer of 1972.

Rather than let volatilities influence their choice of particular stocks, most fund managers used their cash positions as the basic control to lower their volatilities. For example, the manager of the Hanover Equity Fund believed that the major growth stocks, in spite of their historically high P/Es, were still the most attractive opportunities for investment. He scaled down his positions in some of these issues and retained the proceeds in cash, but he did not invest in lower beta stocks. Over the time period covered by Exhibit 7B, he effectively lowered his volatility from around 1.30 to 1.10 by going to over 20 percent cash in his portfolio (of course, most of the "cash" was actually kept in short-term governments and commercial paper). By October, the names in his portfolio had not changed markedly, but his volatility had been reduced by the cash so that it was comparable with other funds in his competitive group. Indeed, the Equity Fund manager believed that the 1.10 reading of the weekly sheets and Exhibit 7B overestimated the current volatility of his fund. He regularly received estimates of individual stock betas from a brokerage house, based upon monthly price data for the most recent five years. Like the other Hanover fund managers, he regularly tracked his portfolio beta based upon the dollar-weighted average of these individual stock betas. On this basis, the beta of the Equities Fund had been reduced to around 0.95 to 1.00 by early October. He believed that there was a substantial lag in the "official volatilities" on the weekly "pink sheets" and performance charts and that over the next month or two, these volatilities would gradually drift down to the 0.95 to 1.00 range.

Most fund managers used the weighted average of individual stock betas to give them better guidelines for controlling the volatility of their funds. In addition, these dollar-weighted average betas could be used as an important tool in their discussions with Arthur Sutter. After a fund manager and Sutter had discussed, agreed upon, and implemented a portfolio change, the official volatility measurements would be slow to respond in picking up this change. It would generally take weeks or months for this change to be effectively monitored by the official volatilities; and in the meantime, without some other measure, there might be some nervous discussions with Arthur Sutter. The dollar-weighted average could be instantaneously changed, of course, by changing the weighting of the individual stock betas to correspond with the new portfolio composition. Portfolio managers often preferred to rely upon these more responsive estimates in discussing their portfolio strategy with Sutter.

The manager of the Ranger Fund had also used cash to lower his fund's volatility over the summer of 1972, from a high of around 2.00 to its current value of 1.20. He had attained the earlier high volatilities with the use of leverage; for example in April, he had invested borrowings equal to about 10 percent of the fund's net assets. Over the summer, he reduced a number of his investment positions and used the proceeds to first eliminate the leverage and then raise cash. At one point in September, he held a 40 percent cash position and in October, the Ranger Fund held 30 percent of its assets in cash or cash equivalents. The remaining 70 percent of the fund was invested in relatively volatile stocks with a dollar-weighted beta of 1.67. Considering his 30 percent cash, the Ranger Fund manager concluded that his portfolio beta was about 1.20, which was consistent with "the official estimate" of beta on the pink sheets.

Throughout this same period, the volatility of the Hanover Fund had remained around its early year level of about 0.90 to 1.00, which placed it somewhat above its competitive group average. Arthur Sutter had been exerting some pressure upon the management team to reduce its volatility; and in October they began to sell off some of the higher beta issues which they no longer had confidence in, to scale their volatility back to an "average" level.

Hanover's use of cash to control volatilities sometimes led to confusion among more traditional investment personnel associated with Hanover. For example, at several times during the fall, directors of Hanover had commented to Arthur Sutter, "You must really be bearish on the market, with 20 percent of the Equity Fund and 30 or 40 percent of our most speculative fund in cash. What kind of market decline are you expecting?" On these occasions, Sutter had replied that the organization was "not really all that bearish; indeed we're probably more neutral than bearish. We just want to keep our volatilities average or somewhat below average for the time being, while still concentrating our assets in the issues our fund managers know best." While this explanation had seemed to satisfy the directors, the issue did tend to be raised again periodically—Arthur Sutter felt he had a long-term educational task to pursue with his directors and other more traditional investors who equated large cash positions with extreme caution.

THE REACTIONS OF THE ORGANIZATION TO THE VOLATILITY SYSTEM

There was some divergence of opinion within the investment organization about the benefits of the volatility measurements and about the system for controlling investment policy. While, in general, most personnel tended to believe these measurements and controls were valuable, there were a number of reservations about their actual use.

The research analysts were not really affected much by the volatility system and indeed were explicitly cautioned not to recommend stocks on the basis of their volatilities. Nonetheless, the beta of an individual stock did tend to have some effect upon the analysts. Because they felt a need to "sell" their recommendations to fund managers, the analysts were somewhat reluctant to recommend high beta stocks at a time when they knew the managers were under some pressure to reduce their portfolio betas. With this exception, they were fairly well insulated from the volatility stem and were not overly concerned with its advantages or drawbacks.

The fund managers, however, were directly affected by the volatility system and actively concerned with its evolution. On balance, they believed it was a useful and effective tool for controlling the investment policy of the funds. Some of the fund managers had reservations about some aspects of the system, though, and several of their comments are recorded below:

> Betas can probably have some constructive influence, but they just aren't that important to a fund manager's performance. Look at the year-to-date performance on the Ranger competitive group (see Exhibit 5D). This year, when the market was generally up, one of the lowest beta funds was up 30 percent and the highest beta funds were down 20 percent, exactly the opposite of what volatilities would suggest. If betas are important at all, they're obviously only a very small fraction of the investment job. And whatever their value, they certainly don't explain the differences in investment performance like they're supposed to. Stock selection, the thing beta enthusiasts shrug off as "alpha," is the important thing.

> Betas are usually a good measure of risk, but sometimes their use can be counterproductive. This summer I got my volatility back down by eliminating some higher beta stocks and holding some cash; but by going to cash, I ended up with a much larger percentage of my common stock investments in those issues that were left. The way I see it, I was more exposed, not less, after I reduced my volatility.

> It's all got this look of science, but we have the Hanover systems of betas which tend to drift; plus I compute two beta estimates from individual stock betas I get from two different brokers. I've then got three estimates of my portfolio volatility, and they're all different, sometimes by as much as 20 percent. How scientific is that?

> There's an awful lot that betas leave out; I'm just not sure they're a good risk measure. At one time some of our performance funds had an enormous percentage of their holdings in mobile homes. I'm sure that was a tremendous exposure in a potentially overpriced industry; but the fund betas didn't seem to be all that high. Our Equity Fund now has almost all 350 million of its assets in a small number of issues in one sector of the market: the high multiple, high growth rate, glamour companies that tend to move as a group. That's why that fund has done so well this year. But all these companies are now selling at record prices and multiples, and the gap between them and

the rest of the market has never been larger. One or two earnings declines in this group could bring down the multiples sharply; just look what happened to Digital Equipment lately, a 20 percent drop in price overnight. It seems to me that the Equity Fund is now in a very exposed posture, and yet the volatility of the fund is really quite reasonable. It seems to me that beta only records past variability without regard for real risk, the risk of substantial changes in the fundamental market valuation of a company or a whole sector of the market. In the past, we've been an "earnings growth at any price" outfit, and that's been one of the great strengths of our stock selections. But it can be a very dangerous philosophy, and particularly right now. I think the betas tend to lull us into a false sense of security on this score.

The beta system is an innovation, and probably a useful tool from Arthur Sutter's point of view. But it also tends to minimize the importance of a fund manager's feel for the market. In doing so, I think it threatens an important part of the investment business and creates an unnecessary tension between the Investment Strategy Committee and the fund managers.

The volatility system itself monitors an important dimension of investment strategy. How else are you going to measure risk? But the real problem is that it isn't applied symmetrically. If your beta is a little on the high side, people just sort of wink and caution you; and besides you can always use a little cash to get it back down and still hold on to your favorite hot stocks. But if your beta is a little low, there's tremendous pressure to get it back up. And cash is no help at all. Suppose I wanted to buy a block of AT&T today, and incidentally I think it's a hell of a good buy right now. My beta is already a little too low, and people would really frown on my picking up a stock like that with a lower volatility yet. Once it has moved, its volatility goes back up again and then you can buy it, but by then you've missed it; it's too late.

If there's a problem, it's not with beta itself, but with our whole system of measuring performance. Year-to-date performance is the yardstick, which means that right now we've all got our eye on the next two and a half months. That's an awfully short time horizon, which could someday generate pressure for short-term performance if we're not careful. Maybe that's partially responsible for a couple of our recent problems with one or two aggressive stocks—too short a time horizon. I'm also not sure that measuring performance relative to some competitive group is appropriate. Who's to say what the appropriate competitive group is? I don't think mine is really right. By our system, if your group is down 30 percent, but you're down only 20 percent, that's great performance. I'm not sure the investor who just lost 20 percent of his savings thinks that's great performance. Maybe we should be more concerned about absolute losses rather than relative performance.

Because our volatility measures have such tremendous lags, fund managers tend to overadjust. Fund managers should be given a lot more time to change their betas, and there'd be less temptation to overmanage the portfolio. Also, betas tend to do some weird things in the short term. If the market starts to move and your stocks aren't participating yet, the betas look very low. Yet it's just in these sectors of the market where there's the most potential gain, not in those sectors which have already moved. Similarly, if the market's dropping like a stone, but your stocks haven't yet (perhaps they've even risen a little), your beta suddenly looks awfully low and that's supposed to be good. But I'm not sure that's not the riskiest place to be in a down market; I'd much rather be in stocks which have already suffered their decline. In the long run, I suppose betas are a useful tool, but they can lead to some strange results when you try to control them in the short run.

Though these comments from fund managers describe some of their misgivings about the volatility concepts, there was no clearly visible pressure to discard the beta measurements. Indeed, most of the fund managers seemed to agree that the betas added a useful dimension to the investment policy of the firm.

FRANK DOWLING'S VIEW OF THE SYSTEM

Frank Dowling was generally pleased with the evolution of volatility measurements at Hanover. He felt that, largely because of top management support, they had become an important tool for controlling risk. He was, however, concerned about a number of issues and problems that their use raised.

First of all, he felt that nonmathematicians tried to read too much into their precision, after all 1.20 wasn't much different from 1.30 in terms of the statistical confidence in the estimates. He was consequently concerned that fund managers might overreact to small changes in their fund's estimated volatility. He hoped that his current weighting scheme was an appropriate compromise between the two dangers of overly noisy portfolio betas to which fund managers might overreact, or overly smooth betas which did not respond quickly enough to known changes in the underlying portfolio.

He was particularly concerned about the extent to which the beta measurements were a reliable proxy for risk. Hanover tended to concentrate its funds in a small number of issues rather than widely diversifying them, and beta was theoretically a reliable measure of total risk only for fully diversified portfolios. Frank had studied this problem of diversification and, in particular, the degree to which the "specific risk" of individual issues could be diversified away with certain numbers of holdings, leaving only the market-related risk measured by beta. It turned out that over 90 percent of the "specific risk" was effectively diversified away when a portfolio was evenly distributed among just 20 independent stocks. Thus, Hanover's policy of concentrating in 25 to 35 stocks was not in and of itself a great problem.

Unfortunately, the small number of stocks in Hanover portfolios were often not really independent, and Frank saw this as a greater problem. For example, at one time one of the more speculative funds had invested about 20 percent of its assets in the mobile home industry, whose stocks tend to move together. Similarly, though the Equity Fund was invested in 30 situations, they were all in the high-growth, high P/E, "glamour sector" of the market. One of Frank's assistants had argued that all these stocks tended to move together, and that in effect the Equity Fund was really invested in only four or five stocks. Although Frank had never seen any firm empirical evidence on this, he was concerned that the "specific risk" of some of Hanover's portfolios might be substantial, in addition to the market-related risk measured by betas.

Frank was particularly concerned about this now because of the concentration in high growth stocks throughout the organization's funds, including even the balanced Hanover Fund. This policy certainly was responsible, in large part, for Hanover's success in the last year; many of these growth stocks had risen to record highs and record multiples. To demonstrate this, the Technical Analysis Department of Hanover had assembled and tracked their own "Hanover Glamour Average," a composite of "glamour companies" considered to be typical of many of Hanover's holdings (see accompanying list). A memo distributed from the Technical Department, shown in Exhibit 8, pointed out that in terms of both absolute P/E multiple and P/E multiple relative to the Dow Jones Industrials, this glamour average was at or near record highs. Frank wondered to what extent these high multiples might be in themselves a significant source of specific risk; for after all, a very high P/E relative to historical norms was certainly one of the conventional warnings of investment risk. The scatter diagram shown in Exhibit 9 illustrated some of Frank's concern. Each of the stocks held in the Equity Fund as of September 30 was plotted as a point in Exhibit 9, located both in terms of volatility (beta) and P/E. Note that the fund was concentrated in relatively high multiple stocks, but these same stocks seemed to have reasonable volatilities. Particularly because these multiples were at or near record historical levels, Frank wondered if beta might not be understating the risk involved for the portfolio as a whole. He wanted to design some empirical studies which would shed light on these issues.

ARTHUR SUTTER AND THE VOLATILITY SYSTEM

Arthur Sutter wanted to reevaluate the system of investment controls and policies Hanover had established, including the volatility measurements used to monitor risk levels. On balance, he believed that this system probably had aided the organization in achieving its investment performance over the past two years and might continue to provide a useful set of information and controls. There had been some problems with fund managers overreacting to the system at first, for example, building their portfolio from a beta book and trading stocks solely because of their betas, but these he thought were largely solved. He thought that fund managers might still overreact from time to time to the volatility measures because they knew he followed these numbers so closely, but he thought this might be a reasonable price to pay for the system.

There were several issues that did concern him, however. The current system of organization and controls appeared to have worked adequately in the bull market of the last two years, but other past organizations had also appeared to be very successful in bull markets, before leading to real problems in a steep market decline. Indeed, the system had been at least partially designed in reaction to the problems that became evident in the market decline of 1969 and 1970. Arthur Sutter thought that the current system was in this sense still very much an untested experiment. He wondered whether it would really help Hanover control their losses in a market decline, or alter their investment policies in a period of unfavorable performance comparisons with other institutions.

He was also concerned about the extent to which the volatility measures were suitable as measures of investment risk. He felt that he really needed a set of simple measures which cut through all the data and separated all the factors of individual stock selection and strategy from issues of overall portfolio risk. He had some doubts that beta was a complete measure of risk, but he wondered what other measures would be appropriate to augment the volatility system.

Arthur Sutter also wanted to evaluate some possible extensions of the beta concepts. He knew that some other organizations were using beta to calculate risk-adjusted performance measures to evaluate their portfolio managers and wondered whether such an extension would be sensible at Hanover.

Also, several studies that had been published recently had suggested that mutual funds should describe their volatility levels in their prospectuses. Basically, Arthur Sutter believed his individual investors did not even understand very simple ideas like net asset values, much less an arcane concept like beta. He believed that for the most part, they would not be well-served by an exposure to these volatility concepts in the prospectus. On the other hand, he was concerned that there might be significant regulatory pressure in this direction in the future, and he thought Hanover and the mutual fund industry would be wise to anticipate this pressure and plan their positions accordingly.

For the present moment, however, he was most concerned with an evaluation of Hanover's own policies and systems as a way of implementing investment strategy and controlling the risk levels of their investors' funds.

Exhibit 1

Funds managed by Hanover and their objectives

Fund name	Objectives (as quoted from the prospectus)	Net assets 9/30/72 ($ millions)
Hanover fund	An open-end mutual investment fund, whose prime objective is to provide a Balanced Investment. The Fund's assets are invested primarily in a diversified portfolio of bonds and stocks. . . .	$306
Hanover Equity Fund	A mutual fund with possible long-term growth of capital and of income as its primary objective.	345
Hanover Growth Fund	A mutual fund emphasizing long-term capital growth as its objective, . . . with current income as a secondary consideration.	411
Ranger Fund	A speculative mutual fund seeking capital appreciation, which intends to employ leverage and short-term trading. . . .	58
Ventura Fund	A speculative mutual fund seeking capital appreciation; current income is only an incidental consideration. . . .	49
Hanover Surety—1	A mutual fund whose primary purpose is current and future income. A secondary purpose is preservation . . . of the shareholder's principal.	43
Hanover Surety—2	A mutual fund whose primary purpose is current and future income. A secondary purpose is preservation . . . of the stockholder's principal.	37

Exhibit 2

Performance records for four Hanover funds (Percent changes in net asset value adjusted for all distributions)

	1965	1966	1967	1968	1969	First half 1970	Second half 1970	First half 1971	Second half 1971	First half 1972	6/30/72 to 9/30/72
Hanover Fund	+11.7%	−3.4%	18.6%	9.4%	−7.3%	−14.6%	18.7%	14.0%	6.2%	6.8%	3.4%
Hanover Equity Fund	+11.1	−0.8	24.2	13.8	−3.8	−22.0	20.3	21.2	8.3	17.1	1.3
Hanover Growth Fund	+27.0	−6.3	34.5	14.9	−14.0	−20.9	18.9	18.5	4.6	13.2	−1.4
Hanover Ranger Fund	—	—	—	+46.5	−24.7	−34.3	16.8	28.6	9.8	28.6	−5.6
S&P 500*	+12.3	−10.0	23.7	10.8	−8.3	−19.4	28.3	9.7	4.0	6.5	4.8

* Percent return including dividends.

Exhibit 3A

Portfolio composition of the Hanover Fund—September 30, 1972 (percent)

Common stocks		51.4%

Chrysler
  General Motors
  Monroe Auto Equipment
	Automotive	8.2%

Government Employees Insurance
  MGIC Investment
  Pennsylvania Life
  U.S. Fidelity and Guaranty
	Insurance	7.7

Exxon
  Lubrizol
  Schlumberger
	Oil and oil services	5.6

Coca Cola
  Disney
  Polaroid
	Consumer products	8.5

McDonald's
  Penney (J.C.)
  Sears,·Roebuck
	Retail trade	5.2

Baxter Laboratories
  Johnson & Johnson
  Schering
	Drugs and medical supplies	4.7

IBM Xerox	Office equipment	4.6
Eastern Airlines TWA	Transportation and equipment	3.7
General Electric	Electrical equipment and electronics	1.8
Other Investments	Miscellaneous	1.4
Convertible bonds and preferred stocks		17.5
Bonds, Notes, and preferred stocks		24.8
Other assets		6.3
Commercial paper, cash and equivalent (net)	6.3	

Exhibit 3B
Portfolio composition of the Hanover Equity Fund—September 30, 1972 (percent)

Common stocks			76.8%
Disney			
Gillette			
Howard Johnson's	Consumer products and services	20.4%	
Monroe Auto Equipment			
Philip Morris			
Ramada Inns			
Tampax			
Anheuser-Busch			
Coca Cola	Food and beverage	15.2	
McDonald's			
Tropicana			
American Express			
MGIC Investment	Insurance and financial services	8.0	
Travelers			
Kresge			
Sears, Roebuck	Retail trade	8.4	
Standards Brands Paint			
Kerr-McGee			
Lubrizol	Oil	7.2	
Schlumberger			
Sedco			
Burroughs			
IBM	Office equipment	8.1	
Xerox			
Avon Products			
Johnson & Johnson	Drugs and hospital supplies	6.3	
Merck			
Schering			
Eastman Kodak	Photography	3.2	
Polaroid			
Short-term U.S. government agency obligations			4.5
Other assets			18.7
Commercial paper, cash and equivalent (net)		18.7%	

Exhibit 3C
Portfolio composition of the Hanover Growth Fund—September 30, 1972 (percent)

Common stocks		81.3%

Eastman Kodak
  Farah
  Ford
  General Motors
  Gillette
  Levitz Furniture
  Penney (J.C.)
  Polaroid
  Reynolds Industries
	Consumer products and retail trade	23.0%

Data General
  Honeywell
  IBM
  Xerox
	Data-processing and office equipment	15.3

ABC
  Howard Johnson's
  Teleprompter
  Warner Communications
	Leisure time	6.2

Delta Airlines
  Southern Pacific
  Southern Railway
  Trans World Airlines
	Transportation	6.1

Baxter Laboratories
  Bristol-Myers
  Miles Laboratories
  Syntex
	Drugs, medical, and cosmetics	5.0

Energy Conversion Devices
  Fairchild Camera
  Westinghouse Electric
  Zenith
	Electronics and electrical equipment	4.4

Kerr-McGee
  Louisiana Land and Exploration
  Schlumberger
	Oil and gas	6.2

Continental
  First Charter Financial
  INA
  MGIC Investment
	Financial services	4.8

Gulf & Western Industries Loews Corporation	Diversified companies	2.8
Cummins Engine Peabody Galion	Industrial and agricultural machinery	3.0

Bandag
  Millipore
  Western Union
	Other products and services	4.5

Corporate bonds		3.4
U.S. government obligations		0.4
Other assets		14.9
Commercial paper, cash and equivalent (net)		<u>14.9%</u>

Exhibit 3D
Portfolio composition of the Ranger Fund—September 30, 1972 (percent)

Common stocks			70.1%
American Express General Reinsurance MGIC Investment Travelers	} Insurance and financial services	14.8%	
Automatic Data Processing Data General General Automation Honeywell Intel National Semiconductor	} Electronics and office equipment	16.2	
Franklin Mint Gillette Philip Morris Polaroid Syntex	} Consumer products and nondurables	13.0	
ABC Bandag IMS International National Chemsearch Teleprompter	} Services	12.3	
McDonald's Ponderosa System Winnebago Industries	} Leisure	8.6	
Murphy Oil Northwest Airlines	} Miscellaneous	5.2	
Other assets			29.9
Cash and equivalent		29.9%	

Exhibit 4
Organization chart

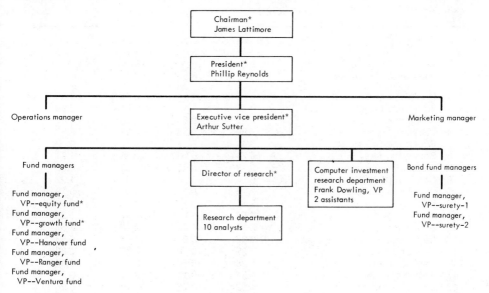

* Member of the Investment Strategy Committee (ISC).

Exhibit 5A
Weekly "pink sheet" for Hanover Fund: Fund performance report for October 13, 1972
(Balanced funds)

	Rank and fund name	Percent change from 12/31/71	Percent change from 10/6/72	Percent change from 8/11/72	Short-term volatility versus market
1	McCormick & Smith Balanced	14.30%	−0.50%	0.63%	0.84
2	Hanover Fund*	9.86	−0.18	0.90	0.95
3	Fisher Balanced Fund	8.74	−0.29	4.83	0.60
4	Pilgrim Fund	7.27	−0.57	1.73	0.75
5	U.S. Security	6.93	−0.19	2.54	0.68
6	Sherwood Balanced	6.91	0.10	1.58	0.57
7	Peterson-Clark Fund	4.67	−0.33	3.64	0.49
8	Equity Mutual	4.40	0.00	3.93	0.66
9	Montgomery-Verdon Mutual	3.93	−0.59	1.76	0.51
10	Danvers A	3.87	0.10	3.43	0.51
11	National Fund	3.40	−0.26	0.80	0.88
12	Investors Security	3.39	0.00	1.53	0.45
13	Philadelphia-Balanced	2.74	−0.08	0.91	0.50
14	Bacron Income	2.36	−0.50	−0.12	0.53
15	Foster Balanced	1.76	−0.12	0.86	0.52
	Average	5.80	−0.23	1.93	0.63

* Dividends excluded in performance calculations.

Exhibit 5B

Weekly "pink sheet" for Hanover Equity Fund: Fund performance report for
October 13, 1972 (Common stock funds)

	Rank and fund name	Percent change from 12/31/71	Percent change from 10/6/72	Percent change from 8/11/72	Short-term volatility versus market
1	Hanover Equity Fund*	16.83%	−1.04%	−2.08%	1.10
2	Waterford Investing	10.16	−0.19	2.31	0.99
3	Associated Stock	9.42	−0.60	0.83	1.01
4	Maryland Fund	7.89	−0.58	−0.12	0.67
5	Sherwood Stock	7.43	−0.14	1.30	0.99
6	Surveyor Stock	6.21	−0.56	1.39	1.01
7	Harvesters-Accum.	5.18	−0.62	1.38	0.88
8	Colonial (A-1)	5.16	−0.35	0.41	1.02
9	Consolidated Fund	3.19	−0.14	3.44	0.73
10	Mackay Equity	2.62	−0.11	3.33	0.58
11	Winchell-Accum.	2.57	−1.02	−2.67	1.25
12	Shelby Fund	2.35	−0.42	4.22	0.67
13	Connecticut Investment	2.32	−0.09	1.66	0.53
14	New England Trust	2.22	−0.16	1.47	0.89
15	Capital Fund	1.28	−0.56	−3.21	0.84
16	Northwest Stock	−1.01	−0.13	2.17	0.71
17	Bacron Fundamental Inv.	−1.52	−0.77	−1.92	0.95
18	Oxford Fund	−4.58	−0.73	−3.47	1.22
	Average	4.37	−0.46	0.58	0.89

* Dividends excluded in performance calculations.

Exhibit 5C
Weekly "pink sheet" for Hanover Growth Fund for October 13, 1972

Rank and fund name	Percent change from 12/31/71	Percent change from 10/6/72	Percent change from 8/11/72	Short-term volatility versus market
1 Spectrum Fund	20.24%	0.18%	2.22%	1.07
2 Weatherall Investors	16.37	0.00	−0.61	1.32
3 New England Growth	17.81	−0.07	−1.58	1.30
4 Hanover Growth Fund*	12.13	−1.14	−2.81	1.17
5 Associated Apprec.	9.68	0.29	−8.11	1.77
6 Surveyor Variable	9.39	−0.66	−0.44	1.26
7 Founders Growth	6.27	−1.03	−5.08	1.33
8 Associated Growth	3.78	−0.17	−13.12	1.78
9 Colonial (A-Z)	3.69	−0.46	−5.45	1.50
10 Newhouser Fund	3.44	−0.60	−4.38	1.27
11 Winchell-Accum.	2.57	−1.02	−2.67	1.25
12 Shelby Fund	2.35	−0.42	4.22	0.67
13 Colonial (A-4)	1.76	0.56	−2.86	1.19
14 Philadelphia Growth	0.74	−0.31	−6.36	1.35
15 Danforth Fund	0.73	−0.40	−4.01	0.96
16 Oxford Fund	−0.48	−0.73	−3.47	1.22
17 Hutchins Fund	−0.65	−1.26	−4.74	1.38
18 Northwest-Growth	−1.14	−0.85	−3.93	1.37
19 Winchell Science	−1.23	−0.38	−4.36	1.31
20 National Growth	−2.31	−0.74	−4.54	1.15
21 Bacron Growth	−7.45	−1.44	−7.29	1.41
Average	4.30	−0.51	−3.78	1.29

* Dividends excluded in performance calculations.

Exhibit 5D

Weekly "pink sheet" for Hanover Ranger Fund for October 13, 1972 (Smaller capital appreciation funds—Ranger comparison)

	Rank and fund name	Percent change from 12/31/71	Percent change from 10/6/72	Percent change from 8/11/72	Short-term volatility versus market
1	Chancellor Fund	34.18%	−1.29%	−3.78%	0.72
2	Hanover Ranger Fund*	21.33	0.00	−4.87	1.20
3	Equity Vista	21.24	−0.49	0.46	1.05
4	Albany National	15.68	−0.24	−0.12	1.43
5	Founders Special	13.47	−0.70	−0.18	0.75
6	Incremental Growth	7.31	−0.21	−3.53	1.12
7	Alpha Fund	6.84	0.20	−14.82	1.78
8	Challenger	5.25	−0.94	−8.97	1.68
9	Investors Apprec. Stock	4.63	−0.48	−0.95	0.71
10	Dixon Equity	4.55	0.00	−2.39	1.29
11	Lafayette Invest.	4.34	0.00	−7.47	1.66
12	Equity Invest.	3.65	−0.17	−6.50	1.05
13	Oxford Leverage	3.55	−1.01	−4.81	1.77
14	Fletcher Growth	3.23	−0.86	−3.78	1.25
15	Professional Invest.	2.88	0.00	−3.98	1.07
16	Newton Fund	2.13	−0.83	−6.03	0.91
17	Philadelphia Special	−1.44	−1.44	−8.85	1.39
18	Capital Leverage	−4.66	−1.26	−11.39	1.34
19	Bacron Capital	−4.78	−1.12	−9.85	1.54
20	Westchester Fund	−5.52	0.76	−9.42	1.29
21	Summit Colonial	−8.30	−1.69	−8.30	1.34
22	Yorktown Capital	−10.86	−0.95	−9.25	0.87
23	Executive Cons.	−14.62	−3.16	−22.32	2.00
24	Greenwich Special	−20.81	0.00	−16.13	1.95
	Average	2.93	−0.66	−6.97	1.30

* Dividends excluded in performance calculations.

Exhibit 6
Exponentially smoothed estimate of a portfolio beta used by Hanover·

Consider a mutual fund whose percentage change in net asset value, Δf, is measured daily and compared to the percentage change in the market as a whole, Δm. For each day i, define the daily ratio of these two percentage, to be b_i:

$$b_i = \Delta f_i / \Delta m_i.$$

Furthermore, on each day i, compute a sequentially updated estimate of beta by:

$$\hat{\beta} = w_i b_i + (1 - w_i)\,\hat{\beta}_{i-1}$$

that is, the updated estimate one day i, $\hat{\beta}_i$, is just the weighted average of b_i and the previous day's updatable estimate, $\hat{\beta}_{i-1}$, where the weight (w_i) is some number between 0 and 1. This sequential updating system provides an estimate which is always a weighted average of previous day's b_i's. For example, consider the special case when w_i is a constant:

$$w_i = w, \text{ for all } i.$$

Then, the updated estimated will be:

$$\hat{\beta}_i = w b_i + (1 - w)\,\hat{\beta}_{i-1}.$$

But we also know that on the previous day

$$\hat{\beta}_{i-1} = w b_{i-1} + (1 - w)\,\hat{\beta}_{i-2}.$$

Therefore, substituting into the previous expression, we get

$$\hat{\beta}_i = w b_i + (1 - w)\, w b_{i-1} - (1 - w)^2\,\hat{\beta}_{i-2}.$$

And continuing this substitution process, we could show that

$$\hat{\beta}_i = w[b_i + (1 - w)\, b_{i-1} + (1 - w)^2\, b_{i-2} + (1 - w)^3\, b_{i-3} \ldots].$$

Or, in summation notation:

$$\hat{\beta}_i = w \sum_{t=0}^{\infty} (1 - w)^t b_{i-t}$$

Thus, this estimate of beta is just the weighted average of all past b_i's, where the weights become exponentially smaller as time recedes into the past. As some distant time, call it t equals zero, the sequential calculations are usually initialized by simply setting the estimate of beta equal to the current b, $\hat{\beta}_0 = b_0$; and then the sequential updating proceeds from that point. In more complex systems of this sort, the actual weighting coefficients, w_i, may be adjusted in time according to the perceived statistical reliability of the b_i's.

Exhibit 7A
Weekly performance chart, 1972—The Hanover Fund (Weekly percentage changes in net asset value absolute and relative to group average)

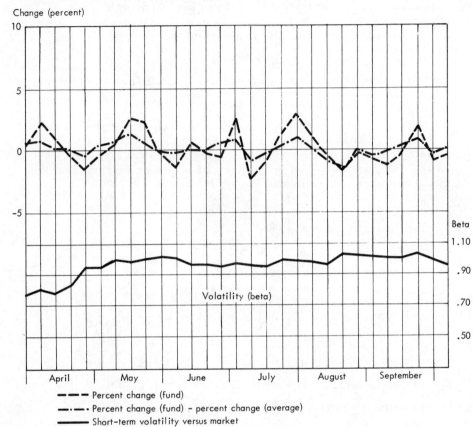

Change (percent)

Volatility (beta)

April   May   June   July   August   September

Beta

– – – Percent change (fund)
–·–· Percent change (fund) – percent change (average)
—— Short-term volatility versus market

Exhibit 7B
Weekly performance chart, 1972—The Hanover Equity Fund (Weekly percentage changes in net asset value absolute and relative to group average)

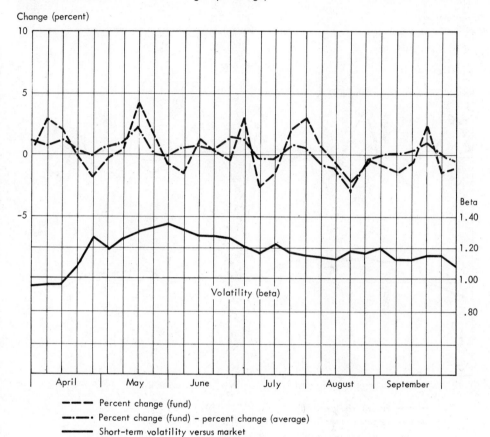

Change (percent)

Volatility (beta)

April   May   June   July   August   September

--- Percent change (fund)
-·- Percent change (fund) – percent change (average)
— Short-term volatility versus market

Exhibit 7C
Weekly performance chart, 1972—The Hanover Growth Fund (Weekly percentage changes in net asset value absolute and relative to group average)

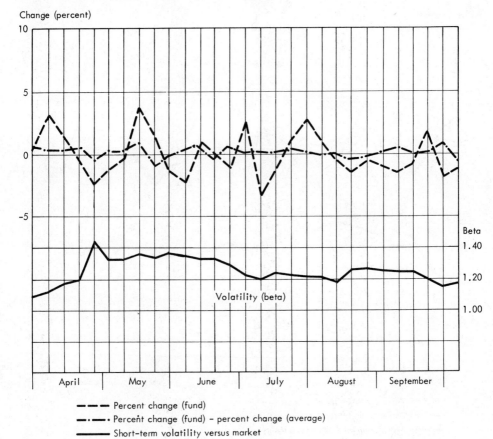

Change (percent)

Beta

Volatility (beta)

```
------  Percent change (fund)
--·--·  Percent change (fund) – percent change (average)
━━━━━━  Short-term volatility versus market
```

Exhibit 7D
Weekly performance chart, 1972—The Hanover Ranger Fund (Weekly percentage changes in net asset value absolute and relative to group average)

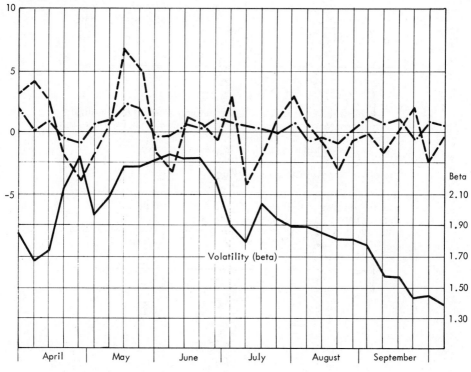

 Percent change (fund)

─·─· Percent change (fund) – percent change (average)

────── Short–term volatility versus market

Exhibit 8

Technical analyst's memo on the gap between the Hanover Glamour Average and the overall market

Date	P/E of Dow Jones Industrials	P/E of Hanover Glamour Average	Ratio
October 3	15.6	56.3	3.61
October 10	15.3	58.1*	3.80†

* Historic range is 25.5 to 62.0.
† Historic range is 1.58 to 3.80.

The most recent results of our continuing study of the Hanover Glamour Average indicates that these glamour companies are now selling at near record multiples, and that these multiples relative to the Dow Jones Industrials are at an all time record.

Stocks in Hanover Glamour Average

Avon Products	IBM	Polaroid
Baxter Labs	Johnson & Johnson	Schering
Burroughs	Kresge	Texas Instruments
Coca Cola	McDonald's	Xerox
Disney	Merck	

Exhibit 9
Scatter diagram of P/E ratio versus volatility for 32 stocks in Hanover Equity Fund (9/72)

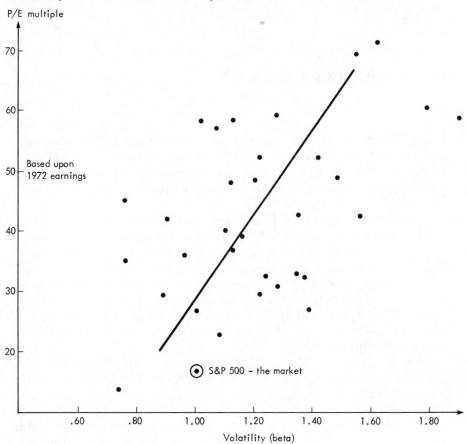

8. The Monroe Corporation

In early July 1976, Willard Hagemen, an outside director of the Monroe Corporation, received an important notice of the next directors' meeting. At that meeting, the directors would be asked to discuss, and hopefully decide upon, a policy for utilizing options within the investment company's overall investment activities.

The Monroe Corporation was a large and well-respected closed-end investment company, whose $110 million of assets were invested primarily in publicly traded common stocks. (See Exhibit 1 for the portfolio mix.) Like other closed-end investment companies, shares in the fund were owned by a wide spectrum of investors and traded in the public markets. For reasons that were never entirely clear, the shares of most of these publicly traded investment companies tended to trade in the markets at a discount from net asset value, and this was currently the case for the Monroe Corporation.

Over the years, the Monroe Corporation had compiled a sound, respectable investment record for its shareholders by its selection of common stocks. Because it held a reasonably diversified portfolio of common stocks, its net asset value had a volatility similar to the volatility for the stock market as a whole. For example, the net asset value per share had increased 31 percent in 1975 (after adjustment for shareholder distributions), compared to the 31.5 percent for the Standard & Poor's 500 Index. By comparison, the year 1975 had been a difficult period for many other institutional investors, whose performances had trailed the S&P 500 Index by substantial margins. In order to provide the continuing investment research and administration needed for the fund's operations, a small staff was employed in New York City. The Statement of Operations for 1975 is shown in Exhibit 1.

The investment staff at the Monroe Corporation had followed the development of the listed options markets for the last several years. As more and more participants were attracted to those markets, and their trading volume grew, options appeared to be rapidly becoming a more attractive investment vehicle. (Exhibit 2 shows current price and volume data for options traded on the CBOE.) After having evaluated various uses of options, the staff had recommended that the investment company proceed with a program of writing covered options. This recommendation is described in detail in Exhibit 3, a memo which accompanied the notice of the directors' meeting.

Willard Hageman was intrigued by the possibilities that options might offer. Through his informal contacts within the investment community, he was aware that a wide variety of institutional investors were now considering their use. In general, most institutional investors seemed to believe that the premiums in the market favored writers of options. A number of "options services" were now being offered to a wide variety of investors. By calculating "theoretical values" for options, often on the basis of rather sophisticated quantitative formulas, these services could evaluate the degree of undervaluation or overvaluation for a particular option. The actual market values of options could often stray substantially from these "theoretical values," indicating potential investment opportunities. The entire field was so new, though, that Hagemen knew of no conclusive evidence on the profitability of trading options with these valuation methods.

In preparation for the upcoming directors' meeting, Willard Hagemen wanted to consider a variety of issues, among them: what were the alternative ways for using options in Monroe's investment policies; how would each of these change the potential risks and return for their shareholders; and finally, should they proceed now with an options program, or continue to monitor the developments in this area carefully, for possible use in future years?

Exhibit 1

The Monroe Corporation

Current Portfolio: June, 1976

Common stock	89%	
Convertible securities	6	
Commercial paper	5	
Statements of operations—1975		
Income		$4,100,612
Dividends	$3,497,824	
Interest	605,788	
Expenses		1,186,355
Salaries	467,105	
Legal and auditing	93,461	
Office facilities and services	192,364	
Transfer agent, registrar and custodial fees	62,650	
Other expenses	298,588	
State franchise and other taxes	72,187	
Net investment income		2,914,257

Exhibit 2

Current quotations on listed options

Chicago Board

Option & price	— Jul — Vol. Last	— Oct — Vol. Last	— Jan — Vol. Last	N.Y. Close
Alcoa .. 40	45 13¾	b	b	53⅞
Alcoa .. 45	68 9	23 9¾	a	53⅞
Alcoa .. 50	133 4¾	22 5¾	19 6¼	53⅞
Alcoa .. 55	40 ¾	59 2⅞	2 4¼	53⅞
Alcoa .. 60	b b	35 1⅜	6 2⅜	53⅞
Am Tel 50	83 6⅝	22 7	11 7½	56¾
Am Tel 55	205 1⅞	118 2-9-16	29 3¼	56¾
Am Tel 60	15 1-16	160 ½	85 15-16	56¾
Atl R .. 80	15 23¾	1 24½	4 24¾	104¼
Atl R .. 90	86 14¼	51 14¾	a	104¼
Atl R .100	184 4¼	88 7	36 9¼	104¼
Avon .. 20	20 17¼	b b	b	47¾
Avon .. 35	42 12¾	a a	b	47¾
Avon .. 40	377 7¾	58 8¾	23 9¾	47¾
Avon .. 45	1266 2 15-16	514 5¼	81 6½	47¾
Avon .. 50	b b	789 2¾	243 3⅞	47¾
B Amer 60	b b	5 1¾	8 2¾	56¾
Beth S .35	57 8½	a	b	43¾
Beth S .40	65 3½	62 6¾	2 5¼	43¾
Beth S .45	144 ¼	171 1¾	32 2-9-16	43¾
Beth S .50	20 1-16	10 ½	b	43¾
Brums .. 10	135 7¼	57 7¾	18 7½	17
Brums .. 15	444 2¼	260 2¾	178 3¾	17
Burl N .35	b b	10 13	1 13¾	47
Burl N .40	77 1¾	3 7¾	10 9¾	47
Burl N .45	141 2¼	78 4¼	44 5¾	47
Citicp .. 30	31 5¾	24 6¾	5 7	35¾
Citicp .. 35	516 ¾	205 2¾	67 3¾	35¾
Citicp .. 40	b b	58 ¾	41 1¾	35¾
Delta .. 35	13 8¾	a	b	43½
Delta .. 40	139 3½	80 5¼	30 6¼	43½
Delta .. 45	171 ¾	130 2¼	39 3½	43½
Dow Ch .45	198 1¼	115 4¼	60 5¾	46¼
Dow Ch .50	75 ¼	481 2 1-16	64 3¾	46¼
Dow Ch .55	2 1-16	150 ¾	32 1¾	46¼
Eas Kd 80	991 8¾	b	b	97¾
Eas Kd 100	1399 1¼	680 7	91 10	97¾
Eas Kd 110	174 ¼	757 3¼	73 5¾	97¾
Eas Kd 120	8 1-16	415 1¾	94 2¾	97¾
Exxon .. 90	45 14⅜	24 15¾	8 16¾	104¾
Exxon .100	238 4⅞	131 7½	25 8½	104¾
Exxon .110	b b	100 2 3-16	39 3½	104¾
F N M .. 15	586 ¼	244 ⅞	429 1 5-16	14¾
F N M .. 20	a a	105 ¼	1 ¼	14¾
Fluor .. 30	5 11¼	a	a	41
Fluor .. 35	35 6	39 6	10 6¾	41
Fluor .. 40	b b	108 4½	78 5¾	41
Fluor .. 45	b b	100 2	74 2¾	41
Ford .. 40	1 16¼	b	b	56¾
Ford .. 45	7 11	2 12	b	56¾
Ford .. 50	209 6½	37 7¾	117 8¾	56¾
Ford .. 60	326 ⅞	300 1 15-16	233 3¼	56¾
G M .. 50	b 16¾	b b	b	66¾
G M .. 60	241 7¼	99 8¾	2 9¾	66¾
G M .. 70	574 ⅜	704 2¾	189 4½	66¾
G M .. 80	a a	94 ½	79 1¼	66¾
Gen El .. 45	7 12¾	b b	b	57½
Gen El 50	97 7½	30 7¾	b	57½
Gen El 55	72 2½	44 4¾	16 5½	57½
Gen El 60	45 3-16	106 1¾	72 3¾	57½
Gif Wn 18½	73 7	b b	b	25½
Gif Wn 20	33 5¾	32 5½	42 6¾	25½
Gif Wn 22½	162 2¾	b b	b	25½
Gif Wn 25	733 ¾	347 1 13-16	178 2¾	25½
Gt Wst .. 20	4 15¾	b b	b	17¾
Gt Wst .. 15	167 2¾	38 3¾	125 4¾	17¾
Gt Wst .. 20	1 1-16	107 ¾	82 1¾	17¾
Halbtn .. 45	22 17¾	b b	b	63¾
Halbtn .. 50	58 13¾	32 14¾	13 15	63¾
Halbtn 53¾	158 10½	a	b	63¾
Halbtn 56¾	221 7¼	59 8½	b	63¾
Halbtn .. 60	b b	74 6¾	12 8	63¾
Homstk .. 30	41 6¾	18 7¼	b	36¾
Homstk .. 35	359 2¼	146 4¾	43 5¼	36¾
Homstk .. 40	641 ¾	260 2	49 2 15-16	36¾
Homstk .. 45	1 1-16	256 ¾	½	36¾
I B M .. 280	179 79½	b b	b	277¾
I B M .. 220	196 50¾	17 62¾	b	277¾
I B M .. 240	380 36¾	20 44	7 48¾	277¾
I B M .. 260	2108 19	376 27¼	29 32	277¾
I B M .. 280	2588 2¾	616 13¾	194 20	277¾
I N A .. 40	40 11	19 41½	4 5¼	38¾
I N A .. 45	40 ¾	60 1¾	7 2¾	38¾
I T T .. 20	60 9¾	15 8½	b	28¼
I T T .. 25	248 3¾	a	4 4¾	28¼
I T T .. 30	227 1-16	282 1¼	218 1 13-16	28¼
In Har .. 20	21 11	a	a	31¾
In Har .. 25	173 6½	87 6½	63 6¾	31¾
In Har .. 30	715 1¼	349 2 7-16	158 2¾	31¾
In Min .. 35	140 1 13-16	77 2¾	51 3¾	36½
In Min .. 40	27 1-16	55 ¾	45 1¾	36½
In Pap .. 40	2 14	13 13	b	71¾
In Pap .. 50	a a	54 5½	8 7½	71¾
In Pap .. 60	a a	25 7¾	a	71¾
John J .. 80	a a	25 7¾	a	84¾
John J .. 90	b b	48 3	6 3¾	84¾
John J .100	b b	5 ¼	a	84¾
Kenn C 30	93 5½	14 6¾	8 6¾	35½
Kenn C 35	332 13-16	158 2 11-16	68 3¾	35½

Listed Options Quotations

Wednesday, July 7, 1976

Closing prices of all options. Sales unit is 100 shares. Security description includes exercise price. Stock close is New York Stock Exchange final price.

Option & price	— Jul — Vol. Last	— Oct — Vol. Last	— Jan — Vol. Last	N.Y. Close
Kerr M 60	58 10¾	a	a	80¾
Kerr M 70	283 1¾	67 12	7 13¾	80¾
Kerr M 80	2 1-16	158 4½	13 7½	80¾
Kerr M 90	b b	a	a	80¾
Kresge .. 30	81 6	4 6¾	b	35¾
Kresge .. 35	187 1¼	91 2 11-16	25 3¾	35¾
Kresge .. 40	10 1-16	44 13-16	13 1¾	35¾
Loews .. 20	28 9⅞	2 7½	b	28¾
Loews .. 25	47 4	5 4¾	5 5¼	28¾
Loews .. 30	61 ¾	37 1 7-16	50 2¼	28¾
M M M 45	37 7¾	17 9¼	a	57¾
M M M 50	212 ¾	143 2¾	24 4¾	57¾
M M M 60	1 1-16	41 ¾	45 1¾	57¾
M M M 70	a a	16 ¼	a	57¾
Mc Don 55	42 7½	46 9¼	1 10½	56¾
Mc Don 60	296 5-16	236 3	117 5	56¾
Mc Don 70	a a	74 ⅞	10 1¾	56¾
Merck .. 60	1 14	8 14½	b	74
Merck .. 70	140 4¾	49 6¾	20 7¾	74
Merck .. 80	34 1-16	114 1½	26 3¾	74
Monsan 70	6 20½	b b	b	90¼
Monsan 80	36 9½	56 12½	13 14	90¼
Monsan 90	209 1¾	78 5¾	27 7¾	90¼
Monsan 100	43 1-16	523 2¾	21 3¾	90¼
N C R .. 25	1 9¼	12 · 10	17 10¾	34¾
N C R .. 30	74 4¾	a	1 6¾	34¾
N C R 35	b b	142 2 15-16	62 4¾	34¾
Nw Air 20	9 12¾	b	b	32¾
Nw Air 25	16 7¾	a	a	32¾
Nw Air 30	25 1-16	b	b	32¾
Nw Air 35	179 ¼	63 1 11-16	14 2¾	32¾
Pennz .. 20	48 14½	a	b	34¼
Pennz .. 25	63 9½	14 10¼	3 10½	34¼
Pennz .. 30	104 4½	65 5¾	50 6¾	34¼
Pennz .. 35	b b	53 2¾	51 3	34¼
Pepsi .. 70	5 9¾	a	a	74¾
Pepsi .. 80	19 1-16	25 2¾	a	74¾
Polar .. 30	157 16¾	120 13¾	21 12½	40¾
Polar .. 35	1817 5¾	463 7½	168 8½	40¾
Polar .. 40	3100 1½	1144 3¾	34 5¾	40¾
R C A .. 15	4 13¾	b b	b	28¾
R C A .. 20	89 8¾	23 9	b	28¾
R C A .. 25	490 ¾	341 1½	54 2¾	28¾
R C A .. 30	365 5-16	441 1 13-16	159 2¾	28¾
Sears .. 60	53 5¾	86 8	9 9½	65¾
Sears .. 70	178 ¼	239 2 9-16	31 4½	65¾
Sperry .. 40	31 10¾	a	a	50½
Sperry .. 45	89 6	2 7¼	1 8½	50½
Sperry .. 50	221 1¾	109 3¾	26 4½	50½
Syntex .. 25	20 8½	10 8¾	31 9¼	33½
Syntex .. 30	1277 3	384 4¾	153 5¾	33½
Syntex 35	806 ·	661 1 13-16	288 2 13-16	33½
Tesoro .. 10	b b	b	b	15¾
Tesoro .. 15	406 ½	180 1 5-16	183 1¾	15¾
Tesoro .. 20	23 1-16	267 ¼	128 ½	15¾
Tex In 100	13 25	2 26½	b	124¾
Tex In 110	122 14¾	10 17	a	124¾
Tex In 120	185 5	53 11¼	a	124¾
Tex In 130	259 ¾	38 5¾	b	124¾
Upjohn 35	116 6¾	8¾	37 1	43¾
Upjohn 40	73a 3¼	244 4¾	76 6	43¾
Upjohn 45	261 ¾	476 2¼	102 3¾	43¾
Upjohn 50	a a	158 15-16	b	43¾
Weyerh 40	39 4¾	5 4¾	b	43¾
Weyerh 45	76 ¼	19 2	23 3¾	43¾
Weyerh 50	a a	27 16¾	5 25	43¾
Xerox .. 45	27 16¾	b b	b	62
Xerox .. 50	400 12	86 15¾	33 14¾	62
Xerox .. 60	1417 2 11-16	8¾ 6½	224 7½	62
Xerox .. 70	13 1-16	955 2¼	19 3	62

Option & price	— Aug — Vol. Last	— Nov — Vol. Last	— Feb — Vol. Last	Close
A E P .. 20	81 2½	b b	b	22¾
A E P .. 24¾	49 5	b b	b	22¾
A E P .. 20	b b	82 2 5-16	a	22¾
A E P .. 25	b b	80 3-16	240 9-16	22¾
A M P 35	a a	1 1¾	3 2	32¾

Option & price	— Aug — Vol. Last	— Nov — Vol. Last	— Feb — Vol. Last	Close
Am Hos 35	13 1¾	10 2¾	a	34¾
Am Hos 40	5 ½	a	7 1½	34¾
Baxter .35	5 6¾	5 6	a	38¾
Baxter ..40	143 1¾	21 2¾	a	38¾
Baxter .45	11 ¾	a	b	38¾
Blk Dk .20	2 4	2 4¾	a	24¾
Blk Dk .25	81 ¾	63 1¾	19 2½	24¾
Blk Dk .30	a a	90 7-16	b	24¾
Boeing .20	b b	15 15¾	b	39¾
Boeing .25	29 10	23 10¾	b	39¾
Boeing .35	29 5¾	36 6¾	11 7¾	39¾
Boeing .40	138 2	43 3¾	14 4¾	39¾
Bois C .35	28 1 11-16	38 2¾	31 3¾	25½
Bois C .30	90 ¼	26 13-16	a	25½
C B S .. 60	27 2	5 3¾	2 5¼	58½
C Data .. 20	6 ¼	63 7¾	b	24¾
C Data .. 25	170 4½	56 5½	19 6¼	24¾
C Data .. 30	470 1¼	375 2½	103 3¼	24¾
Cmw Ed .25	8 ¼	b b	b	29
Cmw Ed 30	39 ¼	216 ½	4 20	29
Coke .. 80	51 5½	27 7½	a	83½
Coke .. 90	66 ⅞	89 3	14 4¾	83½
Coke .. 100	2 1-16	b b	b	83½
Colgat ..25	92 2¾	21 3¾	27 3½	27½
Colgat ..30	130 7-16	97 ⅞	220 1¾	27½
Gen Fd 30	36 ⅝	21 1¼	14 1¾	29
Gn Dyn .40	5 4	28¼	b	64¼
Gn Dyn 45	28 10¾	a	b	64¼
Gn Dyn 50	71 14½	17 15	a	64¼
Gn Dyn 60	168 5¼	33 7⅞	8 9¼	64¼
H Inns .. 10	a a	a	a	14¾
H Inns .. 15	102 11-16	240 1 5-16	125 1¾	14¾
H Inns .. 20	42 1-16	50 ⅜	b	14¾
Hewlet .. 100	12 25¾	b	b	116¾
Hewlet .. 100	40 17¼	6 19½	10 22½	116¾
Hewlet 110	50 8¾	21 12½	18 14½	116¾
Hewlet 120	167 3¾	12 6½	11 9	116¾
Honwll .. 30	3 19¾	b	b	50½
Honwll .. 35	15 16	b b	b	50½
Honwll .. 40	133 11½	5 11½	6 13	50½
Honwll 45	302 7¾	60 7	24 10¼	50½
Honwll 50	1253 3¾	423 5¾	95 7	50½
Honwll .. 60	257 1¼	112 1¾	b	50½
In Flv .. 20	64 1½	a	21 2½	21 3½	25
In Flv .. 30	21 ¼	16 ¾	16 3¾	b	25
J Manv .. 25	7 5¾	1 5½	1	34¾
J Manv 30	80 1¾	28 2¼	7 2¾	30
J Manv .. 35	86 3-16	180 ½	b	30
J Walt .. 30	30 3¾	3 4¾	18 5¼	32¾
J Walt .. 35	49 13-16	a	2 30	32¾
J Walt .. 40	16 ¼	47 1¾	11 1½	32¾
J Walt .. 45	a a	51 3-16	1 ½	32¾
Mobil .. 50	17 8¾	a	a	58¾
Mobil .. 55	219 4¼	a	a	13 7	58¾
Mobil .. 60	240 1½	55 3	15 4	58¾
N Semi 35	24 15¾	b b	b	49¾
N Semi .40	126 10½	26 12¼	5 13¾	49¾
N Semi 45	489 6¾	59 8¾	55 10½	49¾
N Semi 50	1074 3¾	398 5¾	85 7	49¾
N Semi 60	220 5-16	212 1 13-16	b	49¾
Occi .. 10	2 5¾	a	a	17
Occi .. 15	82 1¾	63 2 15-16	50 3¼	17
Raython .. 45	106 ¼	14 13-16	160 1 3-16	17
Raython 50	16 12½	2 13¾	a	62
Raython 60	104 2¾	41 5½	1 7¾	62
Rynlds 60	10 7½	a	a	57¾
Rynlds 60	28 1 1-16	9 2¾	a	57¾
Rynlds .70	1 ¼	55 2¾	b	57¾
Skylin .. 15	71 5	25 5½	a	19¾
Skylin 20	254 1½	140 2	109 2 13-16	19¾
Skylin .. 25	1 ½	60 11-16	b	19¾
Slumb .70	1 16½	7 17¾	b	86½
Slumb .80	35 7¾	19 9½	a	86½
Slumb 90	a a	90 3-16	b	86½
Southn .. 10	5 4¾	a	11 4¾	14¾
Southn .15	170 ¼	219 ½	86 ¾	14¾
St Ind .. 40	a a	2 11	b	51¼
St Ind .. 45	9 6½	3 7	b	51¼
St Ind .. 50	89 2 3-16	30 3¾	14 4½	51¼
St Ind .. 60	a a	10 ¾	b	51¼
Tx Glf .. 20	b b	b	a	33¾
Tx Glf .. 25	7 15-16	17 2 13-16	b	33¾
U A L .. 20	5 7¾	a	2 9½	27½
U A L .. 25	64 3	60 4¾	a	27½
U A L .. 30	68 11-16	52 1¾	b	27½
U Tech 50	25 6½	20 7	3 7½	58½
U Tech 60	44 2¾	39 3½	5 4¾	36½
U Tech 60	b b	108 ¼	3 13¾	36½
Utah .. 50	51 10¾	13 12¾	3 13¼	59½
Utah .. 60	150 3	159 5¾	39 6½	59½
Wilms 20	11 3¾	17 4¾	6 5¾	23¾
Wilms .25	109 11-16	93 1¾	33 2¾	23¾
Wilms .30	25 1-16	44 7-16	b	23¾

Total volume 79,535. Open interest 1,416,662.

Source: *Wall Street Journal*, July 1976.

Exhibit 3
Writing covered options

BACKGROUND

Since call options first began trading on the Chicago Board Options Exchange (CBOE) in April of 1973, listed options markets have expanded very rapidly. Options covering 171 NYSE stocks are now being traded on four securities exchanges; CBOE, Amex, Philadelphia, and Pacific. Total option volume on these exchanges in recent months has been running in the range of 40 to 60 percent of total share volume on the New York Stock Exchange. Open interest covers in excess of 230 million shares.

With growth has come respectability. A number of papers have been published by members of the academic community in support of the view that investment strategies involving the writing or buying of options can be more conservative than the simple strategy of buying and holding common stocks. In July of 1974 the Comptroller of the Currency reversed a previous ruling and permitted national banks and trust companies to write covered options in trust accounts where appropriate. A number of state insurance departments, including New York, have since authorized insurance companies to write options against portfolio stocks. A few pension funds are also writing options even though HR 3052 (the Rosten-kowski Bill), which would permit tax-exempt institutions to treat option profits as investment income instead of as taxable unrelated business income, has yet to be passed. Among closed-end investment companies, United Corp. has already done some option writing and Tri-Continental expects to have a program in effect by midyear.

Much of the increased institutional interest in writing covered call options undoubtedly results from improvements in marketability and standardization of trading procedures instituted by the CBOE. However, it is also likely that unsatisfactory returns from common stock investments over the past eight years and external pressures to improve investment performance have played a major role in stimulating this interest.

RATIONALE

The purpose of writing call options against portfolio stocks is to increase the overall rate of return on portfolio investments. An option program can be designed to minimize (but not eliminate entirely) the possibility of a call being exercised. Option positions are normally closed out through the offsetting purchase of an identical option or, if the stock price has declined sufficiently, allowed to expire.

The assumption that an institution can increase investment returns by writing options rests in turn on the assumption that it can write overpriced options. There is clearly no advantage to writing properly priced options, the result of which would only be to reduce expected investment returns and increase the stability of returns. A similar result could be achieved merely by reducing stock holdings and increasing holdings of cash equivalents.

In order to write options which are in the aggregate overpriced, it is necessary either to have the benefit of a market in which options are chronically overpriced

Exhibit 3 (continued)

or to have the ability to identify overpriced option opportunities. A number of studies offer evidence that options have been generally overpriced in the past or, in other words, that total returns to option buyers have been negative and total returns to option writers have been positive. However, most of these studies cover periods when institutional investor participation in the options market was nonexistent or, at most, minimal. Option buyers then consisted of a large number of individuals willing to exchange the high probability of incurring a small loss for the small probability of obtaining a large gain (the lottery syndrome). Writers, on the other hand, consisted of a relatively small number of sophisticated investors. With the writing of options now rapidly gaining acceptance by the institutional investment community, it appears likely that any prior supply-demand imbalance favoring the option writer is likely to disappear rapidly, if it has not done so already.

There are a number of formulas available for calculating the intrinsic value of options in order to identify those that appear overpriced. All require either an estimate of the probabilities associated with various percentage changes in the price of the underlying stock or an estimate of the stock's volatility. Those requiring estimates of future stock price probability distributions appear to have little value. If one could predict future stock prices with any reliability, that ability would best be directed toward stock selection rather than option writing. Those formulas utilizing volatility data rely on the principal that price volatility associated with a stock tends to be reasonably stable over time. Such formulas, of which the one developed by Black and Scholes is the best known, appear to have merit.

Conceptually, there is appeal in the proposition that options tend to be overpriced when investors are bullish and underpriced when investors are bearish. A disciplined approach to evaluating and writing options should therefore result in writing a greater number of options near market tops than near market bottoms. The accompanying chart, prepared by Value Line, shows option prices expressed

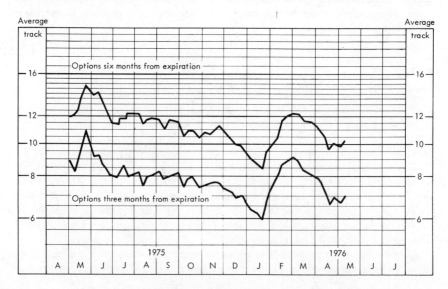

Exhibit 3 (continued)

as a percentage of the market price of the underlying stock. It suggests an availability of attractive option writing opportunities while the market was topping out in May and June of 1975 and in late February and early March of 1976. It also suggests a lack of attractive option writing opportunities in December and January and in late April and early May of 1976.

APPROACH

Any program of covered option writing should be one that is entirely separate from the investment management of the portfolio. In this. respect it should be operated similarly to our stock lending program.

Options should be written against portfolio stock entirely on the basis of the perceived attractiveness of the option without interposing any judgment with regard to the investment merits of the underlying stock or the direction of the stock market. The only criteria to be used in writing an option, therefore, would be the price of the option (premium), exercise price in relation to current market price of the stock, unexpired term of the option, historical volatility of the stock, and dividends expected on the stock during the unexpired option term. No options should be written against stocks of which sale was being considered, but this is the only situation where we now perceive that investment management would impinge upon management of the option writing program.

Option positions should be closed out whenever the price of the option approached its underlying value or when little additional profit potential remained and the price of the stock were near the exercise price. All positions should be closed, therefore, before any significant probability of being exercised occurred. In the event of an unexpected exercise or in the event of an inability to close out a position through some failure in the secondary option market, the required stock should be purchased in the open market without disturbing the portfolio position. Positions with no likelihood of exercise should be allowed to expire.

POTENTIAL RETURNS

At May 31, 1976, the portfolio held 22 stocks for which call options are listed. The total value of these holdings was approximately $36 million, or 33 percent of net assets. If two securities convertible into stocks on which listed options are traded are included, the totals become $42 million, or 37 percent.

Under a fully established option writing program the value of stocks on which options were outstanding might range between 0 percent and 10 percent of net assets, averaging around 5 percent. We are assuming, based primarily upon discussions with options specialists at brokerage firms that a successful options program might provide a net incremental return on the order of 2 to 6 percent annually on the value of the assets against which options are outstanding. On this basis the contribution of a successful program to total investment return could average about 0.2 percent annually over a complete market cycle. An average annual contribution on the order of $200,000 in net premium returns would thus seem to represent an initial order-of-magnitude objective on our current asset base.

Any incremental improvement in investment returns generated by an option writing program would be accompanied by some reduction in the variability of these returns. Option writing profits would be greatest in declining markets, and losses would be incurred in sharply rising markets. A decrease in the variability of investment returns accompanied by an increase in average total returns would represent a tangible improvement in investment performance.

RISKS

Despite all precautions taken to avoid exercise in an option writing program, there is the likelihood that at some time a call would be exercised against a portfolio stock. (Since calls began trading on the CBOE, 74 percent of all options written have been closed out before expiration, 22 percent have expired unexercised, and 4 percent have been exercised.) Although it is contemplated that stock would be purchased to deliver against the call, it is possible that the stock could not be purchased in a single day without materially bidding up the price and increasing the loss on the option. In such a situation there would be a strong temptation to deliver portfolio stock, in which case the option writing program would have interfered with the normal portfolio investment decision process.

In a sharply rising market an option writing program, even if well conceived and well executed, could produce a negative incremental return, thereby detracting from portfolio performance. If the program were then abandoned as a mistake, the portfolio would have absorbed all the disadvantages of writing options without reaping any of the advantages.

It may be that after the methodology of managing an option writing program has been developed no attractive options will be located, or very few. This situation could persist indefinitely if competition among institutional option writers becomes sufficiently intense.

There is no certainty that any formula or procedure adopted for identifying overpriced options will work, or that a sufficiently large incremental return can be earned to justify recordkeeping, commission, and other costs associated with the program.

COSTS

If an option writing program were implemented it would be managed by present personnel. Internal costs would therefore appear to be minimal and confined to those costs associated with increased recordkeeping and additional computer time. Custodial fees would undoubtedly increase, since the bank would be required to issue certificates specifying that shares against which options have been written are being held for our account.

The brokerage commission business generated by an option writing program of the magnitude outlined above could, by our calculations, be equivalent to an increase in portfolio turnover of up to 5 percent. It would be necessary to obtain considerable service from brokers in such areas as setting up procedures, providing continuous screening of available options, and monitoring our outstanding options to avoid being exercised.

Exhibit 3 (*concluded*)

TAXATION—REGULATION

Currently the IRS regards the net premiums received on options which have been closed out or expired as ordinary income. Since such income is not derived from dividends, interest, or capital gains on the sale or other disposition of stock or securities, it does not qualify for inclusion in the 90 percent of a regulated investment company's income which must be derived from these sources. Upon exercise of an option, the gain or loss realized on the stock delivered is long or short term depending upon the holding period for the stock. In this case the premium received for writing the call is treated as an increase in the amount realized from sale of the stock.

HR 1224, a bill introduced by Rep. Abner Mikva (D.–Ill.) has been reported to the House floor by the Ways and Means Committee. Consideration by the full House is expected early this month. The Mikva Bill provides that premiums from expired and closed positions in options written on or after July 1, 1976, be treated as short-term capital gains. The bill would not affect the tax treatment of options exercised. Passage of this bill by Congress would give regulated investment companies greater flexibility in writing options.

9. The Federal National Mortgage Association

There is a basic cyclicality in the residential mortgage market arising from the fact that deposits at savings and loan associations as well as the availability of funds to other mortgage lenders tend to move together over the credit cycle. That is, in periods of tight credit availability, funds available for mortgage lending tend to decline concurrently at all mortgage lenders, while in periods of easy credit availability, these funds tend to increase. In addition, those diversified mortgage lenders, such as insurance companies, commercial banks, and mutual savings banks, which have the authority to lend or invest in other investment areas tend to shift to these other markets in periods of tight credit. One result of this dilemma is the need for secondary mortgage market facilities that do not depend on cyclical credit availability. The oldest and largest institution created to meet this need is the Federal National Mortgage Association (FNMA), or "Fannie Mae." (Exhibits 1 and 2 show FNMA's 1972 income statement and balance sheet. Exhibit 3 presents selected FNMA financial data.)

HISTORIC BACKGROUND

FNMA was originally organized in 1938 as a wholly owned subsidiary of the Reconstruction Finance Corporation to provide assistance to the mortgage market by purchasing from lending institutions residential mortgages insured by the Federal Housing Administration (FHA). In 1948, FNMA was empowered to purchase mortgages guaranteed by the Veterans Administration (VA) as well.

In 1950, supervision of FNMA was transferred to the Housing and Home Finance Agency (HHFA). As a constituent agency of HHFA, FNMA was reorganized in 1954 by enactment of the FNMA Charter Act and charged with three principal functions: (1) the management and liquidating functions, to dispose of its then existing mortgage portfolio; (2) the special assistance functions, to help in the financing of special housing programs and to ameliorate the effects on the housing market of unfavorable economic conditions; and (3) the secondary market operations, which were assumed by the present FNMA, whose purpose was to enhance the liquidity of the secondary mortgage market.

The Housing and Urban Development Act of 1968 amended the Charter Act to partition FNMA into two separate and distinct corporations, each of which was to have continuity as a separated portion of the previously existing corporation. One of these corporations, known as the Government National Mortgage Association (GNMA), remained in the Department of Housing and Urban Development (HUD) and retained the management and liquidating functions and special assistance functions, the two government-financed portions of the previously existing FNMA.

The other corporation, which retained the name Federal National Mortgage Association and the assets and capital structure of the secondary market operations, became a government-sponsored corporation subject to regulation by the Secretary of HUD. The capital represented by privately held common stock then amounted to $140 million and that represented by preferred stock held by the Secretary of the Treasury amounted to about $160 million. FNMA retired the preferred stock, making the common stockholders the sole owners of the corporation.

Although FNMA had become a completely privately owned corporation, the regulatory power retained by the federal government authorized the Secretary of HUD to issue rules and regulations to insure that the purposes of FNMA, as specified in the Charter Act, were accomplished.

The Charter Act nevertheless authorized the board of directors to determine the general policies which govern the operations of FNMA, to adopt and amend the bylaws governing the performance of its powers, to elect the board chairman, and to appoint persons to fill the offices of president and vice president and such other officers as may be provided for in the bylaws. Of the 15 members of the Board, 10 were to be elected annually by the stockholders and 5 appointed annually by the President of the United States. The day-to-day business affairs of FNMA were to be administered by its president as chief executive officer.

Finally, in 1970, the Emergency Home Finance Act empowered FNMA to extend its activities beyond FHA/VA mortgages to the purchase of conventional (that is, not federally insured or guaranteed) mortgages as well.

OPERATIONS

FNMA does not originate any mortgages of its own, but limits its portfolio acquisitions to purchase from such mortgage originators as commercial banks, savings and loan associations, mortgage companies, and other primary lenders it qualifies as eligible sellers. FNMA is also authorized to purchase mortgages insured by the Farmers Home Administration of the Department of Agriculture and mortgages insured by HUD on multifamily housing projects, hospitals, and other health care facilities. However, as indicated in Exhibit 4, FNMA's purchases are predominantly one-to-four family residential mortgages, and the mechanism for these purchases since 1968 has been FNMA's "Free Market System" (FMS).

The Free Market System

The FMS is a competitive auction procedure for "forward commitments" which replaced an immediate and over-the-counter purchasing procedure. FMS auctions for FHA, VA, and conventional mortgages are generally held biweekly. A qualified seller, wishing to make a bid to sell mortgages to FNMA, telephones on the day of the auction and specifies the bid amount and the yield which the seller will accept on the package of loans being offered. In light of the amount of funds it desires to commit to the mortgage market, FNMA determines the lowest yield it will accept at the auction, and every seller that has tendered a bid above this yield is accepted. The selling organization then has a period of four months in which it may deliver all or part of the amount specified in its accepted bid. This is an optional delivery commitment, or "forward commitment" as it is called, and delivery of the mortgages is at the discretion of the seller.

Sellers not willing to accept the possibility of their bid being rejected can make noncompetitive bids which are automatically accepted at the average yield of all accepted offers.

This auction system of "forward commitments" is designed to assure the seller, over the term of the commitment period, of a ready buyer of its mortgages at a preestablished yield, thus giving it flexibility in its mortgage operations.

Fees from auctions are a source of income for FNMA over and above the yields it obtains from mortgages as an investment. These fees are of two types: the offering fee and the commitment fee. The offering fee is imposed only in the case of competitive bids—largely to discourage frivolous bidding. With each competitive bid, a bidder agrees to pay an offering fee of $1/100$ percent of the funds specified in the bid.

The commitment fee is $\frac{1}{2}$ percent of the bid amount accepted. It is payable immediately upon notice of acceptance.

Under the FMS, FNMA has also continued a practice of requiring institutions that deliver mortgages pursuant to FNMA commitments to purchase stock in the corporation. The requirement is $\frac{1}{4}$ percent of the principal balance of the mortgages delivered.

Not all mortgage commitments are issued through the auction. For example, FNMA issues 24-month commitments to purchase mortgages on projects such as apartment developments, nursing homes, and hospitals on a project-by-project basis. It also offers "stand-by" commitments for 12 months on both government-backed and conventional home mortgages. However, pricing of such commitments is related to auction prices and yields. (Exhibit 5 shows yields accepted by FNMA under FMS, 1968–1972.)

A residual supplier of funds

FNMA operates principally as a *supplementary* source of funds to provide liquidity to mortgage originators during periods when mortgage credit from other sources falls short of market needs. An example may best illustrate how FNMA performs this function. When a mortgage banker originates a mortgage, it can be financed with a short-term bank loan, but eventually it will have to be sold to an investor in order to raise funds with which to finance additional mortgage originations. (This origination for resale contrasts with the strategy of other mortgage originators, such as deposit institutions, which use customer deposits to originate mortgages as earning assets for their own portfolios.) The dependence of mortgage companies on interim bank financing makes them, concomitantly, dependent on mortgage investors such as FNMA that will issue them forward commitments, which assure the "take-out" of such financing. The mortgage banker can sell the mortgage to a number of permanent investors, such as savings and loan associations, mutual savings banks, and insurance companies, or to FNMA at the specified yield if a prior "forward commitment" has been obtained. When other permanent investors are in a favorable liquidity position, the mortgage banker is likely to sell mortgages to a primary investor. When interest rates start to rise, however, funds of individual savers tend to shift from deposits at thrift institutions to higher yielding open-market instruments. In addition, many institutional investors similarly tend to shift funds away from the mortgage market to other, higher yielding investment alternatives. With this decline in funds available for mortgage investment, the mortgage banker must increasingly rely on sales to FNMA to obtain the funding to free up the line of credit needed to make new mortgage loans. Hence, FNMA's function is as a residual supplier of funds in the mortgage market. If the mortgage banker were unable to sell the mortgage to FNMA, the mortgage banker would be unable to make any further mortgage loans and the mortgage market would be thus constricted.

Portfolio sales

When credit is easy and there is a plentiful supply of funds at deposit institutions (and at thrift institutions in particular), an institutional demand for mortgages in excess of primary market needs may develop.

Given such demand levels, a number of institutions will often seek to obtain mortgage investments, and this provides an opportunity for the sale of mortgages from FNMA's portfolio. Indeed, in order to provide for such sales, FNMA limits its purchases to mortgages conforming to the requirements of the Federal Home Loan Bank Board (that is, loans not greater than $45,000 for loan to value ratios of 90 percent or less; and loans not greater than $36,000 for loan to value ratios over 90 percent), the chief regulatory authority of savings and loan associations. This policy not only provides saleability of FNMA mortgages to these major mortgage investors, but significantly enhances their marketability to other institutions as well.

On the other hand, in accordance with its Charter Act provision that it maintain liquidity in the secondary mortgage market, FNMA restricts its portfolio sales so as not to adversely affect the availability of money for new mortgages. Thus, it follows a strategy which releases mortgages to the market only under conditions which are characterized by an excess of mortgage money.

The net effect of this sales policy, taken together with FNMA's "supplementary" purchasing policy, is that, buying or selling with alternative swings in the credit cycle, FNMA has emerged over time not as a "dealer" in mortgages (that is, a continuous buyer and seller), but rather as primarily a buyer in most periods, but sometimes a seller in others, as indicated in Exhibit 6.

Financing

FNMA depends heavily on the money and capital markets to obtain funds necessary to support its operations. Toward this end, FNMA has issued several types of corporate obligational securities. These securities are general debts of the corporation and are not identified with any particular collateral. However, classification of these obligations as federal agency securities permits maintenance of an adequate borrowing capacity at favorable interest rates.

One type of security issued by FNMA, short-term discount notes, is comparable to commercial paper. These notes, having maturities ranging from 30 days to 270 days, are distributed through four commercial paper dealers, who also provide a secondary market for them. This form of financing serves as a supplement to FNMA's principal method of borrowing through the issuance of debentures and is used by FNMA to provide operational flexibility. Since short-term rates are typically lower than long-term rates, issuance of discount notes as opposed to longer term obligations can reduce the overall cost of borrowing by FNMA. Issuance of discount notes also permits FNMA to hold off long-term financing until favorable market conditions prevail. Should FNMA have excess funds, the discount notes offer a ready opportunity to retire debt.

Debentures, which are similar to private corporate bonds, are issued for periods from about 3 years to as long as 25 years. In addition to regular debentures, FNMA sells subordinated capital debentures, some of which contain conversion features. Principal and interest on these are subordinated to any payments due on regular debentures and short-term discount notes.

FNMA's borrowing authority is fixed from time to time by the Secretary of HUD. The maximum borrowing authority is expressed as a multiple of the amount of its capital base, which for debt purposes includes outstanding common stock, surplus, and subordinated capital debentures. Subordinated capital debentures may be issued in ratio of $2 to each $1 of common stock plus surplus. At the end of 1972, the maximum borrowing authority in effect was $25 of debt for every $1 of the capital base.

FNMA also has a borrowing authorization with the U.S. Treasury which permits the Secretary of the Treasury, at the Secretary's option, to purchase up to $2.25 billion of FNMA obligations. This borrowing authorization is significant to FNMA's favorable debt costs in that the Treasury can be regarded as a potential source of funds to meet maturing obligations or finance current operations if funds cannot otherwise be raised.

In addition to the Treasury back-up, FNMA also maintains a $600 million line of credit with a consortium of banks. Although rarely used, this line can provide additional flexibility should unusually adverse financial conditions develop.

Finally, FNMA has also obtained long-term funds from the issuance of mortgage-backed bonds. Since the timely payment of interest and principal on these bonds is guaranteed by GNMA, an instrumentality of the U.S. government, such a guarantee invokes the full faith-and-credit of the United States.

FNMA also finances its operations through the sale of common stock. However, given FNMA's 25 : 1 borrowing ratio, equity financing plays a less important role in FNMA than in most other corporations.

Financing strategies

As an issuer of mortgage-related securities, FNMA can attempt to adapt the maturity structure of its liabilities to either the actual maturity of its mortgage assets, or to the expected repayment pattern of these assets. Because most of its purchased mortgages carry maturities of 25 or 30 years, FNMA could choose to fund these mortgages with debt of a comparable maturity. On the other hand, FHA study data indicates, on the basis of repayments from regular amortization, prepayments of principal, and complete loan terminations, that only one half of the original principal value of a portfolio of 30-year mortgages is projected to be outstanding after about 10 to 12 years. If FNMA were to adapt maturities and redemption provisions of its mortgage-related securities to such data, it might maintain a weighted-average debt maturity of around ten years. Of course, mortgage sales from the portfolio could reduce this effective maturity even further, although FNMA has been largely a net purchaser in the past few years.

As an alternative, FNMA can choose to deliberately finance its mortgage portfolio with relatively short debt, exploiting the normally upward-sloping yield curve and thus maintaining substantially larger average margins, but also sustaining the risk that short-term rates may exceed long-term rates at times.

Finally, FNMA can choose to normally finance its mortgage portfolio with relatively long debt matched to its assets but in times of high rates delay the long-term financing by temporarily using short debt, until rates return to relatively lower levels.

FNMA has altered its financing strategy over time. Starting in 1964, the weighted average maturity of FNMA debt obligations declined continuously from 5½ years to 1 year and 3 months in 1970. As FNMA was forced to roll over short-term paper at generally rising rates toward the end of this period, the net earnings from its portfolio were substantially eroded (Exhibit 7). Since this period, FNMA has deliberately attempted to lengthen its debt maturity. Thus, as indicated above, FNMA now follows a policy such that short-term discount notes are used only as a supplement to debentures (whose maturity FNMA has steadily lengthened since 1969, as shown in Exhibit 8).

Exhibit 9 shows FNMA's mix of marketable debt by maturity for the period 1969–1972.

POLICY CONSIDERATIONS

Since FNMA was privatized in 1968, it has, despite government regulation, had much latitude in the conduct of its day-to-day business. Thus, several important policy considerations have become ongoing matters.

Size of support

Before 1968, FNMA's borrowings were often restricted by the Bureau of the Budget in its efforts to constrain the overall size of the fiscal program of the government. However, since FNMA became a private corporation and gained exclusion from the federal budgetary processes, its borrowings have been limited only by its own net worth, its borrowing ratio, and such limitations as the Secretary of HUD might find appropriate. As matters developed, the Secretary has seen fit to authorize FNMA to supply large amounts of credit to the mortgage market. As a result, FNMA's purchases, and therefore borrowings, have risen sharply (Exhibit 6). Given the, at times, large absolute size of these borrowings,

FNMA's reallocation of open-market credit to the mortgage market has posed several potential conflicts between such narrow sector stabilization, on the one hand, and overall economic stabilization and the broad functioning of capital markets, on the other. First of all, FNMA securities have the potential of absorbing savings that would otherwise be placed in thrift institutions, such that not only might there be only a small net gain for the mortgage market, but funds provided could be more costly as well. In addition, FNMA demands may rise the costs to or ration the credit of such less creditworthy borrowers as state and local governments medium-sized and smaller businesses, some consumer sectors, and even some private mortgage borrowers not under the federal umbrella.

FNMA borrowings, if they become too large, could also partially impede both fiscal and monetary policies. One of the larger and faster impacts of restrictive monetary policy tends to be on residential construction, and this impact is to a considerable extent attributable to changes in mortgage credit availability. Insofar as the availability effects on housing are eliminated by FNMA borrowings, monetary policy is blunted. The result could be the need for more restrictive monetary actions and larger swings in interest rates to produce a given effect, and the lags in response could become longer and more costly. Similarly, in terms of fiscal policy, insofar as federal planners fail to integrate into their budget planning the effects of potentially large ongoing borrowings of the de-budgeted FNMA on aggregate demand, federal expenditures for goods and services could exceed levels consistent with the desired degree of restraint.

Timing of support

Another dimension of conflict of private and public roles arises in FNMA's timing of its support to the mortgage market. In principle, FNMA could merely provide a steady and even flow of funds to the mortgage market. However, because of its publicly sponsored role as a buffer to the mortgage market of the cyclical swings in credit availability, FNMA is generally expected to provide funds contracyclically. In order to provide for a profit to its stockholders, though, it must seek to maintain an adequate spread between the cost of new borrowings and the yields on new mortgages. FNMA, in that it funds its mortgage acquisitions through the sale of securities, is faced with the dilemma that the margin between yields on new mortgage loans and yields on new securities often narrows under tight money conditions and can even become negative (Exhibit 10). Thus, FNMA's financing problems can become most acute just when it should give the residential mortgage market the greatest measure of support. Insofar as FNMA attempts to manage its earnings growth, it may depart from the strictly contracyclical role which it would have followed as a federal agency interested only in public sector objectives.

Although FNMA has not moved to the contrary posture of simply funding when rate spreads are greatest, FNMA has modified its contracyclical posture from alternative purchasing and selling to a more steady dominance of purchasing since 1968 and the advent of forward commitments. In recent years, as mortgage companies have increasingly relied on these FNMA commitments as the assurance of a take-out of their borrowings, their business has accounted for from 75 percent to 90 percent of the mortgages sold to FNMA. Thus, with FNMA forward commitments in hand, they have tended not to cut back on originations as they did prior to 1968. Oakley Hunter, president of FNMA, has commented on this development: "Since the institution of FNMA's auction system, we have become relatively less an agency for the purchase of existing mortgages and the subsequent sale of these same mortgages to other investors, and relatively more of an agency to provide take-out money. Fannie Mae has become de facto a permanent lender."

Distribution of support

Since 1970, when FNMA was empowered to broaden the scope of its mortgage market activities to include purchases of conventional mortgages, it has been faced with the question of the appropriate distribution of its support between the government-underwritten and conventional sectors. The conventional sector has almost always been the larger of the two, both in terms of housing starts and net mortgage lending (traditionally about 70 percent of each). Nevertheless, FNMA continues to recognize the FHA/VA market as its "prime responsibility." Indeed, FNMA did not hold its first conventional auction until February 14, 1972, and out of $3.7 billion in mortgage purchases that year, purchased only $55 million in conventional mortgages. One of the public policy arguments for FNMA, as a government-sponsored agency, to provide more intensive assistance to the government-underwritten market is that housing financed with FHA and VA loans on the average serves families of more moderate means. A second consideration is that the government-underwritten segment has been relatively more dependent on such diversified mortgage investors as life insurance companies, commercial banks, mutual savings banks, and, to a minor extent, pension funds. Thus, the FHA/VA sector especially needs a secondary-layer intermediary such as FNMA to counterbalance the periodic shifting from mortgages to alternative investments on the part of these institutions in their characteristic sensitivity to yield differentials.

On the other hand, a conflict arises between these public policy considerations and FNMA's private obligations to its shareholders from the fact that it has been able to earn higher yields on conventional mortgages than on FHA/VA mortgages (Exhibit 5). Because of this, although conventional mortgages should for some time represent only a relatively small percentage of FNMA's total portfolio, FNMA has acknowledged that this percentage may become "larger and larger" and it must continuously consider how much and how soon.

A summary of the policy issues

In summary, then, FNMA must make a continual series of policy decisions regarding the financing of its mortgage portfolio, the amount of support it provides to the mortgage market, and the timing and distribution of that support. And these decisions must be made with due regard for FNMA's responsibility to its private shareholders, its special mission as a government-sponsored corporation charged with providing support to the mortgage market, and a broader view of its effects upon the entire economy and the capital markets within which it functions.

Exhibit 1

FEDERAL NATIONAL MORTGAGE ASSOCIATION
Statement of Income and Retained Earnings, 1972
(000 omitted)

Interest and discount on mortgages	$1,438,482
Portfolio costs	
Interest on borrowings and related costs	1,219,267
Interest on investment in securities	(17,287)
Administrative	13,445
Mortgage servicing fees	78,786
Provision for possible losses	5,425
Total portfolio costs	$1,299,636
Return from portfolio	$ 138,846
Commitment fees	
Home	$ 23,579
Project	21,936
Construction loan participations	1,051
Total commitment fees	$ 46,566
Gain (loss) on sales of mortgages and commitments	$ (779)
Other income	965
Income before taxes	$ 185,598
Provision for federal income taxes	
Currently payable	80,000
Deferred	9,200
	$ 89,200
Net income	$ 96,398
Retained earnings at beginning of period	100,518
	$ 196,916
Less cash dividends declared	14,628
Retained earnings at end of period	$ 182,288
Earnings per share	
Primary	$ 2.17
Fully diluted	1.79

Exhibit 2

FEDERAL NATIONAL MORTGAGE ASSOCIATION
Balance Sheet, 12/31/72
(000 omitted)

Assets

Loan portfolio:

Mortgages, at unpaid principal balances

Insured by Federal Housing Administration (FHA)	$14,624,387
Guaranteed by Veterans Administration (VA)	5,111,647
Insured by Farmers Home Administration (FHDA)	100,000
Conventional, net of reserve for losses	54,433
Total mortgages	$19,890,467
Less unamortized discount	673,291
Mortgages, net	$19,217,176
Participations in construction loans and other	434,692
Total loan portfolio	$19,651,868
Cash and U.S. government and federal agency securities, at cost which approximates market	282,653
Accrued interest receivable	145,119
Accounts receivable and other assets	25,444
Prepaid interest	16,399
Acquired property and claims receivable	193,644
Unamortized debenture expense	30,648
Total Assets	$20,345,775

Liabilities and Stockholders' Equity

Liabilities:

Bonds, notes, and debentures:

Due within one year

Discount notes	$ 1,082,275
Debentures	3,396,100
Mortgage-backed bonds	—
Capital debentures	250,000
Total due within one year	$ 4,728,375

Due after one year:

Debentures	$13,362,110
Mortgage-backed bonds	450,000
Capital debentures	450,000
Convertible capital debentures	248,496
Total due after one year	$14,510,606
Total	$19,238,981
Accrued interest payable	222,995
Accounts payable and accrued expenses	61,984
Mortgagors' escrow deposits	170,423

Federal income taxes:

Currently payable	35,903
Deferred	56,894
Total Liabilities	$19,787,180

Stockholders' Equity:

Common stock $6.25 stated value no maximum authorization: 46,428,209 shares issued (46,086,487 in September, 1973, 45,072,468 in December, 1972)	$ 281,703
Additional paid-in capital	95,301
Retained earnings	182,288
	$ 559,292
Less Treasury stock, at cost—179,259 shares (164,176 in September, 1973, 76,947 in December, 1972)	697
Total Stockholders' Equity	$ 558,595
Total Liabilities and Stockholders' Equity	$20,345,775

Exhibit 3

FNMA total assets and per common share earnings and
dividends, 1963–1972

At year-end	Total assets ($000)	Per common share	
		Earnings	Dividends paid
1972	$20,345,775	$2.17*	$0.33
1971	18,590,634	1.43*	0.27
1970	15,965,316	0.19	0.24
1969	11,017,940	0.63	0.24
1968	7,011,465	0.64	0.24
1967	5,413,545	0.41	0.24
1966	4,334,483	0.26	0.24
1965	2,494,676	0.41	0.24
1964	1,986,253	0.45	0.23
1963	2,096,163	0.45	0.23

* Fully diluted earnings per share for 1972 and 1971 were $1.79 and
$1.36, respectively.

Exhibit 4

Distribution of FNMA one-to-four family/multifamily mortgage purchases, 1971–1972
(Monthly totals)

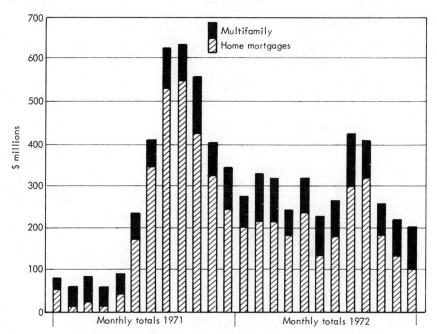

Exhibit 5

Average short-term commitment bid yields accepted by FNMA on
government-underwritten and conventional home mortgages under the FMS,
1968–1972

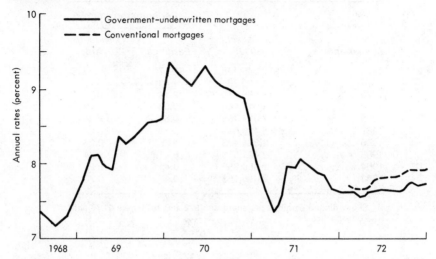

Note: Yields are gross for accepted three-month to four-month commitment bids—before deduction of a 38 basis-point fee paid by FNMA for mortgage servicing.

Exhibit 6
Changes in portfolio versus total flows to home mortgage
market, 1955–1972

Years	Total home mortgages (billions)	Change in FNMA portfolio* (millions)	Change in FNMA portfolio as a percent of total home mortgages
1955	13	$ 86	0.7
1956	11	563	5.1
1957	9	987	11.0
1958	10	255	2.6
1959 ....:...	13	669	5.1
1960	10	853	8.5
1961	12	(31)	(0.3)
1962	14	(25)	(0.2)
1963	16	(785)	(4.9)
1964	15	(65)	(0.4)
1965	15	523	3.5
1966	10	1,877	18.8
1967	13	1,126	8.7
1968	15	1,645	11.0
1969	16	3,778	23.6
1970	13	4,547	35.0
1971	37*	2,299	6.2*
1972	48*	2,000	4.2*

* Includes multifamily mortgages. These mortgages were of limited importance in FNMA's portfolio until 1971 and 1972.

Exhibit 7

FNMA effective interest income rates versus borrowing rates, 1969–1972 (averaged across the entire portfolio)

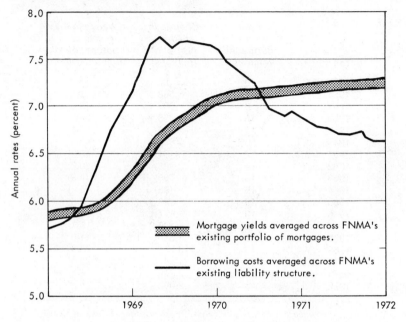

Exhibit 8
Average maturity of FNMA debentures sold in year, 1969–1972

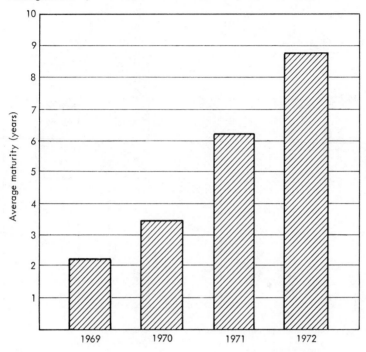

Exhibit 9

FNMA mix of marketable debt, by maturity, 1969–1972

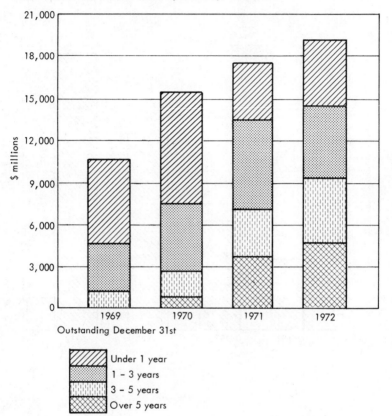

Exhibit 10
FNMA current mortgage yields versus cost of current borrowings, 1969–1972

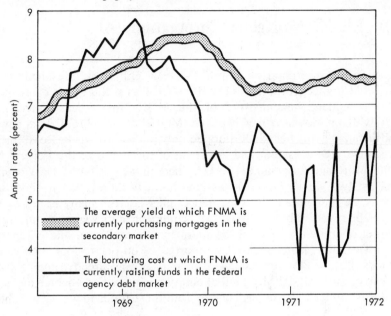

10. MGIC Mortgage Corporation (A)

Early in the afternoon of March 13, 1972, Bill Ross, president of the MGIC Mortgage Corporation (MGIC/MC), was sitting in his office in the starkly modern headquarters of the MGIC Investment Corporation (MGIC/IC) in downtown Milwaukee. MGIC/MC was MGIC/IC's newest subsidiary, having been incorporated only in the past week. Ross, former executive vice president and chairman of the board of the Federal National Mortgage Association (FNMA), had, in fact, arrived from Washington just two weeks before to assume his new duties. Yet in those two weeks, he had already become deeply engrossed in many issues he felt had to be resolved before MGIC/MC commenced its secondary mortgage market operations of issuing commitments to purchase, and purchasing for investment, loans secured by mortgages on one-to-four family residences. But his time for such decision making was already running short. In early April, MGIC/MC's initial equity capital would become available and Ross himself was determined to "put these funds to work" as rapidly as possible.

THE SECONDARY MORTGAGE MARKET

In March of 1972, there were basically two types of lenders in the primary mortgage market. On the one hand, there were institutions such as savings and loan associations and commercial banks which, with the funds of depositors, originated and acquired mortgages largely for their own portfolios.

On the other hand, mortgage companies comprised the second type of primary mortgage lender, which, with interim bank financing, originated mortgages not for their own portfolios, but for sale to other investors. Typically thinly capitalized, most mortgage companies depended on mortgage investors who would issue "forward commitments" (that is, commitments to purchase, on delivery by the seller, a specified amount of mortgages within a certain period of time) to cover some portion of their business. These commitments, by serving as the assurance of a "take out" of the bank borrowings, enhanced mortgage companies' access to bank financing.

In addition to these mortgage companies there were other primary lenders who periodically sold mortgages as well because they were located in mortgage markets which did not generate enough savings to satisfy local demand. Over the last several years, a secondary mortgage market had been evolving out of the purchase and sale transactions between institutions which originated mortgages for their own account, but expected to sell some part of these originations, and institutions which bought mortgages to supplement their own origination activities. These secondary mortgage market transactions were not centrally funneled through any organized exchange, like stock or bond transactions. Rather, a somewhat amorphous set of telephone-based communications systems comprised the "market," one of which was organized and maintained by MGIC/IC.

The development of mortgage insurance had greatly facilitated the development of this secondary mortgage market. The Federal Housing Administration (FHA), created by the National Housing Act of 1934, insured approved mortgage loans made by private lenders, and in addition the Veterans Administration (VA), guaranteed mortgage loans to veterans. In addition to these two federal agency insurance programs, private mortgage insurers had recently been developing, and growing rapidly. Mortgage insurance provided an element of fungibility to residential mortgages and gave the mortgage investor a standard of quality and a measure of protection against credit losses. As a result of both federal, and more recently private, mortgage insurance, the liquidity of the secondary mortgage market had been enhanced.

The other important elements of the developing secondary mortgage markets were such government-sponsored institutions as FNMA, created in 1938 under Title III of the National Housing Act, and the Federal Home Loan Mortgage Corporation (FHLMC), created by the Emergency Home Finance Act of 1970. These institutions raised massive amounts of funds by selling their federal agency debt in the public markets, and thus were able to facilitate the creation, trading, and investment in residential mortgages by channeling these funds into the mortgage market. Rather than originating their own mortgages, these institutions, often using various forward commitment techniques, exclusively purchased mortgages from other originators in a "secondary market." Operating principally as supplementary sources of mortgage funds, they provided critical liquidity to mortgage originators when mortgage credit from other sources fell short of market needs. Conversely, when ease in credit availability brought an overabundance of funds to the thrift associations, these federal agencies might effectively absorb some of these funds by selling mortgages from their own portfolios. Both agencies were empowered by the Emergency Home Finance Act of 1970 to purchase not only FHA/VA-insured mortgage loans, but privately insured mortgage loans as well. Finally, while FNMA dealt principally with mortgage companies, FHLMC, was limited to purchasing mortgages from federally insured deposit institutions and, in fact, dealt principally with savings and loan associations.

MGIC INVESTMENT CORPORATION

The Mortgage Guaranty Insurance Company (MGIC) was established in Milwaukee in 1957 to engage, within the private sector, in the insuring of lenders from losses on residential mortgage loans, much as the FHA and VA did in the public sector. During the Depression, wholesale failures among mortgage guaranty insurance companies had eventually caused them to be legislated from existence. After a law was passed in Wisconsin in 1957 to again permit private mortgage insurance, MGIC was the first company to reenter the field. Although eventually all states passed such laws and other private insurers arose, MGIC was by March of 1972 still the largest private insurer of mortgages in the nation, maintaining what some analysts estimated as a 60 percent share of this market. Private mortgage insurers seemed to be able to "compete" with federal insurance programs because of their relative freedom from constraints, their responsiveness to the market's needs, and their willingness to insure various "nonstandard" mortgages.

As MGIC's business expanded, it diversified into other related insurance activities, and in 1968, MGIC/IC was established as a parent holding company. Through its subsidiaries, including the original MGIC, MGIC/IC continued predominantly in the financial guarantee insurance business. However, in addition to residential mortgage loans, it insured commercial mortgage loans, mobile home loans, and municipal obligations. It also underwrote liability insurance for directors and officers of savings and loan associations. Finally, it was engaged in real estate financing, construction, and development, and owned a 46 percent interest in Firstmark Corporation, a diversified financial services company.

MGIC/IC's revenues from these expanded activities grew steadily from $31,511,000 in 1968 to $73,957,000 in 1971, while income (after tax) for those years increased from $6,536,000 to $16,406,000 (Exhibit 1). Moreover, because of its rapid and steady growth in earnings per share, MGIC/IC had in the past couple of years become a Wall Street favorite, particularly with large numbers of institutional investors. From a low of 11 in 1970, its stock had sold as high as 57⅜ in recent weeks, a price 70 times 1971 earnings per share.

MGIC MORTGAGE CORPORATION BACKGROUND

As part of this diversification, MGIC/IC management had gradually developed the idea of founding a new type of financial institution, to be called the MGIC Mortgage Corporation, as a private sector counterpart to the public sector secondary mortgage market activities of FNMA and FHLMC, that is, to issue commitments to purchase, and to purchase for investment conventional one-to-four family residential mortgages. FNMA and FHLMC had already demonstrated that such an institution could be both valuable for the mortgage market and profitable in itself (at least when financed with federal agency debt). Moreover, MGIC/IC management felt the establishment of this operation at MGIC/IC could exploit certain synergistic relationships as well.

Synergistic relationships

On one hand, the new subsidiary MGIC/MC could reduce its administrative operational, and start-up costs by relying on MGIC's expertise, built up in its previous operations in the mortgage market. Similarly, it could rely on MGIC's experience with individual institutions for evaluation of a potential seller's ability to originate quality mortgage loans and properly service these loans for other investors.

On the other hand, MGIC could gain increased utilization of its residential mortgage insurance product. MGIC/MC would require private mortgage insurance on each mortgage purchased to cover the risk of loss in the event of default by the mortgagor. Insofar as MGIC/MC's secondary market activities increased the demand for private mortgage insurance, such insurance underwriting might be provided by MGIC, thus increasing the revenues and profitability of both MGIC and the parent holding company, MGIC/IC.

With these considerations in mind, MGIC/IC management had become increasingly interested in launching MGIC/MC. Moreover, developments in the mortgage market in late 1971 made such a step seem particularly attractive.

A niche in the market

Although potential sellers of mortgages to MGIC/MC could include such institutions as commercial banks and savings and loan associations, MGIC/IC management had always felt that the operation's principal sellers would be mortgage companies because of their critical dependence on mortgage investors who would issue them forward commitments.

Toward the end of 1971, the FHA instituted a series of additional strictures on its mortgage insuring procedures. Consequently, at this time, mortgage companies began to show increased interest in originating conventional mortgage loans, and concomitantly, in finding expanded secondary market facilities which would enable them to do so. Moreover, considering potential competition for this segment of the market in the closing months of 1971, MGIC/IC management concluded that this was a growing demand that was largely unmet.

Potential competition

By purchasing one-to-four family conventional residential mortgages in the secondary mortgage market, MGIC/MC might theoretically be competing for investments with such large private sector institutional investors as insurance companies, savings and loan associations, mutual savings banks, and commercial banks. However, insurance companies, one of the more important private issuers of forward commitments, had largely restricted their investments to higher yielding large multifamily and commercial properties in recent years; and deposit institutions, being subject to greater fluctuations in the inflow of funds, were generally unwilling to provide forward commitments to other originators. Thus, none of these private sector institutions could provide much direct competition in terms of committing to, and purchasing, residential mortgages from mortgage companies.

In the public sector, both FHLMC and FNMA issued forward commitments. FHLMC, however, was limited to dealing with federally insured deposit institutions and was thus precluded from competing for mortgage company originations. FNMA, in contrast, was the largest investor in mortgage company one-to-four family residential mortgage originations (Exhibit 2); and MGIC/IC management felt that FNMA would be the greatest potential competitor with MGIC/MC. On the other hand, although FNMA had been able to purchase conventional mortgages since 1970, it had not scheduled its first conventional mortgage auction (for commitment bids from sellers) until February 14, 1972. MGIC/IC management believed that although FNMA would probably continue to issue commitments for conventional mortgage originations from mortgage companies, its operations would probably proceed at only a moderate pace for the foreseeable future, and would not significantly impair MGIC/MC's viability and growth in that market.

Having reached these conclusions, MGIC/IC management decided in early 1972 to proceed with the formation of MGIC/MC.

FORMATION OF MGIC MORTGAGE CORPORATION

The master agreement

MGIC/IC management first had to work out details of the contractual arrangements and requirements regarding sales and servicing of mortgages. It was decided that lenders originally approved by MGIC for its mortgage insurance operation would be eligible sellers of mortgages, and that MGIC/MC would specify contractual details in a "master agreement" with each seller.

Under the agreement, an eligible seller would make specific proposals for a commitment from MGIC/MC to buy mortgages on one-to-four family residences, including condominium units. The terms of such proposals would include the type (loan to value ratios), the net annual yield (interest net of servicing fees), and the maximum principal amount of the mortgages involved. If a proposal was acceptable to MGIC/MC, it would issue its commitment to purchase, over a specified time, a specified amount of existing or yet-to-be created mortgages with the net annual yield detailed in the proposal. This commitment would be accompanied by payment to MGIC/MC of a negotiated, nonrefundable fee, called the "commitment fee," which MGIC/IC management felt could be an important element of MGIC/MC's income.

If MGIC/MC issued a commitment, sellers, upon payment of the commitment fee and execution of the commitment contract, would have the option to deliver mortgages which met the conditions of the contract. During the commitment period, sellers could exercise their right to sell to MGIC/MC, retain the mortgages in their own portfolios, or sell the mortgages to other investors. MGIC/IC planned to adopt a commitment strategy such that a significant percentage of the mortgage commitments would lapse, that is, not be delivered to MGIC/MC, thus providing a stream of income from the commitment fees.

Under the terms of the agreement, the seller would normally retain servicing responsibilities for mortgages sold to MGIC. If the seller did not have servicing facilities, it was possible to arrange for servicing by a qualified mortgage servicer.

Financing

It was planned that MGIC/MC would fund its initial mortgage purchases with $10 million in equity provided through MGIC/IC. MGIC/IC management estimated that MGIC/MC could proceed to leverage this capital base, using general MGIC/MC corporate obligations, first up to 10 : 1, and perhaps ultimately as high as 20 : 1. (FNMA, for example, operated with a borrowing ratio of 25 : 1.) While MGIC/IC management did not have an explicit size goal, they believed that it was possible for equity to be eventually expanded to $50 million so as to finance a mortgage portfolio of as much as $1 billion.

MGIC/IC believed that it was important that MGIC/MC be established as a financially independent subsidiary that would stand on its own by issuing general obligation corporate debt to finance its mortgage portfolio. As a result of discussions with a number of interested and important participants in the financial markets, MGIC/IC management thought that MGIC/MC would eventually be able to attain a rating of "Aa" on its debt in public markets. In the meantime, while MGIC/MC was in its first stages, they believed that they might have to depend on private placements of general obligation debt. While it was difficult to estimate the yields MGIC/MC would have to pay on various debt maturities, they believed that the effective debt costs would probably follow a yield curve similar to the yield curve for Aa corporate securities but would be uniformly displaced upwards for all maturities by some unknown "spread" from Aa rates, perhaps on the order of 25–50 basis points (the prevailing yield curve for Aa corporate debt, as estimated by a Wall Street source, is shown in Exhibit 3).

MGIC/IC management decided that MGIC/MC should raise the privately placed or public market funds necessary to finance their mortgage portfolio only after the mortgages were delivered, so as to allow for the lapse (expiration without delivery) of some dollar amount of maturing commitments, but should provide for emergency funding with a back-up of bank credit. MGIC/MC would initially be able to borrow through the parent MGIC/IC, but discussion with MGIC/IC's lead bank, a large New York bank, indicated the types of credit arrangements that would probably become available to MGIC/MC when it established its own credit lines.

Using a syndicate of commercial banks, with the New York bank as the lead bank, MGIC/MC, first, could expect substantial bank lines which would carry the banks' respective prime rates. The New York bank's prime was currently 4.5 percent. These bank lines would require compensating balances of 10 percent of the lines plus 10 percent of the amounts borrowed and would have to be renewed annually.

A more important and secure source of back-up credit from the banks would be a seven-year revolving credit agreement with the bank syndicate, whereby MGIC/MC could borrow some substantial amount, without requirement of compensating balances, at a rate of ½ percent above 120 percent of the lead bank's going prime. Under this agreement, any principal amount outstanding after three years from the execution of the arrangement would be converted to a term loan payable in eight substantially equal semiannual installments (the first due after an additional six months), and bearing a rate of ¾ percent above 120 percent of the lead bank's going prime. This credit arrangement would, in addition, require a commitment fee of ½ percent per annum on the unused portion of the commitment. However, MGIC/MC would have the right, without penalty, to terminate or reduce the commitment under the credit arrangement and prepay any indebtedness outstanding. While it was clear that this bank credit could be quite extensive, particularly if short rates rose, and thus not a particularly attractive method of financing mortgages, MGIC/MC needed a reserve of back-up credit to utilize in case it was for some reason temporarily unable or unwilling to raise funds through general obligation debt. As a matter of policy, it was decided to minimize the actual use of bank debt, but to always have available back-up bank credit equal to the amount of outstanding commitments.

Ross arrives

MGIC/IC management had chosen Bill Ross to be president of MGIC/MC because they felt that his experience at FNMA would be invaluable in their new financial institution. In fact, they had been in touch with him through much of their planning of MGIC/MC.

Therefore, by March 13, Ross had actually been thinking about certain ramifications of a possible "MGIC/MC strategy" for some time. For example, he felt that significant differences between the operation of the public sector FNMA and the private sector MGIC/MC would inevitably emerge. He had been trying to anticipate these differences and consider what their strategic implications might be.

However, since his arrival at MGIC/IC on February 28, he had become increasingly pressed for the resolution of several more specific issues. Thus, this afternoon, after having enjoyed a brief respite during his lunch at the Milwaukee Athletic Club, he continued to turn these issues over in his mind as he had throughout the morning.

ISSUES TO BE RESOLVED

A permanent "holding" strategy versus the opportunities for trading

Ross thought that one basic decision was whether MGIC/MC should commit to a "holding" portfolio strategy or stay more flexibly positioned with relatively liquid mortgages so as to take advantage of possible trading opportunities.

A holding portfolio would be "permanent" in the sense that a given mortgage loan in the portfolio would be held to maturity so as to realize income over the life of the mortgage. These mortgages could hopefully be financed with somewhat lower cost corporate debt so that a modest spread could be "locked-in" for some reasonable period of time, until the mortgage matured or was prepaid by the mortgagor.

In contrast, a more flexible portfolio strategy could also include the possibility of positioning mortgages from a few months to a few years in order to exploit cyclical, seasonal, and geographic factors of supply and demand in the market, which might permit MGIC/MC to realize gains upon the sale of such mortgages at advantageous prices relative to their book value.

Considering the credit cycle, Ross was interested both in the probability of portfolio sales and in the potential for capital gains such sales might present. MGIC/MC's opportunities for portfolio sales and capital gains would arise in the credit cycle out of the coincidence of lower mortgage rates and greater ease in credit availability for mortgage investments at thrift institutions. In times of low open-market interest rates, household savings flowed at substantial rates into thrift institutions. When the inflow of deposit funds available for mortgage investments exceeded mortgage demand as had happened on several occasions in the recent past, MGIC/MC might not only be able to sell mortgages from its portfolio, but to do so at a gain; for insofar as mortgage rates declined with yields on other fixed income securities, prices on mortgages in a secondary market would commensurately appreciate.

Since thrift institutions were the principal mortgage market participants affected by such credit cycle fluctuations, Ross felt that these were the most likely purchasers of MGIC/MC mortgages. Therefore, in order to analyze these cycles, he collated, for the past ten years, annual household savings flows to thrift institutions with annual changes in secondary market yields on FHA-insured one-to-four family residential mortgages on new homes (Exhibit 4). (Yield fluctuations in FHA-insured mortgages would presumably serve as a convenient proxy for yield fluctuations in privately insured conventional mortgages. Although little data were available on privately insured conventional mortgages, they generally sold in the secondary market at yields 10–30 basis points above those of FHA-insured mortgages.)

Superimposed upon these cyclical opportunities, seasonal sales opportunities could arise out of the fact that a greater percentage of loan originations occurred in the summer and fall. Thus, in periods of lesser activity, normally during the winter, demand for mortgages, particularly on the part of savings and loan associations, typically increased.

Finally, the geographic differentials in mortgage demand which arose from time to time could be superimposed upon these cyclical and seasonal factors and could further improve trading potential by allowing MGIC/MC to buy from one area and sell to another (Exhibit 5).

Ross reflected that an important factor in considering the opportunities for trading was that in order to provide for sales, MGIC/MC would, of course, have to purchase relatively liquid mortgages of the type savings and loans were permitted to purchase, often called "conforming mortgages" in the industry. If, on the other hand, he elected a permanent holding strategy, MGIC/MC would not have to be so concerned with portfolio liquidity. This would permit them to purchase relatively nonstandard and hence less liquid mortgages (larger, or with a higher loan/value ratio, or condominium mortgages) which were ignored by thrift institutions and FNMA. These mortgages, in part because of their illiquidity, were generally available at premium yields, often $\frac{1}{8}$ to $\frac{1}{4}$ percent above market yields for "conforming" mortgages. In addition, of course, purchasing these mortgages could be an important dimension which MGIC/MC could use to differentiate its service from that of FNMA.

Another aspect of short-term positioning, moreover, was that this strategy would tend to be more beneficial to the MGIC residential mortgage insurance business since it would entail a more frequent turnover of the MGIC/MC portfolio with the concomitant increased utilization of private mortgage insurance to cover new mortgage purchases.

Finally, Ross considered how his decision might impact the earnings of the parent MGIC/IC. He thought that opportunities for trading could contribute capital gains over a period of years, and thus show higher average returns than the permanent holding strategy. On the other hand, earnings could vary widely from year to year, as selling opportunities did, or did not, present themselves.

Short-term versus long-term financing

Ross was also analyzing his short-term/long-term debt financing decision. He first considered the probable lengths of the alternative terms involved.

While mortgages were almost always originated with a term of 25 or, more likely, 30 years, the "effective maturity" of these mortgages was substantially less. On the basis of normal amortization alone, half the principal value of an 8 percent 30-year mortgage would be repaid by the 23d year. Thus, the "effective maturity" of a mortgage was less than the full term of 30 years. In addition, prepayment and refinancing of mortgages, which were relatively common, reduced the effective maturity substantially further. On the basis of FHA study data, Ross estimated that normal amortization, prepayments and refinancings, and foreclosures combined in such a way that only half of the original principal value of a 30-year mortgage portfolio would be outstanding after about 10 to 12 years. Presumably, if MGIC/MC were to aim at permanently financing a long-term portfolio of mortgages, a weighted-average debt maturity of somewhere around ten years would come as close as possible to matching the asset and liability maturities.

However, if MGIC/MC were to follow a short-term positioning approach for at least some of its mortgages, the "effective maturity" of these mortgages would be reduced substantially further, being equal to the expected holding periods for these mortgages. It was, of course, impossible to predict these holding periods, for they would be initially dependent upon the timing of cyclical swings in the capital markets. Recently, cyclical patterns had recurred rather regularly, however, and Ross estimated that those mortgages which could be traded out of the portfolio would be sold within two to five years.

Having formulated his thoughts on the effective maturities and holding periods of the mortgages, Ross could consider some of the financial options open to him. One of the important variables to concentrate on would be the weighted-average maturity of the general obligation debt that MGIC/MC intended to use to finance its mortgage portfolio.

A conservative option might be to match maturities of the mortgage assets and portfolio debt, although it was not entirely clear just how to implement that in MGIC/MC's case.

A second option would be to finance long relative to the portfolio. This strategy would enable MGIC/MC to benefit from a rise in interest rates. Ross considered, for example, that if the historic uptrend in interest rates were to continue, 25-year to 30-year financing could, over the long term, prove to be especially economical. In addition, this option might be safer with rising rates since it protected against both the inability to sell mortgages which were originally intended for eventual resale and a smaller than anticipated prepayment experience in the portfolio. Long financing would of course have to include some call features to protect against a dramatic downturn of mortgage rates, whereby an accelerated rate of prepayments and refinancings of portfolio mortgages could leave MGIC/MC with substantial borrowing costs and a paucity of possible investments at comparable rates.

A third option would be to finance short relative to the portfolio. This strategy offered the opportunity of exploiting the fact that yield curves were typically upward-sloping as was currently the case (Exhibit 3). Thus, shorter debt could significantly reduce MGIC/MC's over-all cost of borrowing and thereby increase its spread. Finally, Ross noted that financing short in the initial stages had the additional advantage that it would minimize the term for which MGIC/MC would pay the anticipated 25–50 basis point start-up debt cost differential until they could achieve an Aa corporate rating.

On the other hand, any shortening of financing, particularly with debt shorter than five years, would increase the probability of having to refinance with some spread loss in the event of rising interest rates. At several times in the last decade, most recently in 1969–1970, short rates had risen rapidly, rising not only above previous long rates, but also above long rates then existing (Exhibit 6). In fact, FNMA, financing short, had been caught with a negative yield spread on its portfolio during the 1969–1970 credit crunch (Exhibit 7). Ross thought that refinancing in such a position of narrow profits, or even loss, could pose special problems for MGIC/MC. While a government-sponsored institution such as FNMA would still enjoy considerable flexibility, MGIC/MC, a private sector corporation with more limited credit, might be forced to collateralize any debt it issued under such circumstances with mortgages from its portfolio. Were this to happen, MGIC/MC might involuntarily become locked into a "holding strategy" for the period of the debt because they might not be able to sell the mortgage collateral despite what market opportunities might arise.

Length of commitments and their pricing

FNMA was currently making only four-month commitments (although in the past it had offered commitments for a wider range of periods). Many mortgage companies were unhappy with the relatively short span of these commitments, insisting that a longer commitment period would help them to enlarge their operations considerably. Ross felt, therefore, in order to serve the mortgage companies better, MGIC/MC should offer six months as its minimum length commitment period. For such a commitment, he thought that MGIC/MC should obtain a yield of about ¼ percent above the going average secondary market yield for privately insured conventional one-to-four family residential mortgages. For example, these conventional mortgage rates currently stood at 7.65 percent (20 basis points above going secondary market rates on FHA/VA residential mortgages), such that MGIC/MC should be able to obtain a yield of 7.90 percent.[1] Deduction of an estimated 0.38 percent in servicing fees would give MGIC/MC a net annual yield of 7.52 percent. For such a commitment, Ross thought that MGIC/MC should be able to negotiate commitment fees ranging from ½ percent to 1 percent of the specified principal amount of the commitment, depending on particular market conditions. (This commitment fee was a one-time payment, due at the time of the commitment, and not refundable if the commitment were allowed to lapse.)

Along with these six-month commitments, Ross was considering one-year commitments. For these, he thought that MGIC/MC should be able to obtain a yield of ½ percent above going conventional rates, together with negotiated fees ranging from 1 percent to 1¾ percent of the principal amount, again depending on market conditions.

Given the supplementary role MGIC/MC would be playing in the market, that of augmenting the liquidity provided by mortgage companies' other mortgage investors, and the above market yield it would ask for such a service, Ross anticipated that some percentage of the dollar amount of mortgages that could be delivered under a given commitment would usually lapse without delivery. Pricing and length of commitments would, of course, be important determinants of the relative delivery/lapse proportions of a given commitment. For example, from his experience at FNMA, Ross guessed that with both the six-month MGIC/MC commitment priced ¼ percent above market and the one-year MGIC/MC commitment priced ½ percent above market, a 50 percent delivery rate would, on the average, result from stable mortgage rates over the period of the commitment, while pricing even closer to the market in each instance would tend to increase this delivery rate. Ross planned to price his commitments, as indicated above, such that a significant fraction of them would lapse, providing MGIC/MC with profitable fee income.

Unfortunately, considering the characteristic instability of mortgage rates in recent years, Ross realized that no one at MGIC/MC would be able to accurately predict actual mortgage delivery experience for a given

---

[1] These were the approximate current rates for "conforming" or standard conventional mortgages. The more illiquid "nonconforming" mortgages were generally available for approximately a ⅛ to ¼ percent premium above these yields.

commitment period. Throughout the term of commitment, a mortgage company would clearly compare MGIC/MC's previously negotiated rates with the market yields available from other potential purchasers and choose the lowest possible rate. Thus, just as a decrease in rates over a commitment term could result in only a few deliveries, a substantial increase in interest rates could result in a very high percentage of deliveries, perhaps approaching 100 percent. Faced, then, with the potential of wide swings in delivery rates, Ross had to decide what mix of six-month and one-year commitments MGIC/MC should use.

Both commitment periods would be longer and thus more competitive than FNMA's four-month commitments. However, with a one-year commitment, not only were the potential per commitment yield/fee rewards greater, but by offering such increased flexibility to sellers, Ross felt that MGIC/MC was likely to attract a larger share of the market.

On the other hand, the possible delivery percentages and the debt costs at which the mortgages would have to be financed were simply more predictable for shorter periods than longer periods. It was for this reason that Ross had decided against MGIC/MC's offering an 18-month commitment. In trying to project not only mortgage yields and deliveries, but also MGIC/MC's own potential cost of borrowing, Ross did not think that MGIC/MC would be able to obtain a yield/fee return adequate to compensate it for the risks it could be exposed to over such a prolonged commitment period. But in the comparison of six months versus one year, the tradeoff seemed less clear. Therefore, in order to get a feel for the comparative dimensions of risk, Ross analyzed interest rate movements on FHA-insured one-to-four family residential mortgages and on selected long-term and short-term high-grade corporates for the past ten years in terms of net changes over six-month periods (Exhibit 8). He wanted to evaluate the risks and returns of this commitment process and analyze whether the pricing of these commitments (both yield premium and fee) seemed appropriate.

LATE AFTERNOON CONSIDERATIONS

Potential profitability

As Ross prepared to leave for home at the end of the day, he reflected that one determinant of MGIC/MC's potential profitability would be the long-run spread between the costs of borrowed funds and the net yield of its mortgage portfolio, and the factors determining this spread were both multiple and complex.

Starting with the Aa corporate yield curve, which was usually positive, but could change rapidly, particularly in the shorter maturities, MGIC/

MC would initially pay an additional borrowing cost increment on the order of 25–50 basis points.

With such a rate base, MGIC/MC could go either long or short, with significantly varying potential costs. With this funding, MGIC/MC could follow either a permanent holding strategy or remain flexibly positioned to exploit trading opportunities. Holding had the advantage of being more compatible with the purchase of relatively nonstandard mortgages, which would not only allow MGIC/MC to differentiate itself more completely from FNMA, but offered an additional yield of ⅛ percent to ¼ percent over conforming mortgages. Although trading required conforming mortgages, it offered opportunities for capital gains and increased MGIC mortgage insurance business generation.

In purchasing mortgages under either strategy, MGIC/MC could issue either six-month commitments with a proposed pricing structure of a ½ percent to 1 percent commitment fee and a yield of ¼ percent above the market or one-year commitments with a proposed pricing structure of a 1 percent to 1¾ percent commitment fee and a yield of ½ percent above market. These commitments fees could be an important extra source of income, although they had to be balanced off against the ½ percent annual fee MGIC/MC would pay to the banks for their long-term revolving credit agreement.

Finally, MGIC/MC could proceed slowly and maintain a relatively small asset-size portfolio, or by aggressively issuing large forward commitments, attempt to expand rather quickly. MGIC/IC could limit MGIC/MC's equity to $10 million or increase it to $50 million or more.

It was now Ross's job to sort through these factors with their attendant risk/return tradeoffs and develop a coherent overall MGIC/MC strategy. Yet beyond some of these more pressing issues, he felt there were some long-range issues that had to be considered.

Long-range issues

Over the past few years the spread on rates of long-term (30-year) high-grade corporate bonds and residential mortgage loans had declined, and was, in fact, at times negative. This decline continued a long-term trend that began in the 1950s and became more significant in the 1960s (Exhibit 6). Although Ross attributed recent negative spreads to the increased demand for corporate debt financing which he felt was only temporary, he felt that the longer trend reflected a basic change in the nature of a mortgage as an investment. Government and private guaranty insurance had reduced the risk factor, while growth of the secondary mortgage market had further improved the liquidity of mortgage loans. Thus, Ross felt that he had to be concerned with the long-range impact of continued growth of the secondary mortgage market on the potential profitability of

MGIC/MC. However, he believed that given their smaller size, the heterogeneity, mortgages, although becoming more directly comparable to corporates, would, in the long run, always be regarded as less liquid. Although he was not sure of the near term, he felt that when corporate new issue financing abated, recognition of this essential difference in liquidity would restore a more stable spread between long Aa corporates and conventional residential mortgages, perhaps on the order of 50 basis points.

While it was quite difficult to estimate the future long-run profitability of this new type of financial institution, Ross thought that in a condition of stable capital markets, he would generally be able to obtain some reasonably profitable portfolio spread. He was encouraged further by the fact that MGIC/MC could clearly negotiate fees of ½ percent to 1 percent today for six-month "conforming" mortgage commitments at net annual yields of 7.5 to 7.6 percent. These yields were greater than MGIC/MC's potential borrowing costs in today's markets, and it appeared relatively certain that MGIC/MC could at least lock-in a profitable, albeit modest, spread in today's financial environment.

A second issue was the potential impact of MGIC/MC's successful entry into the mortgage market on the behavior of FNMA and FHLMC. If the greater flexibility MGIC/MC could offer sellers resulted in FNMA and/or FHLMC relaxing their own standards to meet the demands of the market, MGIC/MC, with a higher cost of borrowing, might be forced into other market niches where it could differentiate its service. In fact, it was clear that, in the long run, the size of the potential market open to MGIC/MC could be limited to these federal agencies. Ross believed, however, that the realities of the political process in which agencies were often enmeshed would tend to greatly constrain their activities, and that a more flexible private sector institution like MGIC/MC should be able to profitably innovate within those segments of the market that the agencies could not or would not reach.

However, as he left his office, he reflected that although these were important considerations, they were not his immediate concern. For MGIC/IC management was now committed to MGIC/MC's entering the secondary mortgage market. It was his job to decide exactly how MGIC/MC should proceed in its role as a new type of private financial intermediary.

Exhibit 1

Distribution of revenues and income among MGIC/IC's lines of business, 1968–1971
(Thousands of dollars)

	Year ended December 31			
	1968	1969	1970	1971
Revenues				
Insurance business				
Net premiums written				
Residential mortgage insurance	$17,132	$16,434	$15,488	$29,698
Commercial loan insurance	70	328	622	2,058
Lease guarantee insurance	256	544	1,155	2,629
Mobile home credit insurance	—	10	2,142	13,274
Municipal bond insurance	—	—	—	57
Directors and officers liability insurance	—	—	2,024	1,997
Miscellaneous	1,813	4,158	269	5
Total net premiums written	$19,271	$21,474	$21,700	$49,718
Investment income	2,688	4,827	5,727	7,292
Real estate business				
Financing	224	713	6,119	6,835
Construction and development	13,021	14,382	20,854	35,319
Other investment income	301	281	678	71
Income (loss) before income taxes				
Insurance business				
Income (loss) from underwriting:				
Residential mortgage insurance	$ 9,199	$10,916	$10,140	$13,361
Commercial loan insurance	(142)	(17)	78	556
Lease guarantee insurance	(30)	(40)	(32)	(246)
Mobile home credit insurance	—	—	34	(309)
Municipal bond insurance	—	—	—	(235)
Directors and officers liability insurance	—	—	195	843
Miscellaneous	(109)	(56)	(441)	(27)
Total income from underwriting	$ 8,918	$10,803	$ 9,974	$13,943
Investment income	2,585	4,508	4,766	6,545
Total	$11,503	$15,311	$14,740	$20,488
Real estate business				
Financing	10	43	2,419	2,865
Construction and development	767	1,149	2,060	3,543
Total	$ 777	$ 1,192	$ 4,479	$ 6,408
Interest from and equity in net income (loss) of unconsolidated subsidiaries				
Firstmark Corporation	—	—	471	858
Other investment income	289	287	565	63
	$12,569	$16,790	$20,255	$27,817

Exhibit 2

Mortgage loans closed by mortgage companies during 1970 ($ millions)

Size of servicing portfolio ($ millions)	All types	Type of investor*										Inventory without commitment
		Life companies	Mutual savings banks	Savings and loan associations	Commercial banks†	Trusteed funds	MITs and REITs	FNMA	GNMA	Mtg. pools GNMA	Others	
All sizes—total closed	$12,967	$3,181	$997	$2,416	$255	$417	$97	$4,036	$537	$312	$245	$474
One-family	8,479	384	766	2,195	187	234	20	3,728	47	312	153	455
FHA	5,495	196	470	1,331	97	136	13	2,603	47	229	83	291
VA	2,588	90	264	718	48	78	6	1,125	a	83	33	143
Conventional	396	98	32	146	42	20	1	0	0	0	37	21
Multifamily and commercial	4,470	2,781	231	221	68	183	77	308	490	0	91	19
FHA projects	949	65	22	21	2	23	0	308	490	0	18	a
Conventional, multifamily	1,142	845	107	65	17	53	13	0	0	0	30	11
Nonfarm nonresidential	2,379	1,871	102	135	49	107	64	0	0	0	43	7
Farm and ranch	18	16	0	0	0	0	0	0	0	0	2	‡
Servicing not retained	1,827	402	69	417	46	41	19	308	490	0	34	
One-family	502	45	47	352	23	16	0	0	0	0	21	
Other	1,325	357	22	65	23	25	19	308	490	0	13	

* Loans closed by type of investor includes both actual deliveries to investors plus mortgages held in inventory with investor commitment.

† Commercial bank trust departments are included in Trusteed Funds.

‡ Less than $0.5 million.

Source: Data from Table 3, *Mortgage Banking Trends, Financial Statements and Operating Ratios,* Trends Report No. 9, 1970 (Mortgage Bankers Association of America, Economics and Research Department).

Exhibit 3
Aa corporate yield curve, March 1972

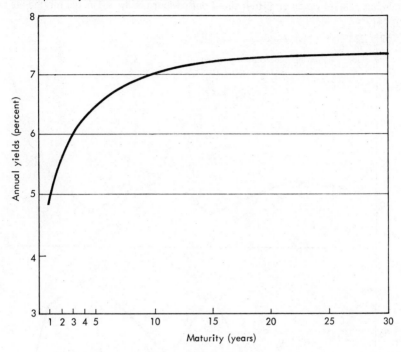

Exhibit 4

Annual household savings flows to thrift institutions versus annual changes in secondary market yields on FHA-insured one-to-four family residential mortgages on new homes

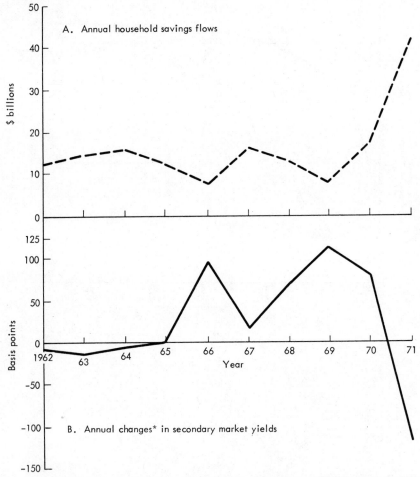

* Difference in basis points between average yield for year and average yield for year preceding.

Exhibit 5
Effective interest rates of conventional
mortgages on new one-to-four family
residences in selected metropolitan areas,
March 1972

Area	Effective rate*
Atlanta	8.02%
Baltimore	7.06
Boston	7.15
Chicago	7.13
Cleveland	7.04
Dallas	7.53
Denver	7.80
Detroit	7.49
Houston	7.77
Los Angeles-Long Beach	7.40
Memphis	7.82
Miami	7.45
Minneapolis-St. Paul	7.70
New Orleans	7.54
New York	7.41
Philadelphia	7.29
San Francisco-Oakland	7.54
Seattle	7.36

* Effective rate reflects fees and charges as
well as contract rate. These are average rates
for newly originated mortgages in the respective
metropolitan area, including the mortgage
organizations of S&Ls and other primary lenders.

Exhibit 6

Yields on FHA-insured one-to-four family residential mortgages on new homes versus yields on selected long- and short-term high-grade corporates

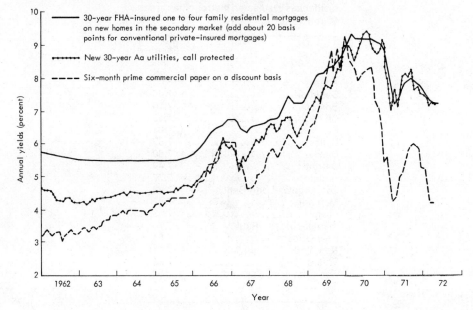

Exhibit 7
Federal National Mortgage Association effective interest income rates versus
borrowing rates (Averaged across the entire portfolio)

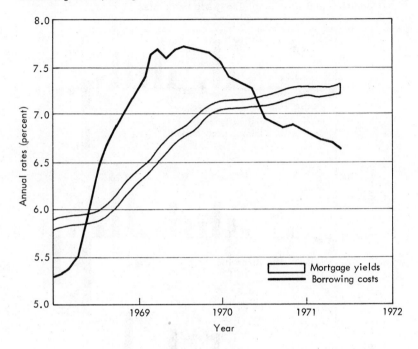

Exhibit 8
Net changes for six-month periods in yields on FHA-insured one-to-four family residential mortgages on new homes and on selected long-term and short-term high-grade corporates

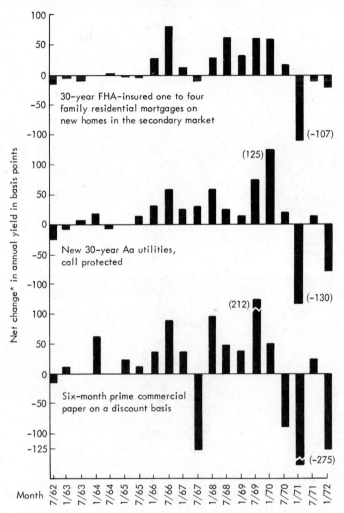

* Difference in basis points between yield for month and yield 6 months preceding.

11. Available Finance Corporation

In late May 1976, Robert Brookes, financial vice president of Available Finance Corporation, was deciding upon a financing plan. Consumer loan demand had been showing signs of renewed life. Available's management expected a continued increase in demand in their consumer loan business for the remainder of 1976, and they were optimistic about 1977 as well. Based on their forecasts, and on the need to refund over $200 million in long-term debt coming due in late 1976 and 1977, Brookes knew that he would have to raise substantial funds in the near future. He would have to decide the form in which the money should be raised (short-term, intermediate, or long-term, for example), in the context of a long-range financing plan for Available Finance Corporation. He was scheduled to present a specific proposal to the Finance Committee at the beginning of next week.

THE CONSUMER FINANCE INDUSTRY

There was about $162 billion of installment consumer credit outstanding in the United States at the end of 1975 (see Exhibit 1).[1] This credit was held both by retailers, who extended credit for the purchase of their own merchandise, and by several types of financial intermediaries, including commercial banks, credit unions, and finance companies. While credit unions lent directly to their membership, banks and finance companies lent both directly to consumers and indirectly through retailers. In the latter case, the credit was extended initially by the retailer, who then sold the note (called "retail paper" or "installment paper") at a discount to the financial institution. Many retailers and automobile companies had established their own "captive" finance company subsidiaries to handle the large volume of credit generated by their business (Sears, Roebuck Acceptance Corporation, for example, which held over $4 billion of consumer credit).

The major types of consumer credit were automobile loans, mobile home loans (conventional real estate mortgages were not classified as "consumer credit"), home improvement loans, revolving credit (credit

---

[1] Excluding 30-day charge accounts.

cards and checking account overdraw privileges), and direct, personal loans (see Exhibit 1 for a breakdown). Interest rates varied with the type of loan (see Exhibit 2); with larger and more securely collaterized loans, such as automobile loans, carrying a lower rate. The consumer finance industry was regulated, by both state and federal governments, as to the types and sizes of loans that could be made and interest rates that could be charged, among other things.

One factor segmenting the market was the convenience nature of most consumer credit. A large percentage of credit was originated at the point of a retail purchase, and most consumers would "shop around" for financing only when making a large purchase. Even then, the market was geographically segmented, with almost all consumer credit being obtained in the individual's immediate area.

Consumer credit was generally of a relatively short maturity, with an average repayment period of less than one year. In 1975, for example, with $159 billion in consumer credit outstanding at the beginning of the year, $163 billion was repaid during the year. During the same year $167 billion in new credit was extended.

As would be expected, the flows of new consumer credit were highly related to both the growth in personal income and consumer durable goods purchases (see Exhibit 3).

THE PERSONAL LOAN BUSINESS

The personal loan business was a segment of the consumer credit industry, distinguished by the fact that the loan was not directly tied to a particular purchase. This segment had traditionally been served by three institutions: banks, credit unions, and finance companies. Among these three institutions, there had been a rather clear differentiation of their respective segments. Credit unions were a major factor in the business (see Exhibit 1), but they could lend only to their membership, and generally concentrated on relatively low rate secure loans. Commercial banks could lend to the public at large, but also tended to concentrate on lower rate, lower risk loans. On the other hand, finance companies generally charged a higher interest rate than both credit unions and banks, and tended to concentrate on the portion of the market where the costs and risks of lending were greater. Lately, however, some of this differentiation was changing. The personal loan business was becoming more competitive as banks and credit unions were expanding the range of loans they would consider. In addition, several very large finance companies had recently been acquired by the holding companies of large money-center banks. Furthermore, some thrift institutions were beginning to enter the consumer credit business in those states where regulations permitted this expansion of their activities. Finally, Available and some other finance companies were now trying to take advantage of recent legislative changes to expand into larger, lower rate, longer term (five to six years) consumer loans, often secured by real estate. In view of all these trends, Available expected continued and increased competition in the future, from banks, credit unions, and others.

While regulations varied from state to state, the typical small loan law that applied to finance companies provided that loans not exceed a four-year initial maturity, and that the interest rate be limited according to the size of the loan. Typically the ceiling rate was 2½ percent or 3 percent per month for loans up to $300, 2¼ percent per month for loans from $300 to $1,000, and was approximately 1½ percent to 1¾ percent per month for loans over $1,000. Within a given state, these ceiling rates were almost always fixed over time, regardless of conditions in the financial markets.

While competition among consumer loan companies was keen, price (interest rate) competition was minimal. Most companies priced their loans at the ceiling rates. Competition focused instead on establishing a recognizable and trustworthy "brand name" and maintaining a chain of convenient, local offices. Consequently, advertising, rent, and personnel costs were major expenses for a large consumer loan company such as Available (see income statement, Exhibit 4), and interest expense was a smaller factor than in other kinds of financial institutions, like commercial banks.

Some of the expenses were relatively fixed costs, at least in the short run, because of the necessity of maintaining a large network of local offices with trained personnel, even when loan demand was low. In addition, many of the costs of actually making a loan, including recordkeeping, credit checking, and collection expenses, were relatively independent of the size of the loan. Thus, small loans were considerably more expensive per dollar than were larger loans.

AVAILABLE FINANCE CORPORATION

Available was one of the largest consumer loan finance companies in the country, with over 1,600 offices from coast to coast, and an advertising slogan ("When money is needed, it's Available!"), familiar to millions of Americans.

Available's principal business was making personal loans under the small loan laws described above, generally at the maximum rate allowed. The typical loan made in 1975 was for about $1,200, had a maturity of about three years and an interest rate of about 1.8 percent per month (the dollar-weighted average of their loan rates had fluctuated between 1.81 percent and 1.84 percent per month during 1971–1975). The customer typically obtained a new loan (generally in an amount larger than their existing balance, which was used to simultaneously pay off the balance of the existing loan and meet new needs) several times before finally paying off all indebtedness; and, on average, customers remained indebted to the company for about 37 months.

At the end of 1975, Available had had almost $2 billion in loan receivables (see balance sheet, Exhibit 5), scheduled to be collected according to the following timetable: 1976, 43 percent; 1977, 31 percent; 1978, 16 percent; 1979, 6 percent; and beyond, 4 percent.

While the receivables balance had grown in recent years (see Exhibit 4), the rate of growth had fluctuated, reaching its recent high in 1972 and recent low in 1975. The last two years had been slow years for the personal loan business in general, as can be seen from Exhibit 1. This was due, at least in Available's case, to a slacking of loan demand as personal incomes and spending dropped drastically in the recession (see Exhibit 3) combined with a tightening of credit standards on the part of the company. Credit standards had been tightened as a management decision, partly in response to the increased cost of new borrowings by the company (see Exhibit 7), and partly in response to an increasing concern over possible credit losses.

Recent increases in personal incomes and durable goods purchases (see Exhibit 3) along with a general feeling that the economy was on the road to recovery, led Available's management to expect a continued increase in personal loan demand. This had been partially confirmed by the large increase in demand for the first few months of 1976 (see Exhibit 1).

Their expectation was for at least a year of increased demand fueled by an economic recovery, coupled with moderate corporate borrowing interest rates. This could lead to not only an opportunity to resume their growth, but to widen their profit margins. Brookes' particular problem was a financial plan to finance this growth.

While long-run expectations for the business were, as always, less clear, management could see two scenarios which bracketed the reasonable outcomes for the foreseeable future. One possibility was a long, uninterupted economic recovery, in which incomes, spending, and consumer loan demand grew steadily while market interest rates remained moderate.

The much more pessimistic possibility was a fairly rapid return to the "stagflation" of the 1973–1975 period, a rapid resurgence of inflation followed by another stagnation of consumer spending. Here, loan demand would undoubtedly fall, while interest rates would rise, eliminating any growth and cutting Available's profit margins.

FINANCING

Available currently had over $280 million in short-term debt, about equally split between bank credit and commercial paper, $1.1 billion in long-term debt, and $566 million in owners' equity (see balance sheet, Exhibit 5). This capital structure was reasonably comparable to the structures of other similar large finance companies, Available's traditional competitors.

The bank debt carried the prime rate. The company had $250 million in unused bank credit lines, maintained partially to back up their commercial paper. They currently were maintaining compensating balances of over $30 million.

Available sold its A-1 rated (the highest credit rating) commercial paper directly, saving the dealer's ⅛ percent fee. Available had not experienced, and did not anticipate, any difficulty in placing its commercial paper at prevailing rates.

The outstanding long-term debt was rated AA and had an average coupon rate of 6.66 percent as of 12/31/75, with the maturity schedule shown in Exhibit 6.

THE CHOICE

To help him with his decision, Brookes had made a chart of recent interest rates (Exhibit 7). In addition, he compiled a list of some recent finance company debt offerings (Exhibit 8).

Most corporate debentures, including the finance company issues in Exhibit 8, contained call provisions favorable to the company. As a partial protection for the investor, the typical provision provided seven to ten years of call protection during which the company could not refund the issue at lower rates. After that date, though, the company could generally call the bonds at its option, usually at a slight premium over par.

One of Available's investment bankers had been suggesting that Available issue a new and different type of long-term debt, with a "put" rather than a "call" provision. While this type of debt had been used in Europe, it was relatively unknown in U.S. financial markets. The investment bankers had proposed 25-year bonds which would not be redeemable at the company's option, but would be redeemable, at par, at the option of the bond holders, starting after the seventh year. The bond holder would thus have the opportunity to redeem the bonds, presumably at a preselected date within the year, in any year from the seventh year until maturity.[1] In essence, these new bonds would be the opposite of most "conventional" long-term bonds. The investment banker suggested that in these times of inflationary fears, this new type of bond would be very desirable for investors, that it could probably be sold with a coupon even

---

[1] To provide for financial flexibility, the bond holder would have to irrevocably elect this redemption at least three months before the actual annual redemption date, thus giving Available at least three months' time during which they would know exactly what fraction of the outstanding bonds were to be redeemed that year.

less than an intermediate-term bond, and that Available was particularly well suited to offer this type of investment.

Brooks knew that substantial funds would be required over the next 18 months. Already in the first four months of 1976, Available's outstanding loan receivables had been increased by well over $100 million, more than double the increase for all of 1975. This increase had been funded by both selling some marketable securities and increasing the company's short-term debt. In addition, some large issues of long-term debt would soon have to be refunded. The principal financing alternatives he was considering were:

1. A greater use of short-term debt, either bank debt or commercial paper. The prime rate was currently 6.75 percent; and the commercial paper rate was 5.38 percent. This short-term financing was currently very inexpensive relative to other alternatives. By financing short, particularly with commercial paper, Available could take advantage not only of these substantial short-run cost savings, but of the long-run tendency for the yield curve to be upward sloping. In addition, since typically almost one half of Available's assets matured within one year, short-run financing would better match the maturities of their assets than their current capital structure, and avoid the potential risks of being locked into expensive longer term financing.

2. Intermediate-term, seven-to-ten-year notes. Earlier in the week another AA rated finance company, Ford Motor Credit Company had sold $125 million of ten-year notes (not callable for seven years) at an 8⅝ percent coupon. Intermediate notes would offer the advantage of assured financing at a known cost over a reasonable period of time.

3. Long-term, callable, 25-year debentures. Ford had sold $125 million of 25-year debentures earlier in the week, along with the 10-year notes. The debentures had carried a 9⅛ percent coupon, and were not callable for ten years. Long-term debt would allow Available to finance at today's interest costs over a much longer period of time.

Additionally, Brookes was intrigued by the new type of long-term debenture suggested by his investment bankers. Its nominal maturity would be 25 years as well, but the redemption option would lie with the bondholder rather than the company. His investment bankers reported some considerable interest in such a security within the investment community and were currently trying to define more precisely what the savings in coupon rate might be. Pending their findings, Brookes was contemplating whether this was a safe and/or appropriate way for Available to finance. In particular, he wanted to make sure that he considered the long-term implications of this new type of security for his future financial planning.

Brookes knew that he would have to formulate a financing plan by the beginning of the next week, which would describe the roles to be played by conventional short, intermediate and long-term debt over the next 18 months. This financing plan would depend in part upon his judgment of what kind of capital structure was appropriate for Available. In addition, conditional upon the investment bankers' report on coupon savings with the new type of debenture, he wanted to decide what role, if any, this debenture should play in the plan. Current conditions in the capital markets seemed favorable for both intermediate and long-term financing. And he wanted to embark relatively soon upon the financing plans which he thought would be appropriate.

Exhibit 1

Aggregate data on the outstandings and flows of consumer credit as of May 1976
(Millions of dollars)

Holder, and type of credit	1973	1974	1975	1975			1976			
				Oct.	Nov.	Dec.	Jan.	Feb.	Mar.	Apr.
Amounts outstanding (end of period)										
TOTAL	148,273	158,101	161,819	158,390	159,200	161,819	160,745	160,094	160,621	162,236
By holder:										
Commercial banks	71,871	75,846	75,710	75,286	75,174	75,710	75,342	75,010	75,103	76,013
Finance companies	37,243	38,925	38,932	38,411	38,642	38,932	38,737	38,660	38,665	39,003
Credit unions	19,609	22,116	25,354	24,706	24,934	25,354	25,250	25,492	26,025	26,403
Retailers[1]	16,395	17,933	18,328	16,444	16,860	18,328	17,771	17,192	16,987	17,060
Others[2]	3,155	3,281	3,495	3,543	3,590	3,495	3,645	3,740	3,841	3,757
By type of credit										
Automobile, total	51,274	52,209	53,629	53,286	53,479	53,629	53,318	53,519	54,117	55,059
Commercial banks	31,502	30,994	30,198	30,259	30,235	30,198	29,862	29,872	30,117	30,682
Purchased	18,997	18,687	17,620	17,848	17,761	17,620	17,500	17,409	17,471	17,742
Direct	12,505	12,306	12,578	12,411	12,474	12,578	12,363	12,463	12,646	12,940
Finance companies	11,927	12,435	13,364	13,203	13,325	13,364	13,407	13,490	13,624	13,869
Credit unions	7,456	8,414	9,653	9,403	9,491	9,653	9,612	9,704	9,908	10,051
Others	389	366	414	421	428	414	437	453	468	457
Mobile homes:										
Commercial banks	8,340	8,972	8,420	8,519	8,502	8,420	8,351	8,279	8,233	8,188
Finance companies	3,378	3,570	3,504	3,498	3,519	3,504	3,464	3,440	3,420	3,409
Home improvement, total	7,453	8,398	8,301	8,374	8,361	8,301	8,263	8,254	8,267	8,300
Commercial banks	4,083	4,694	4,813	4,824	4,827	4,813	4,777	4,757	4,767	4,816
Revolving credit:										
Bank credit cards	6,838	8,281	9,078	8,450	8,500	9,078	9,150	8,987	8,842	8,959
Bank check credit	2,254	2,797	2,883	2,834	2,822	2,883	2,911	2,912	2,876	2,882
All other	68,736	73,874	76,004	73,430	74,018	76,004	75,287	74,703	74,868	75,440
Commercial banks, total	18,854	20,108	20,318	20,401	20,289	20,318	20,290	20,203	20,270	20,487
Personal loans	12,873	13,771	14,035	14,005	13,943	14,035	14,049	14,010	14,034	14,192
Finance companies, total	21,021	21,927	21,465	21,037	21,158	21,465	21,279	21,152	21,078	21,211
Personal loans	16,587	17,176	17,179	16,822	16,942	17,179	17,035	16,952	16,922	17,047
Credit unions	11,564	13,037	14,937	14,559	14,692	14,937	14,878	15,020	15,333	15,557
Retailers	16,395	17,933	18,328	16,444	16,860	18,328	17,771	17,192	16,987	17,060
Others	902	869	956	989	1,019	956	1,069	1,136	1,200	1,125
Net change (during period)[3]										
TOTAL	20,826	9,824	3,719	830	805	894	1,295	1,169	1,513	1,436
By holder:										
Commercial banks	11,002	3,971	−134	309	233	310	208	475	572	561
Finance companies	5,155	1,682	7	36	157	34	260	198	302	347
Credit unions	2,696	2,507	3,237	255	270	471	387	420	514	392
Retailers	1,632	1,538	395	258	84	125	185	58	108	177
Others	341	126	214	−29	61	−44	254	17	16	−43
By type of credit:										
Automobile, total	6,980	935	1,420	389	404	540	488	632	654	710
Commercial banks	4,196	−508	−796	164	163	260	−44	293	239	351
Purchased	2,674	−310	−1,067	76	33	48	40	34	102	166
Direct	1,523	−199	272	88	130	213	−84	259	138	186
Finance companies	1,753	508	929	103	144	89	275	174	230	206
Credit unions	1,024	958	1,239	122	91	184	203	165	192	151
Other	7	−23	48	1	5	6	54	*	−7	1
Mobile homes:										
Commercial banks	1,933	634	−553	−62	−6	−61	−26	−45	−14	−49
Finance companies	462	192	−66	−7	26	−10	−28	−19	−2	−9
Home improvement, total	1,196	946	−100	−6	38	23	106	57	23	18
Commercial banks	483	612	114	23	42	41	30	32	35	27
Revolving credit:										
Bank credit cards	1,428	1,442	798	78	29	−49	107	133	224	134
Bank check credit	479	543	86	17	2	13	23	19	12	32
All other	8,344	5,141	2,133	420	312	440	625	392	615	600
Commercial banks, total	2,479	1,257	213	89	2	107	118	43	75	67
Personal loans	1,491	900	265	119	−6	149	100	33	42	67
Finance companies, total	2,520	906	−462	−27	20	−4	20	49	117	176
Personal loans	1,675	589	−3	−7	15	23	40	114	77	157
Credit unions	1,591	1,473	1,900	127	173	274	173	242	307	228
Retailers	1,632	1,538	395	258	84	125	185	58	108	177
Others	122	−33	87	−28	33	−61	129	*	7	−48

[1] Excludes 30-day charge credit held by retailers, oil and gas companies, and travel and entertainment companies.
[2] Mutual savings banks, savings and loan associations, and auto dealers.

[3] Figures for all months are seasonally adjusted and equal extensions minus liquidations (repayments, charge-offs, and other credits).

Source: *Federal Reserve Bulletin.*

Exhibit 2

Financial rates on selected types of installment credit (Percent per annum)

Month	Commercial banks					Finance companies				
	New automobiles (36 mos.)	Mobile homes (84 mos.)	Other consumer goods (24 mos.)	Personal loans (12 mos.)	Credit-card plans	Automobiles		Mobile homes	Other consumer goods	Personal loans
						New	Used			
1974—Apr......	10.51	11.07	12.81	13.00	17.25	12.28	16.76	......	......	......
May.....	10.63	10.96	12.88	13.10	17.25	12.36	16.86	13.08	18.90	20.54
June.....	10.81	11.21	13.01	13.20	17.23	12.50	17.06	......	......	......
July.......	10.96	11.46	13.14	13.42	17.20	12.58	17.18	13.22	19.25	20.74
Aug.......	11.15	11.71	13.10	13.45	17.21	12.67	17.32	......	......	......
Sept.......	11.31	11.72	13.20	13.41	17.15	12.84	17.61	13.43	19.31	20.87
Oct.......	11.53	11.94	13.28	13.60	17.17	12.97	17.78	......	......	......
Nov.......	11.57	11.87	13.16	13.47	17.16	13.06	17.88	13.60	19.49	21.11
Dec.......	11.62	11.71	13.27	13.60	17.21	13.10	17.89	......	......	......
1975—Jan........	11.61	11.66	13.28	13.60	17.12	13.08	17.27	13.60	19.80	21.09
Feb.........	11.51	12.14	13.20	13.44	17.24	13.07	17.39	......	......	......
Mar.......	11.46	11.66	13.07	13.40	17.15	13.07	17.52	13.59	20.00	20.82
Apr.......	11.44	11.78	13.22	13.55	17.17	13.07	17.58	......	......	......
May.......	11.39	11.57	13.11	13.41	17.21	13.09	17.65	13.57	19.63	20.72
June......	11.26	12.02	13.10	13.40	17.10	13.12	17.67	......	......	......
July......	11.30	11.94	13.13	13.49	17.15	13.09	17.69	13.78	19.87	20.93
Aug.......	11.31	11.80	13.05	13.37	17.14	13.10	17.70	......	......	......
Sept.......	11.33	11.99	13.06	13.41	17.14	13.18	17.73	13.78	19.69	21.16
Oct.......	11.24	12.05	13.00	13.38	17.11	13.15	17.79	......	......	......
Nov.......	11.24	11.76	12.96	13.40	17.06	13.17	17.82	13.43	19.66	21.09
Dec.......	11.25	11.83	13.11	13.46	17.13	13.19	17.86	......	......	......
1976—Jan........	11.21	11.76	13.14	13.40	17.08	13.18	17.25	......	......	......
Feb......	11.18	11.77	13.02	13.24	17.14	13.14	17.37	13.18	19.58	21.13
Mar......	11.13	11.82	13.02	13.13	16.99	13.13	17.48	......	......	......
Apr.ᴾ......	11.08	11.66	12.95	13.16	17.04	......	......	......	......	......

628

Exhibit 3
Consumer credit and the economy

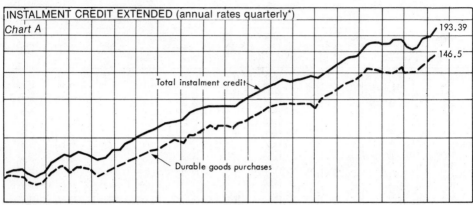

INSTALMENT CREDIT EXTENDED (annual rates quarterly*)

Chart A

193.39

146.5

Total instalment credit

Durable goods purchases

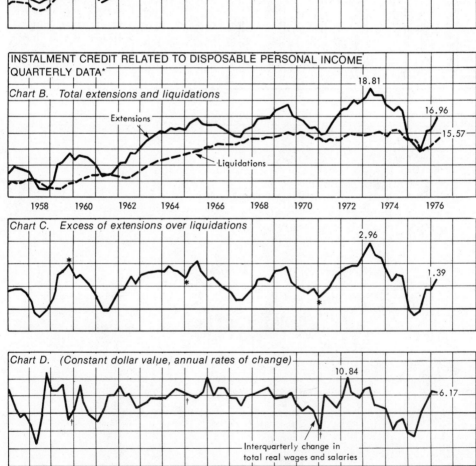

INSTALMENT CREDIT RELATED TO DISPOSABLE PERSONAL INCOME QUARTERLY DATA*

Chart B. *Total extensions and liquidations*

18.81

Extensions

16.96

15.57

Liquidations

1958 1960 1962 1964 1966 1968 1970 1972 1974 1976

Chart C. *Excess of extensions over liquidations*

2.96

1.39

Chart D. *(Constant dollar value, annual rates of change)*

10.84

6.17

Interquarterly change in total real wages and salaries

* Last plotting: Averages for the three months ending March 1976.
† Particularly severe auto or steel strike.
Source: Sears, Roebuck Acceptance Corporation, Interpretation of Consumer Credit.

Exhibit 4
Income statement and loan receivables ($ millions)

	1971		1972		1973		1974		1975	
Revenue	$ 304	100%	$ 331	100%	$ 366	100%	$ 388	100%	$ 383	100%
Less:										
Interest	82	27	92	28	106	29	121	31	109	28
Salaries and employee benefits	73	24	82	25	88	24	91	23	91	24
Provision for credit losses	29	10	34	10	41	11	51	13	55	14
Advertising, rent, telephone and other	49	16	53	16	58	16	62	16	59	15
Profit before tax	71	23	70	21	73	20	63	16	69	18
Profit after tax	38	13	37	11	39	11	33	9	37	10
Loan receivables outstanding at year end (less unearned finance charges)	$1,441		$1,580		$1,701		$1,782		$1,828	
Net increase in loan receivables	$ 74		139		121		81		46	
Annual growth in loan receivables	5.4%		9.7%		7.7%		4.8%		2.6%	

Exhibit 5

AVAILABLE FINANCE CORPORATION
Balance Sheet as of 12/31/75
($ millions)

Assets:

Cash		$ 41
Finance receivables	$2,217	
Less unearned finance charges	389	
	$1,828	
Less possible credit losses	95	
Net finance receivables		1,733
Marketable securities		118
Fixed assets (net of depreciation)		22
Other assets		84
Total Assets		$1,998

Liabilities and Owners' Equity:

Short-term debt		$ 245
Accounts and taxes payable		111
Long-term debt		1,076
Owners' equity		
Preferred stock	$ 120	
Common stock	446	566
Total		1,998

Exhibit 6

Schedule of long-term debt maturities (as of 12/31/75)

By maturity	Outstanding (millions)	Weighted average annual interest rate
1976	$ 123	7.28%
1977	94	5.90
1978	26	8.25
1979	126	8.41
1980	81	7.05
1981–1985	66	6.32
1986–1990	170	4.98
1991–1995	140	5.27
1996–2000	200	7.48
2001–2002	50	7.50
Total	$1,076	6.66

Exhibit 7

Selected interest rates in May 1976 (monthly averages of daily figures)

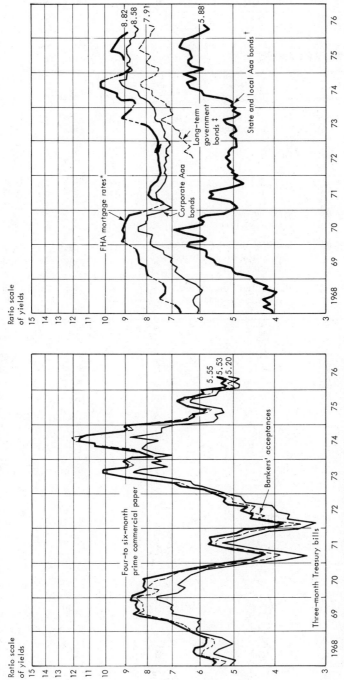

* FHA 30-year mortgages. Dashed lines indicate data not available.
† Monthly averages of Thursday figures.
‡ Average of yields on coupon issues due or callable in ten years or more, excluding issues with Federal estate tax privileges. Yields are computed by this bank. Latest data plotted: FHA, April; Others, May.
Prepared by Federal Reserve Bank of St. Louis. Latest data plotted: May.

Exhibit 8
Recent finance company debt issues

Date	*Rating*	*Company*	*Amount*	*Coupon*	*Nominal maturity*	*1st call date*
5/27/76	AA	Ford Motor Credit Co. (captive finance co.)	125	8⅝%	1986	1983
			125	9⅛	2001	1986
4/14	AA	CIT	100	8⅜	2001	1986
			100	7⅞	1986	1983
3/10	A	Commercial Credit	100	8⅞	1986	1983
			50	8.4	1981	1981
2/24	AA	John Deere Credit Co. (captive finance co.)	100	8	1984	1982
1/28	AAA	General Motors Acceptance corporation (captive finance co.)	200	8¾	2000	1986
			100	8⅛	1984	1982
1/20	AA	Household Finance Co. (personal loan finance co.)	75	8.3	1986	1984
			100	9	2000	1986

Index